SALES MANAGEMENT
Concepts, Practice, and Cases

SALES MANAGEMENT
Concepts, Practice, and Cases

THOMAS R. WOTRUBA

San Diego State University

Goodyear Publishing Company, Inc.

Santa Monica, California 90401

Library of Congress Cataloging in Publication Data

WOTRUBA, THOMAS R.
   Sales management.

  Includes bibliographical references and index.
  1. Sales management. I. Title.
HF5438.4.W67   658.8'1   80-17928
ISBN 0-8302-8130-4

Copyright © 1981 by Goodyear Publishing Company, Inc.
Santa Monica, California 90401

All rights reserved. No part of this book may be reproduced in any form or by any means without permission in writing from the publisher.

Current printing (last digit):

10 9 8 7 6 5 4 3 2 1

ISBN: 0–8302–8130–4
Y–8130–0

Printed in the United States of America

CONTENTS

Questions for Review and Discussion and Notes follow each chapter.

Preface   x

1 INTRODUCTION   1

PERSONAL SELLING: PART OF THE MARKETING SYSTEM   1
   What is Sales Management?   3
   What is the Personal Selling Function?   5
   A Sales Management Model   7
   Challenges to Sales Management Today   12
CONCLUSION   14

2 GOALS FOR SALES MANAGEMENT   16

DEVELOPMENT OF SALES MANAGEMENT GOALS   16
ROLE OF PERSONAL SELLING   22
GOALS AS THE BASIS FOR DECISION MAKING   27
PROBLEMS WITH GOALS   27
CONCLUSION   29

3 MARKET AND SALES POTENTIALS   32

TERMS AND CONCEPTS   32
   Why Use Market Potential Measures: An Illustration   34
MEASUREMENT OF MARKET POTENTIAL   35
MEASUREMENT OF SALES POTENTIAL   43
USES OF MARKET AND SALES POTENTIAL MEASURES   45
OTHER SALES MANAGEMENT USES   47
CONCLUSION   48

4 SALES FORECASTING   52

CONCEPTS AND DEFINITIONS   52
THE SALES FORECASTING PROCESS   53

DEFINING THE PURPOSES OF SALES FORECASTS 53
IDENTIFYING THE DETERMINANTS OF DEMAND 56
OBTAINING DATA 57
SELECTING FORECASTING METHODS 57
CALCULATING THE FORECAST 68
APPLYING FORECAST RESULTS 69
EVALUATING THE FORECAST 69
CONCLUSION 72

5 SALES BUDGETING 76

BUDGETING IN SALES MANAGEMENT 77
NATURE OF SELLING EXPENDITURES 79
DETERMINING THE SELLING BUDGET LEVEL 80
PERCENTAGE OF SALES METHOD 80
ALL YOU CAN AFFORD METHOD 81
COMPETITIVE PARITY METHOD 81
OBJECTIVE AND TASK METHOD 83
RETURN ON INVESTMENT METHOD 85
INCREMENTAL METHOD 86
ALLOCATING THE SELLING BUDGET 87
CONTENTS OF THE SALES BUDGET 88
  Expenditure Categories and Specific Budget Items 88
  Budget Flexibility 89
  Cost Determination 92
ADMINISTRATION OF THE SALES BUDGET 92
  Budgeting Responsibility 92
  Budget Periods 93
  Budget Review and Acceptance 93
CONCLUSION 94

6 TERRITORY PLANNING AND COVERAGE 98

  Benefits of Territories 98
CRITERIA FOR TERRITORY DECISIONS 99
TYPES OF TERRITORY DECISIONS 102
  Determining the Number of Territories 102
  Determining the Location and Boundaries of Territories 109
  Assigning Salespeople to Territories 111
  Allocating Sales Effort to Customers 113
  Scheduling and Routing Salespeople 116
TERRITORY ADJUSTMENTS 118
  Transferring Salespeople 118
  Splitting Territories 118
CONCLUSION 118

7 OBJECTIVES AND QUOTAS FOR SALES PERSONNEL — 123

QUOTAS AND MBO SYSTEMS COMPARED 123
RELATIONSHIPS WITH OTHER SALES MANAGEMENT ACTIVITIES 124
PURPOSES OF QUOTAS AND OBJECTIVES 124
   Provide Incentive for Salespeople 124
   Control Salespeople's Efforts 125
   Evaluate Salespeople's Performance 126
   Limitations in Using Quotas and Objectives 126
FORMULATING QUOTAS AND OBJECTIVES 127
   Selecting Types of Quotas and Objectives 128
   Combining Quotas and Objectives for Proper Emphasis 131
   Determining Levels for Quotas and Objectives 133
   Adjusting Quota Levels 137
CONCLUSION 139

8 PERSONAL SELLING: THE JOB AND ITS ENVIRONMENT — 142

TYPES OF PERSONAL SELLING JOBS 142
USE OF SALESPEOPLE'S TIME 144
THE SELLING PROCESS 145
   Traditional View 146
   New Directions 156
   The Environment of Selling 161
CONCLUSION 165

9 PERSONAL SELLING: STRATEGIES FOR SUCCESS — 168

WHAT MAKES A SUCCESSFUL SALESPERSON? 168
CONTEMPORARY SELLING STRATEGIES AND STYLES 177
CONCLUSION 184

10 SALES ORGANIZATION STRUCTURE — 188

NATURE AND PURPOSE OF AN ORGANIZATION STRUCTURE 188
   Internal Perspective 188
   External Perspective 189
INTERNAL-EXTERNAL TRADEOFF 190
BUILDING A SALES ORGANIZATION STRUCTURE 191
   Identify Market Characteristics 191
   Determine Activities 192
   Establish Positions Needed 193
   Arrange the Structure 202
   Evaluate the Structure 207
CONCLUSION 210

11 HIRING SALES PERSONNEL — 213

DETERMINING HIRING NEEDS   213
  Quantity   213
  Quality   214
  Timing   218
RECRUITING   218
  Recruiting Sources   218
  Recruiting Policy Decisions   220
SELECTION   221
  Selection Tools   221
  Selection Policy Decisions   237
HIRING SALES MANAGEMENT PERSONNEL   238
CONCLUSION   238

12 TRAINING SALES PERSONNEL — 242

NATURE AND PURPOSE OF SALES TRAINING   242
DEVELOPING A SALES TRAINING PROGRAM   244
OBJECTIVES OF TRAINING   244
CONTENT OF THE PROGRAM   247
  Attitudes   247
  Knowledge   248
  Skills   250
ADMINISTRATION OF THE PROGRAM   252
EVALUATION OF TRAINING   258
RELATED TRAINING PROGRAMS   260
CONCLUSION   262

13 COMPENSATING SALES PERSONNEL — 266

CHARACTERISTICS OF A GOOD COMPENSATION PLAN   266
DEVELOPMENT OF A COMPENSATION PLAN FOR SALESPEOPLE   267
  Objectives of a Compensation Plan   268
  Level of Compensation   269
  Methods of Compensation   272
  Testing the Plan   281
  Administration of the Plan   282
COMPENSATING SALES TRAINEES   283
COMPENSATING SALES MANAGEMENT PERSONNEL   264
SALES FORCE EXPENSES AND AUTOMOBILE PLANS   285
CONCLUSION   287

14 MOTIVATION AND SUPERVISION OF SALES PERSONNEL — 290

WHAT IS MOTIVATION?   290
WHAT IS SUPERVISION?   290

FACTORS INVOLVED IN MOTIVATION   291
THE SUPERVISION PROCESS   293
INCENTIVE ACTIVITIES   301
CONCLUSION   305

15 SALES MANAGEMENT EVALUATION 308

ANALYSIS OF PERFORMANCE RESULTS   309
ANALYSIS OF PERFORMANCE EFFORTS   319
ANALYSIS OF PERFORMANCE SETTING   326
DIAGNOSIS, RECOMMENDATIONS, AND ACTION   328
CONCLUSION   330

CASES
  Stonewell Tool Company   336
  Hickok Glass Corporation   338
  Murray Laminating Equipment Company   340
  Webster Tackle Company   342
  Joy Cosmetics   348
  Vidio Star Cable TV Company   350
  Ace Lighting Company   351
  Fastype Company   353
  County Steel and Material Supply Company   355
  G&B Container Corporation   356
  Westerner Sportswear Company   357
  Cosi Cosmetics Company   358
  Accuplate Company   360
  Midwestern Life Insurance Company   362
  The Goodall Tire Company   366
  Doben Rubber Company   367
  Par-Breaker Golf Company   369

ADDITIONAL READINGS   373

INDEXES   374

Preface

Many changes have occurred in sales management since the first edition of this book appeared a decade ago. The orientation of sales management practice has become increasingly profit-focused, strategic, and decidedly professional. Trade journals and academic literature have provided a wealth of new ideas and evidence, much of it with action-oriented implications such as interactive models which guide the salesperson's time allocation. New ideas or applications of older ideas to sales organizations include expectancy theory, Management-By-Objectives, and behaviorally-anchored rating scales. Educational institutions have fostered a revival of interest in this subject as well, especially in helping students to prepare for entry-level positions.

In brief, the personal selling function has gained corporate, academic, and educational status.

These developments are central to this revised edition. Its framework remains as before, based on a logical model of the sales management planning and decision process. But the contents which flesh out this framework contain many changes. The book is entirely rewritten, shorter in total words, and contains more narrative and visual examples to focus on key points and stress the applied nature of the subject. Two new chapters have been added, covering the selling process and sales jobs, to provide a basic but solid treatment of personal selling. Cases have been prepared especially for this book, based on real-world situations known to the author, and covering all the major decision areas encountered by the sales manager. Review questions at the ends of chapters have also been revised, with additional short problems and applications of the key analytical procedures introduced in the chapters.

This edition, like the first, attempts to reflect the available research evidence, company experiences, and significant opinion from an extensive review of printed literature. The references should provide interested readers with follow-up sources for more in-depth pursuit of major topics.

This text is aimed primarily at undergraduate students with a serious professional interest in sales force management. But graduate students in a first sales management course should find the analytical approach challenging as well. Some background in basic business administration subjects such as accounting, management, economics, finance, and marketing will be useful, although experience or strong interest in selling or sales management will certainly overcome any gaps in formal academic background.

I am grateful for the comments and suggestions from many students, and authors who have referenced my prior edition. To have people read one's book is delightful, but to get feedback, especially of a constructive nature, is especially welcome. In particular, the careful and helpful reviews of Doug Dalrymple, Indiana University, and Ed Simpson, Miami University, were of great help, and both produced changes which clearly strengthened the final product. I will always welcome feedback from any reader, because there is so much more to learn.

November 1980   T.R.W.

1 INTRODUCTION

Every business sells something. Whether it be toothpaste, rolled steel bars, landscape designing, or any other type of product or service, the success of the business depends greatly upon revenues gained from sales. Not every business sells in the same way, however. Some companies, such as supermarkets, rely almost totally on advertising, sales promotion, and display as their means of contacting customers and obtaining orders. But the vast majority of business organizations utilize personal selling to some degree to achieve marketing success. It is nearly impossible to buy from U.S. Steel, Xerox, Prudential, Volkswagen, and countless other industrial and consumer goods firms without dealing with a salesperson from those firms.

Advertising, sales promotion, and other means of mass selling are more often partners with, not substitutes for, personal selling. Mass selling gains attention and interest for a company's products or services, while individual salespeople show how these products or services can specifically meet the differing needs and desires of each customer. Advertising can present a message economically to many readers or viewers, but the salesperson can fine-tune that message to fit a particular customer's state of awareness, understanding, and need. Advertising communications can be carefully researched, subject to great quality control, and highly polished in execution. Personal selling communications involve feedback, clarification, and what may be most important, a face-to-face attempt and opportunity to obtain an order. It is precisely the direct, intimate, and flexible nature of personal selling that makes it the predominant aspect of the marketing mix for many companies.

PERSONAL SELLING: PART OF THE MARKETING SYSTEM

While personal selling is important, it is certainly not a panacea. A firm's competitive success depends on the successful functioning and coordination of *all* elements which constitute the marketing system. An outstanding personal selling effort will not overcome problems of poor product quality, inadequate distribution, or improper prices. A company's resources should be apportioned among its marketing elements so that they keep in proper balance. The days are fast disappearing (if not gone altogether) when a "slick-tongued" sales force is charged with "getting rid of" a poorly designed or unworkable product or a product which buyers simply don't want or need. Competitors will step in and devote more attention to providing improved products. On the other hand, the best products in the world will not find their way to users in this competitive economy without effective selling effort.

The marketing system itself has also evolved in those firms which have adopted the marketing concept. The marketing concept is a management philosophy whereby customer satisfaction is the central focus of the firm's existence. Formerly, a company might have relied on its engineering and production expertise to produce items that functioned well, and it was assumed that the market would want these products and would buy them at the price necessary to cover production and distribution costs, overhead, and provide a reasonable profit. If the market didn't want them, the burden was often on the sales force to convince buyers otherwise.

Under the marketing concept, this same company would first attempt to identify what needs and desires exist in the market, and concentrate on filling some of those needs by providing products or services which, as shown by market testing, will be well received by potential buyers. The sales force is sometimes asked for advice on what would better serve their customers' needs, and this advice often influences the firm's new market offerings. Under this approach, the role of the sales force switches from being an adversary with customers to one of being an advocate for customers as well as a consultant and a welcome source of information to customers. A good example of this philosophy comes from the marketing vice-president of Marriott Hotels, which offers facilities for conventions and meetings in its 46 hotels to large corporations, trade associations, tours, and other groups. He stated:

> A lot of hotel developers simply go ahead and build, then tell their salespeople, Here it is; fill it up. We ask our salespeople how big the hotel should be and how many guest rooms it should have. Should it have a big ballroom and just a few conference rooms? Or the reverse? In short, what do they think they can sell?[1]

While customer satisfaction is the primary focus, the marketing concept has two other equally important characteristics which have major consequences for sales management. One is that sales volume is not what management is seeking, but rather it is *profitable* sales volume. In other words, discovering what products will provide customer satisfaction is not sufficient. These products must be produced and sold at a profit. As a result, efficiency becomes a key issue in sales management. For instance, can the salesperson's time be more effectively utilized by improving routing or by scheduling calls on prospects with greater potential?

The other characteristic of the marketing concept involves organizational coordination of all marketing elements. This means that all marketing activities are drawn together within a single organizational home rather than being scattered or attached to various nonmarketing departments. Examples include the credit function, which is sometimes found in the accounting or finance portion of the organization, and inventory control, often located within the production arm of the business. Under the marketing concept, credit and inventory control would be viewed as parts of the overall marketing system, and would be found within the marketing organization. The logic of this arrangement is that organizational coordination is necessary as a foundation for a true marketing system to work. Every element of the system can then more conveniently work together to concentrate on customer satisfaction at a profit through a well-integrated and controlled total marketing plan.

Furthermore, if all elements are together every member in this system, such as the sales manager, can more easily work to maximize the success of the *total* marketing operation rather than seek success for his or her functional area *only*. In systems terms, this latter condition is called suboptimization. An example would occur when a salesperson receives orders from customers based on a promise of early delivery dates. But these dates are impossible for the firm's shipping department to meet without incurring so much overtime that the orders become unprofitable if filled.

What is Sales Management? Define MT

This book is for present and potential sales managers, those persons responsible for some phase of the personal selling function in their firms. A brief look at exactly what sales management is and who is responsible for its activities within an organization is appropriate at this point.

Sales management is a business function involving three major sets of activities: (1) formulation of goals, plans, and strategies for personal selling function; (2) implementation of these plans and strategies for the purpose of accomplishing the goals; and (3) evaluation of goals, and accomplishment and necessary revisions therein. Goals and plans are based on corresponding goals and plans devised at higher levels in the firm. In addition, these goals and plans depend on the importance of personal selling in the firm's overall marketing strategy. Implementation is primarily the duty of the sale force, guided closely by their managers. Evaluation involves control of the selling process as it proceeds, as well as a systematic learning from past experience so that future planning and implementation can be improved.

In practice it is probably impossible to separate these three sets of activities because they overlap and interact in most sales organizations. We will separate them for clarity of understanding in this book, however, but will note often where the overlapping and interacting take place.

The activities comprising the sales management function are carried out by sales managers. Historically, the title of sales manager was used to describe the executive in charge of *all* marketing functions, including advertising, physical distribution, pricing, and any other marketing activities in addition to personal selling. Few such instances remain today as this title now is typically used to describe a manager responsible for the sales force as well as for the planning and controlling of the personal selling function.

Even today, the term "sales manager" is somewhat ambiguous because many varieties of sales managers exist, sometimes even within the same firm. Typically, firms with large and geographically widespread sales forces have more than one level of sales managers. Figure 1.1 presents the sales organization of a publishing company with five levels of sales managers in addition to the senior vice-president of marketing and the sales force itself. Between these levels there are some major differences in duties and responsibilities. Managers near the top—the vice-presidents of sales and the regional sales managers—are concerned with planning and determination of sales strategy, including forecasting, budgeting, and goal setting. They are also responsible for setting policies and guidelines for hiring, training, and compensating all sales personnel subordinate to them.

As we proceed to lower levels of managers, the duties become increasingly concerned with implementation of plans and strategies, the actual carrying out of training and supervision programs, hiring (and firing), developing compensation and special incentive programs, and performing day-to-day evaluation of each salesperson or manager subordinate to them in this organization.

FIGURE 1.1

Example of a Sales Organization with Many Management Levels

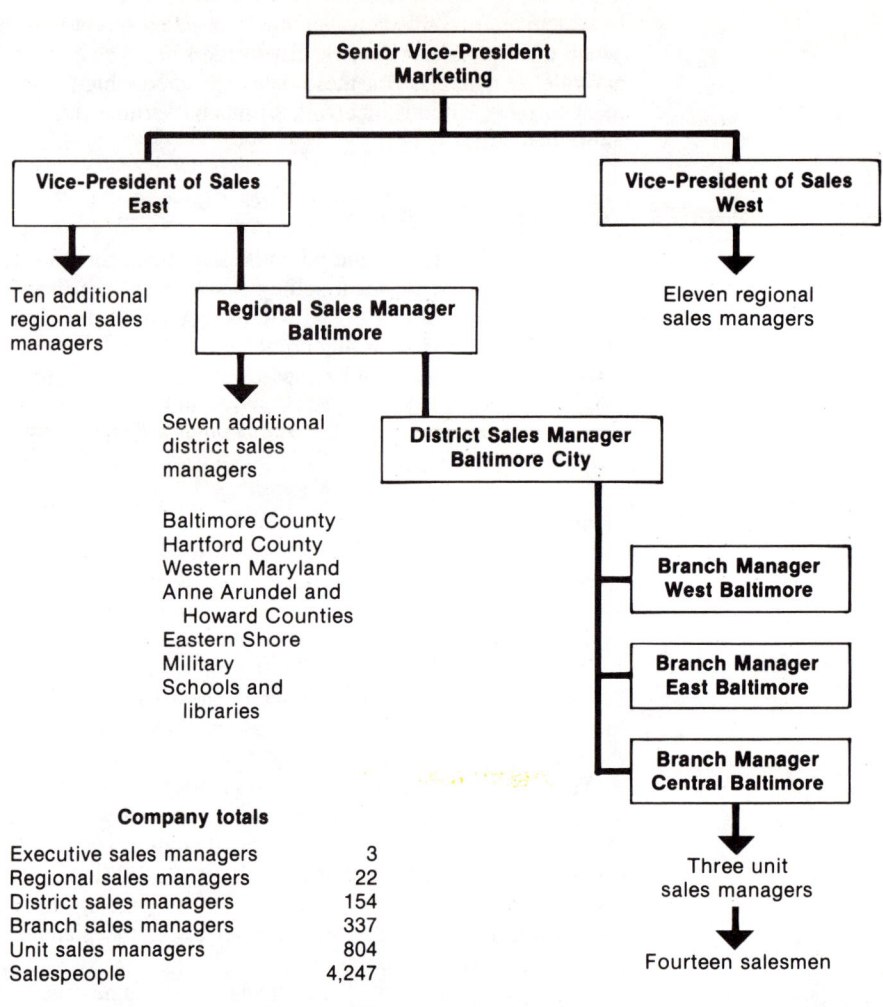

From *Sales Management: A Tactical Approach* by Marvin A. Jolson. © 1977 Litton Educational Publishing, Inc. Reprinted by permission of Van Nostrand Reinhold Company.

Those managers nearest to the sales force, such as branch and unit sales managers in this example, are often called *field sales managers,* though the exact demarcation of which positions are field sales managers is not always consistent among companies. Basically, the distinguishing feature of the field sales manager is that he or she is involved with implementation of plans and strategies, often working directly with individual members of the sales force and sometimes calling on customers as well. Conversely, the higher echelons of sales managers seldom work directly with salespeople, but devote major emphasis to administrative duties such as planning and policy-making as well as to the supervision of other managers. More elaborate discussion of these positions will appear later in the book when we examine the sales organization in detail.

The type of firm illustrated in Figure 1.1 is obviously a large business organization. Firms of other sizes and types carry on personal selling too, of course. In smaller companies with fewer levels of sales managers, all the duties required for effective sales management are still carried out, though perhaps less elaborately since fewer total management hours are available for each task. A small firm, for example, may have only one sales manager to do all the planning, strategy-formulation, policy making, implementation, and evaluation. In an even smaller firm, the sales management duties might be the responsibility of a marketing manager who is in charge of advertising, pricing, product development, and other marketing activities in addition to selling. Furthermore, sales managers in many large firms have responsibilities in addition to those discussed here. For instance, a field sales manager will often be asked to check the credit standing of prospective customers or to manage an entire district office with accounting, storage and shipping, and personnel responsibilities as well as the personal selling operation. But in all these cases, the sales management function is being carried out, though where it rests in the organization and how its component duties may be divided up among specific management personnel will vary among firms of different sizes and circumstances.

Another characteristic of the company illustrated in Figure 1.1 is that its sales force is made up of *outside* salespeople—those who call at the customer's place of business. In contrast, there are *inside* salespeople—those who receive customers at their place of business. The most typical inside salespeople are retail sales personnel, though manufacturers and middlemen also employ inside salespeople who handle telephone inquiries and over-the-counter sales on a cash-and-carry basis. This book is addressed primarily to outside selling situations, although most of the discussion can be applied to inside selling as well.

What is the Personal Selling Function?

What is the personal selling function—the object of sales management attention? While there are many differences in position from one firm to the next, the fundamental activities of personal selling common to most positions are: (1) locating prospective buyers; (2) converting prospects into customers; and (3) monitoring the market and maintaining customer satisfaction.

Locating prospective buyers is a necessary prerequisite to making sales. This activity is often carried out in partnership with advertising and other communications programs. For instance, the firm advertises its products or services in a trade publication, and inquiries generated by the ads are channeled to salespeople for follow-up.[2] Many potential customers do not respond to advertising, however, so the sales force in many firms must uncover prospects in other ways. Prospecting can be done, for example, by careful monitoring of business publications, by inquiry among present customers, by use of directories or membership lists, by attending meetings and trade shows, and just by being well-acquainted with territories.

Once a prospect is identified, some further tasks need to be done. One is to determine exactly what the prospect's needs are and who in the organization are key buying influences and decision makers. Prospects should be researched carefully prior to planning a sales call, so when a presentation is made it is tailored as closely as possible to the prospect's needs, interests, knowledge, and personality. Each salesperson must also estimate the potential sales volume which could be obtained from every prospect in order to plan for the most productive allocation of selling time.

Converting prospects into customers is the payoff in selling, and salespeople are trained to carry out this activity in various ways. Later chapters will examine these ways in more detail, so here we will note the key factors only briefly. The salesperson must establish the prospect's awareness and knowledge of the products or services offered. Equally important, the salesperson must understand the prospect's problems and needs. Only then can the salesperson really know what products or services should be offered. Then these offerings must be described in terms of benefits to the prospect and as solutions to his or her problems.

As noted by the marketing vice-president of Transamerica Corporation, it is the salesperson's job "to exploit the resources of his company in serving the customer."[3] In addition, the salesperson must differentiate his offerings from those of competitive suppliers and must establish the credibility and trustworthiness of the selling firm in the prospect's mind. All of this requires some combination of informing, educating, and persuading by the sales representative together with home office back-up, selling aids, testimonials, and any other assistance which can make the meeting between salesperson and prospect more productive for both parties.

Monitoring the market and maintaining satisfaction of customers is really a two-pronged activity involving follow-up and feedback. Customers may encounter problems with their newly-purchased product or may simply have questions about its use. In many firms it is the sales force which deals with these problems and questions, often in a scheduled set of follow-up calls. Some companies have a special service organization responsible for follow-up after sales. But even in those instances, the astute salesperson will keep in contact with present customers to remain alert to new or changing needs which might be served by additional products or services. Furthermore, the salesperson will benefit by learning how his product functions in this particular setting and how it aids this customer in terms of sales, profits, cost-reduction, or other beneficial ways.

The second prong of this activity is feedback from the market to the home office. Acting as intelligence agents, the sales force can obtain information about competitive strengths and weaknesses, changes in customers' business operations which will influence their buying behavior and needs, and general economic, social, and political trends in regions of the firm's market area.[4] By reporting this information to the home office, the sales force is acting indirectly as agents for its customers and prospects by educating its company how to adjust the company's output to be more in line with upcoming market needs. Done properly, this will clearly aid the sales force in maintaining long-term customer satisfaction by having new products and services available to meet evolving needs.

Beyond these three major activities of personal selling, we should note how the personal selling function is important to the firm. Basically, the sales force is the instrument through which the firm receives the vast majority of its operating revenues. The salesperson is also the main, if not the only, representative of the firm with whom customers and prospects come into contact. Thus, the salesperson *is* the company to many in the marketplace. And this means that to be most effective, each member of the sales force must be knowledgeable about his or her company, its policies, and products, along with an ability to meet and converse with a variety of persons in many different positions and specializations. Few others in any organization need such credentials.

Other factors contributing to the significance of personal selling are evolving technology, which is providing more complex and technically sophisticated products, along with correspondingly more sophisticated and complicated purchasing practices. It is not unusual, for example, for five or six key personnel in a prospect's firm to be influential in deciding on a major equipment purchase or a long-term commitment to buy raw materials or operating supplies. And these five or six persons may include engineers, financial analysts, marketing executives, and production managers, as well as other functional specialists, each of whom has different interests and priorities concerning what benefits the purchase will provide. Needless to say, personal selling takes on new prominence in firms facing these buying challenges.

A Sales Management Model

Sales management is a system of interrelated activities within the broader marketing system. Many decisions must be made by sales managers, such as what kind of training program should be presented to newly-hired salespeople. But these decisions cannot be made in isolation; they depend greatly on other decisions made in the same sales organization. The best type of training program, for instance, depends on the type of persons hired, their backgrounds and experience, the goals and duties established for the sales positions, the budget available, and many other factors.

A flow model of the sales management function has been devised to depict this system. This model identifies the major activities and the key relationships among them. It does not include all the detail and intricacies present in the actual performance of such activities, since that could complicate the model to the point of confusion. In this elementary form the model serves two purposes. First, it shows not only the total scope of sales management activities, but also their sequence. Later activities cannot be carried out effectively until preceding ones are at least under way. Second, since this model represents the scope of sales management, it serves as the outline for the remainder of this book.

The overall model showing all the major activities is presented in Figure 1.2. A more detailed look at each part of the model is shown in Figures 1.3 to 1.5. Since each activity is discussed more fully in subsequent chapters, we will look only briefly at them here.

Goals of the Firm and Role of Personal Selling. The first group of activities involves determining the broad goals of the firm and the role of personal selling within the total marketing strategy. Decisions on these topics generally take place outside the scope of sales management. These decisions are made by the firm's highest executives. Because this component of the model is not strictly within the sales management function, it is set off in Figure 1.2 with a broken line instead of a solid one.

Sales managers must understand these decisions and how they are made, even if they don't participate in them. Broad goals of the firm provide direction to managers in all parts of the organization. These goals are the company's definition of "success" and give each manager guidance in what his area of responsibility must accomplish to be considered successful. Furthermore, to accept the broad goals of the firm without understanding at least generally how they are determined is difficult. Finally, top management's intentions regarding the role of personal selling must be crystal clear to sales managers as well as to others in the marketing organization. Each must know the full extent of his or her responsibilities to avoid unnecessary overlap or working at cross purposes with other functions and elements of the marketing system. Chapter 2 expands on these ideas.

FIGURE 1.2
Overall Sales Management Model

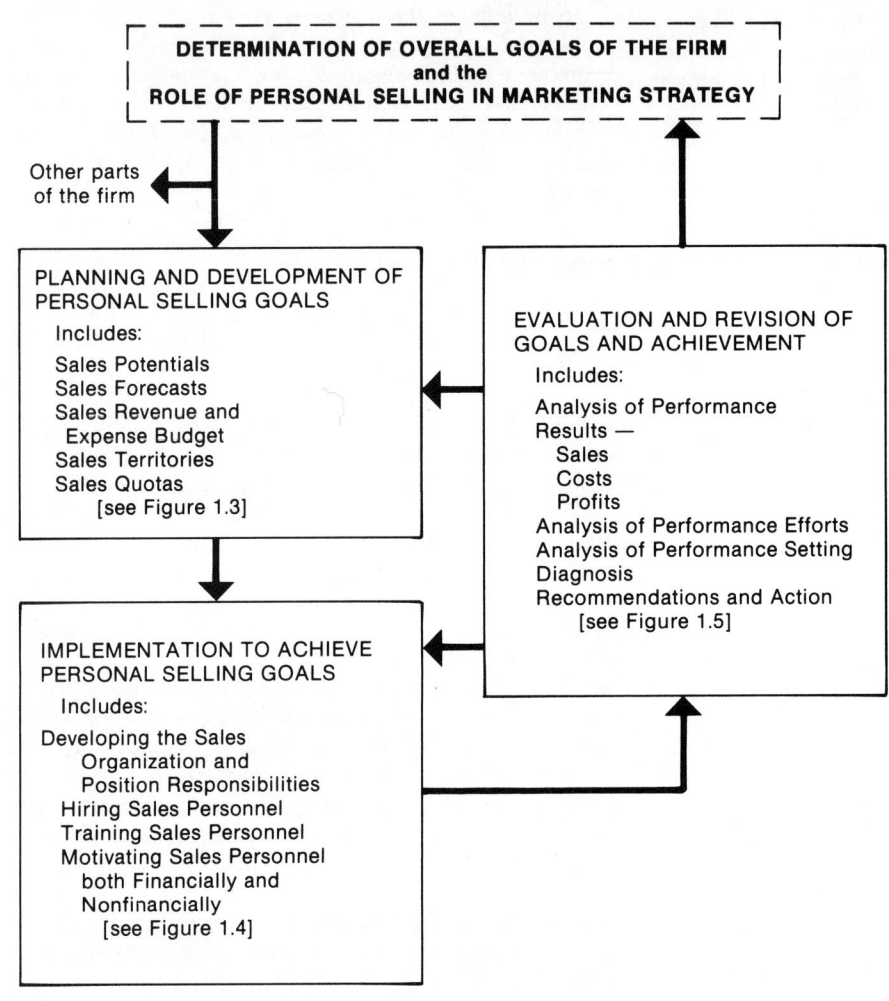

Planning. The first group of activities which is the responsibility of sales management is planning and development of personal selling goals. This component of the model in Figure 1.2 is further detailed in Figure 1.3. The aim of this set of activities is to translate the firm's broad goals into achievable personal selling goals for each individual sales representative. Chapters 3 through 7 discuss these topics in detail.

What Figure 1.3 indicates can be summed up as follows. Sales potentials, which are measures of maximum sales attainable for the company's product in each market and time period, are first determined. Based on these potentials, a sales forecast is developed, followed closely by a budget which translates the forecast into revenue and expense terms. Management scrutinizes the forecast and budget to determine if the level of profit projected is sufficient to meet company goals. Perhaps some

FIGURE 1.3

Planning Component of the Sales Management Model

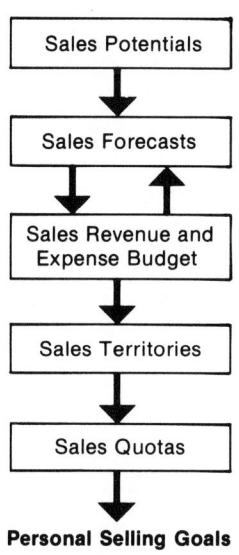

expenses can be reduced, or perhaps an increase in other expenses will bring an even greater increase in sales revenues. The forecast and budget are reworked in tandem until an optimum, but realistic, balance is attained in light of the available sales potential.

Sales territories are then established, or reviewed and revised in an ongoing firm, and quotas are established for each territory. Territories are usually segments of the market assigned individually to each salesperson, and quotas are goals for each territory and salesperson. Quotas, incidentally, can be set up for more than just sales volume. Sometimes quotas are given for activities such as the number of calls expected on new accounts, or financial measures such as maximum expense dollars allowable or territory profit contribution.

Implementation. The second set of sales management activities in Figure 1.2 involves implementation to achieve personal selling goals. As further detailed in Figure 1.4, this component of the model involves activities necessary to develop an organization, to select personnel, and to train and motivate them to accomplish the established goals. Chapters 8 through 14 delineate these tasks more clearly.

In brief, Figure 1.4 demonstrates that implementation starts with the development of an organization structure, one tailored to the needs of the markets served as well as being coordinated with the remainder of the firm. In particular, the responsibilities of each position within the sales organization must be spelled out, as this will influence the types of specialization and methods of coordination needed within the organization structure. Next, sales personnel and sales managers must be recruited and selected. In an ongoing firm, personnel are promoted, transferred, and sometimes fired as well, and all of these circumstances affect staffing needs and decisions.

FIGURE 1.4
Implementation Component of the Sales Management Model

Training occurs after hiring in most sales organizations, and continuous training programs are also offered in many firms for veteran salespeople. Other training needs must be considered for newly-hired or promoted sales managers, and even for customers who must in turn resell the firm's products to others in the distribution channel. Sales personnel must be offered incentives through compensation and motivation programs designed to reward and reinforce goal-achieving efforts. Motivation includes a nonfinancial component termed supervision. Some persons have argued that supervision is not really a distinct phase of sales management, but a combination of training, evaluation, and control. In this book, we will view supervision as the manner in which the job environment is provided to encourage a high level of performance. When effective supervision is coupled with all other activities in Figure 1.4, the result should be a sales force and managers fully able to achieve the goals established for them.

Evaluation. The last group of activities for which sales management is responsible involves evaluation. As Figure 1.2 indicates, evaluation is a comparison of goals and achievements. The purpose of evaluation is to identify areas of significant concern to management, areas where the greatest gaps exist between goals sought and actual achievement of those goals. Both unusually good or poor performance should be singled out, since either can give rise to improved future performance.

Procedures for evaluation are detailed in Figure 1.5. First is the analysis of performance results. Typical measures of results include sales volume, costs incurred to make sales, and profit contributions. As these measures are subdivided into more and more detail, strengths or weaknesses are more likely to be revealed. Sales data, for example, can be subdivided by territory, customer type, product line, and time period. In each case, the results can be compared with goals such as forecasts or quotas, and gaps can be isolated.

Next is the analysis of performance efforts. Some efforts are more quantitative in nature, such as the number of calls made or the amount of time spent on various tasks. Qualitative efforts refer to how well the salesperson carries out his or her

FIGURE 1.5

Evaluation Component of the Sales Management Model

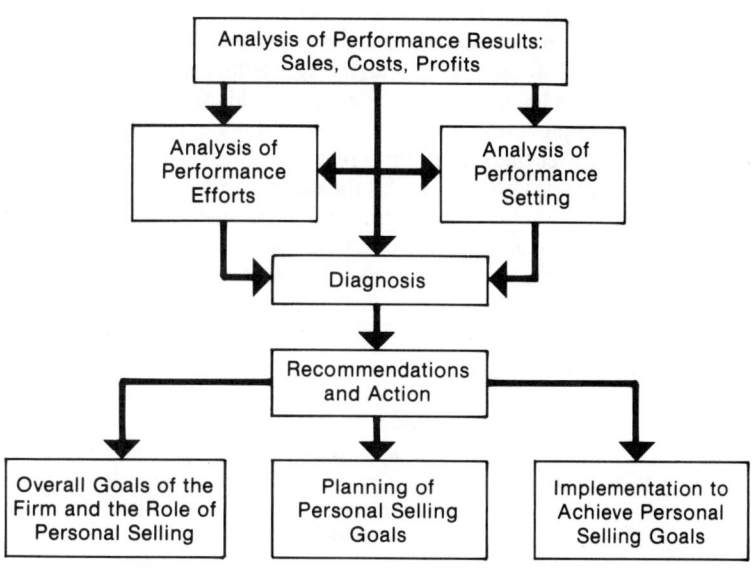

tasks, and these are often measured by judgmental ratings of such items as job knowledge, customer relations, and personal characteristics.

An analysis of the performance setting is the third step. Setting involves conditions under which performance takes place, including goals, policies, procedures, and organization structure. Any of these aspects can be a possible reason for differences between goals and actual attainment of goals. Perhaps selection or training procedures are inefficient, increasing costs unnecessarily. Perhaps compensation policies are ill-defined or quotas unachievable.

Figure 1.5 suggests there is considerable interaction among the three analysis steps. For example, if sales volume is found below expectations for a particular product, this implies that the sales force's efforts should be checked and that the policies and goals relating to this product should be scrutinized carefully as well. If the efforts analysis shows that customers are not getting proper service, this suggests a check on training procedures to determine if customer service is being stressed sufficiently.

The diagnosis step involves interpretation of information uncovered in the previous analyses. Once problems are identified and traced to their source or cause, the sales manager can take action which will improve performance in the following period. Sometimes the action called for is outside the sales manager's scope of responsibility, and he must make recommendations to his superiors, as indicated in Figure 1.2. For instance, top management's goals might be in need of some revision due to new circumstances in the market. These evaluation topics are covered more fully in Chapter 15.

Tradeoffs and Interactions in the Model. This flow model and brief explanation have been kept simple and straightforward for ease of understanding. In reality sales management decisions in any area are highly interrelated with other areas.

We have noted a few such interactions above, between forecasting and budgeting and among the analysis of performance efforts, results, and setting. Many more exist. In fact, an interesting exercise is to pick out any two components from Figures 1.3, 1.4, and 1.5, and try to identify possible interactions between those two components. How does design of sales territories affect the compensation plan, for example? Suppose each territory is not exactly equal in terms of potential business or travel time required to reach customers. Should the salespeople in those unequal territories be paid under the same compensation plan? Would some types of compensation be more appropriate than others under these circumstances?

There are also tradeoffs among the components of this model which add a more realistic complexity to sales management. A tradeoff means that the manager has some options in how to place emphasis among two or more activities. For example, the firm can recruit and hire inexperienced sales representatives, develop a thorough training program, and devise a compensation program that will reward good performers very well but will correspondingly discourage poor performers. Another option is to recruit and hire only highly experienced salespeople, offer only minimal training, and devise a compensation program designed to induce maximum performance from these proven performers. Tradeoffs, like interactions, can be found between many of the model's components. Should management work hard in devising accurate quotas, or should they rely more strongly on close field supervision to guide sales force achievement? Should job descriptions be developed with specific details concerning scope of authority and responsibility allowed, or should responsibilities be left more vague to allow the salesperson opportunities to show leadership and decision-making potential? Such tradeoffs and interaction are inevitable parts of sales managers' day-to-day decision making, and are symptoms of the fact that sales management is really a system of activities.[5]

Challenges to Sales Management Today

Besides fulfilling their responsibilities as defined by the model, sales managers face some major challenges which permeate all aspects of their jobs. We will examine these challenges under the two headings of productivity and professionalism.

Productivity. As the cost of personal selling escalates, productivity becomes a critical managerial problem. The cost of selling is rising at a rapid rate. The average cost of an industrial sales call reached $71.27 in 1975, as compared with only $33.55 in 1965 and $17.29 in 1955.[6] Thus, cost per call has been doubling every ten years, and could approach $150.00 by 1985. Inflation explains some of this cost increase, but certainly not all. Other factors include more complex customer needs and stiffer competition which require more extensive sales force effort per customer. Also involved is the enlarged scope of sales force responsibilities as their positions become more managerial in nature. Customer needs are changing rapidly, and a salesperson must be more alert than ever before to avoid wasting time and effort selling to meet yesterday's needs.

Sales managers have tried various tactics to cope with the productivity challenge. At the extreme, perhaps, is the attempt to replace the high-cost personal salesperson with a lower-cost substitute. Consider the amazement when customers of Ennis Business Forms opened an attaché case sent from Ennis and out popped a mechanical foot-high robot reciting a tape-recorded sales message.[7] Other efforts have been less creative, but certainly at least as effective. Chief among these is the use of new selling tools such as the computer. Computers have become invaluable assistants in laying out and modifying territories, in forecasting sales, and in allocating sales force time among various customers and prospects. To increase sales productivity, for example, Ducommun, a metals distributor, has set up a computerized information system to identify prospects by industry classification in each territory and transmit these prospect names to its sales force. A Ducommun executive noted, "We found we had been missing out on quite a bit of territory. Salespeople have a tendency to go back to the same old folks over and over."[8]

Other efforts at productivity improvement involve more conscientious efforts in many of the sales management activities described in this book. For instance, time studies can be done to determine how a salesperson could better utilize his or her time. Improved measures of sales and profit potential per account can be generated so the sales force can spend more time where sales and profits are likely to be greater. Compensation, training, and motivation programs can be geared more to productivity and profitability rather than simply to sales volume alone.[9] The key to productivity improvement in selling is seldom one of cutting costs, but instead involves directing these costly efforts toward the most profitable market opportunities.

Professionalism. A Bristol-Myers executive summed up the challenge of professionalism recently in this way:

> We have to project to America's young people a truer image of what modern American salesmen and sales executives are doing. The day of the shine and smile has long since gone. The day of hail-fellow, well-met, glib-tongue, two-fisted drinker, constant joke-teller—the classic stereotype of the salesman—is no longer true or valid as an honest representation of America's salesman.[10]

This stereotype of the salesperson has nearly become an American institution. It has been reinforced repeatedly in television shows, movies, plays, comic books, and joke books.[11] As a result, even college students in professional business programs have mixed feelings about the desirability of becoming sales representatives.[12]

Clearly, this stereotype is undeserved today. But concerted effort will be needed by sales and marketing managers to produce a professional image for selling. Adoption of the marketing concept is a step in the right direction, but more specific action is needed. Greater progress will occur as the sales job evolves visibly and substantially toward that of a problem-solver and territory manager. The essence of problem solving is simple: don't sell products or services; sell solutions to customer's problems. If the salesperson's product, service, and talent, combined with home office backup, can solve the prospect's problem (at a profit, of course), then that prospect should be pursued. Therefore, prospects must be sought out who have problems which the sales force can handle, and handle better than their competitors.

Territory management is also a significant departure from the traditional view of the salesperson stereotype. As a territory manager, the salesperson no longer just responds to his superior's memos and commands, but is actually participating in the management and planning of the sales function. Firms which seriously accept the professionalization challenge are designing training programs to convert salespeople-workers into salespeople-managers.[13] Other firms are upgrading their hiring requirements and are placing their territory managers into positions of profit responsibility. At Litton Microwave, for instance, "The salesman is a mini-general manager. Through him, and our mix of dealers, we generate the profits we're looking for. We also have an annual marketing plan for which we need field feedback—sales forecasts, expected expansion and market saturation. So we hire men with experience—professionals."[14]

The challenges of professionalization and productivity are important issues for all levels of sales management. Firms that meet these challenges will certainly become industry leaders both in the marketplace and inside their own organizations, providing rewarding and desirable job opportunities for the highly qualified.

CONCLUSION

Personal selling involves locating prospects for the firm's offerings, converting these prospects into customers, and maintaining customer satisfaction. Managing this selling function requires many interrelated planning, implementation, and evaluation activities which are previewed in the flow model and discussed briefly in this chapter. The upcoming chapters cover each part of this model in sequence, flowing from one activity to another in the same order as they are typically encountered by sales managers.

QUESTIONS FOR REVIEW AND DISCUSSION

1. To what extent are personal selling and advertising interchangeable in a company's marketing strategy?
2. Can personal selling be an important activity for nonbusiness organizations such as art museums and community hospitals? Why?
3. Why do large firms have more than one level of sales management personnel in their organizations? How do the jobs at different levels differ in responsibilities?
4. "Nothing happens until somebody sells something" is an old saying. How true is it?
5. When a business firm adopts the marketing concept, what are some ways this can affect the job of the sales manager?
6. Why is the cost per sales call rising from one year to the next? Does this mean that eventually personal selling will become too expensive for business firms to use?
7. Should the sales manager have a voice in the development of top management goals and plans? Why?
8. What is meant by describing the salesperson as an intelligence agent?
9. What specific action can sales managers take to increase the professionalization of selling? What is the payoff for such management efforts?
10. Discuss the possible interactions between any one sales management activity in Figure 1.3 and another activity in Figure 1.4. Then pick two activities in Figure 1.4 and discuss possible tradeoffs between them.

NOTES

1. James D. Snyder, "Marriott Hotels Keeps That Personal Touch," *Sales & Marketing Management,* May 24, 1976, p. 15.
2. John M. Trytten, "How to Use Advertising to Make Cold Calls," *Sales Management,* June 10, 1974, pp. 53–58.
3. "The New Supersalesman: Wired for Success," *Business Week,* January 6, 1973, p. 45.
4. Dan H. Robertson, "Sales Force Feedback on Competitive Activities," *Journal of Marketing,* vol. 38 (April 1974), pp. 69–72.
5. Further discussion of this point, together with a different version of a sales management flow model, is found in Porter Henry, "Manage Your Sales Force As A System," *Harvard Business Review,* vol. 53 (March–April 1975), pp. 85–95.
6. McGraw-Hill Research conducts a study on the cost of industrial sales calls every two years and the results are reported in *Report 8013, Laboratory of Advertising Performance,* McGraw-Hill Research.
7. "The Battle to Boost Sales Productivity," *Business Week,* February 12, 1972, p. 68.
8. *Ibid.,* p. 69.
9. These and other approaches are discussed in William P. Hall, "Improving Sales Force Productivity," *Business Horizons,* vol.18 (August 1975), pp. 32–42. See also Charles W. Smith, "Gearing Salesmen's Efforts to Corporate Profit Objectives," *Harvard Business Review,* vol. 53 (July–August 1975), pp. 8, 12, 14, 16.
10. "College Grads Urged to Enter Sales," *Agency Sales Magazine,* January 1977, p. 12.
11. A comprehensive review of literature and other sources contributing to this stereotype is found in Donald L. Thompson, "Stereotype of the Salesman," *Harvard Business Review,* vol. 50 (Jan.-Feb. 1972), pp. 20–22 ff.
12. Various studies reinforce this conclusion. See "College Grads Want to be Salesmen if . . . ," *Sales Management,* February 21, 1972, pp. 34–35; and John S. Ewing, "Honesty, Salesmen, and College Students," *Sales & Marketing Management,* May 10, 1976, pp. 73–75.
13. One such training program is described in "Salesmen! Think Management Now," *Industrial Distribution,* January 1976, pp. 59–61.
14. Rayna Skolnik, "Thou Shalt Not Cross Territory Lines at Litton Microwave," *Sales & Marketing Management,* May 24, 1976, p. 37.

2 GOALS FOR SALES MANAGEMENT

What should sales management achieve within the firm? Goals provide the answer to this question. Without clearly articulated goals, there are really no definite criteria for success, no solid standards against which achievement can be measured. Goals provide targets for management; they answer the obviously important question, "Where are we going?"

We need not discuss the importance of goals to the business firm in general, since that is well-argued in many other books.[1] We must, however, put the subject of goals into an operational sales management perspective, since goals are the foundation for decisions made by sales managers and sales force personnel. We start by looking at how sales management goals are developed, what they include, and what specific purpose they serve.

Development of Sales Management Goals

Since sales management is usually at a middle management level within the firm, it is necessary to begin with higher management levels in order to understand the background from which sales management goals are derived. At any given management level, properly set goals will be fashioned after the goals at the next highest level, all the way up to top management and the company president. Large firms with many management levels will have corresponding levels of goals; smaller firms with fewer management levels will have fewer levels of goals. This idea of a system of goals is depicted in Figure 2.1. While there are seven levels in this particular example, the number will vary for each individual firm. Note also that the highest level is not that of top management, since even company presidents and boards of directors must not establish goals which are at odds with national economic, political, and social goals.

National Goals. Although the United States and similar economies are described as "free enterprise," no firm is free to pursue certain goals which conflict with fundamental national goals. Our basic national economic goal is the preservation of the competitive market system, coupled with the desire to promote economic growth in order to raise the general standard of living.[2] Social and political goals relevant to business include the maintenance of personal freedom and equal opportunity as well as the protection of health, safety, and honesty.[3]

FIGURE 2.1

System of Goals from a Sales Management Viewpoint

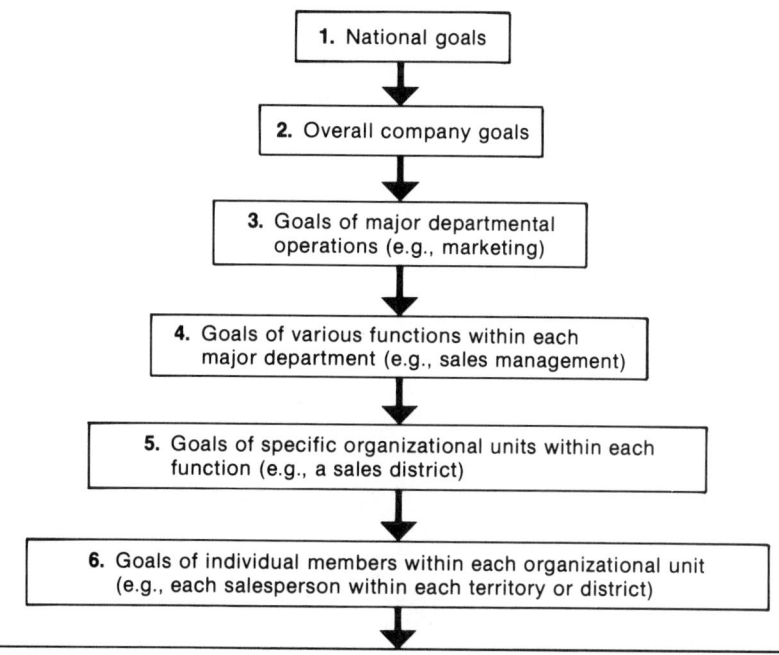

The attempt to implement this framework of goals has resulted in many laws and court decisions at the federal, state, and local levels. And beyond the technical interpretation of laws and statutes lies the area of ethics and how it affects business practices. Because these topics are especially significant to the personal selling function, they are discussed more fully in a separate section later in this chapter.

Overall Company Goals and Marketing Goals. Overall company goals are usually formulated in three related stages: a definition of the nature and purpose of the firm; a set of clearly defined objectives to be attained; and a description of the general strategy to be followed to achieve the objectives.

Goals should provide a unifying blueprint for all departments of the company to follow. Top management is the architect for the work performed by the firm's departments, and each department must follow the same plans if all parts of the business are to mesh properly. As one experienced management consultant put it:

> Without adequate documentation of sales objectives, goals, and strategies at the headquarters, regional, and territory levels, it is almost impossible to mount a sustained improvement program. Invariably, the company with a well-thought-out plan has done its analytical homework. That is, it knows where it stands relative to competition and has ongoing plans to stay ahead or catch up. My own experience over the years (with companies making such diverse products as gloves, domestic water

pumps, and compressor components) confirms that well-documented and implemented marketing plans produce beneficial product results.[4]

Marketing objectives and strategy must coordinate with overall company objectives. For instance, top management might specify an annual 10% growth in total sales revenue as a corporate target. Marketing management would translate that into separate sales growth objectives by major market segments, product lines, and perhaps time periods. At the next goal level, sales management would pinpoint the amount of sales increase expected on each product from each territory and even from certain individual customers.

Sales Management Goals. Sales management goals are developed next in the goal system. As in the preceding levels, goals here also involve purpose, objectives, and strategy. Once the firm's overall marketing strategy has been decided upon, the role of personal selling is established. It is then up to the chief sales executive to understand and translate this role into specific objectives and strategy for the sales organization. Later in this chapter we will discuss the role of personal selling in more detail.

Objectives are established in parallel areas covered by top management and marketing objectives. Figure 2.2 illustrates how three levels of the goal system might appear for a given firm. The eight key areas of overall company objectives used in this illustration have been adopted by many large firms such as General Electric and Westinghouse Air Brake Company.[5]

A more specific set of sales management objectives is presented in Figure 2.3. Univis, Inc., is a manufacturer of lenses and frames for eyeglasses. Their general sales manager's objectives (which they term standards of performance) can each be traced back to one of the eight key areas of overall company objectives noted in Figure 2.2. For instance, under *Section I. Sales Results—Specific,* statements A and C fit under Market Standing; statements B and D belong under Productivity; and statements E through H most likely apply under Profitability (assuming that the sales volume mix is established in proportion to relative profitability among the product lines).

Strategies follow objectives, and must be developed in close coordination with the other components of the marketing mix such as advertising, pricing, and physical distribution. Strategy in personal selling involves the selection of customers and prospects to pursue, the types of sales appeals to use, the kinds of presentations or demonstrations to make, and many other factors. One strategy might involve focusing on product quality in order to downplay price, especially if competitors' prices are lower. Another strategy might emphasize the experience of the producer and product reliability, especially if it is reinforced through a well-coordinated advertising campaign. In general, the strategy used should take advantage of company strengths and competitors' weaknesses, and relate directly to true customer needs.

Goals for Sales Districts, Individual Territories, and Key Accounts. Each succeeding level within the sales organization will have its own corresponding purpose, objectives, and strategy. In some cases, these will be set for the district or territory as a whole. In other cases, individual "key" accounts will be singled out for separate attention because of their large sales volume potential. White Trucks, the division of White Motors Corporation which makes diesel-powered trucks, defines

FIGURE 2.2

Corresponding Types of Objectives at Three Levels of the Firm's Goal System: An Example

AREAS OF OVERALL COMPANY OBJECTIVES	CORRESPONDING TYPES OF MARKETING OBJECTIVES	CORRESPONDING TYPES OF SALES MANAGEMENT OBJECTIVES
1. Profitability	Profit and ROI per product and per market segment; Expenses in dollars and as a percent of sales; Sales volume mix.	Profit contribution as a percent of sales; Sales volume mix in proportion to profitability of product lines; Compensation based on profitability of sales.
2. Market standing	Market share by product, customer group, geographic area; Sales volume growth.	Market share by territory and age of territory; Balance between prospects and customers; Growth of sales organization.
3. Productivity	Cost per dollar sales volume; Percentage of market penetration.	Sales volume per salesman; Sales volume per sales call; Allocation of sales force time among customers and by call lengths.
4. Innovation	New products; Product improvements; Creativity in marketing strategy.	Creative sales techniques; Obtaining market information on customer needs and competition; Organization structure and job specialization.
5. Physical and financial resources	Facilities such as district offices and field warehouses; Equipment; Inventory levels; Pricing; Credit.	Financial qualifications of prospects; Expense control; Resources for customer assistance; Samples; Trade shows.
6. Manager performance and development	Supervisory activities; Audits; Development programs; Decentralization of authority.	Preparing replacements for all management personnel; Career development training; Sales Management audits; Career paths.
7. Worker performance and attitudes	Hiring; Training; Compensation; Incentives; Control; Job Environment.	Initial and continuous training; Participation in decision-making; Opportunity for achieving personal goals; Job environment.
8. Public responsibility	Ethics; Community and public relations; Adherence to the law.	Role of sales personnel in community activities; Training in legal and ethical matters; Professionalism.

such an account as one currently operating 100 or more vehicles out of 10 or more separate locations which handle and haul its own goods.[6]

To illustrate this process, let us examine the approach used by Hooker Chemical Company at the individual territory level. Each Hooker salesperson prepares a written sales plan for each major account or prospect within the territory. Included in the plan is a customer profile, sales volume goal, strategy to be used, and a program of sales action for that particular account.[7] Hooker has developed sales planning manuals which describe twelve specific sales strategies. Three of these, for example, are the technical assistance strategy, cost reduction strategy, and quality strategy. Each salesperson must pick the one strategy best suited to each major account, based on the needs of that account and the strengths and weaknesses of competitors which are likely to seek the same business.

Carrying out goal-setting all the way to individual accounts is a time-consuming process. While the end result provides many benefits, the process of getting there

FIGURE 2.3
Sales Management Goals in Univis, Inc.

UNIVIS, INC.
General Sales Manager

Standards of Performance, 19 _____[a]

Satisfactory performance will be attained with respect to discharging responsibility for this position when:

I. Sales Results—Specific

A. The minimum budget level of _____ for net domestic sales is attained.
B. This sales volume is secured at sales cost of field sales not to exceed _____%.
C. Univis' share of market for all major product classifications has increased in 19_____ over 19_____.
D. Returns on any major product classification do not exceed _____% of sales. Top performance requires a rate of return of less than _____% of sales.
E. Sales of single-vision glass lenses of at least _____ pair of uncuts.
F. Field sales sells a minimum of _____ pairs of plastic lenses consisting of a combination of multifocals and single-vision.
G. Sales of _____ of multifocal lenses are obtained.
H. Domestic frame sales of _____ are obtained.

II. Sales Results—General

A. The field sales department has successfully implemented its man-power and job function program agreed upon at the end of 19_____. This program has:
   1. Provided a better appraisal of the sales workload.
   2. Provided better supervision.
   3. Provided more effective training for supervisors.
   4. Resulted in this agreed-upon expansion of the field force in direct relationship to funds available under sales cost constraints.
B. As UNI-FORM system units are available, priorities for accounts to be sold will be recommended by the General Sales Manager.
C. The sales department has successfully introduced the two new plastic products; both products by year end are leaders in their respective product categories.
D. The sales department has stepped up its sales coverage at the retail level.
E. The sales department has widened its base of frame distribution by having more wholesalers regular users of Univis frames.
F. The sales department has reduced attrition of in-line frame products by increasing the useful selling life of such products.
G. All new frame products for 19_____ have been successfully introduced with a high degree of accuracy in the attainment of forecast levels of sales volume.
H. The sales department has performed and reached its objectives within the framework of company policy, as well as within budgets established for operations for 19_____.
I. Customer relations are maintained at a high level.
J. Additional care is taken in connection with the listing of Univis distributors; Univis customers are convinced that the Univis distribution policy is constructive.

III. Planning—Field Sales Programs
Sales—Tactical

A. Sales presentations properly and effectively recognize all segments of retail market.
B. Sales department has obtained effective and meaningful information covering wholesalers' buying habits.
C. An analysis has been made, during the first quarter of 19_____, of all customers operating either with automatic ordering procedure of frame control program, or both. The analysis is followed by a program which causes an increased number of distributors to operate under these inventory control programs.
D. The sales department has made a careful analysis of results obtained under frame control program, and has made recommendations for pertinent improvements should they be indicated.
E. Univis attendance at trade conventions is better planned, and Univis exhibits designed to attract customers to the Univis booth result in more business at these trade meetings. Each

---

[a]This statement of standards combines in one document the stability of traditional standards with the flexibility of annual job objectives. The measurements made on each major responsibility are relatively stable; the measurement values which will define standard performance will usually change from year to year. Although not shown here, the relative importance of each responsibility is usually indicated by a percentage weighting.

such meeting is based on a specific objective. This objective is to be included in the written report prior to each meeting, along with personnel to attend, budget, and assignment of responsibility.

F. Sales department has solved the expense problem of running sales meetings with increasingly large attendance so that the annual cost of these meetings is contained.
G. The car-leasing program is handled in such a manner that no field personnel are without transportation over one week.
H. Any excess leased car is to be turned back within two months after termination or change of personnel. Should it be expedient not to turn it in, the reason should be outlined in writing to the Vice President for Marketing no later than two weeks after it becomes excess.

Sales—Strategic

A. Sales department has further developed a plan for the recognition of buying power and functional performance by some of its customers, leading to price differentials on purchases made by customers at different levels of performance.
B. Sales department has set forth in written form before year end its overall manpower program for the ensuing five years.
C. Sales department has provided Vice President for Marketing with analysis of the probable future shifting importance of the M.D. optician–O.D. relationship, and what if any new direction Univis should consider.
D. Sales department has provided Vice President for Marketing with updated information about the growth of the second market; the stance taken by competitive manufacturers in relation to the market; and recommendations as to what Univis should consider in its connection.
E. Field sales makes frequent, specific, and formal recommendations for new products.
F. A review is made of current recruiting methods, and a written report evaluating these methods is submitted to the Vice President for Marketing at least twice a year.
G. Review is made of the current salesman-selection system, and a written report evaluating the system employed is submitted to the Vice President for Marketing at least twice a year.
H. A plan is in effect and is working to develop the skills of field personnel to permit promotions and other job vacancies to be filled from within the organization.
I. Effective recommendations are made to improve the servicing of specials.

IV. Supervision and Controls

A. Performance standards for all key personnel to be covered for 19_____ are in existence on the first day of January, 19_____.
B. Performance reviews have been conducted during 19_____ for all people so covered, no later than the last day of the month following each quarter. These reviews have been summarized by the reviewing supervisor and a report given to his supervisor. All reviews establish work plans for the individual being reviewed as required to meet performance standards.
C. Sales department has administered its new compensation plan for all personnel in an intelligent and efficient manner, resulting in a sense of maximum incentive by bonus-eligible individuals reflecting directly on improved results.
D. Sales has instituted and implemented a cost-reduction program which has eliminated waste and duplicate costs in sales operations, and manpower is efficiently utilized.
E. Effective budget controls have been established, are in written form, and are working.
F. Sales personnel are required to perform, and failure to do so results in work plans which improve performance, or the poor performer is replaced.
G. Field activity on the part of territory managers is performed at a minimum average of 4.0 calls per day. Minimum activity on the part of professional representatives averages 7.0 calls per day. Sales calls by all field personnel cost the company no more than $_____ per call.
H. New and improved communication devices are evaluated as pertaining to increased efficiency of the Customer Service Department, and recommendations are made in writing to the Vice President for Marketing.

V. Communications and Inter-Division Cooperation

A. Reports, analyses, and communications in general requested by the Vice President for Marketing are supplied promptly and adequately.
B. There are established procedures for two-way communications between the sales department and other marketing departments; there is evidence that these procedures and communications achieve understanding.

Source: Reprinted by permission of the publisher from Research Study no. 85, *Objectives and Standards of Performance in Marketing Management,* pp. 72–75, by Ernest C. Miller. © 1967 by the American Management Association, Inc. All rights reserved.

requires great discipline on management's part along with a substantial investment in money and effort.[8] Some firms will not devise a goal system, at least formally or systematically, as complete as the one suggested here. But there is evidence that when it is done, solid benefits have been reported.[9] Better coordination occurs throughout the sales organization. Achievement at the territory level corresponds to top management goals. Objectives at higher levels become more realistic when directly tied to districts and territories. Sales effort is planned and used more efficiently, sales potential is more fully developed, and the servicing needs in the district are more adequately fulfilled.

Planning and goal-setting also provide psychological and educational benefits to personnel at these levels. Reports of greater enthusiasm, increasing management ability, and better understanding of company objectives are not uncommon. In fact, experience in developing goals is valuable training for a district manager who will move up the ladder into a higher management position, and likewise for the salesperson aspiring to move into management. The professionalization of selling is increased and improved.

Role of Personal Selling

Personal selling is one of a number of marketing mix components which can be used in a firm's marketing strategy. The chief marketing executive's task is to select which components to use and to also decide how they are to be used. When this task is completed, the role of personal selling, as well as of advertising, packaging, sales promotion, and other marketing mix components, will be defined.

Every firm has considerable latitude in deciding how to assemble its marketing mix and what role personal selling will play. As a result, the role of selling and sales management can vary greatly from one company to the next. Regardless of the firm involved, each manager's decision on the role of personal selling should be guided by answers to the following questions:

1. What information and communication must be exchanged between our firm and our customers and prospects?
2. What are the alternative ways of carrying out these communications exchanges?
3. How effective is each of these alternatives, taking into consideration our customers' needs and expectations, the communications techniques used by our competitors, and the other strategy components we will utilize in our marketing mix?
4. What is the cost of each alternative, or more importantly, what is the cost-effectiveness of fulfilling each communications task with each alternative, taking into consideration customer needs, competition, and coordination with other marketing elements?

For example, a machine tool company which specializes in custom building machines to the specifications of individual customers would have a great need for communications with each customer individually on a broad range of technical, financial, and administrative topics. The precise capability required of each machine must be determined separately for each customer; costs, financing, and credit arrangements have to be worked out; delivery and installation schedules must be agreed upon as well as initial training of operators and servicing of any problems with the new machine. Prior to all these tasks, the customer must be convinced to purchase the machine instead of buying or leasing a standard model offered by a competitor which might not have the precise capabilities desired but which is less expensive and has a track record of reliability. In addition, the competitor might sell its machines through distributors rather than directly, or else might have an inventory in stock in a field warehouse for quick delivery, providing an advantageous distribution difference as well. To what extent can each of these firms rely differently on personal selling, advertising, sales promotion, and nonselling aspects of marketing strategy for their competitive success?

The role of personal selling in each firm is most clearly documented within the job description for that firm's sales position, and is further defined within the firm's sales training program. Subsequent chapters cover these topics in detail. For now, let us look at how some firms differ in the importance they assign to personal selling, and how this importance might change in the foreseeable future.

In a major study of more than 400 large U.S. manufacturers, a top-ranking marketing executive in each firm was asked to indicate the relative importance of each activity in the marketing strategy for a major product of their company.[10] The results, by selected industry groups, are shown in Table 2.1 Three main conclusions can be drawn from this table.

First, there is a wide variation among industries in the importance of personal selling and sales management. Importance varies from a low of 10.7 (points out of 100) in the food, liquor, and tobacco industry to a high of 32.9 in the industrial chemicals industry.

Second, in spite of these wide variations, there is a strong indication that industrial goods manufacturers generally place more importance on personal selling and sales management than do consumer goods manufacturers. For instance, if we compare the average importance score from the four industrial groups with the average score from the five consumer groups, the industrial goods average is nearly 10 points higher (27.3 for industrial goods versus 17.9 for consumer goods manufacturers).

Third, when we compare the scores assigned to personal selling and sales management with scores assigned to other marketing activities, we find that in six of the nine industry categories sales management and personal selling is rated more important than any other individual activity listed. Of course, if the other marketing activities were labeled differently or grouped in some manner, these results might change. But it certainly seems apparent that personal selling and sales management is a major marketing activity in most manufacturing firms, with a significant role to play in overall marketing success.

What about the future? A study was carried out among 150 executives of large U.S. corporations, including company presidents, executive vice-presidents, corporate planning vice-presidents, and marketing vice-presidents. They were asked how individual elements of marketing will change in importance in the next decade. Among the conclusions were that sales management and personal selling will increase in importance, and increase more than will advertising in print or broadcast media, branding and packaging, and other special promotional activities such as trade shows, promotional warranties, and product displays.[11] These expectations of experienced top executives indicate a continuing and even growing importance for the role of personal selling in the future.

TABLE 2.1
Importance of Specific Marketing Activities Among Selected Types of Manufacturers

	INDUSTRIAL GOODS MANUFACTURERS					CONSUMER GOODS MANUFACTURERS				
Marketing Activity	Aerospace and Defense (n = 29)	Capital Goods (n = 127)	Industrial Chemicals (n = 41)	Fabricated Parts and Materials (n = 140)		Consumer Chemicals (n = 13)	Consumer Durables (n = 44)	Petroleum Products (n = 18)	Food, Liquor & Tobacco (n = 30)	Other Non-durables (n = 18)
Sales management and personal selling	19.6	25.3	32.9	31.5		23.4	16.7	22.0	10.7	16.7
Advertising	3.0	6.0	4.5	5.8		14.7	10.2	12.2	19.8	16.5
Other marketing communications	3.7	7.4	4.9	8.2		7.0	9.5	11.9	14.1	11.8
Selection and development of distribution channels	0.5	5.7	3.3	5.4		6.4	12.5	9.3	5.4	10.9
Physical distribution	0.8	4.8	7.8	5.9		5.5	6.5	8.8	9.2	6.9
Product service	16.3	13.4	9.7	10.7		6.4	6.1	4.8	3.4	4.7
Technical R&D and market research	24.6	10.2	9.1	8.2		19.8	13.3	9.2	18.3	15.0
Other product efforts	9.0	7.3	8.1	6.1		3.2	5.2	1.4	4.1	3.1
Pricing	21.6	19.1	19.6	18.3		13.6	19.3	20.6	14.9	14.4
Other marketing activities	1.0	0.8	0.0	0.0		0.0	0.6	0.0	0.0	0.0
Total marketing strategy	100.0	100.0	100.0	100.0		100.0	100.0	100.0	100.0	100.0

Note: Respondents were asked to rate the relative importance of each marketing activity, using a scale of 100 points in total.

Source: Jon G. Udell, *Successful Marketing Strategies in American Industry* (Madison: MIMIR Publishers, Inc., 1972), pp. 82 and 101.

Legal and Ethical Environment

Managers at all levels realize that meeting ethical and legal standards are goals that interrelate with many business decisions. Is a particular action legal? Is it ethical? These questions concern sales managers and salespeople as professionals no matter to what industry or business firm they belong. Professional goals must play at least an equal role with individual company goals in guiding business practices. Over time, an ethical and legal view of correct decision making will be crucial if the organization is to remain viable in the marketplace.[12]

Legal and ethical factors are complex topics, however, and are subject to widely varying opinion and interpretation. We can do no more than introduce the major legal and ethical issues here, since coverage of all the nuances and details far exceeds the scope of this book.

Legal Considerations. All sales activities are subject to legal regulations occurring at the federal, state, and local levels. For instance, federal regulations restricting price discrimination are found in the Robinson-Patman Act of 1936, which is an amendment to the Clayton Antitrust Act of 1914.[13] Perhaps even more important to sales managers is the Federal Trade Commission (FTC) Act of 1914 and its subsequent amendments, the Wheeler-Lea Act of 1938, and the FTC Improvement Act of 1975.[14] Section 5 of the FTC Act declares that "Unfair methods of competition in commerce, and unfair or deceptive acts or practices in commerce, are hereby declared unlawful." Under this law, firms selling in interstate commerce will be investigated by the Federal Trade Commission if their sales representatives make false or misleading statements about a product or a competitor, or offer false buying advantages or confusing and misleading information. Many other federal agencies likewise regulate products and services in specific industries—for example, the Federal Communications Commission, Federal Maritime Commission, Federal Power Commission, and the Securities and Exchange Commission.

At the state level, a major body of legislation adopted in similar form by all states except Louisiana is the Uniform Commercial Code. Article 2 of the Code is specifically concerned with sales transactions such as sales contracts, the passing of title, shipping terms, warranties, and product liability. Of particular interest to sales personnel is the distinction between statements which are considered sales talk or "puffing" when made to prospects versus statements which become warranties. One expert on this subject summed it up as follows:

> The line between warranty and puffing is one that evades specific rules. The problem is that of determining the basis of the bargain—the justifiable expectations of the buyer—and words that are warranties in one situation can be sales talk in another, depending on their impact on the resulting bargain.[15]

The test of whether a salesperson's statements become a warranty is whether those statements induce the buyer to purchase the goods. In other words, if the buyer relies on the statements as "part of the basis of the bargain" (to use the words of the Code), such statements are construed as a warranty rather than just as sales talk or "puffing." To illustrate, a salesman promised a married couple that if they bought a particular new car then on the showroom floor they could have air conditioning installed at a later date. Rather than wait for a factory-installed air conditioned model to be delivered later, the prospects bought the car that was there. A custom air conditioning unit was later installed and didn't work. In fact, it literally fell out of the car. Then the couple learned that the car manufacturer had not installed air conditioning in this particular model for the past eight years and had recommended against custom installation as well. The couple filed suit claiming misrepresentation by the salesman, and the judge agreed, stating, "They obviously relied upon the salesman's statements, and it is clear they had a right to."[16]

Local ordinances concerning selling vary considerably, but perhaps the oldest and best known is the "Green River" type, the first of which was passed in Green River, Wyoming, in 1933. These ordinances generally prohibit salespersons from selling door-to-door unless they obtain a local license or only at the invitation of the householder. "Cooling-off" laws also have been enacted by many communities as well as by state and federal jurisdictions. These regulations allow for a cooling-off period of usually three days during which time the buyer of goods or services from a door-to-door salesperson may change his or her mind, cancel the contract, and receive a full refund of any money paid.[17] Other state and local laws exist concerning unfair sales practices and consumer protection, and a salesperson should become fully aware of all such legislation in effect in his territory by contacting local Chambers of Commerce and Better Business Bureaus.

Other legal issues involve matters internal to the sales organization such as contracts between salesperson and employer, discrimination in hiring and firing, and unfair performance appraisals and compensation schemes. Legal factors have an increasing impact on sales management decisions in such matters, and in the case of hiring in particular have become prominent in influencing recruiting and selection practices. In Chapter 11 we will explore the legal factors affecting hiring in more detail.

Ethical Issues. Ethics relates to personal standards of morality as distinguished from what is legally right and wrong. In the selling profession, as in all professional fields, ethics concerns professionally accepted behavior:

> Professional ethics has to do with morality and refers to the social effects of private action. Together, these rules govern the behavior of members of a profession. Ideally, such rules bind all members of a professional group together—certainly, without such rules no organization could make a claim to the adjective "professional."[18]

In the absence of an agreed-upon definitive code of ethics for salespeople and sales managers, the interpretation of exactly what is professionally accepted behavior is cloudy at best. We have already noted that even under the law a certain amount of "puffing" is considered an acceptable characteristic of the selling process, even though the statements by the salesperson may not be entirely factual or supportable with evidence.

Perhaps we can generalize by saying that an ethical issue is involved when a salesperson or manager suspects that his words or actions might lead another party to a conclusion or action which would have consequences the other party had not anticipated. For instance, a salesperson and prospect talk over the prospect's problem, and then the salesperson praises his or her product's performance though not relating it specifically to the prospect's problem because he or she is not sure of its effectiveness for the prospect's problem. If this leads the prospect to infer that the product will solve the problem, the prospect may buy the product and be subsequently disappointed (and probably angry). Another example would occur when a salesperson obtains some confidential information from a customer so that the salesperson can understand the customer's needs better, and the salesperson subsequently divulges that information to the customer's main competitor in the hopes of gaining favor as well as orders. Sales managers face corresponding ethical issues when they set quotas, develop compensation plans, determine promotions, and make territory assignments.

While specific guidance is difficult, a general rule regarding ethical issues is the "golden rule"—put yourself in the other person's position and honestly determine if this is what you would accept as proper in that position. One thing is certain. If a particular practice deemed unethical by one or more interest groups is continued over time, some legislative solution will probably be attempted. This is what has happened in the cases of "truth-in-packaging" and "truth-in-lending" legislation.

Goals as the Basis for Decision-Making

To a manager or salesperson, the day-to-day function of goals can be easily stated. Goals provide the basis for decision making. How many salespeople should the manager recruit and hire next year? Should the company spend more money on sales training this year or instead use the money for additional bonuses for high performers? Should the sales force make more calls on fewer customers or call on more customers fewer times? These and hundreds of other decisions must be made by members of the sales organization. In each case, the alternative action to be selected should be the one which will best contribute to reaching the organization's goals, bearing in mind legal and ethical factors.

Some firms are becoming more conscious of the function of goals as decision criteria. A recent study noted that "Management's primary objective is to achieve greater compatibility between corporate profit goals and the decisions of salesmen as they cover their assigned territories."[19] If you were the salesperson for one of these firms, your decisions on which products or customers to call on, what products to push, and whom to take to lunch would all be guided by the profit potential of each possible alternative. Other firms which concentrate on achieving greater market share or other types of goals would focus their sales decisions in those directions.

Throughout the remainder of this book we will look at many alternative techniques and policies that can be used in all areas of sales management, such as quota setting, hiring, and training. These techniques and policies become a sales manager's cafeteria of choices. But the specific choice to be made in a given situation must be based on how effectively it contributes to goal attainment. Figure 2.4 shows an example of how a sales manager might analyze four alternative actions he could take concerning sales force size and sales territory assignments. The probable consequences of each action are shown in terms of two major company goals. If you were the sales manager, which alternatives would you choose?

Problems with Goals

There is little doubt that careful development of goals helps a firm toward success. But goals are not a panacea. In fact, managers must recognize and deal with some difficult problems inherent in the use of goals. Three such problems involve conflicts, attainability, and obsolescence.

Conflicts Among Goals. Numerous conflicts can arise concerning goals so that the achievement of one specific objective may not be consistent with the achievement

FIGURE 2.4

Four Alternative Actions Regarding Sales Force Size and Territory Assignments, and How Well Each Will Meet Two Major Company Goals: An Example

Alternative Actions	How well each action will meet company goals of:	
	Increasing Market Share	Maintaining Profit Contribution as a Percent of Sales Volume
Hire more salespeople and add new territories.	May not increase market share since total size of market is now enlarged into areas where competition is established.	Start-up costs of new salespeople and territories may reduce profit as percent of sales.
Hire more salespeople and redivide already existing territories.	May increase sales volume, and if increase is more than that of competitors, will increase market share.	Start-up costs of new salespeople will reduce profits as percent of sales, but more intensive development of smaller territories by experienced salespeople may provide economies of scale leading to offsetting increased profit as percent of sales.
Keep same sales force size, but increase size of territories for each salesperson.	May reduce market share since total market is now enlarged into areas where competition is established; less coverage of present customers makes some accounts more vulnerable to competition.	Start-up costs in new territory sections will reduce profit as percent of sales; opportunities for "cream-skimming" in new territory sections may produce higher profits as percent of sales.
Keep same sales force size and same territory size (i.e., status quo).	Will require weakening in competitors' positions; may be helped with additional special incentives for sales force.	Profit contribution may remain stable unless competition increases; profit may decline slightly if special incentives are given to sales force.

of another. For example, it might be difficult for the sales manager to secure a large increase in sales volume without permitting a considerable increase in cost. In that case, sales volume increase and cost reduction would be difficult to achieve simultaneously. Since it is not always possible to avoid conflicts, management must try to cope with them. One way is to rank objectives into a hierarchy of importance and then use this ranking for resolving conflicts. Another is to assign weights showing the relative importance of each objective. But even ranking or weighting are difficult, since management must come to grips with the conflicts in the process.

A different conflict occurs when company goals conflict with an executive's (or salesperson's) personal goals. A district manager may strongly dislike paperwork, yet be required to file reports or written plans concerning his operation. Such conflicts often lower the manager's motivation to accomplish company goals or even to attempt to recognize and understand them. Sometimes this problem can be met, at least partially, by having individuals participate in setting goals which will affect them directly.[20]

Attainability of Goals. Goals cannot be effective unless they are attainable. A goal which is not feasible to attain can produce detrimental consequences to the firm. Consider what an unreachable sales forecast and impossible quotas can do to sales force morale as well as to cash flow. Yet the inherent attainability of a goal is difficult to establish. Management generally evaluates goals by comparing them with accomplishment. But if accomplishment falls short, management faces the difficult task of determining whether this resulted from improper goals or from insufficient effort to reach them. Even when specific objectives are reached, they may have been set too low to exploit the firm's resources fully.

Sales management personnel are in a most opportune position to contribute to the evaluation of goals. Since many company goals are related directly or indirectly to sales volume, the chief sales executive should play an important role in communicating to top management any unexpected events or gradually changing trends which might affect sales volume and competitive standing. The value of sales managers in goal evaluation has not always been acknowledged by top management, but this should become accepted more widely as firms direct increasing recognition to the role of effective marketing and selling in attaining competitive success.

Obsolescence of Goals. A characteristic of most goals is that they become obsolete. A short-range goal loses its usefulness when it is fully attained, when its underlying conditions change, or when its basic assumptions become clearly incorrect. Under the latter two circumstances, long-range goals also lose pertinence over time and should be updated.

Because goals become obsolete, some managers claim that setting goals in the first place is not worth the effort. A counterargument is that an initially well-defined framework of goals enables all management levels to make subsequent changes in a coordinated manner. Further, the process of setting goals in the first place encourages management to consider the future and what changes might occur. This, in turn, should make the firm better prepared for the inevitable changes that will take place.

CONCLUSION

Sales management goals must be devised to reinforce goals at higher levels of the firm, and must reflect legal and ethical considerations as well. The sales manager must understand overall company goals as well as marketing goals to place the purpose and objectives of the selling function in proper perspective. Selling goals can then be established at the district, territory, and even individual customer levels. The more explicit and refined these goals are, the more effectively they will guide sales managers and sales force members in making decisions among alternative actions.

QUESTIONS FOR REVIEW AND DISCUSSION

1. The top management of a firm in a highly competitive industry has decided that next year's goals should include an increase in market share and an increase in net profits. What problems might this present to a sales manager? What if many of this firm's competitors also decide on similar goals?

2. If you were hired as sales manager in an equipment manufacturing firm, what could you do to learn specifically what goals have been set by higher management?

3. In some firms, the overriding goal is to "do better than last year." Is this an effective goal?

4. What is the difference between goals and strategies?
5. "Don't make your goals too clear, and then you won't have to worry if you don't reach them." What do you think about this advice?
6. Select any five of the sales management goals listed in Figure 2.3 for Univis, and describe what specific marketing and top management goals might give rise to them.
7. Why does the role of personal selling vary from one firm to the next? Should the sales manager push for making selling more important in the firm's marketing mix?
8. What's the difference between legal and ethical standards for judging selling practices? Can you think of some practices that might be legal but not ethical? Ethical but not legal?
9. Review the alternative actions given in Figure 2.4. If you were the sales manager, which action would you decide to take in order to best meet the two goals listed?
10. "It's a sign of good planning when we just barely reach the goals we set." Do you agree? Why?

NOTES

1. See for example, Charles L. Hughes, *Goal Setting* (New York: American Management Association, Inc., 1965).
2. E. T. Grether, *Marketing and Public Policy* (Englewood Cliffs, N.J.: Prentice-Hall, 1966), pp. 1–2.
3. See Mark Massel, *Competition and Monopoly* (New York: Doubleday, Anchor Books, 1964), pp. 16–43.
4. William P. Hall, "Improving Sales Force Productivity," *Business Horizons,* vol. 18 (August 1975), p. 40.
5. These eight areas were originally proposed in Peter F. Drucker, *The Practice of Management* (New York: Harper & Row, 1954), p. 63. Their use by particular firms is noted in Ernest C. Miller, *Objectives and Standards: An Approach to Planning and Control,* Research Study No. 74 (New York: American Management Association, Inc., 1966), pp. 30–36.
6. Roger M. Pegram, *Selling and Servicing the National Account,* Report No. 557 (New York: The Conference Board, Inc., 1972), p. 76.
7. This example is based on a detailed case study in Robert F. Vizza and Thomas E. Chambers, *Time and Territorial Management for the Salesman* (New York: Sales Executives Club of New York, Inc., 1971), pp. 29–40.
8. For further discussion, see Donald W. Jackson, Jr. and Ramon J. Aldag, "Managing the Sales Force by Objectives," *MSU Business Topics,* vol. 22 (Spring 1974), pp. 53–59.
9. William J. McBurney, Jr., *Goal Setting and Planning at the District Sales Level,* Research Study No. 61 (New York: American Management Association, Inc., 1963).
10. Jon G. Udell, *Successful Marketing Strategies in American Industry* (Madison: MIMIR Publishers, Inc., 1972), pp. 41–42.
11. Robert F. Lusch, et al., "The Future of Marketing Strategy," *Business Horizons,* vol. 19 (December 1976), pp. 65–74.
12. Thomas R. Wotruba, "Professional Responsibility in Marketing," *Business Perspectives,* vol. 8 (Spring 1972), pp. 4–7.
13. For a recent review of this regulation and current interpretation, see G. David Hughes, "Antitrust Caveats For the Marketing Planner," *Harvard Business Review,* vol. 56 (March–April 1978), pp. 40–42 ff.

14. A review and implications of this legislation for marketing and sales managers is found in Gerald G. Udell and Philip J. Fischer, "The FTC Improvement Act," *Journal of Marketing,* vol. 41 (April 1977), pp. 81–86.

15. Robert J. Nordstrom, *Handbook of the Law of Sales* (St. Paul: West, 1970), p. 218. Another succinct discussion is found in Bradford Stone, *Uniform Commercial Code in a Nutshell* (St. Paul: West, 1975).

16. "Salesman George Wingfield's Day in Court," *Sales Management,* January 22, 1973, p. 3.

17. A summary of state laws is found in "Cooling It, State by State," *Sales Management,* October 2, 1972, p. 16, and October 16, 1972, p. 32.

18. Albert Haring, "Ethics in Selling," *Ball State Business Review,* vol. 3 (March 1973), p. 3.

19. Charles W. Smith, "Gearing Salesmen's Efforts to Corporate Profit Objectives," *Harvard Business Review,* vol. 53 (July–August 1975), p. 12.

20. Jackson and Aldag, "Managing the Sales Force by Objectives," pp. 53–59.

3 MARKET AND SALES POTENTIALS

Before the sales manager can effectively formulate sales volume, profit, and other goals, he must learn how large a market exists for his company's products or services. If the size of the potential market is unknown, there is no way to determine whether a given sales volume goal is feasible or how difficult it might be to reach it. The ease or difficulty of obtaining a given amount of sales volume affects the amount and type of sales force effort needed and this will subsequently be reflected in selling expenses and profit. Ultimately, the development of all sales management goals in a firm depends on the size and nature of its potential market.

Nearly every firm's potential market is constantly changing and largely uncontrollable by management. Markets are influenced by shifts in the size and composition of the population, changes in levels and distribution of income, and the evolution of new needs and wants within customer groups. If a firm's plans and strategies are to be most effective, they must be based on an accurate identification and measurement of the potential market.[1] Because the market is changing, measurements at regular intervals are necessary, especially as an aid in establishing any pattern or trend likely to develop in the future.

TERMS AND CONCEPTS

A measure or estimate of the size of a potential market is termed a *market potential*. Many different definitions can be found, indicating that no commonly accepted meaning has been attached to this concept.[2] The main point of variation centers on exactly what constitutes a "potential" market for a product. Does it include only sales which are eventually consummated in a particular time period? If so, a market potential measure is a type of forecast. Or does it also include possible sales to prospects who could use the product, but do not buy it within the specified period? In this case a potential market includes prospects who are never approached, prospects who are approached but do not buy, and prospects who are approached but buy less of the product than they could reasonably use. Clearly, a definition of market potential is needed.

Furthermore, *market potential* is often confused with other terms and concepts such as *sales potential, market forecast,* and *sales forecast.* Because these concepts are closely related, it is helpful to define all of them at this point. Comparisons among the definitions should then help clarify their meanings.

A *sales forecast* is an estimate of dollar or unit sales of a product or product line which an individual firm expects in a specified period of time under a given marketing plan.

A *market forecast* is an estimate of dollar or unit sales of a product or product line which all firms together expect in a specified period of time under all the firms' respective marketing plans.

Sales potential is the maximum dollar or unit sales of a product or product line available to an individual firm within a specified period of time.

Market potential is the maximum dollar or unit sales of a product or product line available to all firms within a specified period of time.

There are two main distinctions among these terms as indicated by the column and row headings in Figure 3.1. The first is the distinction between sales and market. The term *sales* indicates that the measure relates to an individual firm, such as a firm's "sales potential" or a firm's "sales forecast." The term *market* indicates that the measures relates to the entire industry of all firms which offer the product or product line, such as an industry's "market forecast" or an industry's "market potential." In economists' terms, the word *sales* identifies a *micro*measure and the word *market* identifies a *macro*measure.

The second distinction is between a forecast and a potential. The term *forecast* refers to expected sales of a product under a given marketing plan. The term *potential* refers to total sales of a product which could be obtained if all possible customers and all possible uses were fully accommodated. Thus, a forecast indicates sales expectations and a potential indicates sales opportunities. If a product's potential is viewed as the summation of all possible customers' propensities to buy, the forecast for that product represents the extent to which a firm or industry seeks out this propensity to buy. A forecast should never exceed a potential, and they should rarely be equal because firms seldom have marketing plans which reach all possible customers. Some customers may be unprofitable to serve, while others are not reached because of imperfections in promotion, distribution, and other elements of the marketing plan.

A lengthier but enlightening definition of market potential has been proposed by a General Electric executive.[3] He divides market potential into two categories:

FIGURE 3.1

Distinctions Among Sales and Market Potentials and Forecasts

	Expectations	Opportunities
Firm	Sales forecast	Sales potential
Industry	Market forecast	Market potential

(1) developed, which includes total industry sales of the product in the upcoming time period, and (2) undeveloped, which includes additional sales obtainable by varying marketing plans and strategies. These categories are also known as prospected versus unprospected, and qualified versus unqualified potential.

This distinction is useful in establishing the boundary of a potential market. For example, suppose a low-income segment of the population desires a high-priced product such as a new Cadillac automobile. If there were no marketing plan conceivable which would allow these persons to buy a Cadillac, this segment would not be considered a part of the car's market potential.

Why Use Market Potential Measures: An Illustration

Measuring the size of a potential market is not a simple task. For that reason, some managers hesitate to get involved with this issue, and sometimes justify their hesitation by questioning the practical significance of the end result. A brief example should help to convince such managers of the use of market potential measurement.

Suppose you are a district sales manager and wish to compare the performance of two salespeople in your district for purposes of year-end evaluation and possible salary adjustment. You examine their sales volume over the past two years and find the following:

	SALES THIS YEAR	SALES LAST YEAR
Benson	$200,000	$180,000
Rogers	$250,000	$220,000

It seems apparent that Rogers is doing the better job, since his sales volume is higher and his dollar increase over last year is greater when compared with Benson. But is this a fair assessment of these two salespeople in their respective territories? Suppose we compare their actual sales with the potential sales available in each of their territories:

	SALES THIS YEAR	SALES POTENTIAL IN SALESPERSON'S TERRITORY
Benson	$200,000	$250,000
Rogers	$250,000	$500,000

It now seems apparent that Benson's performance is at least as good as Rogers' performance, because Benson had a much smaller potential to work with. Benson has captured 80 percent of his potential market, whereas Rogers has obtained only 50 percent of the potential in his territory. Additional sales volume would be increasingly more difficult for Benson to gain than for Rogers, since Benson has a much smaller amount of untapped potential remaining.

The measure of sales potential in this illustration serves as a standard against which to compare actual sales results. It will assist the manager in determining if more sales effort is needed or will be productive in a particular market, and will also help in setting reasonable quotas and in restructuring territories to make them more equal. Without some measure of a market's potential, it also is very difficult to get an adequate assessment of future opportunities to attain sales volume and related goals.

MEASUREMENT OF MARKET POTENTIAL

Market potential can seldom be measured directly from any single source of existing information. The analyst must first identify which characteristics in the market would cause demand to exist for a particular product. These characteristics, such as a particular age group, occupation, or sex, are called determinants of potential demand. Once identified, these determinants indicate what data are needed for calculating market potential measures. Including this first step, the measurement procedure consists of the following:

1. Identify determinants of potential demand.
2. Decide what forms of market potential measures are necessary.
3. Locate sources of data.
4. Calculate the market potential measure(s).

Determinants of Potential Demand. Determinants of potential demand must be identified specifically for each product. Two approaches are used: the judgmental and the empirical.

In the *judgmental* approach, company officials identify characteristics of the market which, based on their experience, judgment, and logic, should correlate with the sales level of their product. Questions such as the following can assist the judgment process: (1) Who or what is the consuming unit of this type of product? (2) What is the amount and type of consumption behavior regarding this product? (3) How desirable is this particular product in the eyes of the market as compared with other ways of satisfying the same needs or wants? The first question identifies the typical customer who has the needs and wants this product can fulfill. The second question concerns the ability to buy and the frequency of purchase. Question three refers to the probability of buying the particular product relative to satisfying the needs or wants in some other way, such as buying a product deemed more desirable in the customer's eyes.

A machine tool company used the judgmental approach in identifying demand determinants for grinding machines. After considering many factors, they agreed on the following:

1. Number and size of metalworking plants using internal grinding machines.
2. Need for new original equipment in industries using grinding machines.
3. Need for replacement equipment in these industries.
4. Funds available in these industries for new equipment.[4]

The *empirical* approach involves identifying relevant demand determinants by means of a statistical analysis or research procedures. For example, a manufacturer of auto seat covers reviewed three hundred factors, ranging from population size to bank deposits and apparel sales per family.[5] A statistical analysis through multiple regression equations pointed out which factors were most closely associated with demand for his company's products. The author has investigated market potential in the cable television industry for a number of years and has discovered through regression analysis how the following demographic variables are related to subsequent demand for cable television:

Demographic variables	Relationship to demand for cable television
Household income	Not significantly related
Family size	Positively related
Single vs. multiple family residence	Not significantly related
Age of head of household	Negatively related
Length of time living in area	Negatively related

The market potential for cable television will be greater in areas of larger families, younger household heads, and higher mobility, but the potential will not be significantly affected by level of income or type of residence.

Combinations of judgment and empirical study can also be employed. Salespersons, for example, can be asked to report to management their ideas of what factors relate to potential demand for their products. A manufacturer of wire rope obtained such information through its sales force, which reported that the amount of wire rope needed was directly related to the number of pieces of construction equipment in use.[6]

Forms of Market Potential Measures. Market potential measures can be developed in two forms. One is a total expressed in dollars or units. The second is a series of relative measures or percentages, each of which indicates what portion of the total market potential falls within a given segment of the total market. Table 3.1 illustrates these two forms and their combination. This firm's market is divided into four territories, and the relative potential measures indicate what percentage of total market potential exists in each territory. When the two forms are combined, the total units, or dollars, of potential in each territory can be determined.

Relative measures may relate to types of market segments other than geographic areas. Industrial marketers, for instance, often compute relative potentials by customer groups, channels of distribution, or types of product application.

TABLE 3.1

An Illustration of Two Forms of Market Potential Measures and Their Combination for a National Manufacturing Firm

Firm's Market Area	FORM OF MARKET POTENTIAL MEASURE		
	Total Measure	Relative Measure	Combination of Measures
Total	6,000,000 units	100%	6,000,000 units
North Central States		26%	1,560,000 units
East Coast States		34	2,040,000
South Central States		18	1,080,000
West Coast States		22	1,320,000

The calculation of each form requires a different type of data. The total measure is based on data in totals only, while the relative measure necessitates a series of data with each component in the series relating to each market segment. Therefore, if the machine tool manufacturer were interested in relative market potentials by state, a corresponding series of 50 figures would be necessary for each demand determinant. In this case, the total number and size of metalworking plants using internal grinding machines is a determinant of *total* potential demand, but *relative* potentials will require that the number and size of these plants be obtained by state, so that each state as a percent of the total can be determined.

Whether management needs both forms of the market potential measure depends on how the information is to be used. Each form is useful for various planning calculations which are considered later in this chapter. Relative measures probably are used more often, especially with new products or in other cases when direct factors concerning the total market are difficult to identify and measure.

Sources of Data. The next step is to locate sources of data for each demand determinant. Two categories of data can be considered: one is secondary data, which includes data collected by anyone inside or outside the firm for a purpose other than that at hand; the other is primary data, data gathered specifically for the problem, in this case, market potential measurement.

Secondary Data. In consumer goods firms, research studies may have been carried out on present customers and their characteristics such as income, age, and other demographic variables. For industrial goods firms, sales records are an excellent source of information because they provide customers' names and addresses, which can be compiled into industrial groups and locations. In addition, research reports on products may shed some light on the desirability determinant of potential demand.

Outside sources of secondary data are so numerous that it is virtually impossible to keep abreast.[7] Trade associations often publish information on sales of their industry by geographic area and carry out many other special market studies. Government agencies publish an immense amount of valuable data. Because of the enormous scope of federal government statistics, the *American Statistics Index* is published annually by the Congressional Information Service and contains a comprehensive index of statistical data available from all federal government agencies. Syndicated services are also available from research companies such as the A. C. Nielsen Co. These companies collect data regularly and sell it on a subscription basis. Additional published sources of data can be found in periodicals, monographs, books, and newspapers. Many of these are indexed in the Business Periodicals Index or in other indexes available in major libraries.[8]

For consumer goods firms, one source in particular is quite popular—the "Survey of Buying Power" published annually by *Sales & Marketing Management* magazine. This source contains population, income, and retail sales data on states, counties, and Standard Metropolitan Statistical Areas (SMSAs), and most cities in the U.S. and Canada. Table 3.2 illustrates the scope of data and the geographic levels on which it is available. Studies comparing data from the "Survey of Buying Power" with the U.S. Census of Population and other Census Bureau data show a close match, indicating that the "Survey of Buying Power" is a reliable and current source of market data.[9]

TABLE 3.2
Example of Data Available from the Survey of Buying Power

GEOGRAPHIC LEVEL	TOTAL POPULATION (THOUSANDS)	% OF U.S.	MEDIAN AGE OF POPULATION	Population by Age Groups (thousands)					HOUSEHOLDS (THOUSANDS)	% OF U.S.
				0–17 YEARS	18–24 YEARS	25–34 YEARS	35–49 YEARS	50 & over YEARS		
Total U.S.	219,768.5	100.0000	30.1	63,207.2	28,965.3	34,427.9	36,039.9	57,128.2	76,904.7	100.0000
California	22,482.0	10.2298	30.2	6,231.4	3,064.4	3,772.5	3,844.2	5,569.5	8,451.5	10.9896
San Diego County	1,783.0	.8113	28.0		17.5	15.7	15.9	23.1	667.0	
Oceanside	64.8	.0295	27.4		16.0	14.2	15.3	23.9	26.4	

	TOTAL EFFECTIVE BUYING INCOME ($000)	% OF U.S.	Effective Buying Income			Households by Effective Buying Income Group (thousands)				
			PER CAPITA	AVERAGE HOUSEHOLD	MEDIAN HOUSEHOLD	UNDER $8,000	$8,000–$9,999	$10,000–$14,999	$15,000–$24,999	$25,000 AND OVER
Total U.S.	1,439,815,449	100.0000	$6,552	$18,722	$16,231	18,037.5	4,604.8	12,555.9	23,641.1	18,065.4
California	166,953,330	11.5955	7,426	19,754	17,186	1,832.0	481.1	1,312.3	2,572.0	2,254.1
San Diego County	12,241,144				15,341			(percents)		
Oceanside	411,152				13,516		6.9	18.0	31.1	20.1
							8.5	19.9	29.0	15.3

	TOTAL RETAIL SALES ($000)	% OF U.S.	PER HOUSEHOLD RETAIL SALES	Retail sales by store group ($ thousands)						BUYING POWER INDEX
				FOOD	EATING & DRINKING PLACES	GENERAL MERCHANDISE	FURNITURE, HOME FURNISHINGS, APPLIANCES	AUTOMOTIVE	DRUG	
Total U.S.	817,461,457	100.0000	$10,630	177,607,447	71,602,628	108,933,704	38,633,807	167,913,413	25,415,251	100.0000
California	91,615,318	11.2073	10,840	19,698,761	9,180,485	12,509,103	4,622,279	16,805,411	3,461,156	11.2058
San Diego County	7,243,673			1,430,850	685,925	1,903,237	377,743	1,394,429	263,757	.8532
Oceanside	236,380			33,043	24,092	31,112	10,559	78,188	3,627	.0289

Source: Data for 12/31/78 from 1979 *Survey of Buying Power, Sales & Marketing,* July 23, 1979. Reprinted by permission from *Sales & Marketing Management* magazine. Copyright 1979.

A useful feature of the "Survey of Buying Power" is the Buying Power Index. This Index is used as a measure of relative potential for many consumer goods which are sold to a wide cross-section of the population, such as popular food and drug store items. It is comprised of three elements: population (weighted 2); effective buying income (essentially the same as disposable income, weighted 5); and retail sales (weighted 3). A weighted average produces the index number for any area, as in this example for the state of California:

		Weight		
Percent of population in California =	10.2298 ×	2	=	20.4596
Percent of effective buying income in California =	11.5955 ×	5	=	57.9775
Percent of retail sales in California =	11.2073 ×	3	=	33.6219
Sum of weights and weighted total =		10		112.0590
Weighted average = 112.0590/10 =				11.2059

About 11.2 percent of the potential demand for these popular consumer goods would be found in California. Products which appeal to more limited market segments will require modification in the makeup of the index to produce a proper set of relative market potential measures.[10]

For firms selling to industrial markets, a companion "Survey of Industrial Purchasing Power" is also published annually by *Sales & Marketing Management* magazine. It includes the number of manufacturing plants, by industry, in the total U.S. as well as in each state and county, and reports an estimate of total shipments of each industrial group by county. From this data, relative measures of industrial market potential can readily be calculated.

In order to facilitate locating, identifying, and comparing data on industrial markets, the federal government has devised a numerical classification system called the Standard Industrial Classification (SIC). All manufacturing and nonmanufacturing establishments which produce a similar product or perform a similar operation are grouped together under the same SIC code number.[11] The "Survey of Industrial Purchasing Power," all government census publications, and most trade and industry periodicals present data in SIC categories.[12]

Primary Data. When accurate and up-to-date secondary data are not available for the demand determinants, and management does not wish to rely on intuition or guesswork alone, primary data must be gathered. The detailed process of obtaining original market data cannot be described within the scope of this book, and we can note briefly some major ways that primary data are acquired for market potential measures.

One approach is a market survey. For example, one firm designed a questionnaire which was mailed to several thousands plants in almost every manufacturing industry. Respondents were asked whether their plant used the product type in question and, if so, how it was used and in what finished products it was incorporated as a component. Additional questions pertained to the approximate amount purchased each year and whether the respondent had any complaints or other comments about the product. Responses to this questionnaire yielded a sample indicating the types and numbers of customers for the product, their purchasing power, and the product's desirability. When this sample was projected to the entire population of industrial buyers, an estimate of market potential resulted.[13]

A second procedure utilizes a test market, which is especially applicable for new products. Parker Pen, for example, spent 15 months testing Systemark, their new writing instrument, prior to full-scale introduction. In a less successful attempt, Best Foods decided to scrap their idea of mayonnaise packaged in a metal tube after a disappointing market test.[14]

Some firms gather data through their sales force. For example, as one spokesman stated,

> We in U.S. Steel have a program designed to estimate, consumer by consumer and product by product, the size of the markets in which we sell. For the basic information we turn to the man who we believe is best qualified to supply it—the salesman. . . . We are only asking the salesman to obtain the best figures that his customer relations, experience, and good commercial judgment make possible. For our purposes these figures have proven quite accurate.[15]

Each salesperson is given records of his previous year's estimate as well as shipments by product to each of his customers. These, coupled with his experience and judgment, give rise to estimates from each salesperson which are consolidated into a total market potential measure. A similar approach is used by the Air Reduction Company, a manufacturer of equipment and gases used in industrial welding and cutting. Management provides suggestions to its salespeople for estimating potential sales, and these suggestions appear in Figure 3.2.

Measuring Market Potential. Once the necessary data, opinions, and other information are collected, market potential measures can be determined. Sometimes it is just a matter of adding up the survey results or projecting the test market findings to the total market area. Other times, additional work is needed to arrive at the total or relative measures. Let us consider the total measure first.

Suppose we wish to determine the total market potential for condominium housing in a particular community.[16] Relevant determinants of demand are households with demographic characteristics most likely related to condominium living (e.g., small families, moderate income, etc.), and the probability that these households would buy a condominium (because of their purchasing power and the product's desirability). Census data, past buying behavior, survey results, and managerial judgment all provide data on these determinants. If the number of households in the relevant demographic groups is 5,870 in the community, and the probability of buying is determined to be .78, then the market potential equals 5,870 times .78, or 4,579 units.

Relative potentials are often based on an index approach, which can be illustrated as follows. Suppose we wish to know what the relative potential demand for microwave ovens is among the seven states in the west north central census region. Table 3.3 illustrates this approach. Demand determinants were identified by judgment in this case. Households is used because this is the basic buying unit for the product. Persons in age group 25–34 are chosen because management believes this is the age group most likely to try new product innovations. Income of $15,000 and over is used because the product is relatively expensive. Sales of furniture, home furnishings, and appliance stores are chosen to indicate where sales of similar

FIGURE 3.2

Suggestions to Salesmen in the Air Reduction Company for Estimating Market Potential

SUGGESTIONS TO SALESMEN FOR ESTIMATING ACCOUNT POTENTIAL

"In many cases it will be possible to obtain the potential purchases of a customer directly from a purchasing agent, buyer or other responsible individual within the account. At times, customer personnel might not be able to give you their anticipated total purchases of the products that you market for 1963, but they might very well be able and willing to give you the amount they have purchased in 1962. With this information, you should be able to come up with a good figure for 1963.

"Potential may also be arrived at through observations made of the type of equipment at the customer's location that either consumes the products we make or could possibly be replaced by products we make.

"It may be possible to relate the number of personnel involved in welding and cutting production or maintenance processes that consume our products to accounts with similar operations where the potential is known.

"Relationships can also be made between the type of the industry and the total number of employees working at an account which closely resembles or corresponds to a similar size plant in a similar industry where the potential is known.

"In some cases, you may have a reliable estimate on the amount of one or two product lines consumed at a specific point which complement or supplement other product lines that we market. It might be possible to arrive at a pretty good estimate of the unknown product line potentials because of their relationship with products of known potential.

"Refer to government contracts and contract awards, as well as requests for bids from accounts in private industry.

"Sometimes, salesmen who sell product lines that are complementary to ours can be quite helpful. For example, a machine tool man may know of an account's plan to buy a certain amount of tools which happen to be used in conjunction with one of our products or processes.

"Chambers of commerce and local utilities, particularly power and light companies, are aware of new companies coming into a particular area before this information is generally available. Local banks also, at times, possess this information; and many times if you have a personal relationship with individuals at basic sources such as this, they might be able to help you get the information you need.

"Dun and Bradstreet reference books and state and local directories can provide valuable information such as the number of employees at specific using points in the event that you do not possess this information. In turn, this information would give you some idea as to what type of our products might be consumed and the amount of consumption."

Source: Reprinted by permission of the publisher and Air Reduction Company, Inc., from *Sales Analysis, Studies in Business Policy, no. 113* (New York: National Industrial Conference Board, Inc., 1965), p. 31.

types of products are more prevalent. Note that these demand determinants can all be measured by using data from the "Survey of Buying Power."

To calculate the index, the data on each determinant must be converted into a series of percentages which total to 100 percent, and each determinant must be weighted to reflect its importance relative to the other determinants. The more closely a given determinant parallels the distribution of market potential among the segments, the greater should that determinant be weighted. Weights can be determined by judgment or can be calculated using regression analysis of survey data or test market results. In this case, let us assume that management judgment produced the weights shown on Table 3.3. A weighted average of the four percents is computed for each state as indicated at the bottom of the table, and the resulting weighted averages are the relative market potential measures. The greatest potential among these seven states is in Missouri with 27.90 percent of the total, whereas the least is in North Dakota with only 3.52 percent of the total.

TABLE 3.3

Example of Relative Market Potential Calculations for Microwave Ovens in the Seven West North Central States

	DEMAND DETERMINANTS (IN THOUSANDS)								Weighed Average Percent and Relative Market Potential
	Households (wt. = 2)		Persons age 25–34 (wt. = 3)		Households with Income $15,000 and above (wt. = 3)		Retail Sales, in Furniture, Home Furnishings, and Appliance Stores (wt. = 2)		
States	number	percent	number	percent	number	percent	dollars	percent	
Iowa	1,025.0	17.0	432.7	16.6	553.4	17.8	428,983	15.1	16.74
Kansas	856.1	14.2	354.0	13.5	440.0	14.1	495,711	17.4	14.60
Minnesota	1,383.8	23.0	659.1	25.2	766.3	24.7	650,595	22.8	24.13
Missouri	1,736.7	28.8	747.7	28.6	856.8	27.6	751,657	26.4	27.90
Nebraska	562.7	9.4	235.1	9.0	284.8	9.2	310,961	10.9	9.52
North Dakota	218.8	3.6	92.6	3.5	103.0	3.3	109,630	3.8	3.52
South Dakota	239.9	4.0	94.3	3.6	102.0	3.3	101,347	3.6	3.59
	6,023.0	100.0	2,615.5	100.0	3,106.3	100.0	2,848,884	100.0	100.0

The weighted average percent is calculated as follows, using Iowa as an example:
(% households × wt.) + (% persons 25–34 × wt.) + (% $15,000+ × wt.) + (% sales × wt.)/sum of weights
(17.0 × 2) + (16.6 × 3) + (17.8 × 3) + (15.1 × 2)/10 = 16.74

Source: Data from *1979 Survey of Buying Power, Sales & Marketing Management*, July 23, 1979.

Some firms are finding the computer useful in measuring potentials. For example, Honeywell has a set of descriptive data on more than 650,000 firms filed in its computer data bank. To identify the potential market for any of its products, management obtains data on a few typical customers, feeds this information into the computer, and asks the computer to pull from its files all the firms which match the present customers' profiles.[17] This can be done for one salesman's territory, for a sales district, or for the entire market area.

One measurement approach used by industrial firms is input-output analysis. It is based on a matrix, or cross-classification table, which shows how change in output of various industries will affect the input or purchase needs of those industries. If your company sells to the automobile industry, an input-output matrix shows you how much more of your product will be required by the auto industry as their sales increase a specific amount.

Combustion Engineering uses a variety of input-output models. Figure 3.3 illustrates one model used by their Refractory Division, in which 24 products are sold to 19 separate markets. As these markets grow, the corresponding demand for each product is measured by the coefficients in the matrix, which are obtained

FIGURE 3.3

Example of Input-Output Matrix Used by Combustion Engineering for Measuring Changes in Demand for Their Products by Industry Markets

Products	\multicolumn{5}{c}{Industry Markets}				
	1	2	3	4	... 19
1		.00023			
2					
3					
⋮					
24					

The matrix relates sales of 24 Combustion Engineering products to changes in output of 19 industry markets to which they sell. Each cell contains a coefficient as illustrated by the .00023 above, which indicates how many dollars of that product (e.g., fireclay brick) are used for each dollar of industry market (e.g., open-hearth steel melting) output.

Source: Reprinted from the *Journal of Marketing Research,* published by the American Marketing Association. Adapted from p. 57 of Elliot D. Ranard, "Use of Input/Output Concepts in Sales Forecasting," Vol. 9 (February 1972).

through interviews with customer industry personnel and a review of trade publications and reports.[18]

The accurate measurement of market potential is certainly not an easy task. But if management forsakes measuring potential demand for this reason, it denies that measurement, even if not perfectly accurate, can be useful. The process of attempting to measure market potential is sometimes as valuable as the final result. Management is forced to consider the specific determinants of demand for its products, thereby gaining more intimate acquaintance with the nature of the market. This procedure is much akin to model building; as succeeding estimates are devised, analyzed, and evaluated over time, management's ability to develop an accurate model will often improve.[19]

MEASUREMENT OF SALES POTENTIAL

In measuring sales potential, the determinants of potential demand also apply, except that they relate to the product of just one firm. The analyst must try to determine what share of total market potential is found in those segments of the total market at which his company's brand is targeted.

When the firm is in the process of measuring market potential, generally only a little more effort is needed to get an estimate of sales potential as well. The two measures can be developed simultaneously using the approach already discussed, but keying the determinants of sales potential more specifically to the firm's target market segments.

To illustrate sales potential measurement, let us examine the process used by Hansen Manufacturing Company, a producer of couplings for power transmission systems.[20] Their three-step process is shown in Table 3.4, and begins by determining the ratio of their sales volume to the number of employees in their customer firms, calculating this ratio separately for each SIC industry group to which they sell. Next, they determine what is the total number of employees within each SIC group in their market area; this includes present customers as well as noncustomers. Finally, they multiply the ratio from Step 1 by the number of employees in Step 2 to produce a sales potential by SIC category. They make these calculations for the market in total as well as for each geographic market segment served by one of their distributors, as illustrated in Table 3.4. This is an example of the statistical series approach to measuring potentials as distinct from the survey and test market approaches.

There is also a more expedient way of estimating sales potential. Since the sales potential for all competing firms must add to total market potential, an analyst can approximate his firm's share by using *indirect estimation*. This method employs the firm's percentage of industry sales and simply applies that percentage to dollar

TABLE 3.4

Calculation of Sales Potential for One Geographic Market Area of Hansen Manufacturing Company

Two-Digit SIC Group	STEP 1				STEP 2	STEP 3
	Number of Present Customer Firms (1)	Current Annual Sales (2)	Number of Employees in Customer Firms (3)	Sales Per Employee (4)	Total Employees in All Firms in Area A (5)	Sales Potential in Area A (4 × 5)
33 Primary metal industries	14	$ 116,551	74,625	$1.56	4,113	$ 6,416
34 Fabricated metal products	22	152,412	60,169	2.53	14,792	37,424
35 Machinery, except electrical	57	503,929	153,670	3.28	15,907	52,175
36 Electrical machinery	24	155,903	80,807	1.93	32,677	63,067
37 Transportation equipment	36	316,878	185,784	1.71	2,024	3,461
38 Professional, scientific, and controlling instruments	9	76,883	22,122	3.48	409	1,423
	162	$1,322,556	577,177	$2.29	69,922	$163,966

Source: Reprinted from the Journal of Marketing Research, published by the American Marketing Association. Adapted from Tables 1 and 4 in William E. Cox, Jr. and G. N. Havens, "Determination of Sales Potentials and Performance for an Industrial Goods Manufacturer," vol. 14 (November 1977), pp. 575, 577.

or unit market potential, preferably by market segment. Thus, if a bicycle manufacturer has 10 percent of all bicycle sales in a given area, he can estimate that his sales potential is about 10 percent of the market potential in that area.

USES OF MARKET AND SALES POTENTIAL MEASURES

Developing Other Measures. Measures of potential demand have many uses in sales management planning and evaluation. To begin with, there are relationships involving market potential, sales potential, and actual sales which provide planning and evaluation bench marks. By comparing certain of these measures in various sequences, three relationships can be developed, namely, sales penetration, market penetration, and market share.

The first is as follows:

1. a. Determine a total sales potential measure.
   b. Determine relative sales potential measures for each market segment.
   c. Allocate the total sales potential measure to market segments according to the relative measures for each segment.
   d. Compare total actual sales of the firm with its total sales potential.
   e. Compare actual sales of the firm in each market segment with sales potential in each segment.

Steps (d) and (e) provide a relationship termed *sales penetration,* which is defined as the extent to which a firm has captured its sales potential. Step (d) gives this information for the firm's market in total, and step (e) provides a sales penetration figure for each of the firm's market segments, such as sales territories or customer groups.

The second relationship is developed as follows:

2. a. Determine a total market potential measure.
   b. Determine relative market potential measures for each market segment.
   c. Allocate the total market potential measure to market segments according to the relative measures for each segment.
   d. Compare total actual sales of the firm with total market potential.
   e. Compare actual sales of the firm in each market segment with the market potential in each segment.

In this sequence, steps (d) and (e) provide a relationship termed *market penetration,* which is defined as the extent to which a firm has captured the total industry's market potential. Step (d) provides this information for the firm's market in total, and step (e) gives corresponding information for each of the firm's market segments.

The difference between sales penetration and market penetration follows from the difference expressed previously between the terms *sales* and *market*. Further distinction is also necessary between market penetration and *market share*. This latter term is used often by businessmen and is defined as the extent to which a firm has captured total actual sales in its industry. We can draw a distinction between another pair of terms, *penetration* and *share*. A penetration measure is based on potential demand, while a share measure is based on actual sales.

Examples of sales and market penetration are shown in Tables 3.5 and 3.6. In each case the firm's total market is divided into four areas as in Table 3.1. From these tables it is also possible to approximate the firm's market share by means of indirect estimation. Nevertheless, a more direct calculation of market share is given in Table 3.7.

Of the two relationships, sales penetration measures are most useful in planning and evaluating because they compare the firm's actual sales with its own sales potential, rather than with the broader measure of market potential. If no sales potentials are available, market penetration measures give the next best indication of effectiveness in capturing potential demand. When total market potential is also unobtainable, the third relationship, which uses total industry sales in place of total market potential, can be developed. The steps are as follows:

3. a. Determine relative market potential measures for each market segment.
b. From secondary data, determine total industry sales.
c. Allocate total industry sales to market segments according to the relative market potential measure for each segment to get an estimate of industry sales by segment.
d. Compare total actual sales for the firm with total industry sales.
e. Compare actual sales for the firm in each market segment with the estimate of industry sales in each segment.

Steps (d) and (e) provide market share relationships. Step (d) gives an overall market share for the firm, which can be compared with each segment's market share from step (e) to determine which segments are performing above or below average. An illustration of this approach to market share measurement is given in Table 3.7.

The validity of the segment measures hinges on the condition implicit in step (c) that such estimates of industry sales for each segment be accurate. This would be true only when the industry is equally effective among all market segments in capturing potential demand. Hence, the segment market share measures would be misleading to the extent that this assumption is incorrect.

Market share measures also might be misleading in another way. Often a territory with a market share higher than the firm's average is evaluated as a good territory. This might be true relative to the firm's other territories, but not true when the

TABLE 3.5
Determination of Sales Penetration for a National Manufacturing Firm

Firm's Market Area	SALES POTENTIAL		Firm's Actual Unit Sales	Sales Penetration
	Percent	Units		
North Central States	24%	120,000	62,400	52.0%
East Coast States	34	170,000	68,700	40.4
South Central States	20	100,000	47,700	47.7
West Coast States	22	110,000	25,700	23.4
Total	100%	500,000	204,500	40.9%

TABLE 3.6 Determination of Market Penetration for a National Manufacturing Firm

Firm's Market Area	MARKET POTENTIAL Percent	MARKET POTENTIAL Units	Firm's Actual Unit Sales	Market Penetration
North Central States	26%	1,560,000	62,400	4.00%
East Coast States	34	2,040,000	68,700	3.37
South Central States	18	1,080,000	47,700	4.42
West Coast States	22	1,320,000	25,700	1.95
Total	100%	6,000,000	204,500	3.41%

territory's sales accomplishments are compared to its sales potential. Since this third relationship does not make use of any total potential measures, it is possible all territories are far below what management desires in market or sales penetration. Conversely, all territories may be penetrating the market very well, so that even the poorest territory is performing well in terms of market share. Therefore, it is difficult to evaluate absolute performance based on market share measures.

OTHER SALES MANAGEMENT USES

Other specific uses of potential demand measures are discussed in later chapters where appropriate. Consequently, only brief mention is made here of other uses which relate particularly to sales management.

Delineation of Sales Territories. Sales territories should be delineated more in accordance with potential demand than with past sales. Provisional territories are often set up to contain equal potential. Then adjustments are made for other factors such as varying travel requirements and different degrees of past sales penetration. Sales potential information assists management also in deciding how many separate territories could be supported by its market.

TABLE 3.7 Estimation of Market Share for a National Manufacturing Firm

FIRM'S MARKET AREA	MARKET POTENTIAL PERCENT	ESTIMATED INDUSTRY UNIT SALES	FIRM'S ACTUAL UNIT SALES	ESTIMATED MARKET SHARE
North Central States	26%	650,000	62,400	9.9%
East Coast States	34	850,000	68,700	8.1
South Central States	18	450,000	47,700	10.6
West Coast States	22	550,000	25,700	4.7
Total	100%	2,500,000	204,500	8.2%

Determination of Sales Budgets. The sales executive must have potential demand data if he wishes to justify budgeting for additional salespeople or more territories. Any major increase in a budget request should be supported by evidence of a probable sales increase. Lacking knowledge of potential demand, the sales executive must often rely primarily on past sales volumes as the basis for budgeting sales effort.

Determination of Sales Quotas. Whether salespeople's quotas can be increased depends largely on the degree of sales penetration in each territory. Furthermore, whether all salespeople's quotas should be equal depends to a great extent on the equality or inequality of sales potential among the territories. Relative differences in territorial potential provide the basis for relative differences in assigned quotas, though quota adjustments are subsequently made for other factors such as varying degrees of sales penetration.

Hiring and Training Salespeople. In the process of measuring potential demand, management becomes acquainted with the types of potential buyers and their uses of the product. This aids in determining what types of persons should be selected for sales positions and what training they need to communicate effectively with customers. If the sales force is utilized to submit information for determining potential demand, this could also affect hiring and training.

Determination of Compensation Plan. Most sales compensation plans include some incentive pay. The extent to which incentive pay is emphasized should bear some relationship to the extent of uncaptured sales potential. If salespeople are paid salary only, increases in their salary might be tied to improvement in their sales penetration.

Supervision and Evaluation of Sales Force Performance. The evaluation of performance is a difficult task at best, but sales potential and sales penetration information can assist the sales manager in judging the effectiveness of his salespeople. The information generated from analyzing potential demand is as helpful in supervision as it is in training. If such information is employed in a positive manner, both the sales force and company can benefit greatly.

CONCLUSION

This chapter presented a framework for understanding and measuring market and sales potentials. Intimate acquaintance with the product, its uses, and its users is necessary along with experience to produce meaningful estimates of potential demand. Because such measures provide the basis for planning and analyzing many other sales management activities, their importance cannot be overstressed. Certainly, the sales manager with no information about his sales or market potential is limiting his own potential for success in subsequent planning activities.

QUESTIONS FOR REVIEW AND DISCUSSION

1. Why are measures of market and sales potential an important basis for sales management planning? Explain, giving examples.
2. The demand for many industrial goods is derived from the demand for consumer

goods. How can this fact be used in establishing market and sales potentials for a firm selling component parts to appliance manufacturers?

3. Suppose you are the sales manager of a firm whose total market is the State of California. You wish to use *Sales & Marketing Management*'s "Buying Power Index" as an indicator of your firm's relative sales potential. From the data in Table 3.2, determine what proportion of your total market's sales potential exists in San Diego County.

4. If you wished to double the importance of the population element in the "Buying Power Index" calculation, what percent of total U.S. buying power, as revised, would exist in California? Use the data from Table 3.2.

5. A firm's controller says to its sales manager, "Market and sales potential measures are fine, but what we really need are measures of profit potential!" How could profit potential be measured? Develop a graph showing sales penetration on one axis and profit potential on the other, and explain their relationship.

6. You are a district sales manager reviewing some performance data on three territories in your district. You put together the following table from fragments of notes and computations:

TERRI-TORIES	TOTAL SALES IN DISTRICT	COMPANY SHARE	INDUSTRY SALES IN DISTRICT	MARKET SHARE	MARKET POTENTIAL IN DISTRICT	SALES PENE-TRATION
North	$ 600	30.0%		33.3%	$2100	
Central	800		$3200			
South		30.0%				33.3%
Total	$2000	100.0%		25.0%	$7500	

Fill in as many of the missing numbers as you can (there are 12 missing). Then draw a conclusion on which territory you think should be able to produce the largest sales increase during the upcoming period, and why.

7. What are some reasons a small electronics firm might not attempt to capture its entire sales potential?

8. A district sales manager has the following data on the district's three territories:

TERRITORY	SHARE OF DISTRICT SALES	MARKET SHARE	SALES PENETRATION
East	30%	30%	30%
Midwest	45%	25%	50%
West	25%	40%	45%

Which territory is performing best?

9. The sales manager of an office furniture producer is about to ask the sales force to estimate the potential demand for desks in their territories. Develop an outline of specific points and suggestions which should be covered in preparing the salespeople for this task.

10. You have just been hired as sales manager for an auto parts wholesaler selling in four market areas. Your boss asks you to formulate an index of how your

potential market is divided among these four areas. The following data are available to you for this calculation:

MARKET AREA	POPULATION	INCOME	AUTO SALES
A	20%	30%	30%
B	30%	40%	30%
C	20%	10%	10%
D	30%	20%	30%
	100%	100%	100%

Describe the steps you would take in using these data to develop your index. Then follow your steps and calculate the index. Which area is the best potential market area for your company?

NOTES

1. Many firms sell more than one product, each of which has a potential market, but for purposes of analysis this chapter focuses on a single product. Services would be analyzed the same way as products.

2. Nine different meanings are presented by Donald R. G. Cowan, "Market Potentials and Marketing Management," in J. C. Halterman and T. C. Meloan, editors, *Market Potentials and the Use of Census Data* (Chicago: American Marketing Association, 1958), pp. 1–3. These and other meanings are discussed in Francis E. Hummel, *Market and Sales Potentials* (New York: The Ronald Press Company, 1961), pp. 6–8.

3. Robert W. Baeder, as quoted in Hummel, p. 7.

4. Francis B. Hummel, "Market Potentials in the Machine Tool Industry—A Case Study," *Journal of Marketing*, vol. 19 (July, 1954), pp. 34–41.

5. Hummel, *Market and Sales Potentials*, pp. 206–207.

6. Harry Leopold, Jr., "Sales Potentials by Customers," in *Marketing Research in Action*, Studies in Business Policy, no. 84 (New York: National Industrial Conference Board, Inc., 1957), pp. 78–79.

7. This brief discussion does not even scratch the surface of all the secondary data sources available. For an expanded discussion, see a recent marketing research text such as Donald S. Tull and Del I. Hawkins, *Marketing Research: Meaning, Measurement, and Method* (New York: Macmillan Publishing Co., Inc., 1976), pp. 118–122.

8. One of the main problems with secondary data is that it becomes outdated quickly, sometimes even before it is published. For an approach to cope with this problem, see Ed Spar, "Measuring the Local Potential of Your Product: Who Says You Can't Get Current Data?" *Sales & Marketing Management*, May 16, 1977, pp. 66–68.

9. Charles Waldo and Dennis Fuller, "Just How Good is the 'Survey of Buying Power'?" *Journal of Marketing*, vol. 41, no. 4 (October 1977), pp. 64–66.

10. Further discussion of this and other indexes can be found in each edition of the "Survey of Buying Power" which is published annually in July.

11. Office of Management and Budget, *1972 Standard Industrial Classification Manual* (Washington: U.S. Government Printing Office, 1972).

12. Robert W. Haas, "Sources of SIC Related Data for More Effective Marketing," *Industrial Marketing*, May 1977, pp. 32–34, 39, 42.

13. Hummel, *Market and Sales Potentials*, p. 117.

14. Sally Scanlon, "Calling The Shots More Closely," *Sales & Marketing Management*, May 10, 1976, pp. 43–44.

15. Speech by Donald E. Stewart to the Thirty-seventh National Conference of the American Marketing Association, Chicago, 1955, as quoted in Hummel, *Market and Sales Potentials,* p. 151.

16. This example is based on Robert B. Woodruff, "A Systematic Approach to Market Opportunity Analysis," *Business Horizons,* vol. 19 (August 1976), pp. 62–63.

17. Thayer C. Taylor, "The Computer in Marketing, Part 11: Sales Force Management," *Sales Management*, March 15,1969, pp. 74–75.

18. This is an oversimplified explanation of a much more intricate process. Detailed discussions are found in Elliot D. Ranard, "Use of Input/Output Concepts in Sales Forecasting," *Journal of Marketing Research,* vol. 9 (February 1972), pp. 53–58; and James T. Rothe, "The Reliability of Input/Output Analysis for Marketing," *California Management Review,* vol. 14 (Summer 1972), pp. 75–81.

19. Further examples of how industrial firms estimate market potential are in Morgan B. MacDonald, Jr., *Appraising the Market for New Industrial Products,* Studies in Business Policy, no. 123 (New York: National Industrial Conference Board, Inc., 1967). See also Walter H. Klinger, "Measuring Market Potential for Industrial Products: An Eight-Step Approach," *Industrial Marketing Management,* vol. 6 (1977), pp. 39–42.

20. This example is based on William E. Cox, Jr. and G. N. Havens, "Determination of Sales Potentials and Performance for an Industrial Goods Manufacturer," *Journal of Marketing Research,* vol. 14 (November 1977), pp. 574–578.

4 SALES FORECASTING

Forecasting future sales volume is a fundamental activity in sales management planning. Forecasts serve as goals to be accomplished, and also provide the basis for planning in many other parts of the firm.

In some companies the sales manager is assigned the complete forecasting task. In others, the responsibility rests with the marketing research department, forecasting committees, or with operating division heads. In larger firms, two or more forecasts are prepared independently in different departments or levels of the organization, and these are then analyzed and reconciled into a final form by top management.

As firms take increasing advantage of computers, more complex techniques have been incorporated into the forecasting process, and these developments require greater use of staff specialists. One report of how the computer is influencing sales forecasting states:

> The machine's renowned prowess as a number cruncher is prompting General Electric and RCA to construct complex econometric models of the total economy that juggle hundreds of equations using thousands of statistics. The output of these models is used by operating divisions as the starting point for their own product forecasts, and by top management as a check on how closely such forecasts jibe with economic reality—or at least the world as sketched by the model builders.[1]

The purpose of this chapter is to provide a *managerial*, rather than *technical*, understanding and appreciation of sales forecasting. Sales managers must utilize forecast information in budgeting, quota-setting, and other activities. This chapter should help the manager use forecast data more intelligently. It is less concerned with constructing forecasts, except in those areas where sales managers are likely to become directly involved in the development of forecast data.

CONCEPTS AND DEFINITIONS

A *sales forecast* has been defined as an estimate of dollar or unit sales of a product or product line which an individual firm expects in a specific period of time under a given marketing plan. Since forecasts are used in further planning and as goals to be accomplished, it is essential that forecasts be set forth in quantitative terms.

Such statements as "Sales should be up a bit next year" or "We'll get our share of the industry's increase" are of little help in sound planning and control.

Further, forecasts should stem from a careful appraisal of expected or planned conditions affecting company sales. The specific marketing plan to be used during the forecast period is of great importance. It is difficult to anticipate the exact results of a given marketing plan, but it is generally true that different marketing plans will produce different sales results. Thus, the forecast should reflect the specific market segments sought, the channels of distribution selected, the pricing policies adopted, and all other aspects of the marketing mix.

While the sales forecast is an end, *sales forecasting* is the means or process of reaching that end. Two essential ingredients of sales forecasting are facts and judgment, since "all modern-day techniques are designed either to limit the area in which judgment must be exercised, or to improve the quality of judgment by reinforcing it with facts."[2] Judgment is emphasized because in the constantly changing economic and competitive environment in which business firms operate the simple extension of past behavior into the future seldom proves correct.

Forecasting forces management to think about the future and especially about what circumstances are likely to change in the forecast period. The facts available usually pertain to past market, economic, and competitive behavior. As such, they aid in analyzing what relationships existed in the past between company sales and other variables. To what extent these relationships will continue in the future is a question which must be dealt with primarily by informed personal judgment. Perhaps the greatest challenge concerns how these two ingredients can best be combined.

THE SALES FORECASTING PROCESS

Effective sales forecasting requires a series of steps both before and after the forecast itself is calculated. A diagram of the sales forecasting process is presented in Figure 4.1. To begin with, forecasts can serve a variety of purposes, and each might require a different kind of forecast or a different form of forecast results. In turn, the most pertinent determinants of future demand differ depending on what kind of forecast is desired. In the forecasting process succeeding steps depend on previous steps. We shall examine these steps in turn.

DEFINING THE PURPOSES OF SALES FORECASTS

One major purpose of sales forecasts is to aid in long-range planning and goal setting. Many business plans and decisions involve long-term commitments such as the purchase of major equipment, warehouses, and plant capacity. Firms facing rapid technological change or fluctuating markets find this a key to their success. In the Chemical Division of Merck & Company, for example, "the remarkably rapid evolution of chemical products from introduction to obsolescence makes accurate long-range sales forecasts of extreme importance, to ensure that the market and profit potentials of a product are long-lived enough to warrant heavy capital outlays."[3] Future personnel and financing needs must also be anticipated early so that they can be obtained at the best opportunities.

FIGURE 4.1
The Sales Forecasting Process

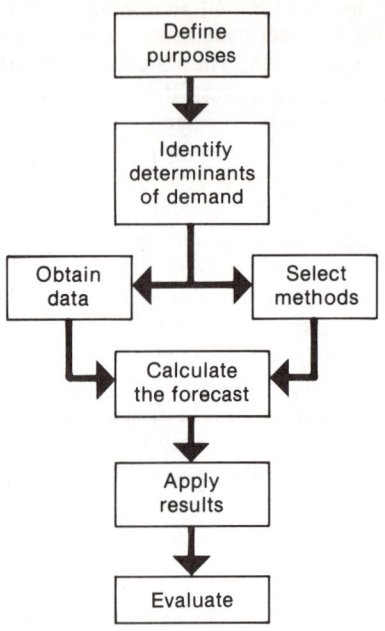

A major long-range concern in sales management is planning for a sufficient number of sales personnel, since the process of recruiting, hiring, training, and providing experience to salespeople is a long one. Long-range sales estimates also help management in setting up territories which will not need frequent changes. Continuous changes will hinder territory development, to say nothing of customer relations and sales force morale. The sales force compensation plan should also take long-term sales growth into consideration so that proper incentives and fair rewards are based on a realistic estimate of sales trends.

The second major purpose of forecast data is to assist in short-range operating decisions. A one-year forecast gives the sales manager a basis for setting annual quotas for each salesperson. Reliable short-term forecasts can also help identify weakening territories or changing economic conditions. These forecasts are essential in evaluating the work of the sales force at the end of the forecast period as well.

To meet these various purposes, many firms generate a large number of forecasts rather than just one. Republic Steel Corporation prepares three sets, including a short-term three-month forecast, a short-term one-year forecast which is revised quarterly, and a long-range ten-year forecast which is updated annually.[4] In the electron tube division of RCA, five-year, twelve-month, and four-month forecasts are made.[5]

Besides differences in time span, other distinctions can be drawn. Since short-range forecasts are guides for operating decisions, they must be stated in considerable detail. A recent study of small, medium-sized, and large manufacturing and service firms shows that nearly two-thirds of them prepare separate forecasts for individual products and product lines as well as for total sales.[6] In addition, over half of these firms apportion their forecasts into monthly time periods, while a few companies go so far as to break the forecast down by weeks and even days. Once forecasts are made, they are then periodically revised, with the majority of firms making these revisions at least four times a year. At General Mills, end-of-month forecasts for each major brand are updated daily![7]

Forecasting as a Planning Process. Apart from the specific uses of forecast data, there is a more fundamental purpose for the sales forecasting process. Forecasting is an integral part of planning, and effective planning requires management to explicitly consider the company's future—its goals, environment, competition, and strategy. Sales forecasting can be viewed as a projection of *what is going to happen to the company,* or it can serve as a vehicle for management to express *what the company is going to make happen* out of the market opportunities available to it. Where forecasting is a projection only, the company is not effectively planning, at least not in a responsible managerial sense. On the other hand, forecasting can serve a vital role in planning when management uses the sales forecast as a type of *simulation.* Alternative forecasts can be prepared which correspond with alternative marketing strategies and assumptions about the environment. From the various resulting forecasts, management can then determine what strategy would produce the best results under each environmental assumption.

For instance, suppose there are two major environmental alternatives (e.g., one that competition gets stronger and the economy slackens, and the other that competition stays the same and the economy strengthens) and three major marketing strategies that the company is considering (e.g., capture customers from competition, obtain sales from new market segments, or continue as at present with no changes). A sales forecast can be made for each alternative combination, and the results might look like this:

ENVIRONMENT	STRATEGY	SALES FORECAST
1. Competition stronger, economy weaker	1. Seek competitors' customers	$5,900,000
	2. Seek customers from new segments	$7,200,000
	3. Continue as at present	$6,400,000
2. Competition steady, economy stronger	1. Seek competitors' customers	$7,000,000
	2. Seek customers from new segments	$6,800,000
	3. Continue as at present	$7,400,000

The sales forecast column represents the "payoff" in sales revenues under each combination of environment and strategy. Management must try to determine which environmental state is most likely to occur, and must also carefully analyze the costs and profitability associated with each sales forecast. How forecasting plays an integral part of planning is evident—these simulations give management additional information to help in deciding what future direction should be taken for this business.[8]

IDENTIFYING THE DETERMINANTS OF DEMAND

What factors influence the level of sales volume for a product or product line? Potential demand must exist before actual sales or revenues can be attained. Sales forecasting might be viewed as pinpointing what part of potential demand will become "actualized" during the forecast period.

What causes potential demand to become actual demand for a company's products? Demand determinants can be grouped into three major categories:

1. Economic and psychological developments affecting market behavior.
2. Company strategy, especially marketing strategy.
3. Competitive and industry conditions.

Economic and Psychological Developments. Purchasing behavior of consumers and industrial buyers often follows cyclical patterns, which reflect economic and psychological changes in the market. Though potential demand may remain relatively constant, actual demand for a product often varies upward or downward according to the stage of the cycle. A forecasting executive in General Foods assessed cyclical changes this way:

> Obviously, a trend among customers to reduce supplies from four to three weeks to improve cash flow may have serious effects on long-range sales forecasting. Conversely, in an economic upturn, many of these negative factors may disappear, opening avenues for increased inventory and greater sales.[9]

Seasonal buying patterns are present for many products as well and should be considered in short-term forecasting. Sales of many consumer goods peak a month or two prior to Christmas, while others sell best in spring or summer months. Industrial firms often time their purchases to avoid building inventories at the end of their fiscal year.

Company Strategy. A more controllable determinant is the firm's competitive strategy, particularly its marketing strategy. One company might emphasize large sales volume through a low-price appeal. Another might devise a strategy requiring less volume at a higher price, with the aim of a more prestigious appeal to a smaller market segment. Variations in other parts of the marketing mix, such as the type of distribution channel used and the amount and type of advertising, will influence future demand. The General Foods executive cites, as an example, "a distributor handling four brands may decide to cut one or two from his line to reduce inventory investment and improve cash flow. A well-timed promotion plan may be the vehicle that saves your product at the expense of competition."[10]

The relationship between marketing strategy and the sales forecast is not only in one direction, however. The forecast can influence company strategy because a forecast projects what revenues will become available for use in the budget. When this two-way relationship is recognized, forecasting may be carried out in two stages. First, a forecast is made based on the best estimates of the influence of company marketing strategy. In fact, a number of forecasts may be made reflecting different strategy alternatives, as we have already noted. Second, company strategy is reassessed in light of the level of expected revenues and new forecasts would be made if the strategy is modified.

Competitive and Industry Conditions. The aggressiveness and effectiveness of competitors' marketing strategies will influence the demand for a firm's product. For instance, as noted by the General Foods forecaster, "If a competitor decides not to pass along increased costs through a price increase, that could result in a great deal of new business for the competitor. If you don't match his strategy, your volume will suffer."[11]

The entry or exit of firms in an industry may also affect an established firm's demand. Competitive pressures might cause a firm to cut back its marketing expenditures in order to replace old production facilities with more technologically advanced equipment. Inter-industry competition can exist as well, as exemplified by the glass, plastics, metal, and paper industries all vying for the container market. This determinant is a major cause of forecasting inaccuracy, since competitive situations always tend towards uniqueness and are difficult to foresee.

OBTAINING DATA

Once the demand determinants are identified, the forecaster must assess their influence on sales. This requires two interrelated steps: obtaining data and selecting forecasting techniques. Whatever data and techniques are chosen, they must not only reflect the determinants of demand; they must also produce the various types of forecasts needed. Data and techniques are the means whereby the forecaster translates demand determinants into sales forecasts of the desired detail and type.

It is difficult to discuss data separately from techniques because the techniques chosen will dictate the kind of data needed. The term "data" is not restricted to quantitative measures only, however. While some forecasting data are definitely quantitative—past sales of the firm and economic measures such as new housing starts or personal income—qualitative factors affecting future sales are potentially at least as useful in effective forecasting. Such qualitative factors include customers' attitudes and expectations regarding future buying, the impact of a firm's new marketing strategy, and the anticipated strength of competitors within the market. There is an increasing tendency to quantify these qualitative factors by using techniques which convert expectations or judgments into probability estimates. Illustrations of some of these techniques follow.

SELECTING FORECASTING METHODS

Many forecasting methods exist. There is no one method or even a small group of methods agreed on and used consistently by one company to the next. For a given firm, the best method to use depends on that firm's product and stage in the product life cycle, as well as the competitive situation it faces and the amount of technical forecasting expertise possessed by its staff.[12]

For instance, sales of a very new product cannot be forecast with a method which relies on historical sales trends and extends these trends into the future. But such a method might be effective for an established product within a stable competitive environment. If we consider that most companies have products in different stages of their life cycles, and face different competitive and economic conditions, and note that over time these conditions will change for any single product, we can draw these conclusions about selecting forecasting methods:

a. The same methods might not be best for all products within a company's product line.
b. The same methods might not be best from one time period to the next for any single product.
c. No one forecasting method may be perfect in fitting the total pattern of conditions which will influence future sales of a given product.

What this means is that forecasting methods must be selected to fit each product's situation—forecasting methods are not good or poor *per se*, but their effectiveness depends on the conditions under which they are employed.

The best way to assess the usefulness or applicability of a forecasting method is to evaluate it in relation to the determinants of demand affecting the product sales to be forecast. Table 4.1 provides a broad overview of these relationships. Note, for example, that a product line whose sales are very sensitive to competitive conditions (e.g., a standardized component part such as ball bearings) will be forecast best by a field sales composite method according to this chart. If competitive conditions are stable, however, but the size of the potential market is changing rapidly, then input-output, regression, and survey methods are best suited for effective forecasting. These latter three methods are not very effective in reflecting

TABLE 4.1

How Well Forecasting Methods Can Reflect Changes in Demand Determinants

	FORECASTING METHODS AND THEIR ABILITY TO REFLECT CHANGES IN DEMAND DETERMINANTS				
	Mathematical Models		Surveys	Judgment and Opinion	
Demand Determinants	Time Series and Exponential Smoothing	Regression		Field Sales Composite	Executive and Expert Opinion
Size of Potential Market	poor	good	good	good to fair	fair to poor
Economic and Psychological Factors Influencing Market Behavior	good in short run; fair to poor in long run	very good with leading variables	good to fair	good	fair to poor
Company Strategy	poor	poor (but good when used as simulation)	poor	fair to poor	very good
Competitive Conditions	fair to poor	good to fair	fair to poor	very good	good to fair

Note: While these relationships hold in general, there will be circumstances in which special adaptations of these techniques or particular types of data will produce better results than indicated above.

the impact of company strategy on future sales, so if company strategy is to be modified in the near future, one or more of these methods should be accompanied by executive opinion or a simulation application of regression analysis.

Without getting overly technical, we will review and illustrate these forecasting methods briefly.

Mathematical and Statistical Models. Mathematical and statistical models represent quantitative relationships between the future sales of a company or product and one or more independent variables. While highly complex models can be developed, nearly every such model evolves from the simpler forms discussed below.

Time series analysis is a statistical procedure using the company's own sales data. It involves isolating and measuring the basic patterns which contribute to fluctuations in sales volume. These patterns are classified as trend (long-term, or secular), seasonal, cyclical, and irregular. The level of sales volume at any point in time is the product of each of these four patterns in combination. If regularities in these patterns are uncovered, they can be extended into the future on the assumption that such regularities will continue.

Figure 4.2 shows how a sales volume graph might be broken down into these four component patterns. Note that trend, seasonal, and cyclical patterns can be extended as indicated by the dotted lines, and when the three extensions are combined, the result is the forecast. The irregular component cannot be extended, of course, because it forms no recognizable pattern. Even extending the cycle is sometimes difficult because the timing of the turning point is seldom easy to anticipate.

Time series analysis does not measure the influence of any specific demand determinants directly. Instead, it assumes that all determinants of sales in the past have been reflected in the patterns of trend, seasonal, cyclical, and irregular factors. The projection of these patterns into the future will also reflect all the determinants, though in the same manner as they influenced past sales.

This method has been described by some forecasters as being "objective," since it is based primarily on statistical techniques and past data rather than on the personal judgment of any individuals. Others have termed it "naive" for exactly the same reason, because the assumption of unchanging patterns is a dangerous one on which to rely in a dynamic and changing economy. The Long Island Lighting Company, a public utility, expresses this view as follows: "Although heavy reliance is placed upon statistical methods involving the study and extension of trends, cycles, and seasonal patterns, the company feels that the application of statistical techniques alone will not necessarily produce a reasonable forecast."[13] Time series analysis seldom should be used as the sole means of forecasting. It does provide an excellent check on other methods, however. Any great differences between the results of this and other methods call for an explanation of the anticipated changes that might account for the deviation from established patterns.

Time series analysis requires extensive computation involving a large amount of detailed past sales data. But this problem can be alleviated by using a computer and a standard computer program developed for this method.[14] For example, an international oil company uses its computer to analyze twenty different time series which include past sales in different market areas. The computer identifies the type of curve which best fits the trend and cyclical data of each series, calculates the seasonal index for each series, and ultimately prints out monthly forecasts for the following two years.[15]

FIGURE 4.2

Sales Volume Broken Down into Time Series Components

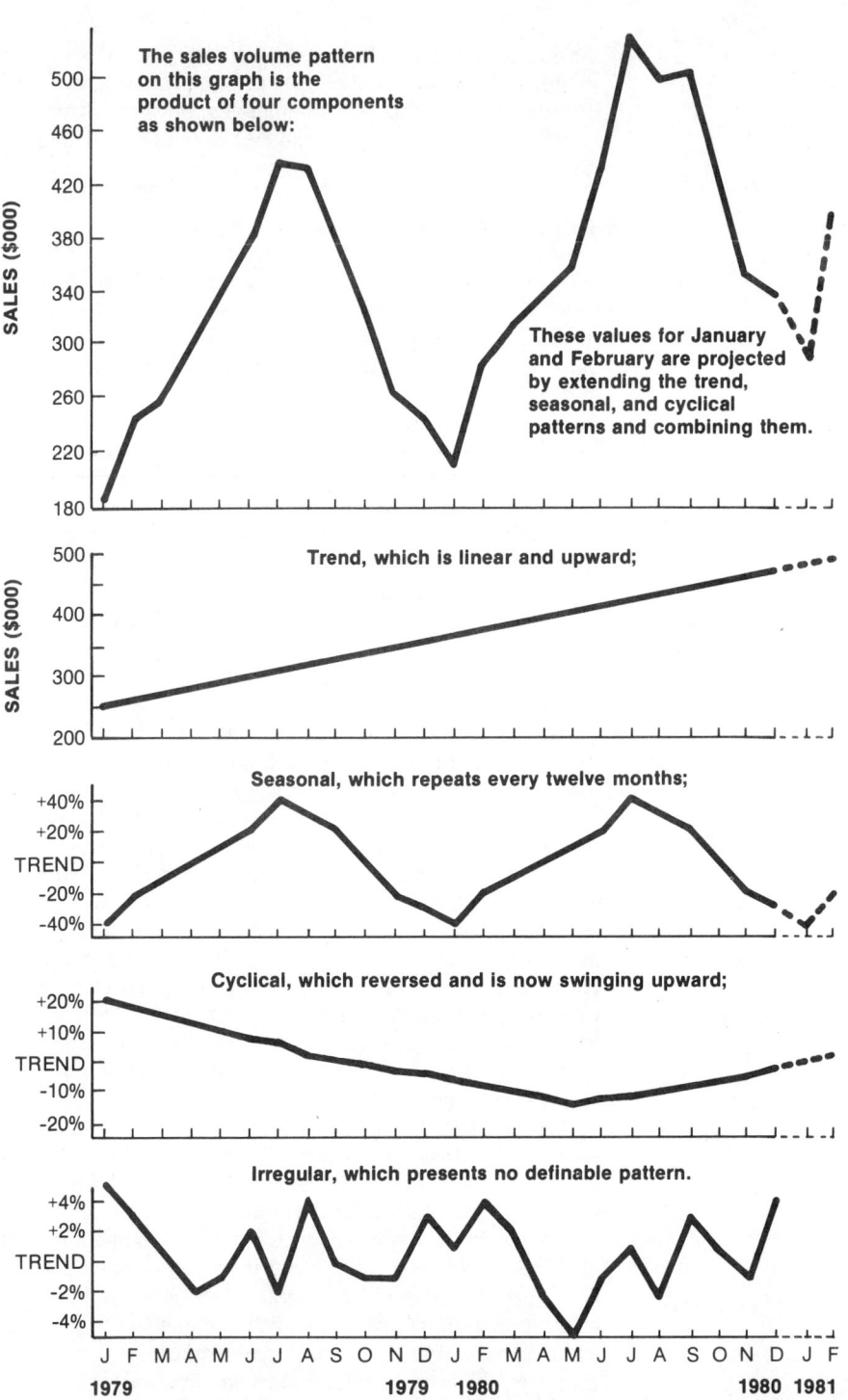

Exponential smoothing is a short-range forecasting method by which sales projections are made one period at a time. In its simplest form, a projection for the next period is made by combining current period sales with the projection for the current period in a weighted average. Translated into equation form, it looks like this:

> Next period forecast =
> (a)(this period sales) $+ (1 - a)$(this period forecast) where $a =$ the weight applied to current sales, often termed a *smoothing constant,* with a value between 0.0 and 1.0

If the sales forecast for the current period was 142 units, actual sales reached 150 units, and the smoothing constant was 0.4, the next period forecast would be:

$$(.4)(150) + (.6)(142) = 145 \text{ units}$$

The most suitable value for the smoothing constant must be determined by the forecaster. In general, lower values are better if sales patterns are stable, whereas higher values produce better results as sales fluctuate more. To determine a more specifically, a series of alternative forecasts, each with a different value of a, can be simulated over past sales periods. Forecast results can then be compared with actual sales results, and the value of a which produces the smallest total absolute deviation between forecast and actual sales should be chosen. In the Sun Oil Company, for example, over one thousand different combinations of weights were tested for sales predictions in each of eight sales districts. These simulations were completed in only a few minutes using a computer, and the best value of the smoothing constant was determined.[16] Such simulations should be carried out periodically to determine if a change in a might improve forecast results, especially when any change occurs in the demand determinants.[17]

Regression analysis involves a mathematical relationship between changes in the level of sales volume and changes in the level of other series of data. A firm might discover, for example, that its sales increase and decrease in the same relative degree as does total employment. In statistical terms, we would say that changes in sales, the dependent variable, are associated with changes in total employment, the independent variable.

In its simplest form, this relationship can be described in a regression equation as follows:

> This period sales $= (a) + (b)$(this period employment) where a and b are constants, often termed *regression coefficients,* which must be calculated in order to use the equation for forecasting

A forecaster can use any series of data as independent variables, but it is logical to concentrate on those series which reflect determinants of demand for the firm's product. Emery Industries, a producer of chemicals for drug and pharmaceutical firms, has discovered a relationship between its sales and consumer expenditures for nondurable goods (a component of Gross National Product).[18] More than one independent variable can be used within the same equation. American Can Company forecasts beer-can demand with a multiple regression equation using income levels, number of drinking establishments per thousand persons, and age distribution of the population as independent variables.[19]

Forecasting with regression analysis requires extending the relationship between dependent and independent variables into the future. We must sometimes forecast values of the independent variable before we can obtain a forecast estimate of sales. As one of its forecasting methods, Monsanto Chemical Company bases sales projections on a combination of production indexes published by the Federal Reserve Board. The company employs a consultant to forecast these indexes and has learned that the closeness of this forecast to actual sales depends considerably on the accuracy of the index forecasts.[20]

The necessity for forecasting values of independent variables sometimes can be eliminated by using "leading" indicators. These are series of data whose movements precede similar movements in a company's sales. Leading indicators are particularly useful if they can signal a turn in the cyclical pattern of company sales. For example, quarterly changes in the national economy lead changes in RCA color television set sales to dealers. So RCA's forecasters monitor key economic series which they project after consulting various outside sources as shown in Table 4.2. Any major changes in these economic series signal upcoming changes in television set sales as well.[21]

Regression analysis can be used also to forecast sales for each of a company's sales districts, provided data for the independent variables are available on a district basis. Eli Lilly and Company forecasts pharmaceutical sales by product groups for each sales district using this method.[22] If the nature of the relationship between sales and the independent variables differs for different districts and products, this requires an individual regression equation for each case.

Surveys. A firm can estimate future sales by asking all its customers or a representative sample what their future buying plans are. Many variations of this survey method have been employed, from the use of a single survey of quick telephone interviews to the maintenance of continuous consumer panels.[23] However, the essence of all these variations is the same: customers are asked to forecast their own future purchases. The reasoning seems quite logical. After all, who should know better than the customer himself how his perception of future conditions will influence his buying?

But many customer surveys have not enjoyed great predictive success. Research design problems occur, such as nonrepresentative samples, and those who do respond may subsequently change their expectations.[24] For example, in a study comparing intentions to purchase with subsequent actual purchase of household durable goods, it was found that almost half of those who planned to buy certain products did not make the actual purchase.[25] More recently, improved predictions have resulted when these were based on purchase probability responses of consumers.[26]

The cost of careful research necessary to produce good survey results precludes the use of this method by many firms. Still, surveys deserve consideration under certain conditions. Entirely new products have no historical sales data, which eliminates the use of mathematical and statistical models. Some markets are narrow enough that a survey of customers need not be extensive. For instance, the sales vice-president of Curtice-Burns' C-B Foods Division described their use of surveys as follows:

> For specialty items such as convenience foods we sit down with the buyer and review his past record and try to determine his requirements. Then we solicit a "booking":

TABLE 4.2

Economic Forecasts Used by, and Made by, RCA in Forecasting Television Set Sales

	PERCENT CHANGE, CURRENT YEAR FROM LAST YEAR					Current Year Unemployment Rate (percent)
	Constant GNP	GNP Deflator	Current Dollar Consumer Durables	Pretax Corporate Profits	Current Dollar GNP (billions)	
Manufacturers Hanover Trust (Nov.)	6.8%H	5.5%	13%	19%	$1659	7.4%
Conference Board (Feb. 9)	6.8H	6.0	19H	31	1697H	7.5
W. R. Grace (Nov. 26)	6.5	6.5H	17	23	1674	7.7
Union Carbide (Jan. 13)	6.4	5.0	18	29	1651	7.8
B. F. Goodrich (Feb. 10)	6.4	5.6	18	26	1684	7.2L
Chase Econometrics (Jan. 27)	6.3	5.9	16	32H	1661	7.7
Mellon Bank (Jan. 30)	6.2	5.7	15	25	1680	7.5
Equitable Life (Feb. 25)	6.0	6.5H	16	25	1680	7.5
Bankers Trust (Feb. 18)	5.9	6.0	16	28	1684	7.8
E. I. du Pont de Nemours (Jan. 28)	5.9	5.7	16	32H	1678	7.6
Schroder, Naess & Thomas (Jan. 30)	5.9	5.8	16	29	1681	7.5
Prudential Insurance (Feb. 26)	5.9	6.0	16	27	1684	7.5
Data Resources (Feb. 3)	5.9	6.1	16	25	1660	7.6
U.S. Trust (Feb. 27)	5.8	5.8	19H	25	1675	7.7
Irving Trust (Feb. 5)	5.8	6.0	18	23	1681	7.6
Wells Fargo Bank (Feb. 18)	5.7	5.2	NA	26	1667	7.8
Security Pacific National Bank (Feb. 26)	5.7	5.5	17	31	1672	7.6
American Express (Dec. 15)	5.7	6.1	15	27	1657	7.6
RCA (Feb. 20)	5.6	5.7	16	25	1672	7.5
General Electric (Feb. 25)	5.6	6.4	16	30	1684	7.7
Lionel D. Edie (Jan. 29)	5.4	5.4	16	25	1667	7.6
C. J. Lawrence (Jan. 23)	5.4	4.5L	13	21	1651	7.8
Dean Witter (Feb. 23)	5.4	5.6	12	23	1669	7.5
A. G. Becker (Dec. 4)	5.3	5.4	8L	22	1641L	8.3H
First National City Bank (Feb. 23)	5.2	5.2	13	14L	1659	7.9
Harris Trust (Jan. 28)	5.1L	5.5	13	24	1662	7.8
Table mean	5.9	5.7	15	26	1670	7.7
Table mean last month	5.7	5.7	15	24	1648	7.8

NA—Not available   H—highest forecast in column   L—lowest forecast in column

Of the 26 forecasts tabulated last time which are included this month, 4 revised real growth down, 14 revised it up, and the rest left it unchanged; 9 revised price inflation down, 9 revised it up, the rest left it unchanged.

Sources: Published and personal communication from the economics departments of the firms listed. RCA Forecast: RCA Economic Forecasting Model, 2/20 current year.

Note: In this and other exhibits relating to this company example, data or projections for national economic factors are based on the most recent figures then released by the government; some of these series are subject to later adjustment at yearly or other intervals.

Source: David L. Hurwood, et al., *Sales Forecasting,* Report No. 730 (New York: The Conference Board, Inc., 1978), p. 120.

not a formal contract but an indication that he will buy our product in 12 months, assuming that the price is right and quality is O.K.[27]

In other cases, selling negotiations take a long time and the continuous contact with these customers makes the survey process easier. National Lead, a producer of titanium and other raw materials, surveys many of its customers by personal interview. Three persons in each customer firm are questioned. Technical research directors are asked how much titanium is incorporated in the products they manufacture. Sales managers are then queried on how many of each product which incorporates titanium is likely to be sold. And purchasing executives are questioned about the total amount of titanium they plan to purchase in comparison with past purchases.[27]

Judgment and Opinion. Two major sources of judgment and opinion are used in devising sales forecasts. These include field sales personnel and top executives.

Field sales composite is a method whereby individual forecast estimates from members of the field sales organization are combined to produce a total company sales forecast. At its simplest, each salesperson is asked to provide an estimate of next year's sales in his or her territory. But a more carefully defined and controlled procedure may increase the value of this method considerably. Such a procedure might involve three steps: preparation, forecasting, and evaluation.

Adequate preparation will conserve the salesperson's time and provide background information which can benefit the accuracy of the forecast. At General Electric, for instance, sales force members are provided a customer demand estimate form listing sales to each of their major customers by product line for the past two years. Space is provided for forecast estimates also by product line for each major customer. Accompanying these forms are instructions which include projected economic trends.[29] Similar procedures are followed in all divisions of TRW, where an internal economic monitoring service supplies all field sales personnel with its interpretation of the economic outlook for the following three years.[30]

Additional information also can be helpful. If past forecasts were included, salespeople can compare them with actual results. By analyzing any major differences, they may be able to sharpen their forecasting ability. If available, market share and sales penetration data also can help guide the salesperson's forecasting.[31]

Forecasting itself comes next. At this step each salesperson should meet with his or her manager to discuss past performance and any factors affecting future sales. After that, salespeople study all the information available, consider changes in their territory and inventory levels of their customers, and then fill in their best estimates of anticipated sales in the spaces provided on the form.

Evaluation is the final step. Each salesperson's manager reviews the forecast estimates submitted by sales force members and makes any necessary adjustments in consultation with the salesperson involved. For example, at InterRoyal Corporation, a supplier of commercial and institutional furniture, this step is carried out by regional managers who ask such questions as: Where will these expected sales come from? Will they come to fruition during the next month or so? What is the probability of getting them?[32]

Some problems which managers must anticipate in evaluating forecasts from the sales force are shown in Table 4.3. In a study of sales force forecasting in 200 firms, each sales manager was asked whether these problems occurred in his or her company.[33] The percent of managers acknowledging each problem in their firm also appears in Table 4.3. Once such problems are detected and resolved, then the manager prepares forecast estimates for the district or region as a whole.

This forecasting method is well suited to reflect the demand determinants of market behavior and activities of competitors. Because the field sales organization is that part of the firm in closest contact with the market and competition, salespeople and field managers can often make a more realistic appraisal of these determinants than can anyone else in the firm. Other advantages can be cited for this method. If they have a voice in the initial forecast, salespeople are more likely to accept quotas based on forecasts. And, since a large sample of individual forecasts is involved, this method may lead to greater reliability in the overall forecast. Even though individual salespeople may produce inaccurate forecasts for their own territory, their errors often offset each other when all individual forecasts are combined. Finally, this type of forecast can be more easily broken down by customer types, territories, and even products if desired.

On the negative side, it takes time for a salesperson to prepare forecasts. This time is expensive, and the cost must be evaluated in terms of the lost sales that might have been made. An opportunity-cost problem is thus posed, in which this method must be weighed against other methods as well as against other uses of sales force time.

Finally, if there is high turnover of personnel in selling jobs this method has less value because experienced salespeople are replaced by those with less experience and less intimate acquaintance with customer and competitive behavior. Records of past forecasts can be made available to new salespeople, but records are never a satisfactory substitute for personal experience.

Executive opinion is a method of sales forecasting which involves soliciting top executives' opinions of what sales will be in the coming period. This method can vary from a simple averaging of the quick estimates of a number of top executives to a structured and planned process involving the study of background information, formal presentations, and group discussions. Many of the firms already cited in

TABLE 4.3
Problems in Sales Force Forecasting

PROBLEM	PERCENT OF FIRMS IN WHICH PROBLEM EXISTS
My salespeople typically forecast low so they can earn more money.	5%
In general, my salespeople are inaccurate forecasters because they lack the information about the company's plans needed to accurately estimate their future sales.	20%
In general, my salespeople forecast high because their optimism outweighs their business judgment.	24%
In general, my salespeople are inaccurate forecasters because they lack the necessary insight into the economic factors that impact their customers' need for our product.	16%
In general, my salespeople forecast just about right.	38%

Source: Reprinted from the *Journal of Marketing*, published by the American Marketing Association. Thomas R. Wotruba and Michael L. Thurlow, "Sales Force Participation in Quota Setting and Sales Forecasting," vol. 40 (April 1976), p. 15.

this chapter use an executive committee in evaluating forecasts devised by other methods. But if an executive committee were to originate its own forecast, a good procedure would include the following five steps:

1. Each participating executive prepares background information, including assumptions about the economy, competition, and the market. Previous relationships between each executive's functional activities and sales might be established. Each executive should gather as much background information as necessary to support his forecast.
2. Each executive formulates a forecast estimate, which should be written and backed up with the evidence he has gathered.
3. All executives meet and in turn present their estimates to the group. Inconsistencies are discussed and, if possible, a consensus reached.
4. When the consensus obtained is not sufficient, the varying estimates must be reconciled to a single projection or to a usable forecast range. Responsibility for this step must be clearly identified.
5. As an incentive, a bonus can be promised to the executive whose forecast proves most accurate.

Executive forecasting can also be refined further by using a probability estimation procedure. For example, suppose two alternative marketing strategies were being considered by top management. Each participating executive can be asked first to state a range of sales expectations from each strategy, and then attach to each expectation a probability estimate that it will be achieved. Table 4.4 illustrates what one executive might provide. If asked only for his best estimate of sales, the executive would probably give $20 million for either strategy. But when alternatives and probabilities are introduced, he indicates that strategy A has the greater chance of producing higher sales, resulting in a higher expected value. This type of analysis can be extended to cover additional strategies, varying levels of competition, and different economic conditions. It also provides an estimate of each forecast's reliability, particularly if the standard deviation of each distribution is computed.

TABLE 4.4
Developing Sales Forecast Estimates with Subjective Probabilities

		PROBABILITY OF OBTAINING FORECAST VOLUME UNDER		EXPECTED VALUE OF FORECAST UNDER	
	Forecast Estimate	Marketing Strategy A	Marketing Strategy B	Marketing Strategy A (1) × (2)	Marketing Strategy B (1) × (3)
	(1)	(2)	(3)	(4)	(5)
	$16,000,000	.05	.10	$ 800,000	$ 1,600,000
	18,000,000	.20	.30	3,600,000	5,400,000
	20,000,000	.40	.40	8,000,000	8,000,000
	22,000,000	.25	.15	5,500,000	3,300,000
	24,000,000	.10	.05	2,400,000	1,200,000
	Expected Value			$20,300,000	$19,500,000

Expert opinion is similar to the executive opinion method, differing primarily in the makeup of the participants. Not all company executives are equal in forecasting expertise, and some nonexecutives such as outside consultants or middle management staff personnel can have a great deal of expertise on a particular product or market. Expert opinion makes use of experts regardless of their executive status, and the results are shown by numerous studies to often be a significant improvement over other group opinion forecasts.[34]

An increasingly popular expert opinion approach involves the Delphi technique.[35] A panel of experts is set up, though panel members remain anonymous to each other and never physically meet. Forecast estimates and supporting arguments are provided in writing by each panelist to a coordinator who summarizes the results and gives feedback to the panel. An additional round of estimates is then carried out, and this cycle is repeated until the divergence of opinion among panel members is significantly reduced or estimates are no longer being changed in response to the prior round's feedback. Anonymity avoids the many problems which often hinder face-to-face committees: pressure from domineering personalities, influence or intimidation from higher-status persons, and reluctance to change one's mind after stating an initial position "in public." A Delphi study to estimate demand for educational services in a new sales territory was carried out by Pace Computing Corporation, and additional questions were included for which the correct answers were already known. Because the panel's estimates on the additional questions were extremely close to the correct answers, the company was optimistic about the validity of the demand estimates as well.[36] Further experimentation with this technique is needed, but so far it holds considerable promise.

Which Methods to Use. Since there are many available forecasting methods, management must decide which to use. No single method can reflect all demand determinants equally well, so some combination usually is necessary. Monsanto, for example, uses regression analysis, seasonal indexes from time series analysis, a field sales composite, estimates from product managers, and a committee comprised of sales, production, purchasing, accounting, and research executives.[37]

The use of forecasting techniques, based on a study of 161 industrial and consumer goods manufacturers and service firms, is shown in Table 4.5. For all firms combined, greatest reliance is placed on executive opinion, and this holds true in the consumer goods and service categories specifically as well. But industrial goods producers favor the field sales composite above all other methods. Mathematical models find strongest support among service firms as compared with consumer or industrial firms, and this study noted that experimentation with mathematical models is on the rise.[38]

Other factors to consider include cost and accuracy of each alternative, usefulness in meeting specific forecasting purposes, and understandability of the method by forecast users. A time series approach is far less expensive than the field sales composite method, but the accuracy of each can differ widely depending on which demand determinants are most critical at the time. And beyond some acceptable level, increased accuracy may be less important than speed, so a particular method is used to give quick results. One example is General Motors, which forecasts new car sales monthly. A GM forecaster noted, "We are in a rapidly changing business and the cost of carrying inventory is high. There's nothing we want less than a lot of old models sitting around when the new ones are coming out. We have a limited

TABLE 4.5

Degree of Company Reliance on Major Sales Forecasting Methods

	DEGREE OF RELIANCE ON FORECASTING METHODS BY:											
	All companies			Industrial Goods Manufacturers			Consumer Goods Manufacturers			Services		
	heavy	moderate	little or none	heavy	moderate	little or none	heavy	moderate	little or none	heavy	moderate	little or none
Executive opinion	48%	32%	20%	47%	34%	19%	53%	24%	23%	42%	38%	20%
Field sales composite	42%	33%	25%	50%	36%	13%	27%	24%	50%	35%	35%	30%
Survey of User Expectations	18%	30%	52%	22%	37%	41%	10%	27%	63%	17%	8%	75%
Time series and Exponential Smoothing	25%	32%	43%	23%	30%	48%	29%	29%	43%	25%	46%	29%
Mathematical Models	15%	19%	66%	12%	20%	69%	11%	24%	66%	32%	12%	56%

Source: S. J. PoKempner and E. L. Bailey, *Sales Forecasting Practices,* Experiences in Marketing Management, no. 25 (New York: The Conference Board, 1970), p. 10.

time for inventory adjustments; hence the production schedule must be very sensitive to market changes."[39]

Finally, the forecaster must consider how well forecast users will accept and understand forecast data computed from various methods. Data from a complex mathematical approach may not be used by some company personnel if they do not understand the method. If they do use such forecasts without fully understanding the limitations and assumptions of the method, their resulting plans and decisions may be faulty. In general, simpler methods are preferred to the more complex whenever equally usable results can be attained.

CALCULATING THE FORECAST

Each forecasting method requires a number of steps in planning, data collection, editing, and analyzing the results. A mathematical model can be run almost instantaneously on a computer, but the quality of the results is highly dependent on obtaining accurate data and preparing them properly to fit the model. Opinion and survey techniques are likewise the product of numerous activities. Consider the following description of a field sales composite method as carried out by an industrial products manufacturer:

Our sales forecast is presently built in this fashion:
a. Based on good statistical information by customer and by product, the sales engineer (salesman) prepares his forecast.
b. It is then reviewed and adjusted in a conference between the sales engineer and his district manager.

c. It is then reviewed in a personal discussion between the district manager and his area manager.
d. It is then reviewed in a personal discussion between the area manager and the general marketing manager.
e. It is then reviewed by the general marketing manager and the vice-president—marketing.
f. It is then reviewed by all the key department heads within the division, including the general manager of the division and the group vice president to whom the general manager reports. At this point, manufacturing capabilities and all economic indicators available to us are used to justify or modify the sales forecast.[40]

The total forecasting process is even more complex in many firms. Numerous departments and individuals participate, several techniques are used which must be reconciled, and a varied assortment of forecasts is turned out. Figure 4.3 illustrates this process in Combustion Engineering. A hierarchy of forecasts is produced from various information sources and forecasting techniques, and within each level of the forecast hierarchy there are more detailed breakdowns which are termed information elements. Figure 4.4 shows another view of the forecasting process in Aluminum Company of America. Here the forecasts (which they call "annual requirements estimates") are the product of a long sequence of steps beginning with the sales force, going to the industry specialists in the firm, then to the product specialists, and finally to the general manager. This sequence starts six months prior to the beginning of each new year.

APPLYING FORECAST RESULTS

Once approved, the forecast is distributed to executives in the firm who use this information in further planning. Production managers translate the results into production and inventory control policies. Personnel managers consider hiring and training needs resulting from the forecast. Traffic managers adjust shipping plans. Purchasing managers formulate buying commitments for needed materials. And sales managers use forecast data in assessing territories, setting quotas, devising compensation plans, and many other areas covered in upcoming chapters.

EVALUATING THE FORECAST

Forecasts are evaluated in terms of accuracy—how close was our forecast to actual sales? One study of 175 firms showed that the average error in consumer goods firms was 6.7 percent, while industrial goods firms experienced an average error of 7.6 percent.[41] The marketing manager at Stouffer Foods summed up a generally accepted goal by forecasters when he stated, "If you can come within 5 percent, you've been pretty accurate."[42]

Perhaps a more meaningful accuracy measure is to compare the forecast *change* in company sales from one period to the next with the actual change, especially when short-term decisions are at stake. This error is likely to be far greater than 5 percent. For instance, a study of one of the nation's largest airlines revealed that projected sales changes were in error by over 50 percent when compared with realized changes over a one-year period.[43]

FIGURE 4.3

The Forecasting Process in Combustion Engineering

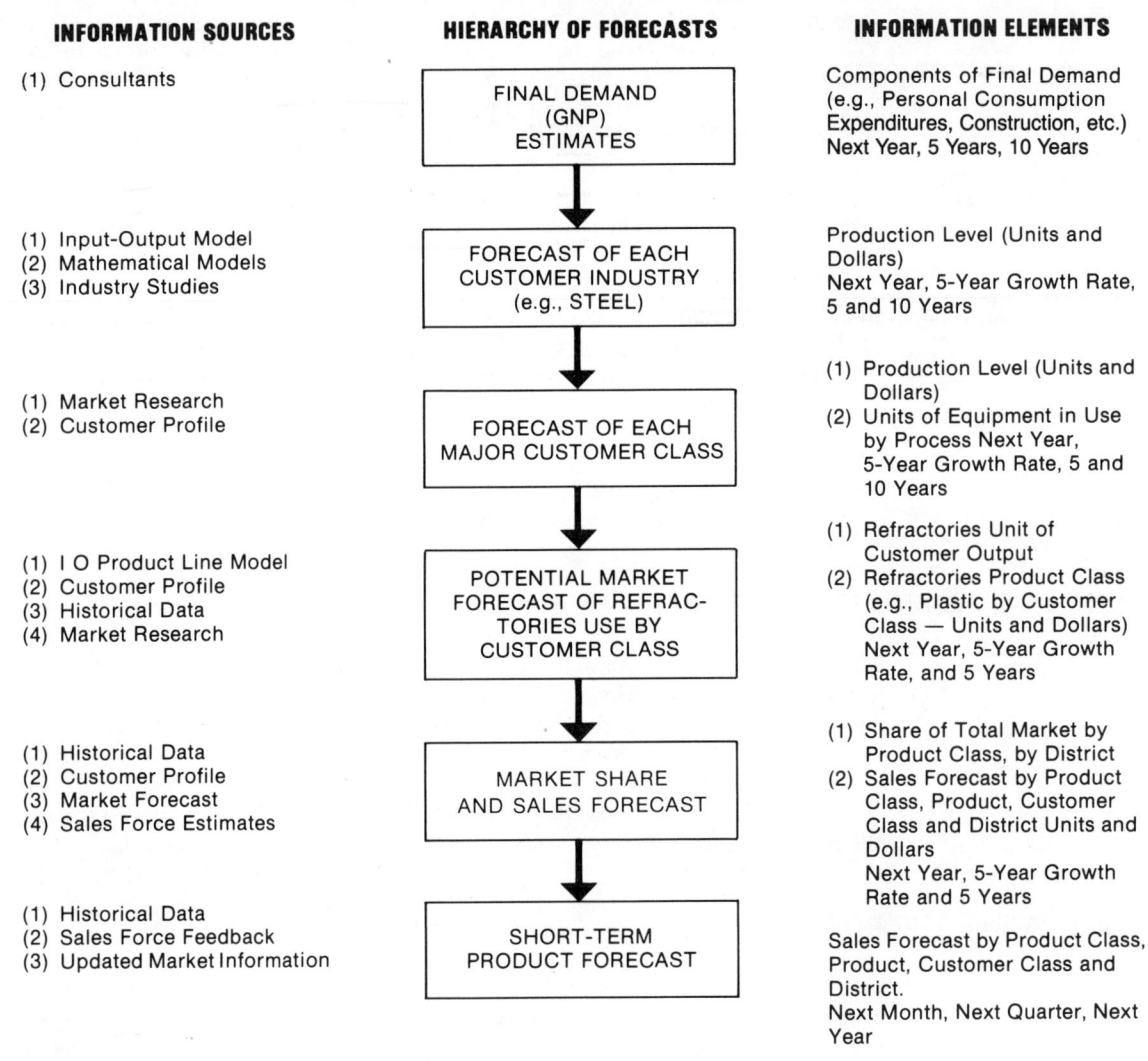

Source: Reprinted from the *Journal of Marketing Research,* published by the American Marketing Association. Elliot D. Ranard, "Use of Input/Output Concepts in Sales Forecasting," vol. 9 (February 1972), p. 54.

FIGURE 4.4

The Forecasting Process in Aluminum Company of America: Preparation of the Annual Requirement Estimate (ARE)

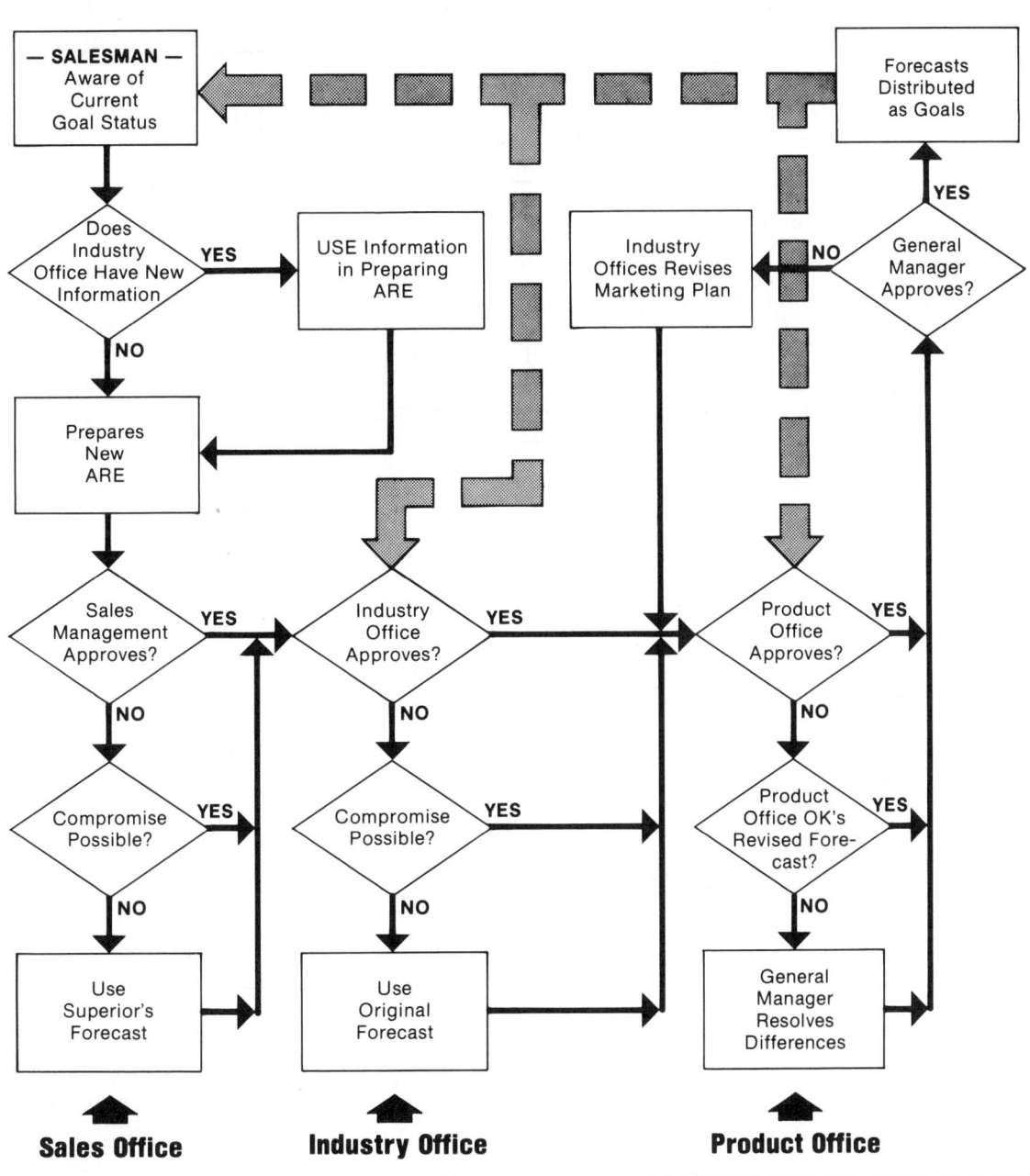

Source: Stanley J. PoKempner, *Information Systems for Sales and Marketing Management* (New York: The Conference Board, Inc., 1973), p. 28.

At times a sales forecast may present an undesirable picture, causing management to attempt corrective action. If corrective action is successful, the original forecast would appear to have been inaccurate. Such a forecast is termed "self-defeating." In an opposite situation, an originally inaccurate forecast eventually might appear to be correct. For example, a forecast which was too low might cause a lack of production and inventory so that higher demand could not be satisfied. The resulting sales volume would be too low, but might match the forecast closely. This is termed a "self-validating" forecast. Evaluating the accuracy of a forecast is not always a straightforward calculation.

While accuracy is important, an even more important criterion in evaluation is the cost to the firm of forecast error. This cost, and associated profit reduction, is a reflection of three factors: the importance of decisions based on the forecast, the proportion of fixed-to-variable costs as sales volume changes, and the ability of the firm to respond or take corrective action when forecast errors become evident.[44] Since many important decisions often rest on a forecast, this cost can be significant.

Sensitivity analysis can simulate the cost and profit consequences of various levels of forecast error. For instance, what would happen to profits if forecast estimates were 10 percent too high, 9 percent too high, 8 percent too high, and so on? If there is some level of forecast error within which profits become largely insensitive, there is no reason to improve forecasting accuracy beyond this level. In general, the firm should spend additional funds for refining forecast estimates as long as the expenditures are less than the resulting reductions in cost of forecast error to the firm.

An evaluation might call for some change in the forecasting process. Before incorporating one or more new methods in the next period's forecast, the forecaster should simulate previous years' forecasts with the new methods to determine what the result would have been in cost and in accuracy. If survey, executive opinion, or field sales composite are the new methods under consideration, such a retrospective test would be impossible, but cost estimates could be made. The old and new methods might be undertaken concurrently in the next period so that a choice can be made on a more directly comparative basis.

CONCLUSION

The sales forecasting process has been presented here in sufficient detail so that a sales manager can analyze forecast results intelligently. If the sales manager has complete responsibility for producing these forecasts for his firm, this chapter provided background to expand his study of the various steps involved. The emphasis here concerned sales forecasting as a major activity in setting sales management goals. Succeeding activities build upon the forecast data. If the forecast is inadequate, the value of subsequent activities will be reduced as well.

QUESTIONS FOR REVIEW AND DISCUSSION

1. What should be included in the ideal forecasting method? Compare this ideal with the methods discussed in this chapter. Which method comes closest to being ideal?

2. What can a sales manager do to motivate the sales force to try to forecast

accurately? Perhaps a review of the model in Figure 1.2 will suggest some areas for possible consideration.

3. As the sales manager for a small electronics manufacturer with seven salespeople, you have obtained the following data to help you make a forecast for the upcoming year:

Extrapolation of trend data from past four years:	$4,200,000
Total of salespersons' territorial estimates:	$3,600,000
Average of opinions of president, chief financial officer, and production manager:	$4,600,000
Average of opinions of four major customers, from which a ratio to their past sales was computed and generalized to your total customer base:	$5,000,000

How would you use these data in arriving at your annual sales forecast? Is there any other information essential to making the forecast?

4. A sales manager can seldom make a good forecast estimate without knowing how many salespeople will be employed during the forecast period. Yet that number will depend on the sales forecast target. How can the sales manager reconcile this circular problem?

5. Discuss some specific sales management applications of both long-range and short-range forecasts. How accurate must the forecasts be before they are useful in these applications?

6. The district sales manager in a firm selling novelty items to wholesalers has been requested to forecast next year's sales for her district. The product line consists of many items sold in large quantities to wholesalers, and there is a slight seasonal variation in sales. What forecasting method or methods should be used?

7. Obtain some monthly sales data from a firm and develop a simple exponential smoothing model. Then discuss the nature and value of this model for that firm.

8. Your firm is a food company selling moderately well-known products through retail grocery stores. Below are three different situations your firm might face. For each situation, pick the best one or two forecasting techniques, and explain why you think they are best for each situation:
    a. Your firm is planning to change the package on one of your standard products (e.g., canned beans), and you need a one-year sales forecast for the product with the new package.
    b. Your firm is going to establish a totally new gourmet food line (10–15 different products under a new brand name), and you need a one-year forecast for the new line in total.
    c. Your firm is planning no major change in product line, but is expecting that economic conditions might decline slightly over the next year, and you want to determine how that might affect future sales.

9. The president of a small manufacturing firm has a simple answer to the sales forecasting process. He believes that the forecast should equal the firm's production capacity, and the sales manager's responsibility is to attain that amount of sales. Evaluate this approach to forecasting.

10. Under what conditions should the sales manager attempt to obtain sales beyond the forecast level? Are there any cases where obtaining sales considerably beyond the forecast level could be detrimental to the firm?

NOTES

1. Thayer C. Taylor, "Econometrics: A Formidable Weapon For GE, RCA, GM, or Nearly Anyone," *Sales & Marketing Management,* November 17, 1975, p. 33.

2. *Forecasting Sales,* Studies in Business Policy, no. 106 (New York: National Industrial Conference Board, Inc., 1963), p. 4.

3. *Forecasting Sales,* p. 61.

4. W. P. Carlin, "Sales Forecasting Operations," in *Marketing Research in Action,* Studies in Business Policy, no. 84 (New York: National Industrial Conference Board, Inc., 1957), pp. 27–30.

5. *Forecasting Sales, op. cit.,* pp. 92–94.

6. These results come from Stanley J. PoKempner and Earl L. Bailey, *Sales Forecasting Practices,* Experiences in Marketing Management, no. 25 (New York: The Conference Board, 1970).

7. Phyllis Daignault, "Marketing Management and the Computer," *Sales Management,* August 20, 1965, p. 54.

8. Another example and further discussion of forecasting as simulation is found in Edward J. Spar, "Using Regression Analysis To Answer the Question 'What If . . . ?'," *Sales & Marketing Management,* October 11, 1976, pp. 78–79.

9. Stephen D. Cole, "Survival Guide: The Ins And Outs Of Predicting Twists and Turns," *Sales & Marketing Management,* November 17, 1975, p. 43.

10. *Ibid.,* p. 42.

11. *Ibid.,* p. 42.

12. One comprehensive study of forecasting offers a detailed comparison and explanation of 18 methods in use today. See John C. Chambers, S. K. Mullick, and D. D. Smith, *An Executive's Guide to Forecasting* (New York: John Wiley, 1974).

13. *Forecasting Sales, op. cit.,* p. 35.

14. Robert L. McLaughlin, "The Break Through in Sales Forecasting," *Journal of Marketing,* vol. 27 (April 1963), p. 46.

15. *Forecasting Sales, op. cit.,* pp. 84–85.

16. *Forecasting Sales, op. cit.,* p. 86.

17. More complex models can be devised to include trend and seasonal patterns. See Frank H. Eby, Jr., and William J. O'Neill, *The Management of Sales Forecasting* (Lexington, Mass.: Lexington Books, 1977), pp. 227–241; and Philip H. Siegel, "Exponential Smoothing for Sales Forecasting: Analysis and Application," *Marquette Business Review,* Winter 1973, pp. 210–217.

18. L. F. Church, "Sales Budgeting," in *Marketing Research in Action,* p. 18.

19. George G. C. Parker and E. L. Segura, "How to Get a Better Forecast," *Harvard Business Review,* vol. 49 (March–April 1971), p. 100.

20. Shea Smith, III, "Forecasting Sales," in *Marketing Research in Action,* pp. 24–26.

21. David L. Hurwood, et al., *Sales Forecasting,* Report No. 730 (New York: The Conference Board, Inc., 1978), pp. 120–122.

22. *Forecasting Sales, op. cit.,* p. 44.

23. See David H. Ahl, "New Product Forecasting Using Consumer Panels," *Journal of Marketing Research,* vol. 7 (May 1970), pp. 160–167; and Robert Ferber, "Sales Forecasting by Sample Surveys," *Journal of Marketing,* vol. 20 (July 1955), pp. 1–13.

24. For example, "inaccurate forecasting" was cited as a severe problem by 40% of the respondents in a study of large national advertisers' use of consumer panel surveys. See David K. Hardin and Richard M. Johnson, "Patterns of Use of Consumer Purchase Panels," *Journal of Marketing Research,* vol. 8 (August 1971), p. 366.

25. Jean Namias, "Intentions to Purchase Compared with Actual Purchases of Household Durables," *Journal of Marketing,* vol. 24 (July 1959), p. 27.

26. J. F. Pickering and B. C. Isherwood, "Purchase Probabilities and Consumer Durable Buying Behavior," *Journal of the Market Research Society,* vol. 16 (July 1974), pp. 203–226; see also F. Thomas Juster, *Consumer Buying Intentions and Purchase Probability,* Occasional Paper no. 99 (New York: National Bureau of Economic Research, Inc., 1966).

27. "Executive Roundtable: Sales Forecasting Emerges As An Indispensable Management Tool," *Sales & Marketing Management,* November 17, 1975, p. 14.

28. *Forecasting Sales, op. cit.,* pp. 31–32.

29. Paul R. Thompson, "Sales Budgeting," in *Marketing Research in Action,* pp. 20–22.

30. Sally Scanlon, "TRW's Forecasts Keep Management On Top Of A Turbulent World," *Sales & Marketing Management,* November 17, 1975, p. 31.

31. For a discussion of how such information might hinder as well as help the accuracy of judgmental forecasts, see Richard Staelin and R. E. Turner, "Error in Judgmental Sales Forecasts: Theory and Results," *Journal of Marketing Research,* vol. 10 (February 1973), pp. 10–16.

32. Richard M. Kahn, "You Don't Have To Be A Colossus To Forecast Accurately," *Sales & Marketing Management,* November 17, 1975, p. 11.

33. Thomas R. Wotruba and Michael L. Thurlow, "Sales Force Participation in Quota Setting and Sales Forecasting," *Journal of Marketing,* vol. 40 (April 1976), p. 15.

34. Roger J. Best, "An Experiment in Delphi Estimation in Marketing Decision Making," *Journal of Marketing Research,* vol. 11 (November 1974), p. 451.

35. Richard J. Tersine and Walter E. Riggs, "The Delphi Technique: A Long-Range Planning Tool," *Business Horizons,* vol. 19 (April 1976), pp. 51–56.

36. Marvin A. Jolson and Gerald L. Rossow, "The Delphi Process in Marketing Decision Making," *Journal of Marketing Research,* vol. 8 (November 1971), pp. 443–448.

37. Smith, pp. 24–27.

38. PoKempner, p. 41.

39. Taylor, p. 38.

40. PoKempner, p. 6.

41. A more detailed discussion of forecasting accuracy, from which these data are drawn, is found in Douglas J. Dalrymple, "Sales Forecasting Methods and Accuracy," *Business Horizons,* vol. 18 (December 1975), pp. 69–73.

42. "Forecasting At Stouffer's: It Helps To Be A Big Boy," *Sales & Marketing Management,* November 17, 1975, p. 41.

43. John J. Clark and Pieter T. Elgers, "Evaluating the Sales Forecast," *Michigan Business Review,* vol. 20 (May 1968), p. 18.

44. Clark and Elgers, p. 19.

5 SALES BUDGETING

While the sales forecast is being determined, the corresponding expenditures necessary to reach that forecast must be identified and budgeted. Budgets and forecasts go hand in hand since these two tools are the key partners in the firm's financial plan. Forecast revenues minus budgeted expenditures must produce the targeted profits as well as market share and other goals desired by management.

Budgeting involves all operations within the firm including the sales department and all other departments. A brief discussion of the purposes of budgeting in a firm will be helpful as background for sales budgeting.[1]

A major purpose of budgeting is to help management plan, and careful budgeting will produce a detailed plan of all operations and tasks in the coming period. Alternatives must be investigated to assure that the best methods and programs will be utilized. If a new product is to be introduced next year, for example, what types and amounts of marketing activities should be used? What should be the relative emphases on packaging, advertising, personal selling, and other aspects of the marketing mix? By attaching costs as well as revenues to alternative programs, management can better select the combination of expenditures that will meet the firm's goals most effectively. This produces an additional benefit as well. Once alternative plans have been evaluated, any ensuing changes can be effected more quickly when needed, thereby reducing crisis planning.

Coordination and communication within the firm are enhanced through budgeting. For example, marketing should not be called upon to sell more than production is scheduled to produce. Management must arrive at a final budget that best harmonizes the divergent needs within the firm. When the final budget is viewed by any member of management, the breakdown of types and amounts of expenditures should clearly express the planned operations in all parts of the firm and how they combine to meet overall company goals.

Through budgeting, cost responsibilities are more clearly identified so that budget variations during the operating period can be traced quickly to the proper departments and managers. Budgeting is not only a planning activity but also a means of control and evaluation. Budgeting can also encourage profit awareness throughout a firm. In his review of departmental budget requests, for example, the general manager of the Health Care Division of Johnson & Johnson stated, "If they fail to meet the profit objectives of the division, the departmental budgets are reworked until they are brought into line."[2] In such an atmosphere, each member of management must present his or her budget request in terms of its overall profit implications. A profit viewpoint is especially critical for the sales manager, since selling costs are often substantial and can have a significant effect on profits.

Effective budgeting involves a great deal more than simply putting together a group of expenditure categories and attaching dollar costs to them—the apparent result when a budget is finally completed. The activity of budgeting truly is a planning and integrating mechanism within a firm. Much of the above discussion can be summarized in this definition:

Budgeting is the planning process whereby management determines the combination of expected revenues and expenditures which will best meet the goals of the firm in the budget period.

In an ideal situation, budgeting produces a detailed statement of a firm's goals and policies in financial terms and reflects the coordinated effort of all management members responsible for carrying out the company's programs and activities.

BUDGETING IN SALES MANAGEMENT

Budgeting for the sales department must begin with consideration of two types of coordination. First is the coordination of sales with other marketing functions. Second is the coordination between budgeting and prior planning activities, especially sales forecasting.

Coordination with Other Marketing Functions. Since personal selling is only one aspect of the marketing mix, budgeting in the sales organization should be done in close communication with budgeting in the other marketing functions. When the various areas of marketing are well coordinated, the expenditures in each should have greater value since they reinforce and complement each other in a synergistic fashion.

Here are two examples of this synergism. One study in a retail music store varied the selling effort and price for a cleaner for 8-track tape players. When price was lowest, regardless of the quality of selling effort employed, a sale occurred 55 percent of the time. When highest-quality selling effort was used, regardless of the price, a sale was made 58 percent of the time. But under conditions of lowest price and highest-quality selling effort combined, a sale occurred 80 percent of the time![3] In another study, a chemical company identified which of its customers were exposed to its advertising and which were not. The cost of selling to each group was then calculated, and this cost was found to be 5 percent *lower* for the group exposed to advertising. In addition, the company's market share was 50 percent higher among the customers in the exposed group![4]

Coordination with Sales Forecasting. In budgeting, the sales manager relies considerably on sales forecast data. Budgeting is usually undertaken with the sales forecast as the starting point for three main reasons.

First, all departments of the firm need a common basis from which to start. A sales forecast, as one measure of the anticipated size of the firm's operations, provides this basis.

Second, a sales forecast allows many expenses to be estimated directly. Such expenses are usually termed *variable costs*. An example is salespeople's commissions, which are often a percentage of their sales.

Third, the sales forecast often is more dependent on uncontrollable factors than are sales expenditures. In this case, it is better to adjust the more controllable expenditures to the less controllable revenues.

Ultimately, however, the level of forthcoming revenues depends on the types and amounts of expenditures incurred. To put it another way, *the budget is a plan for buying revenues with expenditures.* If a firm spends money to add a salesperson, that salesperson will usually increase the firm's total sales. Furthermore, different combinations of expenditures, even when each totals the same dollar amount, can produce different levels of sales volume. So neither forecast sales nor budgeted expenditures can be determined apart. Both must be adjusted until they are consistent with each other and with company goals.

After the initial draft of the budget is completed, the sales forecast should be reevaluated to determine if it is too high or too low. The feasibility of any forecast increase depends on the availability of sufficient sales potential and also on the cost necessary to convert that potential into actual sales. For instance, sufficient potential might exist but it can be captured only at a rising marginal cost. Unless marginal revenues increase in the same proportion, the additional sales would be obtained at decreasing profit per sales dollar, which might be contrary to the firm's overall profit goal. As a general rule, marginal revenues do not change appreciably while marginal costs do change as changes occur in sales penetration. This latter relationship is shown in Figure 5.1.

In this illustration, marginal cost rises at the outset as the firm negotiates initial orders from new customers. Then marginal cost falls, up to some level of penetration (50 percent in this example), because the cost per additional unit of sale declines as the firm gains a foothold in the market. But beyond this level of penetration, each succeeding unit of sale becomes more difficult and thus, more costly to obtain.

FIGURE 5.1

Marginal Cost of Obtaining Sales Penetration Levels

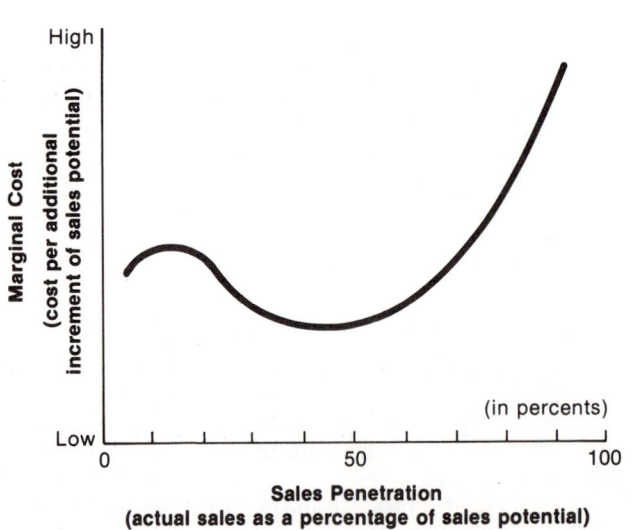

So even if sufficient sales potential is available, the cost of realizing it might become excessive. The exact relationship varies in different markets, but the curve in Figure 5.1 is generally applicable.[5]

This relationship between forecasting and budgeting is exemplified by the procedure used in Cooper-Bessemer Corporation, a manufacturer of engines and compressors. A detailed preliminary sales forecast is prepared by the sales manager and given to the controller, who translates it into a profit-and-loss forecast by using standard costs as well as the judgments of major executives. When finished, the controller submits his estimates to an executive committee, which discusses the assumptions underlying the sales, cost, and profit projections. If adjustments seem necessary, the preliminary forecast is modified and the change is worked into the cost and profit statements until an acceptable set of projections results.[6]

NATURE OF SELLING EXPENDITURES

Under conventional accounting practices, selling expenditures are usually charged in full to the current year's operation of the firm. This treatment implies that such expenses produce their full value during one operating period.

But the value of many selling activities extends much longer. For example, an effective sales training program should benefit sales for several years, and more money spent initially on selection of salespeople might result in better salespeople, higher or more profitable sales volume, and reduced turnover of sales personnel. Some sales efforts may not pay off at all until a later time, so that the value received is delayed considerably after the initial expenditure of funds. This happens when a salesperson calls many times on a prospect with high potential volume before making the initial sale. In these delayed cases, the costs involved produce returns over a longer time in a manner more like that of an asset or an investment. But federal and state regulations, as well as generally accepted accounting principles, require that these items be classified as expenses.[7]

This classification can be detrimental to long-term results, however. It implies that, as "expenses," these are cash outlays which should be reduced as much as possible. The result is sometimes a failure to "invest" sufficiently in certain personal selling activities which seem too expensive if completely written off during the current period. For example, when a sales manager forgoes a more extensive selection or training program now because of high cost, he may face higher turnover or lower sales results in a later period. At that point, increased supervision or sales contests would become necessary in an attempt to improve performance; but the funds diverted to these activities might further reduce the funds available for selection and training of new salespeople.

One firm which formally considers part of its sales budget as an investment is Emery Air Freight, treating two budget items this way. One includes a group of trained sales personnel employed to step into territories vacated through turnover. This minimizes lost sales from interruptions in customer coverage and service. The other comprises a group of salespeople who develop new markets. Together these items account for about one quarter of the company's budget for sales salaries.[8] Typically, however, sales department budget items will be treated as expenses so the sales manager must continually seek ways of convincing higher management of the investment nature of selling activities.

DETERMINING THE SELLING BUDGET LEVEL

The first budgeting decision normally made by a sales manager is to determine how much to spend in total on personal selling activities—the budget *level*. Following that are decisions on how to allocate that total to specific selling activities, how to estimate and classify budgetary costs, and what policies and procedures to set up for budgeting administration. We shall examine the budget level decision first.

Since firms use many types of promotion, the budget level provided for personal selling depends on its relative importance in the promotional mix. As we have already noted, the contribution of personal selling is difficult to isolate from the contributions of other promotional efforts and, indeed, from the other components of the marketing mix.[9] One study sought to determine how management makes these distinctions, but the responses indicated "embarrassed rather than enlightened management" according to the final report.[10] West Virginia Pulp and Paper Company made a buying influences study in which customers' perceptions of the relative importance of different promotional categories were measured. With the results the company set relative budget levels for such promotional types as selling, advertising, sales promotion, and servicing.[11] While such studies are a step in the right direction, their results probably are strongly influenced by the previous budgeting decisions affecting the level of effort for each type.

Many methods are available to assist the sales manager in setting the sales budget level. We shall look first at the methods which are most commonly used (percentage of sales, all you can afford, competitive parity, and objective and task); problems inherent in these methods will be noted, leading to a discussion of methods which are theoretically correct but more difficult to implement (return on investment, and incremental).

PERCENTAGE-OF-SALES METHOD

In determining the total sales budget, many firms use a historical percentage of their selling costs to sales. This method has many variations. One is to apply the percentage to last year's sales volume. For example, if this year's selling costs were 5 percent of last year's sales volume, the budget for next year would be 5 percent of this year's volume. Another variation is to apply this ratio to the sales forecast, so that 5 percent of projected sales becomes the budget level.

A weighted average based on this year's actual and next year's forecast sales is also employed. In this case, 5 percent of the last year's sales might be weighted 0.5 (the weight is a management decision), and 5 percent of forecast sales would then be weighted 0.5. Their weighted sum would then produce the budget amount.

These percentages may be useful guides if management has been satisfied with the past accomplishment of the sales force and if basic sales operations and competitive conditions are generally unchanging. But the logic of this method is weak. Selling efforts are a *cause* of sales volume, but in this approach the level of selling effort becomes the *result* of sales volume. Furthermore, no specific recognition is given to the objectives of selling, and management avoids the important question of whether a higher or lower budget level could improve company profits.

Perhaps the popularity of this method stems from its simplicity. In addition, because expenditures keyed to revenues pose little risk, the amount may be easy to defend in a budget review session. At best, this method offers a bench mark with which to compare the results of other methods.

ALL-YOU-CAN-AFFORD METHOD

It is possible to set the sales budget level on the basis of available funds. This is primarily a residual approach: the sales manager gets what's left after other cost categories have been covered. This method is as weak logically as the first one. Sales efforts become the result rather than the cause of funds available to the firm.

Many firms experience a cyclical pattern in financial liquidity; for them, the selling budget is highest when available funds are high and lowest when funds are low. If there is any benefit in this pattern, it is that higher sales expense serves to reduce company profits and associated income tax in the peak periods and vice versa in the low ones.

This method implies that funds for personal selling will be sufficiently productive at any level. But above some level, diminishing returns are likely. And below some level, it is possible that marginal costs would decrease sufficiently, so that budget funds would generate more profit if some were shifted from other applications to personal selling. This calls for an incremental approach to budgeting, which is discussed later.

Another problem is illustrated by the following example. Suppose management decides to open as many territories as the firm can afford, then later discovers that less funds are available than anticipated, so that cutbacks become necessary under this all-you-can-afford budgeting approach. Since territories have been established and salespeople already hired and in the field, management can only reduce such items as entertainment, travel, and telephone. Such cuts may hamper selling effort to the point where these territories are unprofitable.

COMPETITIVE PARITY METHOD

Under the competitive parity method, the sales budget level is set in relation to competitors' budget levels. One approach is to determine selling costs as a percentage of sales for the industry, and then to apply this percentage to the firm's sales. Finding industry data is not always easy, however, and data which is available often hides differences between companies in their definitions of what constitutes selling expenses.[12] Table 5.1 provides one source which is published annually from a sample of firms in various industries.

In essence, the competitive parity method recognizes that competition affects the productivity of a firm's selling effort. A difficulty, however, is trying to anticipate whether competitors will maintain or change their future budgets in comparison with their past spending. Since competitors' budgets may change, management should analyze the impact of alternative budget levels which competitors might choose. Executive experience and judgment can provide this analysis within a game theory framework. Suppose there are two competing firms in an industry (this can be modified to include one firm and the rest of the industry), and each firm has three main budget alternatives. Management must first construct a matrix which identifies its payoff under each possible combination of its budget levels and those of competition. The payoffs may be stated in sales volume, profits, market share, or any other quantitative measure. Table 5.2 illustrates a game theory matrix with payoffs stated as profit contributions. For example, if the firm budgets $300,000 and competition budgets $450,000, the firm will realize $210,000 in profit contribution.

TABLE 5.1

Some Measures of Selling Costs in Selected Industries, 1977

Industry	Sales Force Selling Expenses as a Percentage of Company Sales			Total Selling Expenses as a Percentage of Company Sales
	Compensation	T&E Expenses	Total	
Consumer Goods:				
Apparel	2.6%	0.9%	3.5%	7.5%
Durable Goods	2.3	1.1	3.4	9.5
Ethical Pharmaceuticals, Surgical Supplies and Equipment	3.2	1.2	4.4	6.4
Food	1.7	0.4	2.1	4.0
Major Household Items	1.1	0.5	1.6	5.5
Proprietary Drugs and Toiletries	4.5	2.7	7.2	13.7
Industrial Goods:				
Automobile & Truck	5.9	1.2	7.1	10.1
Automotive Parts & Accessories	4.0	1.8	5.8	6.1
Building Materials	1.4	0.5	1.9	2.5
Chemicals	1.4	0.7	2.1	2.9
Computers	5.2	N.A.	5.2	4.4
Containers & Packaging Materials	1.5	0.7	2.2	4.1
Electrical Materials	2.9	0.9	3.8	5.3
Electronics	2.6	1.3	3.9	6.2
Fabricated Metals, heavy	1.7	0.7	2.4	3.5
Fabricated Metals, light	2.3	1.0	3.3	4.6
Fabrics	2.3	0.5	2.8	3.0
Glass and Allied Products	1.5	1.0	2.5[a]	3.6
Instruments	3.3	0.9	4.2	10.0
Iron & Steel	0.8	0.3	1.1	1.3
Machinery, heavy	1.3	0.8	2.1	3.3
Machinery, light	2.0	1.2	3.2	5.9
Office and Educational Supplies and Equipment	6.9	N.A.	6.9	13.5
Paper	0.2	0.2	0.4	1.9
Petroleum	3.5	1.0	4.5	5.1
Printing and Publishing	5.0	0.9	5.9	10.4
Rubber, Plastics, & Leather	1.5	0.5	2.0	2.8
Tools & Hardware	4.3	1.3	5.6	9.3

[a] for 1976.

Notes: T&E includes travel, lodging, meals, and entertainment.

Percentages in the first three columns refer to sales made by the sales force.

Total Selling Expense includes compensation of sales force and sales management, travel, lodging, meals, and entertainment, advertising and promotion.

Reprinted by permission of the publisher from *Sales Personnel Report,* 22nd Edition, 1977/78, Executive Compensation Service, © 1978 by AMACOM, a division of American Management Associations. All rights reserved.

TABLE 5.2
Game Theory Matrix for Analyzing Alternative Budget Levels

| Firm's Alternative Sales Budget Levels | PAYOFFS TO THE FIRM IN TERMS OF PROFIT CONTRIBUTION |||
| | Competitors' Alternative Sales Budget Levels: |||
	$150,000	$300,000	$450,000
$150,000	$350,000	$175,000	$100,000
300,000	330,000	225,000	210,000
450,000	320,000	275,00	240,000

Next, management must decide what budget level to select. Various criteria can be used for this decision. One is to note the worst possible outcome for each of the firm's alternative levels and then to select the level for which the worst possible outcome would present the greatest payoff. In this illustration, the best of the worst possible outcomes occurs when the firm budgets $450,000. The worst payoff at that level would be $240,000 which is higher than the worst payoff for any other budget level alternative. This is termed a *maximin* criterion because the firm selects a budget level which maximizes the minimum payoff.

Another criterion is selecting a level which maximizes the maximum payoff or which has the greatest average payoff (that is, the average from all three levels of the competitor's budget). The use of game theory becomes more refined if probabilities can be attached to the competitor's alternative levels, but that is beyond the scope of this book.[13]

OBJECTIVE-AND-TASK METHOD

The budgeting methods examined thus far have one common fault: they fail to reflect the firm's specific selling goals for the budget period. The objective-and-task method attempts to overcome this fault and places selling in its proper role as a cause rather than a result of sales or profits. In brief, this method contains three steps: (1) specify objectives to be attained, (2) designate tasks necessary to reach the objectives, and (3) determine costs associated with these tasks.

An example, patterned after the use of this method by Worthington Corporation, is shown in Table 5.3.[14] Specific promotional objectives are first established and the responsibility for achieving them is assigned to personal selling and to other parts of the promotional mix. Individual tasks are then specified and weighted to reflect their relative importance. Then personal selling's contribution to each task is specified based on its share of responsibility for reaching promotional objectives. The total contribution of personal selling to the overall promotional plan is then calculated—63.5 percent in this example.

A separate analysis is often necessary for each product or market because objectives differ among products or markets. Once the management team agrees on the tasks and corresponding percentages, costs must be determined and evaluated. Suppose the sales manager concludes that $300,000 is necessary to carry out the required personal selling tasks in this example. If projected sales are $10 million, this makes selling costs equal to 3 percent of sales. Past accounting data can be used to evaluate the reasonableness of this percentage.

This evaluation can be carried out still further by comparing alternative uses for these funds. Following Table 5.3, personal selling contributes 63.5 percent of total

TABLE 5.3
Calculating Personal Selling's Contribution to Promotional Tasks

Promotional Task	Relative Value in Total Promotional Plan (in percents)	×	Percent of Personal Selling's Contribution (in percents)	=	Total Personal Selling Contribution (in percents)
Market Development:	Total (20)				
Prospect Contacts	10		50		5.0
Reputation Building	5		20		1.0
Market Education	5		10		0.5
Selling:	Total (40)				
Customer Contacts	5		70		3.5
Arousing Interest	5		50		2.5
Creating Preference	15		80		12.0
Making Proposals	5		100		5.0
Closing the Sale	10		100		10.0
Servicing:	Total (25)				
Follow-up on Sale	10		80		8.0
Handling Problems	5		80		4.0
Keeping Customer Informed	10		50		5.0
Market Information:	Total (15)				
Locating Prospects	5		50		2.5
Competitor Knowledge	5		50		2.5
Market Trends	5		40		2.0
Total	100				63.5

promotional effort, and 63.5 percent of the sales forecast is $6,350,000. Relating this volume to selling costs, the resulting cost to sales ratio is 4.7 percent. Similar calculations are then undertaken for advertising and other categories of the promotional mix. Suppose advertising's contribution to the promotional plan is 26 percent, and the budget necessary to accomplish advertising's tasks is $100,000. The proportion of the sales forecast attributed to advertising is 26 percent of $10 million, or $2,600,000. The cost to sales ratio for advertising is then 3.8 percent. This suggests that advertising is accomplishing its share of the promotional task at less relative cost than personal selling, under the assumption that sales volume is the proper basis for evaluating these costs. Management should then consider whether additional promotional tasks could be shifted to advertising if the shifts can be accomplished at these established cost ratios.[15]

Other calculations can be made using profits as a base rather than volume. For example, if the company's profit on sales equals 6 percent, the following comparisons result:

	Personal Selling	Advertising
Cost	$300,000	$100,000
Sales Attributable to Each Function	$6,350,000	$2,600,000
Profit (6% of Sales)	$381,000	$156,000
Return (Profit/Cost)	1.27	1.56

Since the return on advertising is considerably higher than on personal selling, management should again consider some shifts in funds as long as the tasks originally specified can be satisfactorily fulfilled.[16]

While this method has considerable merit, it can also be misleading. Objectives may be stipulated, budgeted, and achieved without regard for their value. Few objectives are worth achieving unless they make some contribution to profit. A reasonable extension of this method, therefore, is to evaluate and select alternative objectives by comparing the projected costs of each with projected revenues. Under these conditions, the objective-and-task method embodies the process of budgeting defined earlier in this chapter.

RETURN-ON-INVESTMENT METHOD

In the previous illustration, budgeted costs were compared with sales or profits in the same budget period. Yet benefits from selling expenditures are likely to extend beyond this period in a manner similar to the return on an investment. If management regards personal selling as an investment, the budget level decision can be approached from the long-range perspective of capital budgeting.

The return-on-investment method proposes that funds for personal selling should compete with funds for other internal investments in the firm. Investment decisions require that the rate of return over the life of the investment be known. Personal selling investments most likely experience a decreasing return over time, but the rate would be difficult to measure because of the interaction of the many marketing mix variables and fluctuations in competitive conditions. Furthermore, selling effort must be traced to profits, not just sales volume, before making a proper measure of return on investment. All these factors make this method most difficult to put into practice.[17]

Despite these difficulties, a form of return on investment has been used by Sylvania Electric Products to compare alternative sales management actions.[18] To illustrate this approach, termed "Return on Assets Managed" or ROAM, let us assume that a divisional sales manager must decide whether to establish one or more new sales territories. He is considering three locations: Denver, St. Louis, and San Diego. Estimated sales volume in each territory is the same, but costs and profit contributions differ. A ROAM analysis looks beyond the profit results, and recognizes that new territories will generate internal investment which did not previously exist. Two such investment items are accounts receivable and inventories. Thus a proper measure of the productivity of these new territories would be their return on investment (assets).

Table 5.4 illustrates the information necessary to carry out this analysis. The San Diego territory is the best alternative, since it will produce the greatest return on investment. St. Louis offers the largest profit contribution, but would also require the greatest investment of company funds in average accounts receivable and inventories over time. Note that the ROAM computation makes use of two separate ratios. These ratios distinguish between profit rate and investment turnover and are helpful to explain why investments rank differently on return than on profit contribution.

TABLE 5.4
Evaluating Alternative Territory Investments by Their Projected Return on Assets Managed

Projected	Denver	St. Louis	San Diego
Sales	$150,000	$150,000	$150,000
Cost of Goods Sold	80,000	80,000	80,000
Gross Profit	$ 70,000	$ 70,000	$ 70,000
Selling Costs	50,000	36,000	40,000
Profit Contribution	$ 20,000	$ 34,000	$ 30,000
Accounts Receivable	$ 20,000	$ 45,000	$ 30,000
Inventories	25,000	35,000	20,000
Total Investment	$ 45,000	$ 80,000	$ 50,000
Sales/Investment	3.3 times	1.9 times	3.0 times
Profit/Sales	13.3%	22.7%	20.0%
Return on Assets Managed $\left(\dfrac{\text{Profit}}{\text{Sales}} \times \dfrac{\text{Sales}}{\text{Investment}}\right) =$	44%	43%	60%

INCREMENTAL METHOD

Economic theory provides a guide for setting budget levels. To maximize profit, the firm should commit additional funds to personal selling until the added cost of generating one more unit of sale just equals the revenue from that unit of sale. In other words, the budget level should be set where marginal cost equals marginal revenue.

Figure 5.2 illustrates this concept. For convenience, costs other than personal selling are grouped into one category and are assumed constant at $10 per unit for all levels of output. Price is also assumed constant at $30 over all levels of output, resulting in constant marginal revenue. Marginal selling costs decline at low levels of unit sales volume and then rise as sales become more difficult.[19] The optimum is reached at point A where all marginal costs necessary to sell the last unit equal the marginal revenue. Beyond that point the firm's profits will be reduced. Consider for a moment what happens to the optimum point in Figure 5.2 if nonselling marginal costs are rising rather than constant. What if they are declining?

If a firm's funds are so limited that it cannot raise budgets to the level where marginal cost equals marginal revenue, it should allocate funds to selling, advertising, and other categories so that each category's marginal cost generates the same amount of marginal revenue. If advertising and personal selling were the only two cost categories in question, this concept is stated as follows:

$$\frac{MR_p}{MC_p} = \frac{MR_a}{MC_a}$$

where MR and MC represent marginal revenue and marginal cost and the subscripts p and a denote personal selling and advertising.

FIGURE 5.2
Incremental Analysis Relating to Personal Selling Budgeting

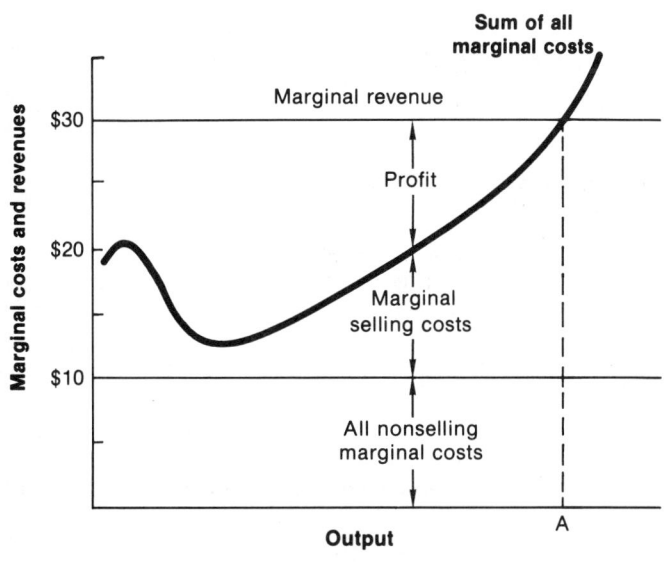

For example, if the last dollar of advertising cost is generating $1.50 of revenue and the last dollar of personal selling cost is generating $2.00 of revenue, funds should be shifted from advertising to selling until the added revenue per dollar cost is equal for each. In this example selling costs are providing more incremental profit than are advertising costs, so a shift in funds would benefit the firm's profits.

From a practical standpoint, incremental analysis is hindered by the problem of estimating marginal costs at various levels of income. Even if these costs could be approximated, they would probably vary over time because of competitors' actions, changes in other marketing activities which interact with selling, and other economic changes. But management should be encouraged to overcome this problem, perhaps with periodic experiments, because the incremental approach puts selling costs in their proper role as the cause, not the effect, of sales volume.

ALLOCATING THE SELLING BUDGET

Through some combination of the above methods, the budget level for personal selling is established. This amount must then be allocated to the various sources of sales volume such as sales territories, customer groups, and product lines. For instance, the sales manager must determine what share of funds each territory should receive for its share of the budget.

These allocation decisions can be guided by many of the same methods we have just reviewed. Percentage-of-sales, competitive parity, objective-and-task, and the incremental method are most applicable, but their same advantages and disadvantages apply here as well. Because these decisions relate directly to territorial planning and coverage, further discussion of sales effort allocation will be put off until Chapter 6. Some administrative aspects of budget allocations, such as who participates in budgeting decisions, are reviewed later in this chapter.

CONTENTS OF THE SALES BUDGET

The budget total must be divided among various expenditure items with specific cost amounts attached to each item. We now look at the basic categories of expenditure items found in most sales organization budgets.

Expenditure Categories and Specific Budget Items

Expenditures can be categorized in different ways. One way is by function performed, such as hiring, training, making sales calls, reporting, and sales administration.[20] Expenses are usually budgeted in terms of the particular item for which they are incurred. A salesperson's salary exemplifies such an expense, since the salary is paid for the services of a salesperson, no matter what functions he performs on his job. These are termed *natural costs* and appear in the income statements of most firms. Budgets made up in a similar manner allow direct comparison with past and future income statements.

Sales budgets using natural costs will include the following categories and items:

1. *Compensation of Sales Force.* The sales force is paid in the form of salary, commission, bonus, or some combination of these, and with numerous variations. In addition, many firms have incentive programs which award merchandise or cash prizes to salespeople. Insurance, pensions, and other fringe benefits also fall in this category.
2. *Travel, Lodging, and Meals.* Most sales jobs require considerable travel, making travel expense a major budget category. Many firms reimburse salespeople for their actual travel and living expense. Others supply an automobile and a fixed sum for expenses which the salesperson must allocate. A few firms place the responsibility for paying expenses directly on the sales force and compensate them additionally. Sales managers, especially at the district and regional levels, also incur travel costs. Some firms pay moving expenses and closing costs in buying a new house for a salesperson being transferred.
3. *Entertainment and Dues.* Salespeople and sales managers are expected, even often required, to develop their acquaintance with customers and prospects in a social atmosphere. These expenses are treated in the same ways as travel and living expenses. Many companies will also pay for memberships and dues in service and professional organizations to encourage their sales personnel to become active in these groups.
4. *Selling Aids.* To assist in the selling job, management prepares brochures, catalogs, price lists, and other printed material. Other aids include product samples, films or slides and projectors, and models or displays. Selling aids also may be training material such as manuals and tape recorders and exhibition material used in trade shows.
5. *Administration.* Compensation for all sales management personnel usually falls in the administration category. The major form is salary, but field sales managers often are paid a small percentage commission, usually termed an *override*, on sales.
6. *Staff.* Staff personnel are specialists employed to advise other members of the organization or to carry out particular activities. An example is a sales trainer.

Firms which sell highly technical or engineered-to-order products may employ technical field assistants in a staff capacity. Larger firms may have staff specialists in budgeting, recruiting, selecting, and other phases of sales management. Not every firm will have staff personnel associated specifically with the sales organization.

7. *Clerical and Secretarial Services.* Persons employed in clerical and secretarial positions deal with correspondence, handle orders, maintain compensation and expense records, file reports, and perform other office duties.
8. *Office.* The office category contains a wide scope of costs, including materials, supplies, equipment rentals, taxes, and insurance relating to the facilities occupied by the sales operation. Telephone expense is included here and often is a large budget item because of calls to and from salespeople, customers, and district or regional offices.

Territorial Differences. In addition, budgets are often subdivided on a territorial basis to allow for competitive, geographic, and other differences which exist among territories. As a result, more precise cost determination is possible, and the budget is more useful in controlling and evaluating each territory's sales operations.

Budget Flexibility

Since personal selling is done in a changing competitive and customer environment, a certain amount of flexibility in plans is necessary for adjusting to varying conditions. For example, an executive of Revere Copper & Brass noted that, upon sensing a rapidly changing business environment, management made over thirty changes in its budget and profit plan with the use of the computer and got a revised plan in less than two days.[21]

Sometimes managers define budget flexibility as meaning cost revisions resulting from changes in sales volume. This is a defensive, though sometimes necessary action. But in the sales operation, budget flexibility must also imply that cost changes should occur with changes in sales opportunities. If a new high-potential market is suddenly discovered in the middle of a budget period, the sales force should not be kept from pursuing it solely because no funds are in the original budget to cover the expense. Budget changes may not only follow changes in sales volume, but should also attempt to bring them about.

Cost Classifications. The impact on the budget of changes in selling plans can be analyzed more easily if budgeted costs are grouped into three classifications:

Variable costs, which vary in some direct ratio to dollar or unit sales.
Fixed costs, which do not change regardless of change in dollar or unit sales.
Semivariable costs, which vary with dollar or unit sales, but not in any systematic manner. These costs might be viewed as partly variable and partly fixed.

Some examples of selling costs classified in this manner appear in Table 5.5. With costs grouped this way, management can now determine whether to pursue new sales opportunities, as the following illustration shows.

TABLE 5.5
Classification of Selected Selling Costs

Variable Costs

Sales Force Commissions
Sales Managers' Commissions and Overrides

Semivariable Costs

Sales Force Expenses
Entertainment
Samples and other Selling Aids
Insurance and Taxes on Payroll of Sales Office and Sales Personnel
Contest Prizes
Training and Sales Meetings
Clerical and Office Expenses
Telephone
Relocation of Transferred Salespeople

Fixed Costs

Salaries of Sales Force, Sales Managers, and Staff Personnel
Rent and Occupancy Expense for Sales Facilities
Insurance, Taxes, and Depreciation of Sales Facilities
Licenses, Fees, Memberships, Dues

Suppose a sales manager discovers a major new potential customer after the budget period has begun. How much more can he afford to spend in order to seek the additional sales volume? After deciding what this additional volume might be, the sales manager should determine what additional variable and semivariable costs would be expected. Other costs besides those for personal selling also must be recognized as in the following:

	ESTIMATED SALES AND COSTS FROM NEW CUSTOMER
Sales	$100,000
Cost of Goods Sold	64,000
Gross Profit	$ 36,000
Variable and Semivariable Costs Other than for Selling	15,000
Contribution to Variable and Semivariable Selling Costs and to Fixed Costs	$ 21,000

If the sales manager believes that less than $21,000 will be needed in variable and semivariable selling costs to obtain the additional volume, he should seek the additional sales.

This analysis could be further refined if the probability of obtaining the additional volume can be determined. This probability comes from management judgment, based on past experience with similar customers and situations. If the probability were estimated at 0.5 for obtaining the $100,000 and 0.5 for obtaining nothing, the expected sales volume increase would be

$$(.5)(\$100,000) + (.5)(0) = \$50,000$$

The sales and cost estimates should then be revised to reflect this lower expected value.

This analysis is misleading, however, because the probability of obtaining the additional sales depends on the amount of selling effort employed. For that reason, a schedule of alternative levels of selling effort (measured by variable and semivariable selling costs) with associated probabilities of obtaining the volume should be determined and the best alternative selected. Table 5.6 illustrates such a schedule. From these data it is clear that $20,000 in additional selling effort would contribute most to fixed cost, so this would be the best level of effort to use. A skeptical manager might question this approach because the probabilities and some of the semivariable costs are subjective estimates. Without question, the estimator's experience and judgment are significant to the outcome of this analysis, but the approach outlined presents at least a framework for making a budget variation decision.[22]

TABLE 5.6
Analysis of Alternative Levels of Selling Effort Directed at a New Potential Customer

Additional Selling Effort (1)	Probability of Obtaining $100,000 Sales* (2)	Expected Sales Volume Increase† (3)	Cost of Goods Sold, and Variable and Semivariable Costs other than for Selling‡ (4)	Contribution to Fixed Costs§ (5)
$ 2,000	.10	$10,000	$ 8,200	−$200
5,000	.15	15,000	12,150	−2,150
10,000	.30	30,000	24,000	−4,000
15,000	.75	75,000	59,250	750
20,000	.95	95,000	73,100	1,900

*Management estimates; $100,000 considered to be maximum volume obtainable from this potential customer.

†These expected values assume that 1.00 − Probability of obtaining $100,000 sales = Probability of obtaining no sales. Probabilities might also be considered for obtaining various sales volumes less than $100,000. In such cases the expected sales volume increase calculations would also change.

‡Accounting estimates.

§Column 3 minus columns 4 and 1.

Cost Determination

Once the specific budget items are identified, the next task is to determine how much cost should be attached to each item. We look first at continuing budget items, those which have been in previous years' budgets.

Fixed costs present little problem because they usually remain the same. Occasionally, the level of fixed costs will change, perhaps because of rent or salary increases, but these changes are usually known in advance.

Similarly, variable costs are easy to determine. They will adjust almost automatically to the sales forecast level. Again, variable cost ratios might change from one year to the next, such as increases in salespeople's commission rates, but these changes also are generally known before the budget period begins.

Semivariable costs are more difficult, since they do not fluctuate systematically with sales volume. But historical relationships between these expenses and other variables can be investigated. Examples of these relationships include travel costs per call and entertainment costs per customer. Changing conditions can make historical relationships invalid, however, so such ratios must be adjusted for trends and anticipated changes. They then provide approximate cost standards, which indicate what expenditures should be under normal conditions for the item in question.

By relating these standards to the details of the forthcoming selling plan, the budget level of semivariable cost items can be estimated as follows. Suppose the number of customers anticipated for the next year is 650. Based on past entertainment cost, number of customers, and cost and entertainment trends, a standard of $20 per customer is established. Therefore, entertainment cost should total $13,000 in the coming year.

When new plans or activities of the sales organization are to be budgeted, cost standards cannot be estimated in the same way. Suppose, for example, that a sales manager wants to begin a system of telephone reports by salespeople to inform him of orders from new or major customers. How much should be budgeted for such an activity? Most likely, the sales manager's judgment will establish this cost level. Or this new system could be installed on an experimental basis in one territory for a short period of time to provide some cost experience. Sometimes trade magazines publish surveys of cost information which can be used as guides.[23]

ADMINISTRATION OF THE SALES BUDGET

Budgeting Responsibility

The administrative process for developing a sales budget varies among firms, but is generally based on one of two sequences. In the "breakdown" sequence, the level is determined first by top management and allocations are then made down the line in the sales organization. The "buildup" sequence occurs when lower echelons of management submit their individual requests which are pooled into an overall budget level subject to top management approval.

Both sequences have advantages. A buildup approach can better reflect market conditions, while a breakdown approach can better reflect a company's financial condition as well as its overall goals and strategy. About one company in five uses both sequences concurrently with a final reconciliation of differences being made by top management.[24]

Whichever sequence is used, each person responsible for budgeted activities should participate in preparing budget requests for these activities. If the firm has a number of field sales offices, each field sales manager should prepare the budget for his or her own segment of the sales operation. For example, in the Health Care Division of Johnson & Johnson, 24 persons each submit their budget proposals; these include the national sales manager, 20 regional and divisional office managers, and specialists for national accounts, trade relations, and sales administration.[25]

Four reasons justify this approach to budgeting responsibility. First, the budgeting is done by persons best qualified to judge the costs necessary to meet their specific needs. A closely related reason is that such decentralization forces the persons involved to plan more effectively in order to justify their budget requests. A third reason involves budget acceptance; a person is more likely to accept a budget if he has had a voice in determining it. Finally, variations between actual and budgeted costs can be traced quickly to the person responsible, so that better control of costs can be maintained.[26]

Budget Periods

For planning purposes, an annual budget is usually prepared. In addition, firms often prepare short-term operating budgets which are used for scheduling and controlling specific activities. The time period covered by an operating budget varies among firms from one to six months, depending on such factors as change in seasonal demand patterns, volatility of costs, frequency of product style changes, and variations in competitive or economic conditions.

Shorter budget periods provide greater flexibility to adjust to such changes. Shorter periods also allow for greater control. If a budget is prepared for each month, variations between actual and budgeted costs can be reconciled monthly.

An offsetting factor, however, is the cost of preparing budgets. This cost is primarily one of executive time which could otherwise be devoted to different activities. Clearly, budget periods should not be so short that the cost of preparing the budget exceeds the value of the additional control and flexibility provided.

Many benefits of short-term budgets can be achieved by reviewing and revising the budget where necessary at selected dates within the budget period. Under these conditions, the budget period and the frequency of budget revisions do not necessarily coincide. The frequency might be once a year, with revisions only at the end of each monthly budget period.

On the other hand, the frequency of budgeting could occur more often than the total period for which budgets are prepared. Suppose a firm budgets for one year in advance, breaking the year into twelve monthly periods. Each month a new budget is drawn up, involving a revision of the first eleven months' figures and the addition of a new projection for the twelfth month. The budget period is one year, but the frequency of budgeting is every month.

Budget Review and Acceptance

After budget requests are developed by each person responsible, the requests must be reviewed and accepted by higher management. Gaining acceptance requires carefully prepared justification, especially for major changes or new items which have not appeared in previous budgets. For instance, a sales manager asking for an addition to the sales force might approach the justification in one or both of the following ways. First, he could indicate the anticipated excess of additional sales revenue over additional cost. Second, he could compare the benefits of hiring new salespeople with the benefits of spending the same funds in other ways, such as on additional sales promotion material.

CONCLUSION

This chapter viewed budgeting as a planning and coordinating mechanism directed toward refining and reaching company goals. Although budgets often start from the sales forecast, the sales budget and the sales forecast often may be modified until they are consistent with each other and yet remain capable of meeting the profit and other goals of the firm. When the sales budget is accepted, it becomes, along with the sales forecast, a statement of goals and policies in financial terms. The remaining planning activities in sales management are primarily concerned with assigning these goals to territories and salespeople.

QUESTIONS FOR REVIEW AND DISCUSSION

1. Why is flexibility important in sales management budgeting? What dangers are associated with budgeting flexibility? How effective is a flexible budget in evaluating the planning ability of a budgeter?

2. A budget increase of $34,000 is contemplated by a sales manager for the purpose of hiring, training, and supporting a new salesperson in the field. What analysis should the manager undertake to demonstrate that this request is reasonable?

3. Find the latest edition of *Sales & Marketing Management*'s "Survey of Selling Costs" in your library, and determine the cost to a salesperson of a three-day stay in each of these cities: Los Angeles, Chicago, and Philadelphia. Make out a budget for this three-day trip to each city, and report your findings and observations to your class.

4. A district sales manager gathers the following data in order to review past budgeting decisions:

	Sales Volume			Sales Budget	
Territory	Last Quarter	This Quarter	Sales Potential	Last Quarter	This Quarter
A	$250,000	$280,000	$500,000	$45,000	$48,000
B	320,000	400,000	400,000	50,000	52,000
C	120,000	136,000	600,000	35,000	38,000

Suppose this manager has a total budget of $145,000 to allocate to these three territories for the upcoming quarter, which is $7,000 more than the total budget for the three territories this quarter. If the goal is to maximize short-run sales volume, how should the total budget be allocated among these three territories, and what expected sales volume should occur? Use the approach suggested by Figure 5-1, and assume the relationships between marginal costs and sales penetration increases will remain the same for each territory as it was over the past quarter. Assume also that it is impractical to cut a territory's budget below what it has been in the past.

5. A sales manager proposes that new territories be budgeted from a long-range return-on-investment point of view, while older established territories be budgeted on a percentage-of-sales basis. Higher management expresses the opinion that the budget for new territories should reflect the all-you-can-afford approach, while established territories should be budgeted on a competitive parity basis. Evaluate these different views.

6. A small industrial firm sells two products, both handled by the entire sales force of six salespeople. You are asked to prepare an annual budget including sales revenues and all sales management expenses. In addition to the sales force, there is one sales executive and a staff of three persons. The following data are to be used:
   a. Total nonmarketing costs—45 percent of sales.
   b. Total nonsales marketing costs (advertising, packaging, other administration)—25 percent of sales.
   c. Total profit desired (before taxes)—20 percent return on net worth of $2,500,000.
   d. Fixed costs:
      Salesperson's salary $ 600 per month per person
      Salesperson's expenses   400 per month per person
      Sales manager's salary   25,000 per year
      Sales staff salary   15,000 per year per person
      Sales department expenses   500 per month
   e. Variable costs:
      Commissions on product A   5 percent of sales
      Commissions on product B   6 percent of sales
   f. Sales forecast:
      Product A $1,500,000 for the year
      Product B $1,000,000 for the year
   g. Industrial data:
      Profit as a percent of sales (industry average) = 15 percent

   On the basis of the forecast provided, will this firm meet its profit goal? Do you feel the sales force will be adequately compensated? What is the minimum sales level that could adequately support this budget and meet the profit goal? What is the next step in this budgeting process?

7. A furniture wholesaler allows its salespeople a fixed percentage of sales obtained for their expenses. Management believes that this approach provides great incentive, because if a salesperson wants more funds to cultivate customers, he or she must earn them through additional sales. This incentive is especially important, management argues, because the sales force is paid by salary only which is of minimal incentive. What do you think?

8. You have been appointed as sales manager for a toy manufacturer. Before budgeting for the next period you discover that every expense item under your responsibility has been stated as a percentage of sales volume and budgeted accordingly in the past. A discussion with your immediate supervisor reveals the following budgeting philosophy: "In this highly competitive industry, every aspect of the business must focus on increasing sales. And when sales increase, every

aspect of the business benefits proportionally." What problems and benefits do you see in such a philosophy?

9. If the sales force is asked to prepare budget requests as well as forecast estimates, should management evaluate these separately or together? If a budget request is lowered, should the salesperson be given another opportunity to submit another forecast?

10. A sales manager is considering opening a new territory and has gathered the following information on three alternative proposed locations:

PROJECTIONS	DALLAS	MINNEAPOLIS	PORTLAND
Sales	$200,000	$200,000	$200,000
Cost of goods sold	110,000	110,000	110,000
Gross Profit	$ 90,000	$ 90,000	$ 90,000
Selling costs	46,000	50,000	45,000
Profit contribution	$ 44,000	$ 40,000	$ 45,000
Accounts receivable	55,000	50,000	35,000
Inventories	40,000	30,000	40,000

The sales manager wishes to choose the location which will provide the best return on investment. Which of the three locations should be chosen?

NOTES

1. Additional discussion of budgeting for the firm in general is found in Jeremy Bacon, *Managing the Budget Function* (New York: National Industrial Conference Board, Inc., 1970).

2. "At Johnson & Johnson, The Sales Budget Gets The Best Of Care," *Sales Management,* May 19, 1975, p. 10.

3. Arch G. Woodside and J. William Davenport, Jr., "Effects of Price and Salesman Expertise on Customer Purchasing Behavior," *Journal of Business,* vol. 49 (January 1976), pp. 56–57.

4. John E. Morrill, "Industrial Advertising Pays Off," *Harvard Business Review,* vol. 48 (March–April 1970), pp. 10, 12.

5. A parallel can be drawn between the level of sales penetration and stages in the product life cycle. See Eberhard Scheuing, "Product Life Cycle as an Aid in Strategy Decisions," *Management International Review,* vol. 9 (1969), p. 115.

6. *Forecasting Sales,* Studies in Business Policy, no. 106 (New York: National Industrial Conference Board, Inc., 1963), pp. 14–15.

7. A persuasive argument for selling costs as investments is found in "The Publisher's Call Report," *Sales & Marketing Management,* February 6, 1978, p. 4.

8. Robert F. Vizza, *Measuring the Value of the Field Sales Force* (New York: Sales Executives Club of New York, Inc., 1963), p. 21.

9. Review Table 2.1 in Chapter 2 as a guide to the sales manager in assessing the contribution of personal selling to overall marketing success.

10. Vizza, p. 16.

11. Vizza, p. 15.

12. Further discussion of this point is found in Earl L. Bailey, "Manufacturers' Marketing Costs," *The Conference Board Record,* vol. 8 (October 1971), pp. 58–64.

13. Further discussion is found in David B. Montgomery and Glen L. Urban, *Management Science in Marketing* (Englewood Cliffs, N.J.: Prentice-Hall, 1969), pp. 121–131.

14. This discussion is an adaptation from the advertising budgeting approach described by a marketing manager of Worthington Corporation (now Studebaker-Worthington). See Cyril Freeman, "You *Can*

Determine Promotion's Role," *Industrial Marketing,* December 1966, pp. 53–56; and his "How to Evaluate Advertising's Contribution," *Harvard Business Review,* vol. 40 (July–August 1962), pp. 137–148.

15. Note that these percentages are stated as averages rather than in marginal (incremental) terms. The latter is more correct, although the difference will not be great if the firm's revenue and cost functions vary approximately in direct proportion to rate of output. This problem will be examined later in the discussion of the incremental method.

16. A similar approach, using "opportunity rates" is described in Sanford R. Simon, *Managing Marketing Profitability* (New York: American Management Association, 1969), pp. 106–111.

17. A more extensive discussion of these problems is in Joel Dean, "Measuring the Productivity of Investment in Persuasion," *Journal of Industrial Economics,* vol. 15 (April 1967), pp. 81–108.

18. The following discussion is adapted from J. S. Schiff and Michael Schiff, "New Sales Management Tool: ROAM," *Harvard Business Review,* vol. 45 (July–August 1967), pp. 59–66.

19. Compare with Figure 5.1.

20. Functional cost analysis is discussed further in Chapter 15.

21. Thayer C. Taylor, "Throwing More Light On Hard-To-See Profit Sources," *Sales Management,* May 19, 1975, p. 41.

22. For another approach which "provides the industrial seller with a method of estimating the chances of success or failure when entering into negotiations for a large sales contract . . . and yields cost and time statistics for the negotiation process," see Monroe M. Bird, et al., "Sales Negotiation Cost Planning for Corporate Level Sales," *Journal of Marketing,* vol. 37 (April 1973), pp. 7–13.

23. A comprehensive and up-to-date source of information on all categories of sales organization costs is the "Survey of Selling Costs," published annually as a special issue of *Sales & Marketing Management.*

24. Vizza, pp. 15–16.

25. "At Johnson & Johnson, The Sales Budget Gets The Best of Care," p. 10.

26. Further discussion of participation in budgeting is found in Charles C. Gibbons, "The Psychology of Budgeting," *Business Horizons,* vol. 15 (June 1972), pp. 47–50; and Henry L. Tosi, Jr., "The Human Effects of Budgeting Systems on Management," *MSU Business Topics,* vol. 22 (Autumn 1974), pp. 53–63.

6 TERRITORY PLANNING AND COVERAGE

Most firms have enough customers to require more than one sales representative. In such cases, the firm's market is often divided into submarkets called territories, and each territory is assigned to one salesperson. Planning can then be adjusted to the needs of each territory rather than for the market as a whole, thereby strengthening the firm's total competitive effort.

Territories are not always geographic areas, although they are usually identified by geographic boundaries. For example, the chief sales executive of Litton Microwave explained, "We have found that the best approach is to make a salesperson responsible for all accounts in a finite territory. For sales efficiency and territory coverage—to maximize call benefits and minimize costs—we stay with a geographical breakdown."[1] But a territory in some firms consists of a list of accounts rather than a geographic area. Maytag uses both territory assignment methods, as noted by its general sales manager:

> Our Los Angeles market essentially consists of Los Angeles and Orange counties, with small portions of Riverside and San Bernardino counties. This area, for Maytag, is covered by eight salesmen. We have one lead salesman who covers eight major accounts. Each of these accounts has multiple outlets or branch stores. This man calls not only on the main buying office of each of these accounts, but also services each of the branch stores. The other seven men in the market are assigned geographical areas, exclusive of these eight principal accounts.[2]

Other companies set up territories which are covered by two or more salespeople, and occasionally a firm assigns two or more territories to a single salesperson. In this chapter, however, the term "territory" refers to that part of the market assigned to one salesperson.

Benefits of Territories

In general, territories provide for organized and systematic market coverage—the responsibility for each customer and prospect is clearly assigned. Each salesperson is more likely to maximize effort with customers and prospects, knowing that any resulting payoff will accrue to him or her rather than to some other member of the sales force. In addition, many salespeople get much satisfaction from having "their own" market responsibility and take great pride in "their own" territory successes.

Customers benefit as well. Over time, a regular salesperson becomes well-acquainted with each customer's needs and policies, leading to more effective service with less total time and bother. In contrast, the new salesperson starts from scratch, needing much more preparation and time from the buyer.

Important economic benefits also occur with territories. Call schedules can be set up for present and potential customers in proportion to their potential sales or profit contribution. Excessive travel time can be eliminated by careful routing, and duplication of calls by two or more salespeople can be avoided. Furthermore, sales, costs, and profits can be compared among territories for purposes of developing standards of good performance. These standards aid in subsequent allocation of sales effort and control of sales expenditures.

Finally, territories aid in hiring and training. Sales personnel can be hired and assigned to match the characteristics of customers in a given territory. Training and supervision can also be keyed to each territory's special demands, improving sales effectiveness.

Exceptions. If the normal customer-salesperson relationship is not continuous, or if customers typically seek out the salesperson first, specific territory assignments may be less beneficial. Selling stocks and bonds or residential real estate are examples. In such cases, a salesperson's territory really consists of the present customers being served, a group which tends to change considerably over time.

Personal friendships may also affect the decision to use territories. Life insurance selling is an example, since a salesperson's friends are often his first major prospects and then his source of leads to additional prospects. In other instances territories are not used because of the time and difficulty involved in establishing them. If their benefits do not override their costs, territories are not justified.

CRITERIA FOR TERRITORY DECISIONS

The effectiveness of a firm's territory structure can be judged on four criteria.

1. Profitability and Other Company Goals. From management's standpoint, profit contribution is a key measure of territory success. In Burroughs Corporation, for example, territories are grouped into profit centers, and profit projections are made to determine what changes are needed in territory boundaries or coverage. As one executive stated, "If you don't like what the numbers show, you try out several configurations until you get an optimal fit."[3]

Other goals such as sales growth and market share must also be reflected in territory decisions. One objective of Best Foods is to cover stores that account for 75 percent of U.S. grocery sales volume. Call patterns are set up for each sales force member based on a computerized analysis of over 32,000 grocery store names, locations, and annual sales.[4] Mutual of New York (MONY) uses a computer to estimate its market share in each county. If an area's share is not large enough, MONY often intensifies its coverage by adding more sales effort there.[5]

What about new territories, particularly in highly competitive areas? It may be one or two years before the territory's sales exceed its costs. A similar problem occurs when customers are so spread out geographically that costs and time involved in travel cannot be supported by expected sales volume. Sales managers often cover such territories with manufacturers' representatives or agents—independent businesspeople who handle related products from noncompeting firms in order to obtain enough sales and commissions to support themselves. Sometimes an agent builds a product's sales volume to the point where it becomes profitable for the producer to use its own salesperson, and in such cases agents lose their jobs to company sales personnel.

2. *Equal and Sufficient Assignments for Salespeople.* From the salesperson's point of view, territories should be approximately equivalent in effort required and opportunity offered. Effort is determined by workload and opportunity comes from sales potential. Assignments requiring noticeably more workload or offering less potential when compared with other company territories may seriously hamper a salesperson's motivation and performance.

Unfortunately, territories equal in sales potential are seldom equal in work load. Because the geographic distribution of customers varies considerably, travel time alone causes work load variations. It is possible, for example, that the states of Nevada, Utah, Wyoming, New Mexico, and Montana together contain the same sales potential as the single state of Washington. Since considerably less travel time would be necessary to cover the Washington territory, the work load in the two territories would be far from equal.

If workload and potential are difficult to equate among territories, is one more important than the other in territory design? Studies have produced mixed evidence on this issue. Examination of a clothing firm's territory structure revealed that both were important factors, but statistical analysis showed that potential was more important than workload in determining sales volume.[6] A study done for Magic Chef, an appliance manufacturer, supported the importance of both also, but concluded that workload was more significant than potential.[7] Because so many other factors influence sales volume, such as competition, pricing, sales force training, and compensation, it is difficult to draw any firm conclusions except that both factors have a demonstrated impact on sales.

Even if territories of equal workload and potential could be determined, they all might be too small or too large. Figure 6.1 shows some of the problems occurring when one or more territories have improper workload and potential. The solutions describe actions taken by some firms experiencing these problems. The resident salesperson, for instance, is a company sales representative who actually sets up an office inside the customer firm and spends all of his time serving that account.

In some cases territories of equal potential are not desirable from management's point of view. Smaller training areas may be set up for new salespeople, who have to prove themselves and earn the right to a larger territory. And if sales personnel differ in ability, territories can be assigned so that the relative potentials in each correspond with the abilities of salespeople.

3. *Customer Response to Selling Effort.* Not all customers respond the same way to selling effort. Suppose it takes five calls per month to obtain maximum sales volume from one set of customers, but only two calls per month to maximize sales from another set of customers. These relationships are called *response functions* or *response curves,* and can be calculated by analyzing sales force call patterns as recorded and submitted in call reports or through experiments. How many customers should be assigned to a salesperson, and how many calls should be made on each account—these are questions of territory size and coverage that can be answered more easily with response curve information.

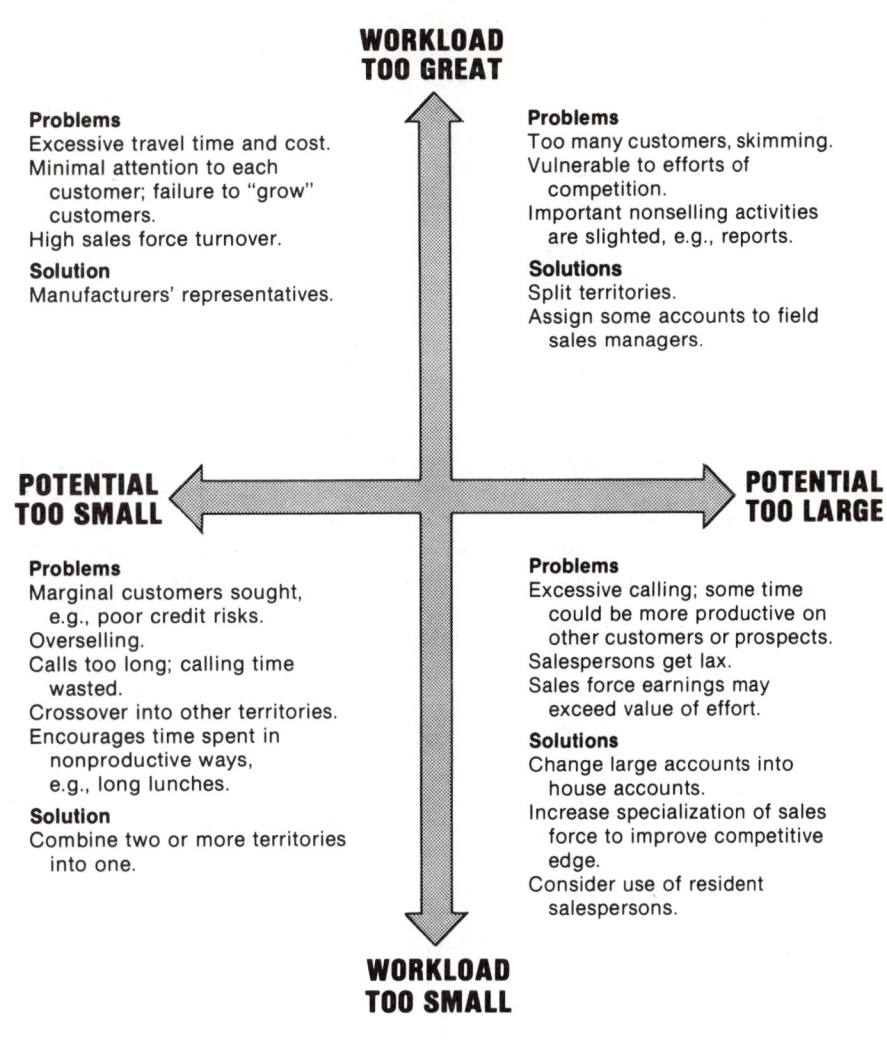

FIGURE 6.1
Problems in Territories with Improper Workload and Potential

Many effort-response relationships can be studied by sales managers. Here are some of the more common ones which firms have used in various combinations:

Response	as a function of	*Effort*
Sales Volume		Size of Sales Force
Market Share		Total Selling Time Spent with Accounts
Profit Contribution		Number of Sales Calls
Conversion of Prospects to Customers		Length of Sales Calls
		Frequency of Sales Calls

For instance, how does sales volume (response) change in a given customer group or market area as the number of sales calls (effort) changes? Or what is the chance of converting a prospect into a customer (response) as more total time is spent (effort) with those types of accounts?[8]

Many firms have run experiments to measure response functions. The Schering Corporation instructed its sales force in five selected territories to increase the number of calls by 50 percent on physicians who last names began with A to K, and to decrease by 50 percent the number of calls on physicians whose last names began with L to Z. Substantial increases occurred in the number of prescriptions written by the A to K group for Schering products, and the company used this data to revamp its territory policies.[9] A specific example of sales volume response to number of calls is shown in Table 6.4.

4. *Stability of Assignments.* Many benefits of territories depend on the stability of territory assignments. Customers get better service if the same salesperson calls on them over time. Salespeople, when they stay in the same territory, develop more thorough customer knowledge and become more valuable contributors to forecasting, budgeting, and other sales organization planning activities. In addition, a survey of purchasing executives showed that 88 percent don't like it when a company switches salespeople on them.[10]

Stability is difficult to achieve. Customers come and go in a particular territory, and many change their demands on suppliers because of growth and diversification of needs. Competitors enter and leave as well, and changes in the firm's own product line will bring about changes in each territory's sales potential.

A major factor which upsets stability is sales force turnover. In some firms, newly-hired sales representatives are promised rapid promotions or transfers for gaining balanced experience. To an ambitious salesperson, three years in the same position may be a long time, tempting him to change employers if his company takes no action. The ensuing dilemma was well summed up by a sales manager as follows, "What we need to do is stop and figure out what our priorities are: to serve customers or provide careers for bright young men."[11]

TYPES OF TERRITORY DECISIONS

A sales manager faces many interrelated territory decisions as shown in Figure 6.2. This sequence of decisions extends from short-range to long-range in effect because a change at any point in the sequence will require changes at all subsequent points. For instance, if the location and boundaries of territories are changed (step 2), changes will have to be made in assignment, allocation of effort, and scheduling as well (steps 3–5). Each decision in this sequence is not totally independent in practice, but we separate them here for a clearer understanding of the problems and techniques involved.

Determining the Number of Territories

Determining the number of territories can be treated as a budget level decision, since each territory established may require considerable cost. Chapter 5 examined methods for setting the overall sales budget level, but here we concentrate on territories only.

FIGURE 6.2.
Sequence of Sales Manager's Territory Decisions Under Various Long- and Short-Range Conditions

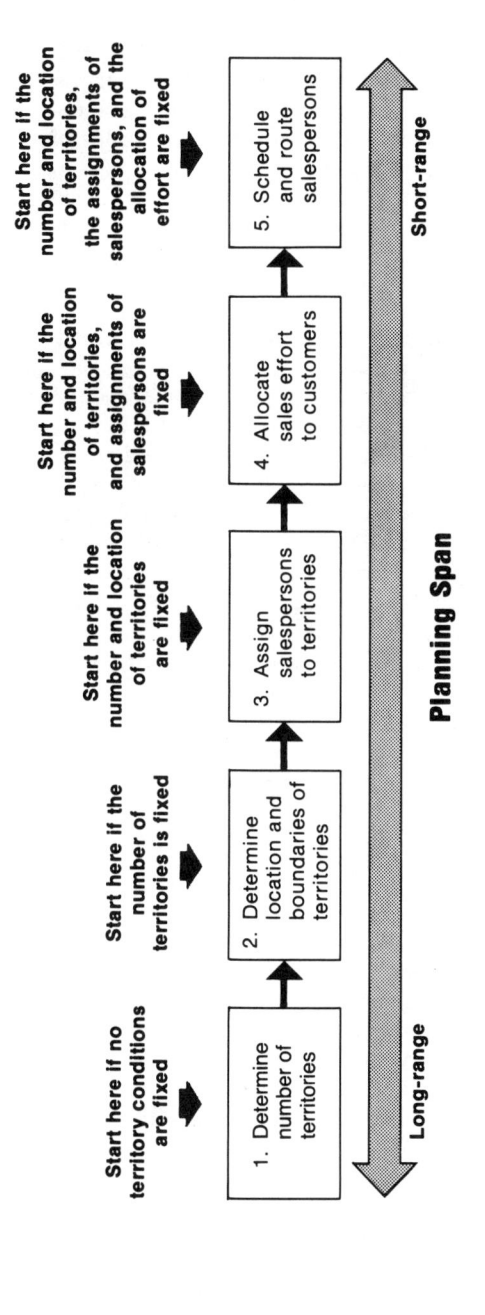

A study of large corporations revealed surprisingly that over half the firms did not have established, formalized procedures to evaluate changes in number of territories or salespeople.[12] In many companies, once the sales force is established the number of territories is based on the number of salespeople employed. This is convenient, but unlikely to be optimum in terms of profit, market share, or sales growth. More logical bases include the amount of available sales potential, the number of customers and prospects to be served, and the contribution to profit which alternative numbers of territories might generate.

Four methods of determining the number of territories are discussed next. Because number of territories is a long-range decision, management may employ these methods more to evaluate its present number of territories than to change it. A change should occur only when the net result will clearly benefit the firm's goal attainment and equivalent results cannot be obtained through changes in subsequent steps as indicated in Figure 6.2.

Work Load Method. The first method is based on the work load each salesperson can handle. By dividing this amount into the total effort necessary to cover the firm's entire market, the number of territories is determined.[13] This method, sometimes termed a buildup approach, consists of the following steps.

1. Establish Total Time Available per Salesperson. Suppose that the selling job requires working an eight-hour day, five days a week. Eliminating four weeks for vacations, holidays, illness, and other emergencies leaves 48 working weeks per year or 1920 working hours (40 hours per week × 48 weeks).

2. Apportion Salesperson's Time to All Required Tasks. A salesperson's time must be divided among all required tasks such as selling, traveling, and nonselling responsibilities. For new territories, the sales manager usually estimates this division of time; for established territories the division can be based on sales force reports or time studies. Suppose the following breakdown of time was established and applied to the average salesperson's total working hours available:

Selling	40%	768 hours
Traveling	30%	576 hours
Nonselling	30%	576 hours
Total	100%	1920 hours

3. Classify Customers According to Selling Effort Required. Next the firm's present and potential customers must be classified in terms of selling effort required. Customers are usually grouped into sales volume categories, although any basis for grouping can be used as long as it distinguishes accounts according to differences needed in selling effort.[14] This can be a tedious task for a firm with many customers and prospects. For example, the National Mills division of U.S. Industries sells to many retail stores. This firm maintains a computerized inventory control system covering each retail customer, however, and as a by-product of this system each customer can be classified according to sales effort needs.[15]

To continue our example, assume that the number of customers (both present and potential) classified by sales volume categories are as follows:

Group 1—Large	210 accounts
Group 2—Medium	650 accounts
Group 3—Small	1100 accounts

4. Specify Length and Frequency of Call for each Category. The sales manager might use response curve information or his own judgment to determine how much time should be spent with the typical account in each group and how often that account should be visited. Potential customers must be considered as well, or else the final number of salespeople will not be sufficient to allow for cultivation of potential accounts.

To continue our example, suppose that present and potential customers are treated equally and the sales manager determines the following call frequencies and call lengths as ideal:

Group 1   24 calls per year × 45 minutes per call = 18 hours per year
Group 2   12 calls per year × 30 minutes per call =   6 hours per year
Group 3   4 calls per year × 30 minutes per call =   2 hours per year

Total time needed to cover all accounts would then be:

Group 1   210 accounts at 18 hours = 3780 hours
Group 2   650 accounts at 6 hours = 3900 hours
Group 3   1100 accounts at 2 hours = 2200 hours

Total   9980 hours

5. Calculate Number of Salespeople Needed. Each salesperson has 768 hours available on average for selling. Total selling time needed to cover present and potential accounts is 9980 hours. By dividing 9980 by 768, the result is 13 territories needed.

The work load method is easy to understand and carry out, and companies have used it with satisfying results.[16] Its major weakness is an implicit assumption that amount of effort is determined by sales volume, when the opposite is true. Furthermore, the analysis is usually based on historical data rather than reflecting possible future changes in customer demand or potential.

Breakdown Method. The breakdown method can be used to estimate the number of territories needed by calculating minimum sales volume required per salesperson and dividing that volume into the total sales forecast. The sales volume per salesperson should be at least a breakeven amount, sufficient to cover direct costs, and can be calculated as follows:[17]

$$\text{Breakeven Volume Per Salesperson} = \frac{\text{Direct Costs For One Salesperson}}{\text{Gross Margin Percentage}}$$

A salesperson's direct costs include compensation and expenses such as travel and entertainment, and the gross margin percentage is total company sales volume minus nonselling costs, expressed as a percentage of sales. For example, suppose the average sales force member earns $20,000 and incurs another $10,000 annually in expenses, making a total of $30,000 direct costs. If the firm's gross margin percentage is 25 percent, the breakeven volume is:

$$\frac{\$30,000}{.25} = \$120,000 \text{ per salesperson}$$

Now the breakeven volume is divided into the total company sales forecast to arrive at the number of territories which this sales forecast can support. If the forecast were $1,700,000, approximately 14 territories would be justified.

Like the buildup approach, this procedure assumes that sales force size is determined by sales volume rather than vice versa. It also produces a breakeven number of territories rather than a number which maximizes profit or at least contributes to a profit goal. Profit contribution can be introduced into this method by varying the gross margin percentage downward or adding to the breakeven volume per salesperson to reflect the profit target desired. Emery Air Freight has adapted the breakeven method in just this way, substituting a measure of "satisfactory" volume per salesperson in place of breakeven volume.[18]

Sales Potential Method. Another popular approach is to base the number of territories on sales potential. For example, Eli Lilly and Company, an ethical drug manufacturer, sells to hospitals, drugstores, physicians, and drug wholesalers. Periodic estimates are made of its sales potential from these customer categories. Management then determines what potential sales volume is sufficient to warrant one salesperson and this amount divided into the firm's total sales potential produces the number of salespeople required.[19]

A more refined version of the sales potential method can be applied in an ongoing sales organization which has territories of unequal potential. Studies have shown that territories with smaller sales potential generate higher sales penetration than do territories of larger potential. If the number of territories is increased, each territory will have a smaller share of total sales potential but the result should be increased sales penetration and higher sales volume.[20]

The first step is to establish the relationship between relative sales potential and sales penetration. Table 6.1 shows what a manager might find in a firm whose territories have evolved to become considerably different in sales potential. Greatest potential exists in the South (territory C), and it has the lowest sales penetration. Conversely, the Southeast (territory B) has the highest penetration but the smallest potential.

Step two is to calculate what might happen if these five territories were redivided into a different number of equal-potential territories. Table 6.2 provides this information, based on the relationships found in Table 6.1. Note that as the market

TABLE 6.1

Sales Volume, Potential, and Penetration in Territories of Unequal Potential

Territory	Sales Volume	Sales Potential Dollars	Sales Potential Percent	Sales Penetration
A. Northeast	$150,000	$ 600,000	12%	25%
B. Southeast	100,000	250,000	5%	40%
C. South	200,000	2,000,000	40%	10%
D. Midwest	125,000	400,000	8%	31%
E. West	175,000	1,750,000	35%	10%
	$750,000	$5,000,000	100%	

TABLE 6.2

Sales Volume, Potential, and Penetration for Various Numbers of Equal-Potential Territories

If this number of territories was established	Each territory would have this relative sales potential	The present territory most similar to these is	Based on that present territory, sales penetration in these territories would be	Total sales volume would be
3	33.3%	E	approx. 10%	$ 500,000
8	12.5%	A	approx. 25%	$1,250,000
12	8.3%	D	approx. 31%	$1,550,000
20	5.0%	B	approx. 40%	$2,000,000

is divided into more territories of smaller potential each, total sales volume will increase.

Step three involves determining whether the sales increase from a larger number of territories is greater than the corresponding cost increase necessary to set up and staff these territories. To illustrate, suppose we compare 8 versus 20 territories. To simplify the accounting procedure, assume that the variable cost of sales equals 50 percent and the cost to field a salesperson equals $40,000. Using these values, the comparison is as follows:

	FOR 8 TERRITORIES	FOR 20 TERRITORIES
Sales	$1,250,000	$2,000,000
Variable costs	625,000	1,000,000
	$ 625,000	$1,000,000
Sales Force costs	8 × $40,000 = 320,000	20 × $40,000 = 800,000
Profit contribution	$ 305,000	$ 200,000

While other alternatives should also be compared, the conclusion from this particular comparison is that 8 is better than 20 territories because eight produces a better profit contribution.

While this method is the best examined so far, it fails to consider that territories of equal potential are likely to contain considerable differences in work load as well as differences in customer response to selling effort. Accounting for these factors is left to the discretion of management.

Incremental Method. In Chapter 5 we discussed the incremental method of budgeting and noted its difficulty in practice. This method has been used successfully in determining the number of territories for the X-ray Division of Westinghouse Electric Corporation which sells medical x-ray film and related equipment.[21]

This method is based on the following premise: the firm's net profit will increase when an additional salesperson is employed if incremental gross profit from the additional sales exceeds the cost of the additional salesperson.

Incremental gross profit was obtained in three steps. First, a model of sales response to the number of salespeople employed was developed, using data from the company's sales districts. It showed that the amount of sales volume contributed by an additional salesperson depended on the previous number of salespeople employed. In other words, an increase from 50 to 51 salespeople in a district produced a different incremental sales volume than did an increase from 60 to 61. So the next step was to determine incremental sales volume from adding one salesperson at various levels of sales force size.

Finally, incremental gross profit was obtained by subtracting cost of goods sold from the incremental sales volume. Assuming that cost of goods sold is 60 percent of sales volume, the following calculation illustrates these steps:

CHANGE IN NUMBER OF SALESPEOPLE	INCREMENTAL SALES VOLUME	COST OF GOODS SOLD FOR INCREMENTAL SALES VOLUME	INCREMENTAL GROSS PROFIT
50 to 51	$100,000	$60,000	$40,000
60 to 61	70,000	42,000	28,000
70 to 71	55,000	33,000	22,000
71 to 72	52,000	31,200	20,800
72 to 73	49,500	29,700	19,800

The cost of an additional salesperson includes fixed costs plus commission on the incremental sales. If fixed costs are $15,000 per salesperson and the commission rate is 10 percent of sales volume, the following incremental costs will result:

CHANGE IN NUMBER OF SALESPEOPLE	INCREMENTAL SALES VOLUME	INCREMENTAL FIXED COSTS PLUS COMMISSION
50 to 51	$100,000	$25,000
60 to 61	70,000	22,000
70 to 71	55,000	20,500
71 to 72	52,000	20,200
72 to 73	49,500	19,950

The proper number of salespeople can now be determined by comparing incremental gross profit with incremental costs:

CHANGE IN NUMBER OF SALESPEOPLE	INCREMENTAL GROSS PROFIT	INCREMENTAL FIXED COSTS PLUS COMMISSIONS	INCREMENTAL NET PROFIT CONTRIBUTION
50 to 51	$40,000	$25,000	$15,000
60 to 61	28,000	22,000	6,000
70 to 71	22,000	20,500	1,500
71 to 72	20,800	20,200	600
72 to 73	19,800	19,950	−150

Adding the seventy-second salesperson contributes $600 to profit, but adding the seventy-third reduces profit by $150. Therefore, seventy-two should be employed.

This approach is the most likely of the four described to produce the optimal number of territories in profit terms. It is less valid, however, in firms using many promotional elements besides personal selling, and it does not account for possible competitors' reactions or for the long-term "investment" effect of personal selling effort.

The latter problem can be alleviated by tracing sales response for more than one year from customers obtained by a new salesperson. After one year, the cost of obtaining sales volume from these new customers might exceed the gross profit obtained. But after a longer period the gross profit might grow to exceed the corresponding cost. This analysis was done by Signode Steel Strapping Company, and the optimum number of salespeople was determined when the three-year cost of sales to new customers just equalled the three-year gross profit obtained from these sales.[22]

Determining the Location and Boundaries of Territories

Once the number of territories is decided, management faces four additional territory decisions which, as we have already noted, are highly interdependent. Computer models are being developed to cope with the complexity of these interrelationships. One such model was tested by a manufacturer of high priced consumer goods with 100 salespeople.[23] The model produced a territory plan by developing a response function, allocating selling effort to customers based on the response function, determining the number of territories and specifying their boundaries, and adjusting for the experience and abilities of sales personnel assigned to each territory. Needless to say, this is a highly complex model, requiring advanced technical training for its effective development and use in any firm. Until such integrated approaches are better tailored for managers understanding, each of these decisions will most likely be approached individually.

The delineation of territorial locations and boundaries is next, though as the above discussion implies, any decision here is preliminary and must be refined in subsequent steps. Two methods can guide the sales manager, one based on work load and the other on sales potential.

Work Load Method. The work load method for locating territories is an extension of the work load method for determining the number of territories. In the example, the average salesperson had 768 selling hours available, so each salesperson would be assigned customers and prospects requiring approximately 768 hours of selling effort in total.

Sales Potential Method. When the number of customers and prospects is large or when prospects cannot be readily identified, the sales potential method is often used to define territorial boundaries. This method includes the following steps:

1. Divide the market into geographical segments called control units.
2. Determine the amount of relative sales potential in each control unit.
3. Group adjacent control units so that their combined relative sales potential includes the proper share of total sales potential for one salesperson.

Control units are small segments of the market used as building blocks for territories. Political units such as counties and states are often chosen as control units for two reasons. They have clear boundaries and are easily located and understood by sales personnel. In addition, statistical data in government publications and other sources usually refer to political units. Any type of geographic areas can be used, however, if sufficient information exists to identify, measure, and combine them accurately.

Control units should also be small enough to permit flexibility in defining territorial boundaries. For instance, if management wishes to adjust territories slightly, a small control unit can be taken in total from one territory and added to another. Some of the more often used control units are the following:

States are suitable when national market coverage is desired with a small sales force. For many companies states are too large, and as a firm grows in sales volume many states have to be broken into smaller units. Other major problems include great variations in size of states and the tendency of customers to ignore state boundaries in their normal trading patterns.

Trading Areas are often useful because, by definition, they include a principal city and surrounding area which encompass natural trading patterns. But trading areas are usually smaller than states and seldom conform directly to political boundaries so that statistical data are difficult to find. Many firms develop their own areas and statistics. Skil Corporation assembles its territories from 500 trading areas as defined by Rand McNally, which publishes trading area maps.[24]

Standard Metropolitan Statistical Areas (SMSAs) have been devised by the Bureau of the Budget to identify major metropolitan concentrations. An SMSA is defined as one or more contiguous counties containing either one city of at least 50,000 population or one city of at least 25,000 population which when combined with the surrounding area totals at least 75,000 population. Over 260 SMSAs have been specified. Although SMSAs do not include all market areas in the U.S., they do pinpoint the areas where greatest demand is likely for most products.[25]

Zip Code areas include over 30,000 five-digit postal zones, each with some degree of economic and cultural homogeneity. These five-digit areas stem from over 300 three-digit centers which include the entire country. Flexibility is a distinct advantage, but far less statistical data are available for Zip Codes than for other control units.

Counties are equal to or smaller than SMSAs, and larger than five-digit but smaller than three-digit Zip Code areas. There are about 3100 counties in the U.S., for which an extensive amount of statistical data are available from federal and county sources themselves. Their size and data availability, as well as their relative permanence, make counties the most popular of all control unit types.

After control units are chosen, the next step is determining the relative sales potential of each. The procedure followed by FMC Corporation is a good example.[26] This machinery producer categorized its customers by SIC code and calculated a consumption estimate per employee for each SIC category. A listing of individual accounts by SIC code and number of employees was then compiled for each state. When the appropriate consumption estimates were applied to each account and totaled for each state, sales potential measures resulted. The final step involved grouping the states into a predetermined number (eight in this case) of territories of roughly equal potential.

FMC used states as control units and constructed a small number of territories. When counties are used, the grouping of 3100 control units into territories is a tedious task. Zip codes and SMSAs present similar problems. A computer model termed GEOLINE has been developed for this purpose and used for delineating territories by CIBA Pharmaceutical Company and others.[27] In brief, the purpose of GEOLINE is to construct a predetermined number of geographically compact territories which are approximately equal on some activity measure chosen by management, such as sales potential or number of sales calls required. Inputs to the model include activity measures and geographic coordinates for each control unit as well as management's choice of territory centers. The model then produces a set of territories around those centers which minimizes total distance required for coverage and equates the territories in terms of the activity measure chosen.

Assigning Salespeople to Territories

Up to this point, territory decisions we have discussed have ignored the varying abilities and characteristics of salespeople. But sales personnel are not all equally effective nor is any one salesperson equally effective in all territories. Sales volume attained will therefore vary depending on the matching of territories and salespeople.

Ability measures for each salesperson can be based on manager judgments, scores on selection or training tests, or performance measures in the field such as a sales-to-call ratio. In the Kaufman Company, an industrial hardware and hand tools distributor, management assesses each salesperson's personality and then assigns them to markets accordingly. A salesman who is "terrific in informal settings but uncomfortable in an office . . . sells to trucking companies and contractors rather than to major industrial firms."[28]

A more structured approach occurs in a consumer goods firm selling primarily to wholesalers and chain stores. Here the sales manager rates each salesperson on seven characteristics:[29]

1. Previous selling experience.
2. Ability to be a self-starter; ability to work alone.
3. Ability and willingness to travel on a regular basis.
4. Good appearance.
5. Ability to work with and supervise brokers in the field.
6. Ability and willingness to cooperate with supervisor.
7. Ability to plan and organize time and work.

The manager then assesses the importance of these characteristics to each customer group. Previous sellling experience might be more important to customer group B than to group A, for instance. So a salesperson scoring high on experience would have a better ability index with respect to group B than to group A, and would be expected to perform better in territories with a larger proportion of group B customers. (All else being equal, of course!)

Armed with ability measures, management proceeds to match territories with sales personnel. To make the match most effective, territories might be adjusted in relation to each salesperson's characteristics. Alternatively, if territories are to remain fixed, sales personnel must be assigned within those constraints so that maximum sales, profits, or other desired objectives are achieved.

Adjusting Territories to Salespeople's Abilities. Suppose we have three territories of equal potential assigned to three salespeople of unequal abilities. The result is unequal sales achieved as the example shows:

TERRITORY	SALES POTENTIAL	SALESPERSON ASSIGNED	ABILITY INDEX	SALES ACHIEVED
A	$200,000	1	1.0	$200,000
B	200,000	2	0.8	160,000
C	200,000	3	0.7	140,000
	$600,000			$500,000

Suppose, however, territories are constructed so that the sales potential of each is proportionate to the ability indexes of the salespeople:

TERRITORY	SALES POTENTIAL	SALESPERSON ASSIGNED	ABILITY INDEX	SALES ACHIEVED
A	$240,000	1	1.0	$240,000
B	192,000	2	0.8	153,600
C	168,000	3	0.7	117,600
	$600,000			$511,200

Sales achievement is increased by dividing sales potential in this manner.

Sales could be increased more if territory A were made even larger, provided that the ability indexes of the three salespeople remained constant. But as a territory is increased in size, a salesperson's ability to capture its potential is likely to decrease. Conversely, the opposite may occur as a territory is reduced in size. In this example, the ability index of salesperson 3 might increase as the size of his territory decreases.[30]

Similar analysis can be done with types of customers. For instance, in the work load example to determine number of territories, accounts were categorized according to size: small, medium, and large. If individual salespeople vary in their ability to handle customers of various sizes, a salesperson who is more effective with a particular customer category should be assigned a relatively larger share of these customers.

To tackle this problem analytically, a computer model has been devised which calculates sales response from alternative sets of accounts to each member of the sales force. The model then determines which accounts should be assigned to each salesperson in order to maximize volume while maintaining territory assignments as closely matched as possible on work load and potential.[31]

Assigning Salespeople to Fixed Territories. When territories are fixed, management should determine the total sales or profit contribution from each combination of territory assignments and select the combination with maximum contribution. To illustrate, suppose there are four territories containing three customer groups in varying proportions. Sales potential for each customer group in each territory is as follows:

TERRITORY	SALES POTENTIAL IN CUSTOMER GROUP			SALES POTENTIAL TOTAL
	1	2	3	
A	200	0	0	200
B	5	80	15	100
C	20	175	5	200
D	0	5	95	100
	225	260	115	600

Each of the four salespeople to be assigned differs in ability with each customer group. Management has devised ability indexes for each in terms of expected sales penetration:

SALESPERSON	ABILITY INDEX WITH CUSTOMER GROUP		
	1	2	3
WW	0.3	0.6	0.8
XX	0.7	0.5	0.2
YY	0.6	0.4	0.7
ZZ	0.5	0.5	0.5

The sales manager computes expected sales per salesperson in each territory by multiplying the ability index times the sales potential for each customer group and summing the products for each territory. Salesperson WW's computations are as follows:

Territory A: 200(0.3) +   0(0.6) +   0(0.8) = 60.0
Territory B: 5(0.3) +   80(0.6) +   15(0.8) = 61.5
Territory C: 20(0.3) + 175(0.6) +   5(0.8) = 115.0
Territory D: 0(0.3) +   5(0.6) +   95(0.8) = 79.0

After similar calculations are made for all salespeople in all territories, a matrix of expected sales volume alternatives is formed as shown in Table 6.3. The solution involves enumerating all possible combinations—twenty-four in this case—and selecting the best one. For this problem the best solution is to assign WW to territory C, XX to A, YY to D, and ZZ to B. In most firms, the number of territories (and salespeople) exceeds four, and manual enumeration can be tedious. For instance, if there are 10 territories to assign to 10 salespeople, the number of possible combinations is 10 factorial, which is 3,628,800. Fortunately, shortcut methods and computer programs are available.[32]

Allocating Sales Effort to Customers

When territories are established and assigned to particular salespeople, the next decision is how much sales effort to allocate to various customers. This analysis has been done for customers in groups as well as for customers individually.

TABLE 6.3
Expected Sales Volume from Each Salesperson when Assigned to Each Territory

Salesperson	EXPECTED SALES VOLUME WHEN ASSIGNED TO TERRITORY			
	A	B	C	D
WW	60.0	61.5	115.0	79.0
XX	140.0	46.5	102.5	21.5
YY	120.0	45.5	85.5	68.5
ZZ	100.0	50.0	100.0	50.0

Allocating Effort to Customer Groups. Response functions form the basis for most allocation decisions, and a simple example of response function analysis is shown in Table 6.4. All customers are grouped together for this assessment, and accounts receiving no sales calls are included because some of them place unsolicited orders sufficient to produce an average order of $10.00. The conclusion that three calls per month per customer is optimum should be used as a guide only, of course, since some accounts are different enough from the "average" to require different treatment.

General Electric is one firm using response functions to guide sales effort decisions. Customers were categorized on the basis of similar characteristics such as type of product purchased or number of employees. Customers in each category were then subdivided according to how much sales time was spent with each. When sales levels were compared among these groups, it appeared that total time spent with all customers could be reduced. As a result, salespeople were able to spend more time seeking new accounts, while sales to present customers remained at the same levels.[33]

General Electric also studied the allocation of effort to prospects. From call reports and other records it was possible to determine how many prospects were eventually converted into customers, how many calls were required, and thus what ratio of calls per conversion was optimum. If, for example, the majority of prospects became customers on the third call, it might be reasonable to drop any prospect not converted on the third or fourth call and to direct the salesperson's efforts to a new prospect.

Linear programming has also been used to allocate salespeople to market areas (branches) as well as to customers within them. In a casualty insurance firm, these two allocations were determined simultaneously by linear programming to check

TABLE 6.4
Simple Response Function Analysis Based on a Salesperson's Call Reports

A REVIEW OF CALL REPORTS BY THE SALES MANAGER PRODUCES THE FOLLOWING DATA:		THE SALES MANAGER CAN THEN COMPUTE THE VALUE OF MAKING ADDITIONAL CALLS:	
If the number of calls per month on a customer was:	The average monthly dollar sales per customer was:	Change in number of calls:	Change in average monthly dollars sold:
0	$ 10		
1	300	from 0 to 1	from $10 to $300 = +$290
2	600	from 1 to 2	from $300 to $600 = +$300
3	1000	from 2 to 3	from $600 to $1000 = +$400
4	1200	from 3 to 4	from $1000 to $1200 = +$200
5	1250	from 4 to 5	from $1200 to $1250 = + $50
6	1050	from 5 to 6	from $1250 to $1050 = −$200

Conclusion: Three calls per customer per month is optimum. Making a fourth call on a given customer does not add to sales as much as using that call as a first call on a new customer (A fourth call is worth $200 in additional sales whereas a first call is worth $290 in additional sales.).

whether the firm's sales personnel were optimally assigned to maximize profit contribution. The conclusions were that the company had correctly allocated its personnel to sales branches, but each branch had devoted too little attention to customers whose policies had large annual premiums.[34] This and related techniques hold promise for assisting management in improving allocation decisions.[35]

Allocating Effort to Individual Customers. The guidance provided by response functions is helpful for the average account, but more refined models exist which help salespeople determine how much effort should be devoted to each individual account with its specific characteristics. In General Electric, for instance, a sample of accounts of various sales volume sizes was drawn, and estimates of account sales potential and sales time spent with each account were obtained. This information was combined in a multiple regression equation to indicate how much time a salesperson should spend on any account according to its potential sales volume (defined as sales volume available to all suppliers) and the share of this volume which General Electric planned to obtain. The resulting equation was:

$$T = .96 + .0048P + .14S$$

where T = Percent of salesperson's time to allocate to the account
$.96$ = minimum percent of salesperson's time to be spent on any account regardless of its size or target share
P = potential sales volume (in thousands of dollars) available to all suppliers
S = target share of that sales volume

If a salesperson has an account with $200,000 potential sales volume and the objective is to obtain 30 percent of that business, the percent of time to devote to that account is computed as follows:

$$.96 + .0048(200) + .14(30) = 5.12\%$$

Management recognized that other factors also influenced these time allocations because the variables in the model accounted for only 70 percent of the variation in time spent with customers. Each salesperson was allowed to apply a plus or minus 30 percent leeway to the computed value for any account.[36]

Other more complex models have also been tested in business firms. Three of these are named ALLOCATE, CALLPLAN, and SCHEDULE, and they are briefly summarized as follows.

ALLOCATE computes how much selling effort should be assigned to customers or prospects based on their sales potential and the level of sales penetration already attained with each account. To use the model, management must supply historical data on the number of sales calls made on each account together with its sales response. Judgments can be used if historical data are not available. A successful application of this model has been reported in a consumer products firm selling to wholesalers and direct retailers.[37]

CALLPLAN determines call-frequency norms for each account which maximize sales minus travel costs over a sales response period. It is an interactive model, allowing the salesperson to participate by providing input data such as the location of each account and the time and cost to reach it, average time per call and number of calls planned for each account and its profit contribution, and judgments on what sales response would occur if different numbers of calls are made than planned. This input information is entered in a typewriter-like terminal connected by telephone line to a computer, and the computer's analysis is printed out within minutes. A salesperson unsure about any input data provided can rerun the analysis quickly using alternative values to learn whether major changes result in call-frequency recommendations. This model was pioneered in Pennwalt Corporation and has since been used successfully in more than a dozen companies.[38]

SCHEDULE is also an interactive model requiring inputs from a salesperson on each account's potential, call-lengths, profit contribution percent, and estimated penetration from three levels of selling effort. A total profit contribution target desired by the salesperson is also supplied to the model, which then responds with the optimum number of calls to be made on each account which will produce that target profit within the scheduling period. This model was tested with a small sales force in a temporary labor firm and produced improved allocations over those in prior use.[39]

Scheduling and Routing Salespeople

Scheduling and routing are primarily short-term problems because sales personnel must often respond quickly to emergency needs of customers and unanticipated moves of competitors. Some firms pay little attention to formal travel schedules for the sales force. But because so much time is spent traveling, attempts to reduce travel time (and thereby increase selling time) can lead to improved sales force productivity. For instance, an analysis of driving patterns by Diamond Crystal Salt produced a reduction in travel of 15,000 miles per year in each territory. As a result, each salesperson could average eight additional calls per week—the equivalent of one extra day each week.[40]

Scheduling and routing plans are encouraged in many firms even though some day-to-day deviations are to be expected. In some companies the sales manager develops the pattern, in others the salesperson is asked to devise his own plan, and in still others it is a cooperative effort. Johnson & Johnson salespeople, for example, are asked to classify all their accounts according to call frequency and call lengths required and then submit to management a schedule reflecting the needed coverage.[41] At Harris Intertype, a printing press manufacturer, management determines the coverage needs for each customer type and supplies the sales force with a "call directory" indicating how each customer and prospect should be covered.[42] Sales personnel and management work together at American Optical Company to devise daily itineraries which are combined into weekly trip sheets covering one year's time.[43]

Models have been devised to assist in these territory decisions. One, a relatively simple computerized model, requires two basic inputs: an expected value of sales volume minus costs from a call on each account, and total time required (travel, waiting, and sales presentation time) for a call on each account. The model then selects the route which will produce the greatest expected value within the total amount of time available. The effectiveness of the model is best in repetitive selling situations where regular routines are followed. When applied to a wholesale liquor route, for example, the expected value per minute of selling time rose to $2.03 from a premodel level of $1.98.[44]

A more complex model, called TOURPLAN, makes a sequence of comparisons between pairs of accounts, selecting the one on each comparison which offers a larger value per cost ratio as long as the ratio exceeds a predetermined critical level. Skipped accounts are reevaluated for future possible routes. When applied in a real territory, the modeled route produced an increase of more than 5 percent in routing efficiency.[45]

A visual solution to the routing problem, called the "outer ring" method, has been proposed which takes place in two stages.[46] In stage 1, as shown in Figure 6.3, an outer ring is created among the customers to be visited, and in stage 2 those inside the ring are connected into the route using as obtuse angles as possible. Underlying this method are the following general principles of efficient routing:

1. Customers in neighboring areas should be visited in direct succession.
2. The order of visits should be selected so the route does not involve sharp angles.
3. The same route should not be used to and from a customer, this being the most acute angle of all.
4. Routes already traveled should not be crossed.
5. The total daily itinerary should be divided up into a route which is as circular as possible.

FIGURE 6.3
The Outer Ring Method of Routing

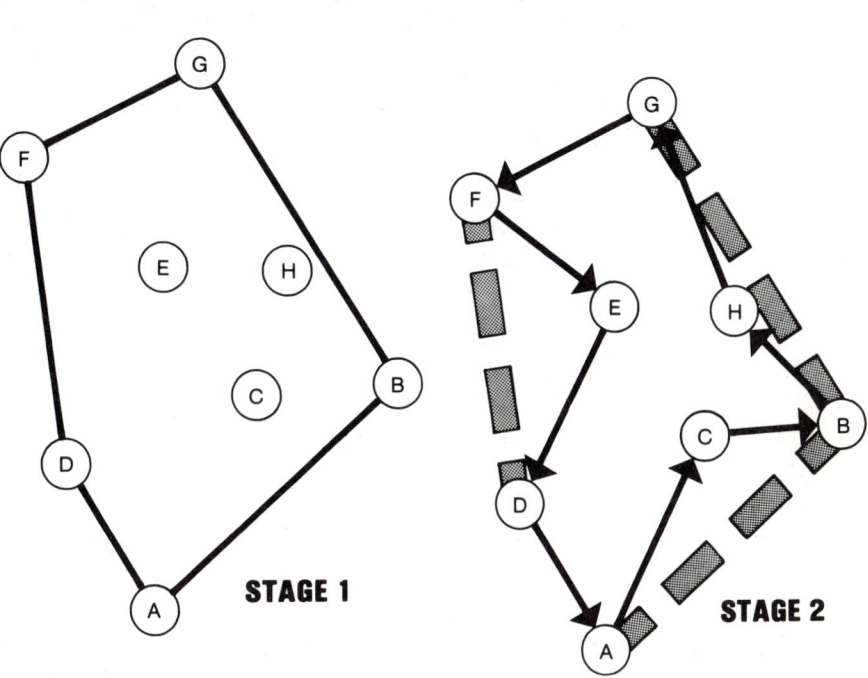

STAGE 1

STAGE 2

Source: Jan Wage, *The Successful Sales Presentation: Psychology and Technique* (London: Leviathan House, 1974), p. 83.

TERRITORY ADJUSTMENTS

In the short run, many territory adjustments are made routinely, such as changes in call-frequencies or in routing plans. But the long-run adjustments such as assigning sales personnel to different territories or splitting present territories are more difficult. Careful handling by management is essential to avoid antagonism and loss of morale in the sales force.

Transferring Salespeople

We have already noted that some salespeople are more effective in one territory than in another. Perhaps one is highly motivated by the challenge of seeking new customers but loses interest when calling on the same customers over and over again. Another may become so entangled in social obligations or community activities that sales effectiveness is hindered more than company reputation or image is helped. In such cases a territory switch might benefit the firm and salesperson as well. On the other hand, stability is valuable to a company and its customers, so a territory switch should be made only after careful weighing of all possible advantages and disadvantages. Certainly the salesperson should have a voice in the decision.

Splitting Territories

Perhaps the most common adjustment facing many firms is reducing the size of territories. As markets grow and marketing efforts improve, each salesperson's work load may expand beyond reasonable limits. Sales managers then face the difficult task of cutting back each territory. The opposite situation—when territories have to be increased in size—usually is a lesser problem because it means an opportunity to cover more customers, make more sales, and increase earnings.

How does a sales manager reduce territories without damaging sales force morale and cooperation? One way is to show the sales force that their level of earnings will not suffer, perhaps by guaranteeing them at least their previous level of earnings for some stated period. If the planned territory reductions will be beneficial to the firm, such a guarantee should not be economically unsound in the long run.[47]

Other justifications have also been used to gain sales force cooperation in territory cutbacks. Smaller territories often mean less travel. In turn, less travel means more time with customers as well as more nights at home. Smaller territories also mean more territories which will call for more district managers and thus increased opportunities for advancement. But no matter what reasons are given, the changes must be presented in a positive way with clear indications of how they benefit each sales force member.

CONCLUSION

Territory determination is a complex activity because it involves a series of interrelated decisions. In this chapter we first discussed criteria which management should consider in making these decisions and then examined some analytical techniques which can be applied to territory problems. Many of these techniques draw on previously established potentials, forecasts, and budgets, as well as analyses of customer response to selling effort. Territories are the production lines of the sales force, and proper territory determination is vital in assuring that the goals and policies developed by management will be effectively achieved in the marketplace.

QUESTIONS FOR REVIEW AND DISCUSSION

1. How often should a sales manager revise the number of his firm's territories?
2. Some firms set aside one or more territories as training areas for new salespeople. Under what circumstances do you think this is justified? For example, would the salesperson's product line influence your answer?
3. Three computer-based sales effort allocation models were described briefly in this chapter: ALLOCATE, CALLPLAN, and SCHEDULE. For any one of these models, look up the noted reference, read the description and applications of the model, and report back to your class a more detailed explanation of how the model works.
4. The sales manager of an industrial chemicals firm has made no formal changes in the firm's territorial arrangement for five years. It has just been learned that the firm's market share has begun to decline, even though sales volume has increased each year. The first thought is to consider some territorial modification. What kind of modification should be explored first?
5. You are a district sales manager and have gathered a representative sample of call activity and orders received from your sales force. You categorize accounts by the number of calls they received during an average month and determine the corresponding average monthly sales volume for each category as follows:

Accounts receiving this many calls per month:	Generated an average of this much sales volume per month:
0	$ 350
1	950
2	1600
3	2100
4	2500
5	2800
6	2900

Your average salesperson has 40 potential customers and can make 60 calls per month in total. How many of these customers should be called on per month, and what is the optimum number of calls per customer to maximize sales volume in the average territory? If these rules were followed, what would be the total sales volume per month in the average territory?

6. Since sales territories cannot be made equal in terms of both potential and workload, management must compromise. If you were a sales manager, which of these two factors do you think is more important to keep equal among territories? Why? What can you do about the inequality in the other factor?
7. A sales manager is examining the firm's territory structure after not reviewing it for more than five years. The following data has been gathered relative to the most current operating year:

TERRITORY AND SALESPERSON	SALES VOLUME	SALES POTENTIAL	
		DOLLARS	PERCENT
A	$ 410,000	$2,000,000	33.3%
B	300,000	1,000,000	16.7%
C	310,000	1,200,000	20.0%
D	330,000	1,500,000	25.0%
E	150,000	300,000	5.0%
	$1,500,000	$6,000,000	100.0%

What would be the expected sales volume and sales penetration from this market in total if the sales manager took the following action:
a. Redivided the market into 4 territories.
b. Redivided the market into 6 territories.
c. Redivided the market into 20 territories.

Which of these three alternatives would be best if the cost of sales equals 50 percent of sales revenue and the cost to field a salesperson per year was $50,000?

8. To allocate the effort of sales engineers among two customer groups, a sales manager has developed the following information:
   a. Number of selling hours available per sales engineer per year = 1000 hours
   b. Number of customers in customer group A per territory = 200
   c. Response model of each customer in group A to selling effort = Profit contribution per customer = $200 + $80 (number of hours of selling effort)
   d. Number of customers in customer group B per territory = 125
   e. Response model of each customer in group B to selling effort = Profit contribution per customer = $300 + $60 (number of hours of selling effort)

The sales manager stipulates that no more than 5 hours be spent with any one customer, and that at least 100 customers in each group be called on. Under these conditions, what allocation would result in maximum profit?

9. The sales manager of a garden tools manufacturer has been asked by top management to submit a plan for opening a new territory so the firm can expand its distribution. It is determined that new territories could be established in four alternative areas. Outline the steps to be taken if an incremental approach to this problem were to be used. Then compare how these results might differ from the results from a ROAM analysis discussed in Chapter 5.

10. Assume your state is the total market area for a general household consumption item such as a broom. Divide your state into four relatively equal sales territories, using the sales potential method for determining territory location and boundaries. Select control units, find a measure of potential for each control unit, and then group the control units into four territories.

NOTES

1. Rayna Skolnik, "Thou Shalt Not Cross Territory Lines At Litton Microwave," *Sales and Marketing Management*, May 24, 1976, p. 34.

2. Gerald E. Ankeny, "Basic Factors in Sales Territory Design—II," *Allocating Field Sales Resources*, Experiences in Marketing Management no. 23 (New York: National Industrial Conference Board, Inc., 1970), pp. 17–18.

3. Thayer C. Taylor, "The Computer in Marketing—Part 11: Sales Force Management," *Sales Management,* March 15, 1969, p. 77.

4. Sally Scanlon, "Best Foods Knows The Score," *Sales & Marketing Management,* May 24, 1976, p. 40.

5. M. A. Brice, "The Art of Dividing Sales Territories," *Dun's Review,* May 1967, p. 98.

6. Henry C. Lucas, Jr., et al., "Sales Response as a Function of Territorial Potential and Sales Representative Workload," *Journal of Marketing Research,* vol. 12 (August 1975), pp. 298–305.

7. David W. Cravens, et al., "An Analytical Approach for Evaluating Sales Territory Performance," *Journal of Marketing,* vol. 36 (January 1972), pp. 31–37.

8. Further discussion of the types of response functions that can be studied is found in Zarrel V. Lambert and Fred W. Kniffen, "Response Functions and Their Application in Sales Force Management," *Southern Journal of Business,* vol. 5 (January 1970), pp. 1–11.

9. Robert F. Vizza, *Measuring the Value of the Field Sales Force* (New York: The Sales Executives Club of New York, Inc., 1963), pp. 50–51.

10. "How Buyers Rate Salesmen: What Makes Them See Red," *Sales Management,* January 15, 1971, p. 23.

11. This quote and additional discussion is found in Mack Hanan, "It's Time to Do Something About Salesforce Turnover," *Sales Management,* February 4, 1974, pp. 47–51.

12. James E. Bell, Jr., and William O. Hancock, "Optimizing Sales Organization Size," *Business Perspectives,* vol. 8 (Winter 1972), p. 19.

13. This method is based on Walter J. Talley, Jr., "How to Design Sales Territories," *Journal of Marketing,* vol. 25 (January 1961), pp. 8–12.

14. Perhaps the best basis for grouping is some measure of profitability such as contribution to profit or return on assets managed. An example of this is found in Sanford R. Simon, *Managing Marketing Profitability* (New York: American Management Association, Inc., 1969), pp. 128–134.

15. Brice, p. 96.

16. For example, its use by Celanese is reported by Brice, p. 93; its use by AT&T and IBM is reported in Robert F. Vizza, *Measuring the Value of the Field Sales Force* (New York: Sales Executives Club of New York, Inc., 1963), pp. 23–24.

17. This approach is based on Robert F. Vizza, *Time and Territorial Management for the Salesmen* (New York: Sales Executives Club of New York, Inc., 1971), pp. 15–16.

18. Vizza, *Measuring the Value of the Field Sales Force,* p. 25.

19. K. F. Griffith, "Establishing Sales Territories and Deploying Sales Man Power," in *Marketing Research in Action,* Studies in Business Policy, no. 84 (New York: National Industrial Conference Board, Inc., 1957), pp. 75–77.

20. Walter J. Semlow, "How Many Salesmen Do You Need?" *Harvard Business Review,* vol. 37 (May–June 1959), pp. 126–132.

21. The following discussion is based on Zarrell V. Lambert, *Setting the Size for the Sales Force* (University Park, Penn.: Center for Research of the College of Business Administration, Pennsylvania State University, 1968). Further encouragement to managers and directions on using incremental analysis are offered in Charles E. Allen, "A Level-Headed Approach to Increasing Sales Force Productivity," *Sales & Marketing Management,* June 13, 1977, pp. 48–51.

22. S. E. Heymann, "Determining the Optimum Size of the Sales Force," in *Marketing Research in Action,* pp. 82–84.

23. Charles A. Beswick and David W. Cravens, "A Multistage Decision Model for Salesforce Management," *Journal of Marketing Research,* vol. 14 (May 1977), pp. 135–144.

24. Harry L. Bullock, "Basic Factors in Sales Territory Design—I," *Allocating Field Sales Resources,* Experiences in Marketing Management no. 23 (New York: National Industrial Conference Board, Inc., 1970), pp. 11–13.

25. A current definition and listing of SMSAs as well as potential SMSAs can be found in the "Survey of Buying Power" published annually by *Sales and Marketing Management.*

26. Michael S. Heschel, "Effective Sales Territory Development," *Journal of Marketing,* vol. 41 (April 1977), pp. 39–43. The FMC procedure described here is similar to the illustration provided in Table 3.4 in Chapter 3.

27. Sidney W. Hess and Stuart A. Samuels, "Experiences With a Sales Districting Model: Criteria and Implementation," *Management Science,* vol. 18, no. 4, Part II (December 1971), pp. P41–P54.

28. "Kaufman Co. Sparkles With a Live-Wire Sell," *Sales & Marketing Management,* January 17, 1977, p. 26.

29. A. Parasuraman and Ralph L. Day, "A Management-Oriented Model for Allocating Sales Effort," *Journal of Marketing Research,* vol. 14 (February 1977), p. 27.

30. This example is adapted from James G. Hauk, "Research in Personal Selling," in George Schwartz, ed., *Science in Marketing* (New York: John Wiley & Sons, Inc., 1965), pp. 238–242.

31. Roy J. Shanker, et al., "Sales Territory Design: An Integrated Approach," *Management Science,* vol. 22 (November 1975), pp. 309–320.

32. This example is based on one used in Mark E. Stern, *Marketing Planning: A Systems Approach* (New York: McGraw-Hill, Inc., 1969), pp. 71–74. A relatively simple algorithm for solving the salesperson assignment problem is found in William R. King, *Quantitative Analysis for Marketing Management* (New York: McGraw-Hill, Inc., 1967), pp. 454–461.

33. Clark Waid, Donald F. Clark, and Russell L. Ackoff, "Allocation of Sales Effort in the Lamp Division of the General Electric Company," *Operations Research,* vol. 4 (December 1956), pp. 629–647.

34. Robert M. Olsen, *Allocating Sales Effort to Branches* (Berkeley, Calif.: Institute of Business and Economic Research, University of California, 1969).

35. For an example of the use of dynamic programming to allocate sales effort to prospects, see Roger A. Layton, "Controlling Risk and Return in the Management of a Sales Team," *Journal of Marketing Research,* vol. 5 (August 1968), pp. 277–282. A goal programming model, which produces an optimum allocation based on multiple objectives, is described in Sang M. Lee and Monroe M. Bird, Jr., "A Goal Programming Model for Sales Effort Allocation," *Business Perspectives,* vol. 6 (Summer 1970), pp. 17–21.

36. Robert W. Baeder, "General Electric's Scientific Method for Helping Salesmen Generate More Sales," *Business Management,* November 1968, pp. 30–33.

37. James M. Comer, "ALLOCATE: A Computer Model for Sales Territory Planning," *Decision Sciences,* vol. 5 (July 1974), pp. 323–338.

38. "Bringing Salesmen and Computers Together," *Sales Management,* June 15, 1971, pp. 26–31. Various versions of this model and its applications are found in the following by Leonard M. Lodish: "CALLPLAN: An Interactive Salesman's Call Planning System," *Management Science,* vol. 18, no. 4, part II (December 1971), pp. P25–P40; "'Vaguely Right' Approach to Sales Force Allocations," *Harvard Business Review,* vol. 52 (January–February 1974), pp. 119–124; and "Sales Territory Assignment to Maximize Profit," *Journal of Marketing Research,* vol. 12 (February 1975), pp. 30–36.

39. Gary M. Armstrong, "The SCHEDULE Model and the Salesman's Effort Allocation," *California Management Review,* vol. 18 (Summer 1976), pp. 43–51.

40. Spencer S. Meilstrup, "Combining Sales Forces," in *Allocating Field Sales Resources,* p. 34.

41. Claire Trieb Slote, "Keying Sales Calls to Profits," *Dun's Review,* November 1960, p. 43.

42. Slote, pp. 43–44.

43. Arthur R. Barrington, "How to Help Your Salesmen Plan Their Travels Better," *Sales Management,* August 5, 1960, pp. 40–42.

44. William Lazer, et al., "Computer Routing: Putting Salesmen in Their Place," *Sales Management,* March 15, 1970, pp. 29–36.

45. James B. Cloonan, "TOURPLAN: A Sales Call Routing and Scheduling Program," Working Paper 9–73 (Chicago: DePaul University, 1973).

46. Jan Wage, *The Successful Sales Presentation: Psychology and Technique* (London: Leviathan House, 1974), pp. 82–83.

47. For a modification of this solution, see Douglas K. Smith, "Painless Way To Split a Salesman's Territory," *Industrial Marketing,* September 1964, pp. 106–109.

7 OBJECTIVES AND QUOTAS FOR SALES PERSONNEL

The final major sales planning activity is setting objectives for each sales organization member. These objectives are called quotas in most firms today, and are assigned individually to each salesperson and often to field sales managers as well. A small but increasing number of companies are evolving from the traditional quotas approach to a management by objectives (MBO) system. MBO typically covers a broader scope of objectives and is based more on joint participation of subordinate with superior than is the quotas approach, although the intention of both is fundamentally the same—to establish performance targets for sales personnel.

QUOTAS AND MBO SYSTEMS COMPARED

Quotas are defined as results expected by management of a salesperson or field sales manager within a specified time period. When applied to managers, quotas usually indicate results expected from that manager's district or branch.

MBO is a process whereby subordinate and superior jointly define the subordinate's goals or results expected through consensus.[1] The MBO process can be distinguished from quota setting in a number of ways.

MBO usually includes objectives for all major job responsibilities as defined in a job description. This may include such topics as selling skills, time management, planning, and reporting as well as sales volume and expense objectives. Typically, an MBO plan will break down objectives and activities by individual customer and prospect, and will list specific strategies planned for each account. Quotas usually will not have this scope or detail, but will focus on sales volume and expense targets in the aggregate or sometimes by product line (as opposed to individual account). Rarely will a quota plan include action steps planned to achieve a sales target.

Joint participation by salesperson and manager is inherent in MBO but not in quota setting. Some firms allow sales force participation in setting quotas but many do not, and this issue is discussed later in the chapter. The aim of participation is to bring about better understanding of company goals by salespeople and to gain a stronger alignment of the sales force with those goals. Through the participation process, both parties can tailor objectives to effectively fit the unique characteristics of each territory. Participation also gives the sales representative's position more of a managerial and professional character since his or her judgment is made more equivalent with that of management. When quotas are used without participation, these advantages are lacking.

Quotas and objectives from MBO have many similarities in types, purposes, and analyses used to formulate them. We will treat them together in most of this chapter, with separate discussion of each only where definite distinctions are necessary.

RELATIONSHIPS WITH OTHER SALES MANAGEMENT ACTIVITIES

Quotas and objectives are the culmination of many planning activities.[2] They are based on higher level goals in marketing and sales management, as translated into sales forecasts, budgets, and profit targets. All subdivisions of the company must reach their quotas if overall company goals are to be reached, so performance evaluations, pay, and promotion opportunities are often dependent on goal attainment. Relationships between quotas, goals, evaluations, and compensation in IBM is clearly summed up as follows:

> The president divided the quotas among the four regions. Like the president, each regional vice-president was responsible for meeting his quotas and was evaluated according to his success in doing so. The regional vice-presidents divided their quotas among the district managers in their regions. The district managers, in turn, divided their quotas among their branch managers, who made the final assignment of quotas to individual salesmen, whose compensation was closely tied to their success in meeting quotas.[3]

Quotas are also closely tied to territory decisions described in the previous chapter. Quotas can be adjusted for territory inequalities in potential or workload, for example. Since selling effort has long-range effects, quotas should not be confined to short-range standards only. Ideally, territories are formulated on this same basis.

Training and supervision relate to quotas as well. Management can diagnose training needs by noting where quota attainment is weak, such as in selling a particular product line. Supervision is aided by quotas when the sales force works in territories distant from the manager's office. Day-to-day communication and control occurs via quotas in these cases where personal supervision is infrequent.

PURPOSES OF QUOTAS AND OBJECTIVES

Quotas serve multiple purposes for both management and sales force. The major purposes are covered in the following three categories.

Provide Incentive for Salespeople

Quotas provide incentive if they challenge the salesperson—both to exceed quota levels and to outperform others on the sales force. But maximum challenge will occur only if quotas are perceived as meaningful and attainable. A quota to set up five displays per week in retail drug stores may not be very important in the eyes of a particular salesperson, for example, so it provides little incentive. Another salesperson may like setting up displays, but five a week seems very easy and not meaningful in terms of what he or she thinks is really a good achievement. A meaningful goal is one which is important to the salesperson's personal satisfaction and one which signifies what the salesperson considers as impressive accomplishment.

Because sales personnel differ in their aspirations and in what they believe are important tasks, participation in quota-setting or in an MBO process can lead to more meaningful goals. In R. J. Reynolds, for instance, the sales representatives set their own goals for sales volume, number of calls, and display placements. According to Reynolds' director of sales, "We've tried goal setting both ways, by having managers do it and by letting the sales rep do it. We find it works better when the rep does it because if the salesperson sets his own goals, he's committed to them and is going to do everything he can to reach them. Also, sales reps continually set higher goals for themselves than we managers would set for them."[4]

Attainability is the other key factor for maximum challenge. Attainability depends on accurate measures of market potential and competitive conditions, and must reflect a realistic appraisal of what is an achievable work load per salesperson. Nothing will damage incentive faster than quotas which are impossible to reach because potential is lacking or the territory is too big to cover even with maximum effort.

Incentive exists directly when compensation is tied to quota attainment. A variety of such plans exist. For instance, a Calumet & Hecla salesperson gets an additional 5 percent of base salary for meeting an annual profitability quota. In IRC, Incorporated, an additional 1 percent of sales is paid for attaining between 90 percent and 100 percent of quota, and 1½ percent is paid for exceeding 100 percent of quota.[5] Even a salary-only salesperson might be motivated to exceed quota if salary raises hinged on such achievement.

Control Salespeople's Efforts

Quotas help management identify problems in a territory or district so they can be investigated and solved as quickly as possible. Suppose a district is reaching only 50 percent of its quota for one product line. Investigation might point out the need for a training session on the competitive benefits or customer applications of that product. Armed with this new information, the sales force can then make amends during the remainder of the year for its early poor achievement.

The best control of sales performance occurs when quotas cover all aspects of the selling job. If a salesperson is expected to do considerable missionary work, for example, a quota for sales volume only can be misleading. One study of sales managers' views on quotas reports that "a volume quota becomes an obsession with salesmen, resulting in a breakdown in control of other activities."[6] To overcome this problem, quotas can be established for those other activities such as servicing customers, collecting past due accounts, or preparing reports and research information.

Sometimes management may feel that its sales force is of sufficiently high caliber that detailed quotas are not needed for all tasks. In such cases, quotas which are assigned must not be so high that meeting them will prevent the sales force from spending sufficient time on other necessary tasks.

An integral part of many MBO processes is the periodic review session between salesperson and manager scheduled at various times during the year to check progress and adjust goals or strategies when needed. Because MBO usually results in action plans as well as objectives to be reached, the control process can be applied to activities as well as goals: Is the plan being followed? Has each scheduled step been carried out? Was it completed on time, at the right place, and with the proper person in the customer's firm?

Evaluate Salespeople's Performance

Sales personnel are often evaluated on how well they met (or exceeded) their quotas. The anticipation of this evaluation is a major incentive to those striving for promotion or pay raises. Branches and districts are likewise judged on quota attainment, and the field sales managers in charge of these units earn promotions and pay increases accordingly. In one division of Sperry Rand, for example, twenty-two separate dollar objectives are set for each sales branch, ranging from sales volume to travel, supplies, and clerical salaries. Effectiveness of each branch is then measured by the percentage attainment of each objective.[7]

Effective evaluation requires that quotas be set accurately. Otherwise it is difficult to judge whether performance gaps reflect the salesperson's ability or poor management planning. Fairness of quotas is a related issue, and often a subject of controversy. Some sales managers believe that quotas are fair when the "weaker" salespeople fail to reach them and the "better" salespeople exceed them.[8] Such quotas are based primarily on market measures without reflecting differences in ability among sales personnel. But if a weaker salesperson is given a lower quota and meets it, his aspirations and motivation are more likely to increase than if he is given a higher quota and then reprimanded for failing to meet it. Quotas set at the *same relative level of difficulty for all sales personnel* constitute the ideal solution for incentive and control as well as for evaluation.

Quotas must also be understandable to those being evaluated. While this may seem obvious, it is sometimes a significant problem. When some performance expectation of management is not clear to the sales force, the chances are that it won't be accomplished satisfactorily. For example, if a quota is set for "new calls," the sales manager should specify exactly what a new call is. Would calling on a previous customer who had not placed an order for a year be considered a new call? Could a sales volume quota be met with sales to a customer who later failed to pay?

The MBO process has some advantage in this case. At the beginning of the year, manager and salesperson meet to discuss the expectations and perceptions of each other concerning the sales job, and they have the opportunity to "clear the air" concerning past confusions or present contentions. As a result, the year-end evaluation should contain no major surprises on what results were really expected.

Limitations in Using Quotas and Objectives

Quotas have limited value when personal selling is of minor influence in the sale, such as when a low price or unusual service is the major deciding factor and the salesperson is mainly an order taker. In other cases selling is a major factor, but it is difficult to attribute sales to the efforts of any one salesperson. Suppose that a firm sells to contractors who in turn recommend the seller's product to their customers. The company's initial sales effort is carried out in the territory containing the contractor's home office, but the final negotiations and purchase may be completed in another territory where the contractor is building for his customer. A similar case occurs when the selling job is carried out by a sales team in which each member specializes in one aspect of the negotiations, and no one is totally responsible for obtaining the order. When the job consists predominantly of missionary work or other nonselling activities, quotas are difficult to devise because qualitative efforts rather than quantitative results are the key to success in such jobs.

When salespeople receive straight commission as their total compensation, the value of quotas is debatable. Skyway Luggage employs twenty commission-only salespeople and uses no quotas, for example. But each Skyway salesperson receives a monthly readout on current sales versus sales a year ago as well as current sales versus sales potential in his territory.[9] While these are not called quotas and are not used as a basis for compensation, they are performance standards used for monitoring progress. Unless some measures like quotas are available, neither manager nor salesperson will know how well each territory is progressing. Even if quotas are not assigned to each salesperson, this does not preclude their use as goals for branch or district sales managers.

For MBO processes to work, supervisors must be effective communicators and know how to give feedback and encouragement to subordinates. Sales managers who are autocratic or uncomfortable in a participative management setting will probably be ineffective in MBO situations as well.[10] Training of these managers may help, but if the sales organization is committed to MBO, candidates for sales management positions should be sought who already have interpersonal skills.

FORMULATING QUOTAS AND OBJECTIVES

Setting quotas and objectives to provide incentive, control, and evaluation is no simple task. Such factors as management's goals, sales force desires, territory characteristics and differences, and market changes over time must all be considered. For clarity, we will examine quota-setting in three separate steps, though in practice these steps are often interdependent. Figure 7.1 depicts the quota-setting process using a format similar to that in Chapter 6 for territory decisions.

FIGURE 7.1
Sequence of Sales Manager's Quota Decisions Under Various Long- and Short-Range Conditions

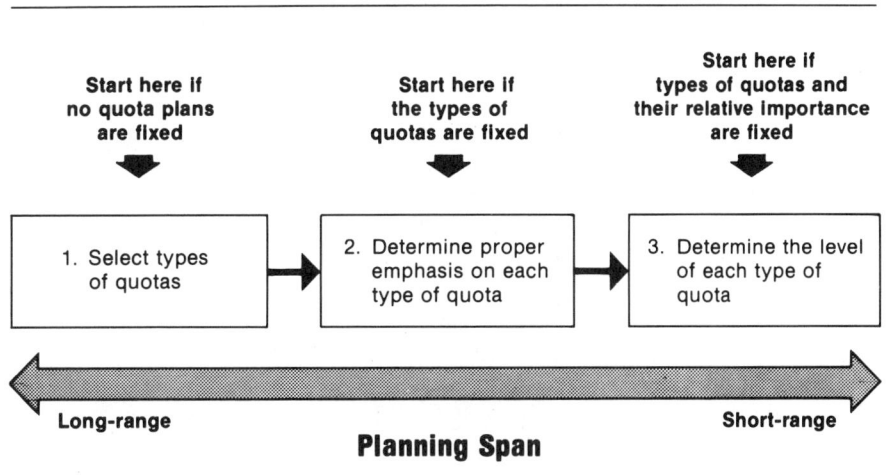

In fact, quota decisions parallel territory decisions at like points in the planning span. The number of territories needed (Step 1, Figure 6.2) depends on how sales effort is to be divided among selling and other tasks (Step 1, Figure 7.1). Short-range territory decisions such as allocating and scheduling calls must likewise coordinate with short-range quota decisions such as what level of sales is needed in each product line to meet a month's quotas.

Selecting Types of Quotas and Objectives

Quotas and objectives for sales personnel can be grouped into sales volume, financial, activity, and professional development categories. Field sales managers often have additional objectives relating to personnel and administration of their branch or district. For any specific sales or management position only those types should be selected which match the job's responsibilities. In a typical MBO process, both participants will write up a list of performance goals corresponding to major job duties. They then meet to reconcile their lists and to align the resulting goals for the subordinate with overall management objectives.

Each category and typical examples are listed in Table 7.1 and are discussed in the following sections.

TABLE 7.1 Types of Quotas and Objectives for Sales Personnel

SALES VOLUME:

in dollars	by product lines
in physical units	by customer types
in points	

FINANCIAL:

expenses, in total or by category
gross margin, in total or by customer type
contribution margin, in total or by customer type
net profit, in total or by customer type

ACTIVITY:

new calls	displays arranged
new prospects	service calls
new accounts	bids made
calls on former customers	dealer sales meetings held
letters to prospects	collections of past due accounts
reactivated accounts	surveys
interviews	reports
demonstrations	meetings or shows attended
time spent per account	

PROFESSIONAL DEVELOPMENT:

selling skills
planning
attitude
preparation for advancement

Sales Volume. Sales volume quotas, the most common in use today, are especially important in growing territories or where a territory's potential is not yet sufficiently captured. In established territories management may emphasize service or profitability rather than sales volume, but sales volume quotas are still useful to maintain a high level of sales penetration.

Sales volume quotas are most often stated in dollars rather than physical units because dollars can be compared directly with other measures such as sales expenses and compensation. Dollars also allow management to aggregate many different types and sizes of products into one total, and such measures can be compared over time even when product lines change.

Unit quotas are applicable when the total product line has only one or a few items or when it is common industry practice to describe products in physical terms. Marriott Hotels' sales force seeks convention business, along with many competitors, and has quotas in terms of room nights—two guests in two rooms for two nights equals four room nights.[11] An advantage of unit quotas is that they need not be recalculated when price change occur, and price inflation does not add to quota attainment.

Point quotas occur when management sets a point value equivalent to a given dollar or unit volume of sales. Point systems are often used to give selective emphasis to particular products. For example, an oil company varies the point value of product lines to direct sales effort to where management feels it is desirable. To deemphasize the sales of gasoline, for instance, its point value is reduced, and the point value is raised for some other product which management wishes to push.[12]

Many firms set dollar or unit quotas for individual product lines. Aggregate quotas are generally used with few products or when the salesperson has little control over the product mix sold. Individual quotas are suitable when one or a few products have relatively high profit potential but are more difficult to sell than other products. The sales force might neglect these items in lieu of the easier-to-sell, lower-profit items if they had only an aggregate quota. Some power tool salespeople in Skil Corporation have more than 150 separate quotas, one for each individual product they sell.[13]

Quotas may also be established to obtain a particular customer mix. Chemical salespeople, for example, may be assigned a few large customers who represent a large share of total sales, along with many smaller accounts. If sufficient attention is not paid to the large customers, their purchases may fall off, causing a large drop in sales volume which may not be compensated for by increased purchases from smaller customers. In this case, quotas by customer can provide an important means of control.

Financial. Financial quotas are one means of guiding a sales force to more profitable sales and of recognizing high-profit performers. When a territory's sales penetration is high, efficiency and cost control should be emphasized more than sales volume increases which might be obtained only at high cost and little or no profit.

Expense quotas are stated as a percentage of sales volume or can be given as an absolute dollar amount. While its purpose is to control excessive spending, an expense quota might encourage excessive cutting of expenses instead. For example, a salesperson may forego opportunities for entertaining prospects and thereby seem less interested than his competitors in their business. To minimize these problems, some firms do not use quotas in a formal sense for expenses, but monitor expense reports to detect any problems. If expense quotas are used, they should be flexible and responsive to varying needs of different territories.

Gross margin and contribution margin quotas are useful when there are marked differences in margins among products sold. Management might calculate the average gross margin percentage for all products in the line and set the quota percentage higher than this average to emphasize the higher-margin items.[14]

Perhaps the major drawback of margin quotas is that salespeople may not have the necessary data to check on their progress within the quota period. Management can achieve nearly equivalent results by setting volume or point quotas for each product line based on its corresponding margin. For instance, a manufacturer of wire and cable sets a point value for each product corresponding with each product's contribution margin, and the salesperson is expected to achieve a point quota through any combination of product sales.[15] Such quotas are easier to understand and the record keeping tasks are simplified.

The net profit quota is ideally the best, for it pertains directly to a major top management goal. It is superior to gross margin and contribution margin quotas because high margin items often require above-average selling and administrative costs, and may not be high in net profit.

Net profit quotas are difficult to use. First there is the problem of calculating net profit produced by a salesperson, which is discussed more fully in Chapter 15. Second, net profit is influenced by many factors not controllable by the sales force, so that their quota performance may reflect factors for which they are not responsible. Firms desiring financial quotas are more likely to use gross margin or profit contribution standards than net profit.

Activity. One purpose of activity quotas is to sustain sales force efforts which have a long-range effect on future sales. An industrial machinery manufacturer, for example, emphasizes the development of new accounts by requiring each salesperson to obtain at least 20 percent of total orders from new customers each year.[16] Without such quotas, the sales force might concentrate on immediate sales to the detriment of future volume.

Activity quotas are also used for nonselling tasks such as reports required and past due accounts solicited. Table 7.1 includes a wide variety of activity quotas and objectives used by many firms. The advantage of these quotas is that performance of activities is often more controllable by the salesperson than is securing sales volume, an important factor when quotas are used for evaluation. A problem is that quantity of activities, not quality of performance, is usually what the quota specifies. If demonstrations or other activities are carried out poorly, they may be of minimal value or even detrimental to the firm.

Professional Development. Professional development objectives, such as "to improve sales presentation techniques," are normally confined to MBO programs because MBO is more likely to incorporate qualitative as well as quantitative goals. If the salesperson (or field sales manager) is seeking a higher management position, MBO is a logical mechanism to identify the achievements needed to qualify and to monitor progress toward that promotion opportunity. A difficulty with these qualitative objectives is in their measurement. How much has the salesperson improved in planning, for example? To cope with this problem, specific steps must be spelled out at the start which, if successfully completed, will indicate success. For instance, the salesperson's planning might be considered sufficiently improved if all monthly route plans are submitted on time and actual routing deviates no more than 10 percent from the plan submitted.

Combining Quotas and Objectives for Proper Emphasis

When more than one quota is used, the salesperson or field sales manager needs guidance on the priorities among these objectives. For example, if the salesperson has a sales volume quota for two separate products, does it matter if he just reaches each quota or instead if he exceeds one significantly but fails to attain the other?

This question of balance or emphasis occurs for two reasons. Market conditions vary among territories, and different emphasis among selling tasks might be needed. Market conditions also vary over time so that what was important in a territory's early years may become less important as a territory matures. In addition, time is a limited resource and sales personnel may not have sufficient time to achieve all objectives to the levels assigned. A salesperson may have enough time at the end of a day to make a call on a totally new prospect or on a former customer, but not both. If there are quotas for each activity, which choice should be made? Often the choice will not be best from management's view but rather will be most convenient or pleasant personally for the salesperson.

The number of quotas assigned should be limited so that all can be achieved. Armour-Dial offers this advice to its managers in preparing for MBO sessions:

> Not only should each objective be realistic, but the *total number* of objectives stated should be realistic and attainable. So many objectives may be stated that their achievement in total, in addition to completing day-to-day responsibilities, is not possible. Two approaches should be used to help solve this problem. First, the priority of objectives should be indicated so that there is clear understanding of which objectives have the most value. Secondly, the supervisor and the employee must exercise careful judgment. They are in the best position to decide how much is enough.[17]

Three approaches can be used to indicate priorities and emphasis: explicit weighting, implicit weighting, and tying quota achievement to compensation.

Explicit weighting. Management can assign each quota a weight corresponding to its relative importance in achieving higher management goals. Weights can be estimated or determined more exactly by various statistical techniques.[18] Hammermill Paper Company, for instance, uses five separate product line quotas and each is ranked in terms of relative profitability so that sales of higher profit products boost performance measures more than the equivalent dollar sales of lower profit products.[19]

Table 7.2 shows an example comparing the performance of two salespeople under a weighted quota plan in which sales volume is considered twice as important as new calls. Overall, both performed equally in this example, but with different weights the calculation would change. (Perhaps different weights would have caused attainment to change also.)

Territory differences can be reflected with different weights in various territories. Suppose a firm's territories range from newly-opened to well-established and three quotas are to be used: sales volume, new calls, and expenses. Management might desire to emphasize the first two in the early years of a territory's development, then gradually shift emphasis to the latter quota as a territory becomes better established. A schedule of quota weights for these territories can be devised as shown in Table 7.3. It requires management to consider long-range territory and

TABLE 7.2
Performance Comparison of Two Salespeople Under a Weighted Quota Plan

		J. JACKSON			
	Quota Level	Attained	Percentage Attained	Weight	Weighted Attainment Percentage
Sales Volume	$150,000	$180,000	120	2	240
New Calls	75	60	80	1	80
				3	320

Performance = 320/3 = 107

		L. PETERSON			
	Quota Level	Attained	Percentage Attained	Weight	Weighted Attainment Percentage
Sales Volume	$160,000	$160,000	100	2	200
New Calls	80	96	120	1	120
				3	320

Performance = 320/3 = 107

quota plans more carefully, but the result should help each salesperson plan better for territory development.

Implicit weighting. Instead of using weights, management might get similar results by adjusting quota levels higher or lower. To increase the importance of sales volume and decrease the importance of new calls, for instance, the sales manager may increase the sales quota level and lower the number of new calls required. This implicit weighting of quotas assumes that salespeople will give more attention to quotas which are relatively high.

This adjustment is not always possible, especially with some financial quotas. To place stronger emphasis on expense quotas it is not necessarily logical to raise or lower their level. Even when levels can be adjusted to imply priorities, a sales force might not react as expected. In one industrial equipment firm the quota on a hard-to-sell product was reduced after sales personnel said they would use the freed time to increase sales of other products. An experiment in a few branches showed the opposite however; that salespeople given reduced quotas on the hard-to-sell product did not attain as much total sales or commission earnings as did a control group with no quota change.[20]

Tying quota achievement to compensation. Many companies have found that compensation serves as an excellent incentive to reach a quota balance desired by management. A large manufacturer of electrical equipment has many divisions sharing one sales force, but found that the sales force were concentrating on a few big-ticket items of selected divisions. Management then established quotas for all product lines of all divisions and devised a bonus plan which would pay those salespeople who met at least 70 percent of the quotas. Management upped the quota requirement to 85 percent after finding that the plan succeeded in producing a more balanced sales mix.[21]

TABLE 7.3
Schedule of Weights for Quota Types According to Age of Territory

Quota Type	AGE OF TERRITORY IN YEARS				
	1–2	3–4	5–6	7–9	10 and over
Sales Volume	50%	45%	45%	40%	40%
New Calls	45	45	40	30	25
Expenses	5	10	15	30	35
Total	100%	100%	100%	100%	100%

Determining Levels for Quotas and Objectives

Once management decides which types of quotas to use and the emphasis on each, the final decision is to set the level of each quota. Table 7.4 presents the most commonly used bases for determining quota levels. We will look at each quota category separately.

Levels for sales volume quotas. Two questions need to be answered to set levels for territory sales quotas: (1) What should be the total of all territories' quotas—should it equal total sales from the prior year, the sales forecast for the coming year, total sales potential, or some value in between? and (2) How should this total be apportioned among territories—in relation to each territory's relative potential, share of past company sales, or some other measure?

TABLE 7.4
Bases for Determining Quota Levels

BASES FOR SALES VOLUME OBJECTIVES:
1. Previous sales for company and industry
2. Sales potential
3. Sales forecast

BASES FOR FINANCIAL OBJECTIVES:
1. Previous financial data
2. Sales management budget
3. Profit and other goals

BASES FOR ACTIVITY OBJECTIVES:
1. Goals and policies of the company, especially for sales management
2. Characteristics of the territory, its customers and prospects, and competition
3. Salespeople's reports
4. Market research data

BASES FOR PROFESSIONAL DEVELOPMENT OBJECTIVES:
1. Job descriptions
2. Time and duty analyses
3. Professional and personal goals of salesperson or manager

The most logical basis for sales quotas in total is an accurate sales forecast, which can be viewed as a collective quota for the sales force. Obviously, sales quotas in total should not exceed sales potential, but some managers might adjust the total somewhere between the sales forecast and sales potential in hopes of raising overall sales force performance. If sales penetration is already quite high in most territories, this adjustment might lead to quotas which prove frustrating or demoralizing. But when sales penetration is low, this boost could pay off in added incentive and sales.

Quotas should seldom be set to match past sales totals unless the firm is in an extremely stable market or desires no growth or increased market share. Past sales might be a reasonable target in a declining market, particularly if the downturn is cyclical and expected to reverse in the near future. Permanent declines call for more drastic marketing action beyond quota adjustments—new product introductions or a complete change in promotion and distribution strategy, for example.

Apportioning the total among territories (or among districts or branches) is done in two ways. The first is a *breakdown* of the total using some type of index. Table 7.5 illustrates how Allis-Chalmers uses an index to subdivide their total company sales forecast among territories. Note that the index itself makes use of all three bases discussed: sales potential, past sales, and sales estimates from each territory's salesperson. The weights are determined by management and may be varied from year to year. For instance, sales estimates would be weighted more heavily if industry and market conditions in the coming year are expected to change significantly.[22]

The second approach involves a *buildup* of separately devised territory quotas into an overall total which is then compared with the sales forecast or other targets. Any discrepancies are then reconciled by adjusting each territory's quota accordingly. Suppose, for instance, that a firm had eight territories and a quota target of

TABLE 7.5

Allocating Company Sales Forecast to Territory Quotas Using a Composite Index

Territory	INDEX COMPONENTS			Quota Index	Dollar Quota
	Percentage of Sales Potential (weight = .5)	Percentage of Past Sales (weight = .3)	Percentage of Estimated Sales (weight = .2)		
A	2.33	2.01	2.40	2.248	$ 562,000
B	1.00	1.00	1.10	1.020	255,000
C	0.53	0.67	0.49	0.564	141,000
.	.	.	.	.	.
.	.	.	.	.	.
.	.	.	.	.	.
.	.	.	.	.	.
Total	100.00	100.00	100.00	100.00	$25,000,000

Source: Adapted from Harold H. Heinecke, "Sales Quotas," in *Marketing Research in Action,* Studies in Business Policy, no. 84 (New York: National Industrial Conference Board, Inc., 1957), p. 64.

$9,600,000 for those territories combined. Individual quotas were set for each territory, and the total of the eight was $10,000,000. Management could then reduce each territory's quota by about 4 percent so that, in the aggregate, they would total the $9,600,000 target.

Waste King Corporation uses a similar approach. Their general sales manager sets individual quotas for each territory, taking into account past sales trends and indicators of sales potential in each territory such as population trends, energy consumption, and trading area indexes. Differences in territory development or intensity of competition are reflected as well so that quotas provide accurate yardsticks for comparing performance of sales force members.[23]

Breakdown and buildup approaches can be used together to gain the benefits of both. The Borden Chemical Company employs an MBO process in which detailed territory plans are devised. Each salesperson ends up with an annual sales quota, subdivided by quarter, on each product line. Factors used by manager and salesperson to arrive at territory quotas are:

1. History of product line sales in the territory for the past three years.
2. "Buying Power Index" (from *Sales & Marketing Management*) for the territory.
3. Marketing objectives for each product line for the year.
4. Timing of promotions for each product line for the year.
5. National and regional advertising for each product line for the year.
6. Breakeven analysis of the 50 top accounts in each territory.
7. Breakeven analysis of salespersons and territory performance.
8. Breakeven analysis of products and product mix.[24]

Levels for financial quotas. The size of the expense budget for a territory is often based on last year's actual expenses (plus an increase for inflation) or on last year's expenses as a percentage of sales, with the same percentage applied to the coming year's sales forecast for the territory. This is similar to the percentage-of-sales method of budgeting discussed in Chapter 5. Waste King sets a "variable sales expense budget" for each territory, which ties allowable expenditures to sales volume levels. The ratio of expense to sales is adjusted for territory differences in costs and travel requirements.[25] A useful source of cost differences among major U.S. market areas is found annually in the "Survey of Selling Costs."[26]

Ideally, expense quotas should be set at levels which lead to optimum results in terms of sales, profit contribution, sales penetration, market share, or any other primary management goal. The desired result is essentially the same as that produced by the incremental method for budgeting. Suppose management is seeking to maximize sales penetration in a group of territories. Expense dollars should be shifted from one territory to another when the overall result will be a sales penetration increase. To carry out this analysis, the sales manager must know how sales penetration responds to changes in expense levels. Response function analysis discussed in Chapter 6 can be applied to this problem as well.

Other financial quotas, such as gross margin or net profit, can be based on corresponding ratios from the total sales management budget. Thus, if the budget projects a gross margin ratio of 40 percent of sales, this same ratio can be applied or modified for each territory. But as we have already noted, profitability is more likely reflected in quotas by using point systems which credit the salesperson with more points for sales of higher profit items or by setting sales quotas for individual products based on their relative profitability.

Levels for activity quotas. Activity quotas are seldom based on quantitative measures or financial analysis. Instead, activity levels are estimated for a territory by analyzing its characteristics, such as the type of customers and prospects it contains, and the activities of competitors. District managers and salespeople themselves are in a good position to know what extent of activities should be toward various accounts to keep pace or to outdo competition.

Analysis of sales force reports can also produce valuable guides. For instance, reported activities were found to correlate with sales volume in the National Cash Register Company.[27] Activity quota levels were set according to those findings, and salespeople were asked to submit progress reports on their activities. Ratios between performance on activity quotas and performance on sales volume quotas were then checked periodically to indicate whether the salespeople were making proper use of their time.

Levels for professional development objectives. In most firms' MBO process, no objective is considered complete until both superior and subordinate agree on how it is to be measured, how much of that measure is expected, and by what particular date.[28] Detailed strategies or steps to achieve each objective are usually included as well. Table 7.6 is based on the MBO process used by General Electric, and shows how specifically objectives and steps to reach them can be spelled out.[29]

TABLE 7.6

Major Account Sales Plan Developed from an MBO Process

			SALES ENGINEER SAM DOAKS		
Major Objective(s)	Measurable Attainable Realistic	Date to Accomplish	Persons Affecting Decision(s)	Planned Steps to Accomplish Objectives	Date to Accomplish
1. Assure continued purchase of product "B" by convincing purchasing agent of the superiority of our paint.		10/1	John Jones *Purchasing Agent*	1. Convince Jones to come to our plant for a visit—make appointment.	9/15
				2. Conduct tour of plant and demonstrate paint finish	10/1
2. Obtain an initial order for product "C" of at least $5,000.		11/15	John Smith *Plant Engineer*	1. Make appointment with John Smith to find current supplier and find out decision maker.	9/5
			Jim Brown *Maintenance Superintendent*	2. Determine whether moisture or aging is most important problem to Smith.	9/5
			John Jones *Purchasing Agent*	3. Get appointment for demonstration of product "C" to Smith, Brown, & Jones.	9/15
				4. Hold presentation and ask for order.	10/1

Source: Robert A. Else, "Selling By Measurable Objectives," *Sales Management,* May 14, 1973, p. 24. Reprinted by permission from *Sales and Marketing Managment* magazine. Copyright 1973.

Field sales managers are also guided by MBO programs which they devise jointly with their superiors. American Greetings Corporation, for example, lists general performance standards for its district sales managers, and each standard is translated into measurable objectives in an MBO session.[30] Two of the many performance standards used are written as follows:

My performance will be up to standard when:

a. I am knowledgeable of competitive activity within the bounds of my district and when no account is lost to competition due to my performance or that of any subordinate.
b. I am training and developing my field manager to be knowledgeable of and capable of performing all the duties of a district manager.

Objectives are jointly devised for these standards using this six point outline:

1. State the established objective for this year.
2. What is the present level of performance to this objective?
3. Next year's objective to achieve the standard or substantial progress toward it.
4. Changes I need to make.
5. Changes my manager needs to make. Training needed, follow through, etc.
6. How performance against objective is to be measured and evaluated.

Adjusting Quota Levels

Quotas are based primarily on management's goals and territory potential, and yet quota accomplishment is also a function of each salesperson's ability and experience. Adjusting quotas to reflect characteristics of individual sales personnel is therefore a final possible step. At IBM, for instance, sales volume quotas are first derived in proportion to sales potential in each salesperson's territory, but then modified to reflect each salesperson's experience.[31]

Adjustments can be made by management using ability indexes as guides, or adjustments can be induced through a participation process such as MBO.

Ability Indexes. In Chapter 6 we examined the use of ability indexes in making territory decisions. If one salesperson has an ability index of 110 and another has an index of 90, quotas might be raised for the first and lowered for the second. Whether the changes should be exactly proportional to the ability measures depends on which purposes for quotas management wishes to stress—incentive, control, or evaluation.

Most quota adjustments are made less formally after considering each salesperson's experience, past performance, and motivation. For instance, different sales personnel respond in various ways to pressure created by increased quotas.[32] At least four alternative reactions are possible:

1. The average sale increases and the standard deviation drops because the salesperson concentrates on the most promising customers.
2. The average sale and standard deviation both increase because the salesperson increases his overall effort.

3. The average sale decreases because the salesperson reacts negatively to pressure.
4. The average sale rises but then drops in subsequent periods because the salesperson borrows sales from future periods.

Knowing which of these reactions occurs in each salesperson, the sales manager can make quota adjustments with more predictable results.

Instead of modifying quota levels, a sales manager might adjust the acceptable amount of variation between quota levels and attainment. If only slight deviation is to be permitted for control and evaluation purposes, quota levels must be set more precisely. But if quotas are boosted to emphasize incentive, management should also consider widening the range of acceptable attainment around these high levels.

Participation. Some managers are skeptical of participation, fearing that salespeople will set quotas too low for easy attainment. Evidence does not support this fear. In one study, about half the firms which use quotas request their salespeople to submit an estimate of quota levels.[33] The managers not requesting quota estimates were asked what errors they expected would occur if such estimates were requested. Their answers were compared with the actual errors experienced by managers who do ask for estimates. As shown in Table 7.7, actual errors were more balanced in direction and smaller in degree than expected errors.

Evidence about MBO practices also does not support this fear. An "informal, loosely managed" MBO system in a hospital products company was improved to one where objectives were specified more formally and performance feedback was given more frequently.[34] Achievement increased significantly on eight of ten per-

TABLE 7.7
Errors Expected versus Errors Experienced when Salespeople Submit Quota Estimates

Direction and Degree of Error	Experience of Managers Who Do Ask for Quota Estimates	Opinion of Managers Who Do Not Ask for Quota Estimates
Direction		
Underestimate	48%	67%
Overestimate	52	33
	100%	100%
Degree		
10% or less	77%	59%
More than 10%	23	41
	100%	100%

Note: Probability from chi-square test < .02 on each comparison.

Reprinted from *Journal of Marketing,* published by the American Marketing Association. Thomas R. Wotruba and Michael L. Thurlow, "Sales Force Participation in Quota Setting and Sales Forecasting," vol. 40 (April 1976), p. 16.

formance standards, and sales volume grew by more than twice the rate of previous years.

Participation can occur in varying degrees. At one extreme, the sales force sets quotas which stand with no management modification. The other extreme occurs when management sets quotas and seeks sales force reaction to them but seldom makes any adjustments in light of the reaction. Most participation policies are somewhere between these extremes.[35] In the Falk Corporation, an industrial components producer, salespeople submit quota estimates to regional sales managers for review, and then to the general sales manager who adjusts them in light of overall industry, customer sales trends and knowledge of the individual salesperson submitting the quota—some are known to be typically optimistic or pessimistic.[36]

CONCLUSION

Quotas and objectives provide incentive for salespeople and, if properly set, aid management in controlling and evaluating sales force performance. In this chapter we examined how quotas depend directly on results from the planning activities covered in the previous chapters on potentials, forecasts, and budgets. Quotas and objectives are translations of top management goals into specific targets and programs tailored to each territory. To be most effective these objectives must be blended with the motivations and desires of each individual salesperson. To help achieve these aims, sales force participation in quota-setting and management by objectives (MBO) programs are becoming increasingly popular, especially as management upgrades the professional status of sales personnel.

QUESTIONS FOR REVIEW AND DISCUSSION

1. How might quotas differ between a firm with well-established products and territories versus a firm with new products and territories in the same industry?
2. Compare and contrast the MBO process with the more traditional method of determining quotas for sales personnel. Why don't more firms use MBO in the sales force? Do you think this use of MBO will increase in the future? Why?
3. Discuss ways in which quotas can be set to emphasize profitability.
4. If a firm uses manufacturers' representatives on a commission-only basis, should quotas be established for these representatives? If so, what purposes would these quotas fulfill?
5. What are two separate approaches a manager can use to help improve the "fairness" of quotas? How does the manager know if the resulting quotas are really fair?
6. The sales manager of an apparel manufacturing company wishes to use activity quotas for her salespeople's calls on new customers. Explain how she might obtain and use response curve data to assist in planning those quotas.
7. You must assign quotas to the five salespeople in your district in order to reach this coming year's $3,000,000 sales forecast for your district. Taking (a) past sales, (b) sales potential, and (c) ability indexes into account from the following table, describe how you would calculate a quota for sales volume for each salesperson:

Sales-person	Last year's sales	This year's sales	Sales potential	Ability index
A	$ 600	$ 750	$1,000	100
B	300	300	1,200	80
C	300	450	1,000	110
D	500	600	1,200	90
E	300	400	600	120
	$2,000	$2,500	$5,000	100 [average]

8. How long should the quota period be? Discuss the merits and disadvantages of setting quotas for year-long periods versus for quarters or even months. In what type of firm would longer quota periods be preferable to shorter periods, and vice versa?

9. If a sales manager wishes to establish some relative measures of each salesperson's reaction to pressure, what characteristics of their behavior should be considered in arriving at the final judgment?

10. Discuss at least two signs which indicate that a quota plan needs revising. Consider the long-range as well as the short-range aspects of the plan.

NOTES

1. General discussion of MBO in sales organizations is found in Donald W. Jackson, Jr., and Ramon J. Aldag, "Managing the Sales Force by Objectives," *MSU Business Topics,* vol. 22 (Spring 1974), pp. 53–59; Richard T. Hise and Peter L. Gillett, "Making MBO Work in the Sales Force," *Atlanta Economic Review,* vol. 27 (July–August 1977), pp. 32–37.

2. In the remainder of this chapter, the term "quotas" will refer to both quotas and objectives from MBO unless otherwise noted.

3. E. Raymond Corey and Steven H. Star, *Organization Strategy: A Marketing Approach* (Boston: Division of Research, Graduate School of Business Administration, Harvard University, 1971), p. 122.

4. Sally Scanlon, "Richard Joshua Reynolds Would Be Proud," *Sales & Marketing Management,* November 8, 1976, p. 45.

5. These and other examples are found in *Incentives for Salesmen,* Experiences in Marketing Management, no. 14 (New York: National Industrial Conference Board, Inc., 1967).

6. Gilbert J. Black, *Motivation of Salesmen through Compensation and Sales Quotas* (New York: Sales and Marketing Executives International, 1968), p. 7.

7. *Sales Analysis,* Studies in Business Policy no. 113 (New York: National Industrial Conference Board, Inc., 1965), pp. 56–63.

8. *Incentives for Salesmen,* p. 67.

9. "Skyway Has Faith," *Sales Management,* April 7, 1975, p. 23.

10. Hise and Gillett, p. 34.

11. James D. Snyder, "Marriott Hotels Keeps That Personal Touch," *Sales & Marketing Management,* May 24, 1976, p. 14.

12. *Measuring Salesmen's Performance,* Studies in Business Policy, no. 114 (New York: National Industrial Conference Board, Inc., 1966), p. 24.

13. Harry L. Bullock, "Market Research Helps Set Quotas," *Industrial Marketing,* July 1962, p. 94.

14. The distinction between gross margin and contribution margin is discussed in Chapter 15.

15. Leslie Rich, "The Controversy in Sales Quotas," *Dun's Review*, May 1966, p. 72.

16. *Measuring Salesmen's Performance*, p. 50.

17. "Appraisal Guidelines," Armour-Dial, Inc., April 1975, p. 160.

18. Numerous multivariate techniques, such as multiple regression, can be used to determine the relative importance of various tasks or achievements in contributing to overall goals. These techniques are discussed more fully in Gilbert A. Churchill, Jr., *Marketing Research* (Hinsdale, Ill.: Dryden Press, 1976), chapters 14 and 15.

19. *Measuring Salesmen's Performance*, pp. 57–60.

20. Leon Winer, "The Effect of Product Sales Quotas on Sales Force Productivity," *Journal of Marketing Research*, vol. 10 (May 1973), pp. 180–183.

21. *Measuring Salesmen's Performance*, p. 24.

22. Harold H. Heinecke, "Sales Quotas," in *Marketing Research in Action*, Studies in Business Policy, no. 84 (New York: National Industrial Conference Board, Inc., 1957), pp. 63–65.

23. *Measuring Salesmen's Performance*, p. 47.

24. Robert F. Vizza, *Time and Territorial Management for the Salesmen* (New York: Sales Executives Club of New York, Inc., 1971), p. 92.

25. *Measuring Salesmen's Performance*, p. 47.

26. Published as a special issue of *Sales & Marketing Management*.

27. Robert F. Vizza, *Improving Salesmen's Use of Time* (New York: Sales Executives Club of New York, Inc., 1962), pp. 27–33.

28. J. Taylor Sims, "Industrial Sales Management: A Case for MBO," *Industrial Marketing Management*, vol. 6 (1977), pp. 44–45.

29. Robert A. Else, "Selling By Measurable Objectives," *Sales Management*, May 14, 1973, pp. 22–24.

30. Management By Objectives Program, American Greetings Corporation, personal correspondence.

31. Corey and Star, pp. 124–125.

32. Charles P. Bonini, *Simulation of Information and Decision Systems in the Firm* (Englewood Cliffs, N.J.: Prentice-Hall, 1963), pp. 65–68.

33. Thomas R. Wotruba and Michael L. Thurlow, "Sales Force Participation in Quota Setting and Sales Forecasting," *Journal of Marketing*, vol. 40 (April 1976), pp. 11–16.

34. Charles M. Futrell, et al., "Benefits and Problems in a Salesforce MBO System," *Industrial Marketing Management*, vol. 6 (1977), pp. 265–272.

35. For an interesting approach where sales force and management negotiate commission rates and quota levels on product lines of unequal profitability, see Otto A. Davis and John U. Farley, "Allocating Sales Force Effort with Commissions and Quotas," *Management Science*, vol. 18, no. 4, part II (December 1971), pp. P55–P63.

36. *Measuring Salesmen's Performance*, pp. 51–52.

8 PERSONAL SELLING: THE JOB AND ITS ENVIRONMENT

What do salespeople do? This chapter and the next investigate personal selling from various points of view. In this chapter we learn of the variety in selling jobs, examine the selling process as it is evolving today, and analyze the environment in which salespeople work. The following chapter reviews various beliefs, as well as evidence, about what produces success in selling, and summarizes the major selling strategies and styles which are in use today.

These chapters have two main objectives. One is to give an organized view of the personal selling function to readers with no previous coursework or formal training in selling. The second is to provide sales managers with a better understanding of the work of their subordinates in hopes that this insight will improve their management effectiveness.

TYPES OF PERSONAL SELLING JOBS

All sales positions are definitely not alike. Selling jobs differ because buying differs from one market to the next. A retail sales clerk in a men's clothing store faces a much different market situation than does a data processing systems salesperson selling to large corporations and government agencies. Furthermore, a sales force is a flexible resource, and management has many options when deciding on what assortment of tasks and responsibilities each salesperson should have. A significant part of this decision depends on what other elements are used in the marketing mix, particularly promotion and communication elements.

To get some idea of how selling jobs vary, we first examine the major bases on which these positions can be compared.

Inside versus Outside Selling. Inside selling exists when the salesperson-customer contact occurs at the salesperson's place of business. Outside selling occurs when the sales force goes to the customer. Most retail store selling is of the inside type, although manufacturers and wholesalers employ inside salespeople as well. For example, a steel service center is a wholesaler of metal and steel materials to such industrial users as welding shops and small manufacturing plants. Customers come directly to the center seeking items in small quantitites or to meet urgent needs, and rely on the inside salesperson for advice and service.[1]

Company Salesperson versus Manufacturers' Representative. We already noted in Chapter 6 that a manufacturers' representative is an independent agent who handles related products of noncompeting firms. Reps, as they are called, are used by new companies or firms with no selling expertise, and are also used in territories where sales potential is not great enough to support a company salesperson. Sola Electric is one firm using reps, and its marketing vice-president explains why: "Because of their other lines, reps know the buyers intimately. And, more importantly, the buyers know them intimately. Mutual trust is long established. In the hands of a good rep, your product has a lot less resistance to overcome, and this is particularly important when you're trying to crack new markets."[2] The main complaint about reps is that they handle too many lines, and no one firm's line gets enough attention.

Tangible Products versus Intangible Services. Intangibles are often more challenging to sell than are tangibles. With no physical product to demonstrate, the salesperson must communicate with words and ideas and rely on the prospect's imagination to experience the benefits of purchase. An architectural firm, for example, may employ someone to sell their professional service of building design. Realtors sell communication and coordination to their property-buying or property-selling clients. With no tangible product to evaluate, the prospect must rely almost solely on a personal assessment of the sales representatative—is he or she likeable, honest, trustworthy, truly interested in my best interests, and so on.[3]

Direct versus Indirect Selling. Indirect selling occurs when persons in the marketing channel are contacted who can influence the purchase of the firm's product. A drug company employs "detail" salespeople to call on physicians in hopes of convincing them to prescribe that company's brands of drugs. Detailing also occurs in calls on government health officials who are deciding on what drugs to sanction under various federal or state health programs. These sales positions require extensive technical training which prepares the salesperson to discuss medical needs intelligently with physicians. For instance, Roche Laboratories' salespeople learn the doctor's world by making rounds with interns and residents at a large metropolitan medical center.[4]

Development versus Maintenance Selling. Some firms have separated the selling process into two sets of tasks—development and maintenance—and made each salesperson a specialist in one or the other. Development tasks involve seeking out new prospects and transforming them into customers. Maintenance tasks include serving existing customers—maintaining the sales relationship by filling reorders, solving delivery or other problems, and monitoring customer satisfaction in general. Specialized development personnel are useful if a firm's products are high-technology or high-cost items and if much preparation and research must precede the sales presentation. A manufacturer of knitting and weaving machines, Textile Machine Works, maintains development specialists for each of its product lines.[5] But many firms have not adopted this distinction because their best sources of increased sales are their present customers.

Promotional Value versus Functional Value Selling. When a large food chain buys many cases of breakfast cereal, it is not because their management wants the cereal but rather because they believe the cereal will resell quickly in their stores and provide a good return on money invested and shelf space used. In other words, the cereal is bought for its promotional value. Conversely, when a hospital buys breakfast cereal, it does so because the cereal fits within the dietary plan devised for its patients. The hospital's purchase has a functional motivation. Many consumer goods bought by wholesalers and retailers are purchased for their promotional value created through advertising and brand name reputation. The salesperson's job is to convince buyers that his product will equal or exceed the financial return available from competitors' products purchased with the same funds and made available on the same shelves.

USE OF SALESPEOPLE'S TIME

Less than half of a salesperson's time is spent in face-to-face calls on customers or prospects. While the use of sales force time varies across companies and among industries, some typical benchmarks are available from research studies. Table 8.1 indicates the average length of a salesperson's day in various industries and what percent of that day is spent in face-to-face selling. The average of 39 percent is slightly less than the 41 percent found in a similar study 13 years before, although the length of the working day has increased an average of 14 minutes over that same time period.[6]

What do salespeople do besides sell? A typical day as reported by consumer, industrial, and service sales personnel (all outside salespeople) appears in Table 8.2. Time spent calling on customers matches the findings in Table 8.1 very well,

TABLE 8.1
Percent of the Salesperson's Day Spent in Face-to-Face Selling, by Industry

Industry	Average Length of Day	Percent of Day in Face-To-Face Selling
Primary Metal	9 hr. 18 min.	48%
Petroleum Refining and Related Industries	10 hr. 6 min.	42%
Fabricated Metal Products	9 hr. 30 min.	41%
Electrical and Electronic Machinery	9 hr. 36 min.	41%
Chemicals and Allied Products	9 hr. 30 min.	40%
Furniture and Fixtures	9 hr. 42 min.	39%
Instruments	9 hr. 30 min.	39%
Rubber and Miscellaneous Plastic Products	9 hr. 42 min.	35%
Machinery, except Electrical	9 hr. 36 min.	34%
Nonmanufacturing Industries	9 hr. 6 min.	30%
Average	9 hr. 36 min.	39%

Source: Report 7023.1, Laboratory of Advertising Performance, McGraw-Hill Research, 1977.

although the participants in the second study reported a longer working day; in excess of eleven hours! It is also possible to calculate the average call length from these results, although that information was not reported originally. For example, consumer products salespeople spend 270 minutes a day, 1350 minutes per week, on 27 calls per week which is an average of 50 minutes per call.

In Chapter 1 we noted that improving productivity is a key sales management challenge, and the data reported in Tables 8.1 and 8.2 reinforce that challenge.[7] Some evidence exists that sales force time is being used more efficiently. The results in Table 8.2 were compared with a similar study four years earlier, and travel time had declined from over 27 percent to 20 percent while telephone time and calling on customers had both increased in this particular analysis.[8]

THE SELLING PROCESS

Although specific jobs differ, the selling process used by nearly all salespeople is basically the same. A comparison among four sales groups, including department store, industrial packaging, gift distributor, and insurance company salespeople, showed the *same types* of tasks performed by each but *different emphasis* on each task from one group to another.[9] For this comparison the selling process was divided into five steps—prospecting, contacting, stimulating, closing, and retaining—plus duties not directly involved in face-to-face selling.

TABLE 8.2

Utilization of Salespeople's Time in a Typical Day

Tasks	CONSUMER GOODS SALESPERSON		INDUSTRIAL GOODS SALESPERSON		SERVICES SALESPERSON		AVERAGE SALESPERSON	
	Minutes	Percent	Minutes	Percent	Minutes	Percent	Minutes	Percent
Calling on customers	270	41.4%	277	38.9%	265	43.8%	273	40.4%
On the phone	35	5.4	73	10.3	100	16.5	62	9.2
Traveling	146	22.4	143	20.1	85	14.0	137	20.2
Paperwork	55	8.4	91	12.8	70	11.6	75	11.1
Meals and Entertainment	82	12.6	71	10.0	30	5.0	70	10.3
Prospecting	40	6.1	41	5.7	45	7.4	41	6.1
Reading specialized publications	24	3.7	16	2.2	10	1.7	18	2.7
Total	652	100.0%	712	100.0%	605	100.0%	676	100.0%
Average number of calls per week:		27		26		48		

Source: "A Day in the Life of a Salesman," *Sales Management*, October 16, 1972, p. 40. The "average salesperson" column has been corrected from the original article. Reprinted by permission from *Sales & Marketing Management* magazine. Copyright 1972.

Following a specific set of steps has traditionally been considered the key to selling effectiveness. Salespeople not sticking to a methodical step-by-step approach find that

> what they can do is often made ineffective by what they don't do. And because they themselves do not see the sale as a sequence of logical steps, they rely on luck and gut feeling to guide them. Admittedly, they can be quite successful. On the other hand, it is more effective to know than to feel: to know exactly what you want to achieve, how to set out for it, and what to do next. Then, where you have failed, you have a standard against which your presentation can be compared and adjusted for improvement next time. Otherwise, the method is without control and the presentation progressively collapses.[10]

The traditional step-by-step approach is still the backbone of the selling process today, so we will look at each step in detail. Following that we will explore some new directions in selling which add to, or modify, the step-by-step approach.

Traditional View

Various lists of steps in the sales process are found in salesmanship books. The following list of six steps is typical.

Step 1. Prospecting. Prospecting involves obtaining names of potential customers. In some companies prospecting is totally a sales force responsibility whereas in other firms the salesperson is supplied with names from advertising or other sources. The marketing manager of Hollingsworth Company, a supplier of motor generators, describes his firm's prospecting system this way:

> Hollingsworth's current customers will comprise the data base, supplemented later by firms replying to four subsequent direct mail promotions. These will be classified as "prospects" and "feelers." A third step will involve culling firms from directories, data banks of outside service houses, and leads developed by salesmen. Each customer and prospect company will be accompanied by as much information as we can gather, including a four-digit standard industrial classification code, number of employees, number of forklift trucks and battery chargers used, title of the buying authority, and the relationship between individual establishments and their corporate entity. Much of the information will be supplied by salesmen, who will also be asked to keep the file updated.[11]

The importance of prospecting varies from one job to the next. Life insurance agents, for example, base their success largely on a constant flow of new prospects. But a medical supplies salesperson might call on only a few large hospitals and clinics which are continuing customers. Where prospecting is important, the sales force must develop a system of obtaining leads. When asked which is the most effective source of new account leads, a panel of salespeople gave these replies:[12]

Source	Percent calling it most effective
Recommendations from customers	38%
Recommendations from business associates	22%
Observation of new business construction	12%
Trade shows	11%
Advertising leads	10%
Conventions	4%
Listings in local, state, and national directories	3%
	100%

Sales leads are not true prospects until their need for the product or service is confirmed. Then the prospect must be "qualified" as to his or her ability and authority to buy. Obviously, calling on an unqualified prospect is a waste of time, and yet many salespeople do it because qualifying prospects is also time-consuming and not always easy. Sources of helpful information about a prospect's needs and authority include credit ratings, business and professional directories, trade publication articles, and even a phone conversation with public relations or switchboard personnel in the prospect's company.

Step 2. Preparation. The preparation step focuses on planning for the call. Whatever information the salesperson has on the prospect must be organized and reviewed, and a strategy for the call must be established.

If the call is to be made on an existing account, that customer file and notes from prior calls should be reviewed. Keeping a customer file is considered essential by many successful salespeople. A typical file format includes a notecard or notebook page for each customer with information on demographic and educational background, interests and hobbies, dominant buying motives, and significant personality traits. This file permits salespeople to remind themselves that the customer they will see this afternoon, for instance, is married with two children at the local university, is an outdoor camping and fishing enthusiast, likes to criticize the city's professional baseball team, especially its manager, is extremely concerned about justifying the cost of purchases if asked by his superiors, and is quite dominant and aggressive in conversation. Armed with this data, the salespeople can tailor their calls much more effectively to fit each buyer's interests and characteristics.

Calls on prospects must sometimes be made without benefit of a customer file, unless a call has been made on the same prospect before and a file entry set up from that call. In a first-time call, it is important to plan the initial minutes to learn about the prospect personally and to adjust the approach accordingly. In addition, one or two early questions might be asked to confirm that the prospect is truly qualified as to ability and authority to buy.

Call strategy can be predetermined to increase selling effectiveness as well. Three guiding questions which the salesperson can ask are:

What needs does this customer have?

How can my products serve them?

How can I convince this customer?

By reviewing all product features, the salesperson should be able to select those which best fit the customer's needs. In first-time calls it is a more difficult task to know which product features are most relevant to a prospect, so that needs and priorities must be explored in the eary stages of such calls. But for ongoing customers as well as for prospects, specific points should be predetermined rather than left to the salesperson's discretion and memory under the pressure of a call. Figure 8.1 illustrates a "Conviction Planning Sheet" for organizing evidence to support a sales presentation. Other elements to plan for include what to say the first few seconds of the meeting, what procedures or visual aids to use in the presentation, and what objections might be raised and how should they be handled.

An important aspect of planning is making an appointment for the call. Calls made with no prior contact are known as "cold calls." Some salespeople thrive under this situation because they have found ways to use the surprise factor in their favor. But most sales personnel dislike cold calls because they are seldom sufficiently prepared, are uncertain about what they are getting into, and as a result are not successful with them. Other problems with cold calls involve time waiting to see the prospect and the impression sometimes received by the prospect that he or she was not important enough to be given the consideration of an appointment. Some cold calls are highly successful. It was a cold call by an Illinois Tool Works salesperson on the vice-president of purchasing for Anheuser-Busch which converted Budweiser to the plastic six-pack carrier replacing the conventional paper container.[13]

Step 3. Presentation. When salesperson and customer meet, what actually happens? How can we describe the process that takes place to bring about a sale? Various theories of the selling process exist, and most salespeople follow one of these theories either instinctively or deliberately as the result of training. We will examine four of these theories.[14]

The *stimulus-response theory* is based on the assumption that buyers make decisions or responses based on statements or actions presented by the salesperson. If the seller can present a series of stimuli which evoke favorable responses, he increases the probability of obtaining an order. A series of questions can be asked which have obvious "yes" answers in hopes that, when asked to buy, the customer will also say yes. Statements used as stimuli by other salespeople include fear when selling life insurance and status when selling automobiles.

Many difficulties exist when using this theory. Different customers react differently to the same stimuli, and the same customer may respond differently under varying circumstances. The customer is considered a passive participant, and any specific buying motives or needs are given no chance to be detected by the salesperson. This theory is extremely simple, and its applicability is limited mainly to selling situations involving low-priced items bought quickly without much purchaser involvement or when the buyer is thought to be easily intimidated. Impulse items in retail stores or carnival sideshow acts are examples of the former, while encyclopedias sold door-to-door in low-income neighborhoods illustrate the latter.

The *selling formula theory* includes several successive stages which the buyer is supposed to experience in a presentation. These stages are often termed *attention, interest, desire,* and *action,* and are expressed in the formula: AIDA. Sometimes a stage of confidence or conviction is placed after interest, and one of satisfaction is added at the end of the formula. The seller plans his presentation using this formula, which he assumes will correspond with the customer's progression of

FIGURE 8.1
Conviction Planning Sheet

Prospect's Name _____ Title _____

Background _____

My Recommendation _____

My Evidence:

I. Our customers have been with us an average of _____ years each.

II. I'll show him these exhibits, samples, models, visuals:

(1) _____ (3) _____

(2) _____ (4) _____

III. I'll give him this third-party evidence from trade journals, professional societies, universities, gov't agencies, etc.:

(1) _____ (3) _____

(2) _____ (4) _____

IV. I'll use these case histories of customers with similar needs:

(1) _____ (3) _____

(2) _____ (4) _____

V. I'll compare his situation with _____

VI. I'll show him these testimonials from satisfied customers:

(1) _____ (2) _____

VII. I've researched these facts about his market, needs, opportunities: _____

VIII. Here are key comparisons between our offer and the competitors': _____

IX. I'll cite this expert opinion, study, survey: _____

Source: Adapted from Carl G. Stevens, "Anatomy of An Industrial Presentation," *Sales Management,* October 1, 1973, p. 34. Reprinted by permission from *Sales & Marketing Management* magazine. Copyright 1973.

mental stages. The presentation is often memorized or at least structured according to a well-defined outline.

Some questions can be raised about this procedure, however. For instance, do all customers actually pass through these stages, and in this order? Does the customer's mind proceed at the same pace as the seller's presentation? This process, like the preceding one, is based on only the seller's view of the sales situation and allows no flexibility in dealing with different customers under varying conditions. It does provide a simple outline which can be useful as a training device. And under circumstances where a salesperson must dominate the meeting with a customer, such as when the product is completely new or unknown to the buyer, this procedure might prove effective.

The *need satisfaction theory* differs significantly from the other two because it is based on the individual customer's needs. The salesperson must first uncover the buyer's needs by encouraging him to participate actively in the conversation. Once the needs are identified, the salesperson must make sure they are understood by the buyer as well. Finally, the salesperson must present his product in a manner directly related to these needs.

This process requires alert and perceptive sales personnel and is seldom amenable to standard formulas and memorized presentations. Contrary to the first two, this approach will benefit from careful preparation to uncover potential customer needs. It presents selling as a two-party interaction and makes the customer an active participant.

The *problem-solving theory* is an extension of need satisfaction, and is based on discovering what problem is at the source of the need. A buyer may not realize how to translate the problem he or his company faces into product or service needs. For instance, a small manufacturer may be paying too much in overtime wages. The buyer and seller together diagnose possible causes of the problem, such as poor production scheduling, faulty plant layout, design or engineering difficulties, or improper work force size. Corresponding solutions are then identified and the best one or more are agreed upon. If the salesperson has prepared carefully for the call, one or more of the solutions will involve products supplied by his firm. But if the most effective solution does not include purchasing his products, the problem-solving salesperson will recommend what's best for the customer anyway.

Problem-solving requires expertise both in the products sold and in the business operations of customers. Often such salespeople are specialized by customer type so they can learn about these customers in depth. Problem-solving also includes customer education, because often the seller must convince the buyers to look at their problems in totally new ways and to understand how new ideas will help solve them. The expertise of a problem-solving salesperson is of little value unless his ideas and analyses are communicated to the customer in understandable terms.

With these theories as background, we turn to the major components of the presentation: the approach or opening, the presentation itself, and the demonstration.

The *opening* sets the tone for the rest of the call, and many salespeople consider it the key factor in selling success. Two types of openings can be distinguished—the preliminary social "chitchat" and the initiation of the sales presentation.[15] Preliminary remarks help to relax the atmosphere, particularly in first-call situations. The salesperson should try to sense how much preliminary conversation each customer wants and attend carefully to what topics interest each customer for later recording in a customer file.

The presentation opening should be planned ahead and tailored to fit that call's overall sales strategy. Typical openers are questions aimed at qualifying the buyer or identifying problems and needs. A Warner and Swasey sales executive indicated "Our opening is to find out all of the customer's manufacturing problems and relate to them. We might ask questions for 15 minutes, 30 minutes, or an hour before we start talking about our line."[16] Other openers which might be tried involve:

Offering a benefit: "Mr. Smith, we have a copying machine that will cut your copying time by at least 25 percent."

Demonstrating something: "Ms. Johnson, I'm going to drop these dishes on the floor and let's see what happens."

Offering a news or success story: "Mr. Morgan, did you hear that Acme Tool Company eliminated all their overtime headaches after installing three of our high-speed punch presses?"

Referring to a mutual friend: "Miss Abramson, your friend, Mrs. Peters at the telephone company suggested that you should see our new personnel records system."

The *presentation itself* is the crux of the selling process. Depending on what theory of selling is guiding the process, the presentation will vary from one extreme to the other in structure. A study among sales executives in a variety of firms examined five types of presentations and how well each achieved sales call objectives.[17] The five types included:

Fully automated. Sound movies, slides, or film strips dominate the presentation. The salesperson's participation consists of setting up the projector, answering simple questions, and/or writing up the order.

Semiautomated. The salesperson reads the presentation from copy printed on flip charts, read-off binders, promotional broadsides, or brochures. He adds his own comments when necessary.

Memorized. The salesperson delivers a company-prepared message that he has memorized. Supplemental visual aids may or may not be used.

Organized. The salesperson is allowed complete flexibility of wording; however, he does follow a company pattern, check list, or outline. Visual aids are optional.

Unstructured. The salesperson is on his own to describe the product any way he sees fit. Generally, the presentation varies from prospect to prospect.

Table 8.3 shows the results, along with the percentage of firms using each type in at least part of its sales force. The organized presentation was rated best, probably because it allows flexibility to adapt to customer reactions while the outline assures completeness and logical sequencing of sales points to be made. With this type of presentation, each salesperson can adjust the delivery to his own personality while the company maintains uniformity in the message content among all sales force members.[18]

Whatever type of presentation is made, a payoff will occur only if the prospect is convinced of the benefits of buying. The presentation must translate the product's features into benefits meeting the buyer's needs. People don't buy automobiles; they buy a means of transportation, a source of power, a status symbol, a mark of achievement. A key task in any presentation is to relate product features to customer

TABLE 8.3

Effectiveness of Alternative Types of Sales Presentations

	TYPES OF SALES PRESENTATIONS				
Objective	Fully automated	Semi-automated	Memorized	Organized	Unstructured
1. Conserve prospect's time	moderate	moderate	low	very high	low
2. Tell complete story	high	high	moderate	high	low
3. Deliver accurate, authoritative, ethical message	very high	high	low	moderate	very low
4. Persuade prospect	low	moderate	low	very high	high
5. Anticipate objections before they occur	moderate	high	low	very high	moderate
6. Facilitate training of salespeople	high	high	very low	very high	low
7. Increase salesperson's self-confidence	low	high	low	very high	moderate
8. Facilitate supervision of salespeople	moderate	high	moderate	very high	low
Percentage of firms using:	9.3%	33.3%	24.0%	85.3%	76.0%

Source: Adapted from tables in Marvin A. Jolson, "Should the Sales Presentation be 'Fresh' or 'Canned'?" *Business Horizons*, vol. 16 (October 1973), pp. 83, 85.

benefits. Armour-Dial sales personnel use a "features-benefits" list similar to that in Figure 8.2 to sell Dial soap, for example.

The *demonstration* is a reinforcement of the sales message which involves samples, pictures, charts, or scaled-down models. Customers usually become more attentive and interested as more of their senses are involved. The salesperson in the automobile showroom urges the prospect to get in the car and take it for a test drive. Perfume counters in department stores have bottles available for customers to sample. The county fair inevitably has a booth in which someone is demonstrating a new kitchen tool which slices, peels, scrapes, dices, cores, and grates. The driving, smelling, and seeing involved in these experiences will often provide the clincher to a sale.

Sales personnel use more sophisticated demonstration devices as well such as films, videotapes, working models of technical products, and statistical graphs and charts of experimental data. If developed properly, these aids will help organize and orient the message to the customer's needs, and will allow the salesperson to concentrate on that particular selling situation without having to worry about what comes next in the presentation. Like the presentation itself, a good demonstration should give prospects ample opportunity to interact—to ask questions, discuss points in more depth, and relate specifically to their particular needs.

Step 4. Answering Objections. Objections can occur at any time in the presentation, and act as blocks to the sale. They are useful to the salesperson because

FIGURE 8.2

A Features-Benefits Comparison for Selling Dial Soap

\	PRODUCT—DIAL SOAP	
FEATURES	**BENEFITS TO THE RETAILER**	**BENEFITS TO THE CUSTOMER**
1. Foil Wrap Bar	Makes entire bar soap section more attractive and calls consumer's attention to "more profitable" deodorant Dial.	Superior wrapper lasts longer and helps bar retain perfumed fragrances.
2. Zip Open Wrapper	No loose wrappers on shelf—consumer satisfaction provides repeat sales.	Ease in opening wrapper, saves fingernails of housewife and helps prevent frustration.
3. 72 Pack Case	Lower labor cost factor. Less chance of O.O.S.	Availability.
4. 4 Colors—Gold, White, Pink, Aqua (1 per case)	Greater choice of colors lessens the chance of consumer going to another store.	Aesthetic value—provides more colors to coincide with bathroom decor.
5. 2 Sizes—Reg., Bath	Choice of size increases total sales in higher profit "deodorant" category.	For use throughout the house.
6. T.V. and Print Advertising	Creates customer awareness which helps maintain existing sales & create additional sales in the deodorant category—advertising rubs off onto other high profit Dial items in H and BA.	Brings attention to formula & quality.
7. Physician Endorsed Formula-TCC & Perfumed	Helps create sales—appeals to all families.	Anti-bacteria—pleasant fragrance—staph control—germicidal.
8. Hard Milled	Minimal damage.	Longer lasting—better dollar value.
9. Deodorant Bar	More sales and greater profit.	Prevents odor and bacteria.
10. Sales Force	Service at shelf—price check—pick up spoils—build displays.	Maintains salable condition of product.
11. National Distribution	Consumer awareness.	Recognizable product.
12. Display Materials	Help create "additional" impulse sales.	Brings customer attention to a value.
13. Promotional Allowances	Additional profits and opportunity to attract more sales.	Better value at lower cost.

Source: Armour-Dial Company.

objections provide feedback and indicate how the prospect is evaluating a sales offer. Objections should be encouraged so the seller can focus attention on points of greatest concern to the buyer.

Objections can be legitimate or simply rationalizations for not buying. If the prospect is properly qualified, objections suggest that something has gone wrong in the communication process. If rationalizations are suspected, the seller might do better to restructure the presentation to be more in line with the buyer's personal interests.

Most objections can be anticipated since they will have occurred in many previous calls. By listing objections experienced and attaching replies to each, the seller will improve his ability to handle these selling opportunities. Of the many techniques for answering objections, a few of the more popular are:

Boomerang: The objection is turned into a reason for buying. If a prospect says, "I'm too busy now," the salesperson replies, "I know your time is scarce, and this product will save you at least a half-hour per day. Why not decide now and save us both the time of another call?"

Yes, but . . .: This objection is not directly denied, but is answered by adding new information. If a prospect says, "Your price is too high," the salesperson answers, "Yes, our machines are slightly more expensive than Acme's, but when you consider that our machines turn out more product per day, the cost per unit produced is very competitive."

Direct denial: The objection is tactfully denied when it is clearly wrong and can be proven so. This is a risky tactic, but can demonstrate the salesperson's knowledge and commitment to his product. If a prospect says, "I hear your adhesives lose strength at high temperatures, so they wouldn't work in our application," the salesperson responds, "You're not the only one who has heard that rumor, but I guarantee you it isn't true. Here, look at these heat test reports we had done by an independent lab on just this point."

Ask questions: The objective is countered with a question aimed at probing for a clearer statement or a concealed reason. This technique is used when the objection is suspected to be rationalization. If the prospect says, "I'm just not sure we can do business with your company," the salesperson replies, "Why do you feel that way?"

Admit and compensate: The objection is a valid one and cannot be denied, but it can be balanced with a strong benefit. The salesperson should hold back a major selling point to use in just this instance. If the prospect says, "Your delivery schedules have been at least two weeks late on the last few orders," the salesperson replies, "I know we've had some problems in the shipping department, and they should be sorted out by now. But don't you agree that our components pass your quality control checks with much better marks than do our competitors' parts?"

Step 5. Closing. Closing the sale by asking for the order is the natural conclusion of the presentation. It is also a difficult step for many salespeople. Few prospects volunteer to buy, and many salespeople fear being turned down as a personal defeat. A marketing manager of FMC Corporation stated it rather strongly: "If there's one single failing in any sales organization, it's that salesmen are incapable of closing. Few people, in fact, have the courage to close."[19]

Experienced sales personnel view the close as having two purposes: to get the order, and to smoke out hidden objections which will detour the sale. If the prospect seems ready to buy, or at least is offering no resistance, a trial close may be attempted even before the presentation is complete. If it produces an objection rather than an order, the seller can reorient the presentation more effectively. If it produces an order, selling time is saved which can be applied to another product. If many sales could be closed sooner, the productivity of selling effort will increase and lead to lower costs per order, improved sales volume, and ultimately, higher profits.[20]

Closing requires initiative by the seller, but it is often aided by careful listening or watching for buying signals—gestures or comments indicating a readiness to purchase. Typical buying signals include picking up the model or product literature for the second or third time, asking to read the contract or asking about delivery schedules, agreement with major selling points or answers to objections (either verbally or by nodding the head), reaching for a pen or pencil, and making notes or calculations on scratch paper (but not doodling!). Buying signals are not guarantees of success, of course, but they do indicate a positive prospect attitude.

Many closing techniques are used, a sampling of which includes:

Summary of selling points: The seller summarizes the major features and benefits of the product, pausing between each one to get agreement from the prospect, and then asks for the order. This approach fits selling situations which have extended over more than one call and may have involved more than one purchase decision maker.

Direct request: The seller asks the prospect to buy (or recommend) the product directly, an approach most effective with decisive buyers and when all selling points and objections have been covered in one relatively short call.

Assumptive close: The seller assumes that the buyer has decided to purchase, and suggests a step that will confirm this assumption, such as filling out some paperwork or asking for a purchase order number. It is useful with prospects who balk at direct decisions, since it requires the prospect to take action only to negate the order.

Alternative choice: The seller asks the prospect which alternative is desired—"Would you prefer the model with the freezer on top or side-by-side the refrigerator?" or "Which of our credit plans best suits your needs in this situation?" This method is effective when many choices exist and the prospect tends to be confused and indecisive. When the choice concerns a minor feature of the product, such as the color of upholstery in an automobile, it is sometimes called a "minor-decision" close.

Balance sheet: The seller lists advantages of the product on one side and disadvantages on the other side, and points out that purchase will be beneficial on balance. The apparent objectivity and honesty of this method often appeals to analytical buyers.

Limited supply: The seller warns that the product is in short supply and may become unobtainable if the buyer waits to purchase, or that price increases will occur soon making immediate purchase of more value. Of course, the possibility of these impending events should be real and not a bluff, and the seller should be prepared to offer some evidence if asked.

Step 6. Follow-up. If a sale does not occur, the salesperson must decide whether to try again. A critical review of the presentation and handling of objections might reveal some room for improvement which can be incorporated into a later call. But if the prospect is not properly qualified or if there is some insurmountable block to a sale, a subsequent call might be useless.

Sometimes a sale is not made, but was not the objective of the call in the first place. For instance, the seller might use a call to learn details of the prospect's business and to explore problems and alternative solutions. Then a second call is used to make a presentation based on the first call's information and discussion. The follow-up step in these cases is similar to the preparation step discussed earlier.

If a sale is made, a follow-up is then in order to maintain good customer relationships. When it is a first sale to a customer, the seller should anticipate some customer anxiety in starting a business relationship with a new supplier. In addition, competitors' sales personnel will undoubtedly visit the customer and raise points which can cause cognitive dissonance, the feeling of doubt whether buying that product was the correct decision. To reduce the anxiety and dissonance, the seller should reinforce the original selling points and benefits and show sincere concern for proper product performance. "Keeping sold" is as important as the initial sale itself, especially early in a buyer-seller relationship.

Other objectives of the follow-up might include the supervision of product installation or adjusting its operation for maximum effectiveness. Sometimes the buyer's personnel will be helped greatly by a short training session in correct product usage and maintenance. If the product is purchased for resale, the salesperson might meet with the customer's sales force and offer assistance in their selling task.

Follow-up can also lead to additional sales in a number of ways. For instance, the customer can supply leads for additional prospects. The customer might also have additional needs which can be explored in hopes that other products will be of use. A follow-up call might also concentrate on establishing an inventory control and reorder system, thereby selling a long-term relationship with this customer.

New Directions

The selling process is not likely to change its basic format drastically. But as technology and customer needs evolve, the selling job evolves in response. Three such changes are occurring today: increased use of computers in the selling process, multiple-level selling to match a growing complexity in the buying process of many firms, and greater use of managerial concepts in selling. Additionally communication and persuasion techniques are improving.

Nearly every salesperson has seen the *impact of the computer* in sales reports, inventory lists, invoicing, and order processing. Far fewer use the computer as an integral part of the selling process. But the computer is being utilized increasingly as a sales tool. For example, Exxon Chemical sales personnel set up a 16-pound briefcase-size computer terminal in a prospect's office, link it to their main computer by telephone, and get answers from it regarding technical and economic aspects of alternative chemical formulations as well as an analysis of the prospect's specific chemical formulation needs. At the end of the presentation, the computer even asks for the order![21] In a similar manner, NCR salespeople can hook up a portable terminal via telephone to data banks at company headquarters and obtain immediate answers on equipment configurations, prices, and delivery dates.[22]

Computer use is not confined to large corporation sales forces. For example, Gastonia Mill Supply Company, an industrial distributor in North Carolina, has used computer-generated data in selling for over ten years. Their president explains: "We do a tremendous amount of research on, and generate a tremendous number of statistics for, the customer so we can show him how our company saves him money by buying from us. What it costs him to buy, keep and use those products."[23]

Firms of all sizes are finding their customers relying increasingly on computer assistance in the buying process. In the case of repetitive purchases, it has been suggested that the seller's task in the future will be to wed computer systems of buyer and supplier. The buyer will mark the quantity desired on punched cards containing a complete material description, and the supplier's computer will process the cards, generate the order, and prepare the invoice.[24]

Multiple-level selling is a process during which several persons in the prospect's organization are contacted by the salesperson, because purchase decisions are influenced by an increasing variety of persons in different functional positions and at different management levels. For example, suppose the seller of fabricating machinery and the related raw materials finds that in a prospect's organization one person buys machinery, another buys raw materials, and to sell both items as a package requires that a third person who supervises the other two must be convinced to coordinate the deal.[25] A graphic example of multiple buying influences is shown in Figure 8.3, describing the process used by New York City government to buy a computer. Seven persons in the buying organization participate in that process, and these persons represent various departments and management levels.

Multiple buying influences provide two major challenges to sales personnel. One is to identify the influential persons in the first place so that they can be called on. A study done for the chemical process industries concluded that salespeople reach only about one-third of the buying influences in their companies, which include chemicals, drugs, fertilizers, paints, petroleum, plastics, and other industrial groups.[26] Another study was done among firms buying material handling and storage systems to determine what functional departments in their firms influenced each of seven steps in the purchase process. Table 8.4 reports those results, showing in what percent of the respondent firms each department was influential in each step. This study not only shows multiple buying influences, but also indicates that not all firms are the same since there is no step in which any one department was influential in 100 percent of the responding firms.

The second challenge is in getting the multiple buying influences to agree on the seller's offering. Suppose purchasing, finance, and engineering represent three buying influences. Each may have quite different priorities in assessing a seller's offering. Purchasing might consider delivery schedules, prices, and shipping policies as highly important whereas finance is most concerned with the profit or return expected from using the product and engineering focuses on the technical, maintenance, and quality control aspects. Since any one seller's offering is seldom tops in all factors, a compromise is usually necessary in the purchase decision. The salesperson who understands how buying influences reach their compromise may be able to direct his presentation accordingly.[27]

As the selling process makes more use of *managerial concepts*, the emphasis on persuasive skills and well-practiced oratory in the presentation gives way to setting objectives, making plans, and analyzing alternatives. The use of MBO as discussed in the previous chapter is one sign of managerial orientation in selling.

FIGURE 8.3

The Decision Process in Purchasing a Computer

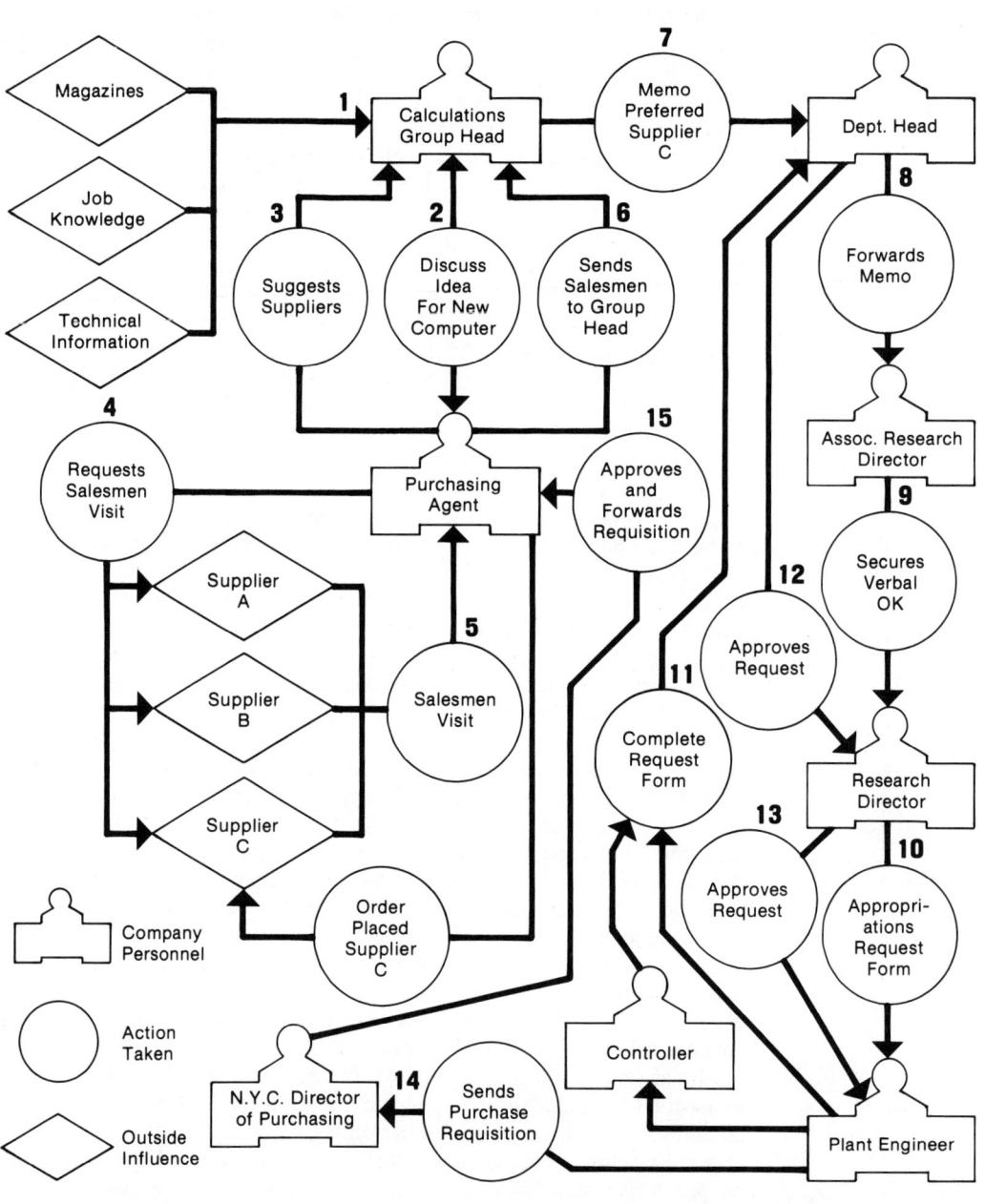

Source: Murray Harding, "Who Really Makes the Purchasing Decision?" *Industrial Marketing,* September 1966, p. 79.

TABLE 8.4

Multiple Buying Influences in the Purchasing Process of Material Handling and Storage Systems

Steps in the purchase process for material handling and storage systems	PERCENT OF FIRMS IN WHICH THESE DEPARTMENTS INFLUENCE EACH PURCHASE STEP							
	Industrial Engineering	Plant Engineering	Purchasing	Production Engineering	Corporate Management	Finance	Others Inside Company	Others Outside Company
1. Identifies need for system.	53%	39%	4%	38%	24%	2%	26%	3%
2. Specifies technical characteristics.	52	49	4	33	13	—	19	4
3. Searches for suppliers.	33	32	64	18	9	1	10	2
4. Chooses suppliers from whom to invite bids.	33	31	61	18	13	2	11	1
5. Evaluates bids from technical and performance standpoint.	46	50	21	29	16	1	17	2
6. Recommends which supplier gets order.	37	38	42	22	20	3	15	1
7. Authorizes final purchase.	11	13	26	8	65	19	15	1

Source: "An In-Depth Study of the Buying Influences for Complete Integrated Material Handling/Storage Systems," Harvey Research Organization, July 1976, p. 8.

The problem-solving theory discussed earlier in this chapter is another. Of course, the presentation remains a key step in selling success, but it changes to become more concerned with the customer's problems and goals, more managerial in its logic, and more analytical rather than persuasive in its strategy. For example, suppose a salesperson calls on two prospects whose main products are in very different stages of their respective product life cycles. Both might have a need for the seller's product, but the prospect with a maturity-stage product is in a totally different set of circumstances than the prospect with an introduction-stage product. They face different levels of market penetration, different competitive and cost situations, and different strategies for long-term success.[28] It takes a managerial orientation in the salesperson to appreciate the difference in position of these two prospects. If the seller's objective is to obtain a given level of sales volume from each over the next five years, the sales plan needed to succeed would certainly differ from one to the other.

Hooker Chemical Company has formalized the managerial approach to selling by requiring all salespeople to prepare a written sales plan for each major customer and prospect. The plan starts with a customer profile, including detailed information about the business such as sales history, competitors and market share, and key buying influences. Separate sections in the plan are devoted to goals, strategies, and action programs to achieve the goals.[29] Compare this approach with the discussion earlier in this chapter about keeping a customer file of personal information on the background, attitudes, and personality of the buyer so that the salesperson can adjust the presentation to these personal characteristics. Both a customer file and a sales plan are useful, but they represent different approaches to the selling process.

A Sales Process Model. An overview of the many factors involved in the selling (and buying) process is presented in Figure 8.4. This model depicts the interaction between salesperson and customer from when they meet to when they part.[30] Note that both salesperson and customer have equal representation, since both participate actively and equally in the process.

FIGURE 8.4

The Sales Process Model

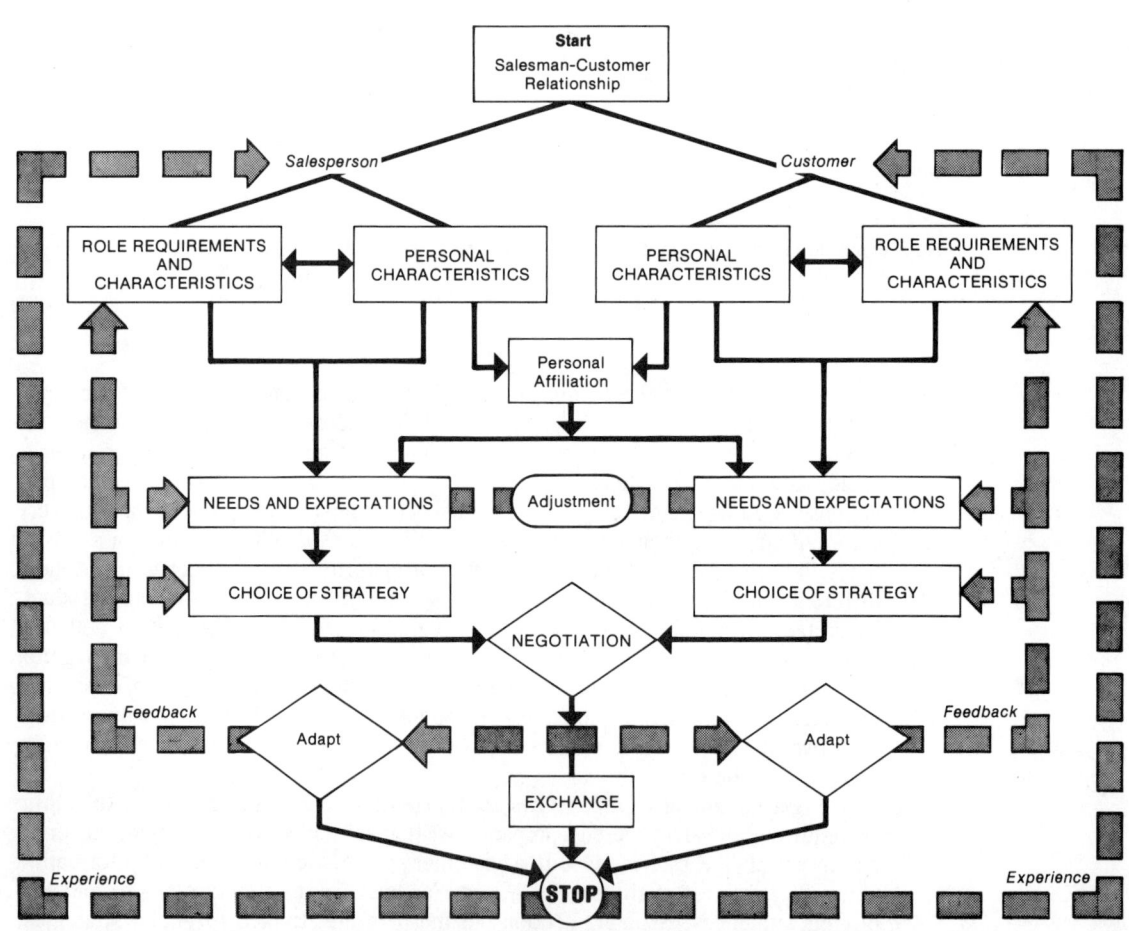

Source: Rosann L. Spiro, et al., "The Personal Selling Process: A Critical Review and Model," *Industrial Marketing Management*, vol. 6 (December 1977), p. 353. Published by Elsevier North Holland, Inc.

Each party brings to the sales process his or her personal characteristics, such as age, height, personality, values, and experiences. Each perceives the other's personal characteristics and, as a result, there occurs some type of personal affiliation—friendship and trust. Each also brings role requirements and characteristics such as responsibilities and authority from his or her organizational position. Role requirements can affect personal characteristics, and they influence needs and expectations from the sales process. It should be clear that if personal affiliation is not positive (e.g., "He just rubs me the wrong way!"), subsequent progress may be hindered greatly.

As each party hears and senses the needs and expectations of the other, adjustments take place. For instance, a dominant salesperson meets a customer who also likes to dominate the conversation, or a customer who needs the assurance of a well-known company reputation may become impressed with a well-prepared presentation by a salesperson from a relatively unknown firm. Buyers may initially seek low price, high quality, and speedy delivery, but sellers may need a higher price for the higher quality products or the speedier delivery service. Each party begins to realize the extent of its flexibility at this point.

Next, the seller and buyer both adopt a strategy intended to produce a favorable exchange. Strategies may include an emphasis on quality, technical assistance, low price, or even an appeal to personal friendship. Based on the strategies chosen, negotiation occurs: a presentation is made, objections are dealt with, and a close is attempted. If the strategies are compatible an exchange takes place. If the strategies are not compatible each party must consider whether to adapt and try again or to stop. Adaptation can occur by changing the strategy, by adjusting needs and expectations, and even by modifying role requirements to the extent possible.

Compared with selling formulas such as AIDA, this model is a highly sophisticated view of the sales process. As such, it is more realistic and useful in helping the salesperson diagnose problems and upgrade performance. Its main limitation is that it emphasizes the *process* rather than the *content* of each stage in the process. Careful preparation and planning prior to the sales process are still critical to successful selling, especially when selling takes a managerial orientation.

The Environment of Selling

Selling takes place in an environment which is unique compared with most other jobs. But the environmental setting is important to understand because it is often a strong influence on the salesperson's behavior. We shall examine this environment in terms of its psychological and social dimensions.

Psychological. Outside salespeople work away from their firm's location and often in isolation from coworkers. They are required to travel from one customer or prospect to the next, and must sometimes be away from home for many days at a time. As part of the job, they may have to seek out prospects with no previous acquaintance. Many circumstances of the job are highly changeable and uncontrollable, such as customers' availability to meet, trends within their business operations, actions of competitors, and even the food, accommodations, and travel schedules to which they must adjust.[31]

The psychological effect of these conditions will often lead to feelings of loneliness, alienation, and frustration.[32] The transient relationships with customers serve to emphasize these feelings, particularly when many sales calls do not succeed in gaining orders. Yet salespeople typically spend far more time with customers or prospects than with members of their own firm, leading to uncertainty about where the salesperson's loyalty and identification really belong.

Inherent conditions of selling make the salesperson particularly susceptible to role conflict—incompatible demands from two or more role partners such as customers, managers, and even family members. The sales representative is often caught in the middle because the selling job is a "boundary" position between two organizations, each with different goals and policies. Sales personnel interact with a large number of different individuals as well—customers and members of their own firms—and the pressures and demands from so many people will certainly produce some conflict. In particular, salespeople who take a problem-solving approach are likely to experience conflict because solutions often require innovative procedure and policy exceptions, upsetting those who desire to maintain the status quo.[33]

The extent of role conflict perceived by sales personnel in ten companies is shown in Table 8.5. On over half the items measured some conflict was indicated by the majority of salespeople. Studies aimed at finding ways of reducing this conflict have not been very successful. One concluded that "The sales or marketing manager can do little to reduce the amount of role conflict experienced by his field salesmen."[34] Some people undoubtedly can cope with role conflict better than others, and some may enjoy its challenges and opportunities, but for most sales personnel, role conflict is detrimental to job satisfaction and performance, and may produce job-related tension and anxiety.[35]

Social. The social setting of the sales job concerns the job's status or prestige. Society characterizes a person by their occupation. To many people, a "salesperson" connotes a rather stereotyped image of low status and ethical standards. Even people in close contact with professional salespeople sometimes reinforce this image. One noted marketing consultant and scholar wrote, "As many of the most productive salesmen are immature or neurotic and, in addition, some are not too well endowed intellectually, a number are chronic problems. Included are many prima donnas with their frequent total disregard for reality. Because of this, they are not to be regarded as wholly rational and responsible citizens."[36] This statement seems rather extreme, but it vividly points out the status position which many salespeople endure.

The occupational status of salespeople can be appraised more objectively by examining the major criteria used to determine status and how they are met in the selling job.[37] Five criteria are commonly used:

1. White collar vs. blue collar occupation
2. Income
3. Freedom and independence on the job
4. Education and training for job entry
5. Power to control others

The first criterion is the placement of the job in the white collar rather than blue collar category. The more creative selling jobs are clearly white collar in nature. Furthermore, selling has been identified as the white collar job most easily accessible to blue collar workers, many of whom undoubtedly become salespeople to gain more status and opportunity to work with higher status people such as their prospects and customers.[38]

TABLE 8.5

Salespeople's Perceptions of Role Conflict

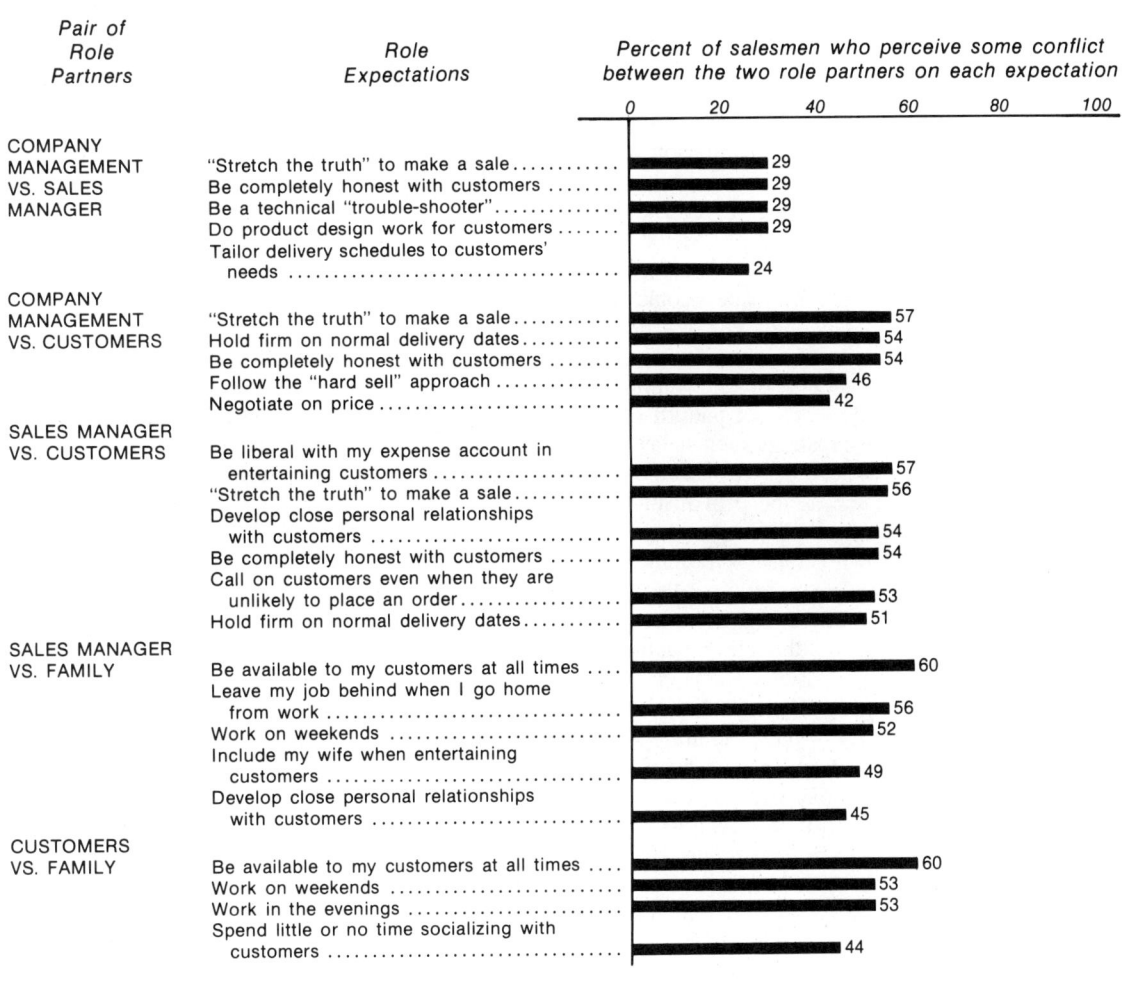

Source: Gilbert A. Churchill, Jr., et al., "The Social Psychology of Industrial Selling: The Salesman's View of His Job," *Perspectives in Business,* no. 1 (Winter 1975–1976), p. 26.

Income is the second determinant of status, and one where many sales jobs score well as many salespeople earn more than their manager, their manager's manager, and sometimes even more than their company's president. But concern over high income varies among sales personnel. While the job can provide extraordinarily high pay to those who are successful, some salespeople view their job as temporary, a stepping-stone to what they consider a more desirable position. This next position may be within the same firm, in a business of their own, or in a job not yet decided upon. In any case, many temporary salespeople think of their job primarily as a means of making as much money as possible.[39] In comparison, the career salesperson is concerned with the noneconomic satisfactions of the job as much as with financial gain.[40]

Stability of income is also associated with status. On this basis, sales jobs which pay primarily by commission might not be as desirable in status as salaried jobs since commission is less secure and more subject to variation. But commission plans offer more opportunities than salary plans for high earnings (as well as greater risks of lower earnings).

The third criterion of occupational status is the amount of freedom and independence associated with the job. We noted above that salespeople work in an environment of considerable freedom and discussed some of the psychological implications connected with this. But this freedom is not the same as independence, since salespeople are quite dependent for success on the cooperation of customers. Sometimes salespeople will describe themselves as really being independent businesspeople, perhaps because of the greater status attached to the autonomy of being one's own boss.

Education and training comprise the fourth criterion for status, and there seems no clearly set pattern for many sales jobs. In contrast, higher status professional occupations such as law and medicine have an entry requirement such as specialized college degrees and the successful completion of examinations. A few selling jobs, such as those in insurance and real estate, have similar requirements, and some industrial firms such as Carborundum and Bethlehem Steel have developed their own extensive training programs to prepare sales personnel with problem-solving and managerial skills.

There is a definite trend among employers to hire college graduates for sales jobs, although one author observed that this practice may be aimed more at raising occupational status than at obtaining required educational background.[41] Some firms hire college graduates as management trainees and place them in a selling job as part of their training. Such educational requirements are not sought for the selling position directly, but for later advancement within the firm. As selling evolves as described earlier in this chapter some clearer educational pattern may emerge as directly beneficial to sales performance.

The final status determinant is power to control the behavior of others. Within the firm's organization, the salesperson usually has no subordinates to control. But salespeople do have the responsibility of influencing prospects and customers to provide orders to the firm. This responsibility is not matched with any corresponding authority or power; the salesperson can only attempt to persuade or convince, not command. Among automobile sellers, for example, a fellow salesperson is considered good "who not only sells but is also adept at manipulating the circumstances of the negotiation so as to assure his control of the sales transaction."[42] Career salespeople especially enjoy the power implicit in persuading a customer to buy. One study of selling as an occupation found that salespeople "agree there is a thrill, a 'kick,' a profound, almost ecstatic sense of satisfaction in the act of consummating a sale."[43] Closing a sale is a mark of power—the personal mastery of one's profession.

Sales managers are concerned about the status of selling. Attempts to upgrade job status include hiring higher educated persons, developing extensive training programs, and replacing the job title of "sales representative" with various others in an attempt to differentiate the sales position in their firm from the stereotyped image of lower-level selling.

Salespeople often appreciate these attempts, although they also recognize that many occupants of selling positions do not really possess the desired "professional" attributes. Furthermore, some salespeople feel a resulting loss of individual importance and independence. Through standardized visual aids, enlarged training programs, and scientifically standardized selection programs, the salesperson may see his job and individuality become more and more controlled by the organization—his personal charisma being slowly deemphasized in favor of greater structuring of the job within the firm.

CONCLUSION

This chapter provided an introduction to the selling process and an overview of different types of sales jobs. Although selling jobs differ from one firm to the next, some underlying similarities were noted. Most salespeople spend less than half their time in face-to-face selling. They typically follow a step-by-step process in selling, consisting of prospecting, preparation, presentation, answering objections, closing, and follow-up. The selling process has been analyzed in various degrees of complexity, from a simple formula view of AIDA to a complex model in which the salesperson's and customer's perceptions, strategies, interactions, and adaptations are equal determiners of the outcome. Changes are occurring in selling, reflecting the impact of the computer, more complex purchasing processes, and more infusion of managerial concepts into personal strategy and procedures. Psychological and social factors associated with sales positions provide some insights into the behavioral environment of selling, a perspective of much importance when devising managerial programs and policies affecting the sales force.

QUESTIONS FOR REVIEW AND DISCUSSION

1. What are the main ways in which selling jobs differ? In what ways are all selling jobs alike? Based on this assessment, do you think that someone successful in one selling job would also be successful in any other selling job?

2. Since less than 50 percent of the typical salesperson's time is spent in face-to-face selling, what could be done to increase the amount of selling time available?

3. What are the advantages of following a systematic, step-by-step approach in the selling process? Are there certain types of selling jobs where this structured approach might be detrimental?

4. Why is it important to qualify a prospect? How much time should a salesperson spend in qualifying prospects?

5. "The purpose for the preparation step in the selling process is to establish a strategy for the call." What is meant by "a strategy for the call"?

6. Develop a sales presentation for any product of your choice using the stimulus-response theory as a guide. Then develop a second presentation based on the selling formula and a third based on the need-satisfaction theory. Try out your presentation on a classmate and analyze which is most effective.

7. Under what conditions would a memorized sales presentation be better than an organized one? Should any salesperson be prepared to use two or more types of presentations in the same market and for the same product? Why?

8. What's the relationship between answering objections and closing the sale? Is it generally easier to close a sale when no objections have been raised by the prospect? Why?

9. What is meant by multiple buying influences? If a salesperson's market includes multiple buying influences, how might this affect each step of the selling process, from prospecting to follow-up?

10. Because of the psychological and social setting of the salesperson's job, do you think there are certain types of persons (i.e., personality types, social classes) to whom a selling job is more suitable?

NOTES

1. See Robert J. Boewadt, "Inside Selling Within the Industrial Marketing Mix: A Role Analysis," in Fred C. Allvine (ed.), Combined Proceedings, 1971 Spring and Fall Conferences (Chicago: American Marketing Association, 1972), pp. 172–175.

2. J. D. Kimball, "Get The Rep's Attention By Giving Him Attention," *Sales & Marketing Management,* February 23, 1976, pp. 52–56.

3. Further discussion of selling services is found in Aubrey Wilson, *The Marketing of Professional Services* (New York: McGraw-Hill, 1972).

4. James D. Snyder, "The Detail Man as Superhero," *Sales & Marketing Management,* March 14, 1977, p. 48.

5. "March Comes in Like a Lion," *Sales Management,* January 21, 1966, pp. 57–58.

6. "Fighting the Clock for More Selling Time," *Sales & Marketing Management,* October 10, 1977, pp. 26–27.

7. A comparison of actual time utilization with sales managers' perception of the ideal utilization of salespeople's time is found in "Getting Your Money's Worth From Your Salesmen," *Industry Week,* April 16, 1973, pp. 30–34.

8. "A Day in the Life of a Salesman," *Sales Management,* October 16, 1972, p. 40.

9. Marvin A. Jolson, "Standardizing the Personal Selling Process," *Marquette Business Review,* vol. 18 (Spring 1974), pp. 16–22.

10. Philip R. Lund, *Compelling Selling* (New York: AMACOM, 1974), p. 2.

11. Thayer C. Taylor, "Finding the Live Ones," *Sales Management,* September 20, 1971, p. 55.

12. "Two Views of Those Vital 30 Seconds," *Sales Management,* October 30, 1972, p. 29.

13. "Cold Calls: The Heat's On," *Sales Management,* February 1, 1970, p. 25.

14. These theories are evaluated more extensively in Robert F. Gwinner, "Base Theory in the Formulation of Sales Strategy," *Business Topics,* vol. 16 (Autumn 1968), pp. 37–44.

15. This discussion is based largely on Porter Henry, "Openings for Every Occasion," *Sales Management,* October 30, 1972, pp. 6–8.

16. *Sales Management,* October 30, 1972, p. 24.

17. Marvin A. Jolson, "Should the Sales Presentation be 'Fresh' or 'Canned'?" *Business Horizons,* vol. 16 (October 1973), pp. 81–88.

18. For further evidence on the number, length, and types of presentations used today, see "What Makes a Good Presentation? It Depends on Where You Sit," *Sales Management,* January 22, 1973, pp. 44–46.

19. *Sales Management,* June 1, 1971, p. 8.

20. A financial analysis of the close is found in Mack Hanan, "The Close and Your Bottom Line," *Sales Management,* June 1, 1971, pp. 21–22.

21. "Portable Computer Terminals and Time-Sharing Network Give Exxon Chemical Reps a Sophisticated Sales Tool," *Marketing News,* March 24, 1978, p. 6.

22. Thayer C. Taylor, "Closing By Computer," *Sales & Marketing Management,* June 13, 1977, pp. 95–96.

23. "The New Business of Selling," *Industrial Distribution,* June 1975, p. 39.

24. H. Lee Mathews, et al., "Selling to the Computer Assisted Buyer," *Industrial Marketing Management,* vol. 6, no. 4 (1977), pp. 307–315.

25. Benson P. Shapiro, "Manage the Customer, Not Just the Sales Force," *Harvard Business Review,* vol. 52 (September–October 1974), p. 132.

26. *Blueprint for Selling: The Chemical Process Industries,* published by *Chemical Engineering,* 1977.

27. John O'Shaughnessy, "Aspects of Industrial Buying Behavior Relevant to Supplier Account Strategies," *Industrial Marketing Management,* vol. 6, no. 1 (1977), pp. 15–22.

28. This is based on Harold W. Fox and David R. Rink, "Coordination of Purchasing with Sales Trends," *Journal of Purchasing and Materials Management,* vol. 13 (Winter 1977), pp. 10–18.

29. Robert F. Vizza and Thomas E. Chambers, *Time and Territorial Management for the Salesmen* (New York: Sales Executive Club of New York, Inc., 1971), pp. 29–36.

30. Rosann L. Spiro, et al., "The Personal Selling Process: A Critical Review and Model," *Industrial Marketing Management,* vol. 6 (December 1977), pp. 351–364.

31. Henry O. Pruden, "The Outside Salesman: Interorganizational Link," *California Management Review,* vol. 12 (Winter 1969), pp. 57–66.

32. Leonard E. Himler, "Frustrations in Selling Activities," in Martin R. Warshaw, ed., *Changing Perspectives in Marketing Management,* Michigan Business Papers, no. 37 (Ann Arbor, Mich.: University of Michigan Press, 1962), pp. 78–83.

33. Orville C. Walker, Jr., et al., "Reactions to Role Conflict: The Case of the Industrial Salesman," *Journal of Business Administration,* vol. 3 (Spring 1972), pp. 25–36.

34. Orville C. Walker, Jr., et al., "Organizational Determinants of the Industrial Salesman's Role Conflict and Ambiguity," *Journal of Marketing,* vol. 39 (January 1975), p. 38.

35. For references, see *ibid.*

36. Robert N. McMurray, *How to Recruit, Select, and Place Salesmen* (Chicago: Dartnell Corporation, 1964), p. 7.

37. The five criteria used here are borrowed from John L. Mason, "The Low Prestige of Personal Selling," *Journal of Marketing,* vol. 29 (October 1965), pp. 8–10.

38. Gerhard W. Ditz, "Status Problems of the Salesman," *MSU Business Topics,* vol. 15 (Winter 1967), p. 69.

39. Raymond W. Mack, "Occupational Ideology and the Determinate Role," *Social Forces,* vol. 36 (October 1957), pp. 39–40.

40. F. William Howton and Bernard Rosenberg, "The Salesman: Ideology and Self-Imagery in a Prototypic Occupation," *Social Research,* vol. 32 (Autumn 1965), p. 283.

41. Ditz, "Status Problems of the Salesman," p. 71.

42. Stephen J. Miller, "The Social Base of Sales Behavior," *Social Problems,* vol. 12 (Summer 1964), p. 23.

43. Howton and Rosenberg, p. 282.

9 PERSONAL SELLING: STRATEGIES FOR SUCCESS

While there is general agreement on the basic steps in the selling process, far less agreement exists on what produces success in selling. In this chapter we first review and assess some basic beliefs of what distinguishes the more successful from the less successful salesperson and note their implications for sales management. Then we describe the major selling strategies and styles which guide professional selling today.

WHAT MAKES A SUCCESSFUL SALESPERSON?

This section must be headed with a question, since there is no single answer with convincing evidence. But sales managers search constantly for some one key factor which can open the door to routine sales success. The issue boils down to this: Is there something about a person—personality, background, actions—which make him or her inherently a better salesperson? We have already noted in Chapter 6 that selling success can be affected by territory assignments as well as scheduling and routing, so those factors are not covered in this discussion. Here the concern focuses on the qualities and actions of the person which affect the sales call.

Many writers and managers have advanced theories about what makes a successful salesperson, and for convenience we will group these into four categories:

1. the *chemistry* view
2. the *traits* view
3. the *behavior* view
4. the *dyadic* view

The Chemistry View. The earliest explanation of selling success involved the belief that good salespeople were "born, not made." This theory held that success came from some inborn and undefined "chemistry"—a gift which empowered salespeople to open doors and close sales. The true nature of this chemistry has always been vague and illusory, making it difficult to define. One manager sought this inborn talent by assessing the manner and appearance of people applying for sales jobs: "The applicant must be a wooer. In one way or another he must be able to set up almost instant rapport with strangers. He must have charisma. Without it, he can't sell."[1]

Others believe that chemistry is a necessary but not sufficient factor in selling success. A consultant specializing in selection and training of sales personnel and managers stressed that good salespeople must be both born and made, but emphasized, "If a person isn't born with the right temperament for selling or management, he will find these jobs very difficult and will usually fail."[2] A study of outside salespeople on the East Coast produced another version of the "necessary but not sufficient" belief, and gave us an additional definition of what chemistry means. This study concluded:

> The salesman defines his expertise as a mixture which consists approximately of one part education (skill of the teachable and learnable sort) to two parts genius (skill of the nature of a gift). A sense for practical psychology combines with an intuitive grasp of the logic of merchandising to form a mysterious amalgam called "general selling ability."[3]

Other attempts to translate chemistry into understandable terms have also occurred. Table 9.1 contains a physiological interpretation of what goes on in the seller's body chemistry, and suggests that success is the result of understanding and channeling this process for positive results. Many authors have written books supposedly sharing their secrets for sales prosperity or personal achievement in general.[4] Many of these books report anecdotes or exhortations about positive thinking and "try, try again" persistence. One researcher reviewed this large body of advice and success stories, and distilled ten identifiable or recurring elements.[5] Many of these key elements fit into the traits, behavior, and dyadic views, but three did not. These three, which are enthusiasm for the job, motivation to succeed, and a need for personal fulfillment, might be considered another interpretation of the meaning of chemistry. But this explanation assumes that selling ability is already "built-in" to the potentially successful salesperson, and potential will become actual success when that ability is unlocked through enthusiasm, motivation, and drive.

TABLE 9.1
The Chemistry of the Close

Without a doubt, closing is the most emotionally loaded part of the sale. Tied into an untidy bundle of anxiety, anger, fear, guilt, the close causes a psycho-physiological maelstrom of gland secretions and nerve janglings.

What actually happens under the salesman's skin as he moves to close a sale? In general, his breathing is deeper, he has a fuller, faster heartbeat, his blood supply shifts from the digestive, eliminative, and sexual apparatus to the brain, sense organs, and muscles. Sugar is released from storage by the liver to give energy support. And then, of course, we have our old friend, adrenalin, which is of critical importance for two reasons: it is a powerful stimulant and alertness sustainer; and the quality of the adrenal secretion determines whether the salesman will have a positive response, like excitement, or a negative one, like anxiety.

Although a salesman cannot possibly keep track of individual glandular and neurological functions that comprise the emotional drive, he can be guided in their use. If a salesman knows all this emotional ammunition is coming his way at the close, he can channel it for maximum effect. In addition to the obvious benefit of increasing sales, learning to use the emotional loads can help avoid such emotion-based illnesses as hypertension. All told, the salesman who knows what's going on under his skin utilizes his principal tool of the trade—himself.

Source: Jane Templeton, "The Chemistry of the Close," *Sales Management*, June 1, 1971, p. 12. Reprinted by permission from *Sales & Marketing Management* magazine. Copyright 1971.

Some evidence exists to support the motivational interpretation of the chemistry view. Two samples of 75 salespeople—one sample of high performers and one of low performers—were compared on a variety of psychological characteristics. The results showed greatest differences between the two groups on self-actualization, which was defined as feelings of self-fulfillment, worthwhile accomplishment, and realizing one's own potential.[6] In simple terms, salespeople perform better when they feel their job is important and their work is stimulating and productive.

Whether self-actualization is the cause or the effect of some underlying chemistry is not known. But the chemistry view does seem related to personal desire, drive, ambition, and motivation in general. Managers who favor the chemistry view, at least in part, will do well to concentrate on hiring persons with a positive appreciation and strong desire for selling and will stress the motivational and incentive factors in the job environment.

The Traits View. Many managers believe that a person's success or failure in selling is related to that person's background, personality, or other traits. This is a less elusive theory than the chemistry view because traits can be defined and measured. Included in the traits category are biographical factors such as age, education, and previous work experience; personality and character traits; intelligence and aptitude as measured by various psychological tests; and generally any kind of measure that can be used to describe and differentiate among people.

Examples of the traits view are not hard to find. The president of an industrial distributor offered this observation: "There are many personality traits that go into the making of a salesman. At the top are tenacity, determination, persistence—traits based on conviction about oneself and the product one sells."[7] A study done among sales and purchasing executives in the brewing and college textbook publishing industries produced a profile of traits describing their version of the "good salesman stereotype."[8] As shown in Figure 9.1, this profile indicates that the good salesperson is halfway between severe and lenient, much more reputable than disreputable, much more optimistic than pessimistic, and so on. Opinions abound, but the real issue is whether these judgments are valid.

The key to the validity of the traits approach lies in finding evidence linking traits with selling success. Will the judgments and opinions hold up when subjected to statistical testing? Many studies have been published on the characteristics of successful salespeople. In the late 1950s a summary of these studies to date concluded that, for salespeople in general, no significant relationship existed between sales success and any one of these: age, personality trait measures, intelligence test scores, character trait measures, level of education, and level of sales activity.[9] A more recent review confirmed those conclusions.[10] But these reviews and other studies did note that sometimes a profile of traits would be useful when applied to specific sales jobs in a particular company. In commenting on three stereotyped traits often associated with sales success—motivated, intelligent, aggressive—a personnel psychologist stated:

> "Motivated": Does the job really offer a chance for immediate advancement? A highly motivated salesman might not stay unless it does. "Intelligent": A too-intelligent man might find it hard to communicate with his customers. "Aggressive": Many selling jobs call for solving the customer's problems; an overly aggressive man might talk instead of listen.[11]

FIGURE 9.1

The Profile of the "Good Salesperson Stereotype"

Source: William R. Darden and Warren A. French, "Dimensions of Salesman Stereotypes and Their Relation to Executive Characteristics," *Social Science Quarterly*, vol. 51 (March 1971), p. 961. Copyright © 1971, University of Texas Press.

The traits approach offers much more promise when one overall stereotype of selling success is discarded, and instead different investigations are carried out specifically for each separate selling job. We noted some differences among sales jobs in the last chapter. One difference involved development versus maintenance selling. Consider how the traits needed for those two types of jobs would vary:

> The crucial talents and skills of the development salesman are qualities that a maintenance salesman requires only to a very limited extent and perhaps not at all—such traits as empathy, a sharp "third ear," introspective skill, and superior intelligence.[12]

Studies in many companies have produced trait distinctions between better and poorer sales producers. The Metropolitan Life Insurance Company found that two biographical factors, level of previous earnings and number of dependents, distinguished high producers from low producers.[13] Success by an oil company's sales personnel was significantly correlated with scores on an intelligence test, a personality test, a social aptitude test, and an interest test.[14] The 3M Company compared two of its sales forces—one calling on retail dealers and the other calling on industrial firms—and found significant differences on both interest and personality test scores.[15] An industrial building materials manufacturer investigated five personality and six biographical traits, and analysis of the results produced the following profile of the successful salesperson in that firm:[16]

> Tall, physically impressive, and energetic.

Good work habits; is perseverant, willing to work long hours, and enjoys solving problems.

Seeks and enjoys recognition from others for selling accomplishments.

Has a broad range of interests, but is not extensively involved in civic and professional organizations.

Not highly educated in a formal manner, but intellectually capable.

May be emotional and somewhat disorganized, but adaptable and flexible in work habits.

Not overly sensitive or perceptive to the reactions and feelings of others.

Views selling as a professional career and has little interest in achieving status beyond the selling position.

The evidence for a traits view of selling success is far stronger when we make separate analyses for specific sales positions. Yet, in a few instances, traits common to selling success in two or more different jobs have been found. Separate studies of automobile, insurance, and mutual funds salespeople produced consistent results when two characteristics—empathy and ego drive—were studied. The best performers scored highest on these characteristics, described as "central dynamisms" made up of patterns of interacting traits.[17] Empathy is the ability to feel as the other person feels, and ego drive is the desire to want and need to make the sale in a personal way more than just for the money earned.

In another study, real estate and private utility sales forces were compared on their "self-other orientation," which is defined as an individual's perception of himself in relation to significant other persons or groups.[18] No significant differences were found between these sales forces, but numerous significant differences did occur when both sales forces were combined and compared with a sample of nonsalespeople. The sales personnel scored higher in self-esteem, social interest, and majority identification (perception of similarity between self and the majority of others), and scored lower on self-centrality (perceiving the environment from the viewpoint of the perceiver rather than the viewpoint of significant others).

Management should be cautious about any stereotypes or opinions they hold concerning traits and sales success. But if supporting evidence can be found in a firm, the traits view has management implications for hiring and job placement. Key traits can be sought in the hiring process, and differences among applicants in background and personality can be matched to different job requirements. We will discuss this topic in more detail when we examine the selection process in a later chapter.

The Behavior View. Because the traits approach has produced mixed results, many managers have sought the secret to selling success in the salesperson's behavior. The behavior view relates sales effectiveness to some action of the salesperson, either verbal or nonverbal. The stimulus-response and selling formula theories described in the previous chapter are based on the behavior view, since they assume customers will react in the desired way if the right behavioral stimuli are presented by the seller.

Selling is certainly a behavioral process, but are there certain key behaviors that excel at eliciting a sale? Again, opinions and examples are not hard to find. One psychologist observed, "Historically, managers focused on traits . . . However, performance actually is determined by the presence of several specific 'behaviors.' These are concrete and measurable. If they exist in a candidate, his success as a salesman is predictable."[19] Among the behaviors noted were persistence, sincere manner of communication, and verbalization of conviction and enthusiasm. A specific behavior termed "sales aggression" has been related to selling situations in which repeat-sale potential differs from high to low. High repeat potential situations are best approached with low aggression presentations (i.e., "soft sell") whereas low repeat sale situations call for high aggression presentations (i.e., "hard sell").[20] No evidence was supplied to support any of these ideas, however.

In an interesting study done for a computer firm, numerous incidents were collected from the sales force and amalgamated into a videotaped "case." Two groups of salespeople—high success and low success—were asked to take turns assuming the salesperson's role, and report what "cues" they discerned while watching these incidents. The high success group reported significantly more nonverbal cues than did the low success group, but both groups were equal in verbal cue reporting. The conclusions were

> First, the salesmen's effectiveness in the face-to-face encounter hinges upon placing full attention on the prospect. This can only be done if the salesman is well prepared. Second, the prospect or customer's nuances may convey more than his speech does.[21]

Another study of the effectiveness of various behaviors was done for Berkshire International, a large hosiery manufacturer. Four general types of sales behavior were identified as follows:

1. Reactive: Salesperson tries to do what the customer wants.
2. Preactive: Salesperson tries to get the buyer to do what the salesperson wants.
3. Interactive: Salesperson influences, and is influenced by, the buyer to attain immediate tactical goals.
4. Proactive: Salesperson influences, and is influenced by, the buyer to attain longer-term strategic objectives.

Through a questionnaire, each of the 450 sales force members was classified as fitting one of the four behaviors. The company sells three brands of hosiery which face different market and competitive conditions. Using sales per store for each brand as a measure of each salesperson's performance, management found that each brand was sold best by sales personnel in different behavior categories. For instance, Berkshire brand was sold best by interactive salespeople while the Dior brand was sold best by proactive salespeople.[22] This study suggests that behavior, like traits, might be best studied specifically for each separate selling job.

Verbal behavior has been investigated far more than nonverbal. A study to compare the impact of sales presentations versus well-known company reputations via advertising showed the value of an effective presentation:

> Against a good sales presentation by a little-known company, a well-known one must also have a good presentation if the customer-getting value of its reputation is to be realized. Conversely, a little-known company, by concentrating strongly on training its salesmen to make good presentations, may be able to make considerable progress toward overcoming the liability of its relative anonymity.[23]

A study of a house-to-house selling organization compared more effective with less effective saleswomen and found the more effective scored higher on communication skills, use of emotional appeals, and dramatization.[24] Conversely, a study of retail appliance salespeople could not trace successful versus unsuccessful sales transaction outcomes to any specific sales behavior differences.[25]

Nonverbal behavior, or "body language," has received little formal study in marketing. But nonverbal cues, as noted in the computer firm study above, can be significant in understanding interpersonal communication and, ultimately perhaps, in closing a sale. Many interpretations of body positions and gestures have been made. For instance, a prospect who draws his shoulders back while talking to the seller is showing suppressed anger; a sitting prospect whose legs are crossed is less responsive to a sales presentation than is a prospect with uncrossed legs; and so on.[26] Future investigations should analyze how well nonverbal behavior supports the verbal; or if a conflict between verbal and nonverbal behavior occurs, is one consistently the more accurate reflection of the communicator's true feeling?[27]

In summary, behavior of both verbal and nonverbal varieties can have an impact on sales results. But there is no strong evidence that one set of behaviors is the panacea for all selling situations. Behavior, like traits, seems situational. If management can discern what behaviors are effective in its particular market, as did the computer firm above, this information can then be incorporated into training programs and supervision sessions.

The Dyadic View. Those who hold the chemistry, traits, or behavior view believe that a salesperson's success depends chiefly on what that salesperson is or does. If that is true, why does a given salesperson succeed with some prospects but not others? A partial explanation of this problem occurs when the situational nature of traits or behavior is accepted. If we carry this logic one step further, we can conclude that success is only partly a result of what the salesperson is or does; success depends also on the other party to the transaction. In other words, what constitutes the "most effective" traits or behavior will change from one sales call to the next. The same traits or behavior will not produce the same results with different prospects.

This reasoning brings us to the dyadic view. A dyad is a pair which is analyzed as a unit. For example, a salesperson and a prospect form a pair of parties to a possible transaction, and the two together form a unit having its own characteristics which can be measured and analyzed. The pair may be internally similar or different in age, sex, attitudes, and many other characteristics. The dyadic view says that selling success depends on the characteristics of this pair of interacting parties. The separate characteristics of each party don't matter, as in the traits or behavior view, but how these characteristics match or compare is what affects the success of the outcome.

Initial evidence for this view occurred in a study of life insurance agents and their prospects.[28] A comparison of the sold versus unsold prospects showed no significant differences on aggregate demographic, personality, or attitudinal variables. But the sold prospects were more like their agents on a variety of characteristics than were the unsold prospects. In other words, the successful dyads were more internally alike than were the unsuccessful dyads. This pattern included many variables: age, height, income, religious affiliation, education, political preference, and smoking habits. In fact, *perceived* similarity for religion and political preference were of greater importance than actual similarity.

Follow-up studies among life insurance sellers have supported the dyadic view.

One study for Equitable Life Assurance focused on age as the only variable, and showed that an unexpectedly high share of each agent's business occurred with prospects within five years of the agent's own age.[29] A subsequent study of a different life insurance firm revealed that the overriding difference between sold and unsold prospects occurred in role congruence—the prospect's comparison of the agent's actual behavior with an "ideal" agent standard. Unsold prospects perceived a large gap between actual and ideal role behavior while sold prospects perceived only a small and not statistically significant gap.[30] Apparently, the better the agent fit (or adjusted to) the role expectations of the prospect, the better were the chances for a sale.

Thus, similarity between salesperson and prospect has been demonstrated as contributing to sales success, and similarity has been studied in various characteristics—demographic, behavior, and attitudes. A different line of research has compared the impact of seller-buyer similarity (a *dyadic* factor) with the degree of expertise of the seller (a *traits* factor). An experiment was set up in a retail paint store to persuade customers to switch to a different-price paint after they had made an initial selection.[31] Two alternative approaches were used by the salesperson—an "expert" approach and an "I'm similar to you" approach. Both induced some switching, but the similar approach was significantly more effective. In another study the opposite conclusion occurred. Customers buying stereo music tapes in a Georgia music store were asked to purchase a tape recorder cleaner kit.[32] Four alternative approaches were used in this experiment, combining either expert or nonexpert with similar- or dissimilar-to-buyer appeals. In the similar appeal, for instance, the salesperson stated having the same tapes as the customer was buying, while in the dissimilar appeal the salesperson stated having no tapes of the type (e.g., classical, rock) the customer was buying. Coupled with that was the product statement demonstrating either expert knowledge or a vague description of how it worked. Table 9.2 shows the results for all combinations of appeals. Again, any appeal produced some sales (the poorest was the nonexpert, dissimilar condition as would be ex-

TABLE 9.2

The Effects of Expertise vs. Similarity in Retail Selling of Tape Recorder Cleaner Kits

	EXPERIMENTAL CONDITIONS AND COMBINATIONS								
	Expert and Dissimilar	Expert and Similar	Non-Expert and Similar	Non-Expert and Dissimilar	Expert	Non-Expert	Similar	Dissimilar	Total
Purchased kit recommended by salesperson	80.0%	53.3%	30.0%	13.3%	66.7%	21.6%	55.0%	33.3%	44.2%
20%	20.0%	46.7%	70.0%	86.7%	33.3%	78.4%	45.0%	66.7%	55.8%
	100.0%	100.0%	100.0%	100.0%	100.0%	100.0%	100.0%	100.0%	100.0%

Source: Adapted from Arch G. Woodside and J. W. Davenport, Jr., "The Effect of Salesman Similarity and Expertise on Consumer Purchasing Behavior," *Journal of Marketing Research*, vol. 11 (May 1974), p. 201. Reprinted from the *Journal of Marketing Research*, published by the American Marketing Association.

pected), but in this case expertise was effective more often than similarity in inducing sales.[33]

Similarity within the dyad has not always directly increased sales. In some cases, studies have shown less decisive results. Wholesale drug salespeople and retail pharmacy buyers were studied, and measures of "ideal" and actual behavior of salespeople were obtained from all parties.[34] Unlike the insurance study noted above, there was no relationship in this case between role congruence and sales volume. One finding did emerge, however; the smaller the gap between ideal and actual behavior as perceived by the buyer, the fewer the number of suppliers he dealt with. A salesperson meeting the buyer's "ideal" expectations well had fewer competitors for that account.[35]

While the dyadic view is relatively new as compared with the traits and behaviors views, it already has some convincing support through the studies noted above. The implications for management are quite different than if a traits or behavior view is followed implying a "one best way." The dyadic view suggests that salespeople be hired who have a variety of different characteristics, and this variation should be guided by the variation among buyers or prospects of the firm. Training programs should concentrate on teaching adaptability and detecting prospects' expectations rather than perfecting a standard approach to all sales presentations. The assignment of salespeople to territories or customers should be sensitive to how effective the resulting dyadic relationship will be. Firms using sales teams might also consider rotating team leadership for different clients, depending on who makes the best interpersonal "fit" with the key person in the buying organization.

Which View Is Best? Our summary of the four views reveals no one key factor producing consistent selling success, but rather some evidence pro and con for each view. To sum it up, we can say that a salesperson's success is probably affected by all of these views—motivation or chemistry, background and personality traits, verbal and nonverbal behavior, similarity to the prospect, and other factors as well—in some combination.

To get the salesperson's view of how these factors rank in importance, a study was carried out among the sales force of Del Monte Corporation.[36] Each of the 208 respondents rated a series of statements on a ten-point scale (10 = extremely important to selling success), and the results were as follows:

	Average Score Among All Salespeople
Chemistry view	9.0
Traits view	8.0
Behavior view	7.4
Dyadic view	6.5

The chemistry view was given top rating while the dyadic view was considered least important by this sales force. When the salespeople were grouped according to performance ratings assigned by their supervisors, no significant differences were found in the ratings among these groups. Better-performing salespeople don't differ from the poorer performers in their views of what produces selling success. The lack of a clear relationship between success and belief in any of these four views suggests that the secret to successful selling—at least one single and simple key factor—is still quite elusive.

CONTEMPORARY SELLING STRATEGIES AND STYLES

While the basic process of selling is not likely to change, the role of the salesperson and the purpose of the selling function itself will adapt to meet changing customer needs and to remain viable in an increasingly competitive marketplace. Changes are occurring in the strategies used to formulate benefits and the styles used to present these benefits to customers. We shall examine five of the most significant trends:

1. Consultative selling
2. Systems selling
3. Negotiation
4. Team selling
5. Territory management

Consultative Selling. Consultative selling means that the salesperson becomes a consultant, customers become clients, and the focus of the sale is not on product benefits but on profit improvement. Consulting with a client differs from selling to a customer in a number of ways. The consultative salesperson must learn how his clients make their profits and must generate ideas to assist in this process. The assistance may come in identifying new market opportunities, technologies, production or administrative processes, or solutions to any problem, but all with the goal of profit improvement through reduced costs or increased revenues.

A consultant sells services and must be an expert in his client's business. The same is true for a consultative salesperson, who differentiates his offering to the buyer in terms of problem-solving ability and analytical expertise. Many trends are causing this selling style to become more widespread.[37] Product standardization is increasing, making product differences a less important competitive advantage. At the same time, new materials and technologies are appearing at a rapid pace, faster than buyers can keep up. Price erosion makes price differences among competitors disappear as major appeals. Instead, service appeals are used to differentiate one supplier's offering from another's. Multiple-level buying decisions, as noted in Chapter 8, have accompanied these changes, requiring a wider scope of expertise by the salesperson in negotiating a transaction.

The net result of these trends has been an upgrading of selling, and consultative selling is a style which has naturally emerged. Firms making the transition from traditional selling have found many internal benefits as well as competitive advantages. "The effect on sales forces has almost always been highly motivational, and sometimes it has been little short of galvanic. Salespeople have seen in consultative selling not only an answer to many of their problems but a career opportunity that offers personal and professional rewards far exceeding those of product salesmanship."[38]

One way to visualize the difference between a consultative and a "traditional" salesperson is shown in Figure 9.2. The consultant enters the picture where the problem is still being recognized and formulated. The consultant might even initiate the problem recognition. By entering at this level, the seller can show how the firm's offerings can solve the problem and produce profit improvement for the client. Conversely, the traditional salesperson (termed a "vendor" in Figure 9.2) enters after the customer develops his or her own solution and formulates exactly what products are needed. The main way the vendor can capture that business is with a competitive price and, of course, the proper product specifications.

FIGURE 9.2

Comparison Between Consultative and Traditional Selling

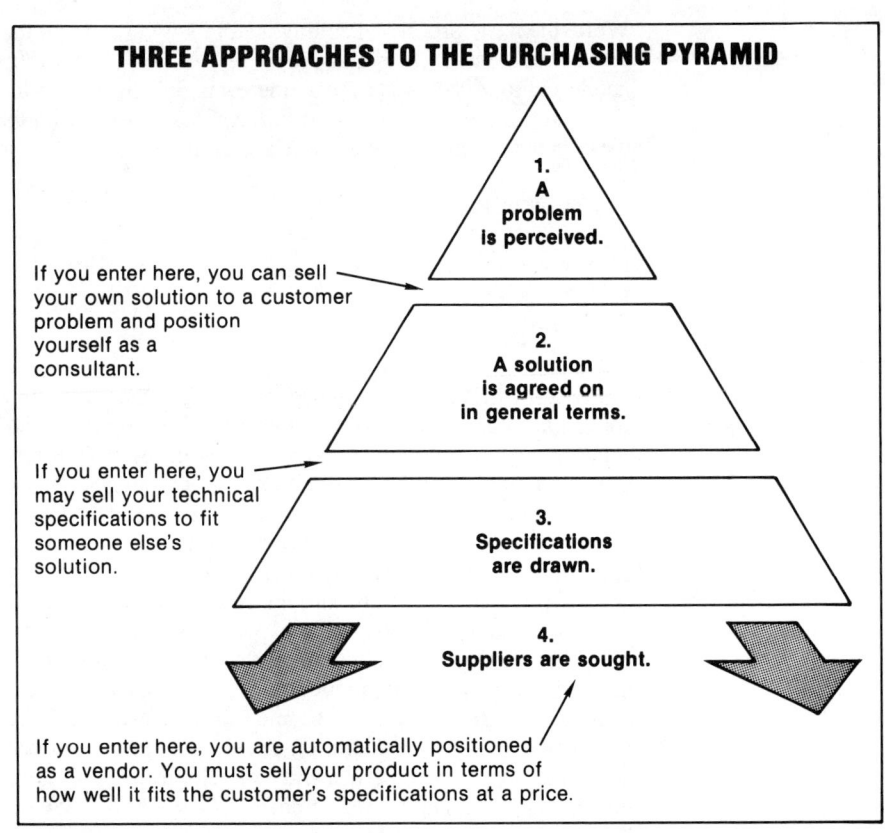

Source: Mack Hanan, "Stick With Being a Vendor And You'll 'Pay the Price,'" *Sales & Marketing Management*, July 12, 1976, p. 58. Reprinted by permission from *Sales & Marketing Management* magazine. Copyright 1976.

One major problem some firms have faced in the transition to consultative selling concerns what problems of a client to tackle. Not all problems will be profitable for the selling firm to solve. There is danger in offering to take on any problems a potential client has to solve. One district sales manager noted:

> For some problems, the solution costs the customer more than the disease. Sure, we could probably cure them. But the customer would go broke paying for the solution. Other problems we can't solve at all. But we don't admit that until after we've plowed bushels of dollars down the drain—dollars that come right out of our profits.
>
> But there's a third result that's the worst one of all. We discover we really *can* solve the customer's problem. And the customer discovers that he really *can* afford the solution. Then, and only then, do we find out there's no payoff. After all that work, there's no profit.[39]

Consultative salespeople must be well-versed in translating problem opportunities into profit opportunities, both for their own firm as well as for their potential clients. Training needs broaden considerably beyond the traditional prospecting, preparation, and other steps in the selling process. The sales vice-president for Olin Chemicals put it this way:

> We're having to train the salesman to talk and think much more about financial matters. In many lines, he's talking more about finance and investments than technical things. He has to know more about economics. He certainly has to know the difference between return on net assets or gross assets, and on new capital.[40]

Systems Selling. Firms use systems selling when, instead of just selling products, they sell products, services, and other administrative assistance—a complete system of benefits necessary to carry out a complex function or process for the buyer. A typical systems seller is Acme Visible Records, which "produces systems for expediting the flow of records for virtually any type of information problem."[41] Acme manufactures business machines and printed forms, and provides services such as diagnosing a prospect's record and information needs and prescribing a package to meet those needs. The recommended package contains Acme's machines and forms, of course, but also includes layout of physical facilities, training of operators, reorder arrangements, and any other services or information necessary to implement and maintain the system. Sometimes, a systems sale will include products or services from other suppliers which are coordinated and obtained by the main systems seller.

Key ingredients in most systems selling are the diagnosis and prescription. The salesperson first seeks permission to survey the prospect's needs. Suppose a vending and foodservice salesperson approached the manager of a large industrial plant with the idea of improving the foodservice to that plant's employees. The salesperson would, if given permission, survey some employees to determine how their present foodservice needs are being met and what they would like in a new or improved service. The salesperson would visually survey the physical location of the foodservice area to learn of space and facilities constraints, and would gather data on the total number of employees by shift and their pay scales. From this information, an analysis of potential demand and cost is made and a proposal is drawn up detailing the survey findings, the recommended facilities and food to be offered, maintenance and servicing arrangements, and the cost and revenue projections, with perhaps some persuasive sidelights on the effect of a new foodservice facility on morale and absenteeism.

While it occurs in most every industry, systems selling has been studied most comprehensively in the marketing of maintenance, repair, and operating (MRO) supplies by industrial distributors.[42] Included in these transactions are not only the MRO items, but also some cost-saving benefits. One is shifting much of the customer's MRO inventory back to the distributor, which saves the customer storage space as well as inventory investment. Other benefits include automatic ordering of items from a preprogrammed schedule, and one-day delivery of other items as needed. The total cost of procurement is lowered as a result, since storage space, investment, and purchasing paperwork and time are all reduced.

To succeed in systems selling, the salesperson must be highly knowledgeable about customer business operations and must be able to analyze and communicate effectively in the survey and proposal stages. Systems purchases are usually subject to approval at high organization levels, requiring the seller to seek out and negotiate with top management personnel. These transactions are usually significant in size, and necessitate conscientious monitoring by the salesperson to resolve problems and ward off any possibility of losing the customer to competition.

Negotiation. The key philosophy underlying negotiation is that both parties in the transaction win, so negotiation is defined as a "win-win" sales strategy.[43] Other strategies which can be contrasted with negotiation are persuasion, accommodation, and compromise.

Persuasion is the subtle imposition of the seller's ideas and desires on the buyer, and implies that the seller must overcome the buyer in some way even when it results in the buyer's best interest. Buyers won by persuasion are susceptible to competitive persuaders who may take away the business. Some critics have likened persuasion to manipulation and its accompanying ethical issues. Persuasion is essentially an "I win" strategy for the seller.

Accommodation implies that one party gives in to the other; hence, it is a one-winner strategy. Compromise means that neither party wins, because the final result includes less than each party wants. Both accommodation and compromise occur under an implied adversary relationship, with both parties viewing that gains for one can occur only with losses to the other:

> One of the major challenges faced by every salesman who uses negotiation is to teach his customers how to relate to him in win-win situations. The vast majority of customers are used to win-lose interactions with salesmen. If the salesman wins, they assume they must lose something. That both the salesman and the customer are winners is an unheard-of experience for them. At the outset of converting them to win-win situations, you'll most likely find them at best skeptical and at worst cynical. This is true despite the fact that they operate on a win-win basis as a matter of course with their doctors, lawyers, clergymen, and some of their accountants.[44]

The basic approach of negotiation is to make the customer into a partner, not an adversary. "Partnering," in turn, produces common objectives of profit improvement for both parties, common strategies for achieving objectives, common risk concerning potential gains or losses, and a common defense against others outside the partnership. Conversations between seller and buyer rely heavily on phrases like "What can *we* do about this problem?" or "Can *we* talk to your chief engineer to see what specific factor bothers him?" or "I think my production people will let *us* come up with a suggested solution to your design requirement." or "Based on our earlier discussions, why don't *we* review the pros and cons of your taking on another supplier?"

Negotiation takes consultative selling one step further, because both parties now merge into one common mission and essentially one common organization (their "partnership"), and respond to each other's individual as well as organizational needs. The buyer benefits from the seller's knowledge, availability, ideas, and support as well as products and services, all aimed at achieving profit improvement and personal success for the buyer within his or her firm. The seller benefits from being able to obtain a premium price for the premium value of services offered, and creates long-term relationships in the process.

Team Selling. In the previous chapter we noted the increase in multiple decision makers within customer firms. The net effect is that purchases are made by a buying "team"—either formally meeting as a group or informally as the influential members report their feelings and recommendations to the purchasing manager. To deal most effectively with the particular interests and questions of each buying team member, a sales team is used. The specialties of those on the sales team usually match those of the buying team. A marketer of jet airplanes for corporate use, for example, includes on its sales team the company president and other top personnel in marketing, operations, logistics, and law.[45] A regional sales manager for General Electric characterized team selling this way: "While personality will always be a factor in selling, the art of persuasion is much less important now. What companies want are hard facts from a team of technical and marketing experts."[46]

Sometimes the entire sales team is present when the presentation is made to the prospect; at other times the team members are contacted at the home office when questions occur for which the salesperson needs more detailed information. A steel company has its sales team divided into three groups:[47]

1. The headquarters sales force, the main selling tool.
2. The sales staffs from each division, which furnish backup support for the headquarters sales staff. Each of the divisional sales staffs is composed of the following divisional people: president; vice-president, sales; production manager plus staff; customer service manager plus expediters and inventory personnel; quality control manager plus staff; technical service manager plus staff; and product and market development manager plus staff, including research.
3. The executive sales staff, a combination of about a dozen top executives who back up the divisional sales staffs and the headquarters sales force.

The sales force requests help from the divisional sales staff when their technical expertise is needed, and can request aid from the executive sales staff to help close sales or to add prestige to social get-togethers with customer personnel.

The steel company illustrates two types of personnel participating on teams. One includes functional specialists, and the other involves high-level executives who have authority to make special arrangements that their subordinates cannot. Figure 9.3 illustrates the pattern of sales calls used by CP Rail, a Canadian Pacific division involving railroad freight sales. This concerted effort occurs with prospects or clients which represent large portions of CP Rail's business, and for which special equipment or pricing arrangements may be tailored to their specific needs.

Team selling is obviously costly and requires a large volume to support the cost of many team members. This strategy fits best with selling large capital equipment or setting up long-term supply relationships.[48] Team selling also requires the utmost in coordination to avoid presenting conflicting impressions to buying team members. Some sales teams may spend as much time communicating among themselves as they do with customers.

Territory Management. The ultimate upgrading of personal selling occurs when selling is viewed truly as territory management. As contrasted with a territory "worker," the territory manager (TM) takes charge by setting objectives, marshalling resources, making decisions, and taking the responsibility for reaching those objectives. The territory worker, on the other hand, waits for guidance on what to do and how to do it. Territory workers take little or no initiative and require close

FIGURE 9.3

Sales Calls Made by Members of CP Rail Selling Team on Client Firms

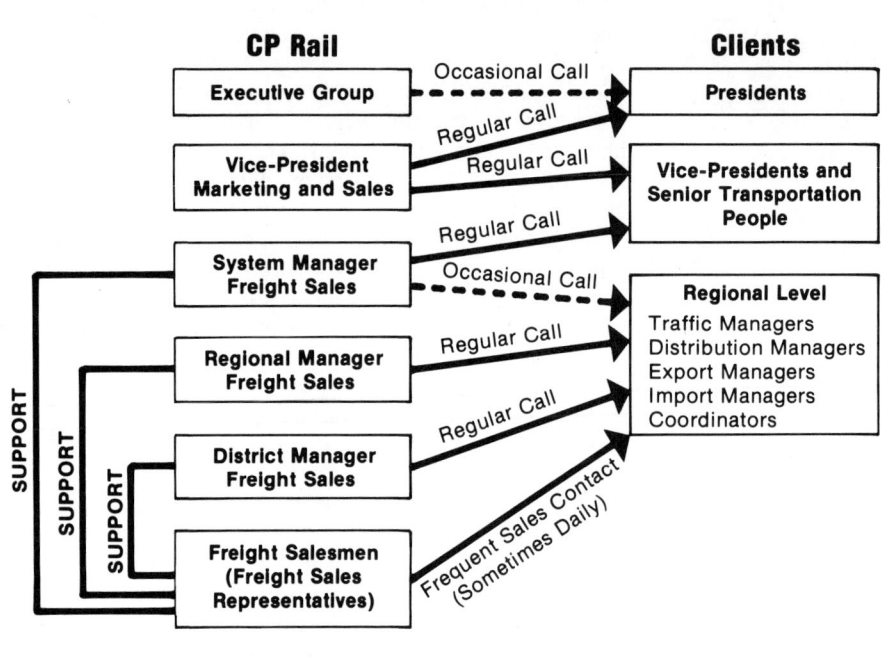

Reprinted, by permission of the publisher from William H. Kaven, *Managing the Major Sale,* Research Study No. 105, © 1971 by American Management Association, p. 79. All rights reserved.

supervision and control. They are quick to look outside themselves to explain performance deficiencies—the price is too high, the buyer was in a bad mood, the economy is down, and so on. The TM doesn't try to make excuses, but rather assumes the responsibility for the problems and moves to fix them. At Diamond Alkali, the territory manager's job is described this way:

> Conducted properly, and viewed from the longer range, the salesman's job is a management job. The Diamond salesman is responsible for the business in his territory, and he operates with some considerable independence and at least without day-to-day supervision. In short, he manages time, territory, and people, including himself. His is a job of planning, organization, integration of effort, and measurement of results, and these are management elements.[49]

Table 9.3 shows some differences between a territory manager and a territory worker. The major factor underlying these differences is a managerial attitude or identification with a managerial role.[50] The TM views his job as consisting of the same activities followed by other managers. As depicted in Figure 9.4 (and suggested in the Diamond Alkali description above), the steps in territory management are as follows:

Planning includes identifying opportunities and deciding on objectives so that the TM will contribute properly to overall company goals. Opportunities occur with

TABLE 9.3

Some Differences Between a Territory Manager and a Territory Worker

THE TERRITORY MANAGER	THE TERRITORY WORKER
Creates a plan, builds an organization, delegates, leads, reviews.	Carries out instructions.
Gets things done through people.	Does the work himself.
Makes things happen.	Waits to be told.
Makes decisions systematically.	Lets others make the decisions.
Thinks money and territory profit.	Thinks sales volume, not profit.
Makes maximum use of support people and programs.	Resents "outside experts" and "home-office stuff."
Thinks of "my territory, my company, my customers."	Thinks of "the company, those customers, the territory."
Believes that he is in control of his future.	Wonders what "they" are going to do to him.

Reprinted by permission of the publisher from Gerard J. Carney, *Managing a Sales Territory,* © 1971 by American Management Association, p. 29. All rights reserved.

new prospects, lost customers, or additional sales to present customers. Careful analysis of strengths and weaknesses of competitive products may indicate opportunites as well. Objectives can then be set for each opportunity segment in terms of sales volume, share of business, profit contribution, or many other measures as discussed in Chapter 7.

Resource analysis is the next step. The TM's main resource is time, so the most productive allocation of time among customers and prospects must be carefully determined. Other resources include present customers who can help in prospecting, writing testimonial letters, and giving references; new customers who will be able

FIGURE 9.4

A Model of the Territory Management Process

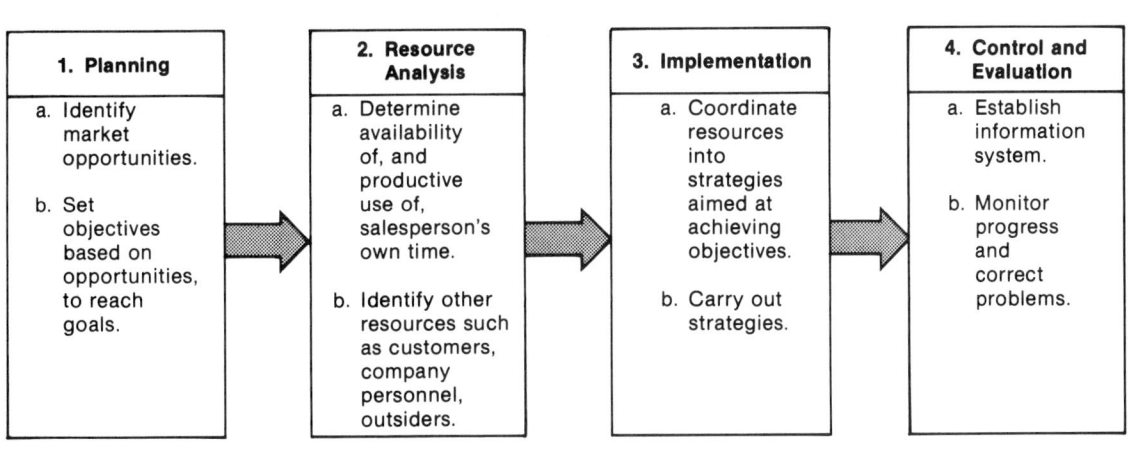

to give similar help; home-office personnel such as technical or service representatives, sales promotion and advertising staff, shipping and office clerks, and many others; and persons outside the firm such as trade associations, librarians, and university researchers. Of course, the TM has no formal authority over these persons, so as in selling situations, he must apply interpersonal skills in these instances to rally others to his programs and ideas.

Implementation of plans via available resources is next. Call schedules are devised and followed, sales appeals are selected and presented, the assistance of others is requested and received. The selling process really becomes a process of managing resources to achieve planned objectives at this step.

Control and evaluation round out the managerial activities of the TM. Achievements are compared with objectives using an information system established by the TM to provide data on sales calls, order sizes, what sales strategies worked and didn't work, expenses, and any other meaningful measures. Often this can be done in coordination with the company's sales reporting system. Then, steps are taken to diagnose and correct problems before they attract the attention of higher management and place the TM in a defensive position.

CONCLUSION

The search for a key to success in selling has produced four different approaches or views which we explored in this chapter: chemistry (or motivation), traits, behavior, and dyadic. Each of these has sometimes found support when studied in experimental or research situations, but on other occasions the support failed to occur. For the present, it seems best to conclude that all four views offer some partial explanation for selling success, and that no one of them should be totally dismissed. Meanwhile, sales managers continue to search and debate.

In response to changing customer needs and buying behavior, many new selling strategies and styles are being adopted by sales organizations. We reviewed five new trends in selling, including consultative selling, systems selling, negotiation, team selling, and territory management. These are not mutually exclusive, since most of them can be employed simultaneously—consultative selling and negotiation or team selling and territory management, for examples. Territory management is perhaps the ultimate development of personal selling towards true managerial status, although its adoption as well as the adoption of any of these styles and strategies is by no means widespread.

QUESTIONS FOR REVIEW AND DISCUSSION

1. If a sales manager believes strongly in the chemistry view of selling success, what impact might this have on that manager's hiring and training programs for the sales force?

2. Suppose you are a sales manager and wish to set up an experiment to evaluate the traits view of selling success. What traits would you investigate, and how would you set up such a study among your sales personnel?

3. Empathy and ego drive have been described as key ingredients for selling success. Are these traits, or are they behavior factors which a salesperson can learn through training and experience? Does it make any difference to the sales manager?

4. What's the difference between reactive and preactive sales behavior? How do these relate to the theories of selling discussed in the previous chapter?

5. Some managers argue that proper dress and grooming are critical factors in sales success. Does this belief correspond best with the traits, behavior, or dyadic view of selling success?

6. How does the dyadic view differ from the traits view? What differences would occur in the sales training programs geared to one view versus the other?

7. If a salesperson believes in the dyadic view of selling success, what are some of the ways he or she can try to "match" the buyer?

8. What is the major advantage a consultative salesperson has over a "vendor"? Does consultative selling differ appreciably from systems selling?

9. Distinguish between negotiation, persuasion, accommodation, and compromise as selling strategies. Does negotiation offer any truly substantial benefits to the buyer?

10. Both team selling and territory management increase the professionalization of selling as noted in Chapter 1. Discuss in what specific ways this happens.

NOTES

1. T. H. Hartman, "Start Right By Hiring Right," *Sales Management,* April 30, 1973, p. 75.

2. Jack M. McQuaig, "How to Pick Winners," *Agency Sales Magazine,* January 1978, p. 10.

3. F. William Howton and Bernard Rosenberg, "The Salesman: Ideology and Self-Imagery in a Prototypic Occupation," *Social Research,* vol. 32 (Autumn 1965), p. 284.

4. See, for example, Napoleon Hill, *Think and Grow Rich* (New York: Hawthorne Books, 1967); Frank Bettger, *How I Multiplied My Income and Happiness in Selling* (Englewood Cliffs, N.J.: Prentice-Hall, 1954); Charles B. Roth, *The Secrets of Success Encyclopedia* (New York: McGraw-Hill, 1965); and Norman Vincent Peale, *Enthusiasm Makes the Difference* (Englewood Cliffs, N.J.: Prentice-Hall, 1967).

5. Walter P. Gorman, "Success Theory for Sales Classes," *Journal of Business Research,* vol. 1 (Fall 1973), pp. 183–192.

6. Robert W. Sweitzer and Dev S. Pathek, "The Self-Actualizing Salesman," *Southern Journal of Business,* vol. 7 (November 1972), pp. 1–8.

7. James W. Fairchild, "Match the Man to the Job," *Industrial Distribution,* October 1976, p. 81.

8. William R. Darden and Warren A. French, "Dimensions of Salesman Stereotypes and Their Relation to Executive Characteristics," *Social Science Quarterly,* vol. 51 (March 1971), pp. 959–969.

9. Samuel N. Stevens, "Selling and the Salesman," in *Aspects of Modern Marketing,* Management report no. 15 (New York: American Management Association, 1958), pp. 85–94.

10. James C. Cotham, III, "Selecting Salesmen: Approaches and Problems," *MSU Business Topics,* vol. 18 (Winter 1970), pp. 64–71.

11. Arthur A. Witkin, "The Myth of the Storybook Salesman," *Sales & Marketing Management,* June 14, 1976, p. 72.

12. George N. Kahn and Abraham Shuchman, "Specialize Your Salesmen," *Harvard Business Review,* vol. 39 (January–February 1961), p. 94.

13. Robert Tanofsky, et al., "Pattern Analysis of Biographical Predictors of Success as an Insurance Salesman," *Journal of Applied Psychology,* vol. 53 (April 1969), pp. 136–139.

14. Thomas W. Harrell, "The Relation of Test Scores to Sales Criteria," *Personnel Psychology,* vol. 13 (Spring 1960), pp. 65–69.

15. Marvin D. Dunnette and Wayne K. Kirchner, "Psychological Test Differences Between Industrial Salesmen and Retail Salesmen," *Journal of Applied Psychology,* vol. 44 (April 1960), pp. 121–125.

16. L. M. Lamont and W. J. Lundstrom, "Identifying Successful Industrial Salesmen by Personality and Personal Characteristics," *Journal of Marketing Research,* vol. 14 (November 1977), p. 525.

17. David Mayer and H. M. Greenberg, "What Makes a Good Salesman," *Harvard Business Review,* vol. 42 (July–August 1964), pp. 119–125.

18. J. H. Scheibelhut and Gerald Albaum, "Self-Other Orientations Among Salesmen and Non-salesmen," *Journal of Marketing Research,* vol. 10 (February 1973), pp. 97–99.

19. Richard E. Rogala, "Ten 'Behaviors' That Pay Off in Sales," *Industry Week,* January 28, 1974, p. 60.

20. Barry J. Hersker, "The Ecology of Personal Selling," *Southern Journal of Business,* vol. 5 (July 1970), pp. 41–46.

21. Gary M. Grikscheit and William J. E. Crissy, "Communication Correlates of Sales Success," *Industrial Marketing Management,* vol. 5 (1976), p. 177. For greater detail of this study, see by the same authors, "Improving Interpersonal Communications Skill," *MSU Business Topics,* vol. 21 (Autumn 1973), pp. 63–68.

22. Peter W. Pasold, "The Effectiveness of Various Modes of Sales Behavior in Different Markets," *Journal of Marketing Research,* vol. 12 (May 1975), pp. 171–176.

23. Theodore Levitt, "Communications and Industrial Selling," *Journal of Marketing,* vol. 31 (April 1967), p. 17.

24. R. Wayne Pace, "Oral Communication and Sales Effectiveness," *Journal of Applied Psychology,* vol. 46 (October 1962), pp. 321–324.

25. Richard W. Olshavsky, "Customer-Salesman Interaction in Appliance Retailing," *Journal of Marketing Research,* vol. 10 (May 1973), pp. 208–212.

26. Peter J. Hampton, "Body Language," *Agency Sales Magazine,* April 1977, pp. 8–10. This article contains a good bibliography for additional reading.

27. Thomas V. Bonoma and Leonard C. Felder, "Nonverbal Communication in Marketing: Toward a Communicational Analysis," *Journal of Marketing Research,* vol. 14 (May 1977), pp. 169–180.

28. Franklin B. Evans, "Selling as a Dyadic Relationship—A New Approach," *American Behavioral Scientist,* vol. 6 (May 1963), pp. 76–79.

29. M. S. Gadel, "Concentration by Salesmen on Congenial Prospects," *Journal of Marketing,* vol. 28 (April 1964), pp. 64–66.

30. Edward A. Riordan, et al., "The Unsold Prospect: Dyadic and Attitudinal Determinants," *Journal of Marketing Research,* vol. 14 (November 1977), pp. 530–537.

31. Timothy C. Brock, "Communicator-Recipient Similarity and Decision Change," *Journal of Personality and Social Psychology,* vol. 1 (June 1965), pp. 650–654.

32. Arch G. Woodside and J. W. Davenport, Jr., "The Effect of Salesman Similarity and Expertise on Consumer Purchasing Behavior," *Journal of Marketing Research,* vol. 11 (May 1974), pp. 198–202.

33. Additional support for this conclusion was found in a laboratory experiment involving college students' perceptions of life insurance agents. See Paul Busch and David T. Wilson, "An Experimental Analysis of a Salesman's Expert and Referent Bases of Social Power in the Buyer-Seller Dyad," *Journal of Marketing Research,* vol. 13 (February 1976), pp. 3–11.

34. Henry L. Tosi, "The Effects of Expectation Levels and Role Consensus on the Buyer-Seller Dyad," *Journal of Business,* vol. 39 (October 1966), pp. 516–529.

35. Another study with mixed results involving department store selling is Gilbert A. Churchill, et al., "Should Retail Salespersons Be Similar to Their Customers?" *Journal of Retailing,* vol. 51 (Fall 1975), pp. 29–42, 79.

36. James E. Puetz, "The Effect of Sales Management Strategy Upon the Success of the Personal Selling Effort," unpublished Masters Thesis, San Diego State University, Summer 1977.

37. Mack Hanan, et al., *Consultative Selling* (New York: American Management Association, Inc., 1970), pp. 16–18.

38. Hanan, et al., p. 19.

39. Mack Hanan, "You Don't Know What Problems Are Until You Become a Problem Solver," *Sales Management,* July 22, 1974, p. 32.

40. "The Salesman's New Job: Drumming Up Supplies," *Business Week,* October 26, 1974, p. 54.

41. William H. Kaven, *Managing the Major Sale* (New York: American Management Association, Inc., 1971), pp. 55–59.

42. William J. Hannaford, "Systems Selling: Problems and Benefits For Buyers and Sellers," *Industrial Marketing Management,* vol. 5 (1976), pp. 139–145.

43. This discussion follows many of the points made in Mack Hanan, et al., *Sales Negotiation Strategies* (New York: AMACOM, 1977).

44. *Ibid.,* p. 20.

45. James E. Skinner, "The Gates Approach to Learjet Sales," *Marketing Insights,* November 11, 1968, pp. 10–11.

46. "The Battle to Boost Sales Productivity," *Business Week,* February 12, 1972, p. 69.

47. Kaven, p. 114.

48. Benson P. Shapiro, "Manage the Customer, Not Just the Sales Force," *Harvard Business Review,* vol. 52 (September–October 1974), p. 132.

49. As quoted in James H. Bearden, "Decision Processes in Personal Selling," *Southern Journal of Business,* vol. 4 (April 1969), p. 189.

50. This discussion is based primarily on ideas from these two sources: Gerard J. Carney, *Managing a Sales Territory* (New York: American Management Association, Inc., 1971); and Robert F. Vizza and Thomas E. Chambers, *Time and Territorial Management for the Salesmen* (New York: Sales Executives Club of New York, Inc., 1971).

10 SALES ORGANIZATION STRUCTURE

The sales organization structure is the home of the firm's personal selling operation. It includes a set of selling and sales management positions and a set of relationships among these positions. The sales organization is a means to facilitate goal accomplishment and not an end in itself. In other words, there is no single organizational pattern which is best for all firms because firms face different market and competitive environments and differ also in the goals they aim to achieve. Likewise as a firm's goals, markets, and competition change over time, its organizational needs will also change. Thus, restructuring or revising the organization is a matter requiring regular attention.

The first section of this chapter includes a brief summary of the nature and purpose of an organization structure, which is followed by a more detailed discussion of the major steps in building a sales organization structure.

NATURE AND PURPOSE OF AN ORGANIZATION STRUCTURE

An *organization structure* can be defined as a framework within which two or more persons each carry out specific tasks in order to reach common goals. It is often described formally with an organization chart and written job descriptions. Traditional management thought has concentrated on the internal relationships within the organization structure. A "mechanistic" viewpoint prevailed whereby the aim was to achieve machine-like efficiency.[1] More recently there has been increasing attention to how the organization must adapt to its external environment to take advantage of new opportunities. This is an "organic" view requiring flexibility, a continued assessment of activities and priorities, and far less concern for the efficiencies resulting from routines. Both internal efficiency and external adaptation must be achieved in some combination, of course, to produce an effective organization.

Internal Perspective

From an internal view, the organization should be efficient, and this is accomplished through specialization, coordination, and authority.

Specialization. Specialization increases as the range of tasks for each position decreases. Task specialization allows the employee to concentrate on a limited number of activities, which results in greater learning, improved performance, and increased efficiency. Sales force members may be specialized by product line, customer type, or other bases discussed later in this chapter.

A second type of organizational specialization is reflected by the fundamental nature of the job—planning, advising, deciding, or doing. Top-management jobs are more concerned with planning; the lower levels in the organization are more involved with doing. Line positions are those with decision-making authority, while staff positions are primarily advisory in nature. This is role specialization, and it exists simultaneously with any form of task specialization found in the organization.

Coordination. Specialization must be accompanied by coordination. As the scope of each position narrows, the need to dovetail their performance into a unified pattern becomes more critical. Coordination is achieved mainly by effective communication. One type of communication is vertical and involves the routine phone calls, memos, and other correspondence which flow up and down the chain of command in the firm. Since many sales organization members are physically separated into regions, districts, and territories, the communication process is sometimes difficult and may produce occasional misunderstandings or fail altogether.

Horizontal communication between functional areas or other specialized segments of the firm is best achieved when positions requiring close coordination are placed near each other within the organization structure. If the need for communication is great, perhaps the form of specialization should be reviewed to determine whether these jobs should remain separated or be redefined with a different form of specialization.

Authority. The final factor influencing organizational efficiency is authority, which is the power ascribed to a position in the organization to give and enforce orders. Authority is necessary to settle disputes, to make decisions, and to ensure coordination.

Authority is usually associated with vertical line relationships in the organization structure—the so-called chain of command which spells out superior-subordinate relationships. Sometimes a functional type of authority exists which gives top executives or other specialists power in matters relating to their functional areas. A salesperson, for example, may receive instructions from the credit manager regarding the granting of credit to various accounts, directions from the traffic manager concerning the shipping of goods, and orders from the sales manager regarding other aspects of the sales job. The danger in functional authority is that of conflicting orders being given to a subordinate by two or more sources.

The responsibilities of any position should be matched with commensurate authority. It frustrates a sales manager to be held responsible for reaching the forecast level of sales, but to be given no voice in determining that level. To some extent all marketing positions lack an equality of authority and responsibility, since they cannot command prospects to buy. Instead, the sales force is sometimes said to have "persuasive" authority achieved through effective selling skills.

External Perspective

While the internal perspective stresses efficiency, the external view is concerned with adapting the organization to the environment in which it operates. The sales organization operates in a dual environment. One part is comprised of its customers or markets; the other is the broader organization structure encompassing the total firm. A sales organization provides the structural link between these two parts.

Market Environment. From a market standpoint, the sales organization should be structured to respond to customer needs in the most effective manner. As markets and their needs change, the organization must change with them to remain effective. Ansul, a producer of fire protection equipment, illustrates this point very well. Special sales forces are created as they identify new market segments. When the assigned task is completed, the special force is disbanded and its sales personnel are assigned to other duties. Ansul's vice president noted that some managers and salespersons don't like this state of flux and leave the company. But, he concluded, "Most of the people who remain understand that we'll stop changing only when the market does."[2]

From this point of view, the organization structure might be interpreted as a constraining rather than as a facilitating mechanism. Firms specialized by product and not by customer, for example, would find consultative selling difficult to undertake in that structure. Or if certain portions of the market required team selling, an organization using individual product specialists might be restricted from serving them adequately. When restricted opportunities begin to outweigh available opportunities, structural adjustment seems strongly advisable.

Organizational Environment. The sales organization must coordinate with other organizational components within the total firm. If an entire company is specialized by product, this specialization would probably occur in the sales organization as well. If top management moves to a more decentralized decision-making philosophy, the sales manager may gain more flexibility in adjusting the sales organization structure and positions.

A key determinant affecting the sales organization structure is the importance of personal selling to total company effectiveness as viewed by top management.[3] When management gives high priority to its sales operation, those planning the sales organization structure may be free to develop one based mainly on market needs. If the sales operation is less significant in management's eyes, its structure is often patterned after the rest of the firm's organizational layout, as much or more so than to fit the needs of the market.

INTERNAL-EXTERNAL TRADEOFF

At their extremes, the internal and external views (i.e., mechanistic and organic) represent opposite ends of a continuum for guiding organizational structure decisions. Efficiency, produced through specialization and clear-cut authority, provides a consistent organizational setting. Routine and predictable are key descriptors of the internal orientation. Effectiveness, however, is produced through adaptability to new opportunities. This requires flexibility, not routines, and authority determined by expertise rather than by location on the organization chart. Adjusting and responding are key descriptors of the external orientation.

Where the firm's markets are stable and the organization's tasks are well-defined, a mechanistic approach will result in high performance. But when markets are changing and the tasks, which are less well-defined, may require modification, the organic approach should predominate. High technology firms with innovative expertise will gravitate toward an organic organization, while raw materials producers might lean toward a mechanistic mode. Management must decide what mix between these extremes is most fitting for its organization.

BUILDING A SALES ORGANIZATION STRUCTURE

We now turn to the process of building a sales organization structure which incorporates both the internal and external perspectives. Five major steps are used to guide this process.

1. Identify market characteristics with which the sales organization must coordinate.
2. Determine activities to be performed.
3. Establish the types and numbers of positions needed.
4. Arrange the positions within a pertinent structure.
5. Evaluate the structure.

Identify Market Characteristics

The sales organization is the major link between company and market. It must be patterned to minimize obstacles that can hinder effective market development and to maximize opportunities to meet the market's needs efficiently and competitively. As stated in a study of General Electric's sales organization, "the starting point for decision making is the customer. *The market determines the type of sales organization.*"[4]

This first step is one of identifying the firm's market segments, the buying behavior of each, and their expectations and needs which the seller must fulfill to be successful. Differences among segments call for correspondingly different selling approaches and organizational patterns. As one executive noted:

> Machine tools and their fixtures are closely allied. But do not try to sell drill bits while you are selling boring mills—not with the same sales force. Industrial disposables don't go to market by the same route as capital machinery. Some of them may end up together on the production floor, but they got there through different buying routes.[5]

The sales manager must be especially alert to changes in buying behavior so that the selling organization can adjust accordingly.[6] Some of these changes now occurring within many buying organizations include:

Centralized purchasing: Chain store and franchise members seldom do their own buying. Even independent businesses are grouping into integrated operations or cooperatives for centralized purchasing efficiencies.

Multiple buying influences: As noted in Chapter 8, more firms are involving more of their personnel in purchasing decisions, and each additional person included has different criteria to guide his or her assessment of a particular seller's offering.

Systems buying: Buyers are increasingly looking to sellers for assistance beyond the product itself, such as in services (e.g., training the user of the product, routine maintenance service) and administrative help (e.g., automatic reorder systems, accounting and financial analysis).

Long-term contracts: Some buyers contract with a single supplier to cover an extended purchase period such as two years. This minimizes the need to negotiate more frequently with numerous suppliers. Typical products in this arrangement include raw materials such as chemicals, operating supplies such as recordkeeping forms, and fabricated parts such as small electric motors or containers.

As these trends develop, purchasers are relying more on salespeople as sources of information rather than simply sources of products. The computer's impact on buying is also growing, as noted in Chapter 8, and this will affect the skills needed as well as procedures for invoicing and inventory control used by sellers.

Determine Activities

Selling Strategy. Having identified buying behavior and needs of customer segments, the sales manager must next determine the necessary activities to be performed. Coordination with other marketing components is essential so that the role of personal selling complements and reinforces their activities such as advertising aimed at the same segments. A case in point concerns Paper Mate which sells to wholesalers, retailers, major chains, and commercial suppliers.[7] Three distinct sets of selling activities are necessary to cover these markets. Major chains require the seller to devise complete promotional programs for a year at a time, and purchases are handled at chain headquarters. Wholesalers and retailers seek merchandising help also, but at a more local level, and actively participate in cooperative advertising to reinforce the national advertising by Paper Mate. This push approach to selling—pushing the product through the channels towards the ultimate consumer—is contrasted with the pull approach used in commercial selling where the task is to convince purchasing agents to request Paper Mate products from their suppliers. Each of these three marketing tasks requires a separate organizational approach.

Marketing Intelligence. Besides selling activities, management must consider other tasks necessary to monitor market changes and make effective adjustments. The responsibility of gathering marketing intelligence has fallen to the salesperson in many firms. Because of their close contact with customers and intimate knowledge of territories, sales personnel are a direct link to useful information about competitive actions, customer behavior, and general market conditions. One study of large diversified industrial companies showed that 90 percent of the firms used the sales force to gather research data.[8] Because this activity requires time which could otherwise be devoted to selling, it is a controversial practice.[9] But many executives believe it makes the sales force better informed and also provides a stronger role for salespeople in company planning and management. The president of White Motor Corporation noted the effects on the sales force after they began providing marketing intelligence: "They feel that they carry more responsibility in the organization. They no longer consider themselves less important than marketing people. In sum, they are once more an integral part of the company's operations."[10]

Management Processes. Management tasks must be accomplished as well. In Chapter 9 we examined the salesperson as a territory manager responsible for planning, analysis, implementation, and control activities. This trend reflects the parallel developments of professional upgrading and increased managerial responsibility in purchasing departments. Managerial tasks necessary to staff, supervise, and coordinate the sales organization must also be determined. A cross-section of 223 firms reported what tasks were considered of primary responsibility in the management of a field sales operation, and these results are shown in Table 10.1. Note that personal selling is included in this table, indicating that for certain customers or markets, selling is considered an important responsibility of managers, in addition to their managerial duties.

Establish Positions Needed

Determining the types and numbers of positions needed in the sales organization is the next step.[11] Since salespeople provide the direct link to the market, their jobs should be established first, followed by sales management positions.

Personal Selling Positions. Two decisions are necessary in defining sales force positions. One concern is the choice between company employed salespeople versus independent representatives (often called reps), agents, or brokers. The second involves what types of specialization to use within the sales force.

Reps, agents, or brokers are a typical choice over company employed salespeople in new markets where expected market share or sales penetration is low, when the company is new and has little marketing or selling experience, or when the cost

TABLE 10.1
Primary Responsibilities of the Field Sales Supervisor in 223 Companies

AREA OF PRIMARY RESPONSIBILITY	TOTAL NUMBER OF MENTIONS
Develop salespeople	198
Plan and monitor territorial sales effort	184
Motivate salespeople	171
Communicate to and from field	166
Hire new salespeople	136
Enforce company policies in field	133
Administer field sales office	124
Personal selling	115
Fiscal responsibilities (budget, expense control, credit)	16
Customer-supplier-distributor relations and service	9
Coordinate with other company operations	5
New business development	5
Other	39

Source: Morgan B. MacDonald, Jr. and Earl L. Bailey, *The First-line Sales Supervisor,* Experiences in Marketing Management no. 17 (New York: National Industrial Conference Board, Inc., 1968), adapted from table 7, page 22.

of obtaining and training needed salespeople is high.[12] Clorox is one firm which has compared both types of selling positions, using brokers in one area of the country and company employed salespeople in another. Advantages of brokers, in the opinion of Clorox's national sales manager, are in achieving broad sales coverage at minimum cost (brokers are paid 5 percent commission on sales), in gaining local market advantage, since brokers already know their territories, and in avoiding turnover within the sales organization.[13] On the other hand, the company employed salesperson has only one boss and sells only one product line, can be more directly supervised and controlled, and can be less expensive beyond a certain level of sales volume.

Sales force specialization results from grouping activities into positions which will best serve the specialized needs of the firm's market segments. Common bases for specialization are geographic location, product line, and customer type.

Customers can be grouped by *geographic location* and assigned to salespeople on this basis. Specialization by location may be more related to efficiency and convenience than to customer needs. But geographic specialization offers some significant advantages. Each territory is clearly defined and the salesperson gains an in-depth knowledge of economic and competitive conditions within that area. Heinz U.S.A. uses an extensive geographic specialization pattern consisting of 400 salespeople grouped into approximately 100 areas, which form 30 districts and which, in turn, are grouped into 6 regions.[14]

Specialization by *product* occurs in firms which make products which are so complex or unique that purchasers need a great deal of assistance in using them. The more training and experience needed for each product, the fewer products each salesperson can become qualified to sell. Some firms which have diversified into totally different product areas will establish a separate sales force for each because of differences in each sales job. Parker Hannifin, which sells auto parts and fluid power components, maintains 22 separate sales forces, each selling a different group of products. They sometimes have as many as six salespeople assigned to a particular customer, but each usually calls on a different buyer whose purchasing responsibilities are specialized in a parallel manner to the sales force.[15]

Specialization by *customer* occurs when significant differences exist in buying practices and product use among major customer types. In this case, the same product is sold by two or more different salespeople from the same firm to different customer types. NCR, a producer of accounting machines, cash registers, and computer systems, uses "vocational" specialization whereby the sales organization is subdivided into three parts each serving a separate customer group.[16] Prior to this approach the organization was specialized by product type, and any one NCR account might have received calls from three different NCR product specialists. A major advantage of customer specialization is the opportunity it provides for consultative selling, since each sales representative becomes an expert in all phases of a customer's business.

Many additional types of specialization are possible. One is *inside* selling in which customers come to the seller's place of business or sellers use the telephone instead of making personal calls in the field. U.S. Gypsum, for instance, uses 23 inside salespeople who concentrate on customers with regular buying patterns and no personal follow-up needs.[17] Other types include *development* selling, in which the salesperson specializes in converting prospects into customers who are then served by regular sales personnel, and *indirect* selling, which involves influencing potential buyers but not making sales directly, as in the case of missionary selling or detailing. These and other types of selling jobs were discussed in Chapters 8 and 9.

More than one type of specialization can be used at the same time. A sales force may be divided on a geographic basis and subdivided into both product and customer specialties. Some of these salespeople, in turn, may be assigned to develop potential accounts while others are responsible for maintaining sales to existing customers. A few may remain at the home office responding to customer-initiated requests or seeking sales by phone. In other words, many types of specialization can be employed by one firm if market size and characteristics recommend it.

Sales Management Positions. The sales management structure depends on a variety of interrelated factors. One way to summarize them is outlined in Table 10.2. Market-oriented factors relate to the type of market served as reflected by the number and type of personal selling positions established. Policy-oriented factors involve internal aspects in the structure, are subject to policy decisions, and provide more control by management. Evaluating factors are used to assess the economic feasibility of any proposed structure. For example, sales and profit potential may be too low to allow as many management positions as desired. In this situation, one or more of the other factors must be considered as possible means for adjustment, such as an increase in span of control or a reduction in the size of the sales force.

Relationships between each of the *market-oriented factors* and the sales management organization structure are easy to see in most cases. A widespread geographic market often requires more field management positions, since there is more area in which supervision and communication must take place. Greater differences in competitive and market conditions from one area to the next necessitate more individualized management attention. As the sales force enlarges in size, more

TABLE 10.2

Factors Influencing the Nature and Number of Sales Management Positions in the Organization Structure

MARKET-ORIENTED (EXTERNAL) FACTORS:

1. Geographic area of market
2. Competitive and market conditions
3. Size of sales force
4. Types of specialization in sales force
5. Nature of sales job and its importance in total marketing strategy

POLICY-ORIENTED (INTERNAL) FACTORS:

1. Decentralization of authority
2. Span of control
3. Competence, training, and experience of managers
4. Use of staff positions

EVALUATING FACTORS:

1. Availability of profitable sales potential
2. Cost of the organization structure
3. Effectiveness and efficiency

managers are needed to provide effective supervision. Increasing specialization in the sales force requires additional managers to oversee each segment of performance. The importance and number of sales management positions will also increase as the selling job assumes a more important place in the marketing mix, because more extensive planning and control of sales operations will be necessary.

Policy-oriented factors require management decisions. The first on Table 10.2 is *decentralization of authority*. How much decision-making authority should be granted to regional or district sales managers? How far should decentralization go—should the salespeople themselves have the discretion to vary prices or credit terms, or should these decisions be made at the district or regional level? Should they be made at the home office without any decentralization? The decentralization philosophy of Skil Corporation is summed up this way:

> We feel that each region, within certain limits, should be operated as a separate business. To this end, we have 16 regional sales managers who make most of the local decisions themselves. They have a voice in nearly all of the decisions made at the home office. What is right in Cincinnati may lay a big egg in Seattle. A manager behind the desk at the home office can't always keep his finger on the local pulse. We keep top-grade men in the field, pay them well, give them a lot of responsibility, and they succeed.[18]

As the selling job becomes more oriented to customer problem solving and individual treatment of each account, there is likely to be an accompanying tendency toward decentralization. One author cites the following conditions as favoring decentralization in the sales organization:

1. Development of new accounts is a primary goal.
2. Customer needs vary greatly among market segments.
3. Customers demand considerable service.
4. Personal selling is the primary factor in the promotional mix.
5. Sales force size is large.
6. The nature of the business requires policy flexibility at the operating level.[19]

The next policy-oriented factor is *span of control*, the number of subordinates per supervisor. The fewer the number of salespeople reporting to a single manager, the narrower the span. In the Heinz U.S.A. organization previously described, six regional managers supervise 30 districts, producing a span of control averaging five to one at this managerial level.

How wide should the span of control be in the sales organization? Smaller spans are usually necessary when subordinates' jobs are more complex and nonroutine and when personal contact is vital. Wider spans often result from increasing decentralization of authority. One study of over 200 sales organizations showed the median number of salespeople per field sales manager was seven, and the median number of field sales managers reporting to the next highest management echelon was five.[20]

The wider the span of control, the fewer manager positions are needed. Consider two organizations, one with a span of 10 to 1 and the other with a span of about 5 to 1. If each organization employed 100 salespeople, they would compare as follows:

Organization with 10 to 1 span

100 salespeople, reporting to
10 field sales managers, reporting to
1 general sales manager.

Organization with 5 to 1 span

100 salespeople, reporting to
20 field sales managers, reporting to
4 regional sales managers, reporting to
1 general sales manager.

The result is a difference between 11 managers versus 25 managers, and a corresponding difference in costs from salaries, overhead, clerical and secretarial assistance necessary, and other administrative expenses.

The feasibility of decentralization and a wide span of control depends considerably on the *competence of field managers*. Top management's concern about this factor should be reflected in selection and training policies and in compensation programs for field sales management positions. Obviously, managers with greater competence can make better decisions and supervise more personnel effectively.

Finally, *staff positions* are often desirable, sometimes even essential, to provide sales managers with technical or specialized assistance. The most common activities involving staff assistants include sales training, sales promotion, and sales analysis or research. One or more staff assistants usually increases a manager's capacity to handle a wider span of control, and this helps offset the additional costs incurred by adding the staff personnel. On the other hand, as a sales force becomes more specialized, the need for specialized staff personnel diminishes. Staff positions may also be less essential with increases in decentralized authority. As managers are freed from routine decision problems, they can concentrate more on planning and analysis, which might otherwise be staff responsibilities. If decentralization is accompanied by a wider span of control, however, the need for staff positions will remain.

This brief discussion shows that the policy-oriented factors are highly interrelated and should not be considered in isolation. Some of the tradeoffs among these four factors are summarized in Table 10.3. For example, if a wider span of control was being considered, it could be achieved effectively if greater decentralization of authority occurred, if field managers of higher competence were obtained (via hiring or training), if more staff assistants became available, or through some combination of these factors.

Position Descriptions. Once the types of positions and their contents have been decided, a position description is prepared for each job.[21] Without a position description, the new salesperson or manager may be unsure about exactly what the job's duties and responsibilities are, which can lead to a lack of coordination and misdirected effort.

The following outline includes the major contents of most personal selling position descriptions:

1. Exact title of the position
2. Objectives of the job
3. Relationships within the organization
4. Duties and responsibilities

TABLE 10.3 Tradeoffs in Constructing the Internal Sales Organization Structure

MAKING THIS ORGANIZATIONAL CHANGE:	REQUIRES OR ALLOWS ONE OR MORE OF THESE ORGANIZATIONAL ACTIONS:
More decentralization of authority:	Wider span of control. Greater competence of field managers. Fewer staff personnel.
Less decentralization of authority:	Narrower span of control. Lesser competence of field managers. More staff personnel.
Wider span of control:	More decentralization of authority. Greater competence of field managers. More staff personnel.
Narrower span of control:	Less decentralization of authority. Lesser competence of field managers. Fewer staff personnel.
Greater competence of field managers:	More decentralization of authority. Wider span of control. Fewer staff personnel.
Lesser competence of field managers:	Less decentralization of authority. Narrower span of control. More staff personnel.
More staff personnel:	Less decentralization of authority. Wider span of control. Lesser competence of field managers.
Fewer staff personnel:	More decentralization of authority. Narrower span of control. Greater competence of field managers.

5. Authority
6. Working conditions, compensation plan, and normal range of pay
7. Promotion possibilities

The exact title of the position is necessary to differentiate it from other selling positions in the firm. Titles may be worded by management to add prestige to positions, hence the importance of conveying them precisely. Objectives of a job include statements of the importance of this position in reaching company goals, in solving customer problems, and in demonstrating personal capabilities. Relationships within the organization include the position to which this position reports and others which report to this one, if any.

The major section of a job description includes the duties and responsibilities of the position, which can be expressed in two ways. One stresses individual tasks while the other focuses on overall results. In the first case a position description might indicate that a certain number of sales calls be made. The second approach might specify what quotas or other goals are to be met. Some combination of the two is typical.

The authority granted to each salesperson, such as to quote price changes, adjust normal shipping schedules, or allow changes in package design, must be clearly stated. Days and hours to be spent on the job, amount of travel, attendance at conventions and trade shows, and vacations are items sometimes spelled out as working conditions. The compensation, such as salary, commission, or bonus, is often indicated. The position to which the jobholder might be promoted is occasionally found in the description as well.

The exact contents of a position description varies considerably from one firm to the next. Table 10.4 describes one of many personal selling jobs at the Armour-Dial Company. Descriptions for sales management positions follow the same basic outline, and Table 10.5 describes an Armour-Dial district sales manager position.

TABLE 10.4
Description of a Personal Selling Position in Armour-Dial Company

POSITION TITLE: DIRECT ACCOUNT SPECIALIST
DEPARTMENT: CONSUMER PRODUCT SALES
REPORTS TO (TITLE): DISTRICT MANAGER

FUNCTION:

The Direct Account Specialist, under supervision of a District Manager, is primarily responsible for the direct sales of Armour-Dial Consumer Products to assigned retail stores such as mass merchandisers, department stores, drug stores, etc. He/She systematically and economically calls on assigned retail stores with the objectives of *selling volume, gaining new distribution* on the full line, *arranging for advertised* and *mass displays* of our promotions, and *developing a good working relationship with store personnel.*

In addition, a Direct Account Specialist is responsible for calling on and selling assigned Wholesale or Direct Buying Headquarter Accounts the full line of Consumer Products.

DUTIES/RESPONSIBILITIES

A. *Retail/Wholesale Sales Volume:* Generate case sales to meet and exceed assigned budgets, previous years sales, and to approach maximum account sales potential. Utilize our product promotions to secure account advertising, the rapid flush-through of deal pack, mass displays, new distribution, and the achievement of special promotion objectives.

B. *Store Conditions:* Maximize sales of ADC products to the consumer by eliminating out-of-stocks, selling and maintaining maximum product distribution, securing the proper position, space and pricing for our items, selling displays, rotating stocks when necessary and removing damaged merchandise from the shelf in accordance with company policy.

C. *Retail Coverage:* Responsible for developing, evaluating, updating and following an effective and economical retail store coverage program in line with company policy.

D. *Expense Control:* Control and if possible reduce "Direct Controllable Cost of Sales Expense" such as automobile, transportation, entertainment, lodging and meals, meetings, samples, telephone and stationery. Follow company policy regarding the expenditure and reporting of the Travel Expense Program.

E. *Company Property:* Follow prescribed maintenance policies for care of company automobile; and keep the sample case, call books, organizer, manuals and other assigned materials in good condition.

F. *Reports and Records:* Prepare and submit *daily reports,* competitive activity and other assigned reports as per instruction; and keep the call books, organizer, operating manual, direct account folders and all other records accurate and up to date.

G. *Personal Development:* Follow a program of self improvement designed to increase present and future job knowledge and skill level.

(continued)

Table 10.4 (continued)

RELATIONSHIPS		
	Internal:	*Assistant to the Zone Manager:* Follows advice and guidance in order to more effectively manage the retail territory and maximize toiletry sales.
		District Manager: Immediate supervisor and contact regarding personal development, performance evaluation, salary administration, personal advancement, sales problems and all phases of company communication.
		Zone Manager: Follows policies, instruction and guidance from Zone Manager.
	External:	*Retail* (Store Manager/Buyer/Aisle Clerk/Chain Store Supervisor): Develop a good working relationship with *all* retail store personnel in order to communicate and accomplish ADC objectives.
		Wholesale (Buyer/Head Buyer/Advertising Manager/Store Set-Up Manager/Buying Committee/Other Key Personnel): Gain an intimate understanding of the overall operation of assigned direct accounts. Cultivate a good working relationship with all personnel responsible for the marketing of ADC products.
	Possible Promotion Ladder:	*From What Positions:* Retail Sales Representative, Grade 9; Sales Representative, Grade 10
		To What Positions: Key Account Supervisor, Grade 12; Assistant to the Zone Manager, Grades 12, 13
	Scope of Responsibility:	*Total Annual Sales Affected:* Direct account sales, retail and wholesale, purchasing (or with the potential to purchase) 50,000 to 100,000 cases per year.

Reprinted by permission of Amour-Dial Company.

TABLE 10.5 Description of a District Sales Manager Position in Armour-Dial Company

POSITION TITLE: DISTRICT MANAGER
DEPARTMENT: CONSUMER PRODUCTS SALES
REPORTS TO (TITLE): ZONE MANAGER

FUNCTION:

A District Manager, under direct supervision of a Zone Manager, is responsible for the sale of Armour-Dial consumer products through the assigned district wholesale and retail accounts. He/She administers efforts of district personnel to achieve and exceed assigned budgets and year-ago sales volume, and personally calls on and sells one or more major district wholesale accounts.

DUTIES/RESPONSIBILITIES:

A. *Sales Volume:* Produce case sales to meet and exceed assigned budgets, previous year's sales, and to approach maximum district sales potential.

B. *Key Wholesale Account Development:* Through personal solicitation and by effective administration of district personnel, the District Manager gains and maintains full distribution of ADC consumer products, secures strong support for promotional programs, implements the Dial 3-Point Space Management Program, conducts periodic business reviews and remains knowledgeable about all phases of the key account business, and makes marketing recommendations to the Zone Manager regarding future promotional needs.

C. *Retail Store Development:* Directs district sales force to minimize sales of ADC products to the consumer by eliminating out-of-stocks; selling and maintaining maximum product distribution; securing the proper position, space and pricing for our items; selling displays;

rotating stocks when necessary and removing damaged merchandise from the shelf in accordance with company policy.

D. *Personnel:* Hires, supervises and motivates district sales personnel. Assigns direct accounts and direct account budgets; evaluates performance; initiates salary increases; recommends qualified sales personnel for additional responsibility and grade promotion; administers the Manpower Management Program; and within company policy, terminates those individuals with unsatisfactory performance. Routinely and systematically works with all district sales personnel in accordance with zone objectives, and becomes knowledgeable regarding each individual sales person's strong points, training needs and overall territory management.

E. *Training of District Personnel:* The District Manager will work with a new hire for a period of at least two days prior to that person being approved for attendance at the Professional Selling Skills Workshop. A report will be submitted to the Zone Manager, that evaluates a) the preparedness of the individual to advance to the Workshop, and b) the training received from the Assistant to the Zone Manager.

Following the sales person's attendance at the Workshop, the District Manager will be responsible for the ongoing training of this individual in addition to all other experienced district personnel. Preparation of reports and distribution to the Zone Manager on individual sales person's strengths and responses to training will be required. An itinerary of training plans will be prepared and forwarded to the Zone Manager two to four weeks in advance.

F. *Coverage:* Develop and manage a coverage program that maintains proper frequency for all chain supervisors, retail stores and direct accounts. Insure that daily calls are arranged in an efficient and economical manner in order to minimize driving expense and loss of productive time.

G. *Expense Control:* Review, control and if possible reduce "Direct Controllable Cost of Sales Expenses" such as: automobiles, transportation, entertainment, lodging and meals, meetings, samples, telephone and stationery for all district personnel. Follow company policy regarding the expenditure and reporting of the Travel Expense Program.

H. *Reports and Records:* Administer the proper preparation, submission and maintenance of reports and records by all district personnel.

I. *Company Property:* Administer the district car maintenance program and the proper care of all materials used by district sales people.

J. *Personal Development:* Follow a program of self-improvement designed to increase present and future job knowledge and skill level.

RELATIONSHIPS:

A. *Internal:*
  1. *District Personnel:* Direct and work closely with all district personnel. Supervise and encourage *effective* communication within the district, with other districts and with the Assistant to the Zone Manager.
  2. *Assistant to the Zone Manager:* Assume the ongoing responsibility for training experienced sales personnel following their completion of the workshop. Help the Zone Manager in the development of the Assistant to the Zone Manager by exposing him/her to all phases of the District Manager position.
  3. *Zone Manager:* Support and follow policies, instructions and guidance from the Zone Manager. Immediate supervisor and contact regarding personal development, performance evaluation, salary administration, personal advancement, sales problems and all phases of company communication.

B. *External*
  1. *Retail:* Supervise the development of good working relationships between ADC and retail store personnel.
  2. *Wholesale:* Gain an intimate understanding of the overall operation of district key toiletry and grocery accounts. Supervise the development of good working relationships between ADC and direct account personnel.

(continued)

**TABLE 10.5
(continued)**

POSSIBLE PROMOTION LADDER:

From What Positions: Account Supervisor, Grade 11; Key Account Supervisor, Grade 12; Assistant to the Zone Manager, Grade 12, 13
To What Positions: District Manager, Higher Grade Zone Manager, Grade 18, 19 & 20

SCOPE OF RESPONSIBILITY:

District Manager

Grade	Total District Dollar Volume
13	Under $3,000,000
14	$3,000,000–$5,000,000
15	Over $5,000,000

Reprinted by permission of Armour-Dial Company.

Arrange the Structure

We have examined the ingredients of the organization, and must now fit them together into a pertinent structure. While almost every sales organization is different, basic forms or types usually exist. But with growth, an organization usually becomes more complex, making its basic type more difficult to recognize. The following discussion presents these basic types in order from the simplest to the more complex as they might evolve in a growing company.

Single-Line. Single-line sales organizations are the simplest, since they include no staff positions and the sales force is not specialized on any basis. Figure 10.1 shows a single-line structure in which four salespeople report directly to the general sales manager.

This type is most appropriate when the firm sells one or a few related products in a geographically concentrated area and needs only a small sales force which can be adequately supervised by one manager. A meat provisioner in a metropolitan

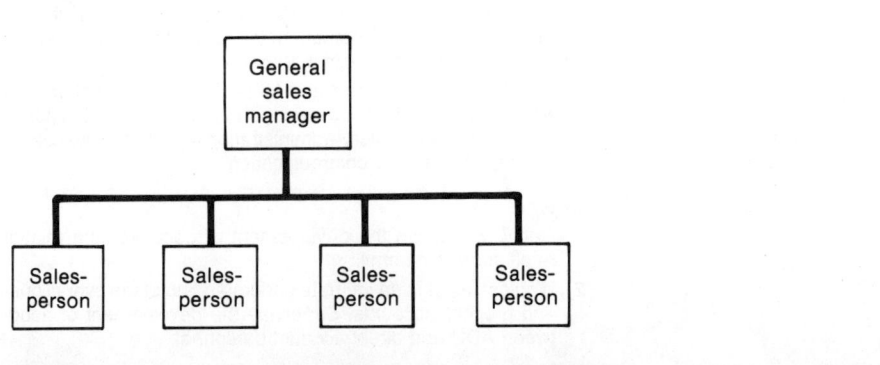

**FIGURE 10.1
Single-Line Organization Structure**

area is a good example. The sales force calls on restaurants and institutional buyers such as hospitals, with each salesperson handling the complete product line.

One-stage Specialization. As a small firm grows, some type of specialization is soon considered. The most common type, illustrated in Figure 10.2, is specialization by geographic location, with a district or regional sales manager in charge of a field office in each major area.

Other bases for one-stage specialization are less common, although product or customer specialization sometimes occurs. If the district sales managers in Figure 10.2 were replaced with product sales managers, a one-stage product specialization would result. Such organization would be appropriate only to firms which have relatively local or concentrated markets. An automobile dealer with separate new car and used car sales forces would be a typical example.

One-stage Specialization with Staff. The addition of staff personnel can benefit a growing sales organization in two important ways without appreciably changing the basic structure. In the first place, staff assistants are one means of allowing a manager's effective span of control to enlarge, as discussed earlier. The general sales manager in Figure 10.2 can increase the number of sales personnel and district sales managers if the assistance of staff specialists were obtained, as shown in Figure 10.3.

A second use can occur in a sales organization which is subdivided by geographic location, but would like some of the benefits from additional specialization. Staff specialists in product lines or customer types can be added in lieu of additional specialization in the sales force itself. Caterpillar Tractor Company makes extensive use of staff specialists, having 20 for various market types such as logging or railroad construction and an additional twelve for particular product lines. These

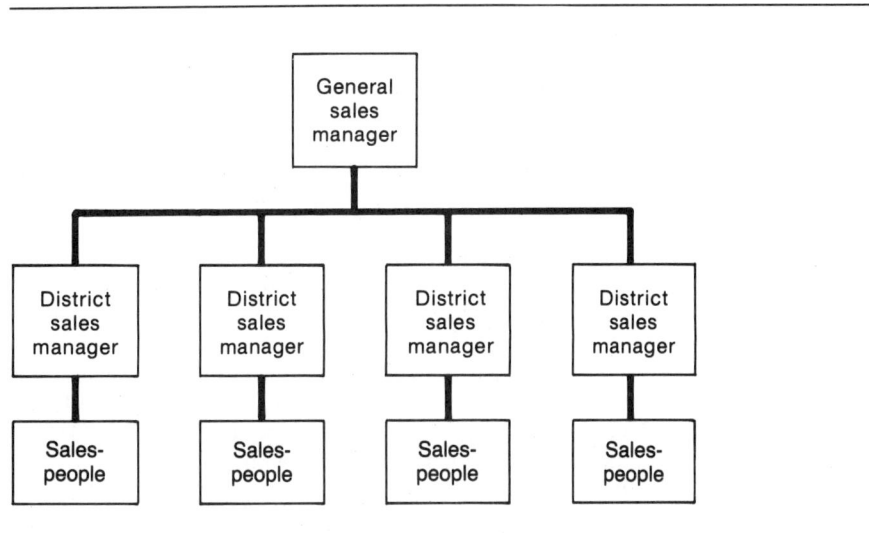

FIGURE 10.2

Sales Organization Specialized by Geographic Region

FIGURE 10.3

Sales Organization with Increased Geographic Specialization and with Staff Specialists

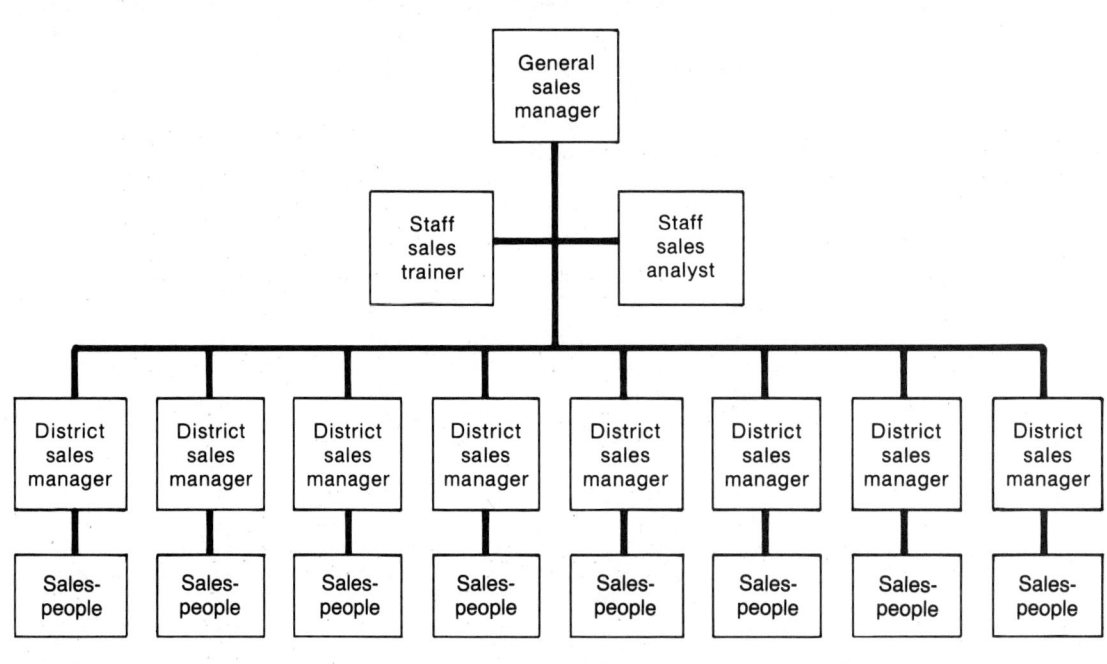

specialists provide research studies for use in product development, engineering, and advertising, and act as a liaison between the salespeople and other departments of the firm.[22]

Two-stage Specialization. The next logical development is two-stage specialization, in which the line organization is subdivided on two separate bases. Figure 10.4 illustrates two alternative sales organization structures which have been segmented by four areas and three customer types, both of which are examples of two-stage specialization.

When two or more stages of specialization are used, a decision must be made concerning the *order of subordination*. Figure 10.4 (*a*) shows customer specialization subordinate to area specialization, and the opposite is true in Figure 10.4 (*b*). How can the better structure be identified?

The first point to consider is coordination, which becomes more difficult as specialization increases. In general, the lower level of specialization should be the one requiring greater coordination. Figure 10.4 (*a*) provides close coordination among all customer salespeople within a single area. Inter-area coordination would be of less significance. An example of this situation is an advertising agency which has major offices in four large metropolitan areas: New York, Chicago, Los Angeles,

FIGURE 10.4
Sales Organization Specialized by Geographic Location and Customer Type:
Two Alternative Structures

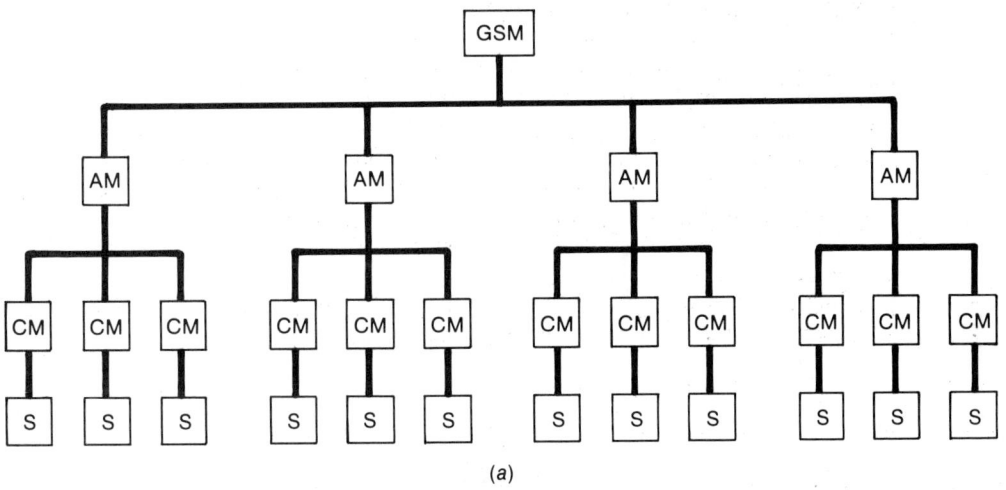

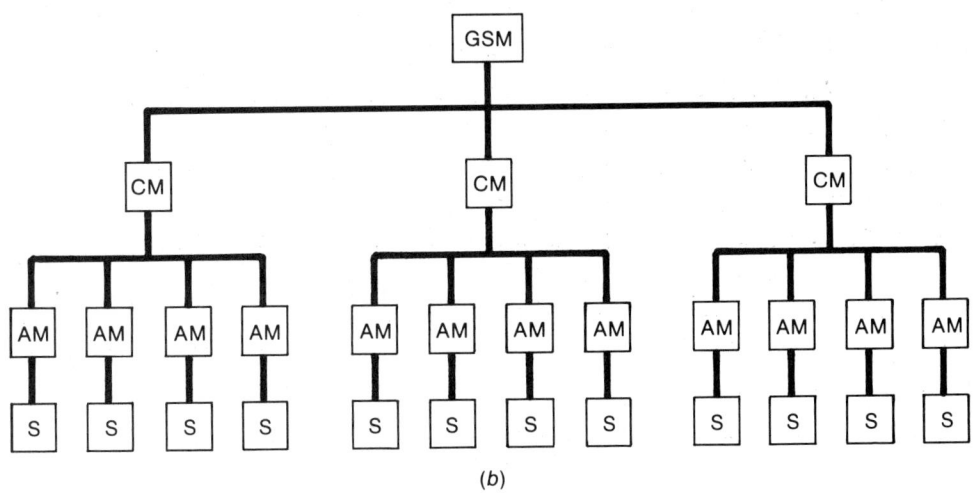

Key: GSM = General sales manager AM = Area manager
CM = Customer type manager S = Salespeople

and Houston. Each office obtains and works with clients independently, but all four try to maintain a balance among types of clients such as industrial goods manufacturers, consumer goods manufacturers, and large retailers or distributors who have local markets. This balance is necessary to ensure efficient use of agency's talent and facilities. Separate types of account executives or representatives (that is, advertising sales personnel) pursue each of these three markets, but they must communicate among themselves often in order to maintain the balance and to avoid obtaining competitive firms as clients.

Figure 10.4 (b) allows close coordination among all areas for each customer type. This basic structure may be used by a large consumer goods manufacturer who sells to major chains directly, to independent wholesalers, and to sizable institutional buyers. Each sales program can be tied together by extensive advertising and sales promotion on a national basis. Maximum marketing effectiveness requires every area sales representative calling on a single customer type to coordinate closely with the advertising and sales promotion directed to their particular market. An integrated marketing effort by product throughout the entire country is best aided when geographic specialization is the subordinate type in the organization structure.

A second point concerns the costs of alternative structures. Figure 10.4 (a) represents the more costly structure because it contains more positions in total and also more higher-level positions which command greater compensation. When an additional stage of specialization is added, cost factors dictate that the stage with the smallest number of categories be placed nearer the top.

Finally, the future direction of organizational growth and change should be considered. Figure 10.4 (b) would more easily allow for further geographic subdivision of territories for any customer market. In Figure 10.4 (a) this kind of modification could not be made without a considerable organizational shakeup, although additional customer types could be singled out in any area.

More Complex Structures. Further evolution into more complex structures can occur in three ways.

One is to continue adding stages of specialization or single positions of a specialized nature such as a development or a missionary salesperson. Staff positions can likewise be increased. The use of staff specialists at the district or regional level instead of the home office is a feasible option as the sales organization grows very large in size.

A second direction is to use staff personnel and give them authority over the sales force in their particular areas of specialization. A sales promotion specialist would have authority over the sales personnel concerning sales promotion strategies. This is termed a *functional* organization, and is illustrated in Figure 10.5. Theoretically, this type of organization is more efficient because communication is faster and more direct from specialists to salespeople. But in a practical sense, functional authority may become confusing to the sales force. Each functional specialist may try to push his plans at the expense of a balanced operation, and may cause conflicting demands on salespeople's time.

A third direction involves a *matrix* organization design composed of two dimensions of specialization—by business function and by marketing program. Each program manager draws upon the functional resources of the firm to implement that program. Figure 10.6 shows a marketing organization of the matrix type. Each sales force member reports to the sales manager as well as to the manager of any

FIGURE 10.5

Sales Organization Specialized by Geographic Location and Customer Type with Functional Authority

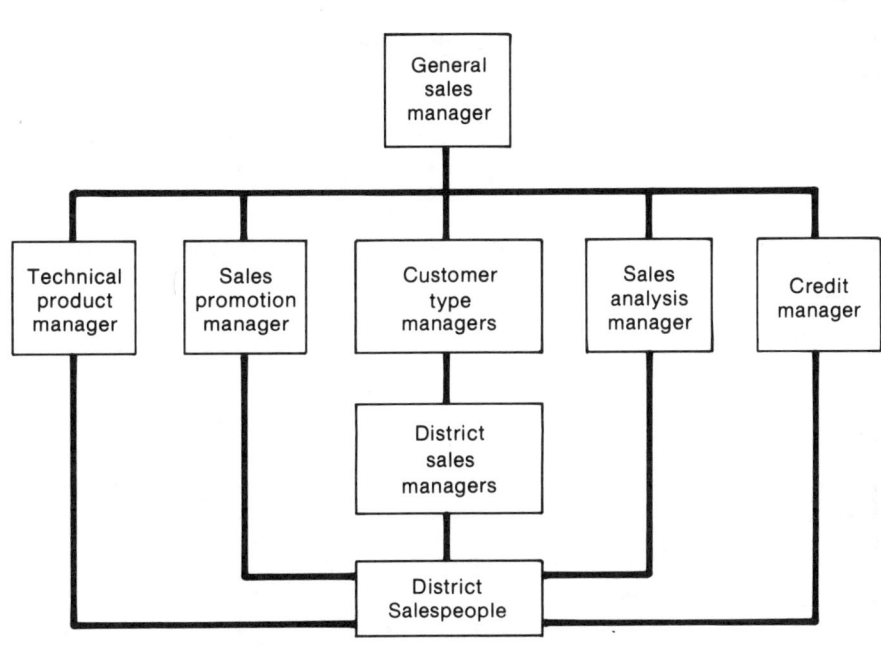

marketing program presently involving the sales force. Coordination problems exist under these conditions also, but firms such as IBM, General Foods, DuPont, and Xerox have moved toward this design because it is truly a market orientation.[23]

Evaluate the Structure

For an ongoing organization, the first four steps discussed in the previous section provide a checklist for evaluating its effectiveness. Are market characteristics correctly identified, activities and positions properly devised to serve the market, and components efficiently arranged to facilitate the firm's mission? If alternatives to the present structure are being considered, or if a totally new structure is being planned, some further criteria for evaluation exist: availability of sales potential, competitors' organizations, the influence of people, and the extent of an informal organization.

Availability of Sales Potential. The size of the organization is influenced by the amount of profitable sales potential available. Increased size brings increased costs, and this necessitates more revenues. For instance, suppose management wished to increase the amount of specialization from geographic only to geographic plus product. If there are three product lines, then three salespeople per geographic area would be required, and sufficient sales potential must be available in each area for each product line to make this change economically feasible. The amount of sales potential limits the extent of specialization.

FIGURE 10.6

Marketing Organization with a Matrix Structure

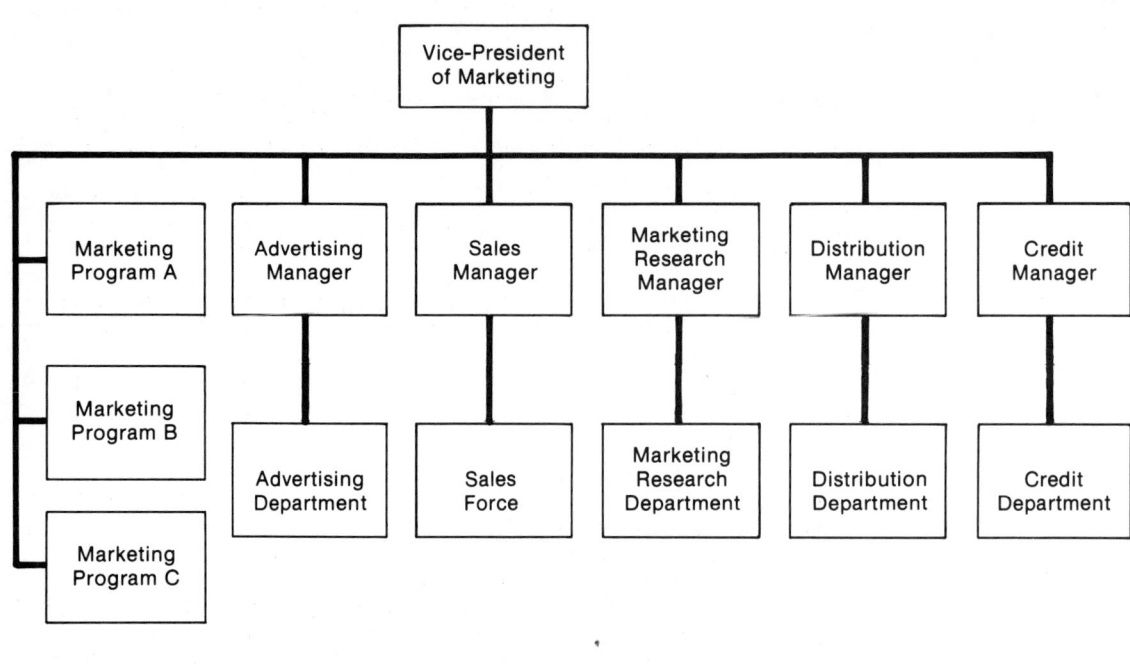

Organization Structures of Competitors. Competitive survival often requires that an organization match or exceed the offerings of its major competitors. If a number of competitors have sales personnel specialized in development selling, perhaps the organization should do the same just to maintain the chances of getting new customers. Instead of matching competition a different strategy for obtaining customers can be tried, such as the use of team selling. In either case, competition provides an impetus to increased specialization and its attendant additions to the organization size.

Influence of People. The influence of people and personal relationships in an organization can be very strong. When a company is first begun, it takes its character largely from the desires of its founders. As a small company grows, it often adjusts its organization structure to the talents of its employees. For example, top management may desire more decentralization of authority, but don't push it because people in middle management positions are unable or unwilling to work with this philosophy.

Sales organizations are especially dependent on the personal nature of the sales force members. A salesperson's personality is sometimes the major means of differentiating one firm's offering from that of a competitor. Newer organizational concepts are beginning to recognize the importance of people. Clearly, an employee's job performance is greatly influenced by his personal needs, and those needs may be better met in one type of organization pattern rather than in another.

Extent of an Informal Organization. The informal organization is the pattern of communications and group associations that actually exists among organization members. It may not, and seldom does, coincide with the formal relationships as expressed in organization charts and job descriptions. Communication efficiency is often enhanced by circumventing formal channels. Speed in obtaining an immediate credit clearance on a prospective customer might be critical in closing a sale. Using normal channels, the request would go through the district manager to the general sales manager, then to the controller, and finally to a credit manager. In an emergency, the salesperson or district manager might contact the credit manager directly. As such emergencies occur more often, some thought should be given to restructuring the formal channels of communication or to a rearrangement of positions.

One study identified the informal communication patterns within a marketing organization, as shown in Figure 10.7. Obviously a formal organization structure

FIGURE 10.7

Informal Communication Patterns within a Marketing Organization

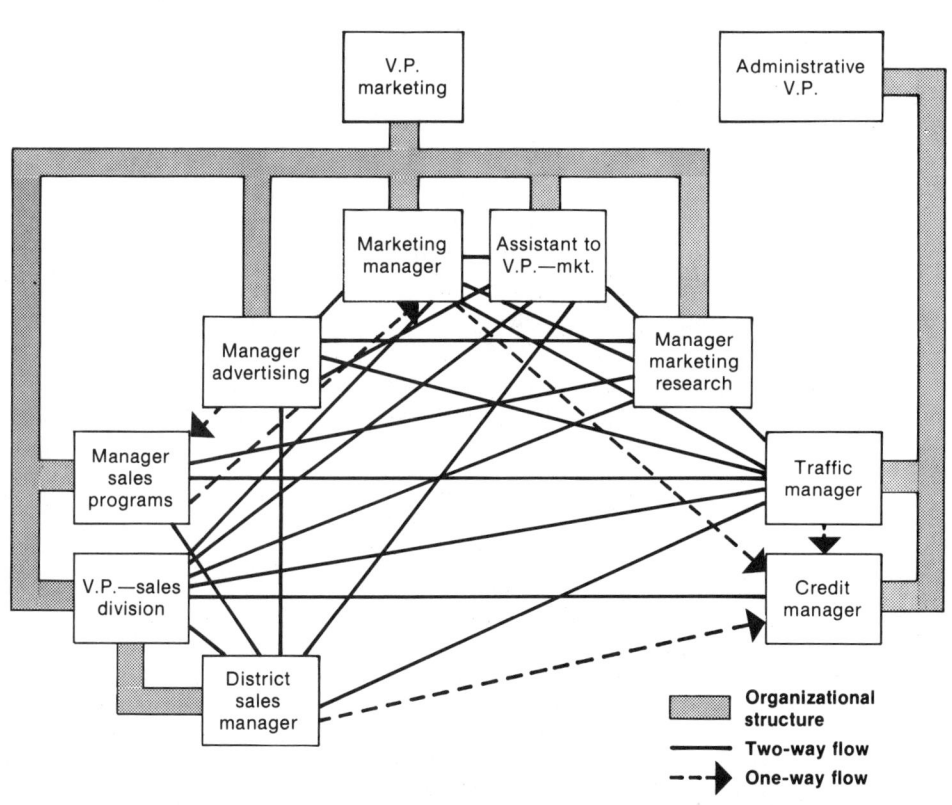

Reprinted from *Journal of Marketing*, published by the American Marketing Association. Adapted from R. Clifton Andersen and Edward W. Cundiff, "Patterns of Communication in Marketing Organizations," vol. 29 (July 1965), p. 33.

cannot easily be developed to reflect all these relationships without being made highly complex and confusing. But perhaps this indicates why matrix structures are becoming more popular, especially among larger firms with numerous specialists.

CONCLUSION

A good sales organization structure is the product of many variables. This chapter has stressed the characteristics of the firm's market as being the most significant. The numbers and types of customers, the potential sales volume they represent, and their buying patterns and service needs provide the bases on which the structure is established. Then internal variables such as the degree of specialization and the extent of decentralization are considered and manipulated to produce a structure which will be both competitively effective and economically feasible. But any organization structure is inert without people, who are also a variable affecting its performance. To realize the value of a good structure, it is necessary to obtain the right kinds of people to fit each job, then guide them towards effective job performance. The next chapter considers the tasks of obtaining sales personnel.

QUESTIONS FOR REVIEW AND DISCUSSION

1. "The organization of the sales operation should match the organization of the market." Give your evaluation of this statement.
2. Since members of the sales organization are often physically decentralized, does this have any significant bearing on how much decentralization of authority should exist in that organization?
3. If a firm produces goods for private brands as well as for its own national brand, how might the sales force be specialized to best handle this situation?
4. How often should a sales manager consider restructuring the sales organization? Consider the distinctions between the long-range and short-range aspects of reorganization.
5. Discuss the internal-external tradeoff in structuring an organization. Give an example of a company which would favor the internal orientation in its sales force. Then give an example for the external orientation.
6. Should field sales managers sell in addition to their management duties? Discuss the pros and cons of giving field sales managers selling responsibility.
7. Suppose you are a district sales manager and have been requested to evaluate and report whether your district operation is too large, too small, or of optimum size. Outline the points you would make in such a report.
8. A large manufacturer (sales of $75 million annually) of industrial tools distributes two separate lines of products. One includes metal-working machine tools used by most firms involved in fabricating metal parts. The other includes portable and hand power tools which pertain more to repair shop operations and lightweight metal fabricating. Some customers buy both lines from this manufacturer, while others make use of only one line or the other.

The total market area for this firm includes the four western states of Washington, Oregon, California, and Arizona, although top management is interested in expanding the market eastward.

The firm has been relying on outside selling agents, but now wishes to employ its own sales force. The present sales organization, exclusive of any field sales force, includes a sales manager; two regional sales offices containing a regional sales coordinator and a customer service manager; and a traveling "missionary" salesperson who visits major customers in order to discover new needs or applications, to provide assistance on special in-plant problems, and to check on the effectiveness of the selling agents.

Devise a sales department organization for this firm including the present personnel and the desired field sales force. State your reasoning and any assumptions necessary to arrive at your answer.

9. As the computer plays an increasing role in sales management, how do you think it will affect the informal organization? Will this effect, in turn, have any significant influence on the formal organization?
10. What is meant by staff specialization in the sales organization? Under what conditions may this be more effective than line specialization?

NOTES

1. Michael B. McCaskey, "An Introduction to Organizational Design," *California Management Review*, vol. 17 (Winter 1974), p. 14.
2. Sally Scanlon, "Ansul Blazes New Sales Patterns," *Sales Management*, December 9, 1974, p. 25.
3. Gerhard W. Ditz, "The Internal-External Dichotomy in Business Organizations," *Industrial Management Review*, vol. 6 (Fall 1964), pp. 51–52.
4. Robert F. Vizza, *Measuring the Value of the Field Sales Force* (New York: Sales Executives Club of New York, Inc., 1963), p. 55.
5. James Girdwood, "Restructuring Sales Territories," in *Allocating Field Sales Resources*, Experiences in Marketing Management no. 23 (New York: National Industrial Conference Board, Inc., 1970), p. 29.
6. Alton F. Doody and William G. Nickels, "Structuring Organizations for Strategic Selling," *MSU Business Topics*, vol. 20 (Autumn 1972), pp. 27–34.
7. Rayna Skolnik, "Paper Mate Flourishes By Making Sure Customers Do, Too," *Sales Management*, May 19, 1975, pp. 15–17.
8. Lee Adler, "Think Twice Before Having Salespeople Take a Flier At Marketing Research," *Sales & Marketing Management*, April 11, 1977, p. 88.
9. Dan H. Robertson, "Sales Force Feedback on Competitors' Activities," *Journal of Marketing*, vol. 38 (April 1974), pp. 69–71.
10. J. N. Bauman, "Rebirth of the Salesman," *Dun's Review*, vol. 91 (March 1968), p. 100.
11. Since determining the *number* of salespeople needed has already been discussed in Chapter 6, we concentrate here on determining the *types* of positions needed.
12. An analytical method to help make this choice is found in C. Davis Fogg and Josef W. Rokus, "A Quantitative Method for Structuring a Profitable Sales Force," *Journal of Marketing*, vol. 37 (July 1973), pp. 8–17; another approach is found in Clyde E. Harris, Jr. and Jimmy E. Hilliard, "Switchover for Bigger Profits," *Sales & Marketing Management*, November 8, 1976, pp. 47–48.
13. Art Detman, "Clorox's Tasty Sideline," *Sales Management*, June 10, 1974, p. 27.
14. Martin Everett, "Heinz Is Changing Sloooow Fast," *Sales Management*, August 5, 1974, pp. 19–24.

15. "Marketers, et cetera," *Sales & Marketing Management,* November 14, 1977, p. 42.

16. Thayer C. Taylor, "Can NCR Cash In?" *Sales & Marketing Management,* February 7, 1977, pp. 30–36. Additional discussion of NCR and other firms using customer specialization is found in Mack Hanan, "Organize Your Company Around Its Markets," *Harvard Business Review,* vol. 52 (November–December 1974), pp. 63–74.

17. "Dial 'G' For Gypsum," *Sales Management,* October 14, 1974, p. 12.

18. Harry L. Bullock, "Basic Factors in Sales Territory Design—I," in *Allocating Field Sales Resources,* p. 15.

19. Adapted from Merrill DeVoe, *How To Tailor Your Sales Organization to Your Markets* (Englewood Cliffs, N.J.: Prentice-Hall, Inc., 1964), p. 32.

20. Morgan B. MacDonald, Jr., and Earl L. Bailey, *The First-line Sales Supervisor,* Experiences in Marketing Management no. 17 (New York: National Industrial Conference Board, Inc., 1968), p. 5.

21. The processes and activities involved in defining the nature of a job are often grouped under the term *job analysis*. This is discussed in greater detail in Chapter 12.

22. Art Detman, Jr., "This Glorious or Alarming Situation?" *Sales Management,* January 21, 1966, pp. 30–31.

23. More detailed discussion of this organizational trend is found in E. Raymond Corey and Steven H. Star, *Organization Strategy: A Marketing Approach* (Boston: Division of Research, Graduate School of Business Administration, Harvard University, 1971); and Mack Hanan, "Reorganize Your Company Around Its Markets," *Harvard Business Review,* vol. 52 (November–December 1974), pp. 63–74.

11 HIRING SALES PERSONNEL

In this and the next three chapters we consider the hiring, training, and motivation of sales personnel. Each of these activities is essential in producing a top-notch sales force. But the importance of initial selection cannot be overstressed because it supplies the raw material from which a productive sales organization is fashioned. A new recruit's abilities can be developed by training, but neither training programs nor incentive plans can completely offset a lack of potential capability in those hired.

Hiring mistakes are costly. Money spent in selection, training, and initial compensation is lost when the newly-hired salesperson realizes the position is unsuitable and departs. Some don't leave, at least not very soon, and their cost is measured indirectly in lower productivity. Incidentally, the salesperson also is penalized, for it is costly to change jobs and adds a note of instability to a resumé.

Hiring decisions involve quantity, quality, and timing needs which must be specified by management. We examine these first, then discuss the recruiting and selection stages in obtaining sales personnel, and end the chapter with some comments on the hiring of sales management personnel.

DETERMINING HIRING NEEDS

Success in hiring depends on how well management specifies and then meets its hiring needs. First, how many salespeople are needed? At the same time, what quality or type of person is most likely to succeed in the selling job? Additionally, when should the recruiting and selection steps be scheduled so the right quantity and quality of salespeople are added to the sales force at the time they are needed? Answers to these questions will provide operational guides for recruiting and selection programs and policies.

Quantity

To determine how many new salespeople to hire, management must (a) establish the total sales force size necessary to meet its goals; and (b) forecast to what extent its present sales force will fall short of meeting that size. Since determining sales force size was covered in Chapter 6, we concentrate here on forecasting how many members of the current sales force will be available.

Turnover and promotions will cause today's sales force to shrink in size over the next year. Studies show that the average turnover rate among a wide cross-section of sales organizations is 10 percent, with nearly 5 percent additional promoted or transferred to new positions.[1] Some turnover should be expected, in fact encouraged, in hopes of upgrading average performance levels. High turnover, however, may suggest an unusual problem in hiring, training, compensating, or motivating the sales force.

To illustrate how to determine the number of people which need to be hired, suppose a sales manager determines that 32 salespeople will be needed next year. The present sales force size is 30, but one will retire and one will be promoted to fill a field management position. Past turnover rates range from 5 percent to 10 percent per year, so the manager judges that two additional people will be lost through termination. With 26 of the present sales force expected to remain, six new recruits must be hired to reach the needed total of 32.

Quality

Perhaps the most challenging task in the entire hiring process is to determine what attributes indicate future success in the job. We examined the relationship between traits and selling success in Chapter 9, and concluded that such qualifications differ from one selling job to the next. There is no standard approach for determining job qualifications (sometimes termed "hiring specifications"). Type and size of sales force, and length of time in business will determine which of the following approaches is most feasible for a particular firm.

Qualifications from the Position Description. A written position description can be analyzed to deduce important job qualifications. For example, the Armour-Dial position description in Chapter 10 (Table 10.4) suggests the following important characteristics: initiative, orderliness, attention to details, and knowledge of basic financial and marketing techniques. The main difficulty with this approach is that such qualifications are hard to define precisely and objectively. Furthermore, it is nearly impossible to determine how much of each trait is desired. How much initiate is necessary for success? Is it possible for an applicant to have too much initiative? Nevertheless, checklists of personal traits based on job duties are devised by many companies and used to rate applicants in the hiring process.

Qualifications from Personal History Analyses. Instead of focusing on *job* duties and responsibilities, the sales manager might compare the *persons* on the job to discover any patterns or comparisons among the good and poor performers at the time they were hired. A careful analysis of the best salespeople might reveal that they shared a common educational background or type of previous work experience. Similar analysis can be done on poor performers, and factors which they shared in common prior to being hired might be considered as negative qualifications or "knockout" factors. A list of such factors devised by Friden, Inc., a business machines manufacturer, included job-hopping, poor credit rating, excess indebtedness, marital troubles, and unexplained gaps in employment.[2]

Studies of only good performers or of only poor performers must be interpreted with caution because factors shared in common within a group may not necessarily differentiate it from another group. All good performers may have been business majors in college, so management is tempted to accept this as a job qualification. But it is possible that most of the poor performers had also been business majors, and if so, this characteristic does not really relate to performance success. A better procedure is to compare good performers with poor performers in the same analysis. If a certain characteristic is found consistently in good performers but is generally not possessed by poor performers, then this characteristic can be associated with success on the job.

As an example, suppose that a firm has personnel records available on 180 salespeople categorized as good performers and on 120 salespeople judged as poor performers. These two groups are compared on amount of education at the time each was hired, as shown in Table 11.1. College graduates were more likely to fall in the good performers category than were those with any other amount of education. In addition, the chance of falling in the good performers category increased as the amount of education increased until college graduation, but decreased with post-graduate education. Therefore, a college degree with no further formal schooling seems to be the most desirable qualification in terms of education.

Similar analysis can be done with other personal history characteristics such as age, marital status, number of dependents, and years of previous experience. Any other measurable characteristics can also be studied to determine possible qualifications. If a firm uses an intelligence test as a part of its selection procedure, the test scores can be compared between good and poor performers in the same way as for education.

Some characteristics may not show appreciable differences between good and poor performers, so these characteristics cannot be used as valid qualifications. Furthermore, results obtained by analyzing salespeople in one position may be entirely different from results pertaining to another position or to a similar job in another company. A major problem with this approach for many firms is the need to have a large number of salespeople to provide reliable results. With a small number, differences between good and poor performers may not be significant when tested statistically. Furthermore, if the sales force does not include any outstanding performers, this analysis will fail to pinpoint characteristics which distinguish the highest caliber salespeople.

Qualifications form Customer Characteristics. To the extent that the dyadic view of selling success is true, a salesperson's effectiveness depends on how well matched he or she is with the buyer in a particular transaction. This matching can occur in physical characteristics such as age or height, in role behavior and expectations such as how a salesperson should behave, in personality, social interests, political

TABLE 11.1

Comparison of Good and Poor Performers on Amount of Education at the Time Each Was Hired as a Salesperson

Amount of Education	Number of Good Performers	Number of Poor Performers	Total	Percentage of Total Who Are Good Performers
Did not finish high school	5	20	25	20
High school graduate	30	50	80	38
Some college	45	15	60	75
College graduate	85	15	100	85
Graduate study	15	20	35	43

attitudes, and in many other possible dimensions. If management can find evidence that matching on some characteristic produces improved success, then those characteristics of customers in the territory can be used as hiring specifications for that particular position. The main problem with this approach is that not all customers in the same territory will be alike. A salesperson who matches one customer well in physical and personality traits, for example, will not match other customers as well if they are different in physical and personality traits. Nevertheless, customer characteristics should be given consideration since it is well documented in many firms that a given salesperson is more effective with some customer types than with others.

Legal Perspective on Job Qualifications. The Civil Rights Act of 1964 was the start of a series of legislation aimed at preventing employment discrimination based on race, color, nationality, religion, or sex. The Age Discrimination in Employment Act of 1967 added age, specifically aiming at discrimination against persons in the 40–65 age group, and the Vocational Rehabilitation Act of 1973 added the handicapped to the groups targeted for nondiscrimination in employment. Guidelines for interpreting the legislation have been issued by the Equal Employment Opportunity Commission (EEOC) and the Office of Federal Contract Compliance (OFCC). Various state laws and corresponding state agencies also exist to enforce the regulations.

We can only briefly summarize the main points from this legislation, which is still undergoing clarifying interpretations. Primarily, it is illegal to use any attributes or personal history characteristics as job qualifications *if* they result in discrimination against persons of a given race, color, religion, nationality, sex, age, or any other minority group *unless* the employer can show that the characteristic used is a "bona fide occupational qualification" (BFOQ). A BFOQ is a qualification essential to performing the job successfully, and the employer must have evidence that the qualification is indeed job-related.

If any qualification is used which results in the selection of a lesser proportion of any one group (e.g., racial, ethnic, sex) than another, the selection process is said to have "adverse impact." A qualification which produces an adverse impact is acceptable only if it is supported by valid evidence as being clearly job-related. Qualifications which do not produce an adverse impact are not subject to legal scrutiny, however.

Suppose a firm requires a high school diploma as a job qualification. This qualification will result in adverse impact if the proportion completing high school differs among racial or ethnic groups. In that case, a high school diploma cannot be a legal hiring qualification unless management has solid evidence that it is job-related—that a person without the diploma will fail to perform the job satisfactorily because of no diploma.

Problems in Developing Qualifications. Since a valid job qualification is one which relates to success on the job, management must first define success before determining what factors relate to it. Many different criteria of selling success have been used, with sales volume being the most popular.[3] But sales volume alone is often not a valid basis for comparing performance because of territory differences in size and potential and because of many other factors uncontrollable by the salesperson which nevertheless affect sales. In one study, the criterion of success used was simply a positive answer by sales managers to the question, "Would you rehire this man if he were a new applicant and you knew as much about him as you do now?"[4] Other firms have used multiple criteria rather than just one.[5] For instance, the success of real estate sales personnel was measured in terms of dollar earnings, number of property listings obtained, and ratings by their sales manager.[6]

Even if management finds satisfactory criteria of performance success, there are other difficulties. While the aim in selection is to identify applicants with potential capability for success, additional factors such as training programs and motivation plans will influence their eventual performance. Two possible ways of looking at this relationship are shown in Figure 11.1. On the left side the effects of each factor are cumulative. Stronger potential capability may result in better training effectiveness, and those two factors in combination influence motivation. All three then interact and combine to produce some level of accomplishment by the salesperson. Mathematically, these three factors are expressed in a multiplicative relationship, indicating that an improvement in any one will multiply the value of the others in its total effect on accomplishment. For instance, training and motivation programs will contribute more to accomplishment if management hires persons with increased potential capability. Note, however, that any attempt to isolate a direct relationship between initial qualifications of potential capability and subsequent performance would be rather tenuous.

On the right side the effects of each factor are viewed in an alternative way as being independent and noninteracting, producing a mathematically additive relationship. If this version is more correct, the effects of potential capability on accomplishment can be traced directly, since these effects will not change even if

FIGURE 11.1
Alternative Views of How a Salesperson's Accomplishment Is Affected by Potential Capability, Training, and Motivation

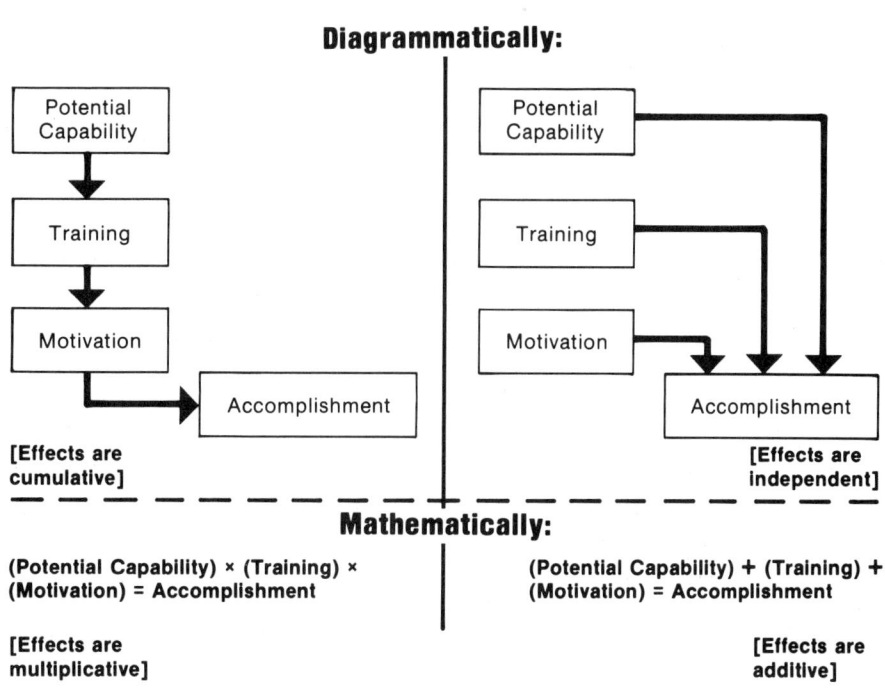

training or motivation programs are changed. Which version is correct? No formal studies have been made, but it would seem unusual if at least some cumulative or interactive effects didn't occur to affect the success of most sales personnel.

A final problem is that of qualification change. Selling jobs and job environments vary over time, and perhaps the successful salesperson hired ten or even five years ago would not be as successful if hired today or five years in the future. For this reason, it is advisable to study trends in the personal history characteristics of successful performers. For instance, the education of good performers at the time they were hired might show a pattern toward higher levels over time.

Timing

Timing is concerned with having the right number of qualified salespeople available when needed. Without proper timing, poor performers might be retained too long because new personnel were not ready, or recently hired salespeople might be given inadequate training to get them into the field more quickly. Sometimes district managers temporarily work an unoccupied territory until a new salesperson is ready, and this detracts from the performance of their regular managerial responsibilities.

Timing requirements are set by working backwards from the time new salespeople are required in the field. Suppose five new sales personnel will be needed next June first. If the company's initial training program takes two months, these five must enter training on April first. When the time normally needed to complete the selection procedure is included, management can set the date at which a sufficient number of applicants must be available to produce the five necessary additions to the sales force.

The significance of accurate timing as well as quantity planning is illustrated in the case of the Equitable Life Assurance Society of the United States, which requires three to five years to prepare a person sufficiently as a member of its active sales force.[7] As a result, personnel needs must be forecast for three years in the future. By analyzing its records, management can estimate what portion of new appointees, as well as of one- two- and three-year salespeople will remain with the company. Then a time schedule covering the next three years is devised to ensure that the number hired this year will be enough to meet the forecast needs of the active sales force.

RECRUITING

Recruiting consists of securing applicants for particular jobs. It does not include, but is followed by, the selection process in which applicants are evaluated and screened for possible hiring. Recruiting can be used as a screening device, however, as we shall discuss later in this section.

Recruiting Sources

Companies use a variety of recruiting sources to obtain sales job applicants. The following sources are those used most often.

Schools and Colleges. College graduates become more desirable as the selling job becomes more complex and demanding. These graduates are also viewed as good potential management personnel and may be hired primarily as management trainees. Many firms pursue this recruiting source by making regularly scheduled visits to college campuses and by meeting with placement officials and faculty members in addition to students. Some firms have also instituted a trainee program for students midway between their junior and senior years. In these cases, the student can learn about a possible career choice with the firm without making an immediate commitment, and management has a chance to learn about a potential employee.

Employment Agencies. Employment agencies are quite popular, but their value is sometimes questioned by sales executives who believe that job seekers go to employment agencies only as a last resort. Many agencies can be of value to the recruiter, particularly those dealing with professional placement or specializing in sales personnel. They not only search for candidates, but can perform initial screening as well. Some firms have found agencies especially helpful in locating qualified minority applicants.

Present Employees. Present employees serve as recruiting sources in two ways. They can be candidates themselves or they can recommend candidates. There are distinct advantages in considering present nonselling employees as sales candidates. The firm already has records on their work, and they in turn understand many aspects of the company and its operations. Of course, success in nonselling jobs does not necessarily mean success in selling. But by studying the performance of salespeople recruited from within the company, management can determine whether the better performers are more likely to come from one area of the firm than another.

Referrals from present sales personnel often produce recruits with considerable knowledge of the job and experience in selling. Some managers hesitate to use their sales force as a recruiting source, however, because they fear a salesperson's pride and morale may be hurt if a suggested applicant is turned down. But because present salespeople can prescreen before recommending candidates, this source can produce more qualified candidates from fewer recruits, and is more efficient than other recruiting sources.

Advertisements. Recruiting through advertising covers a wide range of possibilities. At one extreme is the small classified ad in the daily newspaper. It attracts many responses at low cost, but if the position is not described in detail, only a few of the respondents turn out to be qualified and interested. Trade or professional journals in business and technical fields are much more selective media. While their cost per response is higher than for newspaper advertising, there is a compensating cost saving because fewer unsuitable applicants must be screened.

A debatable issue concerns the use of blind ads, in which the company name is not given. One study compared blind ads with full-disclosure ads and found that the blind ads produced about three times as many applicants. But a higher percentage of applicants from the full-disclosure ads were hired.[8] Blind ads might be favored if an extensive recruiting effort is required or if the firm wishes to avoid informing its competitors that it is experiencing turnover problems in the sales force.

Business or Personal Contacts. Applicants might be located through other contacts such as present customers or suppliers, business associates in noncompeting firms, or persons in various organizations to which the sales executive belongs. If the firm sells to dealers or distributors, some of their employees might consider changing jobs if it means an improved opportunity. Such action should be agreed upon by the customer, however, in order to maintain good business relations.

Voluntary Applicants. Voluntary applicants are often considered excellent candidates because they exhibit initiative and interest in the firm—qualities considered important to selling success. The number recruited this way is usually insufficient for company needs, however, and may also include unqualified persons or those unable to secure other positions. Firms accepting voluntary applicants generally use a short screening form or interview to pick out quickly and inexpensively those with at least minimum qualifications.

Legal Perspective on Recruiting. Recruiting sources must be chosen which, in combination, do not result in discrimination against any groups covered by the Civil Rights Act and subsequent legislation. Furthermore, it is not sufficient just to avoid discrimination, but in many cases the firm is required to seek out and encourage minority group members to apply for positions. Such *affirmative action* programs are required by the EEOC of any firm in which a pattern of past discrimination (whether deliberate or not) is found. The OFCC requires written affirmative action programs from any federal government supplier with 50 or more employees.

Much evidence exists that women and blacks in particular have been affected by discriminatory sales recruiting practices in the past.[9] Reasons given included fear of unfavorable customer reaction (e.g., of white customers to black salesperson) or belief that turnover rates will increase significantly (e.g., from marriage and pregnancy of women, and from job dissatisfaction of women and blacks). Many firms have made special efforts in the past few years to recruit from these minority groups. Numerous individual successes have been cited, and sales managers are learning how to adjust for the different needs and expectations of these employees in company training and motivation programs.[10]

Recruiting Policy Decisions

The main recruiting policy decisions can be expressed in two questions:

1. How many applicants are necessary to meet quantity needs?
2. How many and what recruiting sources should be used to supply this number of applicants?

The number of applicants necessary will vary depending on the recruiting source used. For example, a recent study by Armour-Dial showed the following ratios of applicants to hireds from four recruiting sources:[11]

Colleges:	17 applicants per 1 hired
Employment Agencies:	18 applicants per 1 hired
Newspaper Advertisements:	36 applicants per 1 hired
Sales Force Referrals:	9 applicants per 1 hired

Past ratios for each recruiting source should guide the sales manager in determining how many applicants to recruit from any one source.

Which source to use is a more complicated question. Two main factors to consider are the cost of each source and the success ratio of salespeople hired from each source. Table 11.2 shows how four recruiting sources might be analyzed. Using the Armour-Dial ratios and with a quantity goal of ten new salespeople to be hired, column 3 shows the number of applicants needed if only that source was to provide all ten new hires. When the recruiting cost per applicant is multiplied by the number of applicants needed, and that total is divided by ten, which is the target number of new hires, the recruiting cost per hired is calculated in column 5. Using this column as a guide, colleges are the most costly source while agencies and sales force referrals are the least expensive.

If different recruiting sources typically produce different ratios of successful performers to total hires, this analysis can be carried on. The recruiting source is now a screening device, and the effectiveness of each source in providing successful performers is shown in column 6. The cost to recruit each successful salesperson appears in column 7, and the post-recruiting costs spent on the unsuccessful performers appear in columns 8–10. Based on this analysis, colleges represent the least expensive recruiting source, since its success ratio is best and it requires the least funds spent on unsuccessful performers. Recruiting efforts should therefore be focused on colleges, and if not enough recruits can be generated from this source within the time available, sales force referrals appear to be the next best additional source.

Of course, if the ratios in column 6 were not appreciably different among recruiting sources, the second part of this analysis could be eliminated. In either case, results will be most reliable for large firms which have recruited and hired many salespeople. For smaller firms or those with less recruiting history, such information may be far less reliable since it is based on fewer instances. At best, it should be used as just a guide to assist the sales manager's judgment in recruiting policy decisions.

SELECTION

The selection stage involves evaluating and screening applicants. This is normally done with various tools that measure each applicant's job qualifications.

Selection Tools

Although many different selection tools are in use, they can be categorized into six main groups:

1. Application blanks
2. Interviews
3. References
4. Psychological tests
5. Physical examinations
6. Environmental tests

Firms differ greatly in both choice and utilization of these tools. We first examine how each tool can be used, and then review the policy decisions necessary to formulate a selection program.

TABLE 11.2
Information for Developing Recruiting Policies

Alternative Recruiting Sources	Target Number of New Hires [1]	Ratio of Applicants To Hires [2]	Number of Applicants To Be Recruited [3]	Recruiting Cost Per Applicant[a] [4]	Recruiting Cost Per Hired [5]	Ratio of Successful Performers To Hires [6]	Recruiting Cost Per Successful Hired [7]	Post-Recruiting Cost Per Unsuccessful Hired[b] [8]	Number of Unsuccessful Hires Per Successful Hired [9]	Total Cost of Recruiting One Successful Performer [10]=[7]+[8×9]
Colleges	10	17 to 1	170	$35	$595	1 to 2	$1,190	$5,000	1	$ 6,190
Employment Agencies	10	18 to 1	180	$20	$360	1 to 3	$1,080	$5,000	2	$11,080
Newspaper Advertising	10	36 to 1	360	$15	$540	1 to 4	$2,160	$5,000	3	$17,160
Sales Force Referrals	10	9 to 1	90	$40	$360	1 to 2.5	$ 900	$5,000	1.5	$ 8,400

[a]Includes all direct costs for each source (e.g., travel and related costs for college recruiting; fees, records, and correspondence for employment agencies; media costs for advertising) plus cost of company personnel time, plus administrative costs in corresponding with applicants, processing applications, recordkeeping. The costs used in this example are hypothetical.

[b]Includes out-of-pocket costs of training, compensation, expenses, administration. The cost of lost sales is not included because it is not out-of-pocket.

Application Blanks. In general, the application blank is used to obtain factual information about the applicant. This includes such items as education, work experience, and other personal history characteristics, as shown in the example in Figure 11.2. Some questions traditionally asked on application blanks have been deleted for legal reasons. Examples are questions on marital status and place of birth. In fact, any question which is not job-related, especially if it might tend to identify an applicant's race, religion, age, nationality, or sex, is best removed from the application blank.

This tool can serve three purposes. The first is in determining whether the applicant possesses any particular qualifications required for the job such as educational or experience requirements. Many firms use the application blank in another way; as a guide for questions in an interview. Suppose an applicant indicates membership in several organizations. An interviewer could pursue this topic by asking why the applicant joined each organization, what he or she has contributed to its success, and what values he or she receives from membership. Answers could provide insight into the applicant's personal goals, desires for achievement, and ability to work effectively with others.

The third way of using an application blank is by weighting and scoring the applicant's responses on key items. It is then termed a *weighted application blank*. An applicant's score can be compared with predetermined standards developed through a personal history analysis. A minimum score can be set as a cutoff point, and applicants below this point can be eliminated from further consideration.

A weighted application blank usually is developed as follows: (1) determine which items on the application blank have produced significantly different answers between good and poor performers; (2) develop a scoring system which assigns a point score to each possible answer for each question; and (3) weight each item to reflect its relative importance in predicting sales success. These steps are simply an extension of the personal history analysis previously illustrated in Table 11.1.

All items for which there are adequate records should be considered, since no list has been found which applies to all sales positions.[12] Often, a large proportion of items will not differentiate significantly between the two performance groups. In one company, only 13 of 31 items analyzed proved to be useful.[13]

To determine which items distinguish good versus poor performers, a chi-square contingency test or some comparable type of statistical analysis is essential. For items which do distinguish, a method for scoring responses must also be devised. From the information in Table 11.1, a scoring system can be developed whereby an applicant in a given category will be given a certain number of points. One logical way is to base the number of points on the percentage scores in the last column. For the education item, an applicant might then be scored as follows:[14]

Education	*Points*
Did not finish high school	2
High School Graduate	4
Some College	7
College Graduate	8
Graduate Study	4

FIGURE 11.2

Application Blank for Sales Position, Del Monte Corporation

Del Monte

APPLICATION FOR EMPLOYMENT

Del Monte Corporation
Del Monte Sales Company
An Equal Opportunity Employer

Name (First)	(Middle)		(Last)	Date
Address (Street and Number)				Social Security Number
(City)	(State)		(Zip Code)	Telephone
Type of Work Desired				When can you start?
Have you previously been employed by Del Monte Corporation? Yes / No	Where		When	Who referred you to Del Monte?

EDUCATION	Name and Address	Major Subject	Grade Point Average Over-all	Grade Point Average Major	Grade Point Average No. Pts. A =	Degree Received
High School						
College						
Graduate School						
Other Education						

Scholastic Honors and Activities

WORK EXPERIENCE (Include Military) Employment Dates (Most recent or present job first)	Firm – Address	Type of Business	Your Title and Duties	Salary

Explain Periods of Unemployment

Reprinted by permission of Del Monte Corporation.

OFFICE SKILLS	Typing Speed	Shorthand Speed	Adding Machine/Calculator	Dictating Equipment
Bookkeeping Machine	IBM (Specify Type)		Other	

AFFILIATIONS (Do not include racial, religious or nationality groups)

HOBBIES TALENTS

FOREIGN LANGUAGES	Speak	Read	Write

CHARACTER REFERENCES (Not former employers or relatives)

Name	Address	Occupation

Other Remarks

To the best of my knowledge the above information is correct. I understand that Del Monte Corporation may wish to investigate my character and qualifications for employment by questioning my references and former employers and I have no objection to this. I understand that my employment is subject to a physical examination and a 90-day probationary period.

Signature _____

DO NOT WRITE BELOW THIS LINE

Employed For		
Position Title		
Starting Date	Classification	Salary
Interviewed By		
Company Plans	References Checked	
To Doctor	Date	Report
Employment Information		

After the points are determined, a cutoff score, which indicates how many total points an applicant needs to be considered further in the selection procedure, must be established. If ten items are being scored, the maximum points attainable might be 80, although it is quite unlikely that any applicant will receive the maximum. Again, analysis of past good and poor performers will indicate where this cutoff should be placed. Ideally, the cutoff score should be that at which the fewest possible good performers would be eliminated, while the fewest possible poor performers would be accepted.

Interviews. Interviews are especially appropriate in selecting sales personnel because an interview with its face-to-face contact resembles the actual job situation. A major purpose for using this tool, therefore, is to judge how an applicant handles himself when meeting others. Another purpose for interviewing is to check and expand information obtained through other tools. Unusual or omitted responses on the application blank can be discussed or more details about previous work experience can be explored. A third purpose is to inform the applicant about the job, either directly or in response to questions. Both parties are seeking to make the best decision, and it is to their mutual advantage to clear up any possible misunderstandings before a commitment is made.

More than one interview is often used with each applicant. A short preliminary interview may be held early in the selection procedure to discuss basic job qualifications. After that, as many as three comprehensive interviews are used in some companies so that judgments of more than one interviewer can be compared. Included may be an interview with the applicant's spouse and family members, often in the home or at a dinner engagement. Studies show that family members exert a strong influence on salespeople's job performance and satisfaction. An unhappy spouse is a major cause of quitting the job by many sales personnel.[15]

Much sales selection interviewing is done by field sales managers. They know the position they are hiring for, but are seldom professionally trained in interviewing procedures. To monitor and improve interviewing practices under these circumstances, many firms have carried out research on this part of the hiring process. Typical findings and suggestions for improving the use of the selection interview are summarized as follows.[16]

Type of Interview. At one extreme is the highly structured interview with a set of carefully worded questions in a predetermined sequence. Responses to these questions can be scored similarly to the weighted application blank. The other extreme is a completely unstructured interview in which questions and topics are chosen at random and insure no comparability from one interview to the next. Between these extremes is a semistructured or "patterned" type where the interviewer follows an outline but can deviate from it to pursue a significant topic. The semistructured approach offers the best opportunity to get additional useful information about an applicant. But research shows that the more structured version leads to greater agreement among interviewers and thus more potential for valid selection decisions.

Standards of Comparison. Managers evaluate applicants in relation to other applicants interviewed at the same time. Standards appear to be more relative than absolute—a mediocre candidate would look very strong if interviewed immediately after two or three unfavorable candidates in a row. Standards vary also in response to the immediacy of the need for new salespeople. If a district manager is behind in meeting staffing needs, many applicants may be evaluated as being stronger than they might be if the manager's needs were not as pressing. To provide better uniformity in assessing applicants, some standardized evaluation system is necessary, perhaps built-in to the interview form itself in a summary section.

Interviewer Experience. Contrary to what many managers believe, experience in interviewing is not necessarily beneficial. Interviewers with more experience did not agree with each other any more than did interviewers with less or different amounts of experience in evaluating interviewees. Systematic training is much more important than experience alone in improving performance predictions from interviews. In addition, feedback should be directed to interviewers on how well their predictions matched eventual performance of those hired.

Interviewer Accuracy. How accurately can interviewers recall what an applicant says in an interview? A group of 40 interviewer-managers were given a 20 question test on the factual content of a selection interview, and the average manager missed 10 of the 20 items! Managers scoring the poorest also rated applicants more favorably than did managers with more accurate recall. Note-taking on an interview guide resulted in greater accuracy, and should be considered essential to effective interviewing.

Evaluation of Interview Results. Most interviewers agree on what are the important facts and statements from the interview which should influence their decision. But fewer agree on how to evaluate those facts, and very few agree on how well the applicant will perform the selling job if hired. Specifically, the inter-interviewer correlation on how to evaluate the facts was .62 in one study, but among the same interviewers the correlation on predicting job performance was only .33 for the same applicants. A summary of this research concluded there was "little in the way of optimism for the traditional approach to the selection interview."[17]

In general, interviewing has not fared well when scrutinized carefully as a selection tool. To improve its effectiveness, sales managers should develop specific training programs for their field managers who carry out the hiring process. A structured interview guide with an evaluation procedure and guide for predicting success will also help standardize the interviewing process. Finally, feedback on selection predictions should help the field manager sharpen selection judgments over time. Figure 11.3 shows one interview guide used with sales applicants at Armour-Dial.

References. Most employers check references. A former employer may be contacted with questions covering the applicant's previous job, pay, performance, and reasons for leaving. Names of character references are sometimes requested from the applicant, usually on the application blank, and subsequently contacted. Credit references can be obtained from local credit agencies. There are other investigating agencies which will supply information on an applicant regarding not only credit rating but also financial condition and even personal life.

Three means of obtaining reference information are by personal interview, telephone, and mail. Personal interview is the preferred means, since statements may be made in person which would not be committed to writing. The cost and time involved in such meetings make them less appealing, however. Telephone is the next best alternative, although some people are hesitant to give information by

FIGURE 11.3
Interview Guide, Armour-Dial Company

CONSUMER PRODUCTS SALES
FIRST INTERVIEW GUIDE

Candidate's Name _____ Date & Time _____
Address _____ Phone _____
Interviewed by _____ For (Position) _____

OBJECTIVE Your objective in the 1st Interview is to determine if there is mutual interest and basic reason to proceed to an in-depth 2nd Interview. By discussing education, work history, personal background and interests you will develop a theme regarding the applicant's background. This will provide clues regarding what kind of person and worker the applicant is.

STRUCTURE The 1st Interview will take the form of a brief screening with your time divided as follows:
Introduction — 10%
Body — 80%
Conclusion — 10%

Depending on the time you have available, select questions for discussion of the major areas with this priority:

(1) work experience
(2) education
(3) personal background and interests

You should cover enough of all areas, however, so that you have sufficient information to make initial judgments regarding physical health, driving ability, sales interest and background, work experience and educational level attained. (See "Evaluation" last page).

STEP 1 Have applicant complete application.

STEP 2 Review application and, if available, a resume.

STEP 3 Begin the interview by informing the candidate that this will be a brief discussion regarding his background and experience in order to make an initial determination of interests and that no final decision will be made at this time.

STEP 4 Explain to the candidate that as time permits you will be covering three areas today, Work Experience, Education, and Personal Background and Interests. Indicate that you will be taking notes during the interview to refresh your memory later and not to be concerned. In asking the following questions try to sound as extemporaneous and relaxed as possible.

I. EDUCATION—Discuss reasons for and value of selection of college versus other alternatives, major and minor course work, courses liked and disliked, overall value of Educational preparation and extracurricular activities. For those applicants who have not gone to college or who have not completed a degree, you will have to alter your questioning to the level of education they have attained.

a. When and why did you decide to go to College? _____

ADI-6586

Reprinted by permission of Armour-Dial Company.

b. I see you majored in_____ in College. How did you decide on this as a major? What other possibilities did you consider?

c. What overall value do you think your education has had? (With regard to career plans and personal development)

d. Were you involved in any extracurricular activities in school? What were they? How did you get involved in them and what influence have they had on you?

II. WORK EXPERIENCE—Briefly review key work assignments to date. You should clarify gaps in employment, discuss specific duties, what they liked/disliked about the job, and in what ways the job contributed to their career goals.

1. _____ JOB _____ DATES _____

Tell me about your work experience:

a. How did you get the job and why do you think you were selected over other candidates?

b. What were your major responsibilities?

c. What significant contributions do you feel you individually made?

d. What were your likes and dislikes about this job? Why?

e. How do you compare yourself to others who were in the same or similar job?

(continued)

FIGURE 11-3
(continued)

f. What were your reasons for leaving? _____

2. _____ JOB DATES _____

   a. How did you get the job and why do you think you were selected over other candidates? _____

   b. What were your major responsibilities? _____

   c. What significant contributions do you feel you individually made? _____

   d. What were your likes and dislikes about this job? Why? _____

   e. How do you compare yourself to others who were in the same or similar job? _____

   f. What were your reasons for leaving? _____

III. PERSONAL BACKGROUND & INTERESTS— Ask the candidate to relate his education and work experience to his career goals. Determine his sense of what is required for a successful Sales career and how he fits into it.

   a. How does your education and work experience relate to your career goals? _____

   b. What are some things you feel are necessary for an individual to have a successful Sales career at Armour-Dial? Why do you think a career in Sales at Armour-Dial would be appropriate for you? _____

c. Are there any other factors that we have not yet discussed that you feel would contribute to your success in Sales at Dial. _____

d. Do you have any health problems that would in any way prohibit you from working with us? _____

e. With regard to your driving record, what citations have you had in the last few years and what were they for? Do you have anything in your driving history that might prohibit your operating a company car? _____

f. Driver's license number.

STEP 5   Conclusion: Inform the candidate of the next step and when you will be able to respond to him.

STEP 6   Evaluation: Before making your final determination, review the notes from your interview and consider all the pertinent information you have obtained.

Recommendation
First Interview

Base Requirements

	Above Expectations	Meets Expec.	Below Expec.
Physical Health			
Education			
Driver's Record			
Sales interest/background			
Communication Skills			
Work Record			

OVERALL RATING

○ Recommend 2nd Interview   ○ Questionable   ○ No Interest

_____
Signature

ADDITIONAL NOTES: _____

telephone unless they know the caller or are assured of the legitimacy of the call. Letters are least valuable. Nonresponse is a problem, and many who do respond will not express any critical comments about an applicant in writing. Some employers are modifying the mail approach by using rating scales or forced-choice questionnaires in hopes that eventually they will find patterns of responses that will be predictive of success.[18]

Psychological Tests. Psychological tests typically used in sales force selection are written tests designed to measure such intangible characteristics as intelligence or personality. Sales performance is affected greatly by the salesperson's psychological environment, as discussed in Chapter 8. It is logical, therefore, to try to identify psychological qualifications relating to selling success and then to measure those qualifications in applicants. But psychological tests are controversial and have often been misused in the past. We look first at what types of tests are used, then discuss how they are used (and misused), and note some problems associated with these tests.

Types of Tests. Four main types of psychological tests are used in selecting salespeople. These are:

1. Intelligence tests
2. Aptitude tests
3. Interest tests
4. Personality tests

Many published tests are available in each of these categories, and a few of the more popular tests are listed in Table 11.3.

Intelligence tests measure a person's general ability to learn. They usually include questions about vocabulary, simple arithmetic, and logical reasoning. But the value of these tests in predicting sales success is open to question. The tests may be valid in measuring intelligence, but any direct relationship between intelligence and sales success is not often found. Intelligence may become more important as sales jobs increase in complexity, but the present consensus is that a fairly broad range of intelligence is suitable for many sales jobs. Those scoring below this range may have difficulty in training programs or in analyzing basic customer problems, however. At the other extreme, those with very high scores may become bored quickly if their jobs involve routine work. If such evidence is found through analysis of past successful and unsuccessful salespeople, an intelligence test can be a helpful screening device to eliminate those falling outside the range.

Aptitude tests measure the knowledge or potential ability of a person regarding a particular subject or skill. Thus, a mechanical aptitude test measures a person's mechanical ability. Numerous sales aptitude tests exist, containing questions similar to those in college selling course examinations. Social aptitude tests also fall into this category and are frequently used in selecting sales personnel. A typical question involves a brief description of a social problem with four multiple choice alternatives, one of which contains the "right" answer. Empathy tests likewise fall into the social aptitude category.

The term *sales aptitude test* has also been used to describe almost any type of written questionnaire for which the pattern of answers correlates with selling per-

TABLE 11.3

Selected Names of Psychological Tests Used in Selecting Sales Personnel

INTELLIGENCE TESTS	INTEREST TESTS
Otis Self-Administering Test of Mental Ability	Gordon Occupational Checklist
SRA Verbal	Kuder Occupational Interest Survey
Thurstone Test of Mental Alertness	Motivational Analysis Test (MAT)
	Strong-Campbell Interest Inventory

APTITUDE TESTS	PERSONALITY TESTS
Diplomacy Test of Empathy	Adjective Checklist
Empathy Test (Kerr)	Bernreuter Personality Inventory
Flanagan Industrial Tests	Edwards Personal Preference Schedule (EPPS)
General Sales Aptitude portion of Aptitude Tests for Occupations	Gordon Personal Profile
Sales Aptitude Checklist	Guilford-Zimmerman Temperament Survey
	Sixteen Personality Factor (16 PF)
	Survey of Interpersonal Values
	Thurstone Temperament Schedule

formance. For example, the life insurance industry has devised an "aptitude index" which includes personal history and temperament items. Firms which process large numbers of sales applicants will sometimes hire a consulting psychologist to construct an aptitude test geared specifically to the requirements of the particular job in question.

Interest tests measure how similar an applicant's interests are to the interests of successful persons in specific occupations. Typical questions concern the kinds of hobbies one enjoys and the way one uses leisure time. Answers given by the applicant are compared with answers given by a successful salesperson. The closer they match, the more likely it is that the applicant's interests fit the selling occupation. Interest tests do not measure ability to perform the job, even though it is sometimes assumed that interests are good indicators of motivation. The greatest value of interest tests may be in vocational counseling rather than in performance prediction, although a few firms have found valid relationships between interest test scores and selling success.

Personality tests cover a wide range of characteristics. The meaning of the term "personality" is vague and inconsistent from one person to the next, even among psychologists, because so many different theories of personality exist. Specific personality tests are available which measure temperament, values, social adjustment, emotional stability, and individual behavior characteristics such as aggressiveness, dominance, and persistence. The obvious difficulties in using these tests are, first, in stating precisely what aspects of personality are true job qualifications, and then, in finding tests which measure these aspects correctly.

Unfortunately, many personality tests have been used with little concern for exactly what traits they measure, as long as the terms describing those traits (e.g., aggressiveness) correspond with what management "believes" to be important to selling success. But when these beliefs are not supported with solid evidence, a test may be misused because it lacks proper validation, as discussed further on.

Figure 11.4 shows the directions for example test items of the 16PF, a test of normal adult personality covering a broad range of traits. The 16PF has been properly validated for sales selection by many firms, such as Pfizer and Southwestern Life Insurance. But the score patterns which relate to success are different for each firm, a situation quite common with most psychological tests.

Use of Tests. To meet legal requirements imposed by Civil Rights legislation, and to reflect good managerial practice as well, tests must meet two requirements. First, the test must measure traits which are clearly relevant to job performance, and second, the test scores must be significantly correlated with some criterion of selling success. Tests meeting these requirements are considered valid for personnel selection. There are many types of validity, however, and a meaningful discussion of this topic is beyond the scope of this book.[19] Let us just summarize the issue by saying that a test might be valid in measuring a psychological construct such as personality, but not valid when its scores are related to job performance. Sales managers should not make the mistake of confusing the first type of validity with the second type. Even though a particular test produces excellent measures of personality traits such as aggressiveness or empathy, and even though the sales manager strongly believes that those traits are essential in sales success, the test is not a valid selection tool unless that manager can produce evidence (not opinion) that those traits are job-related and that test scores on those traits do correlate significantly with performance.

Sometimes adjustments in standard tests, such as those listed in Table 11.3, will make the tests more useful. Some personality tests measure 15 or more traits, but perhaps only two or three of these traits show any significant relationship to job performance. Management, with the help of a consulting psychologist, might then select from one or more tests only those items measuring the traits which differentiate good from poor performers. An industrial building materials firm, for example, used items from three different tests to construct a tailor-made test of their own.[20]

Many firms use a battery of tests rather than just one, and they use patterns of scores rather than individual scores as the basis for their selection decisions. It is probably true that success in most sales jobs is the result of many traits which can occur in various combinations. Applicants have strengths in some characteristics which can offset weaknesses in others, so that it is a total profile which might distinguish good from poor performers. A study in two firms confirmed this idea. When 22 separate characteristics were measured and combined into an overall profile, an improvement occurred from 56 percent to 80 percent of the salespeople who were correctly classified as falling in the high, middle, or low performer category.[21]

Problems in Psychological Testing. Numerous problems can occur in testing. Many available tests are designed to measure the same traits, but they produce vastly different results. One study of four different tests measuring achievement motivation concluded that "the various achievement motivation measures are in fact measuring dissimilar constructs."[22] The results from testing depend not only on what traits management wishes to measure, but also on what test is chosen to measure those traits.

Another problem concerns faking by those tested, who may give answers which they feel are appropriate to the job in question rather than answers which truly

FIGURE 11.4

Directions and Example Test Items for the 16PF, a Personality Test

Form C
1969 EDITION R

16 PF

WHAT TO DO: Inside this booklet are some questions to see what interests you have and how you feel about things. On most items there are no "right" or "wrong" answers because people have the right to their own views. All you have to do is answer what is true for *you*.

If a separate answer sheet has *not* been given to you, turn this booklet over and tear off the answer sheet on the back page. Write your name and other information asked for on the answer sheet.

First, read the four EXAMPLES below and mark your answers *on the answer sheet* where it says *EXAMPLES*. Fill in the box completely:

EXAMPLES:

1. I like to watch team games.
   a. yes, b. occasionally, c. no.

2. I prefer people who:
   a. are reserved,
   b. (are) in between,
   c. make friends quickly.

3. Money cannot bring happiness.
   a. yes (true),
   b. in between,
   c. no (false).

4. Adult is to child as cat is to:
   a. kitten, b. dog, c. baby.

In the last example there *is* a right answer—kitten. But there are very few such reasoning items.

Ask *now* if something isn't clear.

When the examiner tells you, start with number 1 and answer the questions. Keep these four things in mind:

1. Give only answers that are true *for you*. It is best to say what you really think.

2. Don't spend too much time thinking over each question. **Give the first, natural answer as it comes to you.** Of course, the questions are too short to give you *all* the information you might like, but give the best answer you can under the circumstances.

3. Answer *every* question one way or the other. Don't skip any.

4. You should mark the *a* or *c* answer *most* of the time. Mark the middle *b* answer *only* when you feel you have to, because neither *a* nor *c* seems to be right for you.

DO NOT TURN PAGE UNTIL TOLD TO DO SO

Copyright © 1954, 1956, 1969, 1978, by the Institute for Personality and Ability Testing, Inc., 1602-04 Coronado Drive, Champaign, Illinois. All rights reserved. Printed in U.S.A. Not to be translated or reproduced in whole or in part, stored in a retrieval system, or transmitted in any form or by any means, photocopying, mechanical, electronic, recording, or otherwise, without prior permission in writing from the publisher. Catalog No. SC 051

Reproduced by permission of the copyright owner.

represent their own feelings and desires. When asked if he would rather go to a party or stay home and read a book, the perceptive applicant may recognize that the first answer is more appropriate for selling and could respond that way regardless of his personal preference. Even when the test's purpose is not apparent, studies show that test takers can "improve" their scores if motivated to do so.[23] Some tests can detect these tendencies and report their extent, such as with the "motivational distortion" score in the 16PF, but even then it is seldom clear what the resulting scores mean.

Other problems in testing concern the possibility of built-in cultural bias and the chance that the test will screen out those who take highly creative or unusual approaches to situations. For all these reasons, proper use of psychological test data requires someone either inside or outside the firm who is properly trained and experienced in this technical area.

Physical Examinations. Near the end of the selection procedure, many firms require a physical examination, which is often viewed as a rejection device only in cases when applicants do not meet the minimum physical qualifications deemed necessary for the job. This examination is also useful to establish the applicant's physical condition at the time of hiring, especially as a check on any later claims for workmen's compensation because of occupationally induced disabilities.

Environmental Tests. An environmental test includes any situation which simulates the job environment.[24] Rapistan, a firm which sells materials handling equipment, assembles all applicants around a table, and each has five minutes to stand up and sell himself for the job. The others then have five minutes to question him and try to punch holes in his arguments. The company's management psychologist explained it this way:

> What I have tried to do is create a communication situation in which the pressure is similar to that of an actual sales call. I expose the man to his own competitors in the act of selling himself. When a man can define his own position, he can define a product to a customer.[25]

A popular method is the field tryout, in which an applicant is assigned to spend time with a salesperson on the job. The applicant can observe actual working conditions, and the salesperson can evaluate the applicant's reactions. Typically, the evaluation concerns ability to meet people, interest and attitudes concerning the work, and the kinds of questions asked and comments made. Studies show far less turnover in sales personnel who have been screened with field tryouts than in those hired without tryouts.[26]

Legal Perspective on Selection. The legal requirements we noted above for psychological tests apply equally to all selection tools. Whatever techniques are being used to assess applicants, they must be job-related and properly validated if their use produces an adverse impact on any racial, ethnic, or other group protected by Civil Rights legislation. Application blanks, interview guides, reference forms, and all other selection tools must be constructed to comply with federal and state laws regarding acceptable preemployment inquiries.

Selection Policy Decisions

Three major policy decisions must be made concerning the selection procedure. These are

1. Which tools should be used?
2. In what order should the tools be used?
3. Under what conditions should minimum qualifications be varied?

Choice of Tools. Each selection tool reflects different characteristics of an applicant, so one might argue that all tools should be used. But the value of a selection tool is in its ability to predict success using validated job-related qualifications. Thus, no selection tool should be used unless it adds to management's ability to predict job performance. Of course, management might try new tools occasionally to assess their validity, but data from these tools should not be used to influence selection decisions until their validity is established.

Cost is also a factor in this decision. Each selection tool raises the total cost of hiring, and management must compare the cost of each with its added helpfulness in the hiring decision. Some sales managers might feel that a particular psychological test costs more to administer and evaluate than it contributes in added information. Ideally, the cost of a tool should be compared with some measure of additional profit traceable to its use.

Order of Use. In most firms, the selection process follows a *successive hurdles* strategy in which some applicants are rejected after each successive tool.[27] For instance, a firm recruits 100 applicants, eliminates half of them from an evaluation of their application blanks, eliminates half of those remaining with an interview, and selects 10 of the final 25 according to their psychological test scores and references. The alternative is to administer every tool to all applicants before any selection decisions are made, and this is sometimes called a *total profile* strategy.[28]

Under the successive hurdles approach, less costly tools should be used early when there are more applicants rather than later after many have been screened out. But the tools used early must be sufficiently valid to produce good screening decisions. In fact, one study showed that the order of use of selection tools is far more related to each tool's helpfulness in making good performance predictions than to its cost.[29] One reason for extensive research with the weighted application blank is that it shows promise on both criteria. With the total profile approach, order of use is far less consequential.

Adjustments in Qualifications. The third decision concerns adjustments in selection qualifications. Once an appropriate set of qualifications has been determined, it is generally advisable not to alter it, but to seek additional suitable applicants. This may not always be possible, however, as in a tight labor market or when an unexpected opening must be filled quickly. Persons hired under these conditions who do not meet one or more qualifications must then be given extra guidance in training and supervision. Alternatively, such emergencies can give management an opportunity to test the validity of its minimum qualification levels.

HIRING SALES MANAGEMENT PERSONNEL

Sales management personnel are typically selected from the ranks of the sales force, so some persons selected for a sales job today may be targeted for a district or regional sales management position in the near future. A basic problem is that qualifications for selling success are not necessarily the same as qualifications for management success. It is unusual, in fact, for top sales performers to become top-flight sales managers. And yet, good performance in selling is often deemed essential for promotional consideration. On the other hand, deliberately hiring salespeople with management trainee qualifications can be frustrating to present managers, because by selecting such people, the manager is guaranteeing turnover in the sales staff as the inevitable promotions occur.[30] In addition, potentially top-notch sales producers might be bypassed if they do not have managerial qualifications or aspirations.

Some firms try to resolve this problem by hiring two types of salespeople—some seeking careers in selling and others desiring management positions with a short "apprenticeship" in selling. The same tools can be used in selecting both, but the tools must be validated separately based on criteria of success specific to each position. Perhaps as the selling job becomes more managerial in nature, qualifications for success in selling and in sales management may become more similar.

CONCLUSION

The process of obtaining sales personnel involves meeting three hiring needs: quantity of personnel needed with the qualifications indicating potential capability available at the times the jobs are open. Once these needs are specified, recruiting and selection procedures can be devised to secure and evaluate applicants for sales positions. Much of this chapter has been devoted to identifying qualifications of potential capability for a given job and to measuring the extent to which applicants possess these qualifications. But the accomplishment of the sales force depends on more than potential capability; this capability must be developed and directed. We turn next to training, which is a major factor in this process.

QUESTIONS FOR REVIEW AND DISCUSSION

1. Discuss three ways in which qualifications for a particular selling position can be determined. Is any one clearly better than the others?
2. To plan hiring needs for next year, a sales manager gathers the following information from company records:

SALESPERSON CATEGORY	ONE-YEAR SURVIVAL RATE	PRESENT NUMBER OF SALESPEOPLE	SALES VOLUME PER SALESPERSON
First-year salespeople	.75	20	$100,000
Second-year salespeople	.85	20	$130,000
Remaining salespeople	.90	10	$160,000

If projected sales for next year are $8 million, and sales volume per salesperson is assumed to remain the same in each category, how many new salespeople should be hired? What other information might be helpful in this decision?

3. How can a sales manager determine what is the best recruiting source? Does the recruiting source make any difference as long as a careful selection process is used?

4. What are the key legal factors influencing the hiring process? Do these help or hinder the sales manager in making effective hiring decisions?

5. A sales manager has hired ten salespeople a year for the past five years, and has been keeping records on the recruitment sources and selection tools employed. A summary of this information is as follows:

RECRUITING SOURCES	NUMBER OF RECRUITS OBTAINED	NUMBER OF RECRUITS HIRED	NUMBER SUCCESSFUL AFTER 1 YEAR
Employment agency	40	12	6
Advertising	100	8	4
Friends and associates	60	30	15

SELECTION TOOLS	NUMBER OF THOSE HIRED WHO SCORED:		NUMBER SUCCESSFUL AFTER ONE YEAR WHO SCORED:	
	"LOW"	"HIGH"		"LOW"
Personal interview	44	6	22	3
Psychological test	40	10	24	1
Scored application blank	35	15	20	5

a. Should the sales manager concentrate on any one or two recruitment sources? If so, which ones?

b. Should the sales manager concentrate on any one or two selection tools? If so, which ones?

c. When comparing the record of recruiting versus selection, can you conclude that the manager should rely more on one than on the other in helping predict success of applicants for the sales job? If so, which one?

6. It has been stated often that the personal interview is one of the least valid tools of selection. Yet in many firms, interviewing is the major method relied on to select sales personnel. Can you explain this apparent inconsistency?

7. A sales manager and a personnel manager are debating the value of a personality test in the selection process. The sales manager is skeptical of the test because its items do not relate directly to any aspects of the selling job. The personnel manager points out that face validity is not necessary to constitute a valid selection device. Evaluate these positions and discuss what might be done to resolve the debate.

8. Review Figure 11.1, which shows two alternative ways in which potential capability,

training, and motivation combine to affect a salesperson's accomplishment. Which way do you think is more correct? What difference does it make?

9. Devise a brief character reference form in which the respondent is asked to rate an applicant on a series of scales. Then discuss how this tool might be validated for use in the selection decision.

10. A chief sales executive follows a policy of always appointing field sales managers from the ranks of the sales force because "We have information on these people and do not have to go through the costly process of selection again." Do you think the policy is sound for the reason given?

NOTES

1. Turnover and advancement rates by industry are found in Derek A. Newton, *Sales Force Performance and Turnover* (Cambridge, Mass.: Marketing Science Institute, 1973), p. 54. Turnover within the first five years is analyzed in David A. Weeks and M. J. Stark, *Salesmen's Turnover in Early Employment,* Report No. 545 (New York: The Conference Board, Inc., 1972).

2. H. Jay Bullen, "How Industry Finds and Hires Salesmen," *Industrial Marketing,* March 1964, pp. 68–69.

3. James C. Cotham, III, "Selecting Salesmen: Approaches and Problems," *MSU Business Topics,* vol. 18 (Winter 1970), p. 70.

4. Arthur A. Witkin, "Differential Interest Patterns in Salesmen," *Journal of Applied Psychology,* vol. 40 (October 1956), p. 338.

5. Carl H. Rush, Jr., "A Factorial Study of Sales Criteria," *Personnel Psychology,* vol. 6 (Spring 1953), pp. 9–24.

6. Thomas R. Wotruba, "Predicting Success of Real Estate Sales Personnel," Working Paper in Marketing, San Diego State University, 1973.

7. "Manpower Dynamics," *Sales Management,* October 1, 1965, pp. 112–114.

8. Marvin A. Jolson, "A Comparison of Blind vs. Full-Disclosure Newspaper Ads for Sales Personnel," *Akron Business and Economic Review,* vol. 5 (Winter 1974), pp. 16–18.

9. Such evidence is reported in David L. Hurwood, "More Blacks and Women in Sales and Marketing?" *The Conference Board Record,* vol. 10 (February 1973), pp. 38–44; and Marvin A. Jolson, "Employment Barriers in Marketing," *Journal of Marketing,* vol. 38 (April 1974), pp. 67–69.

10. The views and experiences of one industrial saleswoman are discussed in "Women Factory Reps? . . . or How Tolerant are Distributors?" *Industrial Distribution,* January 1978, pp. 69–70. Other studies relating to this issue are the following: Leslie Kanuk, "Women in Industrial Selling," *Journal of Marketing,* vol. 42 (January 1978), pp. 87–91; Dan H. Robertson and D. W. Hackett, "Saleswomen: Perceptions, Problems and Prospects," *Journal of Marketing,* vol. 41 (July 1977), pp. 66–71; John E. Swan, et al., "Same Job—Different Views: Women and Men in Industrial Sales," *Journal of Marketing,* vol. 42 (January 1978), pp. 92–98; Paul Busch and Ronald F. Bush, "Women Contrasted to Men in the Industrial Salesforce: Job Satisfaction, Values, Role Clarity, Performance, and Propensity to Leave," *Journal of Marketing Research,* vol. 15 (August 1978), pp. 438–448; Danny N. Bellenger, et al., "Recruiting Black Salesmen," *Atlanta Economic Review,* vol. 27 (March–April 1977), pp. 28–31; and Thomas Reuschling, "Black and White in Personal Selling," *Akron Business and Economic Review,* vol. 4 (Fall 1973), pp. 9–13.

11. Personal correspondence.

12. A list of eighty-six personal history variables found to be predictive of success in various jobs is in George W. England, *Development and Use of Weighted Application Blanks* (Dubuque, Iowa: William C. Brown Company, 1961), pp. 13–15.

13. O. A. Ohmann, "A Report of Research on the Selection of Salesmen at the Tremco Manufacturing Company," *Journal of Applied Psychology,* vol. 25 (1941), p. 22.

14. The details of developing scoring systems are too lengthy to report further. Additional discussion and examples are found in England, pp. 13–27; Warren S. Blumenfeld, "Application Application,"

Atlanta Economic Review, vol. 23 (May–June 1973), pp. 8–13; Melany E. Baehr and Glenn B. Williams, "Prediction of Sales Success from Factorially Determined Dimensions of Personal Background Data," *Journal of Applied Psychology,* vol. 52 (April 1968), pp. 98–103.

15. For one study, see Marvin A. Jolson and Martin J. Gannon, "Wives—A Critical Element in Career Decisions," *Business Horizons,* vol. 15 (February 1972), pp. 83–88.

16. These findings are based primarily on continuing research programs in the life insurance industry as reported in Robert E. Carlson, et al., "Improvements in the Selection Interview," *Personnel Journal,* vol. 50 (April 1971), pp. 268–275, 317.

17. Carlson, p. 273.

18. Allan N. Nash and S. J. Carroll, Jr., "A Hard Look At the Reference Check," *Business Horizons,* vol. 13 (October 1970), pp. 43–49.

19. A good review of various types of validity and their relationships to employee selection tools is found in Gerald L. Bassford, "Job Testing—Alternative to Employment Quotas," *Business Horizons,* vol. 17 (February 1974), pp. 37–47.

20. Lawrence M. Lamont and W. J. Lundstrom, "Identifying Successful Industrial Salesmen by Personality and Personal Characteristics," *Journal of Marketing Research,* vol. 14 (November 1977), p. 520.

21. The technique used was multiple discriminant analysis. See William D. Perreault, Jr., et al., "Use of Multiple Discriminant Analysis to Improve the Salesman Selection Process," *Journal of Business,* vol. 50 (January 1977), pp. 50–62.

22. Thomas R. Wotruba and Karl F. Price, "Relationships Among Four Measures of Achievement Motivation," *Educational and Psychological Measurement,* vol. 35 (Winter 1975), p. 914.

23. James H. Morris, T. R. Wotruba, and R. B. Settle, "Influence of Respondent Sets on Two Objective Measures of Achievement Motivation," *Educational and Psychological Measurement,* vol. 37 (Winter 1977), pp. 1051–1055.

24. The term *environmental test* was suggested by William H. Reynolds, "The Fail-Safe Salesman," *Business Horizons,* vol. 9 (Summer 1966), p. 24.

25. "How Rapistan Ltda. Hired A Salesman," *Sales Management,* September 8, 1975, p. 69.

26. "Precontract Selection and Training: A Study in One Company," Research Report no. 1957–2 (Hartford, Conn.: Life Insurance Agency Management Association, 1957). For another example, see "The Welcome Mat," *Sales Management,* September 15, 1966, p. 45.

27. Thomas R. Wotruba, "An Analysis of the Salesmen Selection Process," *Southern Journal of Business,* vol. 5 (January 1970), p. 45.

28. For a discussion and example of this approach, see Robert J. Small and Larry J. Rosenberg, "Determining Job Performance in the Industrial Sales Force," *Industrial Marketing Management,* vol. 6, no. 2 (1977), pp. 99–102.

29. Wotruba, "An Analysis of the Salesmen Selection Process," p. 50.

30. Ed Roseman, "Hire Salesmen or Future Managers?" *Sales Management,* October 6, 1975, pp. 42–44.

12 TRAINING SALES PERSONNEL

Hiring highly qualified salespeople is much like finding a market with great potential. Both must be cultivated carefully before their possibilities become actualities. And because the firm's markets, products, and selling jobs all change over time, experienced sales personnel need continuing development as well.

A salesperson's ability is cultivated through training, the formal process of developing attitudes, knowledge, and skills which make an employee capable of effective performance. Capability alone does not guarantee good performance. The employee must also be motivated to use that capability in achieving company goals. Motivation is given major attention in the next two chapters.

NATURE AND PURPOSE OF SALES TRAINING

Training vs. Education. Traditionally, training involves the learning of particular skills for a specific job or task. In contrast, education includes learning widely applicable principles, concepts, and methods of analysis without immediate regard for specific utilization of this information. At the extreme, a well-trained person performs a task without having to stop and think about what to do. Education, on the other hand, prepares a person to stop and think effectively about what action is proper in a variety of circumstances. As the selling job becomes more managerial and consultative, and changes in other ways as discussed in Chapters 8 and 9, a sales "training" program will require increasingly larger doses of "education." A major study of sales training noted that

> future training programs for sales representatives will need to be carefully balanced between the objectives of augmenting technical skills and of instilling mature business judgment. In the future, executives say, the exercise of traditional forms of salesmanship will become inadequate. The need instead will be for greater marketing knowledge, rather than just selling ability.[1]

What Training Can and Cannot Do. Even the most effective training program cannot cure all ills in a sales organization. Training is especially suited to provide knowledge and to develop and sharpen specific skills. To a lesser extent, training may be able to boost a salesperson's self-confidence and improve attitudes toward the company, its management, the product line, and countless other factors affecting the selling job. Training (of an "educational" nature) is often effective in helping sales personnel understand many of the whys concerning the selling process, customer-orientation, company policies, and buyer behavior.

But training is not used well when it is compensating for management inadequacies elsewhere. Performance of poorly-qualified salespeople can seldom be rescued with training efforts (recall Figure 11.1). Training will not substitute for a poor compensation plan, for inadequate supervision, or for a poor product line, unreasonable prices, or consistently late shipments. Finally, training cannot gear up a sales force to reach impossible quotas or forecasts. In fact, good training may alert sales personnel to these problems sooner, with the possible result that better potential performers might leave for a different company.[2]

Incidence and Cost of Sales Training. All sales personnel receive training, even if management does not conduct formal programs. Learning occurs informally and sometimes even unknowingly by trial-and-error and by observation. Trial-and-error can occur, for example, when a salesperson adjusts some part of his or her sales presentation in response to failures on previous calls. But trial-and-error adjustments are often made in an almost random manner and may not provide improvement in later calls, especially if the real problem is not correctly diagnosed.

Most companies have training programs for newly hired sales personnel. And the vast majority of firms also have advanced training for experienced sales personnel, though it is much less formalized and extensive than the training given to newcomers to the sales force.[3] But companies differ in the amount of time and dollars devoted to sales training. Table 12.1 shows that industrial products com-

TABLE 12.1
Training Costs and Length of Training Period for Newly Hired Sales Personnel

	Industrial Products Companies	Consumer Products Companies	Service Companies[b]
Average training cost per salesperson, including salary:[a]	$15,479	$11,338	$8,828
Length of training period:			
0 to 6 weeks:	16%	25%	36%
Over 6 weeks to 3 months:	9	16	28
Over 3 months to 6 months:	42	42	27
Over 6 months to 12 months:	33	9	9
Over 12 months:	0	8	0
	100%	100%	100%
Median training period (weeks):	24	16	8

[a] In addition to salary, covers such items as instructional materials prepared, purchased, and rented for training programs; transportation and living expenses incurred during training course; instructional staff; outside seminars and courses; and management time spent with salesmen when it is a part of the training budget.

[b] Includes insurance, financial, utilities, transportation, retail stores, etc.

Source: *Survey of Selling Costs, Sales & Marketing Management*, February 26, 1979, p. 66. Reprinted by permission from *Sales & Marketing Management* magazine. Copyright 1979.

panies spend over $15,000 to train one new salesperson and take an average of 24 weeks to do it. Other types of firms average less in time and money, although the range in training period length varies from less than six weeks to a year or more in all three categories.

Training also reduces sales costs. Trained employees need less time to carry out assignments and achieve job proficiency sooner. Many day-to-day demands on management are lessened as sales personnel become more self-sufficient. Effective training can also reduce turnover and its related costs.

The applicability of training extends beyond sales personnel, and takes in sales managers, trainers, distributors and other customers, and even nonsales employees in the firm. Training is one means of providing coordination among all these groups which are important to sales success. Although we concentrate on training salespeople in this chapter, some closing comments are made regarding training of other groups.

DEVELOPING A SALES TRAINING PROGRAM

Training needs differ from one sales organization to the next, but the process of developing a training program is similar for any firm. Figure 12.1 depicts the steps in this process. First, objectives are formulated which determine the content of the program. Following this, various administrative decisions must be made. Finally, the trainees and the program itself must be evaluated.

OBJECTIVES OF TRAINING

From management's standpoint, training objectives serve to coordinate training with other sales activities and goals. If one such goal is to increase market penetration, the trainees must learn how to carry out this aim in their upcoming territory assign-

FIGURE 12.1

Steps in Developing a Sales Training Program

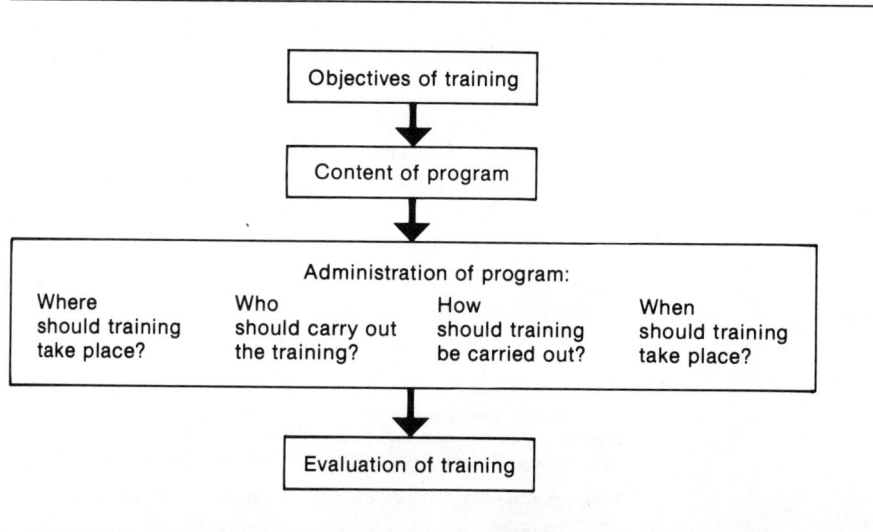

ments. As an important corollary, objectives provide benchmarks for evaluating training results. Thus, does market penetration really increase as the result of this training?

From the trainer's standpoint, objectives stipulate what is to be accomplished; hence they serve as a guide to his duties. Since the trainer must be trained, these objectives aid in organizing learning and provide the means for evaluating his or her work when the training program is completed. Objectives help the trainer focus on the purposes of training rather than only on the process.

The most important party in this situation is the trainee, and therefore objectives must be keyed to trainee expectations and needs. The vice-president of a tobacco company noted that his firm's training procedures have been modified "to reflect a humanistic approach—one that creates an atmosphere and environment where each person can satisfy personal goals, while advancing the company toward our organizational goals."[4] One way to do this is to recast all objectives of training to fit the trainee viewpoint. For instance, nine benefits of training to the salesperson have been listed as follows:[5]

1. Greater job satisfaction
2. Greater job security
3. More promotional opportunities
4. Increased earnings
5. More economic independence
6. Feeling of satisfaction and importance
7. Approval of others
8. Sense of mastery and self-respect
9. Enhanced social standing in the community

By showing how increased market penetration (or whatever management objectives are desired) will provide these benefits, the sales trainer should generate great enthusiasm for learning.

Determining Objectives. Sales training objectives are formulated by carrying out a job analysis and a trainee ability analysis, and then comparing the results to determine gaps which training must fill.

Job Analysis. Job analysis is the identification of skills, knowledge, and attitudes necessary to perform the job successfully. It is based on a careful and systematic collection of information about the job from a variety of sources. One source is company literature, which includes the job description, procedures manuals, and reports circulated among salespeople or issued by salespeople. A second information source involves observation or questioning of present jobholders concerning activities or problems encountered in their work.[6] In fact, an investigator might actually perform the job for a few days to become more intimately acquainted with its demands.

Because sales jobs change as competitors' actions and buying behavior change, job analysis is a continuing need. Some firms will periodically assess the major problems encountered by their sales force in hopes of detecting what changes are occurring that might need attention in the training program. In one study, over 800 salespeople were questioned concerning problems they had with purchasing personnel in customer firms.[7] The salespeople rated buyers as good, fair, or poor on a variety of characteristics as shown in Table 12.2. These salespeople were having problems in getting adequate time for their calls, since the vast majority rated buyers as only fair on this factor. Perhaps an even greater problem occurred with distractions during sales presentations. Sales training attention should now be devoted to these problems—how to arrange calls to get adequate time and what tactics to use to ensure fewer distractions.

Ability Analysis. The extent to which trainees possess the skills, knowledge, and attitudes necessary for their jobs is uncovered by ability analysis. When the abilities possessed are compared with the demands of the job, the result is a pinpointing of training needs. Suppose that through job analysis a sales position is found to demand specific technical knowledge as well as selling skills. Persons hired with technical backgrounds but no selling experience will have different training needs from those with selling experience with nontechnical products.

Procedures used in ability analysis are of two main types. The first is diagnostic tests or evaluations designed to measure knowledge of selling, industry conditions and practices, customer behavior, or any other job-related aspects. Role-playing and business games may also provide indications of training needs, although these devices are more commonly used in the training program itself.

A good example of diagnostic test use is found in the life insurance industry.[8] Agents scoring higher on a product knowledge test were found to have lost a smaller

TABLE 12.2
Salespeople's Evaluations of Buyers

	PERCENT OF SALESPEOPLE WHO RATED BUYERS AS		
	Good	Fair	Poor
Promptness in notifying salespeople when they cannot see them	67%	29%	3%
Giving salespeople adequate time to fulfill purpose of call	19%	77%	4%
Exerting care to reduce distractions while salespeople are making presentation	7%	62%	30%
Having sufficient product knowledge to do a competent job of buying	32%	48%	20%
Assisting salespeople to contact appropriate personnel when buyer lacks sufficient product knowledge	23%	57%	19%
Extent to which buyers are open-minded to new ideas	17%	66%	15%
Reasonableness of buyer's demands when problems of adjustments arise	36%	56%	6%
Dependability in following through on promises	34%	54%	10%
Following ethical purchasing practices	25%	60%	13%
Understanding problems faced by salespeople in performing their sales job	35%	50%	13%
Overall treatment of salespeople	83%	17%	0%

Source: Adapted from Victor P. Gravereau and Leonard J. Konopa, "Attitudes of Salesmen Toward Industrial Buyers and Purchasing Policies," *Journal of Purchasing*, vol. 6 (August 1970), pp. 32–35.

portion of their policies through lapsation. Since the scores related to job performance, this test seemed to be a valid indicator of training needs regarding product knowledge. Whenever tests are used diagnostically, their validity should be established as discussed in the previous chapter.

The second type of procedure relates to a follow-up training program for veteran sales personnel. In this case, the analysis is based on evaluation of past performance in the job itself. One problem with performance evaluation is that weaknesses may stem from causes other than training needs. A poorly devised compensation plan might be encouraging misdirected effort, or unrealistic forecasts may make quota attainment look off-target. But simulations of real selling situations for experienced sales personnel have been used diagnostically by a pharmaceutical firm, for instance.[9]

General versus Specific Objectives. To be most useful, training objectives must be stated as specifically as possible. It does little good to state a general objective of increasing sales or profits. Rather, specific skill, knowledge, and attitude needs must be stipulated, since they can be evaluated much more precisely. If a person's sales do not reach quota, management cannot be sure this indicates a training need or a problem in some other phase of sales management. But if a person lacks some specifically designated product knowledge or selling skill, remedies clearly belong in training.

CONTENT OF THE PROGRAM

Once trainees' needs are determined, the contents of the training program can be assembled. While each firm's program will differ, a composite or "typical" training program will contain three major categories of topics: attitudes, knowledge, and skills.

Attitudes

Positive attitudes in trainees are necessary for maximum training payoff. The sales trainer for Goodyear Tire and Rubber Company noted that many salespeople tend to resist training if they are not convinced of its value to them or are not "in the mood" to accept it.[10] Those who hold the chemistry view of success that good salespeople are born, not made, will also believe that training can do little to overcome lack of inherent talent. But sales abilities have been significantly developed in many company training programs.

Desirability of training is often enhanced with case histories showing how training has benefited other salespeople. Commitment to self-development is essential. The difference between passive acceptance of what is taught and active involvement in learning is the difference between minimum and maximum returns from a training program.

A positive attitude toward selling must be established and reinforced. Trainees must also become infused with enthusiasm about the company, its products, and its customer orientation. Trainees must have confidence in their ability to sell and a desire to succeed. The sales vice-president of Consolidated Cigar puts confidence and motivation at the top of the list of factors essential to selling success.[11] Without such confidence, all the job difficulties and challenges brought out in training sessions will be extremely discouraging.

Knowledge

Professional selling is based on a solid foundation of knowledge. Table 12.3 summarizes the extent of time devoted to these topics in various types of firms.

Company Orientation. The salesperson represents his or her company to customers and prospects, so each sales force member must be well acquainted with company history, organization, and achievements. In particular, each field representative should know company and marketing goals and general long-term objectives. Such understanding will make sales personnel better able to discuss company policies and practices intelligently and to sift out relevant information from the field to pass back to higher management.

Company policies regarding sales and customer relationships are especially important. Each salesperson will face many questions involving such policy areas as pricing, discount structure, and other terms of sale. When customers request special treatment such as product modifications or package changes, the salesperson must be prepared to deal with them.

Market and Industry Orientation. Properly done, the market orientation in a training program can serve two major purposes. One is factual and the other is attitudinal. Facts concerning the firm's markets—their size, buying behavior, needs, technical processes, and so on—must be transmitted to prepare trainees to talk intelligently with customers. But an attitude of customer orientation is a more subtle and difficult training achievement, and requires a far more in-depth understanding and appreciation of customer needs and goals. To meet this purpose, trainees must learn how to diagnose market changes and how to acquire customer information useful in tailoring their company's offerings most beneficially to each buyer.

Industry orientation can range from an historical view of industry development to a present-day (and even projected future) analysis of major competitors, their

TABLE 12.3
Distribution of Training Time for Newly-Hired Sales Personnel

Training Subject	PERCENT OF TOTAL TRAINING DEVOTED TO THIS SUBJECT BY THE AVERAGE COMPANY:			
	Industrial Goods Firms	Consumer Goods Firms	Services Firms	All Companies
Company Orientation	13%	11%	15%	13%
Market and Industry Orientation	17%	20%	13%	17%
Product Knowledge	47%	36%	39%	42%
Selling Techniques	21%	27%	30%	24%
Other	2%	6%	3%	4%
	100%	100%	100%	100%

Source: David S. Hopkins, *Training The Sales Force: A Progress Report,* Report no. 737 (New York: The Conference Board, Inc., 1978), as reported in *Sales & Marketing Management,* March 1978, p. 15.

market shares, and the strengths and shortcomings of their products and service offerings. Attitudes can again be important here. The neophyte salesperson must learn how to respond in situations where his or her products are being compared with those of competitors, especially when the comparisons seem to get overly unfavorable.

Product Knowledge. Product knowledge is of obvious importance to salespeople. In fact, this topic receives the greatest emphasis in training programs as shown in Table 12.3. But trainees should not be taught to amass this information just for its own sake. Rather, the trainee must learn how to use it most effectively in sales situations. As noted in Chapter 8, product features must be translated into customer benefits in terms the buyer can clearly understand. The ultimate purpose of product knowledge is to provide buyers with information pertinent to their needs.

As products become more complicated, and as selling becomes more problem solving or consultative in nature, the product knowledge required is far less than routine. In some firms, sales personnel must customize product specifications to fit a particular customer's circumstances, and then calculate the specific benefits which will occur as a result. Computers aid in this task. For instance, field sales managers in such firms as IBM, Honeywell, and GE can use remote terminals to request information and complex calculations from their home office computer and data base.[12] In these cases, product knowledge involves learning about such on-line information systems.

Selling Techniques. Selling techniques are covered in both the knowledge and skills portions of a training program. Trainees must understand the selling process before they can become truly skilled at selling. Chapters 8 and 9 have already discussed selling in a step-by-step approach as well as some new directions and contemporary strategies, so we will not repeat that discussion here. Each firm selects the approach and techniques which best fit its products and markets, and focuses training attention on these. After proper knowledge foundation, the trainee should be able more quickly to develop selling skills and apply them properly to specific sales situations.

Other Knowledge Topics. Additional topics which are often a part of initial training programs include nonselling activities and time management. Nonselling activities are required of most sales personnel, including keeping records and writing reports to management on personal performance as well as information about customers, prospects, and competitors. Sometimes these activities are tied to a broader marketing information system requiring that the salesperson understand how to use computer equipment and interpret computer output. Some sales jobs call for forecasting territory sales on a regular basis, requiring training in practical forecasting techniques.

Time management is gaining greater attention in sales training programs as management looks for ways to increase sales force productivity. Many firms have found that poor performing salespeople are also those who do little or no planning. In the Chemical Division of McKesson & Robbins, for instance, a time study was done comparing the best performing salespeople with the average and poor performers. Major differences were found and incorporated into the training program, which resulted in significant performance improvement throughout the entire sales force.[13]

Skills

Skills training is primarily putting knowledge into action. Emphasis is on the selling process, and key elements include preparation for a specific sales call and presentation skills. Figure 12.2 depicts these elements as learned by Hooker Chemical sales personnel. Prior to a call, the salesperson reviews the customer sales plan (C.S.P.) previously developed for that specific account. The C.S.P. includes a detailed customer profile, a sales volume goal, a strategy selected from a wide range of strategy options learned in training, a formally written program to be carried out with that customer, and the detailed action of what is to be done, who is to do it, and when and where each action will be accomplished.[14] Then the presentation is planned to follow the sales call formula which is structured into four parts:

1. Reveal customer needs in relationship to Hooker Chemical products and services.
2. Reduce perceptual differences between salesperson and customer by understanding the customer's perception of the situation and proposal.
3. Satisfy customer needs by demonstrating the competitive benefits from Hooker Chemical's products and services in a way that is a pleasant experience for the customer.
4. Ensure satisfaction with the buying decision by follow-up, service, or any other actions necessary.

A major thrust in many sales training programs today is a strong dose of behavioral science skills. Some trainers refer to it as "sensitivity to buyers"—not sensitivity to their purchase needs but to their personal or individual needs. Control Data's training on this topic has two stated objectives: (1) to develop the salesperson's sensitivity to his own and the individual prospect's personality and show how those personalities are likely to interrelate, and (2) to teach which techniques of opening, diagnosing, presenting, overcoming objections, and closing are best suited to particular personalities.[15] Three basic personality types are the focus of this training: the dominant, the detached, and the dependent. Carborundum Company focuses its behavioral science emphasis on the concepts of readiness, empathy, and source credibility.[16] Readiness occurs when the prospect is interested in and willing to discuss the salesperson's proposal. Prospect readiness is aided by the salesperson showing solid preparation and familiarity with the prospect's situation. Empathy involves getting an understanding of the situation through the prospect's eyes so that subsequent conversation can be couched in that frame of reference. Source credibility refers to the confidence and trust placed in the salesperson's words by the prospect.[17] Learning to apply these concepts is a major part of skill-building in Carborundum sales training.

Standardized versus Individualized Training. Training programs can vary from completely standardized to highly individualized content. The standardized approach results in a common program for all trainees. In contrast, individualized programs provide training content tailored specifically to the needs of each trainee. Tailor-made programs require greater administrative time and cost, but offer some offsetting advantages. New salespeople can be hired with diverse strengths, knowing that their individual training needs will be met. With a standardized program, time of some trainees will be wasted by sitting through unneeded sessions, and this could produce attitude and motivation problems as well. The relationship between

FIGURE 12.2

Sales Call Preparation and Presentation in Hooker Chemical Corporation

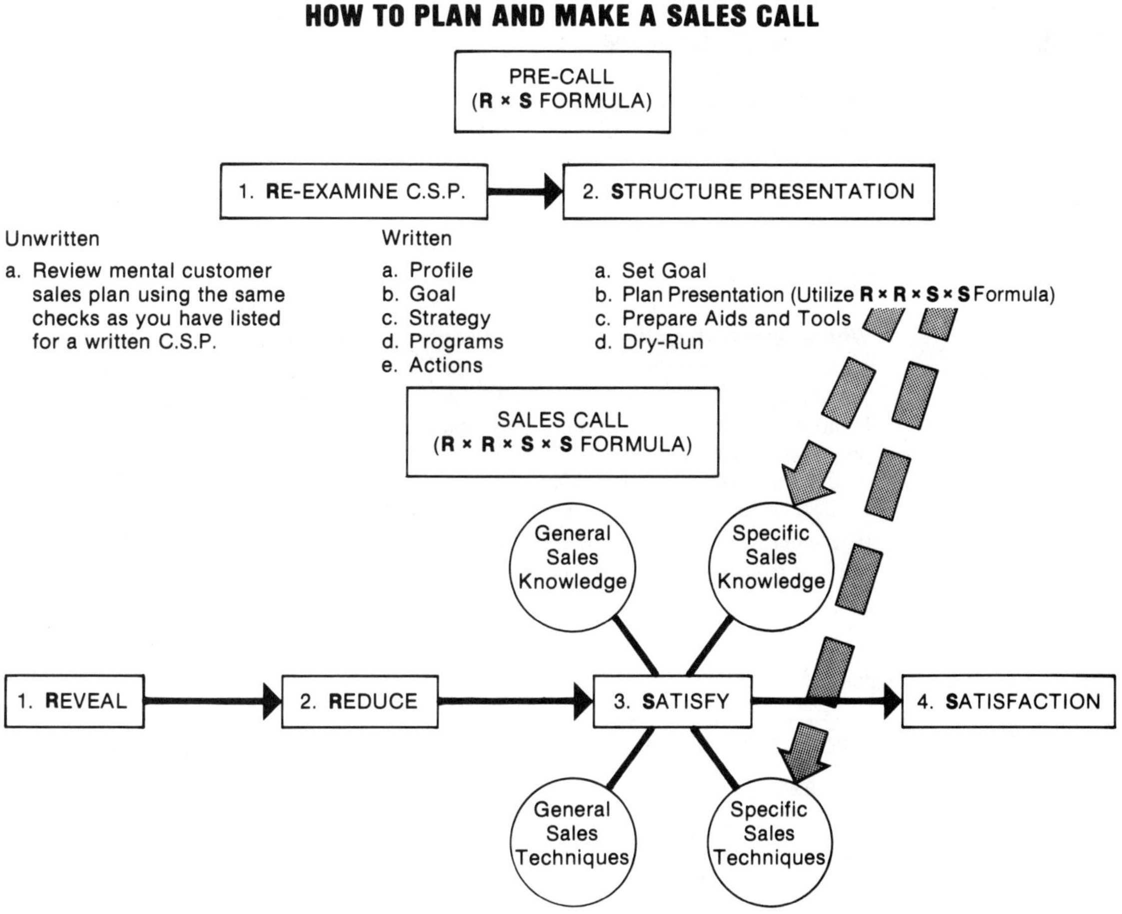

HOW TO PLAN AND MAKE A SALES CALL

PRE-CALL
(R × S FORMULA)

1. **RE-EXAMINE C.S.P.** → 2. **STRUCTURE PRESENTATION**

Unwritten

a. Review mental customer sales plan using the same checks as you have listed for a written C.S.P.

Written

a. Profile
b. Goal
c. Strategy
d. Programs
e. Actions

a. Set Goal
b. Plan Presentation (Utilize R × R × S × S Formula)
c. Prepare Aids and Tools
d. Dry-Run

SALES CALL
(R × R × S × S FORMULA)

General Sales Knowledge / Specific Sales Knowledge

1. **REVEAL** → 2. **REDUCE** → 3. **SATISFY** → 4. **SATISFACTION**

General Sales Techniques / Specific Sales Techniques

Source: Robert F. Vizza and Thomas E. Chambers, *Time and Territorial Management for the Salesmen* (New York: Sales Executives Club of New York, Inc., 122 E. 42nd St., Suite 1014, New York, N.Y. 10017, 1971), p. 73.

training and selection is important to note here. A standardized training program might influence management to recruit new employees with the same training needs. The result is hiring to fit the training program rather than to fit the ultimate job of selling.

Firms with sales personnel of various specializations find that standardized training is not totally effective in meeting the needs of each group. Product specialists need different knowledge and skills than do customer type specialists. NCR, for instance, has what its management calls a "smorgasbord" of 49 different training packages for sales personnel, depending on each trainee's needs and specialization.[18] In addition, different levels of sales positions require correspondingly different training. Del Monte, for instance, has four position levels, each requiring a separate package of training subjects.[19] And even within each of these levels, the trainer may omit one or more training units depending on the trainee's prior experience or background.

ADMINISTRATION OF THE PROGRAM

The administration of a sales training program refers to the questions of who shall carry out the training, and where, how, and when it should be carried out. The who and where aspects relate specifically to organizational decisions, while the how and when aspects are more procedural. All of these questions are at least partially interrelated. For example, the location of training may depend on or influence who the trainer is to be. For ease of discussion, however, these four topics are treated separately.

Where Should Training Take Place? Sales training can occur at one location, or parts can be presented in different places. Location possibilities and their relative popularity are shown in Table 12.4, categorized by centralized and decentralized locations. Many firms use more than one location in order to take advantage of the benefits from each.

Centralized training provides greater consistency in program content, but its cost is high because trainees must be reimbursed for travel and lodging. New sales personnel in all divisions of the Continental Group are brought to the home office in New York for their basic sales training program which is given two or three times

TABLE 12.4

Locations Used for Sales Training

Location	PERCENT OF COMPANIES CONDUCTING TRAINING AT THIS LOCATION			MEDIAN LENGTH OF TRAINING TIME AT THIS LOCATION		
	Industrial Products	Consumer Products	Services	Industrial Products	Consumer Products	Services
Centralized:						
Home Office	91%	69%	100%	2 weeks	3 weeks	2 weeks
Plant Locations	46	0	0	1 week		
Central Facility	37	8	15	3 weeks	2 weeks	4 weeks
Decentralized:						
Field Office	64	77	72	16 weeks	12 weeks	3 weeks
Regional Office	37	23	57	7 weeks	5 weeks	1.5 weeks
Other:						
Noncompany site such as Hotel, Restaurant, Club	18	0	29	1 week		1 week

Source: Sales & Marketing Management Survey, adapted from *Sales & Marketing Management*, February 26, 1979, p. 66. Reprinted by permission from *Sales & Marketing Management* magazine. Copyright 1979.

a year.[20] Advanced training follows at a decentralized location for each division to concentrate on the specifics of each division's products and markets.

When all trainees are brought together, top management and other company specialists can conveniently participate and thus boost attitude and knowledge training greatly. Decentralized locations, on the other hand, involve learning closer to the actual locale of the job and in contact with the field managers who will be the trainees' eventual supervisors. Knowledge of customer buying behavior and competitive conditions, as well as the development of selling skills, might be most effectively taught at a decentralized location by a trainer in tune with local or regional conditions.

A growing number of special training facilities indicates the importance placed on this activity by many firms. Armour-Dial, for instance, has a training center complete with an auditorium, seminar room, research library, videotaping system, television cameras and monitors, electronic and audiovisual equipment, closed-circuit television capabilities, and a simulated supermarket.[21] Other well-equipped centers are operated by Eastman Kodak, Univac, Armstrong, General Motors, and American Republic Insurance, to name but a few. In addition to company operated facilities, there are training centers available for use by any company. Control Data operates 50 learning centers in major cities which are used by such firms as Abbott Laboratories and Aetna Insurance. Desk-top computer terminals allow trainees to obtain answers to specific questions, experiment with alternative solutions to case studies, and engage in other dialogues with the computer.[22] In this way, some of the advantages of centralized control can be maintained via the computer programs prepared for this training while gaining the flexibility and convenience of decentralized locations.

Who Should Train? The question of who should train really requires two separate answers: who should prepare the training program and who should present it? In many companies, the sales manager does both. But the role of the sales training specialist is expanding. For instance, a survey of large firms showed that half had training specialists responsible for administering the sales training program.[23] Many of these are active members of the National Society of Sales Training Executives, a professional organization dedicated to the betterment of sales training. Smaller firms can use outside consultants or prepackaged sales training courses in lieu of a full-time trainer.[24]

Specialists or outside consultants can prepare programs and then either they or company sales managers can administer them. For example, Heinz has sales trainers for each of its six regional sales managers who report to a manager of manpower development but work directly with each region's sales force.[25] On the other hand, Honeywell hired an outside consultant to develop training materials, which were then taught by Honeywell's branch sales managers.[26] Some pharmaceutical firms, including Beecham, Roche, and Schering, contract for the services of a specialized consulting agency which develops customized training in pharmaceutical sales. The consultant's researchers first determine the knowledge level of the sales force and then tailor a self-study program with cassettes, reference manuals, and resource books.[27]

There is good reason to involve sales managers in training, particularly at the branch or district level. They usually have experience which provides relevance and believability in trainees' eyes. These managers will be the trainees' supervisors as well, and supervision requires continual training on the job which must blend with any formal training received. The main problems of using field managers are their lack of time to devote to training and their weakness in teaching skills. Conversely, specialists and consultants are typically effective instructors but often lack the specific experience in a particular firm's selling situation.

How Should Training Be Carried Out? Many methods and techniques are used in sales training. The usefulness of each depends on the objectives of training and the effectiveness of the learning which that technique can produce. An objective of building positive attitudes toward selling may be achieved best with techniques that could not work well in building selling skills. Table 12.5 shows how training directors in large American companies ranked various training methods in achieving major training objectives. It shows that no one technique is best for all objectives.

Lecture is one of the most widely-used training methods because of its economy. Large numbers of trainees can be provided information at one time, although the effectiveness of this method is considered relatively low. At best, lectures are suitable for presenting clear, factual knowledge basic to subsequent training. The lecture method is often supplemented with demonstrations, skits, films, or other visual aids to increase trainees' interest and involvement.

Conference and discussion methods involve two-way communication among participants, and are considered more effective than lectures for most training purposes. A basic feature of discussion is interchange of ideas among participants. As a result of their direct involvement in this process, trainees are more likely to accept the results. When guided by a skilled discussion leader, this method will aid trainees in developing insight and analytical abilities as well as positive attitudes

TABLE 12.5

How Training Directors Rank Training Methods for Achieving Various Objectives

Training Techniques	RANK OF TECHNIQUES' EFFECTIVENESS IN MEETING THESE OBJECTIVES					
	Knowledge Acquisition	Changing Attitudes	Problem Solving Skills	Interpersonal Skills	Participant Acceptance	Knowledge Retention
Case Study	2	4	1	4	2	2
Conference or Discussion Method	3	3	4	3	1	5
Lecture (with questions)	9	8	9	8	8	8
Business Games	6	5	2	5	3	6
Movie Films	4	6	7	6	5	7
Programmed Instruction	1	7	6	7	7	1
Role Playing	7	2	3	2	4	4
Sensitivity Training	8	1	5	1	6	3
Television Lecture	5	9	8	9	9	9

Source: Adapted from Stephen J. Carroll, et al., "The Relative Effectiveness of Training Methods—Expert Opinion and Research," *Personnel Psychology*, vol. 25 (1972), p. 499.

toward learning and their job. Some specific types of conference and discussion methods are the following four: case studies, role playing, business games, and sensitivity training.

Case studies produce best results when they are true situations or problems typical of those trainees may experience on the job. If the situation is fictional, some trainees may dismiss it as being irrelevant and unrealistic. Case studies should be analyzed using underlying principles which the trainee discovers or has previously learned. Reaching an agreed-upon solution is often not as important as a stimulating discussion which helps trainees identify major principles and how they can be applied to selling problems and decisions.

Role playing is a situation where one trainee assumes the salesperson role and another trainee or the instructor takes on the role of a prospect. The trainee-seller then tries his skill by earnestly attempting to go through all selling process steps successfully. A major aim of this method is getting the trainee personally and emotionally involved in the face-to-face selling experience. Armour-Dial uses triad role-playing, for example, in which two of the three persons in the triad take the position of seller and buyer while the third observes, taking notes and offering comments at the end. The three persons then change roles and repeat the process two more times.[28]

Role-playing sessions are often videotaped for later review and critique. Those participating in videotape sessions may become very conscious of the camera, reacting with anxiety or in other atypical ways. Used naively, videotaping and replaying can become very uncomfortable and even destructive to some trainees. Sales trainers using this approach must be well versed in ways of avoiding such problems.[29]

Business games are simulated business situations in which a set of decisions must be made at regular intervals. After each decision the business situation is likely to change. Many games are oversimplified because the number of decisions called for is smaller than would occur in an actual situation. But the advantage of a game is in studying the effects of decisions over time and under uncertain conditions. Decisions normally made once a week or so can be undertaken once an hour or even more often in a game.

Games specifically for sales training are available from a variety of sources. An example is "Sales Strategy," which involves decisions concerning time allocation among selling, planning, prospecting, training, and record keeping.[30] Some games are available in periodicals, such as the "Time and Territory Productivity Game" published by *Sales & Marketing Management*.[31] Most games do not require computer processing and are easily adaptable to various size groups.

Sensitivity training is concerned with increasing the awareness of emotional states and reactions in oneself and in others. A prospect's emotional state may signal the need for different selling if the signal is properly read, even though verbal signals do not support that switch. The salesperson must likewise learn about his or her own emotional patterns and their effect on interpersonal negotiation. Specific techniques used are t-groups and role-playing, with the latter being most popular in sensitivity training for sales personnel.[32] We have already noted how Control Data and Carborundum stress behavioral concepts in their training programs, primarily for the purpose of dealing more effectively with the human or psychological dimension of the sales transaction.

Programmed instruction is the systematic presentation of material to be learned in small doses. Each unit is followed by questions requiring a response from the trainee, and the responses can be checked immediately. When an answer is incorrect, the trainee is told why and referred to that part of the unit where the correct information was presented. Some advanced forms of programmed instruction include branching, whereby a trainee is directed along alternative paths depending on the answers given to key questions.

This method is especially suitable for gaining knowledge and can be adapted to any size sales force and any training schedule. A small firm hiring only a few salespeople and at scattered times throughout the year can build training programs in this format and use them when and where needed. Many large firms also use programmed instruction because it allows each trainee to learn at his or her own pace as well as place—in the territory, at the district office, or even at home. Some types of programmed packages are computerized and require facilities such as Control Data's learning centers. But many are in textbook or looseleaf form and can be studied anywhere, much like a correspondence course.

Audio-visual techniques abound in sales training, and we have already noted the use of videotape recorders with role playing. But videotape is also used to transmit training messages to a firm's branch and regional offices all over the country. American Standard estimated that this approach cut training costs and executive travel significantly when compared with a centralized gathering of all sales personnel. NCR has also made a major commitment to video techniques, equipping its 230 sales offices with videotape equipment and establishing a television production staff of ten at its headquarters.[33]

Other audio-visual techniques include films, slide presentations, and audio tape cassettes. Admiral hired a training specialist to create a series of 10-to-15 minute tape cassettes which are played by sales personnel during their otherwise unproductive time, like driving. At regular intervals, sales personnel receive new tapes focusing on steps in the selling process, product information, and even simulated selling situations. Some tapes are also designed for Admiral's sales force to use in training their retail dealers.[34]

On-the-job training, though not covered in Table 12.5, is a major training method in many sales organizations. In fact, numerous trainers argue that it is the best method of all, particularly for skills training. The training director for Master Builders put it this way:

> On-the-job training is the most effective means of training sales personnel because it brings the training function to its ultimate destination. Because it takes place on real sales calls, with real customers, involving real selling situations, it does not suffer from the artificiality inherent in lecture training or some other very good methods, such as role playing and simulated sales calls using the videotape medium. On-the-job training involves *showing* rather than *telling* the salesperson how to improve. Therefore, there is no question as to its credibility.[35]

This method is not to be interpreted as simply plunging the trainee into the job in a "sink-or-swim" manner. It must be carefully planned so that the salesperson is prepared before the call and aided in an organized manner after the call. A curbstone conference, the common term for after-call coaching, is usually the focal point of on-the-job training. The trainer discusses and analyzes the trainee's performance after each call which they make jointly. On subsequent calls the trainee can try to incorporate the trainer's suggestions and again get immediate post-call feedback.

Other types of training can also be mentioned. Trade schools and colleges offer courses in many business subjects including salesmanship, and some firms reimburse employees for tuition costs if the courses are successfully completed. Correspondence courses are likewise available. Finally, sales manuals are provided by many firms as a major source of information. A manual's contents usually includes a job description and sections on the company, its products, the selling process, and administrative procedures such as keeping records and filing forms.

Multimedia is the term which best describes most training programs, since reliance on one method alone is not typical. Del Monte describes its multimedia program as containing "movies, filmstrips, slides, lectures, tapes, and programmed instruction. The particular medium used for each unit has been selected as the most effective aid for the subject."[36] A well-known training program devised by Xerox Learning Systems comprises three major techniques: paper-and-pencil programmed instruction, programmed tapes, and role-playing.[37] Perhaps the major reason for multimedia use is that attitudes, knowledge, and skills cannot all be taught equally effectively using any single approach.

When Should Training Take Place? For newly hired sales personnel, training can be sequenced in two different ways. One involves completing knowledge and skills training prior to any field assignment. The other involves some field selling experience prior to formal training in hopes that training will then have more meaning. A common approach is to compromise, with part of the formal training deferred until after some on-the-job experience. The effect of this approach was noted as follows:

> Following their initiation into the problems and peculiarities of actually trying to sell their firm's products or services, they come into the classroom training period, as one manager puts it, "loaded with questions based on personal experience in the field."[38]

When initial training is finished, the question of follow-up training must be raised. One authority terms this "upgrading," and distinguishes two types: continuous training and retraining.[39] Continuous training is aimed at helping a salesperson do the same job better—an extension of initial training. It is often done individually and informally by a sales supervisor, though a specific program of material or outlines may be provided if the firm has a training staff. Retraining should occur whenever a person's job requirements change, such as after a reorganization or major change in product line or market targets. Retraining is more likely to involve a formal program similar to initial training but on a smaller scale.

A firm will sometimes tailor one or more follow-up training programs to specific sales force groups. Doubleday, for example, focuses separate training attention on three groups: new hires, those with 5 to 15 years of service, and those with over 15 years of service.[40] But as length of service increases, managers find that training becomes less effective and more challenging. In one study, for example, 10 weekly sessions involving 50 salespeople with 6 months to 6 years of tenure produced least effectiveness in those with the most time on the job.[41] This study concluded that sales training should be completed before habits are formed, and follow-up sessions should be carefully tailored to the needs and problems of the sales group involved.

EVALUATION OF TRAINING

Sales training programs must be evaluated carefully because they are significant in terms of both cost and effect on sales performance. There are two major evaluation questions. First, how well has each individual trainee learned what the program was designed to provide? Second, how effective is the program overall in contributing to improved job performance?

Extent of Trainee's Learning. The first type of evaluation pertains to the trainee rather than to the training program. It parallels the evaluation of a student in a college course. How well has he or she learned the material provided? Trainees should be informed of how well they are progressing, and the trainer must have feedback to tailor the program effectively to meet individual learning needs.

Performance evaluation is covered more fully in Chapter 15, but some evaluation devices can be mentioned here which are used in assessing trainees' progress. These include knowledge quizzes and ratings by the trainer, by the trainee, or even by customers. Figure 12.3 shows a rating form used by Master Builders trainers in assessing on-the-job performance by trainees.

Effectiveness of the Training Program. Some measure of training program effectiveness is necessary for justifying training to higher management. It is possible that more funds should be directed to training if a good payoff can be documented. On the other hand, perhaps more emphasis should be given to other activities such as selection or motivation, especially if training effectiveness proves minimal. Methods of evaluating the effectiveness of a sales training program are the following:

1. Attainment of training objectives
2. Collective pattern of individual trainee's learning
3. Controlled experimentation
4. Surveys
5. Other measures of behavior

Attainment of Objectives. If specific training objectives have been clearly devised, then how well they are achieved is a reflection of training effectiveness. But suppose an objective is to raise sales volume per territory. Can a trainer really claim success if increased volume is achieved? That increase may result from many other causes such as improved products, general economic growth, or weakening competition. Objectives must be stated in precise attitude, knowledge, and skills areas to be most useful for evaluation purposes.

Collective Learning Pattern. When one or a few trainees fail to learn a training topic sufficiently, this is most likely an individual problem. But if the vast majority fail, the problem could very well lie in the program itself, such as in its organization or the trainer's manner of presentation. Test results and ratings can be used collectively to determine if topics are being communicated effectively. This evaluation approach is more diagnostic, however, than one of justifying training in the eyes of management.

Controlled Experiments. Experimental designs are the most valid approach to training evaluation. In brief, this method consists of the following. Two matched

FIGURE 12.3
On-the-Job Training Evaluation Form Used by Master Builders

Salesperson's Name _____ Prospect _____

Time: _____ Date: _____

DID THE SALESPERSON:

	YES	NO		YES	NO
1. Prepare for the call? Did the call show good preplanning?			6. Practice good listening skills?		
2. Have a good opener? Did it get the attention of the prospect?			7. Use visual aids—photos, evidence, proof, back-up data—to substantiate statements, ideas, and claims?		
3. Probe? Ask questions? Use good questioning techniques (who? what? where? when? why? how?) to determine prospect's needs? Handle objections? (Questions can be used in the opening, body, handling objections, and closing.)			8. Overcome objections effectively?		
			9. Was the salesperson convincing?		
4. Keep control of the interview? Stick to the subject? Stay with the objective? Or did the interview wander? Did the salesperson get sidetracked by the prospect?			10. "Benefitize" the presentation? Did the salesperson talk features (facts), or benefits which answer the question, "What does it mean to me, the prospect?"		
5. Use good communication skills? Did choice of words express ideas and concepts so they were clearly understood by the prospect?			11. Accomplish the ojective of the call?		
			12. Ask for the order? A decision? A commitment for further action?		

What was good about the call? (Good Points?)

What could be improved? (Wording, word choice, terminology, expression of ideas, explanation of products, in addition to the above point?)

Source: Anthony K. Gross, "On-the-Job Training Techniques," in Jared F. Harrison (ed.), *The Sales Manager As A Trainer* (Reading, Mass.: Addison-Wesley Publishing Company, Inc., 1977), p. 82.

groups of trainees are identified. One, the experimental group, receives the training to be evaluated, and the other, the control group, does not. After training is completed, the two groups are compared in terms of some criterion of effective performance. Any difference resulting from this comparison can then be attributed to the training given the experimental group, provided that the two groups were well matched at the beginning. Figure 12.4 shows some experiment results from companies using the Professional Selling Skills program by Xerox Learning Systems.

Surveys. Opinion surveys often provide insight into training program problems. Westvaco uses the form shown in Figure 12.5. Prior to a training meeting, each salesperson checks which objectives are important and their degree of importance.

FIGURE 12.4

Results from Training Evaluation Experiments in Companies Using the Professional Selling Skills Program by Xerox Learning Systems

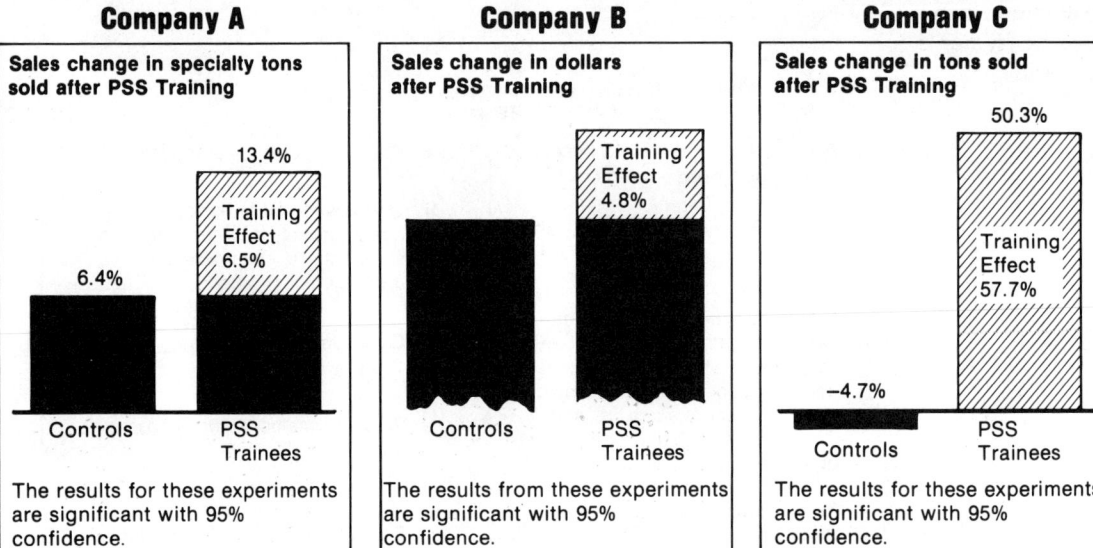

Source: "Professional Selling Skills," Xerox Learning Systems, p. 15.

At the end of the meeting, the manager returns the forms to acquire an evaluation as shown in the last column. Again, this is a diagnostic type of evaluation which serves mainly to help improve future training activities as well as to indicate topics for follow-up programs.

Other Measures of Behavior. Other measures of salespeople's behavior and performance are sometimes used in evaluation, even if they do not relate to specific training objectives. These measures include turnover, sales expenses, levels of sales force morale, and a variety of other performance measures such as number of calls per day or average order size. In general, these measures are not adequate for evaluating training programs and may even be misleading because of the many other factors which influence their outcome.

RELATED TRAINING PROGRAMS

Field sales managers, distributors, and even customers are important training candidates for many firms.

Training Field Sales Managers. Present or potential field sales managers are receiving training in a small but growing number of firms. Separate training of these groups is necessary for two reasons. First, management responsibilities involve

FIGURE 12.5

Form for Planning and Evaluating a Sales Training Program, Used by Westvaco Corporation

Sales Meeting Program: 'The Problem-Solving Salesman'

Your Name: _____

I want to be able to:

	1. Objectives*	2. Degree Of Importance**	3. Degree Of Fulfillment†
1. Improve my ability to recognize customer problems, probable causes, and possible solutions.	✓	20	5
2. Broaden my awareness of the many ways to dig out facts that uncover customer problems.			
3. Acquire a better understanding of the customer benefits our products and services provide.	✓	20	5
4. Make my sales presentations more customer benefit centered, and thus more persuasive.	✓	50	10
5. Acquire a better understanding of the backup help available from company departments in solving customer problems.	✓	10	10
6. Other (specify): _____			
		TOTAL 100	

*Check those objectives that are important to you. (Ignore those that are not.)

**Weight each checked objective for its importance to you, allocating exactly 100 points among all those checked. A total of 100 points *must* be assigned. If you checked only one objective, assign all 100 points to it; if you checked two objectives, spread the 100 points between them, etc.

†Rate each objective you checked from 0 to 10 to indicate how well it was fulfilled. 0 is unsatisfactory; 1-2, poor; 3-4, below average; 5, average; 7, good; 8, very good; 9-10, excellent.

Source: Howard L Bayne, "For A Realistic Training Session, Catch Up With The Sales Force Before And After," *Sales & Marketing Management*, November 8, 1976, p. 95. Reprinted by permission from *Sales & Marketing* magazine. Copyright 1976.

additional tasks beyond those demanded of sales personnel. Second, as the sales management job becomes more complex, selling efficiency and effectiveness grow increasingly vital to competitive success. And yet, management development is often left to the discretion of individual supervisors and to the field managers themselves, since training for these positions is mainly the product of individual needs for widely varying positions. More sales management training comes from external sources—commercial organizations, consultants, and university continuing education courses—than from programs developed within their own firms.[42]

Training Distributors. Many firms which sell to and through distributors find that training their distributors' sales forces pays off in increased distributor loyalty and in boosting sales. In a sense, the training becomes a benefit received by the distributor for handling the producer's line. One such program is offered to construction equipment distributors by American Poclain Corporation.[43] Selling skills are emphasized along with some product knowledge, and the two-day courses make generous use of videotape recording and role-playing techniques.

Training Customers. Customers sometimes need training also so they can use their newly purchased products most effectively. In fact, some producers have found it essential to train customers carefully, thereby minimizing later problems from incorrect product use. Nalco Chemical sells water treatment chemicals used by heavy industrial equipment manufacturers to keep boiler systems operating efficiently. Nalco has found that boiler operators become dependent on the chemical salesperson for troubleshooting boiler problems. As a result, Nalco developed a Boiler Operator Training Program in hopes that more knowledgeable boiler operators will require fewer emergency calls to its sales personnel, calls which detract from total selling time.[44]

Sales Training For Other Company Personnel. Nonsales personnel are sometimes called upon to participate in the selling process. When highly technical products or applications are involved, for example, engineers may be needed to discuss problems with the prospect. If such situations are fairly typical, sales training for the nonsales participants may be of value. To be most effective, training material should be developed and communicated in terms of the language and background of the trainee. To communicate sales problems to engineers, one firm instituted a "marketing technology development program," a part of which was termed "persuasion engineering."[45]

CONCLUSION

Training is an important activity in developing a salesperson's capability. Sales personnel are always learning, whether through formal training programs or by trial-and-error. To give new sales personnel good preparation for their jobs, management must provide a complete and well-organized initial training program. Follow-up training is useful at periodic intervals to maintain and build sales proficiency, especially when there is a change in the job or selling environment.

Although training is important, it is not a panacea. Therefore, training objectives must be defined carefully and every effort made to evaluate training's contribution to sales organization success. While good training opens the way to effective job performance, the salesperson must still be motivated properly to use his or her abilities. The next chapter explores a significant factor in motivation—monetary compensation.

QUESTIONS FOR REVIEW AND DISCUSSION

1. You have been hired to fill a full-time staff position as sales trainer in a firm which employs 150 salespeople. Discuss the activities your job might entail that would require you to utilize your time fully. Consider all aspects of training.

2. The study reported in Table 12.2 suggests some problems which might be addressed in a sales training program. Pick three problem areas from that study and describe how a sales force might be trained to deal with them.
3. What should guide the sales manager in determining the specific objectives of a sales training program?
4. A manufacturer of industrial welding and soldering equipment hires two basic types of salespeople:

	TYPE 1	TYPE 2
Recruited from:	college	competition
Educational background:	marketing	engineering
Sales experience	none	2–4 years

Outline a sales training program which will provide the necessary preparation for these two types. Then discuss how this training program can be evaluated for each type of salesperson.

5. Six months after a new training program was put into operation, a firm's sales began to increase. Is this a valid indication that the training program is effective?
6. A district sales manager is planning a three-day refresher training program for the six salespeople under her supervision. To help plan a program most pertinent to their needs, she is considering sending them a questionnaire which it is hoped will identify these needs. What suggestions would you make concerning the content of this questionnaire? Do you think the questionnaire approach is suitable for this purpose?
7. Based on the findings in Table 12.5, describe what training methods should be included in the ideal sales training program for new sales personnel. Why do companies sometimes use other methods instead of those you identified as best?
8. A major aim of training is to build confidence in each salesperson. Discuss some specific ways in which sales force confidence can be reinforced through training.
9. A sales manager offers this philosophy regarding refresher training: "Training is expensive. It pulls the sales force out of the field and cuts out chances for sales during the training period. So we don't use refresher training unless sales volume is clearly dropping." Evaluate this reasoning.
10. Compare the benefits of decentralized training by district sales managers with centralized training by staff specialists. Which do you feel is generally better, and why?

NOTES

1. David S. Hopkins, *Training The Sales Force: A Progress Report,* Report No. 737 (New York: The Conference Board, Inc., 1978), p. 2.

2. Further discussion of these topics is found in Thomas F. Stroh, *Training and Developing the Professional Salesman* (New York: AMACOM, 1973), pp. 2–9.

3. Hopkins, p. 15.

4. Hopkins, p. 25.

5. Kenneth B. Haas, *How To Develop Successful Salesmen,* 1st paper ed. (New York: McGraw-Hill, Inc., 1957), pp. 98–99.

6. A questionnaire process and analysis of results for a construction materials firm is described in Lawrence M. Lamont and William J. Lundstrom, "Defining Industrial Sales Behavior: A Factor Analytic Study," paper presented at the National Conference of the American Marketing Association, Portland, Oregon, August, 1974.

7. Victor P. Gravereau and L. J. Konopa, "Attitudes of Salesmen Toward Industrial Buyers and Purchasing Policies," *Journal of Purchasing,* vol. 6 (August 1970), pp. 28–39.

8. Paul W. Thayer, John A. Antoinetti, and Theodore A. Guest, "Product Knowledge and Performance—a Study of Life Insurance Agents," *Personnel Psychology,* vol. 11 (Autumn 1958), pp. 411–418.

9. David W. Ross, "Diagnostic Training for Improved Sales Performance," *Personnel,* vol. 31 (March 1955), pp. 473–480.

10. "To Me, Training Is the Lifeblood of any Successful Salesman," *Sales Management,* April 1, 1966, p. 72.

11. John C. Gfeller, "Five Keys to Better Salesmanship," *Nation's Business,* December 1976, pp. 56–58.

12. "The Battle to Boost Sales Productivity," *Business Week,* February 12, 1972, p. 68.

13. Robert F. Vizza, *Improving Salesmen's Use of Time* (New York: Sales Executives Club of New York, Inc., 1962), pp. 15–17.

14. Summarized from Robert F. Vizza and Thomas E. Chambers, *Time and Territorial Management for the Salesmen* (New York: Sales Executives Club of New York, Inc., 1971), pp. 26–40 and 71–76.

15. Sally Scanlon, "Every Salesperson A Psychologist," *Sales & Marketing Management,* February 6, 1978, pp. 34–36.

16. Joseph W. Thompson and William W. Evans, "Behavioral Approach to Industrial Selling," *Harvard Business Review,* vol. 47 (March–April 1969), pp. 137–151.

17. Further discussion of these and other behavioral science concepts is found in Joseph W. Thompson, *Selling: A Managerial and Behavioral Science Analysis,* 2nd ed. (New York: McGraw-Hill, Inc., 1973).

18. Thayer C. Taylor, "Can NCR Cash In?" *Sales & Marketing Management,* February 7, 1977, p. 35.

19. Hopkins, p. 45.

20. "Teaching the 'Deep Sell' At Continental," *Sales & Marketing Management,* August 9, 1976, pp. 49–50.

21. Richard Cooper, "Simulated Supermarket," *Training,* November 1974, pp. 8–12; for a description of other sales training centers see "Sales Training Centers—Educational Wonderlands," *Sales Management,* June 1, 1970, pp. 58–59.

22. "PLATO's Wisdom," *Sales & Marketing Management,* June 1978, pp. 19–20.

23. Hopkins, p. 3.

24. An annotated list of available sales training programs by medium (i.e., audio, video, correspondence, etc.) is in *Training,* October 1975, pp. 36–39, 44–45.

25. Martin Everett, "Heinz is Changing Sloooow Fast," *Sales Management,* August 5, 1974, p. 24.

26. Vincent L. Smith, "Practice Makes (Honeywell) Perfect," *Sales Management,* September 17, 1965, pt. ii, *Sales Meetings,* pp. 98–105.

27. "ROLS: Detailing the Detail Man," *Sales Management,* August 5, 1974, p. 3.

28. Homer Smith, "Armour-Dial Gives Role-Playing a Whole New Meaning With Bedlam," *Sales & Marketing Management,* July 10, 1978, pp. 67–68.

29. A detailed discussion with recommendations is found in Stroh, pp. 138–160.

30. This and other relevant games are available from Didactic Systems, Cranford, New Jersey.

31. July 10, 1978, pp. 33–40. Previous issues contain other games, such as "Salesmanship: The Time-Is-Money Game," in the March 8, 1976 issue, pp. 43–50.

32. Stroh, p. 72.

33. "Selling's 'Global Village,' " *Sales Management,* June 1, 1970, pp. 62–64.

34. *Ibid.,* p. 63.

35. Anthony K. Gross, "On-the-Job Training Techniques," in Jared F. Harrison (ed.), *The Sales Manager As A Trainer* (Reading, Mass.: Addison-Wesley Publishing Company, Inc., 1977), pp. 73–74.

36. "Today's Sales Training Program," Del Monte, September 1976.

37. "Professional Selling Skills," Xerox Learning Systems, p. 4.

38. Hopkins, p. 6.

39. Homer Smith, "To Make Training Click, Train By Objectives," *Sales & Marketing Management,* August 9, 1976, p. 44.

40. Clark Lambert, "In Upgrading, Good Is Better, Better Is Best," *Sales & Marketing Management,* August 9, 1976, pp. 46–48.

41. John Withey, "Training The Older Salesman," *Sales Management,* August 4, 1975, p. 93.

42. Donald W. Jackson, Jr. and J. L. Schlacter, "Educating Today's Sales Managers for Tomorrow," survey sponsored by the Sales & Marketing Executives International, 1977.

43. "Videotape Demonstrations Aid Sales Training Effectiveness," *Industrial Marketing,* December 1977, pp. 42–43.

44. Sally Scanlon, "Nalco's Steamed Up About Customer Training," *Sales & Marketing Management,* August 1978, pp. 40–41.

45. R. P. Andelson, "Harnessing Engineers and Scientists to the Sales Effort," in John S. Wright and J. L. Goldstucker (eds.), *New Ideas for Successful Marketing* (Chicago: American Marketing Association, 1966), pp. 204–215.

13 COMPENSATING SALES PERSONNEL

Careful selection and training can produce a capable sales force, but performance depends on more than capability. The additional factor necessary is often termed motivation, although it is really a combination of incentive and control factors that influence an employee's behavior. This chapter examines compensation of sales personnel and its relationship to motivation. Other incentive and control factors outside the compensation plan are discussed in following chapters.

A compensation plan provides direct and indirect monetary rewards to sales personnel for achieving objectives through the performance of their work. In short, compensation is the incentive to reach objectives. But all salespeople do not respond equally to this incentive. Some differ because of experience or capability. Different responses also reflect differences in motivation. In this sense, motivation refers to the state of needs or wants within the individual that guides his or her behavior. Since individuals' motivations differ, a given compensation plan does not produce a similar reflex-like response from each member of the sales force.

These few comments point out what sales managers sometimes fail to recognize—that a compensation plan does not necessarily supply a salesperson with motivation. Motivation is a force within the person, who will adjust to a given compensation plan by working sufficiently to satisfy his or her income goal. The ideal compensation plan is one which allows both the salesperson's and the company's goals to be reached simultaneously through personal selling effort. But a compensation plan will seldom cause a salesperson's goals to increase.

A second result of a well-designed pay plan is control. Management's task is to devise a plan which directs salespeople to accomplish company goals. This plan thus provides a guide to the most financially rewarding use of sales time. No matter what level of earnings a salesperson aspires to, it must be attained according to directions in the plan. The more one acts in accordance with these directions, the more these actions are reinforced with compensation. And if management has devised the plan carefully, it will induce performance in the best interests of company success.

CHARACTERISTICS OF A GOOD COMPENSATION PLAN

Characteristics of a good compensation plan are noted throughout this chapter, since they influence many aspects of compensation planning and policy. At the start, it is useful to draw together the major characteristics of a good plan, since they serve as a foundation influencing nearly all compensation decisions. Four major characteristics can be identified:

1. The plan recognizes and meets the objectives of all parties concerned.
2. The plan provides fair and competitive earnings.
3. The plan is understood by and acceptable to all parties concerned.
4. The plan can be administered effectively and efficiently.

Well-defined objectives become the criteria for evaluating any compensation plan. Furthermore, the objectives of all parties must be considered—management, salespeople, and customers—as we discuss more fully in a following section.

To be fair and competitive, earnings potential must reflect specific job requirements and the pay for related jobs. A position's pay level determines, in large part, the caliber of persons attracted to it. The pay level must be competitive with alternative job opportunities available to the type of person sought. These and other factors relating to level of compensation are also discussed later in more detail.

If the compensation plan is not understood clearly by sales personnel, it is not likely to achieve its objectives. Each salesperson should realize precisely how efforts or accomplishments will translate into earnings. But understandability must not be confused with simplicity. Emphasis must be placed first on making a plan which will attain objectives, and then on making sure the plan is clear to the sales force. In other words, the plan's effectiveness as a control device should not be foresaken for simplicity. Indeed, some salespeople might resent an oversimplified pay plan which did not truly reflect job complexities.

Coupled closely with understandability is acceptability. If the plan is not acceptable to management and sales force alike, it will seldom produce good results for either group or for their customers.

Problems of administrative effectiveness and efficiency are discussed later, so it is sufficient here to say that the plan must operate as well in practice as it appears to on paper. As computers are used more widely by firms in order processing, invoicing, and sales analysis, it is logical to extend their use to sales force pay calculations as well. This action would make feasible the administration of more sophisticated pay plans than might have been attempted in the past.

DEVELOPMENT OF A COMPENSATION PLAN FOR SALESPEOPLE

The development of a sales force compensation plan is presented here as if it were a totally new formulation. In reality, most action on such plans is in the form of revision. Major revision of an ongoing compensation plan is much like a totally new formulation, however. Thorough evaluation of any plan requires an analysis of all steps in its development. Figure 13.1 indicates the five major steps that form a framework for compensation decisions. These are

1. Specify objectives which the plan is to fulfill.
2. Determine the level of compensation required.
3. Select appropriate methods of compensation.
4. Test the plan.
5. Provide for administration of the plan.

Each of these steps will be examined in order.

FIGURE 13.1
Sequence of Compensation Decisions

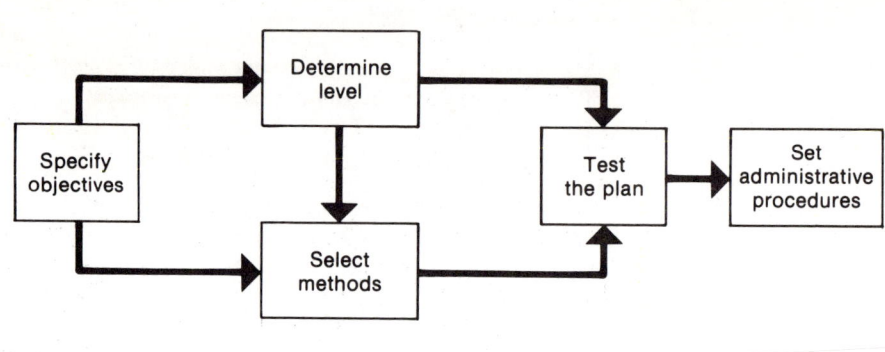

Objectives of a Compensation Plan

A good compensation plan is defined as one which meets its objectives, so the most logical first step in the plan's development is to specify those objectives. This initial step is also a source of perplexing compensation problems because a variety of objectives must be considered. To begin, three parties—sales personnel, management, and customers—are involved and the objectives of each are not necesssarily the same.

Salesperson's Objectives. Some salespeople desire considerable security in earnings. Others are willing to risk low earnings if, at the same time, they have the opportunity for high, even unlimited, income through a plan emphasizing incentive pay. A related objective is to avoid being penalized for factors beyond a salesperson's control. Selling effort may not pay off during unusual economic downturns, for example, or following delivery of a run of defective products.

Some sales personnel take a long-range view of their earnings goals, seeking to reach a particular level within, say, five years. Others are more interested in current earnings. Some managers try to uncover very specific objectives, such as one salesperson's desire to buy a new car this year, and then translate that objective into the amount of effort and results needed under the salesperson's prevailing pay plan.

Management's Objectives. Long-range management objectives focus mainly on profitability. Thus, compensation for sales personnel is being viewed more and more as a reward proportional to the profitability of their sales efforts. More specifically, these objectives may be stated in terms of greater sales emphasis on the higher-margin products or in terms of obtaining new customers of some minimum potential order size. Profitability also can be increased through more effective use of company manufacturing facilities, and this is often accomplished by selling a balanced line of products which will keep all production facilities operating at their most efficient levels.

Short-range management objectives often relate to specific products, customer types, or territories. One objective might be to capture quickly a significant market share for a new product, or another might entail the introduction of a new service in a particular territory in hopes of attaining a stronger competitive position.

Other management objectives often incorporated into compensation plans are

1. Encouragement of cooperation among members of a selling team.
2. Minimization of the incidence of small orders.
3. Encouragement of the performance of nonselling duties.
4. Maintenance of sound credit practice.
5. Reduction of expenses.
6. Minimization of price cutting by salespeople.
7. Attraction of high-caliber salespeople.

Customers' Objectives. From the customer's view, a major objective is maintaining a proper inventory level as opposed to being over- or undersold. Customers also desire proper service and quick attention when problems occur regarding such things as delivery or product performance. Pay plans which discourage after-sale service or periodic review of a customer's satisfaction may cause many customers to turn elsewhere for their needs.

Changes in Objectives. Not only are there multiple objectives, but many of these objectives change over time. Markets change, as do the needs of sales personnel and management. As a result, a pay plan which is satisfactory under today's conditions may be ineffective a year from now. Of course, if a major change occurs very often the plan becomes confusing and costly to administer, and morale can suffer.

How Many Objectives? The number of objectives for a compensation plan could be large. But this does not mean that all of these objectives should be incorporated into every plan, because the more there are, the less likely each is to be met effectively and the more likely conflicts will occur. Management should consider whether some objectives should be sought more through training or supervision than through the compensation plan. Four or five major objectives is generally considered the limit if the pay plan is to be reasonably effective.

Level of Compensation

The level of compensation for a particular job usually refers to the average earnings of all those in that job. Every salesperson in a given job for any one company does not earn the same pay; there can be a wide range reflecting differences in experience and ability. The level of compensation might then be viewed as the mean or median earnings within this range.

An alternative view relates level of compensation to the worth of the job itself rather than to job performance. The level then becomes an absolute rather than a relative measure and may not coincide with the average earnings of those employed in that job. If all the firm's salespeople were unusually good performers, for example, the average of their earnings might exceed the compensation level normally associated with the job. In fact, this differential is encouraged when the pay plan includes a significant incentive portion.

In any case, an average earnings level defines the target income for average acceptable performance in a particular position.[1] Once the level is established, methods of compensation can be selected to provide that amount of pay. The level indicates how much the average salesperson is worth, and the methods of compensation define how a salesperson will earn that pay. Three approaches to determining compensation level involve job evaluation, levels of pay for similar jobs within the industry, and levels of pay for other jobs within the same firm.

Job Evaluation. Job evaluation is a systematic method of determining the importance of a specific job within an organization and its value in terms of earnings it should command. Many approaches are used. One is simply to rank each of the jobs according to its value to the firm. It is best to have a number of qualified judges independently submit sets of rankings. The results can then be reconciled, if necessary, and a hierarchy of jobs obtained.

Another approach is to rate all jobs on a number of common factors, such as mental requirements, skill requirements, responsibility, physical requirements, and working conditions. Each job is given a score on each factor, and the sum of all the ratings produces a total point score which places the job at a relative position within the total range of jobs. Sometimes the point scores are related to dollar values of pay per month or per year. For example, each point might stand for $10 of pay per month. If a given sales job received a total point score of 140 this would indicate that the average qualified jobholder should be paid $1400 per month.

In many firms, job evaluation has not been applied to sales positions. Some managers believe that a sales job cannot be compared with others because it contains too many intangibles and unique features. Others believe that job evaluation is suited only for positions paid by salary with no incentive pay opportunities. In spite of these feelings, there are many instances where job evaluation has been applied successfully to sales positions.[2]

Industry Levels. Some sales managers establish pay levels in relation to what other firms pay for similar jobs. If the pay offered is much below this "going rate," the firm may have difficulty in attracting or keeping good performers. On the other hand, if the level offered is too far above the industry average, overcompensation results. This, in turn, can increase selling costs, which would lead to high prices, reduced profits, or both. Some firms prefer to offer slightly above-average pay levels in hopes of reducing turnover or attracting above-average personnel, such as those with beneficial previous experience or unusually desirable educational backgrounds.

Table 13.1 reports recent trends in compensation level for four typical positions within a sales hierarchy. Other sources provide mean or median earnings and ranges by industry and product type.[3] Many difficulties are involved in using such surveys.[4] Because of inflation, compensation averages become outdated quickly, even before they get into print. In addition, many sales jobs differ considerably even within the same industry; and an average may not be applicable to a firm's specifically defined selling job. Nevertheless, a measure of the market value of the sales job should be considered at least as a bench mark.

Other Jobs in the Firm. The relationship between the salesperson's pay and that received by others in the same firm should also be considered. Discrepancies within the sales organization itself can be a particular problem. For example, a good salesperson may eventually surpass the district manager in earnings, producing an awkward superior-subordinate relationship. Furthermore, those qualified for a management position might not accept a promotion if it means a cut in pay. Table 13.2 shows how pay levels compare among selling and sales management positions in various types of firms.

TABLE 13.1
Trends in Level of Compensation for Various Personal Selling Positions

	TOTAL COMPENSATION PAID TO THE AVERAGE			
Year	Sales Trainee	Regular Salesperson	Senior Salesperson	Sales Supervisor
1972	$ 9,141	$12,628	$16,654	$18,667
1973	9,495	14,350	17,052	20,255
1974	9,895	15,126	19,566	22,100
1975	11,975	17,114	21,766	25,720
1976	12,588	17,592	22,768	26,143
1977	13,750	19,410	24,003	28,919
1978	15,217	20,252	26,530	31,575
1982 (est.)[a]	21,480	27,860	36,228	44,898

Includes sales personnel for consumer goods, industrial goods, services, insurance, transportation, and utility firms.

[a] Not included in original source, but estimated by the author based on the average annual rate of increase per year in each category over the period 1972–1978.

Reprinted by permission of the publisher, from *Sales Personnel Report,* 23rd Edition, 1978/1979, © 1979 by AMACOM, a division of American Management Associations. All rights reserved.

Additional Factors Influencing Pay Levels. Many other factors influence pay levels. One is the general compensation structure within the community where a salesperson is employed. This is really a reflection of the cost of living which differs considerably among metropolitan areas.[5] If the sales force is unionized, there is probably some predetermined average or minimum level specified by a governing agreement. In some cases, the individual's bargaining strength has as much impact on his or her pay level as does the nature of the job itself. This is especially true for salespeople who are long-time employees with proven ability.

Problem of the Level Drifting Too High. It sometimes happens that sales force pay levels drift too high in proportion to the value of their jobs relative to other jobs in the company. Many factors influence the ease of selling as a firm develops its position in the marketplace. For example, products are improved and companies strengthen their reputation through advertising and technical service. The result is a boost in sales volume which, when coupled with higher prices from inflation, produces higher commissions and bonuses for the sales force. Under such conditions, a soft drink distributor's sales representatives reached a pay level of $150,000 per year![6] Are such earnings true reflections of the value of the job to the firm? Should sales force pay even increase in the same proportion as sales volume, or should compensation costs decline as a percent of sales dollars to reflect increasing productivity?[7] And if sales force pay does go up, why not the pay of advertising, research, and product managers in the same proportion?

Sales force pay levels sometimes drift disproportionately high because some sales managers believe that higher pay motivates better performance. As noted earlier in this chapter, such reasoning is not necessarily sound. In fact, higher pay levels may reduce productivity since a salesperson can earn as much as previously but with less effort.

TABLE 13.2

Levels of Compensation for Selling and Sales Management Positions as Compared with the Marketing Vice-President's Pay

	COMPARISON BY SIZE OF FIRM						COMPARISON BY TYPE OF PRODUCT		Comparison in All Sales Forces Combined
	$250 Million or More	$100– $249 Million	$50– $99 Million	$25– $49 Million	$10– $24 Million	Less than $10 Million	Consumer Goods	Industrial Goods	
Vice-President Marketing	100.0%	100.0%	100.0%	100.0%	100.0%	100.0%	100.0%	100.0%	100.0%
General Sales Manager	69.2%	69.8%	70.8%	63.6%	75.4%	81.7%	72.8%	72.5%	70.1%
Regional Sales Manager	54.7%	51.5%	55.1%	62.4%	70.4%	60.0%	62.7%	68.1%	64.2%
District Sales Manager	46.6%	36.2%	48.4%	62.3%	60.1%	n.a.	51.8%	68.7%	56.1%
Field Sales Manager	35.0%	37.8%	42.0%	46.0%	56.6%	62.9%	44.2%	50.5%	46.7%
Field Salesperson	22.2%	24.6%	31.2%	35.2%	45.1%	53.3%	32.0%	39.7%	35.0%

Source: Calculated from data in David A. Weeks, *Compensating Salesmen and Sales Executives,* Report no. 579 (New York: The Conference Board, Inc., 1972), pp. 2–3.

The best solution to this problem is to plan to avoid it initially.[8] Based on a long-range sales forecast and company marketing plans for the coming years, management must attempt to structure a pay plan which will not produce excessive earnings at a future date. The alternatives are to tolerate levels which are too high or to cut sales force pay periodically. The former is not appealing from a profit viewpoint, and the latter will surely cause morale problems and turnover within the sales force.

Methods of Compensation

As stated earlier, methods of compensation define the ways in which salespeople receive their pay. We first review the alternative methods available, noting their general attributes, the incentive and control features of each, and measurements necessary to implement them. We then discuss the tasks of choosing and combining methods into a total plan. The compensation methods examined are:

1. Salary
2. Commission
3. Bonus
4. Expense payments
5. Fringe benefits

Salary. A salary is a fixed payment for a period of work time. Many sales managers believe that a salary produces a feeling of company loyalty within the sales force since it treats them the same way as management personnel are paid. It is also easy to understand and provides a steady income.

Since it is a fixed payment the salary method may not present a strong incentive for increasing effort. Rather, the salary portion of a pay plan is usually viewed as providing security in terms of regularity and stability of earnings. Incentive can result from frequent management appraisals of each salesperson's performance and corresponding salary adjustments. But such appraisals seldom occur more often than annually.

The salary method gives management flexible control of sales force activities. For example, one salesperson might be asked to concentrate on obtaining new customers one month, performing nonselling tasks the next month, and soliciting repeat business the third month. But the salary method does not ensure that these various tasks will be carried out. Often, such control requires close supervision. On the other hand, salary plans have been highly successful with salespeople with a solid formal education who are carefully selected and trained to function with minimal supervision.

Situations appropriate for salary occur when the sales force has little control over the amount or timing of a sale. Some industrial sales are conditioned largely on the success of the customer's business, for instance. In other cases, the sales force does not sell directly. The sales personnel director for Philip Morris provides an example:

> The Philip Morris salesperson has very little control over shipments into his territory. Although he can sell a few cartons to fill in a retailer's stock, distributors do the real selling. Our rep's job is to merchandise.[9]

Salary is best suited to cases where personal selling is a minor factor in the customer's decision. Salary is also used where the time span between initial sales contact and final buying decision is extensive. This occurs, for example, when the product is very costly, highly technical, made to order, part of a larger system of products in an extensive installation, or some combination of these. Salespeople for aerospace manufacturers are paid primarily by salary. In other cases, sales result from the effort of two or more company representatives as a team and it is impossible to single out the individual contribution of each.

Measurements necessary to carry out the salary method present little problem. Time is the basis of payment. The unit of time which constitutes a pay period is subject to management decision. Monthly periods are common when salary is the only method used, but variations exist.

A more difficult problem concerns measurements necessary for adjusting one's salary level. Many approaches exist for evaluating performance, and Chapter 15 explores these in more detail. For salary adjustments, many managers devise some overall rating of general performance while others relate salary change to sales volume achieved or simply length of service. Maryland Cup, a producer of paper and plastic products for food and beverage services, pays salary plus bonus on sales over quota, and any bonus earned becomes the salary increase for the following year. But a salesperson who fails to make quota receives a corresponding salary cut under this plan.[10]

Commission. Pay calculated as some percentage of sales volume or profit achieved by the salesperson is called commission. In contrast to salary, which is payment for time, commission is payment for some specific unit of accomplishment.

Commission methods are designed to provide incentive. At the same time, the commission method encourages feelings of independence by the salesperson because rewards are tied directly to his or her own efforts. Incentive pay methods allow high performers to be rewarded more quickly in proportion to their achievements. In fact, high achievers are often attracted to firms with straight commission (i.e., commission only) plans. Muzak is one such firm, and its president noted, "Commission plans offering a potential for high earnings, which our plan does, attract the good salesperson. We have good salespeople."[11]

Straight commission plans have some major disadvantages. Pay can be affected greatly by conditions the salesperson cannot control, such as economic swings or price changes. The feelings of independence often make a commission-only sales force difficult to manage, particularly when nonselling tasks are required. Long-term territory development needs often lose out to short-term sales results. In addition, straight commission plans have not been able to attract college-educated recruits needed for today's problem-solving style of selling and for tomorrow's sales management jobs.[12] The high earnings potential associated with this plan is also changing. While commission-only salespeople generally earned more than those under other pay plans, recent studies show straight commission sales forces are no longer superior in pay.[13]

Commission methods provide management with a fixed type of control over the sales force. Tasks will be achieved for which commissions are paid. Cost control is also fixed. On the downside, payments are not made unless sales or profits are achieved. Thus, new firms or those in relatively weak financial position often favor this plan. But on the upside, commissions are paid as sales increase for whatever reason—improved economy, effective advertising, product improvements—regardless of the impact of personal selling efforts. It is difficult to improve the productivity of selling effort under a straight commission plan during periods of increased demand, since commissions go up proportionately (whereas salaries remain more fixed).[14]

Every commission method is made up of four separate components: the base, or type of performance for which the commission is paid; the rate, or relationship between amount of pay and measure of performance; the starting point, at which the calculation of commission payments begins; and the payment period, which defines the timing of payments to sales personnel. These components are summarized in Table 13.3. The large variety of alternatives makes the commission method adaptable to many situations, as the following discussion shows.

Bases for Commission Payments. The vast majority of commission plans are based on net sales volume in dollars or units produced by the salesperson. But an increasing number of firms base at least part of total pay in relation to a salesperson's profit contribution. For instance, in a cross-section of U.S. manufacturing firms studied, 41 percent reported sales compensation plans specifically designed to emphasize profitability.[15] Olin's Film Division is one case. Management assigns a "factor" to each of its 22 products reflecting each product's profit margin, and sales force commissions are based on factored sales volume. Therefore, if one product's factor is 0.3, then sales of 10,000 pounds of that product are worth 10,000 × 0.3 or 3,000 points. Commissions are paid on total points achieved from all sales combined.[16] This approach solves one problem—that of keeping actual profit margins confidential. Other problems of profit-based plans involve accounting difficulties related to calculating profitability measures for individual products, and administrative time needed to update and communicate changes in profitability measures.

Commissions may also be based on activities performed, such as demonstrations, calls on new accounts, and others as noted in Chapter 7. In fact, all bases discussed

TABLE 13.3

Components of the Commission Method of Compensation

BASES FOR COMMISSION PAYMENTS	STARTING POINTS FOR COMMISSION PAYMENTS:
1. Dollar or Unit Sales Volume, gross or net.	1. Zero Sales, Profits, or Activities.
2. Gross Margin, Contribution to Profit.	2. Some Percentage of Quota.
3. Activities or Efforts.	3. Break-even Level of Sales Volume.
4. Quotas, which may include above bases.	4. Multiple Starting Points.
RATES OF COMMISSION	PAYMENT PERIODS FOR COMMISSION EARNINGS:
1. Fixed, Progressive, Regressive.	1. Prior to when earned—drawing accounts.
2. Gross versus Net.	2. At time of order or payment for order.

3. Constant versus Variable with regard to
  a. products
  b. customers
  c. territories
  d. order sizes
  e. profit margins
  f. new versus repeat business
	3. At regular intervals, such as weekly or monthly.
	4. In equal installments.

can be incorporated into a quota plan which becomes the base on which commissions are calculated. Earnings would then be determined in proportion to the percentage of quota attained.[17]

Commission Rates. A great variety of commission rates can be employed. To begin, rates can be fixed, progressive, or regressive. With a fixed rate, the same percentage commission is paid at all levels of sales volume (or whatever base is being used). A progressive rate means that commission percentages increase as volume increases. Johns-Manville uses a progressive rate for incentive purposes, which they term an "accelerated" commission on sales beyond quota. For instance, a salesperson may earn 0.5% on sales volume up to quota, but 2.5% in commission on sales volume above quota.[18] Regressive rates involve lower percentage commissions as volume increases, and are used when additional sales presumably become easier to make because of other effective marketing effort or economic improvement, or are used to dampen the effect of windfall sales achieved from little or no effort by the salesperson.

Rates can also be distinguished in gross versus net terms. A gross rate indicates that the salesperson is expected to pay his or her own expenses and maintain his or her own tax records. Under a net rate, expenses are reimbursed and not included in normal commission payments.

Finally, rates can vary according to products, customers, territories, order sizes, and profit margins. Some firms also pay a different percentage commission for new business than for repeat orders. Variable rates can be used to distinguish between more and less profitable business. Fibreboard, for example, calculates gross profit for each customer account, and pays higher commission percentages for the more profitable accounts.[19]

Starting Points For Commission Payments. If commission is the only compensation method used, the starting point is usually set at zero sales (or whatever base is used). But when commission is combined with salary, the starting point is sometimes set at a higher level. For example, both Olin and Johns-Manville use salary plus commission in their pay plans, but Johns-Manville pays commission on all sales while Olin pays commission only after the salesperson reaches quota. To help determine a proper starting point, some managers calculate a break-even level of sales volume necessary to cover the salary and direct expenses of each salesperson.

Greater flexibility is provided when management uses two or more commission components with separate starting points. For instance, a dual commission approach has been proposed in which a "maintenance" commission is paid on sales volume above some predetermined level of market penetration common to all territories, and an "increase" commission is paid on volume in excess of the territory's previous sales level.[20] Other approaches might start commissions on new products or new customers sooner than commissions on repeat business or old products.

Payment Periods. Some commissions are paid before they are even earned. This type of arrangement is usually called a drawing account, and it works as follows. Salespeople are allowed to draw a specified amount of money as a charge against future earned commissions. Subsequently, as commissions are earned, the account is cleared. Two basic variations are common. One, a *guaranteed* drawing account, does not require the salesperson to pay back the full sum of the draw if earned commissions do not reach that amount. It is similar to a salary and its incentive value is somewhat reduced, although a psychological incentive remains for the salesperson to try to earn what has already been received.

The second is a *nonguaranteed* drawing account which requires that the full amount be paid back—if not during the current pay period, then during the following one—much the same as a loan. A nonguaranteed account retains incentive value, but if a salesperson becomes too far overdrawn, incentive may be lost because future earnings must be used to pay what is owed rather than to provide current income. In many such cases the salesperson quits, and unless there is a clear agreement about responsibility for overdrawn accounts, the company is likely to lose the uncollected amount.

Many sales managers believe the best time to pay commission is immediately after it is earned. In psychological terms, this provides reinforcement immediately for desired performance. In practice, however, this is done very seldom because of the administrative difficulties which would result. It is more common to accumulate commissions earned and pay the balance at regular intervals such as monthly or biweekly. Longer time periods will reduce the psychological reinforcement effect.

A few firms use an installment approach whereby commission earnings are credited to the salesperson's account as they are earned, but a fixed sum is paid each month to provide stability in income. In months when actual commission earnings are low, income will come from high commission months. Burroughs uses a slightly different installment approach. Their salespeople's commissions are paid in 24 monthly installments from the time earned. The objective is to encourage salespeople to continue servicing their accounts, and also to avoid the chance of someone quitting or slacking off after one big sale.[21]

Bonus. A bonus is a payment for exceptional accomplishment or for achieving a specific objective such as obtaining 50 new accounts this year. The bonus differs from a commission in two ways. First, a bonus is paid less often—typically once a year as opposed to once a month for commission. In fact, in many firms a bonus is purely discretionary by management and not a regularly recurring part of the pay plan. Second, commissions are usually some percentage of sales while a bonus is typically a percentage of salary.[22] Kaufman Company, an industrial hardware distributor, pays both commission and bonus. Commissions are based on sales volume from small accounts and profits from large accounts. Bonuses are given for meeting specific objectives, one of which is to convince major accounts to accept a systems contract whereby Kaufman will routinely replenish inventory needs.[23]

The bonus adds flexibility to a compensation plan because it can be changed to meet short-term objectives without changing the basic compensation plan. There is a danger that sales personnel may overemphasize bonus objectives to the neglect of the regular objectives of the pay plan. Once a bonus scheme is adopted, it is difficult to drop it from the total plan without causing some discontent among the sales force.

Some firms use the bonus method as a group stimulus rather than individual incentive. If all salespeople in a district meet their quotas, each would receive a bonus of some fixed amount or predetermined percentage of base salary. A group reward is probably best used in cases involving team selling rather than for salespeople working singly. Otherwise, the best performers are actually penalized if weaker salespeople do not perform up to par.

The bonus method involves two major measurement problems. The first involves setting the fund of money to be available for bonus payments. Some firms set aside a predetermined sum in their budgets for this purpose. But because the amount is predetermined rather than related to current performance, its incentive value is limited. A better approach might be to base the bonus fund on a percentage of sales, profits, or some other measure of current performance. This provides incentive because the amount of bonus money will vary in proportion to sales force efforts.

The second measurement problem concerns the basis for calculating payments to sales personnel. Factors used in this calculation are shown in Table 13.4 from a study of 100 firms using bonus plans. Many firms use more than one factor, and some are measured subjectively through managerial judgment. In a typical case, each salesperson's performance is rated on each factor in the bonus plan, and bonus earnings are divided in proportion to the resulting ratings. Figure 13.2 illustrates a popular procedure used to calculate bonus earnings for sales force members.

Expense Reimbursement. Expense payments are not actually considered compensation, but expense arrangements are usually included in the compensation agreement because they depend on the methods of pay used. For example, commission-only salespeople are often required to pay their own expenses, while salaried personnel are reimbursed by the company for expenses incurred. Expenses can also influence compensation if expense quotas are used as the basis for commissions or bonus plans. Typical expense plans and policies are discussed in more detail later in this chapter.

Fringe Benefits. Salespeople paid partly or totally by salary generally receive a larger package of fringe benefits than do their commission-only counterparts, though this difference is lessening. Fringe benefits are a way of building company loyalty as well as attracting and keeping top-notch individuals in the sales force. A recent study showed that a typical benefit package would cost the salesperson at least

**TABLE 13.4
Performance Factors Used in Bonus Plans**

Factor	Measured Objectively	Measured Subjectively[1]
Increased over-all volume	96	2
Balanced volume categories	47	4
Expense control	29	9
New accounts	28	11
Territory growth	21	15
Profit contribution of a sale	18	1
Type or class of account	12	8
Promotional activity	11	16
Credit handling	8	13
Length of service	4	7
Season or timing of the sale	4	9
Report handling	3	22
Product knowledge	2	23
Personnel selling effectiveness	2	28

Column header: NUMBER OF PLANS INCLUDING FACTOR

[1]Subjective measures were mentioned by 38 of the 100 plans.

Source: David A. Weeks, *Incentive Plans For Salesmen,* Personnel Policy Study No. 217 (New York: National Industrial Conference Board, Inc., 1970), p. 42.

$1,500 per year.[24] Benefits supplied, in order of their popularity, by the firms in this study included:

Fringe Benefit	*Percent of Firms Providing*
Hospital insurance	99%
Life insurance	92%
Accident insurance	85%
Moving expense reimbursement	65%
Salary continuation program	62%
Educational assistance	60%
Pension plan	56%
Personal use of company car	52%
Club or association membership	38%
Profit sharing	36%
Dental insurance	25%
Stock purchase	18%

FIGURE 13.2
Procedure for Calculating Bonus Earnings

I. INCENTIVE FUND ALLOCATION

The bonus fund, if any, will be allocated by a point system. Points will be assigned for each sales function quarterly, using the attached point allocation form.

The total maximum number of points attainable is the product of the number of participants times the maximum points for all sales functions. The bonus fund available divided by this total maximum number of points will establish a monetary value per point. Individual participant's total points will be multiplied by this dollar value/point to calculate his point system bonus payment.

II. POINT SYSTEM

In order for the company to achieve its sales objectives each individual must conscientiously strive to achieve superior performance in the following functions:

1. New account development.
2. Maintenance and improvement of established accounts.
3. Promotion of new and/or specific products.
4. Emphasis on sales of high-profit items.
5. Emphasis on profit element in all sales.
6. Reporting and record keeping.
7. Feedback of market trends and competitive intelligence.
8. Knowledge of job (products, pricing, competition, potential customers, etc.)
9. Customer relations.
10. Personal qualities (attitude, interest in work).

A point rating of 10 to 0 is used to rate performance against each duty. Points awarded for performance of each duty will be based on quantitative information available from Call Reports, Customer Call Records, Monthly Operating Statements, etc., and on judgmental factors.

Regional Managers will rate Field Salesmen but the points awarded will be co-ordinated by the Sales Manager. For example, Salesman "A" in Western Region and Salesman "B" in Eastern Region both capture two new machinery accounts. The Sales Manager must insure that the performance points awarded by the Regional Managers for performance of Sales Duty (2) are equal in both cases; however, if the two new accounts in Western Region result in twice as much business, then this salesman should have a higher point rating awarded for performance of Sales Duty (1) and (4). The Regional Managers will be rated by the Sales Manager.

Source: David A. Weeks, *Incentive Plans for Salesmen,* Personnel Policy Study No. 217 (New York: National Industrial Conference Board, Inc., 1970), p. 60.

Which Methods to Use? The sales manager must now decide which method or methods will best meet the compensation objectives established. Ideally, the plan should be tailor-made for each salesperson, each territory, and even for each customer. But in a practical sense, industry standards and measurement problems must be considered which will make the plan competitively attractive and administratively feasible.

Although many different varieties of methods exist, three basic types of plans are commonly used: salary-only, commission-only, and combinations of salary, commission, and bonus. Table 13.5 reports the incidence of these plans among broad categories of companies. When compared with previous studies, these results show an increasing preference for the already-popular combination plans and the greatest decline in straight-commission plans. No doubt these patterns reflect changes in the nature of the selling job as discussed in earlier chapters. Note, however, that all types of firms are not alike—considerable differences exist between consumer, industrial, and other types of firms.

TABLE 13.5
Types of Sales Compensation Plans in Use by Various Categories of Firms

Type of Plan	PERCENT OF COMPANIES USING PLANS			
	Consumer Products Companies	Industrial Products Companies	Services and Other Companies	All Companies Combined
Salary-only	13.8%	23.9%	41.9%	23.7%
Commission-only	10.6	4.7	8.1	6.1
Combinations	75.6	71.4	50.0	70.2
	100.0%	100.0%	100.0%	100.0%

Reprinted, by permission of the publisher, from *Sales Personnel Report,* 23rd Edition, 1978/1979, Executive Compensation Service, © 1979 by AMACOM, a division of American Management Associations, All rights reserved.

In selecting methods for a particular firm, the sales manager might consider whether each of three types of compensation is necessary. These include a *fixed* portion, such as salary, which would provide management with flexible control and sales personnel with some level of security; a *general incentive* portion, such as commission, which would be based on the accomplishment of continuing tasks of long-range duration; and a *special incentive* portion, such as a bonus, which would relate to short-range objectives likely to change periodically. Once the need for all or some of these types of compensation is clearly established, the next step is to determine their relative proportions and set down the details of the plan.

Combining Methods into a Total Plan. The details of the plan begin with establishing a pay level for the average salesperson. Suppose that from a job evaluation, and considering industry pay levels, a sales manager sets this level at $20,000. Now, by what methods is this amount to be paid?

Since the majority of plans use a combination of fixed and incentive pay, a major decision concerns the proportion of each type. A split of 80 percent salary and 20 percent incentive is most popular, though a 70 percent/30 percent split is close behind.[25] The relative amount of fixed and incentive pay depends on many conditions, including the type of product sold, the nature of the market and competition, and management's objectives. Table 13.6 presents some guides concerning this split under varying conditions.

Following our example, suppose that the sales manager decides 30 percent of the average pay should be in incentive form. This means that 70 percent, or $14,000 per year, will be the average salary component. The remaining $6,000 must then be divided into general and special incentive components. After evaluating the long-range objectives relating to incentive pay, the manager decides on an average bonus figure of $1,000 per year, with the remaining $5,000 tied to a commission plan. (Alternatively, the manager could decide that any bonus payment would be over and above the total $20,000.)

The sales manager must now set the commission base, rate, and starting point. If sales volume is the base, a logical approach is to forecast the sales volume expected of the average salesperson. With a base of gross margin, some measure of forecast gross margin would be necessary. Assuming that volume will be the

TABLE 13.6 Conditions Influencing the Proportion of Incentive Pay to Total Pay for Salespeople

Condition	CONDITIONS UNDER WHICH PROPORTION OF INCENTIVE PAY TO TOTAL PAY SHOULD BE	
	Higher	Lower
1. Importance of salesperson's personal skill in making sales	considerable	slight
2. Reputation of salesperson's company	little known	well known
3. Company reliance on advertising and other sales promotion activities	little	much
4. Competitive advantage of product in terms of price, quality, etc.	little	much
5. Importance of providing customer service	slight	considerable
6. Significance of total sales volume as a primary selling objective	greater	lesser
7. Incidence of technical or team selling	little	much
8. Importance of factors beyond the control of salesperson which influence sales	slight	considerable

Source: Adapted from Richard C. Smith, "Financial Incentives for Salesmen," *Harvard Business Review*, vol. 46 (January–February 1968), pp. 114–115.

base, let us suppose that the average salesperson is expected to sell about $250,000 during the coming year. If the starting point is decided at zero dollars, the commission rate would be $5,000 divided by $250,000, or 2 percent. If a starting point higher than zero dollars had been chosen, it would require a larger commission rate in this example.

Additional details can now be worked out. For example, should the rate be the same on all products? Should it be fixed, progressive, or regressive as sales volume increases? The base for bonus payments must also be specified, and this depends on the particular objectives for which the bonus is to be used this year.

Testing the Plan

Any new or revised compensation plan should be tested before it is put into operation. One way is to simulate what results the plan would have produced had it been in operation during the previous pay period. For instance, how would each salesperson have fared? In a large sales force, a sample of high and low earners could be chosen and their pay calculated as if they had been under the proposed plan. Of course, sales performance might have differed under another plan. One study at International Harvester demonstrated this clearly; after the compensation plan was changed, the projected profit increase did not occur because some salespeople did not respond to the new plan as predicted.[26] But this backwards projection will usually point out any major earnings problems from the new plan. Budgets, sales-expense ratios, and gross margins can also be calculated and compared with what actually happened. Finally, management should consider what impact the plan might have had on customer treatment.

If possible, the plan should be tested in actual operation in one or a few sales districts. This can be carried out as an experiment, after which the results of the new and old plans can be compared among similar territories. If sales personnel in the test area object to being used as "guinea pigs," they can be paid with whatever plan—old or new—produces more income for them.

Administration of the Plan

Any compensation plan must be administered properly to be fully successful. The following are some key administrative decision areas regarding pay plans.

Splitting Commissions. The necessity for splitting commissions results when a single sale involves two or more salespeople. This can occur when an order is taken by one salesperson at the buyer's central purchasing office, but the delivery and servicing of the account is done by another salesperson in a different territory at the buyer's branch office. Ideally, the commission should be split according to effort expended, but in practice this criterion is difficult to measure and probably varies from one instance to another. Many firms have written policies on split commissions, an example of which is shown in Figure 13.3. Others require negotiation between management and sales personnel in each case.

Windfalls and House Accounts. A windfall sale is a large order placed from the salesperson's territory but resulting from little or no effort by the salesperson. In some cases, the commission from one large order could support a salesperson for many months. How much should a salesperson benefit when no effort has been exerted?

Many companies which expect to experience windfall sales have some provision in their pay plan to limit earnings under these circumstances. One approach, already noted, involves regressive commission rates. In other companies, management and salesperson negotiate on the disposition of the windfall commission. If the windfall

---

FIGURE 13.3
Policy on Splitting Commission Payments by Bergen Machine & Tool Company, Inc.

"(1) Origin of Written Order (Commission: 45% of 15% commission)
   NOTE: If purchase order should materialize in other than territory that sales representative is working and he, the sales representative, is directly responsible for the actual closing, he, the sales representative, will receive the 45% commission, rather than the sales representative in territory of origin of written order. This only applies if company policy of customer requires all purchase orders to be materialized in other than the sales representative's territory who was and is completely responsible for the actual sale.
(2) Installation Location (Commission: 30% of 15% commission)
(3) Engineering (Commission: 15% of 15% commission)
   NOTE: If Engineering is accomplished by the sales representative responsible for the written order, this 15% will be credited to him. If Engineering is required at installation location and is accomplished by local representative at the installation location, he will receive the 15% Engineering commission. If no Engineering is accomplished, then the 15% will go to the sales representative responsible for the written order.
(4) Servicing (Commission: 10% of 15% commission)
   NOTE: This 10% will be credited for installation location sales representative, as it will be his obligation to service the account in the future after completion of installation."

Source: "The Split Commission," *Agency Sales Magazine,* December 1976, p. 7.

is expected to continue into future pay periods, typical practice is to increase quotas to reflect these sales.

A highly controversial method of dealing with windfall sales is for management to take over the account as a house account, service it from the home office, and pay no commissions in its sales. This practice can be abused, especially when a salesperson has invested extensive effort in building that customer even though no previous sales had occurred. To avoid misunderstandings, criteria for an account to become a house account should be designated in advance. And in fairness to sales personnel, the servicing of house accounts should not be made their responsibility unless some form of compensation covers the work.

Territory Shifts. Another difficult situation may occur if a salesperson is shifted from one territory to another which is lower in potential or otherwise not as appealing. In such cases, pay is often guaranteed for a given period of time, no matter what amount is actually earned in the new territory. Some firms also provide an additional pay premium for major cost-of-living increases in the new area, and many pay moving costs as well and reimburse against any loss from the sale of a house in the former location.

Introducing a New Plan to the Sales Force. A noted student of sales management once observed that sales personnel suspect any change in their compensation plan, because they believe management would try to pay less if possible.[27] When any major change in a compensation plan is to be initiated, management must try to minimize sales force apprehension. This sometimes can be achieved by presenting the plan clearly in written form with examples of pay calculations for each salesperson. Individual or group meetings are effective means of explaining significant changes, so that comparisons with the old plan can be made and questions answered. It is always desirable to obtain sales force reactions prior to final implementation. This helps ensure that important objectives of sales personnel have not been overlooked.

COMPENSATING SALES TRAINEES

The level of earnings for trainees depends on such factors as educational background of trainee, type of sales job in question, and the amount of previous selling experience. Studies show that trainees with MBAs receive at least $5,000 more than bachelor's degree holders, and MBAs with technical undergraduate degrees average about $1,000 more in starting pay than those with nontechnical degrees.[28] Table 13.1 reports the average compensation of sales trainees.

Compensation methods for trainees often depend on the type of training they receive. Firms which provide formal training programs usually pay by salary only. Other types of training emphasizing on-the-job learning are sometimes accompanied by an incentive portion in the pay plan. For example, a trainee might be assigned to an experienced salesperson on an apprentice basis. During the first month, the trainee might be paid no commission; in the second month he or she would be given 5 percent of the total commission earnings of the pair; in the third month, 10 percent of the total; and so on. After a year, both would be earning about equal shares of the total commission obtained, and at that point the trainee would become a regular salesperson. An alternative approach involves paying by commission with a guaranteed drawing account, and gradually reducing the guarantee as the salesperson gains experience.[29]

COMPENSATING SALES MANAGEMENT PERSONNEL

Level of pay for each job in the sales management hierarchy must reflect the value of that job to the firm as well as competitive pay levels and the other factors discussed earlier. As one moves up the line in an average sales organization, Table 13.2 shows how pay will increase at each level. But there are considerable differences from one company to the next, depending on scope of job tasks and responsibilities. For instance, is the field sales manager expected to sell, and if so, is pay for selling determined separately from pay for management responsibilities?

Most sales managers receive the majority of their pay in salary, with incentive pay about 15 percent of total compensation.[30] The type of incentive varies from one management level to the next. As shown in Table 13.7, profit-based incentives become more predominant at higher management levels. Green Giant provides an example of an incentive plan for district managers based partly on profitability and partly on sales volume. Each product is assigned points, and point quotas are set each quarter based on past sales, profitability, and production capacity. Managers whose districts exceed each quarterly quota as well as the cumulative year-end quota earn bonuses paid annually.[31]

When commission is used, it can be based on the manager's own sales or those of his sales force. In the latter case it is termed an override. But profit-based commission plans are gaining in popularity. Motion Industries, an industrial distributor, pays each sales office manager a commission on monthly net profit earned in his office. In addition, a year-end bonus is awarded based on the manager's use of money as determined by return-on-investment calculations.[32]

TABLE 13.7
Incidence of Incentive Pay at Various Sales Management Levels

	PERCENT OF FIRMS WHICH GIVE INCENTIVE PAY TO THESE POSITIONS:				
Type of Incentive	Vice-President	General Manager	Regional Manager	District Manager	Field Sales Manager
Profit/Cost based	53%	40%	29%	15%	17%
Sales volume based bonus	11	16	28	49	39
Sales volume based commission	2	5	5	9	17
No incentive used	34	39	38	27	27
	100%	100%	100%	100%	100%

Source: Adapted from David A. Weeks, *Compensating Salesmen and Sales Executives,* Report No. 579 (New York: The Conference Board, Inc., 1972), p. 7.

SALES FORCE EXPENSES AND AUTOMOBILE PLANS

Typical company philosophy about expenses of sales personnel is that the amounts spent be "reasonable." Many companies prefer to avoid a specific definition of what is a reasonable amount, perhaps because it varies among different locations, times of year, and depends on the expected benefit to be derived. Most firms have developed methods of expense control and have adopted a particular expense plan which reimburses for specifically identified items.

Expense Control. Sales managers' concern for expense control stems from the ease of shifting personal expenses into business expenses which are reimbursable. Such shifting results essentially in adding to a salesperson's pay. Management might make estimates of how much shifting occurs and consider this amount as part of total compensation, but that avoids solving expense control problems.

The most popular method of control is simply the review and approval of each expense item by the salesperson's immediate supervisor.[33] Existing expense account budgets usually guide these approvals. Some salespeople are supplied credit cards, which provide detailed records of costs incurred. Other control methods vary with the expense plan used, as discussed below.

The Internal Revenue Service exerts considerable influence on expense control. For example, the IRS requires detailed records on the amount, time, and place of the expense; the business purpose of the expense; and, in the case of entertainment or gifts, the business relationship of the employee to persons entertained or receiving gifts. Salespeople must keep records or receipts of travel and lodging costs which identify time and place of departure, destination, and number of days involved. Specific tax regulations change periodically and seem to increase in complexity, requiring specialized and updated advice.

Expense Plans. Three basic expense plans are used either singly or in combination by most companies. In the first, or *direct reimbursement* plan, the salesperson is reimbursed for all allowable expenses as long as their amounts are reasonable. Payment is usually contingent upon receipts or detailed records supporting the claims.

In the *advances* modification, salespeople are advanced a sum of money to be used for expense purposes. The amount advanced may depend on forecast sales or previous expenses in the territory. Detailed records and receipts are still required to prove that the advanced amount was used. Expenses are not necessarily limited to the amount of the advance, but additional expenses must be approved before being reimbursed.

Under the third system, *predetermined allowances,* the salesperson is given a specific predetermined sum to allocate as effectively as possible among all expenses. The amount given may depend on past or forecast sales volume or be determined on the basis of territory size. Sometimes this allowance is not separately identified, but is included as part of total compensation, usually in salary. Each salesperson must then keep records to support personal income tax deductions for business expenses. This method is the least popular of the three expense plans.

Expenses Allowed. Table 13.8 indicates company policies regarding various expense items. Undoubtedly there are variations from one company to another and

TABLE 13.8

Company Policies Regarding Expense Items

ITEMS USUALLY REGARDED AS REIMBURSABLE EXPENDITURES FOR SALESPEOPLE

Expense Item	Normally Percent	Only On Special Occasions Percent	Never Percent	Expense Item	Normally Percent	Only On Special Occasions Percent	Never Percent
Air transportation				Personal entertainment	4.5	20.5	75.0
First class	7.3%	67.5%	25.1%	Doctor/dentist while away			
Coach	96.4	2.7	0.9	from office	4.5	24.1	71.4
Charges for excess				Travel expenses for wife	0.9	69.5	29.6
baggage	53.4	35.2	11.4	Postage/telephone/			
Travel insurance	12.6	5.4	82.0	telegraphs to home	69.5	23.5	7.1
Cocktails—salesperson				Valet/laundry while away			
alone	30.7	14.7	54.6	from office	58.2	31.6	10.2
Cocktails—with customer	86.7	10.2	3.1	Barber/manicurist/bootblack			
Taxis or other local				while away from office	4.1	11.3	84.7
transportation	96.9	2.6	0.4	Theft/loss/damage to			
Gratuities and tips	96.9	1.8	1.3	personal effects while			
Temporary secretary while				away from office	17.2	41.2	41.6
away from office	10.3	53.1	36.6				
Office supplies/equipment							
while away from office	41.7	43.0	15.4				

ENTERTAINMENT EXPENSES REGARDED AS ALLOWABLE FOR SALESPEOPLE'S BUSINESS PURPOSES

Expense Item	Normally Percent	Only On Special Occasions Percent	Never Percent	Expense Item	Normally Percent	Only On Special Occasions Percent	Never Percent
Restaurants	96.5%	3.1%	0.4%	Club dues	25.2	33.8	41.0
Nightclubs	39.0	48.9	12.1	Movies	22.6	33.6	43.8
Sporting events	37.7	46.6	15.7	At home	14.5	55.5	30.0
Cocktail parties	30.5	55.2	14.3	Hunting/fishing trips	12.8	42.0	45.2
Theatre	28.4	47.3	24.3				

Note: May not add up to 100% because of rounding

Source: "Survey of Selling Costs," *Sales & Marketing Management*, February 21, 1977, p. 21. Reprinted by permission from *Sales & Marketing Management* magazine. Copyright 1977.

from one situation to the next. In particular, practices vary depending on the type of compensation methods employed, with commission-only salespeople generally having fewer expense reimbursement opportunities.[34]

Use of Automobiles. Since most salespeople travel mainly by automobile, a number of important decisions regarding their use of automobiles must be made. Two considerations are important: what is the most economical way to provide transportation; and what is most satisfying to salespeople in terms of morale and to the company in terms of its image.

The solution used by most companies is to supply the sales force with company-leased cars. Next in popularity are two plans, one in which the employee's own car is used and expenses for business use of the car are reimbursed, and one in which the company owns the car supplied to sales personnel. Other less popular plans involve employee-leased cars, a fixed monthly allowance for transportation, and the use of rental cars.[35]

CONCLUSION

The compensation plan is one means of channeling a salesperson's motivation towards attainment of company goals. These goals, as well as the needs of sales personnel and customers, must be translated into specific compensation objectives. A plan is then developed in which the level and methods of compensation are selected to meet those objectives. This chapter presented some approaches to determining the proper level of pay and also discussed various methods of compensation in terms of their incentive, control, and measurement aspects. Problems in administering the plan were also noted, and compensation of sales trainees was given a brief look. Expense plans and typical practices in the use of automobiles for the sales force rounded out this chapter. Compensation is only one means of stimulating and controlling a sales force. In the next chapter we examine additional ways of directing salespeople's efforts toward effective performance.

QUESTIONS FOR REVIEW AND DISCUSSION

1. If a salesperson is happy with the level of compensation received, does it matter what methods of compensation are used to reach that level?

2. Design a compensation plan in which the average salesperson should earn $20,000, of which $8,000 is to be earned in commissions. The average salesperson's annual sales volume is expected to be $400,000 divided equally among two products, but product A has a gross margin of 40 percent whereas product B's gross margin is only 20 percent. The company's territories are well-established, and sales increases from one year to the next are possible but difficult to obtain because of tough competition. Once you have designed the plan, calculate the annual earnings of a salesperson who sells $250,000 of product A and $200,000 of product B.

3. Two district managers are discussing the merits of a commission-only compensation plan. One states that it is the best plan under good economic conditions. The other argues that it is best under poor economic conditions. Could they both be right?

4. In some firms the level of expense money allowable for each salesperson is a straight percentage of that salesperson's sales volume. Is this a good policy?

5. Some salespeople argue that commissions should not be based on gross margins or other profit-oriented measures because the sales force has no control over the margin or profitability of any product. Is this a good argument?

6. Distinguish between compensation methods in terms of fixed versus flexible control. Under what circumstances is one more desirable than the other?

7. A general sales manager is considering a change in sales force compensation plan to reduce the large pay difference among salespeople. Up to now, each has been paid a $500 monthly salary plus 5 percent commission on sales volume. The proposed plan calls for the same salary but a regressive commission rate as follows: 5 percent on all sales up to $200,000, 4 percent on all sales between $200,000 and $300,000, and 3 percent on all sales above $300,000. The following information on three members of the sales force is readily available:

SALESPERSON	LAST YEAR'S EARNINGS	FORECAST SALES FOR NEXT YEAR
Baker	$18,000	$260,000
Garcia	$16,000	$220,000
Washington	$23,000	$360,000

Using this information, evaluate the proposed change.

8. In an attempt to even out a pronounced seasonal pattern in sales, a sales manager suggests that her sales force be paid extra commission in months with a below-average seasonal index. The advertising manager counters that an advertising boost be budgeted for those months instead, making it easier for the sales force to sell. How should this problem be approached, and what additional information might be helpful prior to a decision?

9. Design an experiment to determine whether salespeople should be reimbursed for taking customers to nightclubs, sporting events, and theaters. Is there any other basis which might be used to make this decision?

10. Should district sales managers earn commissions based on sales volume of the salespeople in their district? What other types of incentive pay might be considered for district sales managers?

NOTES

1. Marginal analysis provides another way of determining compensation level. The number of salespeople employed will usually affect the value of each position; thus, the marginal worth of the last sales position filled might be used as a basis for compensation level. See Chapter 6 for the incremental method for determining the number of territories.

2. Elmer W. Earl, Jr., *Determining Salesmen's Base Pay—a Role of Job Evaluation,* Studies in Personnel Policy, no. 98 (New York: National Industrial Conference Board, Inc., 1948), pp. 7–35.

3. Dartnell Corporation now publishes such surveys biennially. Other sources include American Management Association, The Conference Board, Research Institute of America, and *Sales & Marketing Management.*

4. A detailed discussion of using such surveys is found in John K. Moynahan, "Surveys Can Help You Plan Your Sales Compensation Program—Up To a Point," *Sales & Marketing Management,* June 13, 1977, pp. 134–137.

5. A table of living costs for selected metropolitan areas is found annually in *Sales & Marketing Management*'s "Survey of Selling Costs."

6. This incident is described in a more detailed discussion of sales force pay levels in Richard C. Smyth, "Financial Incentives for Salesmen," *Harvard Business Review,* vol. 46 (January–February 1968), pp. 111–114.

7. This question is discussed in detail in William P. Hall, "Improving Sales Force Productivity," *Business Horizons,* vol. 18 (August 1975), pp. 32–37.

8. Some long-term ideas which will gradually bring pay levels in line with market growth are discussed in John K. Moynahan, "How to Correct an Incentive Plan That Pays Salespeople Too Much," *Sales & Marketing Management,* August 29, 1977, pp. 112–115.

9. "Philip Morris: It Pays To Tailor Compensation To The Selling Job," *Sales & Marketing Management,* August 23, 1976, p. 12.

10. "No Paper Tigers Need Apply," *Sales & Marketing Management,* August 1978, p. 39.

11. Rayna Skolnik, "Straight Commission Keeps Muzak's Sales In Tune," *Sales & Marketing Management,* August 23, 1976, p. 39.

12. David A. Weeks, *Incentive Plans For Salesmen,* Personnel Policy Study No. 217 (New York: National Industrial Conference Board, Inc., 1970), p. 4.

13. John P. Steinbrink, "How To Pay Your Sales Force," *Harvard Business Review,* vol. 56 (July–August 1978), p. 114.

14. Hall, pp. 36–37.

15. Weeks, p. 12.

16. "Olin's Sales Force Gets The Point(s)," *Sales & Marketing Management,* August 23, 1976, pp. 40–41.

17. For a plan which tied sales commissions to quotas determined by salespeople themselves as well as to management's objectives, and which was successfully implemented in IBM Brazil, see Jacob Gonik, "Tie Salesmen's Bonuses to Their Forecasts," *Harvard Business Review,* vol. 56 (May–June 1978), pp. 116–123.

18. Sally Scanlon, "Johns-Manville Builds a Better Pay Plan," *Sales & Marketing Management,* August 23, 1976, pp. 10–14.

19. "Using Paper Profits As An Incentive," *Sales & Marketing Management,* May 19, 1975, p. 6.

20. John K. Moynahan and Donald K. Spies, "A Commission Plan With Something for Everybody," *Sales & Marketing Management,* August 23, 1976, pp. 32–38.

21. Personal correspondence.

22. Weeks, p. 63.

23. "Kaufman Co. Sparkles With A Live-Wire Sell," *Sales & Marketing Management,* January 17, 1977, p. 26.

24. Steinbrink, pp. 120–121.

25. Steinbrink, p. 115.

26. Rene Y. Darmon, "Salesmen's Response to Financial Incentives: An Empirical Study," *Journal of Marketing Research,* vol. 11 (November 1974), pp. 418–426.

27. Harry R. Tosdal, "Administering Salesmen's Compensation," *Harvard Business Review,* vol. 31 (March–April 1953), p. 72.

28. Based on annual studies by Abbott, Langer & Associates, Northwestern University Placement Center, and College Placement Council.

29. Additional ideas are discussed in James F. Carey, "Paying The Sales Trainee," *Sales & Marketing Management,* August 23, 1976, pp. 43–49.

30. David A. Weeks, *Compensating Salesmen and Sales Executives,* Report No. 579 (New York: The Conference Board, Inc., 1972), p. 7.

31. "More Green At Green Giant," *Sales & Marketing Management,* October 11, 1976, pp. 15–16.

32. "Profitry in Motion," *Sales Management,* September 17, 1973, p. 3.

33. "Survey of Selling Costs," *Sales & Marketing Management,* February 21, 1977, p. 23.

34. A comparison of expense practices by type of compensation plan is found in Steinbrink, p. 119.

35. Further assessment of these alternatives is found in Don Korn, "To Buy, To Lease, To Reimburse?" *Sales & Marketing Management,* October 10, 1977, pp. 55–62. In addition, some firms are using company airplanes as alternative transportation methods. See "Taking Off," *Sales Management,* August 4, 1975, pp. 46–51.

14 MOTIVATION AND SUPERVISION OF SALES PERSONNEL

The performance of sales personnel depends on many factors we have already discussed—job qualifications, training, and compensation. But as time on the job grows, day-to-day performance will depend increasingly on how stimulating the job is and on how well it satisfies the salesperson's motivational needs. Understanding and meeting these motivational needs for the purpose of improved performance is the focus of this chapter. Since financial compensation has been covered in Chapter 13, this discussion will concentrate on nonfinancial aspects of motivation.

WHAT IS MOTIVATION?

Motivation is a force or pressure based on an individual's needs and wants that gives rise to his behavior. It is what directs a person to spend effort on some tasks but not others. Motivation is highly complex because it reflects the totality of a person's experiences and aspirations. It involves the whole person, and separating the aspects of motivation which apply to one job alone or to any other single activity or role is extremely difficult.

A salesperson will work hard at his job as long as it provides opportunities to meet his needs. But if these opportunities decrease, as often happens when one's needs change, job-related effort will also decrease and nonjob activities will gain higher priority to provide satisfaction.

WHAT IS SUPERVISION?

The sales manager's challenge is to establish and maintain a job environment which is fulfilling and stimulating to the sales force, thus encouraging a high level of performance. We will use the term *supervision* to describe this management process. In a narrow sense, supervision is sometimes viewed as the working relationship between subordinate and superior. While this personal relationship is important, it is only one of many aspects in the total job environment which affect motivation.

Supervision involves all management actions geared toward meeting the motivational needs of sales personnel. In this sense, managers do not "motivate" people directly—managers devise a job climate which fits their subordinates' needs. The key is to meet company needs at the same time. One writer put it this way:

You can't motivate people. That door is locked from the inside. You can create a climate in which most of your people will motivate themselves to help the company to reach its objectives.[1]

FACTORS INVOLVED IN MOTIVATION

Because it is so complex, we can gain a better appreciation of motivation by reviewing some of the major factors involved. From a managerial viewpoint, we are interested especially in how these factors relate to job performance.

Company Goals. Does the mere stating of company goals have a motivating impact on sales force behavior? In general, sales personnel work to attain their own goals. If meeting company goals is, in fact, an important personal goal to one or more sales force members, then company goals may be strong motivators. But usually management tries to translate company goals into personal objectives as noted in Chapter 12 on training and Chapter 13 on compensation. An MBO process is sometimes used to bring personal and company goals into alignment, as noted in Chapter 7, by encouraging sales personnel to participate in setting objectives and quotas.

Job Satisfaction. Most managers are interested in maintaining a high level of job satisfaction among their sales personnel. This reflects both a humanistic concern (i.e., we want our workers to be happy) as well as a desire for better performance (i.e., happy workers are more motivated to be better performers). But studies have not always found that satisfaction and performance are directly related. For instance, one study of a national producer of wood products concluded that circumstances which foster higher sales performance may not be conducive to high satisfaction.[2] In another study, this one of steel strapping salespeople, the opposite results occurred.[3]

One reason for inconsistent findings may be that job satisfaction is a complex of many other factors and is not always measured the same way. In one study of more than 400 sales personnel from ten different companies, job satisfaction was found to be a composite of seven factors:

1. *The job itself:* e.g., challenging, exciting, sense of accomplishment.
2. *Fellow workers:* e.g., are they responsible, intelligent; do we get along well together.
3. *Supervision:* e.g, does our manager try to get our ideas on things and provide us with things we need to do our job.
4. *Company policies and support:* e.g., company benefits, sales training, promotional support.
5. *Pay:* e.g., level compared with other companies, incentive to increase sales.
6. *Promotion and advancement:* e.g., opportunities for, and a fair basis for promotion.
7. *Customers:* e.g., do they respect my judgment, are they fair.[4]

The importance of these factors to an individual is a gauge of that person's motivation. Suppose promotion opportunities are a salesperson's high-priority need. A job with good promotion opportunities should then be highly motivating to that salesperson.

Role Ambiguity and Role Conflict. Another set of factors which affect job satisfaction and performance are role ambiguity and role conflict. Role ambiguity occurs when salespeople do not clearly understand how to perform their jobs because they are unclear about what is expected of them by those with whom they interact. Role conflict occurs when salespeople believe that others expect them to behave in conflicting ways. An example of role ambiguity occurs when a salesperson is unsure about how best to use expense account funds; role conflict occurs when the salesperson believes customers want to be entertained lavishly but management wants entertainment expenses cut to the bone.

Many studies have focused on these two factors. In one, the results indicated that job satisfaction would increase if role ambiguity was reduced.[5] Another showed that role conflict reduced job satisfaction.[6] In the study of steel strapping sales personnel, both role ambiguity and role conflict were related to lower performance levels.[7] In general, a job which is unclear or presents conflicting demands is less likely to satisfy the jobholder, to meet his or her motivational needs, and to induce top-level performance.

Pay. Pay is certainly an important factor in motivation, but sales managers sometimes overvalue its impact. Economic rewards satisfy only a part of an employee's total needs. In one study salespeople were asked if they would quit work or continue after receiving a large inheritance. Over 90 percent said they would continue, even though their economic needs would be met without that job.[8]

To what extent does pay motivate sales personnel to higher performance levels? When International Harvester changed its sales compensation plan, sales force reaction was carefully monitored and the conclusion drawn was that

> each salesman has in mind (consciously or not) a certain income level he wants to reach, given a specific remuneration scheme which is offered to him. Then, he adjusts his level of activity to reach this income. When the remuneration structure is altered, the salesman reconsiders the amount he wants to earn and consequently readjusts his effort.[9]

A change in pay plan which offers more income incentive for increased effort may not produce the increased effort if sales personnel are satisfied with existing earnings levels. In fact, an increase in commission rate may produce decreased effort since less sales volume is necessary at higher commissions to reach a given income target. A study of life insurance agents went one step further and found that the better performers were those with the stronger desire for recognition rather than those with the stronger desire for more pay.[10]

One's Life in General. Performance on the job is affected by problems and circumstances off the job. Worrying about a family problem can certainly divert one's attention from work. A recent analysis of sales motivation observed:

> When you improve an individual's closing technique, you might get 10 percent more sales volume. If you resolve someone's problem with a teenage son, or help the individual accept the problem, so that his or her concentration is not diverted, sales can increase by 25 percent to 50 percent.[11]

Should sales managers be concerned about the off-the-job lives of their sales personnel? This is a touchy issue, requiring managers to assess the tradeoff between respect for personal privacy and responsibility for job performance. One writer suggested that sales force management in the future must not be only limited to professional development but must concentrate increasingly on total human resource development.[12] However this matter is resolved, it will remain a major factor affecting sales force motivation.

THE SUPERVISION PROCESS

As already noted, effective supervision involves establishing and maintaining a job environment that encourages a high level of sales force performance. Management sets performance expectations which will meet company goals. What is achieved is a reflection of the personal goals of sales force members. It is the meshing of expectations and achievement which is the key to supervision success.

Supervision must not be regarded as the remedy for ills in other sales management areas such as hiring or training. A manager may be tempted to use weekly sales meetings rather than careful selection or a solid training foundation to induce good performance. But the effectiveness of meetings or other supervisory activities will be based on the potential capability of those hired and the training they have received.

We will examine the supervision process in three steps. The sales manager must:

1. Gain an understanding of what motivation is.
2. Measure motivational needs of sales personnel and assess their job environment.
3. Develop motivational programs to improve job performance.

Understand Motivation. Many motivational programs do not succeed because they are misdirected. A manager hears about some contest or incentive program that really fires up another sales force, applies it to his own firm, and watches it fizzle. It doesn't work because the two sales forces have different motivational needs. But if the sales manager understands motivation, he should be able to diagnose his own sales force situation and devise programs that are on target.

Understanding motivation involves a two-part learning process of study and application. The manager must first study a basic theory of motivation, and second must solidify this learning by "testing" the theory through observation and analysis of sales force members. To see how this works, let us consider a simple motivation theory devised by Maslow.[13]

Hierarchy of Needs Theory. Maslow's theory states that basic human needs are organized into a "hierarchy of prepotency." This means that some categories of needs take priority over others, and when the higher-priority needs are substantially satisfied, the needs next in priority (or potency) appear and guide the person's behavior. When satisfied, needs cease to be sources of motivation, so that a person's motivation at any one time stems from the highest-priority needs in the hierarchy which are not yet sufficiently satisfied.

The hierarchy of needs suggested in this theory is as follows, from highest to lowest priority:

1. Physiological needs, such as food and sleep
2. Safety needs, such as protection, security, and order
3. Belongingness and love needs, such as acceptance and affection

4. Esteem needs, such as achievement, status, and recognition
5. Self-actualization needs, such as self-fulfillment or doing well what one is potentially fitted for

This theory is sometimes criticized as being far too simple, but it does provide a foundation for observing sales personnel and learning to recognize motivational differences. Through informal conversation, the manager can determine which position in the hierarchy of needs best fits each salesperson. For example, one salesperson might be very vocal about gaining recognition both on and off the job—by pushing for a more prestigious job title, by seeking acclaim or publicity in community or professional activities, even by the type of car driven or clothes worn.

Expectancy Theory. A more complex but also more realistic theory of sales force motivation is termed expectancy theory and is diagrammed in Figure 14.1. In this theory, motivation is based on two factors:

1. The relationship expected by the salesperson between effort devoted to a particular task and the achievement resulting on a particular performance measure. For instance, a salesperson might expect that making five calls per week on new

FIGURE 14.1

Expectancy Theory of Sales Force Motivation

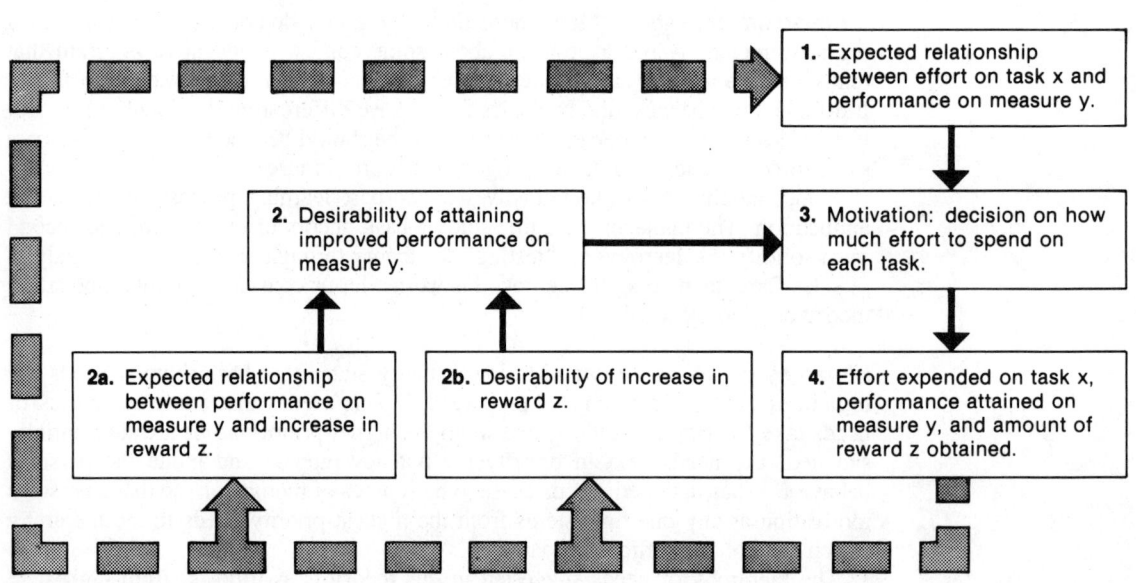

Reprinted from *Journal of Marketing Research*, published by the American Marketing Association. Adapted from Orville C. Walker, Jr., et al., "Motivation and Performance in Industrial Selling: Present Knowledge and Needed Research," vol. 14 (May 1977), p. 162.

prospects will result in a 50 percent chance of meeting the quota set for sales of a newly introduced product, while eight calls per week on new prospects will result in a 95 percent chance of meeting that quota.
2. The desirability to the salesperson of attaining that improved performance. This estimate of desirability is dependent on two subfactors:

2a. The relationship between improved performance and increase in one or a variety of different rewards which might be gained as a result. The salesperson might expect that meeting the quota for sales of the new product will assure him of special recognition in the company's monthly newsletter and might help in getting a year-end bonus of $500.

2b. The desirability of those increased rewards. Here the salesperson must consider the desirability of newsletter recognition and the desirability of the $500 year-end bonus. The desirability of additional recognition and pay will depend on how much this salesperson currently is acquiring these rewards and how strong is his need for more.

Each sales force member evaluates these factors and subfactors for all tasks confronting him (off as well as on the job) and their corresponding expected rewards, and decides how to direct his efforts as indicated in box 3. The actual effort-performance-reward relationships are then experienced as shown in box 4, and become inputs to future evaluations by the salesperson. All of this happens very quickly, informally, and even subconsciously in the salesperson's mind. While this theory is more realistic and comprehensive than Maslow's, it is obviously more cumbersome to apply through informal observation. But there is considerable research, both completed and ongoing, which is making expectancy theory more understandable and applicable to the practicing manager.[14]

Measure Motivational Needs. As the understanding of motivation grows, the manager can move to the next step involving measurement of motivational needs and job environment. A variety of approaches have been used, and we will examine some examples of these using formal and informal measurement.

Formal Measurement. The most popular measures concerning motivation are usually related to *job satisfaction* and its components. A study at 3M illustrates this approach. All 3M salespeople were surveyed with a mail questionnaire. Some of the survey topics which earned positive results were the following:

87 percent of the respondents called their work "challenging."

83 percent reported leaving work often with a feeling of having done something worthwhile on the job.

74 percent rated their individual morale as high.

On the negative side, many respondents felt the company was not doing a good job of providing them with career information, and that the job required too much paperwork and too much time on other things besides selling.[15] A job satisfaction questionnaire has been devised specifically for sales personnel and tested for validity and reliability in a variety of firms ranging from machine tools to computers to cleaning supplies.[16] A sample of questionnaire items, divided by job satisfaction components, is shown in Table 14.1. Respondents are asked to reply to each item

TABLE 14.1

A Sample of Items on the Sales Force Job Satisfaction Questionnaire

Component	Total number of items	Sample items
The job	12	My work is challenging. My job is often dull and monotonous. My work gives me a sense of accomplishment. My job is exciting.
Fellow workers	12	The people I work with get along well together. My fellow workers are selfish. My fellow workers are intelligent. My fellow workers are responsible.
Supervision	16	My sales manager is tactful. My sales manager really tries to get our ideas about things. My sales manager doesn't seem to try too hard to get our problems across to management. My sales manager sees that we have the things we need to do our jobs.
Company policy and support	21	Compared with other companies, employee benefits here are good. Sometimes when I learn of management's plans I wonder if they know the territory situation at all. The company's sales training is not carried out in a well-planned program. The company is highly aggressive in its sales promotional efforts. Management is progressive.
Pay	11	My pay is high in comparison with what others get for similar work in other companies. My pay doesn't give me much incentive to increase my sales. My selling ability largely determines my earnings in this company. My income provides for luxuries.
Promotion and advancement	8	My opportunities for advancement are limited. Promotion here is based on ability. I have a good chance for promotion. Regular promotions are the rule in this company.
Customers	15	My customers are fair. My customers blame me for problems that I have no control over. My customers respect my judgment. I seldom know who really makes the purchase decisions in the companies I call upon.

Reprinted from *Journal of Marketing Research,* published by the American Marketing Association. Gilbert A. Churchill, Jr., et al., "Measuring the Job Satisfaction of Industrial Salesmen," vol. 11 (August 1974), p. 258.

using a five-part scale ranging from "strongly agree" to "strongly disagree." Another popular job satisfaction instrument which has been used in sales organizations is the Job Descriptive Index (JDI) which measures satisfaction with five areas of a job: type of work, pay, opportunities for promotion, supervision, and co-workers.[17]

A second measurement focus is the *job environment*. This is a logical counterpart to job satisfaction, since the manager must determine what factors in the job environment relate to high versus low levels of job satisfaction. In particular, those aspects of the job environment which are controllable by management should be assessed, since those are the factors management can adjust to improve satisfaction. A questionnaire to measure the job environment might include the following factors:[18]

1. *Closeness of supervision:* how closely are job activities structured, monitored, and directed?
2. *Influence in determining standards:* to what extent do salespeople have input in determining standards used to control and evaluate their performance?
3. *Frequency of communication:* how often do salespeople and managers communicate in person, by phone, or in writing?
4. *Authority structure:* how many departments in the firm can influence a salesperson's activities and can approve or reject a sale?
5. *Demand for innovation:* to what extent is the salesperson required to deal with unique situations without receiving sufficient assistance from the company?
6. *Role ambiguity:* to what extent are salespeople unclear about what is expected of them by others?
7. *Role conflict:* to what extent do salespeople believe others expect them to behave in conflicting ways?

From studies carried out to measure both job environment and job satisfaction, some specific managerial conclusions could be drawn for the firms involved. One conclusion, for example, was that sales personnel were more satisfied when they experienced closer supervision, although not necessarily more frequent contact with their managers. In addition, job satisfaction was greater under conditions of more active participation in determining standards, but the number of departments influencing salespeople's activities did not affect their job satisfaction. Of course, different firms are likely to experience different results.

A third measurement approach is more ambitious, and involves the major *components of expectancy theory*. A life insurance company devised questionnaires to measure the desirability of twenty different rewards to the sales force (box 2b in Figure 14.1), the expected relationship between performance and rewards (box 2a), and the expected relationship between efforts and performance (box 1). Sales goals for each insurance agent were used as the performance measures. Through a rather complex analysis, management discovered which of the twenty rewards were the best motivators and which were perceived as not related to performance or efforts by the sales force. For instance, earning membership in a sales club, such as the "$1 Million Club" for those selling one million dollars in annual volume, was found to be a significant motivator.[19]

Informal Measurement. Informal measurement is simply a continuation of the observation and conversation approach discussed under the first step. Maslow himself suggested that motivational level can be judged by a person's complaints which indicate unmet needs of importance to the complainer.[20] In other words, a "hierarchy of grumbles" exists which parallels the hierarchy of needs. Table 14.2 shows some typical grumbles which might occur at each need hierarchy level. As one's lower level complaints are satisfied, higher level complaints emerge reflecting the higher-level needs which have now taken priority. By categorizing a salesperson's grumbles, a manager can determine where in the need hierarchy that salesperson is positioned.

**TABLE 14.2
Measuring Motivational States of Sales Force Members Using the "Hierarchy of Grumbles"**

MASLOW HIERARCHY POSITION	TYPICAL "GRUMBLES" AT THIS LEVEL
Physiological	The heat in our apartment doesn't work. Do you know what it costs to feed a family of four nowadays? The office is always cold.
Safety, Security	I never know where I stand with my boss. One day he's happy with my work and the next day he's mad. Somedays I think he's out to get me fired.
	Customers sure are fickle. You think you've got a good thing going with one of them and then one day they turn around on you and give the order to someone else. I sure wish I could keep going with my established customers better than I do. Finding new ones is hard, and it's a real bother.
Belongingness, Social	This job must be pretty tough because the people in this office sure are unfriendly. The way they snap at me some days, you'd think I was their worst enemy. It sure would be a lot more pleasant around here if everybody was a little more friendly.
Esteem, Recognition	Nobody seems to understand how well I'm doing in this tough territory. Just last week I thought for sure I had won the monthly recognition award for adding six new major customers, but somehow Johnson got it instead. I wonder what you have to do around here to be really appreciated?
Self-actualization	Some days I feel I'm doing my job well, but other days I know I really blow it. I wish I knew what to do to really get better at my work. If only my boss or my friends would be really honest with me, I think I could get to the top.

Develop Motivational Programs. An effective motivational program meets two criteria. First, it offers attractive rewards keyed to sales force needs, and produces a better job environment and job satisfaction. Second, the extra sales force effort it triggers is aimed directly at achieving management objectives. In other words, both sales force and management benefit. Dictaphone devised a program aimed at controlling field sales expenses, Heinz offered incentives for improving profit contribution, and Textron's program focused on getting new accounts.[21] Once management sets its objectives, the program's details should be worked out to offer the sales force as appealing an incentive as possible. Of course, motivation is a continuing process, whether management has a special goal singled out or just wishes to maintain top selling effectiveness. In the latter cases, motivational programs must be geared to producing results which reinforce management's regular goals.

Motivational programs can be implemented with three basic approaches. The most detailed occurs when managers relate to each salesperson as an *individual*. A second occurs when the sales force is divided into *groups,* and the third involves treating salespeople *all alike* for motivational purposes.

Individual Approach. The individual approach requires the manager to adjust his or her "supervision" (i.e., the job environment) to the unique needs of each salesperson. If done correctly, this should maximize sales force effectiveness. But the price is great in time and personal involvement on the manager's part. A district manager with twelve salespeople would need to plan and keep track of twelve separate motivational strategies.

One suggestion for carrying out the individual approach involves offering a cafeteria of rewards from which each salesperson can choose. These rewards range from the more traditional color television sets and vacation trips to more leisure time (e.g., two free afternoons a month), a more prestigious car, or even more money. Each salesperson earns performance "points" and can spend them on whatever rewards best meet his or her needs at that time.[22]

Another idea is in the form of a guide to the sales manager as depicted in Figure 14.2. Based on Maslow's hierarchy, this guide shows what types of pay, nonfinancial incentives, leadership relations, and so on are best suited to persons at each stage of the need hierarchy. A salesperson at the safety level would be best satisfied by pay which is more in salary than in incentive, by nonfinancial incentives which are more tangible and practical than intangible and psychological, and so on across the diagram. It is up to the manager to translate these guides into specific rewards and activities for each salesperson. In one firm, for example, each salesperson could choose, within limits, what proportion of his total pay would be in salary and what proportion would be in commission.[23]

Group Approach. In the group approach, sales personnel are categorized into several distinct groups, and separate motivational programs are applied to each group. The key question involves what basis to use for grouping. Careful mea-

FIGURE 14.2

Guide to Devising a Motivational Climate for Individual Salespeople

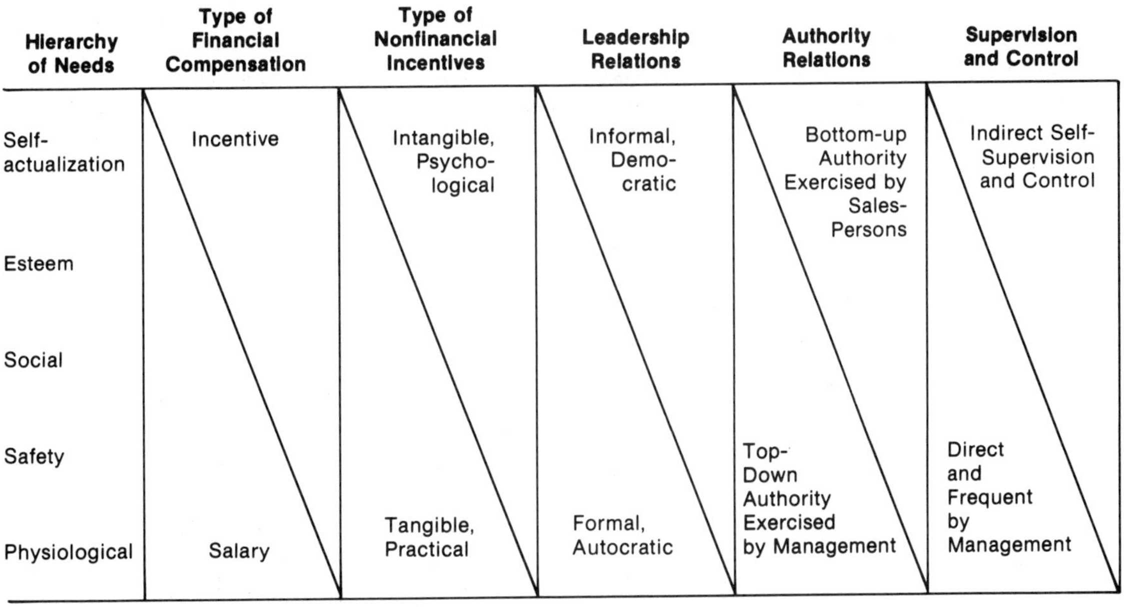

Hierarchy of Needs	Type of Financial Compensation	Type of Nonfinancial Incentives	Leadership Relations	Authority Relations	Supervision and Control
Self-actualization	Incentive	Intangible, Psychological	Informal, Democratic	Bottom-up Authority Exercised by Salespersons	Indirect Self-Supervision and Control
Esteem					
Social					
Safety					
Physiological	Salary	Tangible, Practical	Formal, Autocratic	Top-Down Authority Exercised by Management	Direct and Frequent by Management

Source: Adapted from Roger E. Dewhurst, et al., "Managerial Goals and Individual Needs in Salesmen's Compensation Plans," *Atlanta Economic Review*, Georgia State University, vol. 19 (April 1969), p. 16.

surement can help the manager identify groups with common sets of needs. If, for example, needs were related to length of time in a sales career, four groups might be distinguished: trainees, salespeople, senior salespeople, and master salespeople. Table 14.3 shows some suggested components of a motivational program geared to these four groups. Not only does job title and its associated status change, but changes also occur in pay, recognition, and communication practices. Note some of the similarities between this plan and the one outlined in Figure 14.2. In essence, the trainees are considered more involved with the lower levels of the need hierarchy while the master salespeople are nearer the opposite end seeking esteem and self-actualization.[24]

The group approach is used by Doubleday & Company with three, rather than four, sales force categories. New hires, those with 5–15 years of service, and those with over 15 years of service are each handled in a different manner in Doubleday's "upgrading" program. With new hires, the emphasis is on training, realistic goals, and clear feedback. Those with 5–15 years of service are given management de-

TABLE 14.3

Motivational Program Geared to Sales Force Groups—An Example

Title and Time	Pay and Benefits	Recognition and Communication
Trainee. Suggested period of product and sales training is 0–6 months. At completion he receives a promotion or separation.	Base hiring salary, no change while in this status. No bonus eligibility. Uses basic car. Not eligible for trips, contests, or similar rewards.	No vacation. Primary contacts during training through training personnel. Communications through trainers dealing with planning, sales techniques, role playing, competitive product, and formal progress reports.
Salesperson. Can be hired directly or moved from trainee status. Typically 3–5 years in this capacity, then either a promotion or career status.	Incremental raise on graduation from trainee status. Productivity raises. Bonus or incentive limited to 10% over salary. Eligible for contests.	Standard vacation, periodic home office sales meetings. Communications through training in more detailed competitive analysis, advanced closing techniques, etc. Introduction to general company problems and actions.
Senior Salesperson. 5–7 years in this category. Three choices: marketing management, master salesperson, or career status as senior salesperson.	Bonus with 30% limit on salary. Middle range car. Eligible for all regular contests plus special contests for senior and master only.	Standard vacation. Periodic sales meetings plus special sessions with middle managers. More personal communication, sometimes from upper management. Special peer sessions within sales meetings. Broad-base company bulletins.
Master Salesperson. A terminal title and position. Top 20% of sales force.	High salary, no limit on bonus. Premium cars. All contests plus special awards and premium trips.	Managerial discretion on vacations, home office visits. Attend all routine sales meetings. Act as upper management resource for broad-base planning and strategy. Presents successful sales experiences to others. Periodic dinner with the president.

Source: Adapted from Herbert Mossien and Eugene H. Fram, "Segmentation for Sales Force Motivation," *Akron Business and Economic Review*, vol. 4 (Winter 1973), pp. 8–9.

velopment opportunities while those with over 15 years of service are offered rewards emphasizing sales achievement, loyalty, experience, and for assisting in training new hires.[25]

All Alike Approach. All salespeople are treated alike when a single motivational program is used throughout the entire sales force. Widely differing needs among sales force members will moderate the effectiveness of this approach unless the motivational program is very broad in scope or taps some motivational needs common to the majority of salespeople. But job enrichment studies have shown that "enriching" the job environment can have a widespread positive effect on performance. Basic components of job enrichment include opportunities for personal achievement and its recognition, more challenging and responsible work, and greater chance for advancement. In one sales force, a job enrichment program was devised whereby each sales representative (a) was no longer required to write a report on each customer call; (b) was given authority to settle many customer complaints; (c) was given authority to adjust prices up to 10 percent at his or her discretion; and (d) was given improved assistance from the firm's technical service department when requesting information from a prospect or customer. The result of these and other changes produced a significant increase in sales volume and job satisfaction, with no offsetting decline in profitability feared from possible overuse of the pricing discretion.[26]

Another firm using this approach is Black & Decker. Its marketing vice-president defined the goals of their job enrichment program as "using the maximum capabilities of an individual by bringing him into the picture with a full range of motivating factors."[27] Black & Decker's motivational program includes seven factors:

1. Salary—higher than average.
2. Growth potential—many advancement opportunities in the sales force and other marketing areas.
3. Self development—educational assistance program with tuition reimbursement.
4. Training—frequent training activities for salespeople at all experience levels.
5. Communication—complete communication regarding marketing programs, new product developments, and overall goals.
6. Responsibilities—each salesperson is asked for idea development, to aid other salespeople, to develop managerial potential.
7. Recognition—numerous means of formal recognition such as company meetings and newspapers.

In seven years of implementing this program, dollar sales per sales force member have tripled. Of course, what succeeds in one firm may not do well in another.

INCENTIVE ACTIVITIES

Incentive activities are the building blocks of motivational programs. The variety is extensive, limited only by the imagination of management. We shall look at four major categories which, in one form or another, have proven useful in many firms:

1. Contests
2. Meetings
3. Recognition
4. Promotion opportunities

Contests. A sales contest is a competition in which salespeople are rewarded for specific achievements beyond those normally covered by the regular compensation plan. If used often throughout the year they may be viewed as simply another part of the compensation plan. But contests are more effective if geared to one or a few specific short-run objectives. If their use does not become routine, a well-designed contest can supply a change of pace which builds enthusiasm throughout a sales force.

Contest planning begins with setting objectives. For example, companies have devised sales contests

- To obtain greater volume per call
- To build better product displays
- To get a renewal of business from former customers
- To promote special items
- To introduce a new product or line
- To ease an unfavorable inventory position

Salespeople view contests as opportunities to fulfill personal needs such as a desire for recognition. So while management's purposes define the goals of a contest, it is the needs and motivation of the sales force which determines the contest format, rules, and prizes. For example, Regina devised a contest to increase the number of outlets carrying its Electrikbrooms. The contest format was a lottery in which each sales agent got one chance for each new account opened. Three winners received Caribbean cruises, and the rest earned double commissions on all new account reorders for six months.[28]

Any sales manager considering contests should be aware of their possible problems. One is cost. Most contests require management time in planning as well as clerical expense in keeping separate contest records and providing periodic reports to the sales force. Sales personnel also may spend more than normal recordkeeping time in tabulating their contest progress.

Another problem concerns sales force behavior during the contest period. Sales personnel may concentrate on contest goals to the detriment of other responsibilities. For example, they may overstock their customers in order to get contest credit for larger orders. Sometimes sales during a contest occur only because they have been "borrowed" from sales which normally would have been made in later periods.

Contests have losers as well as winners. While the winners may receive a morale boost, losers may be less motivated than before the contest. This problem can be minimized by careful planning to ensure all participants a reasonably good chance of winning a prize. Salespeople who realize they are not going to reach their contest quotas are likely to give up before the contest is even half over.

Meetings. Nearly all firms have meetings of sales and management personnel at regular intervals. Some meetings aim at inspiration and encouragement of the sales force through entertainment, rousing speeches, and even singing and audience participation. Electrolux, for instance, holds national meetings for its top sales personnel which include awards dinners, fashion shows, product demonstrations, and even competitions among sales personnel for the tables they will occupy during the convention period.[29]

Other meetings are geared more towards training and updating the sales force about new products, advertising programs, and other company developments. Still other meetings focus on communication and problem-solving among marketing personnel. A Del Monte meeting included product managers as well as sales personnel for the purpose of promoting teamwork and building better coordinated plans.[30] Inspiration, training, and problem discussion all can have incentive value for sales personnel under the proper circumstances, and meetings also are short-run means of building motivation through increased job involvement and raised aspirations.

Sales meetings, like contests, should be planned to achieve one or more specific objectives. These must be defined in detail to provide a basis for evaluating whether the meeting was a success. For example, it is seldom enough to say that a particular meeting is to inspire the sales force. Rather, the purpose of the meeting should be stated in measurable terms, such as to produce a specific increase in sales volume or a reduction in sales expense.

Many other decisions are also necessary. How often should meetings be held? Between two and four times per year is most popular, although the range extends from one per day to less than one a year.[31] Where should meetings be held? Location possibilities include the local or district office, the centralized home office of the firm, and resorts or large hotels. Costs and time involved must be evaluated in light of the benefits anticipated from such meetings. Other decisions relate to the length of each meeting, its program and scope of coverage, the selection of participants, and the administration of all the details involved in setting up and carrying out the meeting.[32]

Recognition. Recognition is a relatively simple but effective incentive. Consider this scenario:

> The lights go out. Conversation stops. Dr. Pete Franz, Director of Marketing, steps behind a podium into the spotlight. Dramatically, he reminds the audience of 90 salespeople and their managers what it takes to become a Supersweet Trail Blazer: outstanding performance in such areas as planning, credit control, sales volume, and dealer training.
>
> As Dr. Franz announces, "Our first Trail Blazer is . . . ," a spotlight flashes among the tables and fastens on the winner. Applause. A drum rolls. The winner, led by his sales manager, strides to the stage. His manager replaces the jacket he's wearing with a Trail Blazer's white Palm Beach blazer. Sales administrator Richard W. Wacholz reads the winner's accomplishments to the hushed audience. He hands the Trail Blazer a plaque. More applause. Then the winner steps aside to a place of honor while nine other Trail Blazers bask in their moment of glory.[33]

Firms can provide recognition in many ways. Table 14.4 indicates the usage of various recognition methods and their popularity in the opinion of sales managers. R. J. Reynolds is one firm where recognition is a major incentive for the career salesperson. As noted by their sales vice-president, "We've found that recognition is one of the best things we have to keep him happy."[34] Reynolds uses five specific methods of recognition: letting younger salespeople work with him; giving him more responsibilities such as a big account; writing up his work in our sales department house organ; writing letters of congratulations for special accomplishments; and a pat on the back.

**TABLE 14.4
Usage and Popularity of Sales Force Recognition Methods**

Method	Percentage Who Use	POPULARITY RATING BY USERS		
		Very Popular	Popular	Not Very Popular
Wall plaques	72.5%	43.2%	51.3%	5.5%
Trophies	39.2	45.0	50.0	5.0
Publicity—company	33.3	52.9	35.3	11.8
Membership in special sales club	25.5	38.5	61.5	0.0
Jewelry	23.5	50.0	33.3	16.7
Special meetings with top executives	21.6	63.6	27.3	9.1
Publicity—trade	19.6	60.0	30.0	10.0
Publicity—hometown	17.6	55.6	11.1	33.3
Special business cards	17.6	22.2	55.6	22.2
Other*	15.7	100.0	0.0	0.0

*Personalized gifts, cash, trips, nonpersonal merchandise, clothing.

Source: *Sales & Marketing Management,* April 12, 1976, p. 45. Reprinted by permission from *Sales & Marketing Management* magazine. Copyright 1976.

Promotion Opportunities. The opportunity to advance in an organization is a definite incentive for many employees, especially those with high ability and potential—the kind management usually wants to retain. To make promotion opportunities an effective incentive, management must spell out clearly what types of jobs can become available to the successful salesperson and how those jobs can be reached. The progression from one job opportunity to the next is called a career path. One large sales organization with a small product line has laid out the following career path for newly hired salespeople:

Trainee	Government sales representative
Junior salesperson	Sales supervisor
Sales representative	District sales manager
Senior sales representative	Regional sales supervisor
Specialty sales representative	Regional sales manager
Industry sales representative	Division sales vice-president

Every manager in this company started as a sales trainee and progressed through this career path.[35]

Learning how to reach each job in a career path usually requires a definite program to *acquaint* prospective jobholders with the type of work involved and to *train* them in the duties and responsibilities necessary to succeed. Royal Typewriter has devised its Royal Management Institute program to achieve these objectives. The program contains four levels. At level one the present salesperson becomes a candidate and studies sales leadership fundamentals. Those who succeed and remain interested progress to level two, planning and participating in recruiting and other managerial tasks. Graduation to level three involves the candidate in broader marketing planning and in building a marketing study. At level four candidates become field sales supervisors responsible for hiring, training, and supervising new sales personnel. During the course of this program, many good salespeople learn that they don't want to pursue management careers, and they redirect their energies to developing their professional selling skills.[36]

CONCLUSION

Effective supervision of sales personnel involves identifying each salesperson's needs and goals and then providing a job environment which meets these needs as well as company goals at the same time. Understanding motivation is a fundamental step in supervision. Only then can management devise motivational programs with a high degree of effectiveness. Incentives such as contests or recognition plans will then be most suitably tailored to gain the maximum boost in job satisfaction and sales performance.

This chapter concludes the second major part of sales management: implementation to achieve personal selling goals. In this part we have examined the selling process, the sales organization structure, and recruiting, selection, training, compensating, and supervising sales personnel. Whether management has been successful in setting and implementing its goals is dealt with in the remaining chapter on evaluation.

QUESTIONS FOR REVIEW AND DISCUSSION

1. Distinguish between motivation and supervision. Then explain how incentives are used to tie supervision and motivation together.
2. Does the motivation of a man in a salesman's role differ from his motivation in other roles such as father, Boy Scout leader, or golfer?
3. For salespeople with a high need for safety and security, what policies should management consider regarding the following:
   a. Length of the quota period.
   b. Frequency of performance review by the district manager.
   c. Type(s) of compensation methods.
   d. Method(s) of sales forecasting.
4. Discuss the relationship between job satisfaction and performance. How do they influence each other? Will salespeople who are more satisfied with their job also be better performers?
5. Sales contests are sometimes effective in temporarily overcoming seasonal slumps in sales. If a contest works in these situations, why does a slump occur without it? In other words, what is missing when the contest is not used? Is a contest the only answer?
6. Devise a questionnaire to measure job satisfaction for the selling job in Armour-Dial Company described in Chapter 10. Then discuss how you would use the results from this questionnaire if you were an Armour-Dial sales manager.
7. Compare the "individual," "group," and "all alike" approaches to devising motivational programs. Make up a chart assessing the pros and cons of each approach.

8. Discuss some approaches to providing a need-satisfying environment for members of a selling team involved in long-term negotiations with buyers of high-cost production systems. Consider the needs of individual team members as well as of the team as a unit.

9. A district sales manager prepares the following memo to his sales force:

   Sales in this district have not kept pace with overall company sales for the last three months. Some of you have complained that our prices are higher than Johnson Company's prices. Since there are no plans to cut prices at this time, I must urge you to emphasize the higher-quality aspects of our line. After all, if our prices were lower than competition's, what need would there be for the high-caliber sales force we have in this district?

   Would you consider revising any of this communication to make it more effective?

10. One sales manager expresses the following philosophy: "We take care to check the motivation of sales recruits at the hiring stage. Anyone not highly motivated to work in our kind of job is just not hired. That way we don't have any motivation problems." What do you think about this view?

NOTES

1. Kenneth A. Kovach, "Improving Employee Motivation in Today's Business Environment," *MSU Business Topics,* vol. 24 (Autumn 1976), p. 12.

2. Henry O. Pruden and R. M. Reese, "Interorganization Role-Set Relations and the Performance and Satisfaction of Industrial Salesmen," *Administrative Science Quarterly,* vol. 17 (December 1972), p. 605.

3. Richard P. Bagozzi, "Salesforce Performance and Satisfaction as a Function of Individual Difference, Interpersonal, and Situational Factors," *Journal of Marketing Research,* vol. 15 (November 1978), p. 526.

4. Gilbert A. Churchill, Jr., et al., "Measuring the Job Satisfaction of Industrial Salesmen," *Journal of Marketing Research,* vol. 11 (August 1974), pp. 254–260.

5. James H. Donnelly and J. M. Ivancevich, "Role Clarity and the Salesman," *Journal of Marketing,* vol. 39 (January 1975), pp. 71–74.

6. Gilbert A. Churchill, Jr., et al., "Organizational Climate and Job Satisfaction in the Salesforce," *Journal of Marketing Research,* vol. 13 (November 1976), p. 328.

7. Bagozzi, p. 526.

8. Nancy C. Morse and Robert S. Weiss, "The Function and Meaning of Work and the Job," *American Sociological Review,* vol. 20 (April 1955), p. 197.

9. Rene Y. Darmon, "Salesmen's Response to Financial Incentives: An Empirical Study," *Journal of Marketing Research,* vol. 11 (November 1974), p. 424.

10. Richard L. Oliver, "Expectancy Theory Predictions of Salesmen's Performance," *Journal of Marketing Research,* vol. 11 (August 1974), p. 250.

11. Research Institute of America, *Motivating Salespeople, 1977 Style,* as quoted in *Marketing News,* February 11, 1977, p. 11.

12. Leslie M. Dawson, "Toward a New Concept of Sales Management," *Journal of Marketing,* vol. 34 (April 1970), pp. 33–38.

13. This discussion is based on A.H. Maslow, *Motivation and Personality* (New York: Harper & Row, Publishers, 1954), pp. 80–106.

14. A good summary and bibliography are found in Orville C. Walker, Jr., et al., "Motivation and Performance in Industrial Selling: Present Knowledge and Needed Research," *Journal of Marketing Research,* vol. 14 (May 1977), pp. 156–168.

15. "Happy At 3M," *Sales & Marketing Management*, June 14, 1976, p. 12; and "Sad At 3M," *Sales & Marketing Management*, September 13, 1976, p. 28.

16. For further details, see Gilbert A. Churchill, Jr., et al., "Measuring the Job Satisfaction of Industrial Salesmen," *Journal of Marketing Research*, vol. 11 (August 1974), pp. 254–260.

17. Patricia C. Smith, et al., *The Measurement of Satisfaction in Work and Retirement* (Chicago: Rand McNally & Co., 1969). For an application of the JDI to sales management, see Paul Busch and R. F. Bush, "Women Contrasted to Men in the Industrial Salesforce: Job Satisfaction, Values, Role Clarity, Performance, and Propensity to Leave," *Journal of Marketing Research*, vol. 15 (August 1978), pp. 434–448.

18. This discussion is based on Churchill, et al., "Organizational Climate and Job Satisfaction in the Salesforce," *Journal of Marketing Research*, vol. 13 (November 1976), pp. 323–332. See also Orville C. Walker, Jr., et al., "Organizational Determinants of the Industrial Salesman's Role Conflict and Ambiguity," *Journal of Marketing*, vol. 39 (January 1975), pp. 32–39.

19. Oliver, pp. 243–253.

20. A.H. Maslow, *The Farther Reaches of Human Nature* (New York: Penguin, 1976), Chapter 18, "On Low Grumbles, High Grumbles, and Metagrumbles," pp. 229–238.

21. Sally Scanlon, "A New Role for Incentives," *Sales Management*, April 7, 1975, p. 41.

22. David M. Gardner and K. M. Rowland, "A Self-Tailored Approach to Incentives," *Personnel Journal*, vol. 49 (November 1970), pp. 911–912.

23. Frederick E. Webster, Jr., "Rationalizing Salesmen's Compensation Plans," *Journal of Marketing*, vol. 30 (January 1966), p. 56.

24. This example is based on Herbert Mossien and Eugene H. Fram, "Segmentation for Sales Force Motivation," *Akron Business and Economic Review*, vol. 4 (Winter 1973), pp. 5–12. A related analysis is found in Marvin A. Jolson, "The Salesman's Career Cycle," *Journal of Marketing*, vol. 38 (July 1974), pp. 39–46.

25. Clark Lambert, "In Upgrading, Good is Better, Better is Best," *Sales & Marketing Management*, August 9, 1976, pp. 46–49.

26. William J. Paul, et al., "Job Enrichment Pays Off," *Harvard Business Review*, vol. 47 (March–April 1969), pp. 66–68.

27. John I. Leahy, "Total Motivation = Top Performance," *Sales Management*, April 30, 1973, pp. 12–13.

28. "Regina Beats the Bushes," *Sales & Marketing Management*, August 1978, p. 24.

29. "Electrolux's Truly Golden Jubilee," *Sales Management*, July 22, 1974, pp. 21–24. For another vivid description of this type of sales meeting, see Dorothy E. Peven, "The Use of Religious Revival Techniques To Indoctrinate Personnel: The Home Party Sales Organization," *Sociological Quarterly*, vol. 9 (Winter 1968), pp. 97–106.

30. Ron McWilliams, "Sales Managers and Product Managers: Strangers When They Meet," *Sales & Marketing Management*, November 14, 1977, pp. 66–68.

31. Data on frequency of sales meetings is found in David S. Hopkins, *Training the Sales Force: A Progress Report*, Report No. 737 (New York: The Conference Board, Inc., 1978), p. 16.

32. A monthly publication available to help answer many of these problems is *Successful Meetings*.

33. Sally Scanlon, "Let's Hear It For Recognition!" *Sales & Marketing Management*, April 12, 1976, p. 42.

34. Sally Scanlon, "Richard Joshua Reynolds Would Be Proud," *Sales & Marketing Management*, November 8, 1976, p. 46.

35. Thomas F. Stroh, *Training and Developing the Professional Salesman* (New York: AMACOM, 1973), p. 244.

36. Frank Masi, "How to Turn Good Salespeople into Good Sales Managers," *Training*, July 1976, pp. 20–22.

15 SALES MANAGEMENT EVALUATION

Evaluation involves a comparison of goals and achievements. The sales manager first uncovers any major gaps between goals sought and results attained. Reasons for these gaps are then diagnosed, and ways to counter them are devised and incorporated into upcoming plans. At its best, evaluation is a systematic process of learning from experience. This process should enable the manager to identify weaknesses in planning as well as in performance. A gap between quotas set and quotas achieved, for example, can stem from faulty quota setting as well as from ineffective selling. In addition, both positive and negative gaps should be investigated so that upcoming plans can capitalize on strengths as well as overcome weaknesses.

Evaluation programs will vary somewhat from one firm to the next, but a serious and well-organized approach will contain the ingredients in this five-step program:

1. Analysis of Performance Results. This first step includes the analysis of sales volume, its associated costs, and the resulting profit contributions of various market segments.
2. Analysis of Performance Efforts. Included in the second step is analysis of quantitative and qualitative measures of sales force efforts, such as time utilization and the quality of sales calls or demonstrations.
3. Analysis of Performance Setting. The third step involves a review of the factors influencing efforts and results. Included are goals of the sales organization as well as policies, procedures, and the organization structure which make up the total sales operation.
4. Diagnosis. After problems and strengths are uncovered in the above steps, diagnosis involves interpreting this information to identify causes for both problems and strengths. Diagnosis is the translation of symptoms into reasons.
5. Recommendations and Corrective Action. The payoff in evaluation occurs through recommendations and corrective action leading to improved performance and planning. Some actions require higher management decisions, such as a proposed change in the firm's forecasting process. Other changes can be implemented directly by the sales manager, such as a modification of the training program.

ANALYSIS OF PERFORMANCE RESULTS

Major categories of performance results include sales, cost, and profit, and we examine these in turn.

Sales Analysis. Sales analysis is the gathering, classifying, comparing, and studying of company sales data.[1] All companies must gather and classify sales data to maintain necessary accounting records, although accounting reports must often be recast to be most useful to the sales manager.

Format of Sales Analysis. Systematic sales analysis follows the framework shown in Figure 15.1. The specific format produced for any firm is the result of four questions:

1. What constitutes a sale?
2. In what units should sales be measured?
3. How should sales volume be subdivided or categorized?
4. What standards can be used to evaluate the results?

When does a sale occur? Is it when an order is taken, when an order is shipped, or when the customer pays the invoice? When NCR gets an order for a computer, more than a year may pass before the machine is installed and revenue is received, so NCR uses cash receipts as their primary definition of when a sale occurs.[2] In general the most popular choice is at time of shipment.[3] But whatever choice a particular manager makes, it should be maintained so that comparisons of sales volume over time are consistent. All three could be used and comparisons among the three might prove useful. For instance, how much sales volume is lost because orders are unfilled? Is the rate of cancelled orders higher for one territory or product line than for others?

Measurement unit options are best illustrated with the example in Table 15.1. The questions below the table point out some of the complexities in analyzing even a simple set of sales data for three products over two years. Product A increased the most in dollars, but did not increase in units, so the sales increase is all traceable to a price increase. Product B also went up in dollar sales but increased in unit sales as well and, in fact, experienced a price decrease (price = dollar sales divided by unit sales). Product C unit sales remained the same although dollar sales declined because of a price reduction. Apparently the market for each of these products responds quite differently to price changes.

In general, dollars are the most common choice because dollar sales can be compared directly with other financial measures such as costs. Also, dollar sales of various sizes, models, or colors of one product or groups of products can be combined into one category. But when a company sells through a variety of distribution channels, each of which pays a different price, dollar sales measures would not give a good comparison of the channels' relative importance. And if significant price changes occur, as noted above, sales should be measured in both dollars and units so that changes in physical unit sales can be identified separately from the effects of price changes.

Categories of analysis chosen by the manager will depend on the firm's breadth of product line, organizational structure, selling strategy, and other factors. Most

FIGURE 15.1
Framework for Sales Analysis

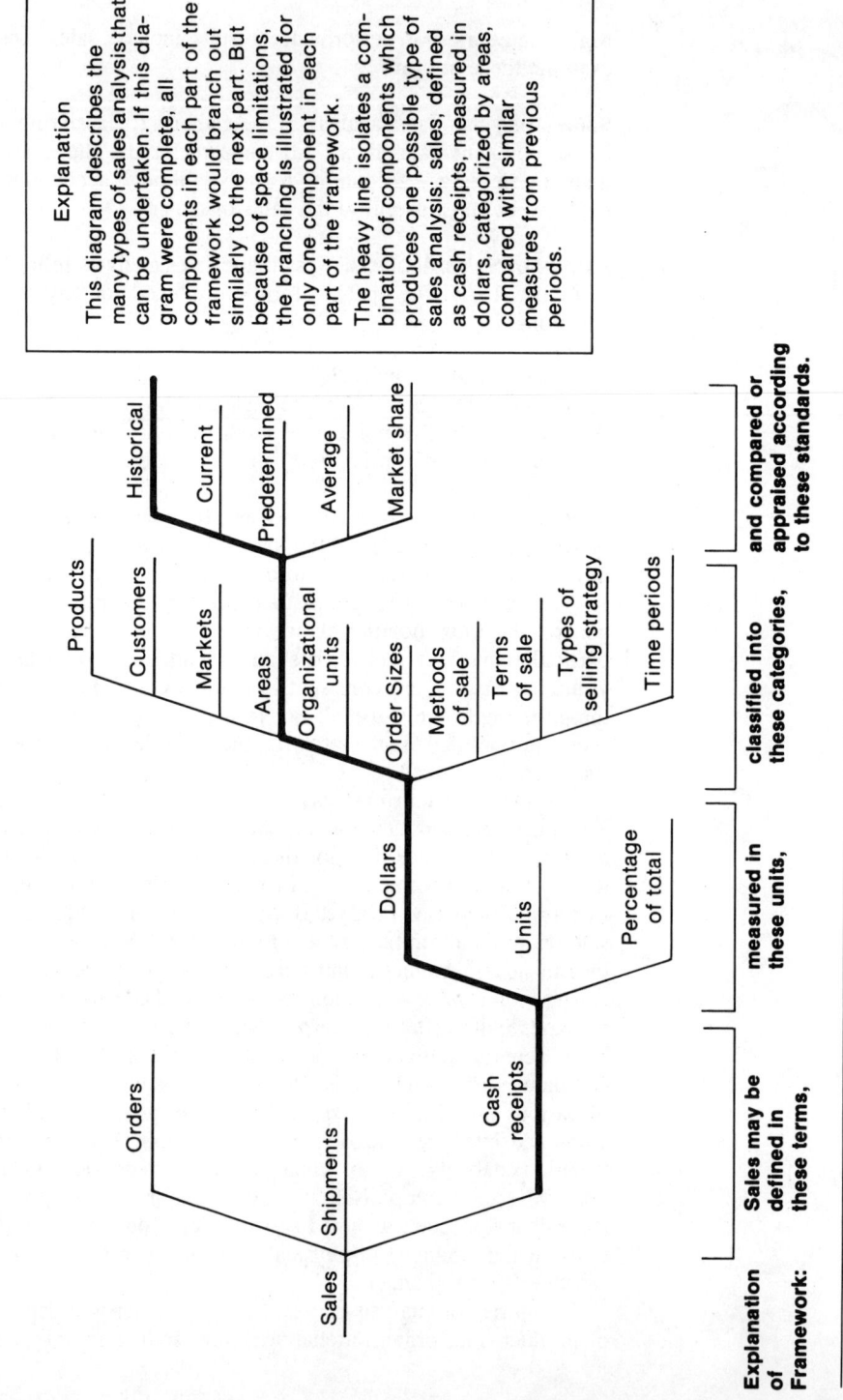

TABLE 15.1

Illustration of Measurement Unit Options in Sales Analysis

Products	LAST YEAR'S SALES				THIS YEAR'S SALES			
	Dollars (000)	Percent	Units (000)	Percent	Dollars (000)	Percent	Units (000)	Percent
A	$ 250	25%	100	20%	$ 400	33%	100	17%
B	500	50	200	40	600	50	300	50
C	250	25	200	40	200	17	200	33
	$1000	100%	500	100%	$1200	100%	600	100%

Which product's sales went up the most in dollars? in units? as a percent of total?

Which product went up in dollars but down in price? down in dollars but up in price?

Which products increased because of price more than unit volume? unit volume more than price?

---

firms will subdivide total sales volume by products or product lines, by major customer types, and by territories or geographic areas. Once these categories are chosen, the manager must decide on the extent to which each category should be further subdivided in order to provide detailed information. Guidelines for this decision stem from two general principles regarding patterns in sales data: the *iceberg principle* and the *concentration principle*.

The iceberg principle is named as such because total sales figures, like the visible portion of the iceberg, reveal only a fraction of the larger problem. The more subdivisions made in any category of sales analysis, the less opportunity there is for concealing undesirable results. For instance, suppose a firm sells six product lines and its total sales is right on target with its forecast at $5 million. No apparent problem seems to exist. But management decides to subdivide its sales into two categories as follows:

PRODUCT LINES	ACTUAL SALES	FORECAST	DIFFERENCE
A, B, and C	$2,300,000	$2,500,000	−$200,000
D, E, and F	2,700,000	2,500,000	+ 200,000
Total	$5,000,000	$5,000,000	—

From this information, the sales manager might become a little concerned with products A, B, and C, but might be quite pleased with products D, E, and F. However, if a more detailed breakdown were undertaken, these results might unfold:

PRODUCT LINE	ACTUAL SALES	FORECAST	DIFFERENCE
A	$1,000,000	$1,000,000	—
B	700,000	750,000	− 50,000
C	600,000	750,000	− 150,000
D	1,000,000	500,000	+ 500,000
E	1,500,000	1,000,000	+ 500,000
F	200,000	1,000,000	− 800,000
Total	$5,000,000	$5,000,000	—

Apparently the previous conclusions were misleading. Product lines D, E, and F were all way off target and should be investigated further to determine why they diverge so much from their forecasts. Conversely, product line A and possibly B seem to require no further immediate attention.

The concentration principle (sometimes called the "80–20" principle) is named because a large proportion of any firm's sales and profits (e.g., 80 percent) is usually concentrated on a small proportion of customers and products (e.g., 20 percent). One study of large national manufacturers showed that the top one-third of their customers provided over 75 percent of their sales, and the top one-third of their products contributed nearly 75 percent of their sales.[4] An illustration of the concentration principle as it applies to order sizes is shown in Table 15.2. While only about 20 percent of the orders are for $500 or more, they account for nearly 85 percent of sales revenue. Management should subdivide any sales category sufficiently to identify the key products or customer types (or order sizes) which provide the largest share of company sales. Once identified, these key customers and products should become the targets for increased sales force effort. For example, based on such an analysis, USV Pharmaceutical reduced the number of accounts called on by its sales force from 400,000 to only 70,000 of the highest-potential accounts. Because each account could now receive more sales calls, the company's sales volume increased 250 percent over a four-year period.[5]

The final sales analysis question involves the selection of standards. Standards are necessary to assess the effectiveness of any sales volume measure. Without standards, it is impossible to conclude whether a given level of sales represents good or poor performance. Many types of standards can be used, either singly or in combination:

1. *Historical.* Historical standards are simply the sales for a previous period of the products, customer types, or other subdivisions in question. These figures are then compared with the sales of the same subdivisions in the current period, as

TABLE 15.2
Concentration Principle Applied to Order Sizes for Orders Received in One Month

Size of Order	Number of Orders	Percentage of Total Orders	Sales Value	Percentage of Total Sales	Average Sales Value per Order
under $10.00	477	17.2	$ 2,599	0.3	$ 5.45
$10–$24.99	462	16.8	8,607	1.0	18.63
$25–$49.99	558	20.3	21,059	2.4	37.74
$50–$99.99	388	14.1	29,798	3.4	76.80
$100–$199.99	151	5.5	23,450	2.7	155.30
$200–$499.99	156	5.7	50,039	5.7	320.76
$500–$1,000.00	209	7.6	163,559	18.7	782.58
over $1,000.00	352	12.8	576,588	65.8	1,638.03
	2753	100.0	$875,699	100.0	$ 318.09 overall average

Source: Adapted from Curtis J. Blecke, "The Small Order Problem in Distribution Cost Control," *NACA Bulletin,* June 1957, p. 1280; as reprinted in William A. Terrill and Albert W. Patrick, *Cost Accounting for Management* (New York: Holt, Rinehart and Winston, Inc., 1965), pp. 657–658.

illustrated in Table 15.1. Historical comparisons can be misleading, especially when previous sales figures represent unusually high or low volume. Sometimes more than one previous period is used to establish a trend.

2. *Current.* Sales in one subdivision can be compared with sales in another subdivision of the same category for the current period. For example, how do this month's sales in territory X compare with sales in territory M? Such comparisons will be of little value unless the expected results in each subdivision are similar. The concentration principle uses current standards to pinpoint key subdivisions.
3. *Predetermined.* Predetermined standards are those devised at the beginning of a period to indicate expected or ideal performance. A quota or forecast are common examples.
4. *Averages.* The average of all subdivisions' sales is calculated, such as the average territory or the average product, and compared with sales of each individual territory or product. One value of averages is that they can serve as a check on other standards. Average performance well below or above a predetermined standard would be cause to review the feasibility of that standard as well as the effectiveness of performance.
5. *Market Share.* Though not a standard in the sense we have been using, a market share measure is often employed as a basis for comparing performance. A major problem is in finding industry sales figures that correspond to the subdivisions being analyzed. What are industry sales in territory M or to customer type C, for instance? Normal sources of industry sales, such as trade associations or government publications, seldom provide such details, and special research studies might often be necessary to calculate such standards.

It is important to specify how much deviation between actual results and the standard can be tolerated before additional investigation is warranted. In general, any deviation is significant if its investigation leads to an increase in profitability. In other words, the results of the study should produce greater revenue than the cost involved. Management's experience from prior investigations should help determine what constitutes a significant deviation.[6]

Sources of Sales Data. The most common source of sales analysis data is invoices, which normally identify the customer and location, amounts and types of product bought, terms of sale, date of transaction, shipping method, and salesperson who obtained the order. Other records such as order forms, credit records, company forecasts, and industry trade association reports may also be useful.[7]

Source documents must be designed and prepared so that necessary information is easily available for processing. Suppose one category of sales analysis requires tabulation of sales by customer types. If customers are to be classified by SIC codes, then these codes must be added to each invoice before the data is extracted from the invoice and punched into a data processing card or stored in a data base awaiting sales analysis tabulation.[8]

Limitations of Sales Analysis. Sales attainment is not necessarily indicative of profitability or efficiency of performance. For instance, one of the easiest ways to increase sales volume is at the expense of profits—by cutting prices or by spending more in an effort to capture sales. Nevertheless, sales volume is a direct and understandable measure of performance, and with proper planning and budgeting sales analysis can help in the control and direction of sales effort.

Managers must be careful not to jump to conclusions from sales analysis reports. These reports seldom provide reasons for problems or unusually good performance. They simply point out what needs further investigation. Suppose, for example, that a district manager discovers one member of his sales force is significantly below quota on a particular product line. Many possible explanations could exist:

1. The product is competitively weak, either in price or quality.
2. Customers who would normally buy this product have less need for it than anticipated.
3. Customers for this product are suffering a business decline.
4. The salesperson is doing a poor job of selling this product either by not calling on the right prospects, by not presenting it properly, or by pushing other products to its disadvantage.
5. Advertising and other promotional support for this product have not been forthcoming in this territory.
6. The quota for this product was set too high.
7. Delivery of this product has been too slow, causing canceled orders.

A problem revealed by sales analysis cannot be solved until further investigation clarifies what really is the problem's source. This sometimes requires additional sales analysis. If, for instance, the first explanation above were true, other salespeople would most likely be having similar problems with the product. If the third explanation were true, a customer type analysis should reveal that these customers are buying less than expected of many products. By proper cross-classification of sales data, it may be possible to eliminate some alternative explanations, or, conversely, to support them.

Cost and Profit Analysis. Cost analysis can be defined (to parallel the definition of sales analysis) as the gathering, classifying, comparing, and studying of company marketing cost data. When sales and cost data are combined, profit analysis occurs. Cost data are not sought solely for the purpose of measuring profits. A major purpose for accurate cost information is in planning marketing activities such as pricing, budgeting, and setting commission rates for the sales force. Cost standards established for these planning purposes are also used in cost control and evaluation. For instance, how efficient is our selling operation? Is our cost per call or cost per order increasing? If so, can we get it under control by redirecting our sales force to higher potential customers? Profit analysis is extremely useful in evaluating territory and product performance, in uncovering unprofitable market segments, in calculating year-end bonuses, and generally in directing the development of marketing strategy. It is not unusual for a firm to discover that 20 percent of its products are unprofitable or that many smaller sales volume territories are contributing more profit dollars than are some larger sales volume territories.

Format of Cost and Profit Analysis. The detailed procedures of cost and profit analysis are complex and even controversial, but we can gain a basic understanding of the procedure and its resulting output by looking at it in four steps:

1. *Cost Classification.* Costs are classified by type, since different types of costs receive different treatment.
2. *Functional Cost Analysis.* Costs associated with the personal selling function are identified and computed, and the total is used to evaluate the overall function.

3. *Segment Cost Analysis.* Costs associated with each category of sales volume (termed segments in cost accounting) are identified and computed, and the total for each is used to evaluate that segment.
4. *Segment Profit Analysis.* Profitability for each segment is measured in one or more ways, and the results are evaluated.

In the first step, each cost is classified as either fixed or variable and also as either direct or indirect. A variable cost is one which changes as sales volume changes.[9] Sales force commissions are variable costs if they are based on sales volume. Salaries are fixed costs since they do not change with sales volume fluctuations. Fixed costs may become variable in the long run, as illustrated by annual salary raises given to salespeople as a reward for sales volume increases. Direct costs are those incurred for, and traceable to, specific segments of sales such as territories, products, or customers. Indirect costs (sometimes called common costs) are incurred for more than one segment and cannot easily be apportioned to each of the segments involved.[10] Some costs are direct with respect to one segment but indirect in other segments. Consider a salesperson's salary. It is a direct cost to that person's territory, but indirect with respect to customers and products sold.

Step two is the calculation of the cost of the personal selling function. Many costs are easily identified as selling costs—sales force salaries, commissions, expenses. But others are not so easily identified because they are shared in common among a number of functions. For instance, rent, utilities, and taxes are all indirect costs if sales, advertising, research, and other department's personnel share the same facilities. To allocate these costs properly to each function, some basis of allocation must be used which indicates what portion of each cost is incurred for each function. Rent, for example, might be allocated based on what percentage of total floor space is occupied by each function's operation.

When finally determined, personal selling cost is compared with various measures of personal selling accomplishment. Some of the measures which can be used are number of orders obtained, number of calls made, and dollars of sales volume obtained. Suppose total selling cost is $423,900 for a given accounting period, and selling accomplishment during that period is measured as follows:

Number of orders	=	3,660
Number of calls	=	7,280
Sales volume dollars	=	$4,710,000

These analysis measures can then be calculated:

$$\text{Selling cost per order} = \frac{\$423{,}900}{3{,}660} = \$115.82$$

$$\text{Selling cost per call} = \frac{\$423{,}900}{7{,}280} = \$58.23$$

$$\text{Selling cost per sales dollar} = \frac{\$423{,}900}{\$4{,}710{,}000} = \$.09$$

By comparing these results with similar previous period measures or with standard costs, the sales manager can determine whether further investigation is required. Such might be the case if the cost per call has increased substantially. But sometimes strategy changes are employed which are expected to bring about cost changes. For instance, the sales force might have been directed to concentrate more on larger customers, and since these calls take more time fewer calls can be made and the cost per call will increase; but the cost per sales dollar should decline as a result of larger orders.

In step three, each category isolated in sales analysis is now a candidate for a cost examination. If sales volume was categorized by territory, by product, and by customer type, a parallel cost analysis can be made by territory, by product, and by customer type. In cost analysis terminology, these categories are called segments.

Costs which are variable and direct are easily attached to their respective revenue segments. But costs which are both fixed and indirect are often impossible to attach except arbitrarily. Consider again the salary of a salesperson selling three different products to 20 customers. What proportion of that salary should be charged as a cost against the revenue coming from each customer or each product? A logical test for charging a segment with a cost is one of "escapability"—the cost should disappear if the segment was eliminated. In this case, what part of the salary would be reduced if one of the customers was no longer served, or if one of the product lines was dropped by the company? If no part of the salary would be reduced, then the cost is not escapable with respect to those segments. One view is that only escapable costs should be charged to segments, while others believe that all costs should be charged somewhere since all costs have to be covered by revenues to achieve profitability. This is part of the controversy in marketing cost analysis.[11]

Determining segment costs is a big job because it involves costs from all departments and organizational units of the firm, not just from the sales organization. Costs must be obtained from manufacturing, purchasing, administration, engineering, and all other functional areas including those in marketing. Proper segment cost analysis requires a carefully organized system of monitoring and retrieving cost data, often implemented with computers.[12]

Without getting involved in the details of all these costs, let us examine what the sales manager can learn from the results. After assigning direct and variable costs to each segment, and after allocating any common costs agreed upon by management, the sales executive can compare segment costs with measures of segment accomplishment. Following our previous example, suppose that of the 7,280 calls made, product A was presented in 1,240 calls and product B was presented in 6,620 calls (this totals to more than 7,280 because both products were presented on some calls). If the segment cost of product A was $682,000 and the cost of B was $3,893,450, our costs per call by product are:

$$\text{Product A} = \frac{\$682,000}{1,240} = \$550$$

$$\text{Product B} = \frac{\$3,893,450}{6,620} = \$588$$

A corresponding look at sales volume per call would help put these measures into perspective. If, from sales analysis, the revenues for product A were $790,000 and for B were $3,920,000, we would have obtained $637 revenue per call from A and $592 revenue per call from B. Product A calls are therefore producing higher revenue at lower cost than are product B calls. The sales manager might want to investigate further to determine if shifts in call patterns could be made to take advantage of more product A call opportunities.

Step four takes us into profit measures by segment. Because of the controversy in treating indirect fixed costs, various profit measures have been suggested, each having a slightly different label.[13] The following accounting statement format sums up some of these measures:

	Segment revenues
minus	Segment variable costs
equals	Segment contribution margin
minus	Segment direct fixed costs and/or controllable costs
equals	Segment profit contribution
minus	Segment indirect fixed costs
equals	Segment net profit

Since segment net profit requires arbitrary prorating of indirect fixed costs among segments, we will concentrate on profit contribution measures as being the most useful for comparing profitability among segments. Pillsbury uses such measures, for example, obtained monthly on each of its sales regions and on each product within each region.[14]

To continue our example, let us look at two ways of examining segment profit contribution measures. One is to look at each segment independently, one at a time. For instance, we can examine the profitability of each product, then look at the profitability of each territory, then each customer type, and so on. Table 15.3 illustrates this analysis for two succeeding years, with year 2 corresponding to our ongoing example. It shows that all segments are profitable, with product A, territory 2, and customer type Z being the most profitable in their respective categories.

The second way is to cross-classify segments so that we can see the profitability of product A sold to customer type W in territory 1, and so on. Table 15.4 presents

TABLE 15.3

Profitability of Segments Analyzed Independently

YEAR 1	PRODUCT A	PRODUCT B	TERRITORY 1	TERRITORY 2	CUSTOMER TYPE W	CUSTOMER TYPE X	CUSTOMER TYPE Y	CUSTOMER TYPE Z
Sales	$750,000	$3,050,000	$1,650,000	$2,150,000	$950,000	$700,000	$750,000	$1,400,000
Variable costs	465,000	2,531,500	1,306,500	1,690,000	746,500	560,000	591,000	1,099,000
Direct fixed costs	177,600	501,400	305,100	373,900	175,500	129,600	141,900	232,000
Segment profit contribution	$107,400	$17,100	$38,400	$86,100	$28,000	$10,400	$17,100	$69,000
YEAR 2								
Sales	$790,000	$3,920,000	$2,110,000	$2,600,000	$1,220,000	$890,000	$890,000	$1,710,000
Variable costs	489,800	3,253,600	1,686,200	2,057,200	966,400	719,800	703,000	1,354,200
Direct fixed costs	192,200	639,850	374,450	457,600	216,600	157,850	177,050	280,550
Segment profit contribution	$108,000	$26,550	$49,350	$85,200	$37,000	$12,350	$9,950	$75,250

TABLE 15.4
Profitability of Segments Analyzed Via Cross-Classification

PRODUCT A	CUSTOMER TYPE W		CUSTOMER TYPE X		CUSTOMER TYPE Y		CUSTOMER TYPE Z	
	TERRITORY 1				TERRITORY 2			
	Year 1	Year 2	Year 1	Year 2	Year 1	Year 2	Year 1	Year 2
Sales	$ 200,000	$ 220,000	$ 100,000	$ 90,000	$ 150,000	$ 170,000	$ 300,000	$ 310,000
Variable costs	124,000	136,400	62,000	55,800	93,000	105,400	186,000	192,200
Direct fixed costs	45,000	46,100	24,100	23,300	35,500	41,250	73,000	81,550
Segment profit contribution	$ 31,000	$ 37,500	$ 13,900	$ 10,900	$ 21,500	$ 23,350	$ 41,000	$ 36,250
PRODUCT B								
Sales	$ 750,000	$1,000,000	$ 600,000	$ 800,000	$ 600,000	$ 720,000	$1,100,000	$1,400,000
Variable costs	622,500	830,000	498,000	664,000	498,000	597,600	913,000	1,162,000
Direct fixed costs	130,500	170,500	105,500	134,550	106,400	135,800	159,000	199,000
Segment profit contribution	$ (3,000)	$ (500)	$ (3,500)	$ 1,450	$ (4,400)	$ (13,400)	$ 28,000	$ 39,000

Note: Territory 1 contains only customer types W and X; territory 2 contains only customer types Y and Z.

Source: This and the previous table are adapted from Frank H. Mossman, et al., *Financial Dimensions of Marketing Management* (New York: John Wiley & Sons, 1978), p. 45.

this analysis. It reveals some definite weaknesses, with the most dramatic one involving product B sold to customer type Y in territory 2. What other suspicions should this table arouse in a sales manager's mind for further investigation?

Sources of Cost Data. The company's accounting department is the source of most data for cost and profit analysis. In fact, any cost and profit analysis reports desired by the sales manager are typically generated by the accounting personnel. Marketing research departments and the sales force itself might be called upon to make time studies or other measurements which can be used in allocating indirect fixed costs.[15] The sales manager has prime responsibility of defining what cost and profit information is desired, and then explaining these desires clearly to accounting personnel.

Limitations of Cost and Profit Analysis. Cost analysis, like sales analysis, identifies symptoms for further investigation. If a product line is unprofitable, the solution to this problem is not easy because the problem itself is not always clear. Further investigation must delve into why the product line is unprofitable. Is it priced too low? Is the sales force giving it enough attention? Or is it getting too much attention with customers who have no need for it? Is it inferior compared with competitors' products? Should the line be dropped? Improved? Redesigned? Cost and profit analysis does not answer these questions, but helps focus management attention where these questions should be asked.

Other limitations stem from the difficulties in measuring marketing costs. Since marketing activities are not standardized, but rather vary as competitive and economic conditions change, these conditions make consistent cost determinations extremely challenging and accurate cost forecasting nearly impossible. In addition, the indirect nature of many marketing expenditures produces controversy in how to calculate segment cost and profit measures.

ANALYSIS OF PERFORMANCE EFFORTS

Sales managers generally agree that a salesperson has far more control over efforts than over results, making efforts a more fair basis of evaluation. Sales volume, costs, and profits are all often affected by factors outside the salesperson's control, such as shipping problems or economic swings. But efforts, such as the number of calls made or days worked, are far more controllable. If a salesperson's efforts fall short of reasonable standards, the problem is more likely to be the person than outside uncontrollable factors.

There is also a time lag between sales efforts and results as measured in orders or dollar volume, so an appraisal of current performance may not be complete if based on results alone. This doesn't mean that results should be disregarded, because the purpose of efforts is results! But it does mean that efforts may be a better measure of performance in a short-term appraisal period than results which may not all be in yet.

Efforts have both a quantitative and qualitative dimension. Two sales force members might produce nearly equal amounts of effort, yet the first outsells the second because of more effective demonstrations or servicing. If both dimensions are not adequately measured, a manager might mistakenly assume that *more* calls will improve the second salesperson's performance whereas in reality it is *better* calls that are needed.

Major categories of efforts include time and duty analysis, other activity measures, and performance appraisals. We will look at these one at a time.

Time Analysis. Time analysis involves a systematic study of how much time salespeople allocate to the many elements of their total job. When time utilization patterns are compared between better and poorer performers, it is possible to determine how poorer performers might reallocate their time to become more productive.

Three steps are involved. The first is to define job elements in terms of activities in which the salesperson spends time. In one study, ten such elements were identified and grouped into essential and nonessential categories as shown in Table 15.5. The second step is to select which salespeople are to be studied. When the sales force is very large or when the study is being done for the first time, a sample of better and poorer performers is usually selected so that comparisons can be made between these groups.

The third step involves time measurements. One way is for time study observers to accompany each salesperson for a period of one or more full days, although the presence of an observer may produce atypical behavior or embarrassment to the salesperson. Management at Atlantic Refining Company approached this problem by asking its salespeople to introduce the observer and explain his presence at each call in a manner they felt most suitable to the customer.[16] An alternative approach is to ask the sales force to report their own time utilization. In the IBM Data Processing Division, for example, ten percent of the sales force are asked every six months to indicate their time spent in one full day on each of a series of activities listed on a report form.[17]

Time studies produce valuable results for most sales managers. Table 15.5 is typical of these findings, which show that better salespeople spend a larger portion of time in essential tasks and spend a larger portion within that time in selling activities. Poorer salespeople spend more time in nonessential tasks such as waiting for interviews. Such information is useful in improving training and supervision programs.

Duty Analysis. Duty analysis often accompanies time analysis, although each has a distinct purpose. Time analysis aims at increasing efficiency whereas duty analysis is concerned with improving effectiveness of selling time.

Most duty studies focus on the content of the sales call. Three types of relationships have been studied between what a salesperson does on the call and what results occur:

1. The number of items mentioned and the number sold per call.
2. The number of items mentioned and sold by type of selling appeal.
3. The number of items mentioned and sold by type of selling method.

In the wholesale drug company study, the relationship between the number of items mentioned and sold was determined from 575 calls as follows:

NUMBER OF ITEMS MENTIONED PER CALL	NUMBER OF ITEMS SOLD PER CALL
Less than 10	1.4
10–19	3.3
20–29	5.7
30–39	6.5
40–49	7.8
50 and over	9.4

This seems to confirm the rather logical assumption that as the number of items mentioned increases, so does the number of items sold.

The Atlantic Refining Study investigated the effectiveness of selling appeals, and produced the following results:

APPEAL	EFFECTIVENESS	FREQUENCY OF USE
Stock needs	44%	23%
Salability	23	2
Profitability	25	9
Availability	23	1
Quality	15	3
No appeal	10	62
		100%

TABLE 15.5
Results of Time Analysis for a Wholesale Drug Company

Element of Call	TEN MOST EFFICIENT DRUG SALESMEN		TEN LEAST EFFICIENT DRUG SALESMEN	
	Minutes	Percentage	Minutes	Percentage
Promotional Selling	11.2	30.5	8.5	24.9
Dealer Assistance	0.3	0.8	0.8	2.3
Want Book Selling	8.6	23.4	4.3	12.6
Collection and Adjustments	2.4	6.5	1.7	5.0
Sales Promotion	1.7	4.6	1.3	3.8
Miscellaneous	0.8	2.2	0.5	1.4
Total Essential Time	25.0	68.0	17.0	50.0
Await Interview	3.7	10.1	5.0	14.6
Broken Interview	4.5	12.2	6.5	19.0
General Conversation	2.7	7.3	4.8	14.1
Idle Time	0.9	2.4	0.8	2.5
Total Nonessential Time	11.8	32.0	17.1	50.0
Total Call	36.8	100.0	34.2	100.0

Source: James H. Davis, *Increasing Wholesale Drug Salesmen's Effectiveness* (Columbus, Ohio: Bureau of Business Research Monograph no. 48, The Ohio State University, 1948, p. 79).

When the appeal used was the customer's need for the item to complete his stock, 44 percent of the items mentioned were sold. But for nearly two-thirds of the items mentioned by salespeople, no reason for buying was given the customer. Furthermore, the quality appeal was low in effectiveness but used more than other more effective appeals.

Similar results have been found in studying the effectiveness of selling methods. In this aspect of its duty analysis, Atlantic Refining discovered the following:

SELLING METHOD	EFFECTIVENESS	FREQUENCY OF USE
Stock Checking	45%	13%
Selling with Samples	34	2
Selling with Reasons but without Aids	28	18
Selling with Printed Matter	14	23
Selling without Reasons or Aids	11	44
		100%

This information is interpreted the same way. For example, selling without reasons or aids was least effective but was used most often. Such findings can help explain why sales results are lower than expected, and can provide valuable input to sales training and motivation programs.

Measurements for duty analysis are made by observers or from self-reports by salespeople, as is done in time analysis measurement. One study of department store selling involved the use of small wireless microphones carried in each salesperson's pocket, which transmitted a verbal record of each customer conversation to a receiver behind the counter which tape recorded it for later analysis.[18] In this particular case, management was able to determine that a purchase typically did not follow a price-oriented discussion, whereas discussions about styling, delivery, or the warranty were far more likely to evolve into a purchase.

Other Activity Measures. Many specific activities not covered in time and duty analysis are also indicators of salesperson effort. The number of calls made per day, for example, may be a useful measure when trying to diagnose reasons for unusually low sales volume. In chapter 7 we discussed activity quotas, and Table 7.1 listed some popular types of activities measured.

If activity quotas are defined at the start of a period, they become standards for appraisal. If quotas are not set, the sales manager can still use activity measures. For example, suppose the average number of calls per day in a sales force is four, but one salesperson who is not reaching his sales volume quota averages only three calls per day. If his territory is typical in terms of travel time and distance, management should investigate whether his number of calls can be increased. If, on the other hand, his number of calls was above average, management might question whether those calls are being made on customers of unusually small potential or whether his selling effectiveness needed improvement. In either case, the use of an activity measure helps the sales manager narrow down a problem investigation to fewer likely causes.

Activity measures are usually obtained through *call reports*. Many firms ask their sales force to file a separate report on each call, indicating the date, length of call, products discussed, person or persons called on, action resulting from the call, and other items of information on that account.[19] Other firms require daily or weekly summaries. Some companies have experimented with tape-recorded reports which the salesperson can record on cassettes while driving from one call to the next. But the level of consistency in report content and the time necessary to transcribe the results at the home office are drawbacks to this method.

Computerized systems have also been devised, such as CRIS (Complete Retail Information System) at Del Monte and REACH (Retail Achievement Report) at Pillsbury.[20] Del Monte salespeople use preprinted forms for each store called on, check responses on such topics as inventory level, displays, and prices, and send the forms to headquarters where they are processed and turned into computerized summaries.[21] Such reporting systems involve much market and competitive information in addition to sales force activities.

Asking the sales force to report on their own activities has its problems. Reporting diverts time from other tasks, and management must weigh the value of information received against the value of other achievements which could occur in that same time, such as additional sales calls. The value of that information also depends on the accuracy and timeliness of such reports. One study showed that reporting accuracy depended on how the sales force was compensated (poorer reporting under commission-based plans) and on whether any formal recognition was provided to good reporters. Timeliness was best when the sales force believed management used the information and especially when the information produced help in improving selling effectiveness.[22] Management must consider its reporting needs when designing compensation and motivation programs.

Efforts-Results Relationships. Time and duty analysis usually involves a comparison of efforts with results, and other activity measures can be analyzed in a similar manner. One such ratio is sales volume per call, which is a measure of productivity. If volume per call is low, it may indicate that not enough time is being spent on each call or that low-potential customers are getting too much attention. Another productivity measure is the "batting average"—the ratio of orders taken to calls made. If only ten orders are produced in 100 calls, that salesperson's batting average is ten percent. Comparisons among individual sales personnel will show where further investigation of calling effort might be most productive.[23]

Efforts-results comparisons can also be used to assess the sales force as a whole. Suppose the number of calls by all district sales personnel is calculated and divided by customer categories as follows:

CUSTOMER CATEGORY	NUMBER OF CALLS BY SALES FORCE	PERCENTAGE OF TOTAL CALLS
Largest Five Accounts	460	5.5
Other Large Accounts	2650	31.5
Medium Accounts	2445	29.0
Small Accounts	2865	34.0
Total	8420	100.0

Then the amount of sales to these customer categories is compiled for comparison:

CUSTOMER CATEGORY	AMOUNT OF SALES	PERCENTAGE OF TOTAL SALES
Largest Five Accounts	$3,456,000	36.9
Other Large Accounts	3,650,000	39.0
Medium Accounts	1,285,000	13.7
Small Accounts	969,000	10.4
Total	$9,360,000	100.0

The distribution of calls differs greatly from the distribution of sales, indicating possible opportunities from a reallocation of calls among customer types. Before drawing this conclusion, the district manager should consider such factors as sales potential by customer category and the cost per call by customer type.

Performance Appraisal. Selling performance is affected by many factors which differ among territories and change over time. One such factor involves competitors' efforts, and another is local economic conditions. Quantitative measures and ratios cannot easily be adapted to reflect the individuality of each selling situation and must be supplemented by qualitative appraisals to give a properly balanced assessment of efforts. Such appraisals are based on the judgment of the salesperson's supervisor.

Supervisors continually judge their subordinates' efforts in an informal way, often without explicitly recognizing it. Input to this informal process comes from every contact and any other feedback received about the salesperson. Passing comments made by other sales personnel about salesman Smith, newspaper articles about Smith's civic activities, and conversations with Smith about customers as well as favorite baseball and football teams all influence this appraisal.

The dangers and shortcomings of this process are clear. Some inputs may be irrelevant to Smith's job performance. Other relevant factors may escape the supervisor's attention. Seldom will the boss obtain comparable information about all sales force members, so that fair and consistent appraisals cannot possibly result. And lack of objectivity, known as personal bias, is inevitable, particularly when appraisals are developing informally and even subconsciously.

Improving qualitative evaluation can occur only when the process becomes systematic. A systematic appraisal procedure starts with the setting of objectives, then incorporates techniques directly relevant to the objectives sought, and clearly identifies the items of behavior or performance on which each salesperson is to be judged.

Objectives. While the overall objective of evaluation is to improve the selling function, there are some particular objectives for appraising individual salespeople. One is to aid in personnel decisions, such as promotion or salary increases. Another concerns personal development—finding ways of strengthening present job performance or preparing for an advanced position in a career path. Sometimes there is the additional objective of validating selection or training techniques, in which certain types of efforts provide the criteria for desired performance.

Techniques. Different objectives call for different techniques, such as relative versus absolute rating. Relative evaluation typically involves ranking salespeople on a series of items. Ranking systems are suitable for identifying who is most promotable from a group of sales personnel, for example. Absolute evaluation occurs when each salesperson is rated according to standardized quality levels of performance. Figure 15.2, the appraisal form used by Del Monte, involves absolute measures. Numerical values allow the rater to add the points and arrive at an overall score for each person rated. Point scores are useful when the appraisal objective is to determine who gets how much salary adjustment or to decide how to split a bonus fund among all district sales personnel. Some sales managers believe that numerical scores imply a quantitative precision that is unrealistic.

Items. The items to be included again depend on the objectives for appraisal. If the purpose is to identify promotable salespeople, some items should relate to management tasks such as planning and organizing. If evaluation is aimed primarily at improving present job performance, the items should include key responsibilities and tasks in the present job as spelled out in the position description.

One appraisal method which places special attention on the item-development process is called Behaviorally Anchored Rating Scales (BARS).[24] Critical incidents of effective and ineffective sales behavior are described by sales personnel and grouped into performance categories. A second group of salespeople and managers reviews this grouping and assigns each behavior item a rating on a scale of one to ten representing low to high performance effectiveness. Items which are assigned widely varying scale positions by the raters are eliminated, and the remaining items

FIGURE 15.2

Form for Performance Appraisal of Sales Personnel Used by Del Monte Corporation

Below Average	+	−	Good	+	−	Very Good	+	−	Outstanding
1	2	3	4	5	6	7	8	9	10

PERFORMANCE APPRAISAL

Indicate by your rating from 1 to 10 (considering above scale and explanation in instructions) the degree to which the individual meets the following standards and objectives.

RESPONSIBILITIES	PERFORMANCE STANDARD/OBJECTIVE		RATING
CALL ACTION & RESULTS			
Distribution	• Attains acceptance on authorized items with accounts, and overall distribution growth with them.	D | R	
Volume	• Capitalizes on opportunities to sell events, displays, ad features & influence volume orders.	D | R	
	• Attains overall volume growth with all accounts.	D | R	
Goals	• Achieves: Total Del Monte volume goal	D | R	
	• Individual item volume goal	D | R	
	Distribution goals	D | R	
Shelf Management	• Checks, & records distribution, out-of-stock, shelf impact and pricing objectives.		
	• Presents shelf change suggestions.	D | R	
	• Effects change in line with shelf management objectives.	D | R	
	• Corrects shelf housecleaning problems.		
Merchandising	• Proficient with merchandising ideas & methods.		
	• Keeps prepared for merchandising with P.O.S. & other material.		
	• Productively handles store sets & revamps.		
SELLING SKILLS/ATTRIBUTES			
Sales Planning	• Analyzes all retail/direct accounts for distribution/volume opportunities.		
	• Utilizes market/account information (i.e., CRIS, SAMI, Majors, Dollar Volume Summary).		
Presentations	• Follows store call plan and sales formula, incorporates samples and other visuals in sales presentations.		
	• Information and visuals are imaginative, creative, effective and personalized.		
	• Develops product knowledge & uses in presentations along with samples.		
	• Presents in a professional manner using engineering of agreement.		
	• Handles objections, describes features, advantages and benefits, and obtains the close.		
Human Relations	• Tactful; sensitive; respected; maintains cooperative & constructive relations with all associates.		
Trade Relations	• Knows all appropriate direct/retail personnel. Maintains cooperative & constructive relations with them.		
	• Prompt to deal with problems. Shows initiative in selling & servicing assigned accounts.		
	• Familiar with each account's business philosophy including merchandising methods & private label/national brand attitudes.		
Communications	• Attentive listener.		
	• Clear & convincing speaker.		
	• Writing is clear, concise & legible.		
ADMINISTRATIVE SKILLS/KNOWLEDGE			
Authorized Accounts	• Maintains current list; account changes submitted according to CRIS procedures.		
Records & Reports	• All records, S.C.R's, D.I.P., account diary & account record forms, orders & reports accurately maintained & submitted on time.		
Territory Coverage	• Prepares effective retail/direct call plan and routing.		
	• Maintains high ratio of calls vs. plan, and allocates time efficiently.		
Company Policies	• Understands, supports & implements appropriate company consumer & trade policies.		
Company Auto	• Properly follows maintenance and operating procedures as outlined in Auto Fleet Manual/Training Unit.		
Competition	• Seeks out competitive information; is aware of product lines, prices & promotion activities.		
	• Promptly reports competitive findings & recommends appropriate action.		

Reprinted by permission of Del Monte Corporation.

and scales form the appraisal instrument. Figure 15.3 is an example of one such scale out of perhaps a dozen in a typical appraisal system. While this procedure requires considerable preparation, it has the advantage of sales force participation, provides specific tailoring of evaluation to key job activities, and is a clear indication of what is necessary to improve one's ratings by just looking at the scales.

ANALYSIS OF PERFORMANCE SETTING

Performance setting includes the conditions, circumstances, and constraints under which sales force performance takes place. This phase of evaluation concentrates on the work of sales managers. In essence we are asking to what extent unusually good or poor performance is really attributable to management's goals, policies, or procedures. For instance, it is possible that some quotas are not reached because they have been set unrealistically high. Failure to reach the sales forecast in total may not be the fault of the sales force. Rather, the fault may lie in the methods and procedures used to devise the forecast.

Performance is also influenced by factors outside management control, such as competitors' activities, economic conditions, and changes in customer buying patterns.[25] But in this discussion we will concentrate on controllable factors, including sales managers' activities, procedures and methods, and goals and policies guiding the sales operation.

Sales Managers' Activities. Field sales managers and others in the sales management hierarchy are crucial factors in the performance setting because their activities and communications represent "the company" to the sales force. A careful assessment of how field sales managers set their priorities and spend their time might point out why particular sales force efforts or results were misdirected. Some district sales managers place high priority on going into the field themselves to make sales, which leaves less time for administrative tasks such as planning and evaluation. This practice may add to district sales volume, but it can cause badly needed training or supervision to be neglected.[26]

A management activity study was carried out in a large industrial chemical firm to identify what field sales managers felt were their key duties, how they allocated their time, and why.[27] The results showed that they considered some tasks, such as personal selling, to be more important than did their superiors, while other tasks such as recruiting, training, and evaluating sales personnel were considered less important by the field managers than their superiors. In particular, the field managers believed profitability would be positively affected with more time spent in district meetings, with an increase in time spent prospecting, and with an increase in total number of accounts. But other data in the study revealed that none of these relationships held true for this particular company.[28] Different results will occur for different firms and perhaps even for the same firm at two different times, but most firms will gain useful insight from such studies.

Procedures and Methods. All sales management activities involve procedures and methods. Without periodic evaluation, some procedures may become inefficient or unproductive but, nevertheless, remain in operation. An evaluation of procedures is called methods study, and consists of four essential steps:[29]

1. Record all relevant facts about the existing method.
2. Examine those facts critically and in ordered sequence.

FIGURE 15.3

A 'BARS' Performance Appraisal Scale and Its Behavioral Items

Scale Topic: Promptness in Meeting Deadlines

VERY HIGH

This indicates the most often than not practice of submitting accurate & needed field sales reports.

10.0 — Could be expected to promptly submit all necessary field reports, even in the most difficult of situations.

9.0

8.0 — Could be expected to promptly meet deadlines comfortably in most report completion situations.

7.0

6.0 — Is usually on time and can be expected to submit most routine field sales reports in proper format.

MODERATE

This indicates the regularity in promptly submitting accurate & needed field sales reports.

5.0

4.0 — Could be expected to regularly be tardy in submitting required field sales reports.

3.0

2.0 — Could be expected to be tardy and submit inaccurate field sales reports.

1.0 — Could be expected to completely disregard due dates for filing almost all reports.

VERY LOW

This indicates irregular & unacceptable promptness and accuracy of field sales reports.

0.0 — Could be expected to never file field sales reports on time and resists any managerial guidance to improve this tendency.

Reprinted from *Journal of Marketing*, published by the American Marketing Association. A. Benton Cocanougher and John M. Ivancevich, "'BARS' Performance Ratings for Sales Force Personnel," vol. 42 (July 1978), p. 92.

3. Develop the most efficient method.
4. Install the proposed method and maintain it by regular routine checks.

Methods study can be applied to procedures used by sales personnel as well. For instance, one firm had accumulated a file of 1,200,000 prospects from which each salesperson extracted sales leads on a manual and almost random basis. No system was used to evaluate the prospects in terms of sales potential or profitability.

But as the result of a methods study, the company established a prospect priority system, and at the same time realigned territories to be more equitable in sales potential. A sales information storage and retrieval system was also devised which gave feedback to management on call patterns and territory progress. Sales increased 40 percent in each of the two years after this system was installed.[30]

Goals and Policies. Goals and policies are guides to performance, and can be evaluated on three levels. First, are goals or policies needed where none now exist to help guide decisions? Perhaps sales volume goals must be specified in greater detail, such as by product line, to direct proper effort to higher margin items. Or perhaps policies are needed regarding types and amounts of expenses allowable for the sales force.

A second level concerns existing goals and policies which are unclear to sales personnel. A study in pharmaceutical sales forces found that performance was better when goals were clearer, when the relationship between rewards and performance was more direct, and when the salesperson perceived more personal influence through participation in goal setting and work planning.[31] The third level involves goals and policies which may be unfair or dysfunctional. Consider a policy that states when a customer's sales volume reaches a particular level, that customer becomes a house account with no more commission to the salesperson who nurtured the account. Won't sales force members be tempted to ease up in selling accounts which are approaching this level to avoid losing the commission, even though the accounts may have much greater sales potential?

DIAGNOSIS, RECOMMENDATIONS, AND ACTION

The payoff in evaluation occurs through proper diagnosis of problem causes followed by action to overcome problems and capitalize on strengths. Diagnosis is more a matter of tying together the right pieces from prior evaluation steps, rather than carrying out any additional analysis. A problem is identified, such as failure to attain a product line forecast. Then all the possible causes for this problem are tested from other data gathered. Is the sales gap centered in one or a few sales personnel, or is it consistent throughout the entire sales force? Is it a high-cost product line? Has it received enough attention in sales force calls? Have effective appeals been used? Was the forecast properly calculated? Was the forecast communicated clearly to the sales force? Was the product neglected in training or supervision programs? The same process applies in diagnosing the cause of unusually good performance.

An example of a more formal approach involves a study done by Magic Chef.[32] Differences in territory performance can have many possible causes, as illustrated in Figure 15.4. To incorporate all these factors, management devised a multiple regression model in hopes of determining statistically which factors had the greatest impact on performance. The total number of accounts assigned was found to be most influential, followed by territory potential, company experience, workload per account, and the salesperson's effort.

Recommendations and action can involve a multitude of directions and will vary widely among companies, depending on their specific problems and circumstances. Three major categories of action include most of the possibilities. One is reallocation of effort. This entails shifting amounts of time spent from one activity, product line, or customer category to another. For example, Babcock & Wilcox devised a

FIGURE 15.4

Factors Considered in the Magic Chef Study of Sales Territory Performance

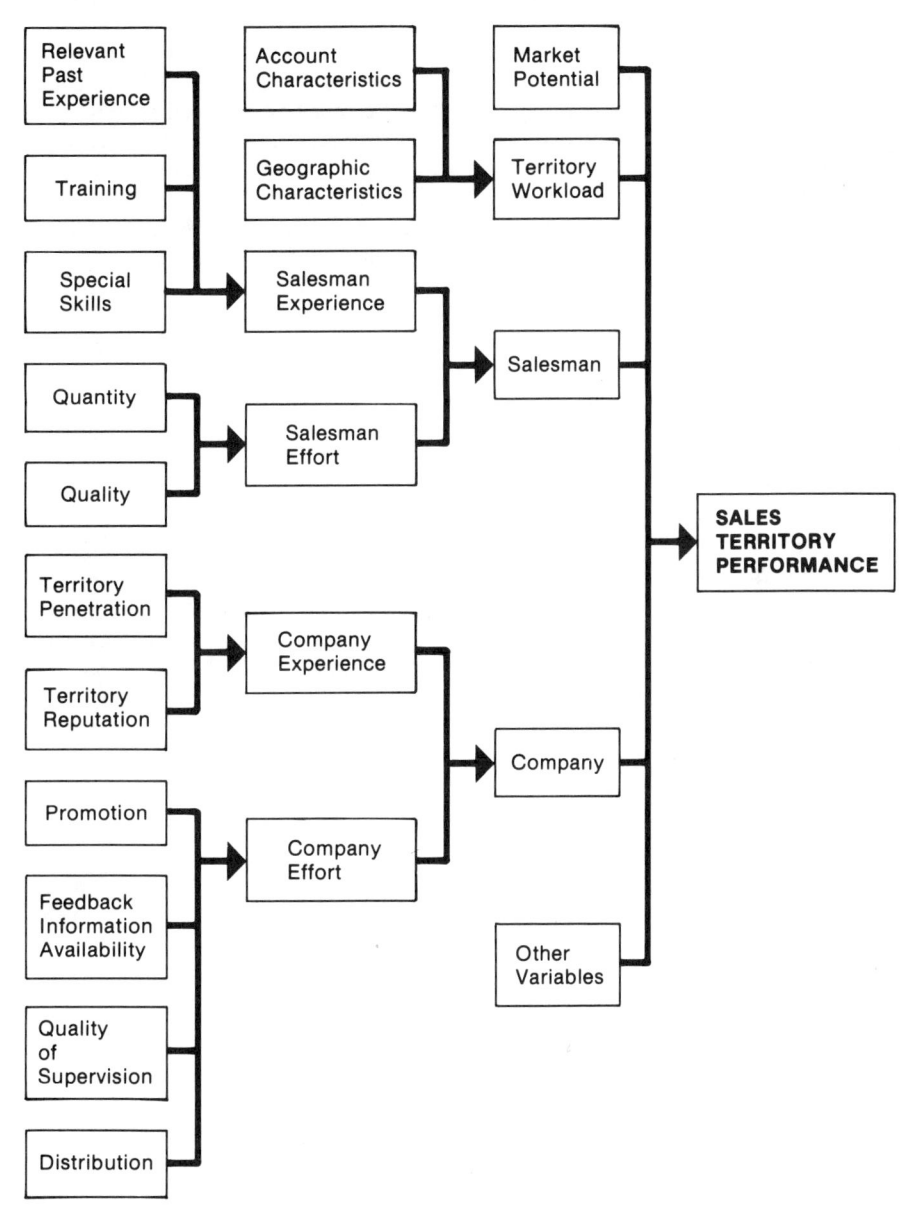

Reprinted from *Journal of Marketing,* published by the American Marketing Association. David W. Cravens et al., "An Analytical Approach for Evaluating Sales Territory Performance," vol. 36 (January 1972), p. 32.

"sales action program" based on evaluation information from sales, cost, and time analyses. Total selling effort was reallocated to maximize the number of planned as well as unplanned sales calls, and to minimize cost and travel time.[33]

A second category involves personal development. Changes in the content of training or supervision programs may be necessitated, and the sales job itself might require some modification to keep effectively competitive. Personal development also means grooming employees for promotion and working in MBO programs to increase the professional character of the selling job.

Changes in the performance setting constitute the third action category. Should new training methods be tried? How can inconsistencies or conflicts among policy statements be reconciled? Should a minimum order size policy be established, or should credit policies be adjusted in light of changing economic conditions or competitive pressures? This category sometimes includes changes beyond the authority of the sales manager, and will require recommendations to higher management. The credit and order size questions may fall in that category, as would possible changes in product lines or in corporate forecasting procedures. Any such recommendations require careful and detailed justification—top management is not always an easy customer to sell!

CONCLUSION

We have now come to the end of our coverage of sales management as outlined in the first chapter. Since evaluation leads to planning, and planning gives way to implementation, we are ready to cycle back to the beginning. Of course, there is actually no clear beginning or end, since many sales management activities occur simultaneously and even continuously. This book should help guide present and aspiring sales managers past the pressing day-to-day demands to a logical, comprehensive, and professional view of sales management.

QUESTIONS FOR REVIEW AND DISCUSSION

1. A major purpose of sales analysis is to help management in directing sales effort more effectively. How can sales analysis uncover evidence of misdirected sales effort?

2. A district sales manager has collected the following information about his three sales territories. What conclusions can he draw, and what other information should he seek?

Territory	Relative Sales Potential	Percentage of District Sales	Index of Performance
1	40%	50%	125
2	25	20	80
3	35	30	86
Total	100%	100%	

3. What types of cost and profit analysis would be most useful for the following decisions:
   a. To consider dropping a product from the product line
   b. To consider splitting a particular territory
   c. To establish a minimum order size policy
   d. To set sales force commission rates by product

4. Some evaluation data obtained by the chief sales executive of a small industrial firm are the following:

	This year	Last year
Number of orders by the sales force:	2,900	2,600
Number of sales calls:	6,200	5,800
Sales volume:	$2,200,000	$2,000,000
Cost of the personal selling function:	$ 112,100	$ 102,700

Indicate at least two useful evaluation measures the manager can derive from these data, and compute them. What further action or steps by the manager do these data suggest?

5. In a newly established company or division, one of the major tasks of the sales force is building a reliable reputation for its company. Discuss how this task might affect the evaluation of sales force performance.

6. Which of the following measures of a salesperson's performance do you think is most valid? Why? Which do you think is least valid?
    a. Average sales volume per week
    b. Supervisor's rating of overall performance
    c. Batting average
    d. Average order size
    e. Number of new accounts obtained
    f. Sales-expense ratio

7. The Atlantic Refining duty analysis noted in this chapter produced the following results:

Strategy	Effectiveness	Frequency of Use
Stock checking	45%	13%
Selling with samples	34%	2%
Selling with reasons but without aids	28%	18%
Selling with printed matter	14%	23%
Selling without reasons or aids	11%	44%
		100%

What is the batting average of this sales force now? What would the batting average be if half the calls using no reasons or aids were switched and equally split among "selling with samples" and "stock checking"? If the average call costs $40 and the average order size is $200, what additional profit contribution would this switch provide? Assume this analysis covers 2000 total calls.

8. Three purposes for evaluation have been identified in this chapter:
    a. To aid in making personnel decisions
    b. To aid in developing salespeople's abilities
    c. To aid in validating selection and training techniques
    Discuss how the results of time analysis can be used to meet each of these purposes.

9. A sales manager of a large packaged foods company is evaluating her sales force to determine who should get the annual "star sales pro" award. Two finalists have been determined, and their performance profile is as follows:

	Smith	Robertson
Number of orders per month	30	40
Total sales volume per month	$75,000	$80,000
Number of sales calls per month	50	60
Number of service calls per month	25	20
Market penetration	25%	30%
Average rating by customers on overall effectiveness of sales effort (1 = poor, 5 = excellent)	4.2	3.8
This year's sales volume as a percent of last year's sales	120%	115%
Ratings by supervisor on overall sales ability (1 = poor, 5 = excellent)	3.8	4.2

If you were the manager with this information, how would you go about determining the winner? Based on your approach, who would receive the award, and why?

10. Discuss some ways in which management can demonstrate to its sales force the usefulness of information supplied by their call reports.

NOTES

1. *Sales Analysis,* Studies in Business Policy no. 113 (New York: National Industrial Conference Board, Inc., 1965), p. 3. The term *sales analysis* is sometimes used to include costs, profits, and sales efforts as well, but that broader meaning is not employed here.

2. Thayer C. Taylor, "Can NCR Cash In?" *Sales & Marketing Management,* February 7, 1977, p. 32.

3. David A. Weeks, *Incentive Plans for Salesmen,* Personnel Policy Study No. 217 (New York: National Industrial Conference Board, Inc., 1970), p. 24.

4. Harry D. Wolfe and Gerald Albaum, "Inequality in Products, Orders, Customers, Salesmen, and Sales Territories," *Journal of Business,* vol. 35 (July 1962), p. 300.

5. Robert F. Vizza and T. E. Chambers, *Time and Territorial Management for the Salesmen* (New York: The Sales Executives Club of New York, Inc., 1971), p. 97.

6. A more formal approach, involving the use of statistical control charts, is found in Burton D. Seeley, "Interpretation of Sales Data for Action," *Akron Business and Economic Review,* Vol. 3 (Spring 1972), pp. 35–42.

7. A more detailed list of sources is found in *Sales Analysis,* p. 68. See also Frank H. Eby, Jr., *Sales Analysis: Concepts and Applications* (New York: AMR International, Inc., 1971), pp. 36–47.

8. For further discussion of the data processing involved, see Stanley J. PoKempner, *Information Systems for Sales and Marketing Management,* Report No. 591 (New York: The Conference Board, Inc., 1973).

9. In Chapter 5 we also looked at "semivariable" costs, but that category is omitted here to avoid complicating an already complex subject.

10. Rather than direct versus indirect, costs can be classified as controllable versus uncontrollable

with respect to the segment in question. See Patrick M. Dunne and H. I. Wolk, "Marketing Cost Analysis: A Modularized Contribution Approach," *Journal of Marketing*, vol. 41 (July 1977), pp. 83–94.

11. For further discussion, see John J. Wheatley, "The Allocation Controversy in Marketing Cost Analysis," *University of Washington Business Review*, vol. 30 (Summer 1971), pp. 61–70.

12. Such systems are discussed in Frank H. Mossman, et al., *Financial Dimensions of Marketing Management* (New York: John Wiley & Sons, 1978), Chapters 3 and 5.

13. For instance, each of the following four sources uses different terminology and a different approach to segment profitability: Dunne and Wolk; Stephen L. Buzby and L. E. Heitger, "Profit Oriented Reporting for Marketing Decision Makers," *MSU Business Topics*, vol. 24 (Summer 1976), pp. 60–68; Charles W. Smith, "Gearing Salesmen's Efforts to Corporate Profit Objectives," *Harvard Business Review*, vol. 53 (July–August 1975), pp. 8–16; and W. J. E. Crissy, et al., "Segmental Analysis: Key to Marketing Profitability," *MSU Business Topics*, vol. 21 (Spring 1973), pp. 42–49.

14. Thayer C. Taylor, "Throwing More Light On Hard-To-See Profit Sources," *Sales Management*, May 19, 1975, p. 42.

15. For an example, see R. E. Bailey, et al., "Time Allocation of A Pooled Industrial Sales Force," *Industrial Marketing Management*, vol. 5 (1976), pp. 343–350.

16. Noble Hall, "Setting Standards To Improve Sales Performance," in *Rating and Developing the Sales Force* (New York: American Management Association, Inc., 1952), p. 30.

17. Robert F. Vizza, *Improving Salesmen's Use of Time* (New York: Sales Executives Club of New York, Inc., 1962), p. 13.

18. Allan L. Pennington, "Customer-Saleman Bargaining Behavior in Retail Transactions," *Journal of Marketing Research*, vol. 5 (August 1968), pp. 255–262.

19. Further discussion and examples of call report forms are found in E. Patrick McGuire, *Salesmen's Call Reports*, Report No. 570 (New York: The Conference Board, Inc., 1972); and *Sales Management*, August 18, 1975, a special issue on sales control forms.

20. For a brief description of REACH, and of its predecessor in Pillsbury called SOAR, see James M. Comer, "The Computer, Personal Selling, and Sales Management," *Journal of Marketing*, vol. 39 (July 1975), p. 28.

21. "Del Monte Sells By The Numbers," *Sales Management*, March 17, 1975, pp. 3–7.

22. Thomas R. Wotruba and Richard Mangone, "More Effective Sales Force Reporting," *Industrial Marketing Management*, vol. 8 (June 1979), pp. 236–245.

23. Other ratios are discussed in J. Porter Henry, "Failing At The Controls," *Sales Management*, June 11, 1973, pp. 25, 28–29.

24. A. Benton Cocanougher and J. M. Ivancevich, " 'BARS' Performance Rating For Sales Force Personnel," *Journal of Marketing*, vol. 42 (July 1978), pp. 87–95; William B. Locander and W. A. Staples, "Evaluating and Motivating Salesmen with the BARS Method," *Industrial Marketing Management*, vol. 7 (1978), pp. 43–48.

25. Monitoring external factors is discussed more fully in Francis J. Aguilar, *Scanning the Business Environment* (New York: Macmillan, 1967).

26. This problem, as well as the general subject of evaluating field sales managers, is discussed in Robert T. Davis, *Performance and Development of Field Sales Managers* (Boston: Division of Research, Harvard Business School, 1957), pp. 185–215.

27. Eric N. Berkowitz, "Organizational Perceptions of Sales Managers," *Industrial Marketing Management*, vol. 7 (1978), pp. 37–42.

28. Eric N. Berkowitz and J. L. Ginter, "Time Management of Sales Managers," *Industrial Marketing Management*, vol. 7 (1978), pp. 250–256.

29. For the complete discussion from which this is summarized, see John O'Shaughnessy, *Work Study Applied to a Sales Force* (London: British Institute of Management, 1965), pp. 13–41.

30. Jeffrey H. Wecker, "An Approach to Higher Profits with Reduced Selling Costs," *Industrial Marketing*, December 1977, pp. 56–58.

31. Charles M. Futrell, J. E. Swan, and J. T. Todd, "Job Performance Related to Management Control Systems for Pharmaceutical Salesmen," *Journal of Marketing Research*, vol. 13 (February 1976), pp. 25–33.

32. David W. Cravens, R. B. Woodruff, and J. C. Stamper, "An Analytical Approach for Evaluating Sales Territory Performance," *Journal of Marketing*, vol. 36 (January 1972), pp. 31–37. Additional data on this study is found in Cravens and Woodruff, "An Approach for Determining Criteria of Sales Performance," *Journal of Applied Psychology*, vol. 57 (1973), pp. 242–247.

33. Charles E. Bergman, "All Out For Productivity," *Sales & Marketing Management*, March 14, 1977, pp. 52–59. For another approach, see Bruce M. Smackey, "A Profit Emphasis for Improving Sales Force Productivity," *Industrial Marketing Management*, vol. 6 (1977), pp. 135–140.

CASES

CASE 1 Stonewell Tool Company

The Stonewell Tool Company is a well-established firm in the Southwest United States. It has been making quality tools and equipment for many years, and has a good reputation among industrial buyers. A recent top management change produced a reorientation of company goals which up to now had stressed conservatism, stability, and a satisfactory return on investment. A younger and more aggressive new company president has appeared on the scene, and has clearly stated that growth is to be the key goal for the next few years, and with the larger sales volume will come more production efficiencies and corresponding profit improvement as well.

Tim Moore, the firm's general sales manager, began to assess how this intended growth would affect the sales organization. Up to now, Stonewell had employed its own sales force in only one region of the country, consisting primarily of California, but also with some coverage in Arizona and Nevada. Washington and Oregon had been covered for Stonewell by a manufacturer's representative who also handled other noncompeting lines of tools and electrical components. The mountain states of Colorado, Wyoming, Utah, Montana, and Idaho were covered by another manufacturer's rep. No other market areas were being sold at this time.

Tim's assessment was that Jim Harrington, the Washington and Oregon rep, had done a far better job of establishing Stonewell's reputation and in gaining sales than did Craig Pine, the Mountain States rep. He based this conclusion on a comparison of the two areas for the past year as follows:

	RELATIVE PERCENT OF MANUFACTURING ACTIVITY	RELATIVE PERCENT OF STONEWELL'S SALES	DOLLAR SALES OF STONEWELL PRODUCTS
Northwest Area (Harrington)	55%	71%	$500,000
Mountain Area (Pine)	45	29	200,000
	100%	100%	$700,000

Tim reasons that the best area to seek a more rapid sales increase is the Northwest since it had a larger potential than the Mountain area and also because Stonewell had a stronger foothold there already. To generate growth would require a company sales force in place of a manufacturer's rep. Tim believes, based on Stonewell's sales experience in California, that at least ten times as much sales volume is available in the Northwest if a strong sales effort was made. He believes that if he could triple the sales in the Northwest, he will more than meet the new president's expectations, and might even get a raise or at least a good bonus.

Tim figures that two full-time company salespeople can produce the sales target he desires. Informal conversations with his sales personnel in the California territories indicate that none of them is particularly interested in moving to a new territory in the Northwest. They are all well-established in their communities and have little desire for trying to build up another territory, particularly under the eager eye of the new president. An alternative Tim has is to hire two new salespeople, but he feels that new company representatives will not be able to reach the sales increase he wants within a year. Training normally takes six weeks to three months. Even after that, it takes more time to really master all the applications of the product line and to become fully acquainted with a new territory. Besides, the costs of hiring, training, and setting up two new salespeople will probably exceed $50,000 without even considering their salaries for the first year. This extra cost would reduce the impact of any sales increase, especially if the increase is small due to new personnel learning the business and the territory.

Tim then began to think about what Jim Harrington would do when he found out he had lost the Stonewell line. Could he find another line similar to Stonewell's quickly and take away some of the customers? If so, sales projections will have to be toned down quite a bit. Tim realizes that a third alternative is to hire Harrington as a full-time Stonewell salesperson. He calls Harrington to try to sound him out.

After a two or three minute conversation about sales in general, Tim states, "Well, Jim, it sounds like things are going pretty well for you. Have you ever thought about working full-time for one of your principals?" Harrington replies, "I'd sure be dumb to do that. Why give up a good thing? You and six other producers depend on me, and that's a good feeling. Anyway, I make as much money as you do, probably. You don't make more than 75 grand, do you? Besides, being independent is great. I bet you'd do it if you could."

After the conversation ends, Tim feels confused and discouraged about whether growth was such a good thing after all, and about whether he has any really good options left. In fact, as he leaves the office, the thought crosses his mind for a brief moment that maybe he will have to cover that Northwest area himself.

QUESTIONS

1. What is the problem Tim is trying to solve? Has he identified all the alternatives?
2. Should he have given Harrington a straightforward offer? Should he still do it?
3. Why should he consider the Northwest rather than the Mountain area as the best source of sales growth?

CASE 2 Hickok Glass Corporation

The Hickock Glass Corporation is headquartered in New Haven, Connecticut. The firm manufactures a variety of glassware products, with primary emphasis on drinking glasses. Most of the products are geared for supermarket and variety store sales, although Hickok does make a few lines for gift purchases in department stores and specialty shops. The firm has recently expanded into plastic materials for glassware and in the near future is planning more diversification into cookware suitable for microwave oven use.

Hickok has 15 sales territories throughout the U.S. The newest of these territories has been established for five years, while some older territories have been unchanged for 15 years or more. All territories have boundaries which match state boundaries because of the convenience of getting market data by state. Total company sales for the year just ended were almost exactly $8 million, up 7 percent from the year before. Price increases alone should cause this coming year's sales to increase nearly 9 percent, but with a sales penetration nationally of only about 40 percent a larger sales increase is expected.

In June 1979 Roger Sloan joined Hickok as national sales manager after having worked his way up the ranks to regional sales manager for a nationwide kitchenware producer. Sloan's next six months were spent reviewing past sales trends and analyzing individual territory performance in addition to his day-to-day administrative duties. He met with the three district managers twice in that time—first just to get to know them and to learn about any particular problems in their market area, and second, about four months later, to discuss with them some of his goals and observations about their territories and past performance. Since he was brought into his position from the outside rather than from within (and thus over the heads of the district managers), Sloan was aware that he was "on trial." As a result, he felt it important to be sure about his facts and figures before proposing any new directions or changes in existing sales operations.

Sloan's last meeting with Jake Phillips, the Southern District manager, left him particularly puzzled. He and Jake discussed future growth possibilities and ways of "turning on" the sales force to improve penetration, but felt that Jake really wasn't on his side in trying to improve sales. Jake noted more than once how he and his sales team were "old pros" in their territories, and knew the real potential of their market because they had all been on the "firing line" for more than ten years together.

Somehow, Sloan wasn't convinced that the Southern District was performing as well as they could. He began looking into available data and company records which might help assess the potential and performance of territories in the Southern District. Each of the firm's 15 territories was originally targeted to have between six and seven percent of total sales potential, but an updated study of sales potential per territory had not been done for five years. Since all territories had been producing sales

Cases

volume in nearly equal amounts, Sloan's predecessor didn't think it necessary to spend time updating territory potential measures. Instead, the previous manager installed a compensation plan which paid an attractive salary plus 1 percent commission on all sales above quota, hoping that this provided incentive and would minimize sales force turnover. The same plan is still in effect.

From the "Survey of Buying Power" and other sources, Sloan pieced together an analysis of territories in the Southern District. His investigation pointed out two territories in particular that seemed poor performers. One included the states of Texas, Oklahoma, and Arkansas, though Jake referred to it as "Texas and the leftovers." The other included the five states of Kansas, Nebraska, Iowa, Missouri, and Illinois. Jake didn't consider this a truly "Southern" territory although it was assigned to the Southern District (the other districts were the Northeast and the West).

Sloan put some figures on paper for these two territories:

	PERCENT OF TOTAL COMPANY SALES VOLUME	PERCENT OF TOTAL U.S. HOUSEHOLDS	PERCENT OF TOTAL U.S. INCOME	PERCENT OF TOTAL U.S. RETAIL SALES
Texas*	5.7	5.8	5.9	6.7
Oklahoma	0.3	1.4	1.2	1.3
Arkansas	0.2	1.0	0.8	0.9
Territory Total	6.2%	8.2%	7.9%	8.9%
Kansas	0.2	1.1	1.1	1.1
Nebraska	0.1	0.7	0.7	0.7
Iowa	0.2	1.3	1.3	1.3
Missouri	0.9	2.3	2.1	2.2
Illinois*	4.3	5.1	5.7	5.6
Territory Total	5.9%	10.5%	10.9%	10.9%

*Home state of salesperson assigned this territory.

Sloan felt that these two territories were not holding their own for the potential they had. The thought crosses his mind to redivide these two territories into three, add a new salesperson, and get better sales penetration overall as a result. He wonders how the two salespeople now in the territories will react. He doesn't know them personally, but can see that this action might hurt their chances of making quota and thus the extra commissions. Their records showed that each had earned about $2,000 in commissions this past year. Each sales force member had received equal quotas in the past, and Sloan wonders if this, too, should be changed.

QUESTIONS

1. Based on the information given, determine the relative sales potentials for the two territories. Then compare each territory's relative potential with its sales volume percentage. Do you agree that the territories are not producing as well as they should?

2. What might be some reasons for lower productivity in these two territories?
3. If you were given the task to redivide these two territories into three, how would you do it? What would your final result be? Into which territory would you assign the new salesperson?
4. What other approaches might Sloan consider for improving sales volume in the Southern District?

CASE 3 Murray Laminating Equipment Company

Atch Murray, the founder and general manager of Murray Laminating Equipment Company, was reviewing his firm's recent sales forecasting experience in hopes of finding some way to get better accuracy in his sales projections. Murray Laminating is a highly specialized producer of laminating equipment sold to manufacturers for binding metal, plastics, and woods to a wood base. Furniture, appliance, and office equipment producers have been the company's major markets. Atch himself invented the original machine and had started building and selling it in 1969 in a two-man operation with his college roommate, Jed Riley. But Jed went on to law school, so Atch decided to establish a full-fledged business.

The machine was simple to assemble, once the proper materials were bought and shaped, so Atch leased a small space in an industrial park, hired a production foreman and a crew of two workers, and took over the selling job himself. Sales grew rapidly, causing Atch to hire additional salespeople, and the sales force increased to a total of 20 in 1977. Not all sales force members were full-time employees of Murray Laminating, however; a few sold other, noncompeting lines. By 1978 the product line had also grown to include three models of laminating machines, with the latest added for the 1978 season. Each model was geared to a particular set of laminating applications, although they could interchange with some loss of efficiency.

This rapid growth had produced some problems. How much finished goods inventory to carry, what stock of raw materials should be on hand, and how to time purchases so that sufficient cash would be available to take advantage of discounts were some of these problems. To maintain his price advantage over all major competitors, Atch felt these were key factors in the success of his business. Atch had always stressed growth to his sales force, and had tried to hire salespeople with strong motivation and high energy levels. Straight commission was the compensation plan used, which Atch believed would give the greatest incentive and keep operating costs controlled.

Beginning in 1978, Atch asked each sales force member to submit a forecast for the upcoming year in his or her territory. The procedure was somewhat informal. Atch gave each salesperson the following request in early December 1977:

MEMO TO: Robert Adams

FROM: Atch Murray

SUBJECT: To help us plan better for the coming year, I would like each sales rep to make a carefully thought out estimate of what you will sell in your territory for 1978. Since we will now have three products, make an estimate for each one separately, then add them all together for a total.

Put your forecasts directly on this form and return it to me *before Christmas:*

Forecast for:	Number of Units
Model 23:	_____
Model 100:	_____
Model 450 (new):	_____
Total:	_____

Atch thought that asking for individual product lines would make each salesperson spend more time on the request and produce a better total. He also believed that errors in one product forecast might be offset by balancing errors in another, again making the total more accurate. The total was most important in his opinion because each model used nearly identical parts except for some size and shape differences which were made in the production process. All three models were priced within 15 percent of each other as well.

This procedure was followed for the next three years, but Atch has mixed feelings about how much it had helped. He felt that too much capital has become tied up in inventory, and the company has experienced some tight periods of cash flow during which he had to borrow from the local bank. He was hoping that these forecasts would get better, but had never taken the time to analyze the process or the results in detail. So after the 1981 projections were all received from the sales force, Atch took a day after Christmas to dig out all the past forecasting data he had collected. He summarized it all as shown on the table.

QUESTIONS

1. How should Atch evaluate the results from this sales forecasting process? What specific measures or comparisons should he make?
2. How accurate have the results been? Is the accuracy improving? What might be some reasons for the change in accuracy?
3. Evaluate the procedure used to carry out this forecasting process. Could it be improved? If so, how?

MURRAY LAMINATING EQUIPMENT COMPANY

Sales Force Forecasts Compared With Actual Sales

Salesperson and Year Joined Company	1978 Forecast	1978 Actual	1979 Forecast	1979 Actual	1980 Forecast	1980 Actual	1981 Forecast
Adams, R. (76)	145	117	145	123	150	131	162
Atwood, L. (75)	203	194	215	209	225	218	234
Cabases, R. (72)	355	359	380	376	396	395	408
Damberger, J. (77)	120	91	125	109	130	118	155
Feldman, M. (74)	225	219	237	232	255	246	260
Gedney, E. (72)	280	288	295	289	320	322	335
Inacio, M. (76)	148	124	152	133	160	137	169
Irish, K. (75)	250	232	252	243	260	254	272
Lambert, F. (77)	100	78	110	93	125	112	140
McCaig, G. (71)	285	289	300	310	325	324	332
Mulky, D. (76)	190	155	190	171	200	186	205
Oberg, O. (73)	268	262	275	271	288	285	295
Portillo, G. (72)	345	351	355	358	368	367	373
Salkowski, A. (77)	110	87	115	96	130	113	135
Sherman, L. (75)	185	177	200	192	201	193	210
Strong, W. (73)	320	310	335	328	342	336	350
Tidrick, J. (76)	165	143	180	159	192	176	202
Usher, J. (77)	140	115	155	126	165	129	180
Waldeck, G. (71)	340	332	355	353	362	359	370
Yee, E. (72)	302	307	318	319	325	325	336
Totals	4476	4230	4689	4490	4919	4726	5123

4. Based on your evaluations above, what do you think would be a realistic forecast for 1981?

CASE 4 Webster Tackle Company

The Webster Tackle Company is an old, established fishing tackle manufacturer located in Wisconsin. Traditionally, sales had been made primarily to wholesalers who would resell to sporting goods retailers. In the last few years, however, a strong shift has occurred in fishing tackle distribution with chains and discount stores capturing a large consumer market share. In turn, these chains and discount stores buy directly from manufacturers through central or headquarters buying offices for all their stores in a geographic region or even for the entire country. Webster has tried to shift its selling effort to match this trend, but its sales manager, Don Lopez, has not been satisfied with the results. In particular, Lopez felt that sales growth is not keeping pace with the growth rate in the economy and especially with the leisure activities boom which took place during the early and mid 1970s. Sales in 1962, for example, were $7,845,000 and in 1979 had grown only to $8,786,000.

Webster had developed seven sales territories by 1962, and has not changed its territorial makeup since that time, as shown on the accompanying map. Some of these territories have been in existence much longer, covered during that time by long-time Webster personnel. A brief summary of each territory and its history is as follows:

1. Northeast Territory, including

Connecticut	New York
Maine	New Jersey
Massachusetts	Pennsylvania
New Hampshire	Delaware
Rhode Island	Maryland
Vermont	District of Columbia

Salesperson: Charlie McClosky, a native New Yorker selling for Webster for 22 years. Charlie started in the territory in 1957 as its first salesperson and has developed many long-standing customers. Now 53 years old, Charlie complains occasionally about how hard selling has gotten and how tough it is to travel in the "crowded East."

2. Southeast Territory. Includes

Virginia	Mississippi
West Virginia	Alabama
North Carolina	Georgia
South Carolina	Florida
Tennessee	

Salesperson: Billy Brown, who lives in Birmingham, Alabama, and comes from an old Southern family. Billy took over the territory in 1960 when it was 10 years old and gave it a sizeable boost in sales. Now 44, Billy seems still quite energetic and is very happy with his territory.

3. East Central Territory. Includes

| Indiana | Kentucky |
| Ohio | Lower Michigan |

Salesperson: Hans Fogel, an ex-steelmaker from Gary, Indiana, who is an ardent fisherman and loves to travel. Hans started in 1961 and has maintained an average sales record as compared with the company as a whole. He was given Kentucky as a part of his territory in 1962 since management felt it was being neglected by Billy Brown who had it included in the Southeast. Hans is now 60.

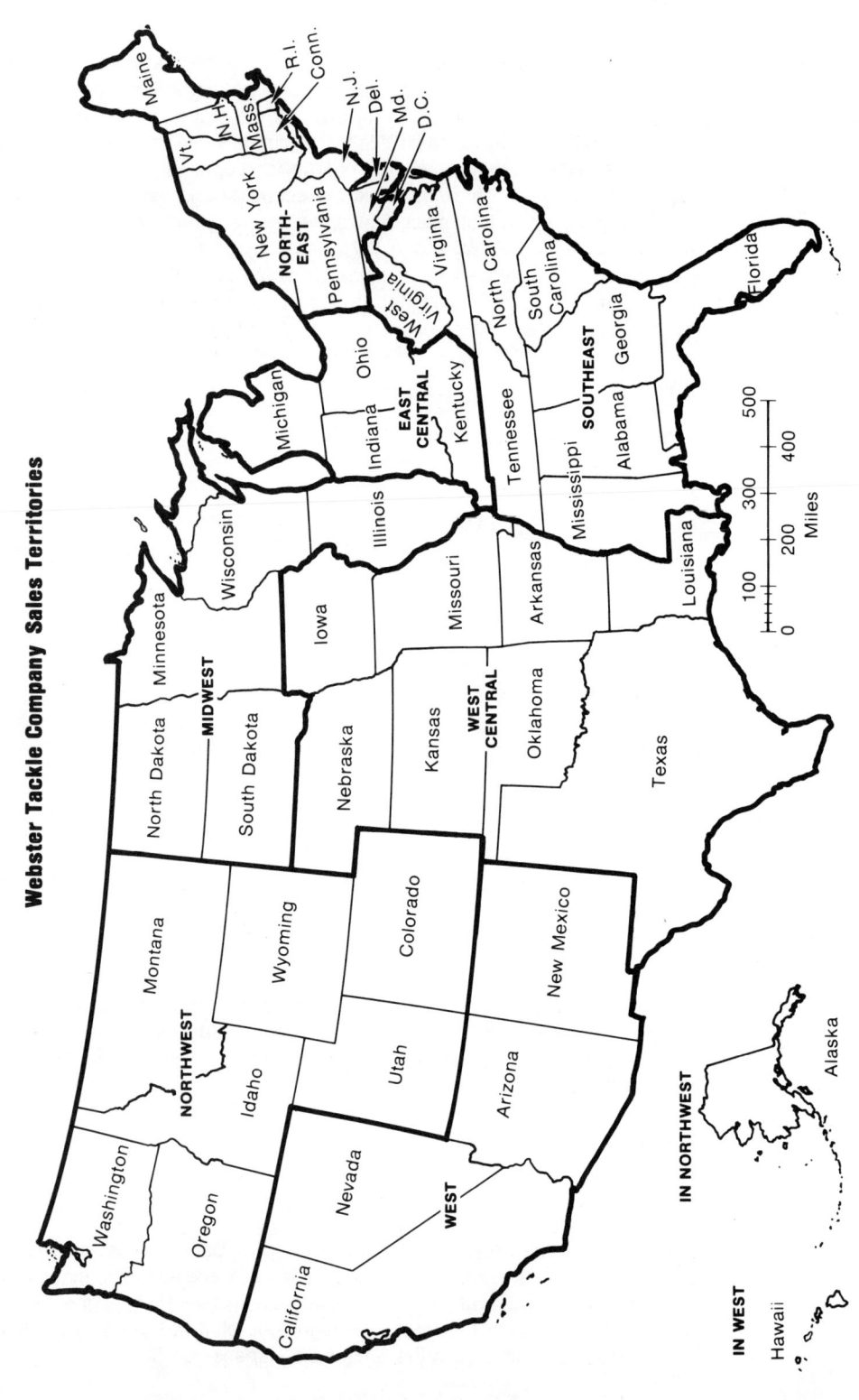

4. Midwest Territory. Includes

North Dakota	Wisconsin
South Dakota	Illinois
Minnesota	Upper Michigan

Salesperson: Al Barrows, a native of Northern Wisconsin whose family owns a small summer resort. Al took over the territory, the company's oldest, in 1951. It is considered somewhat of a "plum" because it is the company's home territory. Other salespeople believe that Al gets credited with a lot of business he doesn't really earn because nearby customers call in orders and even occasionally visit the manufacturing plant. Al is 63 and will retire in two years.

5. West Central Territory. Includes

Iowa	Oklahoma
Nebraska	Arkansas
Kansas	Texas
Missouri	Louisiana

Salesperson: Abby Hendrix, a 31-year-old outdoors lover from Dallas. She began working for Webster in 1972, taking over the territory from another Dallas native who retired after building a great sales record over the previous 18 years. Abby was a physical education major in college and is eager to maintain the business she inherited in the territory.

6. Northwest Territory. Includes

Washington	Colorado
Oregon	Montana
Idaho	Wyoming
Utah	Alaska, added in 1973

Salesperson: Harry "Hap" Hazard, the newest sales force member, who acquired the territory after it was split off the West territory in 1973. Hap was an outdoors writer for a Washington newspaper, and got this position through his friendship with Dirk Olson, Webster's Western sales rep who was then covering this area. This territory was considered almost too small by Lopez, but Hap convinced him that the large amount of fishing activity in these states could support an ambitious salesperson like himself. Hap is 32.

7. West Territory. Includes

California	Nevada
Arizona	New Mexico
Hawaii, added in 1973	

Salesperson: Dirk Olson, a transplanted Midwesterner who worked in Webster's home office until offered the opportunity to establish a West Coast market in 1958. Now 50, Dirk has become a happy Californian, although he has cut down on his travel greatly in the last few years. When the territory was split in 1973, Hawaii was added to Dirk's responsibility but he has been there only twice in the subsequent six years. Travel and shipping costs, he claims, do not make Hawaii a very desirable market.

Don Lopez feels it is time to review the total territory structure, particularly in light of the fact that a couple of his sales personnel will be retiring within the next few years. In addition, he is encouraged by the results from splitting the West territory five years ago, and wondered whether any other territories might benefit from splitting.

To help organize his review, Lopez gathered some data on the territories for 1979, the year just ended. Since fishing has broad popular appeal, he believes that measures of total population for these territories will be good indicators of relative market size, and found such data in the "Survey of Buying Power" from *Sales & Marketing Management* magazine. He also recorded the "Buying Power Index" values for his territories and, after examining other data available from the same source, decided to add their "1983 Buying Power Index" projections to his review as well. As a basis of comparison, he dug out 1962 data on sales and population for the territories as they now were divided. The accompanying table presents the data he put together.

QUESTIONS

1. Evaluate the present territory structure. Should the number of territories be changed? The boundaries? Any other changes?
2. How should the data be used to help Lopez make any territory change decisions. Would any additional market data be helpful? What data, and why?
3. If you were Lopez, what further information would you like to have on each sales force member to help in making sure that your territory decisions will benefit both the company and the salesperson involved?

WEBSTER TACKLE COMPANY

Territory Analysis

	1962		1979			1983
	Percent of U.S. Population	Percent of Company Sales	Percent of U.S. Population	Buying Power Index	Percent of Company Sales	Projected Buying Power Index
NORTHEAST TERRITORY:						
Connecticut	1.44	1.92	1.43	1.54	1.01	1.45
Maine	.52	1.68	.50	.46	1.05	.46
Massachusetts	2.90	3.09	2.64	2.68	2.87	2.58
New Hampshire	.33	.20	.40	.41	.01	.42
Rhode Island	.47	.81	.43	.41	.52	.41
Vermont	.21	.15	.22	.21	.02	.20
New York	9.27	4.44	8.16	7.99	4.76	7.46
New Jersey	3.53	.85	3.34	3.64	.65	3.56
Pennsylvania	6.20	3.93	5.38	5.28	3.88	5.15
Delaware	.26	.10	.27	.28	.04	.28
Maryland	{1.77	{.89	1.90	1.91	.72	1.93
District of Columbia			.31	.35	.06	.33
	26.90	18.06	24.98	25.16	15.59	24.23

	1962		1979		1983	
	Percent of U.S. Population	Percent of Company Sales	Percent of U.S. Population	Buying Power Index	Percent of Company Sales	Projected Buying Power Index
SOUTHEAST TERRITORY:						
Virginia	2.25	.67	2.37	2.27	1.21	2.35
West Virginia	.94	.28	.86	.75	.53	.78
North Carolina	2.50	.72	2.56	2.27	1.07	2.43
South Carolina	1.32	.20	1.33	1.14	.45	1.21
Tennessee	1.94	2.29	1.99	1.81	2.36	1.91
Mississippi	1.15	.77	1.10	.91	.32	.93
Alabama	1.78	3.59	1.72	1.51	3.61	1.57
Georgia	2.18	3.39	2.33	2.14	3.40	2.22
Florida	3.10	1.70	3.99	4.20	1.92	4.65
	17.16	13.61	18.25	17.00	14.87	18.05
EAST CENTRAL TERRITORY:						
Lower Michigan	4.33	3.66	4.10	4.31	3.87	4.11
Indiana	2.57	1.30	2.44	2.46	1.49	2.30
Ohio	5.55	3.51	4.90	4.95	3.83	4.57
Kentucky	1.62	2.00	1.60	1.43	.94	1.49
	14.07	10.47	13.04	13.15	10.13	12.47
MIDWEST TERRITORY:						
North Dakota	.34	.03	.30	.27	.04	.27
South Dakota	.37	.04	.32	.28	.08	.26
Minnesota	1.88	3.78	1.84	1.81	3.97	1.75
Upper Michigan	.09	.06	.09	.07	.11	.09
Wisconsin	2.18	8.48	2.14	2.13	8.37	2.16
Illinois	5.64	5.80	5.14	5.56	4.35	5.33
	10.50	18.19	9.83	10.12	16.92	9.86
WEST CENTRAL TERRITORY						
Iowa	1.47	1.45	1.33	1.30	.98	1.27
Nebraska	.76	.27	.72	.70	.09	.67
Kansas	1.19	1.06	1.08	1.08	.42	1.05
Missouri	2.34	4.88	2.21	2.16	4.72	2.09
Oklahoma	1.25	3.01	1.33	1.26	2.63	1.31
Arkansas	.95	1.76	1.00	.88	1.14	.95
Texas	5.54	10.09	5.99	6.17	9.64	6.48
Louisiana	1.82	3.50	1.81	1.62	3.11	1.69
	15.32	26.02	15.47	15.17	22.73	15.51

(continued)

WEBSTER TACKLE COMPANY

Territory Analysis (continued)

	1962		1979		1983	
	Percent of U.S. Population	Percent of Company Sales	Percent of U.S. Population	Buying Power Index	Percent of Company Sales	Projected Buying Power Index
NORTHWEST TERRITORY:						
Utah	.52	.38	.60	.54	.59	.58
Colorado	1.02	2.31	1.23	1.26	3.01	1.37
Washington	1.60	.99	1.72	1.84	1.99	1.81
Oregon	.99	1.06	1.12	1.08	1.87	1.17
Idaho	.37	.12	.41	.37	.36	.39
Montana	.37	.20	.36	.32	.29	.33
Wyoming	.18	.01	.20	.20	.06	.21
Alaska[a]	—	—	.19	.24	.25	.26
	5.05	5.07	5.83	5.85	8.42	6.12
WEST TERRITORY:						
California	9.48	7.68	10.23	11.21	9.67	11.20
Arizona	.81	.56	1.10	1.07	.72	1.21
New Mexico	.53	.34	.56	.51	.65	.53
Nevada	.18	.00	.30	.34	.22	.37
Hawaii[a]	—	—	.41	.42	.08	.45
	11.00	8.58	12.60	13.55	11.34	13.76
Total of all Territories	100.00	100.00	100.00	100.00	100.00	100.00

[a]Not covered in 1962.

CASE 5 Joy Cosmetics

Joy Cosmetics has been in operation for seven years, and this past year has attained national distribution and strong brand recognition. Joy produces a wide line of cosmetics for the teenage market. To remain competitively strong, Joy has come out with ten or more new products a year. The company retails its merchandise in selected chain and drug stores as well as major department stores throughout the U.S. To handle its sales, they have divided the market area into ten regions with up to six territories in each region depending on its size and growth.

Last year company sales reached $195 million, and the goal for this year is $225 million, a sales increase of $30 million which is to be evenly distributed among the ten regions. The new "Baby Soft" and the new "Allergetic" lines, which will be introduced in the spring, will account for $20 million of the increased sales goal. The remaining $10 million is expected to come from price and volume increases in sales of existing products plus other new products in existing lines.

Connie Applby, the sales manager, received a complaint from Jerry Parmely, one of the regional sales managers. It seems that two of his salespeople, Stuart and Hogarth, complained that their last year's sales quotas were too high, and they found it impossible to meet them. As a result, they missed any chance for a salary increase, which is only considered for those who at least reach their annual sales quota. Because they have been with the company since it started, Parmely decided to pass their complaints along to Ms. Applby. Parmely told Applby that his region in total had come very close to meeting its sales goal, and he had no particular complaint about the two who did not reach their sales quota.

Ms. Applby pulled the past sales records for Parmely's region. She observed that two salespeople (Stuart and Hogarth) did not meet their quotas, but two (Smith and Nunez) had exceeded theirs by a good margin. She also noted that, up to now, quotas were set by all regional managers in the same way, applying a fixed percentage increase to the previous year's sales for each salesperson. If the region had to increase sales by 10 percent, then each salesperson was asked to increase sales by 10 percent as well.

She then asked Parmely to dig further into other market measures for these six territories and to try to come up with a more equitable way of devising quotas. But any new procedure should not damage the strong drive shown by Smith and Nunez, she cautioned. As soon as he had a method to propose, she wanted to review it to see if it might be adopted by all the regions.

Parmely collected whatever available data he could find on the six territories, and put it into this table:

JOY COSMETICS
Analysis of Region Six Territories

Sales-person	PAST YEAR				Sales Potential ($ millions)		Sales Penetration	Age of territory	Length of Sales-person's employment	Present salary
	Quota ($ millions)		Sales ($ millions)							
	$	%	$	%	$	%				
Evans	3.50	17.9	3.52	18.0	9.3	16.3	38%	4 years	4 years	$28,000
Hogarth	4.40	22.4	4.00	20.5	6.0	10.5	67%	7	7	$35,000
Nunez	3.00	15.3	3.45	17.6	15.0	26.3	23%	4	2	$22,000
Reilly	2.90	14.8	2.93	15.0	9.8	17.2	30%	5	3	$25,000
Smith	2.90	14.8	3.15	16.1	12.0	21.1	26%	2	2	$21,000
Stuart	2.90	14.8	2.50	12.8	4.9	8.6	51%	7	7	$35,000
	$19.60	100.0	$19.55	100.0	$57.0	100.0	34%			

QUESTIONS

1. What factors from the table should Parmely use in devising more equitable quotas?
2. Using these factors, calculate a set of quotas for the upcoming year to reach a total regional goal of $22.6 million in sales.
3. Do you think that tying salary increases to quota attainment is a good practice for this company?

CASE 6 Vidio Star Cable TV Company

The Vidio Star Cable TV Company is newly formed to provide cable television to Lemonville, California, a city of 75,000. The company has recently spent $1,000,000 (much of it borrowed) for vehicles, facilities, and equipment to start operations. Another $600,000 is budgeted for operating expenses the first year. Of this amount, $200,000 is allocated for sales expenses and training.

Vidio Star plans to break even within five years but hopes to do so in three or four. Management estimates their proposed $25 initial installation fee charged to customers will just cover costs directly attributable to the installation. The $8.50 per month service charge will apply to other expenses and ongoing maintenance.

Jim Swanson was hired for $25,000 per year to hire, train, and supervise the sales force. Swanson's previous employer had been an established cable TV firm in a small, wealthy resort community. There he had supervised four full-time salespeople older than himself.

Swanson studied data Vidio Star had compiled. Lemonville's population projection is 5,000 more people each year for the next five years. Each household averages 2.5 people. The city has a small university with 6,000 students and consequently, many apartments with younger tenants. The city is currently served by only two television stations, but weak signals can be received from eight channels in cities 125 miles or more distant. Vidio Star projected 80 percent of the households as their potential market. They expect 60 percent market penetration within five years and feel that 40 percent should be attainable the first year.

Drawing on his past experience, Swanson figures a full-time salesperson should average 12 personal calls or 24 telephone sales calls per day. Six of the 12 first time personal calls should result in sales while only 4 telephone calls (with occasional personal call follow-ups) should be successful. Swanson believes the successful first call ratio will improve after a few months as word-of-mouth advertising by satisfied customers will help sell potential customers. Also, more unsolicited call-ins requesting service should also be realized.

Swanson knows that commission basis only, paying their own expenses, and $10 commission per sale, are industry standards for full-time sales personnel. Training, sick leave, paid vacations, and other fringe benefits should cost about $2,500 per salesperson per year. However, he also believes that college students, working on a part-time, independent contractor basis, might work for $5 commission. His training and supervision costs and employee turnover will be greater but the alternative deserves further investigation.

The company's general manager gives Swanson three weeks to present a detailed staffing, job description, training, and compensation plan which will fall within his first year budget. He is also asked to submit tentative budget and sales projections for each of the full five years.

QUESTION

1. Devise the plan and projection requested by the general manager.

CASE 7 Ace Lighting Company

Ace Lighting Company produces a wide assortment of commercial and industrial lighting. Most of its products can be grouped into two main categories:

1. Fluorescent lamps, which include various lengths of tubes to use in lighting work areas in factories, offices, and schools. Different colors can be produced by coating the inside of the tubes with chemical compounds. For instance, a zinc silicate coating will result in green light. Most fluorescent applications are for regular "white" light, however. Compared with tungsten, fluorescent lighting is more economical to operate. Ace is also experimenting with fluorescent panels in addition to tubes for lighting whole ceilings or walls, but the panels are not yet available in its catalog.
2. Neon lights, which is a term used to describe gas-filled tubes that glow from electricity flowing through the gas. Neon is only one type of gas used in this product line, and it produces a red color light. Other gases produce other colors, such as blue light from argon. These tubes can be shaped in a variety of ways, and are often used for advertising and display signs. One unique application is the use of krypton-filled lamps which produce light flashes to mark airport runways.

Ace does not make tungsten bulbs for home use because its management feels that competition would be too intense from the other well-known and highly-advertised light bulb producers such as G.E. and Sylvania. But the product development department has been most interested in establishing a mercury vapor product line because its technical and medical applications fall into growing markets. For instance, ultraviolet rays from mercury vapor lights kill bacteria and thus have numerous medical uses. Also some forms of mercury vapor (and sodium vapor) lights have increasingly been used to light city streets and highways because of their intense light output and low operating costs. Besides, the production process and technical problems are quite similar to those for fluorescent lighting, an area of technical and competitive strength for Ace.

The company has grown steadily during its eight years of existence, and top management has decided to expand its market coverage nationwide after being limited to the Northwest for five years and, three years ago, to the entire West Coast. Ellen Vanell, the sales manager since the company's founding, now faces the task of enlarging her ten-person sales force to one of approximately 40 necessary for proper national coverage. Up to now, each salesperson sold all products to all customers in an assigned territory. Ellen believes that national expansion provides an opportunity to consider some sales force specialization besides just geographic territory assignments.

A review of the major customer types sold by Ace during the past three years revealed a broad cross section. Manufacturers, wholesalers, and retailers purchased fluorescent lighting, and its primary use was for office, shipping, and production areas. Government agencies were also big buyers of office lighting. Ellen believes that these customer groups will be good prospects for mercury vapor lights when that product will be finally introduced in two or three years. Retailers and some manufacturers were also neon lighting customers for advertising and display uses.

Ellen also realizes that some salespeople are not equally effective in selling to all types of customers and all types of products. She has learned through informal conversations that many salespeople find it hard to adjust to sometimes vastly different buying procedures. Government agencies, for example, often require complicated bids and technical proposals whereas manufacturers are more concerned with service and maintenance arrangements. In particular, she has found that some of her sales force members are very interested in selling neon lighting for advertising applications because they enjoy the challenge of designing shapes, working with colors, and solving the technical problems unique to many jobs.

Ellen requested from accounting a breakdown of sales from the past two years by product line and customer type. She is hoping to find some useful guides for devising specialization patterns. The report reached her desk with the following summary:

PERCENTAGE DISTRIBUTION OF ACE LIGHTING SALES—PAST TWO YEARS

Customer Types	PRODUCT LINES		
	Fluorescent	Neon	Total
Manufacturers	30%	9%	39%
Wholesalers, Distributors	5%	5%	10%
Retailers, Services	6%	16%	22%
Government (Federal, State, Local)	23%	3%	26%
Miscellaneous	1%	2%	3%
Total	65%	35%	100%

After examining these results, Ellen called Dick Stone, the chief accountant, to determine if he had any available data on profitability by customer types or product lines. Since the accounting department had never done a full-fledged cost accounting analysis for marketing, Stone replied that all he had were "guesstimates." He believed that the neon line was more profitable than the fluorescents, though the fluorescents sold more. He also stated that government business was quite profitable once Ace got established as a particular agency's supplier, but the process of negotiating initially was quite costly in sales force time as well as in the backup needed from accounting and engineering personnel in the home office to prepare proposals and answer questions and meetings.

QUESTIONS

1. What are some possible ways to specialize Ace's sales force as it expands to cover the entire country?
2. What are the pros and cons of each alternative?
3. Which alternative would best allow future product line expansions without upsetting the organization structure?
4. Devise an organization chart which includes 40 salespeople divided into four regions, using the specialization pattern(s) you think best.

CASE 8 Fastype Company

The Fastype Company was formed as a subsidiary of a large business machines corporation to produce and sell a major new product line throughout the country. Fastype management has determined that it needs 25 new salespeople within the next two months who will be located in major metropolitan areas across the U.S. The sales positions are largely creative or developmental in nature and involve selling word processing systems which can be quite productive for a number of companies, but which are also quite expensive.

The parent corporation has had the following results from its use of various sales personnel recruiting sources in the recent past:

	NUMBER RECRUITED	NUMBER HIRED	RATIO OF HIRED TO RECRUITED	NUMBER SUCCESSFUL	RATIO OF SUCCESSFUL TO RECRUITED
Sales Personnel Agencies	30	20	67%	13	43%
Universities	20	10	50%	7	35%
Referrals by Current Sales Staff	25	6	24%	3	12%
Business Associates' Referrals	26	12	46%	7	27%

While the use of agencies specializing in sales personnel has been the most successful source in the past, it is also quite expensive. Management feels that it must minimize agency fees at this time because of the company's tenuous economic position. They are even considering running advertisements and attempting to screen the people applying themselves, although they have no past experience along these lines.

The sales manager knows of a group of 13 salespeople experienced in this type of selling who are willing to join Fastype for the "right offer" but other executives question the loyalty and longevity they would receive from this group if hired. Management believes that longevity is a key factor to selling success over the next five to ten years as the market for their systems develops.

In the past, the parent company has used screening interviews and later one or two in-depth interviews, as well as many available types of tests. They have had only moderate success with the test predictions in the past, and are concerned whether such tests will be useful for this group at all because of the difference in Fastype's market and product. Because of time pressures, there is no opportunity to use a large number of selection tools. They are also concerned as to recent rulings on the legality of tests and other selection techniques.

The parent company's training program in the past has been quite extensive and oriented primarily toward training each individual at his own pace and in the areas of training most needed. No totally standardized program existed. For budgeting reasons, management wished to minimize training costs initially in Fastype. For this reason also, the newly-appointed sales manager is considering whether it might be more efficient to hire seasoned successful sales personnel.

QUESTIONS

1. What are the sales manager's major options in recruiting, selection, and training?
2. What are the cost tradeoffs among these options?
3. Besides the current hiring and training problems, what should the sales manager be thinking about to make future hiring and training more productive?

CASE 9 County Steel and Material Supply Company

County Steel and Material Supply Company is an industrial supply company which has enjoyed a reputation for quality service in its three-state market area for the last 75 years. John Evens had been owner and general manager for the last 20 years, during which the company had grown steadily. John has just recently retired and gave control of the firm to his son-in-law, Hank Alsos, who had five years selling real estate since getting his college degree in marketing.

County Steel employs five salespeople with assigned territories which are approximately equal in geographic area and sales potential. All five have been with the company as long as John Evens has owned it. They have always worked on a combination salary and commission plan, and their total earnings last year averaged $36,000. One-third of their earnings came from the salary portion of their pay.

The salespeople's duties include about 60 percent direct selling. The other 40 percent includes attending city council and chamber of commerce meetings, talking with prospective builders and existing customers, and attending manufacturers' training sessions, as well as other civic and social functions. Territory assignments have remained the same for many years, and each salesperson has built very close relationships with their customers.

As one of his first actions, Hank implemented a $50,000 advertising program in order to increase County's market share during the current fiscal year. The first quarter following the advertising increase produced disappointing results. Studies indicated that potential customers were aware of the ads and were willing to consider County Steel as a supplier. But the sales force had taken advantage of very few of these increased opportunities.

In pondering his next move, Hank drew these conclusions:

1. The existing salespeople have reached a point in their careers where they are not motivated by increased sales potential and earnings opportunities.
2. One or more new salespeople will have to be added to capitalize on the new sales opportunities, but this might require a reshuffling of existing territories which would be upsetting to the veteran sales force.
3. Finding sales recruits who are knowledgeable about County's broad product line is tough, and no formal training program exists since no new salespeople have been trained for at least 20 years.

QUESTIONS

1. What are Hank's options? What should he do next?
2. Was the advertising program a good idea? Was the advertising effective?
3. If you had been given this business by your father-in-law, what would you have done as your first action?

CASE 10 G & B Container Corporation

Two years ago, G & B Container Corporation changed from one national sales force selling all company products to five specialized sales organizations, one for each major product line. These lines included (1) disposable nonfood containers, (2) food and drink containers, (3) temperature controlling containers, (4) reusable containers, and (5) multiproduct, multiuse containers. Each line has its own technical and marketing problems as well as a different set of competitors and potential customers.

The five divisions resulting from this reorganization now each have a marketing manager. Reporting to each of these managers is a division sales manager responsible for field selling, and a product group manager who supervises the work of product management teams. These teams develop programs for advertising, product design and development, customer service, and pricing.

A major problem for G & B has been to recruit and keep top performers in the field sales organization. Phil Davis, Chairman of the Board, was quoted as saying, "Thirty years ago sales was treated as a tough but good job. Now the kids coming out of school don't seem interested in sales. The job is treated as just a stepping stone to management. In our company, where sales has always been the key to success, we've had trouble getting and keeping the kind of people we want."

As the company has gotten larger, it has hired many business school graduates and placed them in selling positions as part of their management training program. To get high caliber people, G & B has offered above-average salaries, and to keep them from moving to other companies, G & B has promoted many of them into management positions even before they were considered ready. Even so, nearly 80 percent of the newly-hired college grads have been lost over the past two years. Those offered positions into the product management teams were more likely to stay with G & B compared with those offered sales management positions.

At the annual get-together of G & B sales personnel, the five managers began discussing their problems of sales force turnover and difficulty in getting good district sales managers "from the ranks." The more they talked, the more they thought that the problem stemmed from the higher management policy of hiring for management training rather than for professional selling or sales careers. They decided to set up a meeting with the five division marketing managers to see if these problems could be attacked in a more unified way across all five divisions.

The corporate vice-president of marketing attended that meeting as well, and directed the early discussion to the company's success in attracting good people to the management training program, but strongly questioned why so many of these "high caliber and high-potential future executives" were being disenchanted on their first job with the company, and strongly hinted that the fault lay with the sales managers who were unable to keep them enthusiastic about G & B. One of the marketing managers noted that "Maybe people were being placed into jobs for the wrong reasons." A sales manager suggested that "Some of these new recruits consider sales a second-class job and product management a first-class job because it got the big play during the hiring process that attracted these people in the first place."

The vice-president was annoyed at these comments, and challenged the marketing and sales managers to "clean up their act" so that the turnover would slow down. He also conceded that if they could present a new hiring and training plan fully acceptable to himself and top management, he would consider it, but only if it will keep up the flow of high-caliber management trainees.

QUESTIONS

1. Why is there so much turnover?
2. Should the hiring process for management trainees be separated from the hiring process for sales personnel?
3. Is selling a good background experience for future company managers? Should these management trainees be treated any differently than those more oriented to careers in selling? Consider training, compensation, and other personnel policies.

CASE 11 Westerner Sportswear Company

The Westerner Sportswear Company is a well-known manufacturer specializing in men's western apparel. The owner and president, Cal Williams, started the company twenty years ago after a successful five years selling for a large suburban automobile dealer. Westerner's market was limited to Southern California until four years ago when Cal decided to expand to the seven Western states.

Westerner currently holds 25 percent of the western apparel sales in their seven-state market. Cal and his sales manager, Tom Burgess, feel that they should have at least 40 percent of the market if their five-person sales force was properly motivated.

The two salespeople who have been with the company for over 15 years produce the highest sales volume. But Tom knows that their jobs have become quite easy, selling to primarily major customers like large chains and department stores on a maintenance basis. Most of their selling occurs in two major cities. Annual income of each has been about $60,000 in each of the last two years. The two-part compensation plan includes $9,000 a year salary with the remainder a fixed commission paid on sales volume at the same rate regardless of the product line sold. Expenses are paid by each sales force member, and they must maintain their own expense records for tax purposes.

A third salesperson of five years has been working long hours in her two-state area. As a result, her annual income has grown to $40,000. The fourth salesperson has been with the company for two years and the fifth for one year. Their total incomes from salary and commissions last year were $17,000 and $16,000 respectively. Both seem eager to increase their sales and find new customers.

Two years ago, Williams and Burgess decided to increase commission rates from 4 to 5 percent to give greater incentive. This increased the two veteran salespeople's income but their sales did not rise appreciably. The middle salesperson increased her sales by $200,000, however, and the other two were not employed prior to this increase.

Still unsatisfied, Williams and Burgess decided this month to pair up each veteran salesperson with one of the two rookies. Their plan is to have the two work together in the newer territories for two months in an effort to increase sales and gain new customers. Williams and Burgess felt that the two should share the additional commissions from any sale to new customers on a sixty-forty basis with the more experienced salesperson receiving the 60 percent. After the two-month period, any repeat business will be credited totally to the rookie's account.

QUESTIONS

1. Evaluate this "buddy" plan through the eyes of the rookie salespeople. How do you think the veterans will like it?
2. What other motivational techniques might be considered to achieve more market share?
3. Was the commission rate increase a good idea?

CASE 12 Cosi Cosmetics Company

Cosi Cosmetics, located in Boston, manufactures a line of quality hair care products. Established in 1972, the company has been growing steadily but slowly, though the expectations of top management include increasing sales growth over the next few years as Cosi's products become better known, accepted, and even demanded by consumers. The products, primarily shampoos, rinses, and conditioners, are sold to beauty supply stores throughout the Northeastern U.S. under the name "NUTRESS" by the company's twelve salespeople who travel from the home office and live in Boston.

Mike Gunnerson, sales manager for Cosi, was concerned by a problem involving Scott Green, one of the company's salespeople. Green had been with the company since its start, and prior to that he worked for a similar firm out of a branch office in Boston. He is 52 years old, married, and has two children. His son Tod recently graduated from college and has taken a job selling life insurance. Susan, his daughter, is a college senior and recently became engaged to be married following graduation. His wife is not employed but does volunteer work for one local hospital and other civic organizations. The Greens have lived in Boston in the same house since they were married. Between his salary and commissions, Scott Green managed to earn over $35,000 this past year, and he had averaged at least $30,000 for each of the past ten years.

Six months ago, Cosi hired a new vice-president of marketing, Victor Christman, who instituted a new salary program for the sales force. Previously, a base salary was paid per month depending on length of employment and the remainder was earned in commissions. Scott Green received a monthly base salary of $1,000 under this plan. Christman believed that if future sales expand at the rate expected, the switchover to salary will save the company money over time, since sales force compensation will not grow in direct proportion to sales volume as happens with commissions. So the payment of commissions was discontinued and the sales force was paid salary only. Scott Green's salary was set at $34,000 per year, the average of his last three years' earnings. As part of the new plan, salary increases will be based on an annual performance review, and granted to those salespeople meriting a raise. No specific performance benchmarks are set as yet, since Christman and Gunnerson need more time to figure out exactly what efforts and results they wish to emphasize for the upcoming year.

After three months under the new pay plan, Gunnerson notes that sales in Scott Green's territory have decreased. An examination of Green's "itinerary schedule" report for the current three month period compared with the prior three month period reveals that his number of calls was down by 20 percent. Gunnerson concluded that Green was making fewer calls and possibly working fewer days, or else spending more time on each call. But after a few phone calls to old-time customers, Gunnerson learns that Green was calling less often and has begun to be more of an order-taker than an enthused and helpful sales representative. In fact, one customer asked Gunnerson whether Green was experiencing any "personal" problems which would divert his attention from his work, since he didn't seem to be his old self lately.

Gunnerson feels that he has to take some action on this problem. He set up a meeting with Scott Green to discuss Green's sales decline. Green was quite vague in his first reaction to the situation. But after the conversation progressed for about 20 minutes, Green observes that "Everyone around here seems to think that big sales increases are just automatically going to happen. I don't think so, and never did. If Christman thinks sales are going to skyrocket, he doesn't know very much about my territory at least. If you guys are counting on this sales boom to carry us over the next few years, I guess my experience is that it's not going to come that easy."

When asked about his number of calls, and why they were down, Green smiled slightly and said, "I figured it shouldn't take as many calls as it used to if sales are going to shoot up like everyone says. Besides, it's time I got some payoff from all my past hard work with these customers, so I've been bothering them a little less than usual, but enough to remind them that I'm still around. You guys don't want me making a pest of myself, especially when sales are supposed to be coming in bigger and better anyway."

Gunnerson points out quite calmly that calls shouldn't be cut back if it means neglect of customers. In fact, that will only lead to better opportunities for competitors. Furthermore, Gunnerson stated emphatically, "Sales will be only as good as our selling effort—if you guys in the field start taking the sales jump for granted, it's going to backfire on us all. We sure want to see you and all our salespeople earn a raise at the performance review, but we need to show better than we've been doing so far."

The two men parted after this half-hour encounter. Gunnerson made a special mental note to watch Green's progress closely, especially his itinerary schedule for the next few weeks. He also feels that it would be wise to check the itinerary schedules of the rest of the sales force to see if any of them are slowing down as well. Since Gunnerson is scheduled to have lunch with Christman later in the week, he decides that would be a good time to discuss the problem and get the vice-president's views.

QUESTIONS

1. What do you suspect are the real reasons why Green's sales and calls have declined?
2. Can Green's sales decline be turned around? If so, how?
3. Why should the vice-president of marketing become involved in this problem?
4. How else might the compensation plan have been revised to control the possibility of the sales force earnings level drifting too high? Should it be controlled at all?

CASE 13 Accuplate Company

The Accuplate Company was considering the adoption of an incentive compensation plan for its sales force. The company is in the business of photoplate engraving and color plate making, and serves a large metropolitan market in the midwest. Its sales force has two general sources for their business: existing buyers whose requirements have been assigned to a salesperson by management, and buyers whose photo-engraving requirements have been solicited by the individual salesperson's own creative efforts. It is each salesperson's duty to seek ways to improve the company's service to customers. Counselling customers about the preparation of their copy and the mechanical construction of the engravings is an important part of this work. At the time this plan was under consideration, sales personnel were being paid a straight salary and were reimbursed for a limited amount of expenses and local travel.

Darius Portet, the sales manager, believed that each sales force member should stress particular activities and qualities that are critical to the operation of the business. From his conversations with his sales force and with others in the firm, Darius identified these qualities and their relative values and developed the following proposed plan.

COMPENSATION PLAN FOR ACCUPLATE SALES FORCE

This plan is based on the fact that a photo-engraving salesperson's worth to the company stems from (a) the amount of established business serviced, (b) experience in this industry, (c) ability to cooperate with the company's policies and with company personnel, and (d) energetic coverage of the potential market. These four qualities are not all of equal value, however, as indicated:

sales volume = 50%
experience = 25%
cooperation = 20%
coverage = 5%

To compensate fairly for the qualities that each salesperson has developed, this plan proposes that performance in each of these areas for the immediate past six-month period be assessed and that salary for the coming six-month period be based on the results of that assessment. This is to be done in the following manner:

(a) Sales volume. A salesperson's ability to (1) efficiently service the existing customers assigned and (2) maintain a volume of business consistent with the potential available shall be valued in terms of points. The scoring is to be figured on this basis, where average refers to the performance of the sales department as a whole.

Above average	=	50 points
		40 points
Average	=	30 points
		20 points
Below average	=	10 points

(b) Experience. The salesperson's worth in experience is to be determined primarily in terms of length of employment. The average length of the entire sales force is worth 15 points. Maximum is 25 points, and is awarded to the salesperson with the firm the longest.

(c) Cooperation. Average is worth 12 points. Maximum score is 20 points.

(d) Coverage. Average is worth 3 points. Maximum score is 5 points.

Therefore, each salesperson's individual score, for any given period, shall be based on ratings assigned for these four qualities in total. The total sum of points represents each salesperson's value to the firm. A standard unit of income (at present $300) will be paid for each point scored. Therefore, someone scoring 50 total points will be paid $15,000 for the next six months (50 × $300).

Score shall be determined by a board composed of the manager, the sales manager, and the office manager. Each salesperson is to be advised of the reasons for his or her scoring so that weaknesses can be worked on and improved.

QUESTIONS

1. What will the average salesperson earn under this plan per year?
2. If you were a salesperson in this firm, would you support this plan?
3. How is the compensation level determined in this plan? What basic compensation methods are being proposed?

CASE 14 Midwestern Life Insurance Company

Art Lewis, the recently hired general sales manager of Midwestern Life Insurance Company, had just completed his own personal "audit" of the sales organization he inherited after taking over this job. He formerly worked as a regional sales manager for a major food processing company, and feels it is very important to determine where his priorities should be placed for greatest early impact on improving selling effectiveness. In discussions with other company management, as well as with his district agents (i.e., district sales managers), and a few long-time salespeople, he concludes that sales force motivation is a key area for action. Turnover rates of 15 to 20 percent a year are typical for the past five years, and they seem to stem from a lack of challenge or excitement on the job rather than from poor hiring or initial training. At least, these are the opinions of most of the people he talked with. The vast majority of those salespeople who did remain taper off in sales after four or five years, and seem to be content with the earnings level they reach in that time.

The cost of replacing those who quit plus the "imputed" cost from lack of sales growth by those who remain is enormous, in Lewis's opinion, and he concludes that this problem deserves his top priority. He contacted an outside agency specializing in sales motivation to study Midwestern Life's sales force and to propose a plan to reduce the motivation problem.

After two months of study and analysis, Al Whittington, the outside consultant, is ready to make a proposal for action to Lewis. At a meeting in Lewis's office Whittington outlined his suggested plan which consists of three parts:

1. First, Lewis must get an accurate reading of the motivational "climate" in the sales organization and any specific motivational problems that currently exist. To do

this, a group of personal interviews must be made. Ideally, each salesperson should be interviewed, but because the company employs nearly 100, Whittington concedes that 50 interviews might be enough as long as a representative sample can be guaranteed. The contents of the interview will be guided by the interview form prepared by Whittington and shown to Lewis at this time.
2. Outside interviewers should be used rather than present company personnel. Two reasons for this include (a) motivation interviewing requires a professionally trained person skilled in interviewing and in understanding motivational concepts and nuances which would be missed or misinterpreted by less skilled interviewers; and (b) the interviewees will be more honest with an outsider than with one of their superiors in the company, especially when it comes to discussing problems or gripes which they have about the company or about their job.
3. The results will then be reviewed and analyzed for logical action to improve the motivational state of the sales force. Whittington notes that his consulting firm was fully experienced and prepared to do this, but that Lewis could try to do it himself if he felt qualified enough and had the amount of time necessary to do an effective job. To give some idea of how the results would be interpreted, Whittington gave Lewis the following guide to interpreting the interview results:

INTERPRETATION OF INTERVIEW RESULTS

Goals: This area of questioning would help determine the future of the individual in the company, as perceived by that individual. A man or woman who seeks a higher position within the company would be considered one who wishes to stay with the company and strive for improvement. This individual will be at least somewhat satisfied with the company and how it is run in addition to the satisfaction with the ability to advance. A response indicating content with the present position, or indicating a possible departure from the company, could foretell no strong satisfaction, or even dissatisfaction, with the company's ability to provide for career development. Perhaps a review of company promotion plans, or even a change in the plan, is needed. It would be strongly indicated if a majority of respondents answered along these lines.

Any change in goals or objectives could be indicative of either job satisfaction or dissatisfaction. Looking forward to a long career, and deciding not to stay, would definitely indicate some dissatisfaction. Again, a look at company policies would be in order, changing points which seem to cause the most disharmony or dissatisfaction.

The ideal job would elicit many varied responses, and so the company should look at what constitutes a good job and see if any of the features can be incorporated into company positions. Good ideas would help to improve working conditions, as long as one person's heaven wasn't another person's hell.

Security: A salesperson who appreciates changes in his environment would be good to use in new or enlarged territories. One who dislikes change would probably do better in small, stable territories. These points can become important when it comes to assigning people to fill vacancies. The length of time to keep a job would indicate how long people feel it is necessary to prove themselves in one position or how soon change is necessary to keep from stagnating. This information could lead to timetables for salesperson rotation, or for promotion. A fresh individual may be all that is necessary to enlarge a territory or increase sales volume. Job security reduces anxiety and tension. People secure in their jobs will probably perform better. Any negative responses to this question should be investigated to determine ways

MIDWESTERN LIFE INSURANCE COMPANY
Proposed Motivation Interview Guide

Motivational Area	Interview Questions	Responses and Comments
GOALS	1. What do you see yourself doing five years from now? 2. Have you changed any personal plans or goals since starting this job? 3. What is your ideal job?	
SECURITY	1. Do you like changes in your environment? 2. How long should someone keep a job? 3. Do you feel secure in your job?	
STATUS	1. Is your spouse happy with your job? 2. Does your job rank equally with your friends' jobs? 3. What three people count most with you?	
JOB ENVIRONMENT	1. Are you challenged by your job? 2. What do you find most attractive about your work? 3. What do you find least attractive? 4. Are you getting enough supervision?	
JOB COMPENSATION	1. What rewards do you get from your job? 2. What matters most, recognition or a bonus? 3. How important is your job to the success of this company? 4. Do you get paid enough?	

to improve security, such as by giving more responsibility (or in some cases, less) or by providing a more relaxed atmosphere when dealing with sales personnel and their problems.

Status: A spouse who is satisfied with an employee's position would probably be satisfied with the company and its policies. If a spouse were not satisfied, the reason(s) could be explored so that possible changes could be considered. This might be accomplished by improving benefits for family members, for example, or by making the spouse and family more active in some way with the company.

The second and third questions of this section would be harder to deal with in terms of appropriate actions. Perhaps you can determine what factors give the job its level of importance, and what the salesperson personally thinks of the job. If he or she feels it is too low in status, the reasons should be explored to see if any actions can be taken to reduce this feeling. Parts of the job which enhance self-esteem could be expanded upon, to incorporate them into more company positions.

Job Environment: The first question will elicit mainly yes or no answers. These should be explored to determine which factors challenge a person and which factors tend to make one lazy or get bored. Some tasks are necessary and cannot be dropped, but affirmative tasks which reinforce an individual could be expanded upon.

The most and least attractive aspects are really self-explanatory. All you must do is analyze them to see what can be changed or removed (in the case of Leasts) or expanded and refined (in the case of Mosts). This is the chance to tailor the job to the individual, and to get rid of unnecessary actions. This goes hand in hand with the challenging part of the job.

People can differ in their need for supervision, and their responses to this question will help you tailor the amount of supervision to the individual. It will also be useful in judging the overall amount to supply to the sales force as a whole.

Job Compensation: The questions in this section will help you determine what the salesperson feels he or she is worth to the company. From this information, sales contests can be planned (if enthusiasm for this aspect is present), bonus plans instituted, and recognition plans could be developed in the form of letters or plaques of recognition or whatever the general consensus felt was needed. The value and magnitude of a "fair and just wage" could be determined. Any factors which introduced job dissonance (in other words, factors which prove detrimental to a salesperson's well-being) could be identified and corrective measures taken. Perhaps this area would consider any problem not previously mentioned. In addition, the importance of money to overall job satisfaction could be evaluated. Several studies by organizational behaviorists suggest that money is not the motivating factor we used to think it was. Other factors, such as self-esteem and recognition, have proved to be more important in many cases.

QUESTIONS

1. Evaluate this procedure for improving sales force motivation. What are its strengths and weaknesses?
2. Do you think that outside interviewers are better than company personnel for this purpose? If so, what does that suggest about a motivational problem in itself?
3. What difficulties would you anticipate if this procedure were carried out? Consider the mechanics of the procedure as well as the analysis of the results and the conclusions drawn.

CASE 15 The Goodall Tire Company

The Goodall Tire Company is a Midwestern-based producer of automobile, truck, and other heavy-duty tire products. Two years ago, to counteract a leveling sales volume, the company expanded its market into the Eastern area of the U.S., giving it full national distribution. This move was made after careful analysis showed that the East offered large sales potential even though competition was well-entrenched there. Ten new salespeople were hired, recruited primarily from sales forces of dealers and distributors that Goodall sold to in the Midwest and West. The starting salary of $18,000 attracted many applicants, although Tom Scully, the general sales manager, planned to switch all the Eastern sales reps to a predominantly commission plan after they became established in the second or third year.

Sales have grown in the past two years after the expansion move, but Tom was disappointed in the overall results. Total sales for the year just ended were $5,500,000 from a national sales potential estimated at $12,000,000. He asked Burt Haradman, his sales analyst, to prepare some comparisons among the three major sales areas of the country, and received this report:

AREA	SALES POTENTIAL	PERCENTAGE OF SALES VOLUME	INDEX OF PERFORMANCE
West	35%	35%	100
Midwest	20%	40%	200
East	45%	25%	56
	100%	100%	

After reviewing these results, Tom felt the West and Midwest were performing up to standards or better. But the East, in his opinion, had not made sufficient inroads into its potential. He asks Burt to prepare an analysis of the districts in the East region:

DISTRICT	SALES POTENTIAL	PERCENTAGE OF SALES VOLUME	INDEX OF PERFORMANCE
New England	25%	40%	160
Mid Atlantic	60%	20%	33
South Atlantic	15%	40%	267
	100%	100%	

Tom concluded the problem to be the Mid-Atlantic district. He gathered the following data about each salesperson from Donna Salvati, Mid-Atlantic district sales supervisor:

SALESPERSON	SALES POTENTIAL	PERCENTAGE OF SALES VOLUME	INDEX OF PERFORMANCE
Bill Glick	40%	20%	50
Jean Thompson	35%	25%	71
Harry Gomez	25%	55%	220
	100%	100%	

Tom now thinks it is time for a meeting with his sales supervisor and her sales force in the Mid-Atlantic district to discuss their performance. He asks Burt to prepare a list of questions to help guide the discussion at this meeting and to shed further light on how to improve this situation.

QUESTIONS

1. If you were Burt, what questions would you propose that Tom ask of each person in this meeting? What would be the purpose of each question?
2. What other useful data can be extracted from the analyses already made and reported above?
3. What are some options Tom should consider for future action prior to the start of the meeting?

CASE 16 Doben Rubber Company

The Doben Rubber Company is a large producer and seller of rubber footwear, including tennis and basketball shoes, galoshes, and ski boots. The nationally advertised line is sold through 10,000 chain and independent stores and mail order houses in urban and rural districts in all parts of the country.

The company maintains 35 sales branches in major U.S. cities, and employs 275 salaried salespeople who are assigned exclusive territories and sell the full line to wholesalers and chains. Their accounts are of two types. The first include "regular" accounts handled entirely by individual salespeople. The second are "house" accounts which include larger customers such as most of the chains and large mail order houses, and are sold directly by the branch managers.

Presently the performance appraisal of each salesperson is done somewhat informally by the branch manager, who considers sales volume, effort, cooperativeness, and standing with the trade as the four major factors. Bonuses are given to the top 20 percent of the sales force in each branch based on these appraisals. Terminations result occasionally as well. When a territory vacancy occurs, the branch manager involved offers it first to the salesperson with the best performance appraisal the previous year. If turned down, it is offered to the salesperson with the second best appraisal, and so on. Salary increases are based primarily on sales volume growth produced by each salesperson, however, regardless of the appraisal results.

Not all branch managers are happy with this system, and some rate all their sales personnel essentially equal to "avoid bad feelings," as they put it. In such cases, available bonus money is split equally among all branch salespeople, and vacated territories usually go to the salesperson first finding out about them. Other branch managers base their judgments on sales volume alone because it is an "objective" measure. Many sales force members are unhappy about this system as well.

Ray Vaughn, a recently appointed branch manager, suggests that the only fair way to evaluate performance is on the basis of each salesperson's direct selling costs and sales results. The costs will include salary and expenses. Salary will be measured as a percent of gross sales to arrive at compensation cost. Travel and other expenses will also be determined as a percent of gross sales. The combined salary and expenses will also be computed as a percent of gross sales to give a total sales cost for each salesperson. Total number of calls per salesperson will be considered in relation to that person's total cost to find cost per call.

Ray believes that this method of appraisal will eliminate the bias of subjective judgments and the inequalities of judging on sales volume alone. It will focus on sales force efficiency, a key factor in overall company success. He presented top

Proposed Performance Appraisal Method

Sales-person	Gross Dollar Sales	SALARIES Dollars	Percent of Gross Sales	EXPENSES Dollars	Percent of Gross Sales	Salaries Plus Expenses as Percent of Gross Sales	Number of Calls	Cost per Call
Art	$ 123,672	$10,000	8.1	$ 4,442	3.6	11.7	58	$249
Karen	153,894	5,200	3.4	1,630	1.1	4.5	212	32
Wayne	36,644	3,600	9.8	none[a]	—	9.8	none[a]	—
Boris	130,988	4,800	3.7	2,722	2.1	5.8	111	68
Carol	133,022	4,400	3.3	3,556	2.7	6.0	115	69
Ken	135,990	5,000	3.7	1,800	1.3	5.0	135	50
Simon	396,100	10,534	2.7	228	0.1	2.8	96	112
Total	$1,110,310	$43,534	3.9	$14,378	1.9	5.8	727	$ 80
House	800,256							
Grand Total	$1,910,566							

[a] Inside salesperson.

management with an example of his plan from an analysis made for seven of his salespeople during the past three months he had been a branch manager. A summary of his presentation is shown on the table.

QUESTIONS

1. Is the proposed plan an improvement over the current appraisal system? What are the strengths and weaknesses of Ray's plan?
2. Who is the best salesperson of the seven in the sample analysis? Why?
3. What could be done to make the proposed plan even better?

CASE 17 Par-Breaker Golf Company

Par-Breaker is a national distributor of four lines of golf-related products, including golf clubs, accessories, shoes, and clothing such as gloves, shirts, and slacks. The company manufactures some of these products and purchases others to be sold under its name. The sales force calls on two customer classes, sporting goods stores and wholesalers, and specialty pro shops. Salespeople are paid a straight commission plus their travel expenses.

Jack Fitzgerald, the company's sales manager, had just returned from a three-day executive development program at the state university which focused on sales force development. Jack became very enthused about trying some type of "management-by-objectives" system among his fourteen salespeople. He feels that an MBO program could give the year-end evaluations a real purpose. Up to now, the evaluations were made, but little was done as a result except to consider the possible firing of a salesperson whose performance was distinctly poor. No one had been fired for at least the last eight years Jack was sales manager. As a result, the evaluations were considered little more than an empty exercise, and Jack felt that an MBO program based on these evaluations might turn them into positive, forward-looking challenges to each salesperson.

Fortunately, it was year-end evaluation time again in Par-Breaker, so Jack could try out his new idea almost immediately. He decided to pick two performance evaluation records and review them carefully in hopes of coming up with an overall procedure and some specific steps for implementing the MBO process. In general, he felt that three basic steps were essential:

1. Salesperson and manager (himself) each review the salesperson's past year's activities and identify strengths and weaknesses;

2. Both parties meet, discuss their interpretations, and reconcile any differences;
3. Together both parties develop a plan of objectives for the salesperson for the upcoming year which will then be assessed at the end of that year when these steps will repeat.

The evaluations Jack chose were those of Tom Chandler and Vinnie Wardlow. Tom has been with the company for ten years, and Vinnie for five. Jack believes they will be most willing to cooperate in his new program because their earnings have increased steadily over the past few years and they are well-respected sales force members in the eyes of management and the other salespeople. The normal evaluation data gathered each year is shown in the attached table for these two salespeople.

As Jack reviewed the evaluations, he made the following observations and wrote down some notes:

"Tom worked fewer days, made fewer calls, and took fewer orders than Vinnie. Tom also spent more money and traveled far more miles. However, we should make some allowances for this because Tom's mountain states territory is more spread out geographically than Vinnie's east coast area.

"Tom's batting average is certainly adequate, and his average order size is more than satisfactory. In fact, it is amazingly high compared with Vinnie's. However, this can probably be explained because the large market potential in Tom's territory in comparison with the number of customers evidently located there would naturally result in high average sales.

"Tom is making a little over three calls per day which is low in comparison to Vinnie. But it doesn't seem too far out of line to cause any action to be taken in light of his territory characteristics. The large number of miles per call is again indicative of the territory.

"Tom's cost per call and cost per order do seem unusually high, however. He worked 20 fewer days than Vinnie. Granted that he traveled 15,000 miles more than Vinnie, but the cost of those miles at 16¢ a mile would be about $2,400, which still leaves quite a difference to be explained between their total expense amounts. Maybe we should discuss how Tom is spending his money, since expenses should be related more closely to the number of days worked and miles traveled.

"Apparently Tom has a more difficult time getting orders from sporting goods stores than from pro shops, although his average sale to sporting goods stores is pretty high. Another thing is that he seems able to sell golf clubs better than clothing. This may just reflect Tom's basic interests, preferring to talk about golf clubs and golf balls rather than about shoes, gloves, and slacks.

"Probably the main problem with Vinnie is his inability to sell to pro shops. He is closing only about 40 percent of the calls he makes on them while the company average is about 65 percent I think. On the other hand, Vinnie has a super batting average with sporting goods stores. Perhaps he speaks the language of the store owner but doesn't communicate very well with the golf expert. Maybe Vinnie is not sufficiently trained in technical aspects of golfing to answer the questions and gain the confidence of the golf professional.

"Vinnie's expenses seem to be well in line with the company average, and his calls per day are probably sufficient. He isn't getting as much market penetration as he should, but he hasn't been selling as long as most of the others either."

PAR-BREAKER GOLF COMPANY

Evaluation of Salespersons Chandler and Wardlow

	TOM CHANDLER			VINNIE WARDLOW		
	Customer Types			Customer Types		
	Stores	Pro Shops	Total	Stores	Pro Shops	Total
Sales ($000):						
Clubs and Accessories	80.1	40.3	120.4	40.1	15.1	55.2
Clothing	110.5	70.5	181.0	80.8	34.6	115.4
Total	190.6	110.8	301.4	120.9	49.7	170.6
Calls Made:	302	403	705	492	394	886
Orders Taken:	148	356	504	444	157	601
Days Worked:			220			240
Expenses:			$12,250			$ 8,096
Miles Travelled:			60,150			44,380
Market Potential (000):						
Clubs and Accessories	400	100	500	200	100	300
Clothing	600	400	1,000	400	200	600
Total	1,000	500	1,500	600	300	900
Average Order ($):	1,288	311	598	272	317	284
Batting Average:	.490	.883	.715	.902	.398	.678
Calls per Day:			3.20			3.69
Miles per Call:			85			50
Expenses/$Sales:			4.1%			4.7%
Cost per Call:			$17.38			$ 9.14
Cost per Order:			$24.30			$13.47

In conclusion, Jack thought for the next year he should try to get Tom to work a few more days. Perhaps it was understandable that Tom is tempted to do a little loafing, because he has an annual income of over $30,000 and is leading the sales force in sales. But Tom's territory has considerable sales potential and we should discuss how to capture more of it. Also, we should try to get Tom to sell more to sporting goods stores. With Vinnie, the main focus should be on why pro shops are such an obstacle. Maybe he could use additional instruction on the technical aspects of golfing.

Having drawn these tentative conclusions, Jack wrote a short memo to his two salespeople explaining the new MBO program's three steps. Along with the memo he sent each a copy of their own evaluation data, and asked them to come up with some constructive suggestions for their own performance improvement for next year. He also set up a meeting with each one individually in his office in three weeks.

QUESTIONS

1. Is Jack's idea of an MBO program a good way of using the evaluation data?
2. From the sales force standpoint, is this a good way to start an MBO program?
3. Assess the performance evaluation data and Jack's observations from it. Are there any other factors which are important to consider? What other possible conclusions would you draw if you were Jack prior to your meeting with each salesperson?
4. What obstacles might you expect to a successful implementation of this MBO program?

ADDITIONAL READINGS

The following are selected new books and articles which are not referenced in the text chapters. These sources offer some of the latest ideas and research findings on sales management topics.

Plannning

ABERNETHY, PAUL L., JR., "Setting Performance Objectives Requires Lots of Give and Take," *Sales & Marketing Management,* May 19, 1980, pp. 86–91.

DARMON, RENE Y., "Setting Sales Quotas with Conjoint Analysis," *Journal of Marketing Research,* vol. 16 (February 1979), pp. 133–140.

RYANS, ADRIAN B., AND WEINBERG, CHARLES B., "Territory Sales Response," *Journal of Marketing Research,* vol. 16 (November 1979), pp. 453–465.

SPIRO, ROSANN L., AND PERREAULT, WILLIAM D., JR., "Factors Influencing Sales Call Frequency of Industrial Salespersons," *Journal of Business Research,* vol. 6 (January 1978), pp. 1–15.

WALTON, JOHN R., "A Comparison of Opinion and Regression Forecasting for an Industrial Product," *Industrial Marketing Management,* vol. 8 (1979), pp. 281–285.

Implementation

ADKINS, ROBERT T., AND SWAN, JOHN E., "Increase Salespeople's Prestige with a New Title," *Industrial Marketing Management,* vol. 9 (1980), pp. 1–9.

BAGOZZI, RICHARD P., "Performance and Satisfaction in an Industrial Sales Force: An Examination of their Antecedents and Simultaneity," *Journal of Marketing,* vol. 44 (Spring 1980), pp. 65–77.

BONOMA, THOMAS, V., AND JOHNSTON, WESLEY J., "The Social Psychology of Industrial Buying and Selling," *Industrial Marketing Management,* vol. 7 (1978), pp. 213–224.

DARMON, RENE Y., AND SHAPIRO, STANLEY J., "Sales Recruiting—A Major Area of Underinvestment," *Industrial Marketing Management,* vol. 9 (1980), pp. 47–51.

DOYLE, STEPHEN X., AND SHAPIRO, BENSON P., "What Counts Most in Motivating Your Sales Force?" *Harvard Business Review,* vol. 58 (May–June 1980), pp. 133–146.

DUBINSKY, ALAN J., "Recruiting College Students for the Salesforce," *Industrial Marketing Management,* vol. 9 (1980), pp. 37–45.

FUTRELL, CHARLES M., "Salesmen and Saleswomen Job Satisfaction," *Industrial Marketing Management,* vol. 9 (1980), pp. 27–30.

KOLGRAF, RON., "Strategies of Territory Management," *Industrial Distribution,* November 1978, pp. 35–40.

MILLER, MARY LYNN, "Motivating the Sales Force," *The Conference Board Information Bulletin,* no. 64 (1979).

MOYNAHAN, JOHN K., *Designing an Effective Sales Compensation Program* (New York: AMACOM, 1980).

MUNSON, J. MICHAEL, AND SPIVEY, W. AUSTIN, "Salesforce Selection That Meets Federal Regulation and Management Needs," *Industrial Marketing Management,* vol. 9 (1980), pp. 11–21.

SPIRO, ROSANN L., AND PERREAULT, WILLIAM D., JR., "Influence Use by Industrial Salesmen: Influence-Strategy Mixes and Situational Determinants," *Journal of Business,* vol. 52 (July 1979), pp. 435–455.

WEITZ, BARTON A., "Relationship Between Salesperson Performance and Understanding of Customer Decision Making," *Journal of Marketing Research,* vol. 15 (November 1978), pp. 501–516.

Evaluation

ADKINS, ROBERT T., "Evaluating and Comparing Salesmen's Performance," *Industrial Marketing Management,* vol. 8 (1979), pp. 207–212.

JACKSON, DONALD W., JR., AND OSTROM, LONNIE, "Grouping Segments for Profitability Analysis," *MSU Business Topics,* vol. 28 (Spring 1980), pp. 39–44.

LAMBERT, CLARK, *Field Sales Performance Appraisal* (New York: John Wiley & Sons, 1979).

STEPHENSON, P. RONALD, ET AL., "Delegating Pricing Authority to the Sales Force: The Effects on Sales and Profit Performance," *Journal of Marketing,* vol. 43 (Spring 1979), pp. 21–28.

General

BAGOZZI, RICHARD P. (ED.), *Sales Management: New Developments From Behavioral and Decision Model Research* (Cambridge: Marketing Science Institute, 1979).

Journal of Personal Selling and Sales Management, commencing in winter 1980.

INDEXES

AUTHOR INDEX

Abernethy, P. L., 373
Ackoff, R. L., 122
Adkins, R. T., 373
Adler, L., 211
Aguilar, F. J., 333
Ahl, D. H., 74
Albaum, G., 186, 332
Aldag, R. J., 30, 31, 140
Allen, C. E., 121
Allvine, F. D., 166
Andelson, R. P., 265
Andersen, R. C., 209
Ankeney, G. E., 120
Antoinetti, J. A., 264
Armstrong, G. M., 122

Bacon, J., 96
Baeder, R. W., 122
Baehr, M. E., 241
Bagozzi, R. P., 306, 373
Bailey, E. L., 68, 74, 96, 193, 212
Bailey, R. E., 333
Barrington, A. R., 122
Bassford, G. L., 241
Bauman, J. N., 211
Bayne, H. L., 261
Bearden, J. H., 187
Bell, J. E., 121
Bellenger, D. N., 240
Bergman, C. E., 334
Berkowitz, E. N., 333
Best, R. J., 75
Beswick, C. A., 121
Bettger, F., 185
Bird, M. M., 97, 122
Black, G. J., 140
Blecke, C. J., 312
Blumenfeld, W. S., 240
Boewadt, R. J., 166
Bonini, C. P., 141
Bonoma, T. V., 186, 373
Brice, M. A., 121

Brock, T. C., 186
Bullen, H. J., 240
Bullock, H. L., 121, 140, 212
Busch, P., 186, 240, 307
Bush, R. F., 240, 307
Buzby, S. L., 333

Carey, J. F., 289
Carlin, W. P., 74
Carlson, R. E., 241
Carney, G. J., 183, 187
Carroll, S. J., 241, 254
Chambers, J. C., 74
Chambers, T. E., 30, 167, 187, 251, 264, 332
Church, L. F., 74
Churchill, G. A., 141, 163, 186, 296, 306, 307
Clark, D. F., 122
Clark, J. J., 75
Cloonan, J. B., 122
Cocanougher, A. B., 327, 333
Cole, S. D., 74
Comer, J. M., 122, 333
Cooper, R., 264
Corey, E. R., 140, 141, 212
Cotham, J. C., 185, 240
Cowan, D. R. G., 50
Cox, W. E., 44, 51
Cravens, D. W., 121, 329, 334
Crissy, W. J. E., 186, 333
Cundiff, E. W., 209

Daignault, P., 74
Dalrymple, D. J., 75
Darden, W. R., 171, 185
Darmon, R. Y., 289, 306, 373
Davenport, J. W., 96, 175, 186
Davis, J. H., 321
Davis, O. A., 141
Davis, R. T., 333
Dawson, L. M., 306
Day, R. L., 122

Dean, J., 97
Detman, A., 211, 212
DeVoe, M., 212
Dewhurst, R. E., 299
Ditz, G. W., 167, 211
Doody, A. F., 211
Doyle, S. X., 373
Drucker, P. F., 30
Dubinsky, A. J., 373
Dunne, P. M., 333
Dunnette, M. D., 185

Earl, E. W., 288
Eby, F. H., 74, 332
Elgers, P. T., 75
Else, R. A., 136, 141
England, G. W., 240
Evans, F. B., 186
Evans, W. W., 264
Everett, M., 211, 264
Ewing, J. S., 15

Fairchild, J. W., 185
Farley, J. U., 141
Felder, L. C., 186
Ferber, R., 74
Fischer, P. J., 31
Fogg, C. D., 211
Fox, H. W., 167
Fram, E. H., 300, 307
Freeman, C., 96, 97
French, W. A., 171, 185
Fuller, D., 50
Futrell, C. M., 141, 334, 373

Gadel, M. S., 186
Gannon, M. J., 241
Gardner, D. M., 307
Gfeller, J. C., 264
Gibbons, C. G., 97
Gillett, P. L., 140
Ginter, J. L., 333
Girdwood, J., 211

Index

Goldstucker, J. L., 265
Gonik, J., 289
Gorman, W. P., 185
Gravereau, V. P., 246, 264
Greenberg, H. M., 186
Grether, E. T., 30
Griffith, K. F., 121
Grikscheit, G. M., 186
Gross, A. K., 259, 265
Guest, T. A., 264
Gwinner, R. F., 166

Haas, K. B., 263
Haas, R. W., 50
Hackett, D. W., 240
Hall, N., 333
Hall, W. P., 15, 30, 288, 289
Halterman, J. C., 50
Hampton, P. J., 186
Hanan, M., 121, 166, 178, 186, 187, 212
Hancock, W. O., 121
Hannaford, W. J., 187
Hardin, D. K., 74
Harding, M., 158
Haring, A., 31
Harrell, T. W., 185
Harris, C. E., 211
Harrison, J. F., 259, 265
Hartman, T. H., 185
Hauk, J. G., 122
Havens, G. N., 44, 51
Hawkins, D. I., 50
Heinecke, H. H., 139, 141
Heitger, L. E., 333
Henry, J. P., 333
Henry, P., 15, 166
Hersker, B. J., 186
Heschel, M. S., 121
Hess, S. W., 122
Heymann, S. E., 121
Hill, N., 185
Hilliard, J. E., 211
Himler, L. E., 167
Hise, R. T., 140
Hopkins, D. S., 248, 263, 264, 265, 307
Howton, F. W., 167, 185
Hughes, C. L., 30
Hughes, G. D., 30
Hummel, F. E., 50
Hurwood, D. L., 63, 74, 240

Isherwood, B. C., 74
Ivancevich, J. M., 327, 333

Jackson, D. W., 30, 31, 140, 265, 373
Johnson, R. M., 74
Johnston, W. J., 373
Jolson, M. A., 4, 75, 152, 166, 240, 241, 307
Juster, F. T., 74

Kahn, G. N., 185
Kahn, R. M., 75
Kanuk, L., 240
Kimball, J. D., 166
Kaven, W. H., 182, 187
King, W. R., 122
Kirchner, W. K., 185
Klinger, W. H., 51
Kniffen, F. W., 121
Kolgraf, R., 373
Konopa, L. J., 246, 264
Korn, D., 289
Kovach, K. A., 306

Lambert, C., 265, 307, 373
Lambert, Z. V., 121
Lamont, L. M., 186, 241, 264
Layton, R. A., 122
Lazer, W., 122
Leahy, J. I., 307
Lee, S. M., 122
Leopold, H., 50
Levitt, T., 186
Locander, W. B., 333
Lodish, L. M., 122
Lucas, H. C., 121
Lund, P. R., 166
Lundstrom, W. J., 186, 241, 264
Lusch, R. F., 30

MacDonald, M. B., 51, 193, 212
McBurney, W. J., 30
McCaskey, M. B., 211
McGuire, E. P., 333
McLaughlin, R. L., 74
McMurray, R. N., 167
McQuaig, J. M., 185
McWilliams, R., 307
Mack, R. W., 167
Mangone, R., 333
Masi, F., 307
Maslow, A. H., 293, 295, 297, 299, 306, 307
Mason, J. L., 167
Massel, M., 30
Mathews, H. L., 167
Mayer, D., 186
Meilstrup, S. S., 122
Meloan, T. C., 50
Miller, E. C., 21, 30
Miller, M. L., 373
Miller, S. J., 167
Montgomery, D. B., 96
Morrill, J. E., 96
Morris, J. H., 241
Morse, N. C., 306
Mossien, H., 300, 307
Mossman, F. H., 318, 333
Moynahan, J. K., 288, 289, 373
Mullick, S. K., 74
Munson, J. M., 373

Namias, J., 74
Nash, A. N., 241
Newton, D. A., 240
Nickels, W. G., 211
Nordstrom, R. J., 31

Ohmann, O. A., 240
Oliver, R. L., 306, 307
Olsen, R. M., 122
Olshavsky, R. W., 186
O'Neill, W. J., 74
O'Shaughnessy, J., 167, 333
Ostrom, L., 373

Pace, R. W., 186
Parasuraman, A., 122
Parker, G. G. C., 74
Pasold, P. W., 186
Pathek, D. S., 185
Patrick, A. W., 312
Paul, W. J., 307
Peale, N. V., 185
Pegram, R. M., 30
Pennington, A. L., 333
Perreault, W. D., 241, 373
Peven, D. E., 307
Pickering, J. F., 74
PoKempner, S. L., 68, 71, 74, 75, 332
Price, K. F., 241
Pruden, H. O., 167, 306
Puetz, J. E., 186

Ranard, E. D., 43, 51, 70
Reese, R. M., 306
Reuschling, T., 240
Reynolds, W. H., 241
Rich, L., 141
Riggs, W. E., 75
Rink, D. R., 167
Riordan, E. A., 186
Robertson, D. H., 15, 211, 240
Rogala, R. E., 186
Rokus, J. W., 211
Roseman, E., 241
Rosenberg, B., 167, 185
Rosenberg, L. J., 241
Ross, D. W., 264
Rossow, G. L., 75
Roth, C. B., 185
Rothe, J. T., 51
Rowland, K. M., 307
Rush, C. H., 240
Ryans, A. B., 373

Samuels, S. A., 122
Scanlon, S., 50, 75, 121, 140, 211, 264, 265, 289, 307
Scheibelhut, J. H., 186
Scheuing, E., 96
Schiff, J. S., 97
Schiff, M., 97

Schlacter, J. L., 265
Seeley, B. D., 332
Segura, E. L., 74
Semlow, W. J., 121
Settle, R. B., 241
Shanker, R. J., 122
Shapiro, B. P., 167, 187, 373
Shapiro, S. J., 373
Shuchman, A., 185
Siegel, P. H., 74
Simon, S. R., 97, 121
Sims, J. T., 141
Skinner, J. E., 187
Skolnik, R., 15, 120, 211, 289
Slote, C. T., 122
Smackey, B. M., 334
Small, R. J., 241
Smith, C. W., 15, 31, 333
Smith, D. D., 74
Smith, D. K., 122
Smith, H., 264, 265
Smith, P. C., 307
Smith, R. C., 281
Smith, S., 74, 75
Smith, V. L., 264
Smyth, R. C., 288
Snyder, J. D., 15, 140, 166
Spar, E., 50
Spar, E. J., 74
Spies, D. K., 289
Spiro, R. L., 160, 167, 373
Spivey, W. A., 373
Staelin, R., 75
Stamper, J. C., 334
Staples, W. A., 333
Star, S. H., 140, 141, 212
Stark, M. J., 240
Steinbrink, J. P., 289
Stephenson, P. R., 373
Stern, M. E., 122
Stevens, C. G., 149
Stevens, S. N., 185
Stewart, D. E., 51
Stone, B., 31
Stroh, T. F., 263, 264, 307
Swan, J. E., 240, 334, 373
Sweitzer, R. W., 185

Talley, W. J., 121
Tanofsky, R., 185
Taylor, T. C., 51, 74, 75, 97, 121, 166, 167, 211, 264, 332, 333
Templeton, J., 169
Terrill, W. A., 312
Tersine, R. J., 75
Thayer, P. W., 264
Thompson, D. L., 15
Thompson, J. W., 264
Thompson, P. R., 75
Thurlow, M. L., 65, 75, 138, 141
Todd, J. T., 334

Tosdal, H. R., 289
Tosi, H. L., 97, 186
Trytten, J. M., 15
Tull, D. S., 50
Turner, R. E., 75

Udell, G. G., 31
Udell, J. G., 24, 30
Urban, G. L., 96

Vizza, R. F., 30, 96, 97, 121, 141, 167, 187, 211, 251, 264, 332, 333

Wage, J., 117, 122
Waid, C., 122
Waldo, C., 50
Walton, J. R., 373
Walker, O. C., 167, 294, 306, 307
Warshaw, M. R., 167
Webster, F. E., 307
Wecker, J. H., 333
Weeks, D. A., 240, 272, 278, 279, 284, 289, 332
Weinberg, C. B., 373
Weiss, R. S., 306
Weitz, B. A., 373
Wheatley, J. J., 333
Williams, G. B., 241
Wilson, A., 166
Wilson, D. T., 186
Winer, L., 141
Withey, J., 265
Witkin, A. A., 185, 240
Wolfe, H. D., 332
Wolk, H. I., 333
Woodruff, R. B., 51, 334
Woodside, A. G., 96, 175, 186
Wotruba, T. R., 30, 65, 75, 138, 141, 240, 241, 333
Wright, J. S., 265

COMPANY INDEX

Abbott Laboratories, 253
Acme Visible Records, 179
A. C. Neilsen Co., 37
Admiral, 256
Aetna Insurance, 253
A. G. Becker, 63
Air Reduction Company, 40, 41
Allis Chalmers, 134
Aluminum Company of America, 69
American Can Company, 61
American Express, 63
American Greetings, 137, 141
American Optical, 116

American Poclain, 262
American Republic Insurance, 253
American Standard, 256
Anheuser-Busch, 148
Ansul, 190, 211
Armour-Dial, 131, 141, 152, 153, 199, 200, 201, 202, 214, 220, 221, 227, 228, 229, 230, 231, 253, 255, 264, 305
Armstrong, 253
Atlantic Refining, 319, 320, 321, 331
AT&T, 121

Babcock & Wilcox, 328
Bankers Trust, 63
Beecham, 253
Bergen Machine & Tool, 280
Best Foods, 40, 99, 121
Bethlehem Steel, 162
B.F. Goodrich, 63
Black & Decker, 301
Borden Chemical, 135
Bristol-Meyers, 13
Burroughs, 99, 276

Calumet & Hecla, 125
Carborundum, 162, 250, 255
Caterpillar Tractor, 203
Celanese, 121
Chase Econometrics, 63
CIBA Pharmaceutical, 111
Clorox, 194, 211
Combustion Engineering, 42, 43, 69
Consolidated Cigar, 247
Continental Group, 252
Continental, 264
Control Data, 253, 255
Cooper-Bessemer, 79
CP Rail, 181
Curtice Burns, 62

Dartnell, 288
Data Resources, 63
Dean Witter, 63
Del Monte, 176, 224, 252, 257, 265, 303, 322, 324, 325, 333
Diamond Alkali, 182
Diamond Crystal Salt, 116
Dictaphone, 298
Didactic Systems, 264
Doubleday, 257, 300
Ducommun, 13
DuPont, 63, 207

Eastman Kodak, 253
Electrolux, 302, 307
Eli Lilly, 62, 106
Emery Air Freight, 79, 106
Emery Industries, 61
Ennis Business Forms, 12
Equitable Life, 63, 175, 218

Exxon, 166
Exxon Chemical, 154

Falk, 139
Fibreboard, 275
First National City Bank, 63
FMC, 110, 111, 154
Friden, 214

Gastonia Mill Supply, 155
General Electric, 18, 33, 52, 63, 64, 74, 114, 115, 122, 136, 181, 191, 249
General Foods, 56, 57, 207
General Mills, 55
General Motors, 67, 74, 253
Goodyear, 247
Green Giant, 284, 289

Hammermill Paper, 131
Hanson Manufacturing, 44
Harris Trust, 63
Harris Intertype, 116
Heinz, 194, 196, 211, 253, 264, 298
Hollingsworth, 146
Honeywell, 249, 253, 264
Hooker Chemical, 19, 159, 250, 251

IBM, 121, 207, 249, 289, 319
Illinois Tool Works, 148
International Harvester, 281, 292
InterRoyal, 64
Irving Trust, 63

Johns-Manville, 275, 276, 289
Johnson & Johnson, 76, 93, 96, 97, 116

Kaufman, 111, 122, 277, 289

Litton Microwave, 14, 15, 98, 120
Long Island Lighting, 59

McKesson & Robbins, 249
Magic Chef, 100, 328, 329
Manufacturers Hanover Trust, 63
Marriott Hotels, 2, 15, 129, 140
Maryland Cup, 273
Master Builders, 256, 258, 259
Maytag, 98
Mellon Bank, 63
Merck, 53
Metropolitan Life, 171
3M, 171, 295, 307
Monsanto Chemical, 62, 67
Motion Industries, 284
Mutual of New York, 99
Muzak, 274, 289

Nalco, 262, 265
National Cash Register, 136

National Lead, 64
National Mills, 104
NCR, 154, 194, 212, 251, 264, 309, 332

Olin Chemicals, 179
Olin Film, 274, 275, 276, 289

Pace Computing, 67
Paper Mate, 192, 211
Parker Hannifin, 194
Parker Pen, 40
Pennwalt, 116
Pfizer, 234
Philip Morris, 273, 289
Pillsbury, 317, 322, 333
Prudential, 1, 63

Rand McNally, 110
Rapistan, 236, 241
RCA, 52, 54, 62, 63, 74
Regina, 302, 307
Republic Steel, 54
Revere Copper & Brass, 89
R. J. Reynolds, 125, 303, 307
Roche, 143, 253
Royal Typewriter, 304

Schering, 102, 253
Security Pacific National Bank, 63
Signode Steel Strapping, 109
Skil, 110, 129, 196
Skyway Luggage, 127, 140
Sola Electric, 143
Southwestern Life Insurance, 234
Sperry Rand, 126
Stouffer Foods, 69, 75
Sun Oil, 61
Sylvania Electric Products, 85

Textile Machine Works, 143
Textron, 298
Transamerica, 6
Tremco Manufacturing, 240
TRW, 64, 75

Union Carbide, 63
Univac, 253
Univis, 18, 20, 21, 30
U.S. Gypsum, 194, 212
U.S. Industries, 104
U.S. Steel, 1, 40
U.S. Trust, 63
USV Pharmaceutical, 312

Volkswagen, 1

Warner & Swasey, 150
Waste King, 135
Wells Fargo Bank, 63
Westinghouse Air Brake, 18

Westinghouse Electric, 107
Westvaco, 259, 261
West Virginia Pulp & Paper, 80
White Motors, 18, 192
Worthington, 83
W.R. Grace, 63

Xerox, 1, 207
Xerox Learning Systems, 257, 259, 260, 265

SUBJECT INDEX

Ability analysis, 246–247
Ability index
   in adjusting quota levels, 137–138
   in assigning salespeople to territories, 111–113
Activities
   evaluation of, 322–323
   quotas for, 130
Adverse impact, 216
Advertising compared with personal selling, 1
Affirmative action, 220
Age Discrimination in Employment Act, 216
AIDA, 148
ALLOCATE, 115
American Statistics Index, 37
Application blanks, 223–226
   weighted, 223–226
Aptitude tests, 232–33
Audiovisual techniques, 256
Authority
   decentralization of, 196
   equality with responsibility, 189
   formal vs, persuasive, 184, 189
   line vs. functional, 189
Automobile, salesperson's, 286–287

Batting average, 323
Behavior view of selling success, 172–174
Behaviorally anchored rating scales, 324, 326, 327
BFOQ, 216
Blind advertisements, 219
Body language, 174
Bonus, 276–277, 278, 279
Branch sales managers, 4
Brokers, 193–194
Budget
   definition of, 78
   see also Sales budgets

Budgeting
  definition of, 77
  purposes of, 76–77
  see also Sales budgeting
Business games, 255
Business Periodicals Index, 37
Buying signals, 155

Call frequency, 102, 105
Call length, 105
Call reports, 322–323
CALLPLAN, 115–116
Career path, 304
Case studies, 255
Centralized purchasing, 191
Chemistry view of selling success, 168–170
Civil Rights Act, 216
Clayton Antitrust Act, 25
Closing the sale, 154–155
Cognitive dissonance, 156
Commission
  base, 274–275
  defined, 273
  payment periods, 276
  rates, 275
  splitting payments, 282
  starting point, 275–276
Compensation level
  compared among sales organization positions, 271, 272
  defined, 269
  drifting too high, 271–272
  methods of determining, 270–271
Compensation methods
  bonus, 276–277, 288, 289
  combining into a total plan, 280–281
  commission, 273–276
  expense payments, 277
  fringe benefits, 277–278
  salary, 272–273
  which to use, 279–280
Compensation plan
  administration of, 282–283
  characteristics of, 266–267
  control provided by, 266, 273, 274
  incentive provided by, 266
  introducing to sales force, 283
  and motivation, 266
  objectives of, 268–269
  for sales managers, 284
  for sales trainees, 283–284
  steps in developing, 267, 268
  testing or evaluating, 281–282
Computer
  in allocating sales effort, 115–116
  in call report analysis, 322
  in cost analysis, 316
  in market potential measurement, 42
  routing salespeople with, 116–117
  in sales forecasting, 52, 59, 61
  in sales territory decisions, 104, 109, 115–117
  in sales training, 253
  impact on selling process, 156–157
Concentration principle, 312
Conferences for training, 254–255
Consultative selling, 177–179
Contests, 302
Control units, 109–110
Cooling-off laws, 26
Coordination
  through budgeting, 77
  in organization structure, 189, 190
Correspondence courses, 257
Cost analysis
  controversy in, 316
  data for, 318
  definition of, 314
  format of, 314
  limitations of, 318–319
  standards in, 315–316
  types of, 314–317
Costs
  direct vs. indirect, 315
  escapable, 316
  fixed, variable, and semivariable, 89–90, 315
  functional, 314–315
  marginal
    related to sales penetration, 78
    related to marginal revenues, 86–87
    related to number of territories, 107–108
  natural vs. functional, 88
  segment, 315
  see also Selling costs
Curbstone conference, 256

Decentralization of authority, 196, 198
Demand determinants, 35–36, 56–57
Delphi technique, 66
Detail salesperson, 143
Development vs. maintenance selling, 143, 194
Diagnosis in evaluation, 328
Diagnostic tests, 246–247
Direct vs. indirect selling, 143, 194–195
District sales managers, 4
Drawing accounts, 276
Duty analysis, 320–322
Dyadic view of selling success, 174–176

Efficiency vs. effectiveness, 190–191
Efforts
  methods of evaluating, 319–323
  quantitative vs. qualitative, 319
  relationships with results, 323
Ego drive, 172
Empathy, 172, 250
Entertainment expenses, 286
Environmental tests, 236
Equal Employment Opportunity Commission, 216, 220
Ethics
  see Sales management, ethical considerations
Evaluation
  definition of, 308
  as major sales management responsibility, 10–11
  program for, 308
  recommendations from, 328–330
Executive opinion forecasting, 65–66
Expectancy theory, 294–295, 297
Expenditures
  see Costs
Expense payments
  automobile plans, 286–287
  in compensation plan, 277
  control of, 285
  items allowed for, 285–286
  plans for, 285
Expert opinion forecasting, 66
Exponential smoothing, 61

Federal Trade Commission Act, 25
Field sales composite forecasting, 64–65
Field sales managers, 4
  hiring of, 238
  responsibilities of, 193
  training of, 260–261
Follow-up after the sale, 156
Forecasting
  see Sales forecasting
Forecasts
  distinguished from potentials, 33
  see also Market forecast, Sales forecast
Fringe benefits, 277–278

GEOLINE, 111
Goals
  as basis for decision making, 27–28
  benefits of, 22
  evaluation of, 328
  of the firm, 7
  for key accounts, 18–19
  marketing, 17–18
  motivational value of, 291
  national, 16–17
  problems with, 27–29
  of sales districts, 18
  of sales management, 16–22
  see also Quotas

Index

Green River ordinances, 26

Hierarchy of grumbles, 297–298
Hierarchy of needs, 293–294
Hiring sales managers, 238
Hiring salespeople
   quality needs in, 214–218
   quantity needs in, 213–214
   timing requirements in, 218
   see also Recruiting, Selection
House account, 283

Iceberg principle, 311
Implementation as major sales
    management responsibility, 9–10
Incentive
   via contests, 302
   via meetings, 302–303
   via promotional opportunities, 304–305
   via recognition, 303–304
   via regular compensation, 266
Informal organization, 209–210
Input-output analysis, 42–43
Inside vs. outside selling, 142, 194
Intelligence agents
   see Salespeople
Intelligence tests, 232
Interactions, 11–12, 77, 124, 217
Interest tests, 233
Internal Revenue Service, 285
Interviews
   evaluation of, 227
   guide for, 228–231
   standards for, 226–227
   type of, 226

Job analysis, 245–246
Job description
   see Position description
Job enrichment, 301
Job environment
   measuring, 296–297
   see also Supervision
Job evaluation, 270
Job qualifications, 214–218
Job satisfaction, 291
Job titles, 300
Jobs
   see Personal selling jobs, Sales
     managers
Judgment
   in forecasting, 53
   in budgeting, 91

Knockout factors, 214

Lecture, 254
Legal factors
   see Sales management, legal
     environment

Management by objectives
   see MBO
Manufacturers representatives, 100,
   101, 143, 193–194
Marginal costs
   see Costs
Market forecast, 33
Market penetration, 45
Market potential
   definition of, 33
   determinants of, 35–36
   developed vs. undeveloped, 34
   measurement of, 35–43
     data for, 37–40
     empirical approach, 35–36
     judgmental approach, 35
     using computers, 42
     using input-output analysis,
      42–43
     using sales force, 40–41
   relative vs. total, 36–37
   uses of, 45–48
   why use, 34–35
Market share
   definition of, 45
   distinguished from penetration, 45
   interpretation of, 45–46
   measurement of, 46
   as performance standard, 313
Marketing concept, 2
Marketing system
   see System, marketing
Matrix organization, 206–207, 208
MBO
   definition of, 123
   distinguished from quota-setting,
     123
   for field sales managers, 137
   see also Quotas
Meetings
   see Sales meetings
Methods study, 326–328
Motivation
   activities providing, 301–305
   definition of, 290
   factors involved in, 291–293
   measuring, 295–298
   programs, 298–301
   theories of, 293–295
   understanding, 293–295
Multimedia training methods, 257
Multiple buying influences, 157, 159, 191

National Society of Sales Training
   Executives, 253
Negotiation, 180

Objections, 152, 154
Objectives
   see Goals, Quotas

Office of Federal Contract Compliance,
   216, 220
On-the-job training, 256
Organization structure
   definition of, 188
   mechanistic view, 188
   organic view, 188
   see also Sales organization structure
Override, 88, 284

Participation by salespeople
   in market potential estimation,
     40–41
   in quota setting, 138–139
   in sales forecasting, 64–65
Pay
   as a factor of job satisfaction, 292
   see also Compensation level,
     Compensation methods,
     Compensation plan
Performance appraisals
   improving, 324
   items in, 324–326
   objectives of, 324
   techniques, 324
   for training program objectives, 247
Performance efforts
   see Efforts
Performance results
   see Cost analysis, Profit analysis,
     Sales analysis
Performance setting, 326–328
Personality tests, 233–234, 235
Personal life, impact on job
   satisfaction, 292–293
Personal selling
   contemporary strategies and styles,
     177–184
     consultative selling, 177–179
     negotiation, 180
     systems selling, 179–180
     team selling, 181, 182
     territory management, 181–184
   environment of, 161–165
   function of, 5–7
   jobs
     boundary nature of, 162
     occupational status of, 162–164
     types of, 142–144
   role in marketing strategy, 7, 22–24
   see also Selling process
Physical examinations, 236
Planning as major sales management
   responsibility, 8–9
Position descriptions
   contents of, 197–199
   examples of, 199–202
   use in hiring, 214
Positions
   personal selling, 193–195

Positions (continued)
  sales management, 195–197
  in sales organization structure, 193–201
  see also Personal selling jobs, Sales managers
Potential capability, 217
Potentials
  distinguished from forecasts, 33
  see also Market potential, Sales potential
Preparation for the sales call, 147–148, 149
Presentation
  demonstration, 152
  opening, 150–151
  outline example of, 251
  theories of, 148–150
    need satisfaction, 150
    problem solving, 150
    selling formula, 148–150
    stimulus-response, 148
  types of, 151–152
Productivity
  see Sales management, challenges today
Professionalism
  see Sales management, challenges today
Profit analysis
  defined, 314
  limitations of, 318–319
  measures, 317
  by segments, 317–318
Programmed instruction, 255–256
Promotional value vs. functional value selling, 143–144
Promotion opportunities, 304–305
Prospecting, 5, 146–147
Psychological tests
  adjusting content of, 234
  battery of, 234
  diagnostic use of, 246–247
  names of those used in selecting salespeople, 233
  problems in using, 234, 236
  types of, 232–234
  use of, 234
  validity of, 234
Puffing, 25–26

Quotas
  adjusting for ability, 137–138
  compared with MBO systems, 123
  combining and weighting, 131–133
  definition of, 123
  fairness of, 126
  levels of, 133–137
  limitations on using, 126–127

participation by salespeople in setting, 138–139
purposes of, 124–126
  control, 125–126
  evaluation, 126
  incentive, 124–125
steps in setting, 127–128
types of, 128–130
  activity, 130
  financial, 129–130
  professional development, 130
  sales volume, 129

Rating forms, 324–326, 327
Reaction to pressure, 137–138
Readiness, 250
Recognition, 303–304
Recruiting
  legal perspective on, 220
  policy decisions in, 220–221
  as screening process, 221, 222
  sources, 218–220
References, 227, 232
Regional sales managers, 4
Regression analysis
  in allocating sales effort to customers, 115
  in evaluating territory performance, 328–329
  in forecasting, 61–62
Reports
  see Call reports
Reps
  see Manufacturers representatives
Resident salesperson, 100, 101
Response curves, 100–102, 114, 115
Response functions
  see Response curves
Return on assets managed, 85–86
Robinson-Patman Act, 25
Role ambiguity, 292
Role conflict, 162–163, 292
Role congruence, 175
Role playing, 255
Routing, 116–117

Salary, 272–273
Sales analysis, 309–314
  data for, 313
  definition of, 309
  format of, 309–313
  limitations of, 313–314
  standards in, 312–313
Sales budget
  administration, 92–93
  allocating among categories, 87–88
  determining level of, 80–87
  flexibility, 89–91
  periods, 93
  review and acceptance, 93–94

  methods
    all-you-can-afford, 81
    competitive parity, 81–83
    incremental, 86–87
    objective-and-task, 83–85
    percentage-of-sales, 80
    return-on-investment, 85
  steps in, 80
  see also Budgeting
Sales forecast
  applying results, 69
  calculation of, 68–69
  definition of, 33
  determinants of demand, 56–57
  evaluation of, 69, 72
  purposes of, 53–55
  self-defeating and self-validating, 72
Sales forecasting
  data for, 57
  definition of, 53
  methods, 57–68
    delphi technique, 66
    executive opinion, 65–66
    expert opinion, 66
    exponential smoothing, 61
    field sales composite, 64–65
    regression analysis, 61–62
    surveys, 62–64
    time series analysis, 59–61
    which to use, 67–68
  as planning, 55
  process, 53, 70, 71
  as simulation, 55
Sales management
  challenges today
    productivity, 12–13
    professionalism, 13–14
  definition of, 3
  ethical considerations, 26–27
  legal environment, 25–26
  system of activities, 7
Sales managers
  compensation of, 284
  evaluating activities of, 326
  levels of, 3–4
  responsibilities of, 3–5
Sales manuals, 257
Sales meetings, 302–303
Sales organization structure
  activities performed in, 192–193
  and competence of field managers, 197, 198
  cost of, 206
  decentralization of authority in, 196, 198
  environment of, 190
  evaluation of, 207–210
  factors influencing management positions in, 195–197

Index

functional relationships in, 206–207
influence of people on, 208
informal relationships in, 209–210
market influence on, 191–192
positions needed in, 193–201
span of control in, 196, 198
specializations in, 193–195,
 203–206
 order of subordination, 204–206
staff positions in, 197, 198
steps in building, 191
types of, 202–206
Sales penetration
 definition of, 45
 marginal cost of obtaining, 78
 measurement of, 45
 used as an ability index, 113
Salespeople
 inside, 5
 as intelligence agents, 6, 192
 outside, 5
 resident, 100, 101
 theories of successful, 168–176
  behavior view, 172–174
  chemistry view, 168–170
  dyadic view, 174–176
  traits view, 170–172
 time utilization by, 144–145
Sales potential
 definition of, 33
 measurement of, 43–45
 method of determining number of territories, 106–107
 method for determining territory location and boundaries, 109–111
 uses of, 45–48, 207
Sales presentation
 see Presentation
Sales promotion, 1
Sales territories
 see Territories
Sales training
 administration of, 252–257
  how to train, 254–257
  when to train, 257
  where to train, 252–253
  who should train, 253–254
 content of
  attitudes, 247
  knowledge, 248–249
  skills, 250
 continuous and retraining, 257
 cost and cost savings of, 243–244
 evaluation of, 258–260
 experiments for evaluating, 258–259, 260
 for field sales managers, 260–261
 incidence of, 243
 length of programs, 243–244

methods and techniques
 audiovisual, 256
 business games, 255
 case studies, 255
 conference and discussion, 254–255
 correspondence courses, 257
 lecture, 254
 multimedia, 257
 on-the-job, 256
 programmed instruction, 255–256
 role playing, 255
 sales manuals, 257
 sensitivity training, 255
 trade schools, 257
 videotape recording, 255, 256
 nonsales personnel, 262
 objectives of, 244–247
 program for, 244
 specialized facilities for, 253
 standardized vs. individualized, 250–252
 what it can and cannot do, 242–243
 see also Training
SCHEDULE, 116
Screening, 221
Segments in cost analysis, 316
Selection
 legal perspective on, 236
 policy decisions in, 237
 tools
  application blanks, 223–226
  environmental tests, 236
  interviews, 226–227, 228–231
  physical exams, 236
  psychological tests, 232–236
  references, 227, 232
 see also Hiring salespeople, Hiring sales managers
Self-other orientation, 172
Selling costs
 categories of, 88–89
 determination of, 92
 expenses vs. investments, 79
 as percent of company sales, 82
Selling process
 model of, 160–161
 new directions in, 156–160
  computer influence, 156–157
  managerial concepts, 157–160
  multiple-level selling, 157
 steps in, 145–156
  answering objections, 152–154
  closing, 154–155
  follow-up, 156
  preparation, 147–149
  presentation, 148–152
  prospecting, 146–147
Sensitivity analysis, 72

Sensitivity training, 255
Simulation in sales forecasting, 55, 16PF, 233, 234
Soft sell, 173
Source credibility, 250
Span of control, 196–197, 198
Specialization
 customer, 194, 204, 205
 functional, 206, 207
 geographic, 194, 203, 204, 205
 product, 194
 role, 189
 task, 188–189
 see also Personal selling jobs
Stability of territory assignments, 102
Staff positions, 197, 198, 203–204
Standard Industrial Classification, 39
Standards of performance, 312–313
Strategies of sales management, 18–19, 192
Suboptimization, 3
Supervision
 definition of, 290
 process of, 293
Survey of Buying Power, 37, 38, 39, 41
Survey of Industrial Purchasing Power, 39
Survey of Selling Costs, 97, 135
Surveys in forecasting, 62–64
Systems
 goal, 16–17
 marketing, 1, 2, 3
 sales management, 7
Systems buying, 191–192
Systems selling, 179–180

Tangibles vs. intangibles selling, 143
Team selling, 181, 182
Territories
 allocating effort to customers, 113–116
 assigning salespeople, to, 111–113
 benefits of, 98–99
 decision criteria for, 99–102
 definition of, 98
 location and boundaries, 109–111
 number of, 102–109
 problems with improper workload or potential, 101
 reasons for not using, 99
 scheduling and routing, 116–117
 splitting, 118
 stability of, 102
 transferring salespeople among, 118
Territory management, 181–184
Time, salespeople's use of, 144–145
Time analysis, 319–320
Time management, 114–116, 181, 249
Time series analysis, 59–61

TOURPLAN, 117
Tradeoffs, 11–12, 197–198, 217–218, 243
Trade schools, 257
Trading areas, 110
Training
  customers, 262
    definition of, 242
    distributors, 262
  vs. education, 242
  see also Sales training
Traits view of selling success, 170–172
Transferring salespeople, 118
Trial close, 155
Turnover, 214

Uniform Commercial Code, 25
Unit sales managers, 4

Validity, 234
Videotape recording, 255, 256
Vocational Rehabilitation Act, 216

Wheeler-Lea Act, 25
Windfall sales, 275, 282–283
Workload, 100, 101, 104–105, 109

Zip code areas, 110